NTC's
THESAURUS
of
EVERYDAY
AMERICAN
ENGLISH

NTC's THESAURUS

of

EVERYDAY AMERICAN ENGLISH

Anne Bertram

Printed on recyclable paper

NTC Publishing Group
Lincolnwood, Illinois USA

1996 Printing

© 1995 National Textbook Company,
a division of NTC Publishing Group, 4255 West Touhy Avenue,
Lincolnwood (Chicago), Illinois 60646-1975 U.S.A.
Manufactured in the United States of America.

5 6 7 8 9 0 VP 9 8 7 6 5 4 3 2

Contents

About This Thesaurus

The English language has an enormous vocabulary—larger than any other language now spoken or ever spoken. The largest of the English language dictionaries contain more than hundreds of thousands of entries. While it is unlikely that anyone would ever encounter all the words in English, a well-educated person can expect to encounter 20 to 40 percent of them in the course of a lifetime. The challenge to the learner of English is as enormous as the size of the language's vocabulary.

Writers have the enormous task of finding the correct words among all those available, and readers also have an awesome task in understanding the words that the writer has chosen. Successful word choice in writing is based on being able to assemble a group of "competing" words and use some rational basis for choosing between them. Both a dictionary and a thesaurus can aid in this task. Dictionaries and thesauruses—*thesauri* is also correct—are two of the most important guides to learning how to deal with the large and complex vocabulary of the English language. But people who try to use a thesaurus to make themselves look like better writers usually end up looking like worse writers than they really are. Simply substituting a word you do not know for a word you do know is risky writing at its worst. Thesauruses and dictionaries provide a roadmap through a huge vocabulary, but unless they are used properly, the result can be worse than getting lost. Writers and readers who understand these word-finding tools will benefit the most from them.

Whereas dictionaries deal with word meaning by providing a definition for each word in isolation from other words, thesauruses deal with word meaning by showing words that are related to one another in meaning. Of course, some dictionaries also show synonyms, making them similar to thesauruses in this regard. Further, some thesauruses also indicate word meaning, but that is never their primary purpose. Yet, thesauruses present writers with a special problem. Used improperly, they can lead to the choice of the wrong word or a word that is not quite suitable for the use to which it is being put. This problem is usually due to a desire on the part of the writer to appear to have a far more extensive vocabulary than is actually the case. Some thesauruses increase the likelihood of this kind of error by presenting short lists of alleged synonyms—with no indication of meaning—that really do *not* share the same meaning, and sometimes do not even share the same part of speech with one another. Thus, the first important rule in using a thesaurus is to come to a thorough understanding of each word that might be chosen for use in writing.

The random selection of synonyms is no replacement for the practice of assembling a list of words with similar meanings and making a thoughtful and informed judgment about which one will do best what the writer wants to do. Choosing the most appropriate and most effective word is a skill that can be learned through practice. This thesaurus is a modest collection of synonyms and closely related words organized in a fashion that will encourage the user to make sensible and rational word choices through the use of *any* good dictionary or thesaurus. It is designed to help ground the learner in *building good word choice habits*. Toward this end, the entries often include contrastive meanings, providing the user with a convenient source of words and meanings to allow practice in building effective word choice skills. The definitions are meant to distinguish one word in the list from the other words in the list. The full sentence examples given with each entry will prove more useful than tight and concise definitions for learners.

To The User

There are some important things to remember in using a thesaurus. Word choice is very important in writing. The goal is to choose the words that convey the exact meaning that you want. You can do this best by assembling a group of "competing" words and then learning enough about the words to allow you to choose between them. This thesaurus is organized to make this task easier.

Each main entry in the thesaurus contains a group of three to seven synonyms or "competing" words. These words are each defined *in terms of the other words in the group.* When using a thesaurus, you should remember that many of the simpler words in English do not have synonyms. For example, *run* is an important word, but there are no synonyms for it. There are words that mean similar things, such as *race, gallop, trot,* and *jog,* but these don't have exactly the same meaning. *Run* and each of these words is substitutable *only in certain contexts.* To further illustrate the specific use of each word, there are two examples of the use of each member of the group of words. The first word in the entry is often a word that has a *core* meaning that can be used in defining the other words in the group.

Remember that working with words—writing and reading—is real work. Understanding the different senses of words is an essential part of this work. Whenever you do not understand the words being used, you should consult a dictionary. By using this thesaurus, you will gain skills in evaluating word meanings and choosing the right word for a particular situation.

A

a short time ago   See the entry for *lately.*

abandon   (*verb*) to leave someone or something and never go back. □ *Alice abandoned the broken-down car on the side of the road.* □ *Vincent abandoned his family and ran off to join the circus.*

    • **defect**   to *abandon* your country or political party. (Often with *from.*) □ *The famous dancer decided to defect and come to live in the United States.* □ *Many people defected from the party after its leaders grew too extreme.*

    • **desert**   to *abandon* someone or something that needs you. □ *Most of George's friends deserted him after he admitted to stealing the money.* □ *Robert's self-confidence deserted him the instant he stood up to give his speech.*

    • **drop**   to *abandon* a friend or a project. (Informal.) □ *Helen and I used to be good friends, but then she dropped me.* □ *Irene suddenly dropped her demand to lead the team.*

    • **maroon**   to *abandon* someone in a place, such as an island, that is difficult to leave. □ *The ship's crew marooned the captain on a tiny desert island.* □ *My mom didn't come to pick me up; I was marooned at the shopping mall.*

    • **walk out on**   to *abandon* a relationship or someone who shares a relationship with you. □ *Art's first wife walked out on him.* □ *How can you walk out on me after everything we've been through together?*

abdicate   See the entry for *resign.*

abduct   See the entry for *kidnap.*

abhor   See the entry for *hate.*

abide   See the entries for *bear, stay.*

ability (*noun*) skill; the energy or knowledge to do something. (See also the entry for *mastery*.) □ *You can't get a job as a secretary if you don't have the ability to type.* □ *Maria has a surprising ability to remember faces.*
  • **capability** a proven or tested *ability*. □ *This cannon has the capability to fire over great distances.* □ *The actor had a well-known capability to mimic people accurately.*
  • **capacity** the *ability* to do something you may never have done before; how much of an *ability* you have. □ *The new job tested Tom's capacity for hard work.* □ *Tom seems to have a limitless capacity for learning new songs.*
  • **power** the energy or strength to do something. □ *After the great battle with his arch-foe, the superhero lacked the power to stop the speeding train.* □ *I don't think my car has the power to get up this steep hill.*

abolish See the entry for *cancel*.

abominate See the entry for *hate*.

aboveboard See the entry for *honest*.

abrade See the entry for *scrape*.

abrupt See the entry for *sudden*.

abscond See the entry for *steal away*.

absent See the entries for *missing, unaware*.

absolutely See the entry for *certainly*.

absolve See the entry for *pardon*.

absorb (*verb*) to suck or soak something up. □ *A sponge absorbs liquid faster than a paper towel.* □ *Maria quietly absorbed everything Tom told her.*

  • **assimilate** to *absorb* something and make it a part of you. □ *The scientist observed that the organism had completely assimilated the nutrients into its system.* □ *So much information was presented in the lecture that Philip could barely assimilate it all.*
  • **soak up** to *absorb* something thoroughly. □ *The carpet soaked up a tremendous amount of water.* □ *I lay on the beach, soaking up the sunshine.*
  • **take in** to *absorb* something passively and quietly. □ *Sue didn't say much, but her wide-open eyes took in everything around her.* □ *There was so much to see in the museum that I couldn't take it all in.*
  [→contrasting word: *expel*; see also: *drink, learn*]

absorbed (*adjective*) paying deep attention to something. (Usually with *in*.) □ *I'm sorry I didn't hear you knock; I was absorbed in the book I was reading.* □ *The two friends were absorbed in a card game.*

• **engrossed**   thoroughly *absorbed*. (Usually with *in*.) □ *Martha is so engrossed in trying to fix the toaster that she's barely aware of anything around her.* □ *Joe was engrossed in the TV program and didn't hear his dad come in the door.*
• **intent**   determined to do something; eager and *absorbed*. (Usually with *on* or *upon*.) □ *Rita is intent on finishing her painting; she wants to have it ready for the show next week.* □ *Intent on winning the bicycle race, Susan hardly noticed the pouring rain.*
• **rapt**   so *absorbed* that nothing can distract you; so *absorbed* that you seem to be in a trance. □ *Tom paid rapt attention to the music through the entire concert.* □ *Jan is rapt in her video game again.*

absorbing   See the entry for *interesting*.

absurd   See the entry for *meaningless*.

abundant   See the entry for *plentiful*.

abuse   (*verb*) to treat someone or something very badly; to use something in the wrong way. □ *I hated the way Mr. Jones abused his dog.* □ *The TV program showed the many dangers of abusing alcohol.*
• **maltreat**   to treat someone or something extremely badly. □ *Jane left her husband because he maltreated her.* □ *The hospital staff was punished for maltreating the patients.*
• **mistreat**   to treat someone or something badly. □ *You can tell that Jim mistreats his guitar; just look at all the scratches on it.* □ *The children liked the baby-sitter because she never mistreated them.*
• **misuse**   to use something in the wrong way. □ *You must not misuse the gas stove; it might cause an explosion.* □ *The doctor sternly told me not to misuse the drugs she had prescribed.*
[→see also: *hurt, slander*]

academy   See the entry for *school*.

accede   See the entry for *consent*.

accentuate   See the entry for *stress²*.

accept   See the entry for *get*.

accepting   See the entry for *resigned*.

accident   (*noun*) something that happens that you could not have predicted; something unfortunate that happens. □ *I didn't mean to spill the orange juice; it was an accident.* □ *There was a terrible accident on the highway and traffic was backed up for miles.*
• **chance**   something that happens that you could not have predicted; an opportunity for something to happen. □ *I didn't expect to meet Donald downtown; we ran into each other by chance.* □ *Give me a chance to finish telling the story!*

• **coincidence**   two things that happen that you could not have predicted; an unusual or lucky *accident*. □ *By coincidence, Edith and Jim were looking for the same book in the library.* □ *Do you really live in the same apartment building as me? What a coincidence!*
• **happenstance**   something that happens by *accident*. (Old-fashioned.) □ *The two travelers regarded their meeting on the lonely road to be a most fortunate happenstance.* □ *An unlucky happenstance robbed Sarah of all the money she had inherited.*

accolade   See the entry for *tribute*.

accompanist   See the entry for *musician*.

accompany   (*verb*) to go with someone or something. □ *Grandma wants me to accompany her on her next car trip.* □ *Donald always accompanies his sister when she goes out.*
• **attend**   to *accompany* someone in order to take care of him or her. □ *Several maids attended the princess whenever she appeared in public.* □ *Mrs. Hall needs a nurse to attend her all the time.*
• **escort**   to *accompany* someone formally or to a formal event. □ *The colonel escorted Miss Jones into the ballroom.* □ *Two policemen escorted Smith to the courthouse.*
• **go along (with)**   to *accompany* someone. (Informal.) □ *Can I go along with you when you go shopping?* □ *Let's ask Tony to go along.*
• **usher**   to *accompany* someone in order to show him or her where to go. □ *Esther ushered the playgoers to their seats.* □ *A secretary ushered me into Ms. Jones's office.*

accomplish   See the entry for *achieve*.

accomplished   See the entry for *experienced*.

account for   See the entry for *explain*.

accumulate   See the entry for *collect*.

accurate   See the entry for *right*.

accuse   See the entry for *blame*.

accustomed   See the entry for *familiar*.

acerbic   See the entry for *sarcastic*.

ache   See the entry for *hurt²*.

achieve   (*verb*) to do something successfully; to complete something. □ *The team achieved a stunning victory.* □ *I hope to achieve my goals.*
• **accomplish**   to *achieve* something successfully. □ *Frank accomplished everything he set out to do.* □ *No one knows how she manages to accomplish so much so quickly.*

• **attain**   to *achieve* something through hard work or after a long time. □ *Our dog has attained a ripe old age.* □ *At last, George attained a high-ranking position in the company.*
• **reach**   to *achieve* a particular goal. □ *Helen wants to reach a high level of prosperity.* □ *Irene can't wait to reach the age of twenty-one.*

acid   See the entry for *sour*.

acknowledge   See the entry for *admit*.

acquiesce   See the entry for *consent*.

acquire   See the entries for *get, learn²*.

acrobatic   See the entry for *agile*.

act   (*noun*) something that is done. (See also the entry for *rule*.) □ *Jean's running away from home was a desperate act.* □ *Saving the drowning child was an act of heroism.*
• **action**   an *act*, emphasizing movement or activity. □ *This crisis calls for immediate action.* □ *I enjoyed the movie's exciting action.*
• **deed**   a noteworthy *act*. □ *Many stories, songs, poems, and movies have celebrated the deeds of Robin Hood.* □ *The villain in the play was punished for his evil deeds.*
• **feat**   a difficult *act*. □ *Kevin can perform incredible feats upon the trapeze.* □ *Getting an A from that strict Mr. Smith is quite a feat!*
• **stunt**   a dangerous *act*, usually performed to impress people. □ *We held our breath as the daredevil attempted the next stunt.* □ *Larry broke his arm when he tried to do a stunt on the jungle gym.*

action   See the entry for *act*.

active   See the entry for *busy²*.

actor   See the entry for *entertainer*.

actual   (*adjective*) real; really existing. □ *We will never learn the actual truth about what happened that night.* □ *I didn't want my friend to know my actual feelings.*
• **exact**   *actual* and precise. (See also the main entry for *exact*.) □ *I suspect that Philip is not telling the exact truth.* □ *His answers to all the questions were exact.*
• **factual**   *actual* and having to do with facts. □ *Is that a factual story, or did you make it up?* □ *Jim gave a very factual account of the accident to the newspaper reporter.*
• **literal**   *actual* and not exaggerated; exactly as stated. □ *That's the literal truth; I'm not exaggerating!* □ *Sue takes everything, even fairy tales, in a literal way, so she believes that frogs can talk.*
[→contrasting word: *figurative*]

acute   See the entry for *sharp*.

ad   See the entry for *commercial*.

adage   See the entry for *saying*.

adaptable   See the entry for *flexible*.

add up   See the entry for *count*.

additional   See the entry for *extra*.

address   See the entry for *speech*.

adequate   See the entries for *enough, satisfactory*.

adhere   See the entry for *stick¹*.

adherent   See the entry for *supporter*.

adjacent   See the entry for *near*.

adjust   See the entry for *arrange*.

administrative   See the entry for *governmental*.

administrator   See the entry for *authority*.

admit   (*verb*) to say that something unpleasant is true. (Sometimes with *to*.) □ *I must admit that I did not enjoy the movie.* □ *Cheryl would not admit that she had stolen the money.* □ *She would not admit to the theft.*
   • **acknowledge**   to agree that something is true. □ *Art acknowledged that Carrie was his sister.* □ *The author acknowledged that many people had helped her write her book.*
   • **concede**   to *admit* something grudgingly. □ *The politician had to concede that he had been involved in shady activities.* □ *Donald conceded that his mission had failed.*
   • **confess**   to *admit* to having done something wrong. (Sometimes with *to*.) □ *I confess that I ate the cake you were saving for dessert.* □ *At last, the prisoner has confessed to the crime.*
   • **own (up)**   to *admit* to having done something wrong. (Sometimes *own up to*. Informal.) □ *George owned that he shouldn't have borrowed my bike without asking permission.* □ *If you took my earrings, you had better own up to it.*

admonish   See the entry for *urge*.

adorable   See the entry for *cute*.

adorn   See the entry for *decorate*.

adroit   See the entry for *flexible*.

advance   (*verb*) to go ahead; to move forward. (See also the entry for *lend*.) ☐ *The army advanced into enemy territory.* ☐ *Weeds are advancing into my garden at an alarming rate.*

  • **go forward**   to *advance* deliberately. ☐ *We decided to go forward with our plan.* ☐ *The general ordered the troops to go forward despite all opposition.*

  • **proceed**   to *advance* in an orderly way; to continue *advancing*. ☐ *After you arrive at the airport, get a taxi and proceed to the hotel.* ☐ *Everyone worked together, and the job proceeded as planned.*

  • **progress**   to *advance* toward a goal. ☐ *I'm afraid that Dad's sickness is progressing.* ☐ *Vincent's novel is progressing slowly.*

  [→contrasting word: *retreat*]

advantage   See the entry for *benefit¹*.

advantageous   See the entry for *convenient*.

adventure   (*noun*) an exciting experience; a dangerous undertaking. ☐ *Our helicopter ride turned out to be a real adventure.* ☐ *Jan is so imaginative that she makes even a trip to the grocery store seem like an adventure.*

  • **exploit**   a heroic *adventure*. ☐ *Bob couldn't wait to read about the superhero's latest exploits.* ☐ *The movie is all about the explorer's most famous exploit.*

  • **escapade**   a wild *adventure*. ☐ *The audience laughed at Pinocchio's escapades.* ☐ *Mark's latest escapade—setting off firecrackers indoors— got him in serious trouble.*

adversary   See the entry for *enemy*.

adversity   See the entry for *problem*.

advertise   (*verb*) to inform the public about something, usually in order to interest people in buying it. ☐ *The company advertised its new product on TV and radio.* ☐ *What do you think is the best way to advertise this sale?*

  • **promote**   to *advertise* in order to get someone or something started or accepted. ☐ *The author appeared on several talk shows, promoting his new book.* ☐ *Kay did everything possible to promote her business.*

  • **publicize**   to inform the public about someone or something. ☐ *We rented a billboard to publicize our services.* ☐ *The mayor's meeting with the youth club was highly publicized.*

  • **tout**   to *advertise* aggressively and persistently. ☐ *If I see one more commercial touting that yucky soft drink, I'll scream!* ☐ *The movie was touted as the best adventure movie of the decade.*

  [→see also: *announce*]

advertisement   See the entry for *commercial*.

advise (*verb*) to tell someone what you think is the best thing to do. □ *Because the weather was so bad, the authorities advised everyone not to travel.* □ *I would advise you to be polite to our hosts.*
- **counsel** to *advise* someone through discussion with him or her. □ *The president's aides counseled him against signing the bill into law.* □ *Mother always counseled us to save as much money as we could.*
- **recommend** to *advise* someone strongly. □ *I recommend turning down the volume on the TV.* □ *Art recommended that we think it over carefully before making a decision.*
- **suggest** to *advise* someone indirectly; to *advise* someone about something by giving hints. (See also the main entry for *suggest*.) □ *Rose suggested that we spend the day at the beach.* □ *If you are going to the Chinese restaurant on the corner, I suggest ordering the egg foo yong.* [→see also: *tell*]

adviser See the entry for *guide*[1].

aerobics See the entry for *exercise*.

affable See the entry for *friendly*.

affected See the entry for *artificial*.

affection See the entry for *love*.

affix See the entry for *stick*[2].

affluent See the entry for *rich*.

aficionado See the entry for *fan*.

afraid (*adjective*) in fear of something. □ *When I was little, I was afraid of the dark.* □ *Don't be afraid; I'll protect you.*
- **alarmed** alert and agitated because you are *afraid*. □ *I was alarmed at the sudden noise.* □ *We were all alarmed when the stone came crashing through the window.*
- **frightened** made *afraid* by something. □ *Stanley began to whimper like a frightened animal.* □ *The eerie noises in the old house made us feel frightened.*
- **petrified** so *afraid* that you cannot move. □ *I was petrified when I felt the touch of a cold hand on my neck.* □ *When the principal told me to enter her office, I was too petrified to obey.*
- **scared** *afraid*. (Informal. Use *frightened* or *afraid* in writing.) □ *Are you scared of snakes?* □ *My sister is scared of clowns.*
- **terrified** very *afraid*. □ *I knew something was wrong when I saw Emily's terrified face.* □ *Linda is terrified of monster movies.*

aftermath See the entry for *result*.

age See the entry for *time*.

agenda   See the entry for *plan*.

aggressive   (*adjective*) demanding; willing to fight for what you want. □ *The coach says we have to be aggressive if we want to win.* □ *I don't like Charlie's aggressive behavior.*

> • **competitive**   naturally *aggressive;* taking pleasure in being *aggressive* or in winning. □ *It's no fun to play games with Jim; he's too competitive.* □ *Mary succeeds because she is competitive.*
>
> • **forceful**   able to get results by being strongly *aggressive.* □ *When the teacher says things in that forceful way, we all obey her.* □ *Kevin is quite forceful; he can make anyone do what he wants.*
>
> • **self-assertive**   willing to speak out for what you want; not letting yourself go unnoticed. □ *You must be more self-assertive if you want people to listen to you.* □ *Mark manages to be self-assertive without being pushy.*

agile   (*adjective*) able to move easily, quickly, and gracefully. □ *Cats are very agile animals.* □ *Tom's agile fingers flew over the computer keyboard.*

> • **acrobatic**   *agile* and able to do physical stunts. □ *Philip is very acrobatic; you should see him do handsprings.* □ *Doris made several acrobatic moves as she tried to keep from slipping on the ice.*
>
> • **nimble**   *agile;* moving lightly. □ *Eddie crossed the creek by taking nimble jumps from rock to rock.* □ *After watching Fran run through the obstacle course, we were all impressed at how nimble she is.*
>
> • **spry**   *agile* and energetic. (Usually used to describe elderly people.) □ *Grandpa may be eighty-five, but he's still quite spry.* □ *John bounded up the stairs in a surprisingly spry way.*

agitated   See the entry for *excited*.

agonize   See the entry for *worry*.

agony   See the entry for *distress*.

agree   (*verb*) to have the same opinion as someone else; to say you are willing to do something. (Usually with *with* in the former case; usually with *to* in the latter.) □ *I agree with everything you've said.* □ *George agreed to meet me at the library.*

> • **assent**   to say you are wholeheartedly willing to do something. (Usually with *to.*) □ *We told Evelyn our plan and she assented to it eagerly.* □ *The committee asked Harold to resign from office, but he did not assent.*
>
> • **concur**   to have exactly the same opinion as someone else. (Formal. Usually with *with.*) □ *Kay thinks that this is a boring book, and I concur.* □ *Fran concurred with Eddie's opinion that the music was too loud.*

• **consent**   to say you are willing to do something; to give someone permission to do something. (Usually with *to*. See also the main entry for *consent*.) □ *Mr. Green would not consent to driving the children to the mall.* □ *Laura could go on the field trip only if her parents consented.*
• **go along with**   to have the same opinion as someone else. (Informal.) □ *Mary is very sensible; I usually go along with whatever she thinks.* □ *Jim wanted to put a tack on the teacher's chair, but no one went along with his idea.*
[→contrasting word: *disagree*]

agreement   (*noun*) a promise that two or more people or groups make to each other. □ *Mark and Tom made an agreement to meet on the basketball court every Saturday at three.* □ *My sister and I have an agreement about who does the dishes every night.*
• **compact**   a formal *agreement.* □ *The two countries made a solemn compact to end the war.* □ *Susan and Eddie made a compact, promising to take care of each other's children in case one of them should die.*
• **contract**   a formal, legal *agreement,* often a written *agreement* to do something or to pay someone to do something. □ *The contract says you must finish the work by this deadline.* □ *The star signed a contract to make six more movies for a million dollars apiece.*
• **covenant**   a solemn *agreement.* (Formal.) □ *According to the covenant they had made, the two nations could never make war on each other again.* □ *In the Bible, there are many stories in which God makes a covenant with his people.*
• **pact**   a solemn, often secret *agreement.* □ *My friend and I made a pact, and now we are blood brothers.* □ *The criminals made a pact, swearing never to betray each other.*

aid   See the entry for *help.*

ailment   See the entry for *sickness.*

aim   See the entries for *goal, mean².*

air   See the entry for *tune.*

alarmed   See the entry for *afraid.*

alert   (*adjective*) watchful and ready to respond quickly to a threat. (See also the entry for *warn.*) □ *The security guard stayed alert all night.* □ *The deer were alert, looking and listening for any signs of a predator.*
• **attentive**   very watchful; paying close attention. □ *The students were not very attentive during the lecture; in fact, several of them fell asleep.* □ *The attentive father watched his sick child carefully.*
• **on guard**   ready to respond to a threat. (Also *on one's guard.*) □ *After the robbery attempt, everyone at the bank was on guard all the time.* □ *Be on your guard when you walk down the street at night.*

• **vigilant**   watchful; fully awake. (Formal.) □ *Thanks to the vigilant police officers, the thief was caught before she could get inside the building.* □ *The watchdog was very vigilant; he barked at the slightest noise.*
• **wary**   cautious, watchful, and suspicious; ready to respond quickly. □ *It is usually a good idea to be wary of strangers.* □ *The wary fox heard the hunters coming and ran away before they could get close.*
• **wide-awake**   fully awake; brisk, watchful, and ready to respond. □ *We could never sneak anything past the hall monitor; she was always wide awake.* □ *Mark had a wide-awake look on his face.*

alien   See the entry for *strange.*

alight   See the entry for *land.*

alike   See the entry for *equal.*

all right   See the entry for *good.*

allege   See the entry for *claim.*

alley   See the entry for *road.*

allocate   See the entry for *distribute.*

allow   (*verb*) to give someone permission to do something; to agree that someone may do something. □ *Doug's parents only allow him to watch one hour of TV every day.* □ *The school rules do not allow students to fight on school grounds.*
• **authorize**   to *allow* something legally; to give someone the legal power to do something. □ *Bob discovered that he could not start a business in town unless the town council authorized it.* □ *The principal authorized Mrs. Hall's plan for a field trip.*
• **let**   to *allow.* (Informal.) □ *The teacher won't let us leave the class-room until we have cleaned up after ourselves.* □ *Do your parents let you stay out late on weekends?*
• **permit**   to *allow* something officially. □ *The curfew law does not permit young people to be out after ten at night.* □ *Jan thinks that smoking should not be permitted anywhere.*
[→contrasting word: *forbid*]

alloy   See the entry for *mix.*

allude to   See the entry for *refer to.*

allure   See the entry for *attract.*

almost   (*adverb*) not entirely but very close to; everything but. □ *I have saved almost enough money to buy a car.* □ *Carrie almost didn't get to go on the trip.*
• **just about**   very close to; everything but. □ *George just about lost his temper.* □ *We have just about enough pasta to feed two people.*

• **nearly**   close to; near to. □ *Donald nearly fainted when he learned he was the winner.* □ *Nearly three hundred people came to the concert.*
• **not quite**   close to but not entirely. □ *They spent not quite a thousand dollars.* □ *It's not quite warm enough to go swimming.*
• **practically**   extremely close to. □ *Eddie owns practically all of the houses on this block.* □ *Fran practically threw a fit because she couldn't go with us.*

alphabetize   See the entry for *sort.*

alter   See the entry for *change.*

aluminum   See the entry for *metal.*

amalgamate   See the entry for *mix.*

amass   See the entry for *collect.*

amaze   See the entry for *surprise.*

amble   See the entry for *walk.*

amiable   See the entry for *friendly.*

ample   See the entries for *enough, plentiful.*

amulet   See the entry for *charm.*

amuse   See the entry for *entertain.*

amusing   See the entry for *funny.*

ancestor   (*noun*) someone you are descended from, usually one who lived in the distant past. □ *One of my ancestors came to the United States from Ireland in 1702.* □ *Helen says that Theodore Roosevelt is an ancestor of hers.*
• **forebear**   an *ancestor* who lived in the very distant past. □ *I am trying to find out what life was like for my forebears in the country where they were born.* □ *Helen is reading a biography of her famous forebear.*
• **forefather**   an *ancestor* of an earlier time. (Formal or poetic.) □ *We must strive to live in a way that would make our forefathers proud.* □ *What inspired our forefathers to their greatest achievements?*
• **progenitor**   anyone you are descended from. (Formal.) □ *Jim seems to have inherited all the worst qualities of his progenitors.* □ *The king and queen were the progenitors of a noble line of descendants.*

anecdote   See the entry for *story.*

angry   (*adjective*) strongly displeased or upset. □ *The rude waiter really made me angry.* □ *Kay was so angry that her face turned red.*
• **enraged**   violently *angry;* full of rage. □ *Lenny was so enraged at being teased that he started screaming at the people who were teasing him.*

□ *After they showed the offensive movie, the TV station got calls from hundreds of enraged viewers.*
• **furious**   wildly, fiercely *angry;* full of fury. □ *It really makes me furious when people ignore me.* □ *When Tom heard what Mary was saying about him, he was furious.*
• **incensed**   passionately *angry* and annoyed. (Formal.) □ *Fran was incensed at the callous way the doctor treated her.* □ *When I saw that the cats had shredded my expensive new curtains, I was utterly incensed.*
• **irate**   intensely *angry.* (Formal.) □ *Irate customers crowded into the store, demanding their money back.* □ *Sue was irate when her favorite TV show was canceled.*
• **mad**   *angry.* (Informal.) □ *Sometimes my parents really make me mad.* □ *I have to get home on time or my mom will be mad.*
[→see also: *indignant*]

anguish   See the entry for *distress.*

animal   (*noun*) a living thing that can move by itself. □ *The koala bear is a rare animal.* □ *Many people keep some kind of animal as a pet.*
• **beast**   any *animal* other than a human being; a human being who behaves very badly. (Old-fashioned.) □ *The enchanted forest was filled with many strange beasts.* □ *Winslow was a beast and a coward, and everyone disliked him.*
• **being**   an *animal* or spirit; an unfamiliar kind of *animal,* as in *a being from another planet.* □ *I've heard that some kind of mysterious being inhabits that ruined building.* □ *We do not know what kind of beings we might encounter on other planets.*
• **creature**   an old-fashioned word for *animal;* an unusual *animal.* □ *The lost kitten cried pitifully, but no one stopped to help the poor creature.* □ *The mad scientist made a frightful creature in his laboratory.*
• **varmint**   a bothersome *animal.* (Folksy.) □ *I wish someone would catch the varmint that's been pulling trash out of my trash cans.* □ *If that stray dog comes around here again, chase the varmint away.*

animation   See the entry for *energy.*

announce   (*verb*) to tell the public about something. □ *The mayor announced that she would run for reelection.* □ *The club president announced that the next meeting would be on Saturday at six P.M.*
• **declare**   to *announce* something formally. □ *The principal declared that Monday would be a holiday.* □ *The president officially declared Donald a hero.*
• **herald**   to *announce* something (usually something good) that is about to happen. □ *A flood of TV commercials heralded the premiere of the new movie.* □ *The newspapers heralded the celebrity's arrival.*

• **proclaim**   to *announce* something formally and impressively. □ *The king proclaimed that his son would marry the princess.* □ *I hereby proclaim you to be the winner.*

• **trumpet**   to *announce* something proudly or loudly. □ *Elizabeth trumpeted her son's victory throughout the neighborhood.* □ *Fran was fond of trumpeting her own accomplishments far and wide.*

[→see also: *say, advertise*]

annoy   (*verb*) to disturb someone repeatedly; to disturb someone so much that he or she loses patience. □ *The noise from the construction site is starting to annoy me.* □ *Gayle's unending questions annoyed her father.*

• **bother**   to *annoy* or worry someone. □ *Don't bother me while I'm trying to work.* □ *It bothers me that no one ever seems to take me seriously.*

• **bug**   to *annoy* someone. (Slang.) □ *Nothing bugs me more than noisy neighbors.* □ *Stop bugging me about the money I owe you.*

• **irk**   to *annoy* someone in a tiresome way. □ *It irks Harold when people misspell his name.* □ *She's always late. It really irks me to have to wait for her.*

• **irritate**   to *annoy* someone so that he or she gets upset. □ *Don't poke the dog; it only irritates her.* □ *It irritates me when the dog won't stop barking.*

• **pester**   to *annoy* someone deliberately and repeatedly. □ *Jay pestered Kay until she gave him what he wanted.* □ *Dad told us to quit pestering him about going to the movie.*

• **vex**   to *annoy* someone very much; to make someone confused and upset. (Somewhat old-fashioned.) □ *If you hadn't vexed the dog so much, she wouldn't have bitten you.* □ *This chemistry problem is really vexing me; I have no idea how to solve it.*

answer   (*verb*) to say or do something in response, particularly in response to a question. □ *I asked the little boy where he lived, but he didn't answer me.* □ *Tom answered our teasing by sticking out his tongue at us.*

• **counter**   to *answer* with an opposing point of view. □ *"No one should have to learn to write letters; it's a useless skill," said Irene. "It's not useless; for one thing, you sometimes have to write letters to apply for a job," Joe countered.* □ *Whenever Kevin disagrees with what you say, he always counters with a clever remark.*

• **reply**   to *answer;* especially, to say or write something in response. □ *I'm sorry it has taken me so long to reply to your letter.* □ *"Is anyone here?" I called into the dark room. "Only me," a voice replied.*

• **respond**   to *answer* or react. □ *Laura waited for someone to respond to her S.O.S.* □ *Mary seems to be unconscious; when I called her name and shook her, she didn't respond.*

• **retort**   to *answer* wittily or cuttingly. □ *"You're the ugliest person I know," Nancy said to Otto. "At least I'm not stupid like you," Otto*

retorted. □ *Whenever the teacher reprimands Paula, Paula retorts and gets herself in even more trouble.*
• **return**   to *answer* quickly or playfully. □ *"Is anyone at home?" Dad asked as he came in. "Only us chickens," we returned.* □ *When someone in the audience heckled him, the comedian returned a funny reply.*

antagonist   See the entry for *enemy.*

anthem   See the entry for *song.*

anticipate   See the entry for *expect.*

antics   See the entry for *practical joke.*

antidote   See the entry for *cure.*

antiquated   See the entry for *old-fashioned.*

anxiety   See the entry for *distress.*

anxious   See the entry for *uneasy.*

apartment   See the entry for *house.*

apathetic   See the entries for *indifferent, removed.*

ape   See the entry for *copy¹.*

apparatus   See the entry for *device.*

apparel   See the entry for *clothing.*

apparent   See the entry for *clear.*

appear   See the entries for *come, seem.*

appearance   See the entry for *looks.*

appease   (*verb*) to give someone what he or she wants in order to calm him or her. □ *The burglar appeased the watchdog by giving it a big piece of meat.* □ *The baby threw a tantrum, despite all our efforts to appease her.*
• **conciliate**   to calm people or groups who are arguing, especially by negotiating with them. (Formal.) □ *Art did his best to conciliate his two brothers, who hadn't spoken to each other for years.* □ *The negotiators were able to conciliate the rebels with the existing government.*
• **mollify**   to give someone something in order to calm him or her; to soothe someone. □ *Dad was very upset when I decided to leave home, but I mollified him by promising to call once a week.* □ *Carrie mollified Ben by assuring him that she would fix or replace everything she had broken.*
• **pacify**   to make someone calm, at least for a time. (Formal.) □ *You can pacify the dog by speaking softly to him.* □ *The boss tried to pacify her restless employees by promising better working conditions.*

• **placate** to calm someone who is angry by giving something to him or her. □ *We placated the teacher with sincere apologies and promises to do better on the next assignment.* □ *Donald is so angry that I'm afraid there's nothing I can do to placate him.*

• **propitiate** to calm someone who might hurt you by sacrificing something to him or her. (Formal.) □ *The villagers propitiated the storm god by sacrificing a small animal.* □ *Eddie gave his bicycle to his big brother in an attempt to propitiate him.*

appetite See the entry for *hunger.*

applaud See the entries for *cheer, praise.*

apply See the entry for *use.*

appointment See the entry for *date¹.*

appreciate See the entry for *like.*

apprehend See the entries for *capture, understand.*

apprehensive See the entry for *uneasy.*

approach (*verb*) to get nearer and nearer something. □ *As we approached the mansion, we could see that all the windows had been broken.* □ *Do you recognize the man who is approaching us?*

• **come close to** to *approach*; to almost do or reach something. □ *When we saw familiar landmarks, we knew we were coming close to home.* □ *The car came close to hitting the tree.*

• **draw near** to *approach*; to come as close as possible. □ *Only when we drew near the store did we realize that it was closed.* □ *All of Kay's children drew near her to comfort her.*

• **near** to *approach*; to come near. (Formal.) (See also the main entry for *near.*) □ *Linda felt more and more desperate as the deadline neared.* □ *As Mary neared the house, she sensed that all was not well.*

appropriate See the entries for *proper, take.*

approve (*verb*) to think or say that something is satisfactory. (Sometimes with *of.*) □ *The teacher approved Tom's idea for building a model of the pyramids.* □ *Sue does not approve of men wearing earrings.*

• **endorse** to *approve* something publicly; to tell the public you support something. □ *The mayor endorses the plan to build a bridge over the river.* □ *The company wanted a rock star to endorse their product in a TV commercial.*

• **OK** to *approve* something officially. (Slang.) □ *Before I take a week's vacation, I have to get the boss to OK it.* □ *The phone company OKed my putting in a new phone.*

• **sanction**   to *approve* something officially or legally; to authorize something. (Formal.) □ *This new law sanctions the construction of new buildings within city limits.* □ *The government does not sanction the buying and selling of endangered animals.*

apt   See the entry for *likely.*

aptitude   See the entry for *talent.*

aqueous   See the entry for *liquid.*

arbitrary   See the entries for *random, unfair.*

arbitrate   See the entry for *mediate.*

archaic   See the entry for *old-fashioned.*

ardent   See the entry for *dedicated.*

ardor   See the entry for *enthusiasm.*

area   (*noun*) a space; a piece of ground. □ *I want to build a house in this open area.* □ *This map shows the area where the ruins were found.*
• **neighborhood**   the *area* near something. □ *The shoe repair shop is somewhere in the neighborhood of the post office.* □ *Philip moved to a new house in the neighborhood of his old apartment.*
• **region**   any *area;* an *area* with specific boundaries, such as a country or a state. □ *Wildlife is abundant in this region.* □ *The people of that region are famous for their style of cooking.*
• **vicinity**   the *area* around something. □ *There are several good restaurants in the vicinity of the movie theater.* □ *The police questioned everyone who was in the vicinity when the crime occurred.*
[→see also: *place*]

argue¹   (*verb*) to talk about both sides of an issue. □ *John and Susan argued the question of whether the minimum wage should be raised.* □ *Both lawyers argued the case very well.*
• **debate**   to *argue* in a formal, orderly way. □ *Tonight, the presidential candidates will debate the issue of public housing.* □ *We must debate what to do about this crisis.*
• **deliberate**   to *argue* carefully and in a reasoned way. □ *The contest judges deliberated for a long time before coming to a decision.* □ *Tim and Jan never just turn on the TV; they always deliberate about what to watch.*
• **discuss**   to *argue* calmly and conversationally. □ *Dad is willing to discuss raising my allowance.* □ *If I have a problem, I usually discuss it with my friends.*

argue²   (*verb*) to fight verbally about an issue. □ *I hear my neighbors shouting at each other; they must be arguing again.* □ *Anna and Charlie seem to argue about every little thing.*

• **bicker**   to *argue* childishly; to *argue* about something unimportant. □ *Now they are bickering about who got the larger slice of cake.* □ *Yesterday they bickered about who should be the one to answer the phone.*

• **dispute**   to *argue;* especially, to *argue* passionately. (Formal.) □ *The opponents disputed hotly until someone intervened.* □ *Donald will dispute with anyone who denies his right to own a gun.*

• **quarrel**   to *argue* seriously or violently. □ *The two sisters love each other, but they can't seem to stop quarreling long enough to say so.* □ *Bob quarreled with his neighbors twenty years ago and hasn't spoken to them since.*

• **squabble**   to *argue* noisily about something unimportant. □ *Stop squabbling over whose turn it is and just play the game!* □ *On the lawn, a little group of sparrows squabbled over a hunk of bread.*

• **wrangle**   to *argue* noisily and angrily. (Usually with *over.*) □ *After their parents died, the brothers wrangled over which one of them should inherit the house.* □ *The two countries wrangled over a small piece of territory.*

argue³   (*verb*) to express an opinion and present facts in support of it. □ *The speaker argued against the existence of UFOs.* □ *The writer of the article argued that all third-graders should study Latin.*

• **assert**   to express an opinion forcefully. □ *The expert asserted that the painting was a forgery.* □ *Eddie asserts that his opponent is a liar.*

• **contend**   to express an opinion although someone opposes it. □ *The reporter contends that UFOs are extraterrestrial visitors.* □ *Fran claims that eating fish makes her smarter, but George contends that what you eat has nothing to do with how smart you are.*

• **maintain**   to hold on to an opinion even though someone opposes it. □ *I have heard all the opposing evidence, but I still maintain that Francis Bacon wrote all of Shakespeare's plays.* □ *Although her friends scoff at her, Fran maintains that eating fish three times a day will raise her IQ.*

aria   See the entry for *song.*

arid   See the entry for *dry.*

aristocratic   (*adjective*) upper-class; having high social rank. □ *Helen's aristocratic manners always impress people.* □ *Jay has an aristocratic taste for all the finer things in life.*

• **patrician**   coming from an *aristocratic* family. (Formal.) □ *Kevin's coarse behavior would have disgraced his patrician ancestors.* □ *Laura has such exquisite manners and speaks with such perfect grammar that I suspect she comes from a patrician background.*

• **refined**   having *aristocratic* manners and good taste. □ *Mary behaved very carefully at the tea party since she knew she was among very* *refined people.* □ *Tom's tastes were quite refined; he insisted on being surrounded by beautiful things.*

• **well-bred**   coming from an *aristocratic* family; showing good manners. □ *Philip is so well-bred that he never forgets to send thank-you notes.* □ *Well-bred children would never behave that way.*

aroma   See the entry for *smell.*

aroused   See the entry for *thrilled.*

arrange   (*verb*) to put something in order; to put something into a pattern. □ *I arranged the furniture in the living room so that it would be easier to see the TV.* □ *Stanley arranged the soda cans into a neat pyramid.*

• **adjust**   to *arrange* something so that everything fits; to move or change things so that they fit or work. □ *Tom adjusted the footstool until he could rest his feet on it comfortably.* □ *The mechanic adjusted a few screws, and the engine started running smoothly.*

• **order**   to *arrange* something in a sensible pattern. (See also the main entry for *order.*) □ *Jan ordered all the cans in her kitchen cupboard so she could find everything easily.* □ *I went through the file and ordered the letters according to when they had been received.*

• **organize**   to *arrange* something in a way that makes everything work well together. □ *I will have to organize all the clutter on my desk before I can get any work done.* □ *The woodcarver had organized all her tools and kept each one in its proper place.*

arrangement   See the entry for *pattern.*

arrest   See the entry for *capture.*

arrive   See the entry for *come.*

arrogant   See the entry for *conceited.*

article   See the entry for *thing.*

artificial   (*adjective*) not real; pretended. □ *Because they were filming a movie about the North Pole in the summertime, the filmmakers had to use artificial snow.* □ *Those aren't real flowers; they're artificial.*

• **affected**   deliberately *artificial;* pretended for effect. □ *Gayle's shyness is entirely affected; she's really a very bold person.* □ *Helen spoke in an affected, babyish way.*

• **assumed**   pretended for a particular purpose. □ *In the enemy country, the spy used a number of assumed names.* □ *Irene didn't want her friends to ask why she was upset, so she behaved with an assumed cheerfulness.*

• **contrived**   clumsily *artificial.* □ *Jill's reaction to the surprise party seemed awfully contrived.* □ *When I asked Kay why she was late to the party, she gave me some kind of contrived excuse.*

• **counterfeit**   *artificial* but pretending to be real. □ *The criminals planned to turn out thousands of dollars' worth of counterfeit coins.* □ *Experts disagree over whether the statue is counterfeit or genuine.* [→contrasting word: *genuine*]

ascend   See the entry for *climb.*

ascertain   See the entry for *learn¹.*

ask   (*verb*) to say something to someone in order to get information. □ *I need to ask someone how to get to the library.* □ *"What's for dessert?" Larry asked.*
   • **inquire**   to *ask.* (Formal.) □ *May I inquire where you purchased your hat?* □ *The investigator inquired if anyone had heard a disturbance.*
   • **interrogate**   to *ask* many questions systematically and thoroughly. □ *The police officers interrogated the suspect thoroughly.* □ *When I got home, Mom interrogated me about where I had been and whom I had been there with.*
   • **query**   to *ask;* to pose a question. (Formal.) □ *"Are you the head of the household?" the salesperson queried.* □ *Dad queried me as to my brother's whereabouts.*
   • **question**   to *ask* one thing after another; to *ask* because you are doubtful. □ *The detective questioned everyone who had seen the accident.* □ *I question Mary's motives for doing me this favor.*

ask for   (*verb*) to try to get something by saying that you want it. □ *Tom asked for a video game for his birthday.* □ *You can't expect people to give you something if you don't ask for it.*
   • **request**   to *ask for* something courteously and formally. □ *The neighbors requested us to keep the noise down.* □ *Several people in the audience requested their favorite songs.*
   • **requisition**   to *ask for* something officially. (Formal.) □ *The Navy requisitioned several new warships.* □ *My boss told me to requisition a new supply of ballpoint pens.*
   • **solicit**   to *ask for* something you need for a business or a cause. □ *Sue is soliciting donations for charity.* □ *Philip found he could not repair his car by himself, so he solicited the help of his friends.*

aspect   See the entry for *looks.*

aspirant   See the entry for *candidate.*

aspire to   See the entry for *hope.*

assail   See the entry for *attack.*

assassinate   See the entry for *kill.*

assault   See the entry for *attack.*

assemble   See the entries for *build, collect, get together.*

assent   See the entry for *agree.*

assert   See the entries for *argue³, claim.*

asset   See the entry for *benefit¹.*

assets   See the entry for *property.*

assignment   See the entry for *lesson.*

assimilate   See the entries for *absorb, learn².*

assist   See the entry for *help.*

associate   See the entry for *partner.*

association See the entry for *organization.*

assorted   (*adjective*) mixed; made up of many different kinds. □ *Please give me half a pound of assorted jellybeans.* □ *These mittens come in assorted colors.*
> • **diverse**   made up of many very different kinds. (Formal.) □ *The book contains pictures of the diverse wildlife on the island.* □ *The movie appealed to diverse groups of people.*
> • **miscellaneous**   made up of many different kinds all mixed together. □ *The menu listed tea, milk, and miscellaneous soft drinks.* □ *The library has ten thousand books and a few miscellaneous videotapes.*
> • **various**   made up of different kinds. □ *Roger tried various headache remedies, but none of them seemed to help.* □ *The coach led us through various different exercises.*

assume   (*verb*) to think that something is true even though you have not checked it out. □ *I assume that Mom will get home from work at the usual time.* □ *Because Susan had stolen things in the past, everyone assumed she had stolen the money.*
> • **presume**   to *assume* something before you know any facts. □ *Nobody asked if I knew how to drive; they just presumed that I could.* □ *I presume that everyone here knows who George Washington was.*
> • **suppose**   to *assume* something, especially for the purpose of an argument. □ *Suppose that Susan did steal the money; what could she have done with it?* □ *When I heard the door open, I supposed that Mom had come home.*
> • **take for granted**   to *assume* something firmly and unquestioningly. (Informal.) □ *Tommy took it for granted that he would always be the best student in the class.* □ *Jan took for granted that her friends would like her no matter what she did.*

assumed   See the entry for *artificial.*

assure   See the entry for *promise*.

assured   See the entry for *certain*.

astonish   See the entry for *surprise*.

astound   See the entry for *surprise*.

astute   See the entry for *wise*.

at ease   See the entry for *comfortable*.

at peace   See the entry for *content*.

athletic   See the entry for *strong*.

atom   See the entry for *whit*.

atrocious   (*adjective*) extremely bad, cruel, or evil; very bad or unpleasant. □ *We must punish the person who committed these atrocious murders.* □ *Anna's manners were thoroughly atrocious.*
   • **heinous**   *atrocious* and hateful. (Formal.) □ *The heinous crime shocked everyone.* □ *The doctor's heinous carelessness cost several people their lives.*
   • **monstrous**   *atrocious* and shocking. □ *I couldn't believe that a sweet old lady could do such a monstrous thing.* □ *Nothing could excuse the monstrous way those people treated their victim.*
   • **outrageous**   *atrocious* enough to cause anger. □ *Most people agreed that the discriminatory law was outrageous.* □ *The governor was found guilty of an outrageous abuse of power.*

attach   See the entry for *join*.

attack   (*verb*) to do something violent to someone, either physically or verbally. □ *The cat attacked the lizard and killed it.* □ *The newspaper article attacked the mayor, damaging her reputation.*
   • **assail**   to *attack* someone with repeated blows. (Formal.) □ *The boxer assailed his opponent with a shower of blows.* □ *A series of newspaper articles assailed the mayor's reputation.*
   • **assault**   to *attack* someone brutally or suddenly. □ *Someone sneaked up from behind Bob and assaulted him.* □ *Several people have been assaulted in that part of town.*
   • **fall upon**   to *attack* someone suddenly. (Old-fashioned.) □ *The wicked knight fell upon our hero and wounded him sorely.* □ *Bandits fell upon the traveler, beat him, and took everything he had.*
   • **have at**   to *attack* an opponent or a problem; to start *attacking* something. (Somewhat poetic.) □ *Sir Fred gave a battle cry and had at the Questing Beast.* □ *I've put off doing my homework for too long; I'd better have at it.*
   [→see also: *fight, battle*]

attain   See the entry for *achieve.*

attempt   See the entry for *try.*

attend   See the entries for *accompany, watch.*

attention   (*noun*) the ability to put your mind to something; the act of putting your mind to something. (Often used in the expression *to pay attention,* to put your mind to something.) □ *If you don't pay attention to the instructions, you won't be able to do this.* □ *It has come to my attention that Sylvia has not been doing the dishes when it is her turn.*
> • **concentration**   deep *attention.* □ *Even the softest sound could break the chess player's concentration.* □ *Tom has amazing powers of concentration; nothing seems to distract him.*
> • **focus**   careful, centered *attention.* □ *Nancy gave her whole focus to solving the math problem.* □ *Repairing watches requires dexterity and steady focus.*
> • **interest**   excited, curious *attention.* □ *The scandal captured everyone's interest.* □ *The cat's interest was attracted by the dangling string.*
> • **notice**   *attention* that is attracted suddenly; observation. (Formal. See also the main entry for *notice.*) □ *Philip's strange behavior escaped his friend's notice.* □ *The controversial book got plenty of public notice.*

attentive   See the entries for *alert, considerate.*

attire   See the entry for *clothing.*

attract   (*verb*) to influence someone or something to come toward you. □ *I've heard that red flowers attract hummingbirds.* □ *Rita's screams soon attracted a crowd.*
> • **allure**   to *attract* someone by offering something pleasant. □ *The health club allured people by promising that exercise would make them healthy and beautiful.* □ *The catalog allured customers with gorgeous pictures of the merchandise.*
> • **draw**   to *attract* someone strongly. (See also the main entry for *draw.*) □ *The ice-cream seller could draw all the children in the neighborhood just by ringing his bell.* □ *The popular movie drew enormous audiences.*
> • **entice**   to *attract* someone by making him or her hope for something; to lead someone on. (Formal.) □ *The delicious smells of cooking food enticed us into the restaurant.* □ *The spy enticed many important men to tell her their secrets.*
> • **lure**   to *attract* someone by fooling him or her. □ *The Venus flytrap lures flies inside it and then eats them.* □ *The possibility of winning millions of dollars lured many people into buying lottery tickets.*

attractive   See the entry for *cute.*

auburn   See the entry for *brown.*

audition   See the entry for *test*.

august   See the entry for *grand*.

auspicious   See the entry for *convenient*.

authentic   See the entry for *real*.

author   See the entry for *writer*.

authoritative   See the entry for *masterful*.

authority   (*noun*) someone who has legal power. (Usually used in the plural. See also the entry for *expert*.) □ *When I saw someone break into the house next door, I notified the authorities at once.* □ *The con artist soon got into trouble with the authorities.*

> • **administrator**   an *authority* in charge of managing something. □ *Mr. Black is the administrator in charge of this department.* □ *An administrator must make hundreds of decisions every day.*
>
> • **bureaucrat**   an *authority* who holds an office; often, an *authority* who cares more for following the rules than for getting anything done. □ *The high-ranking bureaucrat had to resign her office because of rumors that she had been stealing from the company.* □ *The bureaucrat at the motor vehicles office refused to give me a driver's license because I didn't have all the right signatures on my application.*
>
> • **executive**   an *authority* in charge of running something. □ *The chief executive of the company decided to hire six new managers.* □ *Carrie started out as a file clerk, but was steadily promoted until she became an executive.*
>
> • **higher-up**   an important *authority;* an *authority* in a superior position. (Informal.) □ *I wanted to go on vacation this week, but some higher-up decided that I shouldn't.* □ *I have to ask the higher-ups for permission for anything I do.*
>
> • **official**   a government or business *authority*. □ *An important official in the mayor's office has told the press that the mayor will not run for reelection.* □ *The company officials must vote in order to make any big changes in company policy.*

authorize   See the entry for *allow*.

autocrat   (*noun*) a ruler with unlimited power. (Formal.) □ *Dad is the autocrat in our household; we have to do everything he wants.* □ *The elected ruler took on more and more powers until he was, for all practical purposes, an autocrat.*

> • **despot**   a ruthless *autocrat*, especially one of royal blood. (Formal.) □ *The rebels planned to overthrow the despot and take over the country themselves.* □ *After the queen had all her opponents murdered, her people regarded her as a despot.*

• **dictator** a cruel *autocrat,* not of royal blood. ☐ *The dictator did not care how badly the citizens suffered, as long as he had everything he wanted.* ☐ *Secret police worked for the dictator, ferreting out all the plots against him.*

• **tyrant** a cruel or brutal *autocrat.* (Poetic.) ☐ *Everyone in the country was a slave to the evil tyrant.* ☐ *The nobles banded together and planned to assassinate the tyrant.*

automated See the entry for *automatic².*

automatic¹ (*adjective*) done without thinking or without being aware of doing it. ☐ *Fluffing up his tail is my cat's automatic response to being frightened.* ☐ *When anyone says, "How are you?" Frank gives the automatic reply, "Fine, and you?"*

• **instinctive** done without thinking about it; done because it is the natural thing to do. ☐ *The cat's instinctive strategy is to run away from danger.* ☐ *Some birds have an instinctive ability to find their way home.*

• **involuntary** done without wanting or meaning to do it. ☐ *I gave an involuntary shudder when I stepped inside the cold, dark room.* ☐ *I heard George's involuntary gasp when the cold shower hit him.*

• **knee-jerk** done without thinking about it. (Informal.) ☐ *Whenever Grandpa sees someone driving badly, his knee-jerk response is that it must be a woman.* ☐ *Joe's knee-jerk reaction is to try to help anyone who's in trouble.*

• **reflex** done without being conscious of doing it. ☐ *When the doctor tapped my knee, my leg swung in a reflex motion.* ☐ *Harold hits back immediately when anyone hits him; it's almost reflex behavior with him.*

• **spontaneous** done suddenly and without thinking about it. ☐ *Irene was so excited that she gave a spontaneous yell.* ☐ *The actors enjoyed the children's spontaneous reaction to their performance.*

automatic² (*adjective*) done by a machine that can move by itself. ☐ *Just pop a potato in the automatic french-fry machine, and french fries come out the other side!* ☐ *Kay thinks that the cars of the future will be entirely automatic; you won't even need to steer them.*

• **automated** entirely *automatic.* ☐ *The factory is almost completely automated; only a few people work there, and all they do is oversee the machines.* ☐ *Laura has an automated phone that dials the numbers for her.*

• **mechanized** *automatic,* although formerly done by people; machine-like and monotonous. ☐ *There are no announcers at this modern, mechanized radio station, only tape machines that play the music.* ☐ *Mary had a very mechanized daily routine that never changed in the slightest.*

• **push-button**   so *automatic* that you only have to push a button to make it work. (Informal.) □ *The saleswoman demonstrated the easy, push-button operation of the microwave oven.* □ *The tailor delighted in his new push-button sewing machine.*

automobile   See the entry for *vehicle.*

autonomous   See the entry for *independent.*

average   (*adjective*) typical; true of most people or things. □ *How many children does the average family have?* □ *My school was no better or worse than most other schools; it was about average.*

• **common**   average; often seen; not special in any way. □ *Sparrows and starlings are very common birds in most cities.* □ *Cats and dogs are the most common house pets.*

• **normal**   average; not strange in any way. □ *Jane may throw a lot of tantrums, but that's normal for a two-year-old.* □ *Eddie was a normal child; no one could guess that he would be a genius when he grew up.*

• **ordinary**   average; everyday; not different in any way. □ *Nothing exciting happened today; it's been an ordinary day.* □ *The new neighbors seem like ordinary people.*

• **regular**   average; habitual. □ *I had my regular lunch: a cheese sandwich and a bowl of tomato soup.* □ *The tornado certainly interrupted our regular routine.*

• **usual**   average, familiar, or habitual. □ *Let's not go to the usual place for summer vacation; let's go somewhere different.* □ *My usual doctor is on vacation, so I'll have to get an appointment with someone else.*

avid   See the entry for *dedicated.*

avidity   See the entry for *enthusiasm.*

avoid   (*verb*) to keep from coming into contact with someone or something. □ *Avoid getting the shampoo in your eyes; it really stings!* □ *Fran seems to leave the room whenever I come in; I think she's trying to avoid me.*

• **keep away from**   to *avoid* something; to stay away from something. (Informal.) □ *Keep away from the fire so you don't get burned.* □ *Keep away from George; he's in a bad mood.*

• **shun**   to *avoid* someone or something. (Formal.) □ *Mr. Jones shunned anyplace where he might meet his former wife.* □ *Everyone who had heard the rumor about Ida began to shun her.*

• **steer clear of**   to *avoid* something entirely. □ *Mama taught me to steer clear of any kind of gambling.* □ *You'd better steer clear of Jay; he's got a bad reputation.*

[→see also: *bypass, dodge*]

away   See the entry for *missing.*

awesome   *(adjective)* causing you to feel wonder and fear. □ *The evil magician had awesome powers.* □ *When we reached the top of the hill, we saw an awesome sight below: the entire city had been destroyed.*
* **formidable**   awesome and difficult to overcome. (Formal.) □ *Rebuilding the city was a formidable task.* □ *In this issue, the superhero will meet his most formidable enemy yet.*
* **impressive**   great and awesome; making you feel impressed. □ *The army gave an impressive show of force.* □ *Kay wrote a very impressive computer program.*
* **intimidating**   awesome; causing you to feel small and helpless. □ *The new teacher's appearance was quite intimidating.* □ *Several intimidating guards and fences stood between the prisoners and freedom.*

awful   *(adjective)* very bad. □ *Who's making that awful noise?* □ *The cafeteria food was just awful.*
* **dreadful**   frightening and awful; very bad or unpleasant; causing great dread. □ *The villain gave a dreadful scream as he fell off the cliff.* □ *After the earthquake, the house was a dreadful mess.*
* **horrible**   shockingly awful. □ *The movie was so horrible that I couldn't stand to watch the whole thing.* □ *Nancy makes horrible threats but never carries them out.*
* **terrible**   awful; very unpleasant. □ *I spent the weekend with my uncle and had a terrible time.* □ *That barber did a terrible job of cutting my hair.*

awkward   See the entry for *clumsy.*

awry   See the entry for *crooked.*

azure   See the entry for *blue.*

B

babble (*verb*) to talk rapidly and without making any sense. □ *Sue ran into the room, babbling something about an explosion.* □ *The baby babbled happily, and all the grown-ups babbled back at her.*
- **fume** to *babble* angrily. □ *Philip can't seem to stop fuming about the rude way he was treated.* □ *It won't do any good to fume about it; why not write a formal letter of complaint?*
- **prate** to *babble* on and on; to *babble* boastfully. (Formal.) □ *What's he prating about now?* □ *Here comes Mrs. Hall, prating about all the great things her kids have done.*
- **rant** to talk loudly and in a way that attracts attention. □ *Rita was embarrassed by the way her boyfriend kept ranting about the football game.* □ *Dad ranted about my bad behavior for two solid hours.*
- **rave** to talk crazily and wildly. (See also the main entry for *rave.*) □ *Don't pay any attention to Susan; she's just raving and isn't making any sense at all.* □ *Tom, nearly hysterical, raved that everyone hated him and that he wanted to kill them all.*

baby See the entry for *spoil¹*.

backer See the entry for *supporter.*

backslide See the entry for *revert.*

bad (*adjective*) not good; of low quality. □ *Something in the refrigerator smells bad.* □ *I liked the plot of the movie, but the acting was bad.*
- **lousy** quite *bad.* (Slang.) □ *Jan's in a lousy mood today.* □ *I was in such a hurry that I did a really lousy job.*
- **vile** disgustingly *bad.* □ *That's the most vile book I've ever read.* □ *The coffee looked disgusting and tasted vile.*
- **wretched** extremely *bad.* □ *Bill had stomach flu and felt wretched.* □ *The weather has been wretched all week; the sun hasn't come out once.*
[→see also: *awful*]

bad-mouth   See the entry for *slander*.

badland   See the entry for *wilderness*.

baffle   See the entry for *puzzle*.

bag   (*noun*) a thing made of flexible material and used to carry things in; in particular, a suitcase or a purse. □ *The clerk put my groceries in a bag.* □ *The photographer carries his equipment in a leather bag.* □ *Rose packed her bag and called a taxi.*
> • **case**   a *bag* made of rigid material. (See also the main entry for *case*.) □ *I put my guitar into the case and latched it shut.* □ *The typewriter fitted neatly into its case.*
> • **pack**   a *bag* that can contain many things; a *bag* that you can carry on your back. (See also the main entry for *pack*.) □ *I rolled up my sleeping bag and jammed it into my pack.* □ *The peddler's pack contained everything from saucepans to hair ribbons.*
> • **pouch**   a small *bag*. □ *Kathy carries her money in a little pouch she wears around her neck.* □ *Jenny kept the silver spoons in a special cloth pouch.*
> • **sack**   a large *bag*; a paper *bag*. □ *It takes a whole sack full of grass seed to cover our front lawn.* □ *They carried the sacks of groceries upstairs to their apartment.*

bait   See the entry for *tease*.

bake   See the entry for *cook*.

balance   See the entry for *rest*.

ballad   See the entry for *song*.

band   See the entries for *stripe, team*.

bang   See the entries for *clash, pound*.

banner   See the entry for *flag*.

bar   See the entries for *block, forbid, stripe*.

barbecue   See the entry for *cook*.

barbed   See the entry for *pointed*.

barely   (*adverb*) only just. □ *The settlers had barely enough food to survive the winter.* □ *Laura was so dirty that I could barely recognize her.*
> • **hardly**   barely; almost not. □ *Don't scream so loud; I hardly touched you.* □ *Mark isn't my friend; on the contrary, I hardly know him.*
> • **scarcely**   barely; not quite. (Formal.) □ *Nancy is scarcely ever permitted to stay awake till midnight.* □ *There are so many things to do that I scarcely know which to do first.*

• **slightly**   *barely;* only to a small degree. □ *The tabletop is slightly scratched.* □ *Sue opened her eyes slightly.*

bargain   (*verb*) to discuss back and forth in order to reach an agreement about something; usually, to discuss what you think the price of something should be. (Usually with *with.*) □ *Philip bargained with the car salesman until they agreed on a price.* □ *Roger had to bargain with the teacher to get a passing grade.*
 • **dicker**   to *bargain* in a quarrelsome way; to *bargain* over something unimportant. □ *The vendor and I dickered for fifteen minutes, and I finally got him to reduce the price by a few cents.* □ *Susan and Jane are dickering over whose turn it is.*
 • **haggle**   to *bargain* aggressively. □ *You have to haggle with the vegetable sellers if you want to get a good price.* □ *Vivian likes to haggle to see if she can get things cheap.*
 • **make a deal**   to *bargain;* to make a promise. (The former is slang; the latter is informal.) □ *The criminal tried to make a deal with the police officers.* □ *I'll make a deal with you. You do my laundry, and I'll wash the dishes for you.*
 • **negotiate**   to *bargain* formally or reasonably; to meet with someone in order to *bargain.* □ *Andrew tried to negotiate with Steve to see if he could get him to change his mind.* □ *The diplomats met to negotiate an end to the war.*

barge   See the entry for *boat.*

bark   See the entry for *snarl.*

barrel   (*noun*) a large container shaped like a drum or a cylinder. □ *The farmer collected rain water in a barrel.* □ *The general store sold barrels of flour.*
 • **cask**   a *barrel.* (Old-fashioned.) □ *Samuel invited us to drink from a cask of rare wine.* □ *The sailors opened their last cask of water.*
 • **hogshead**   a large *barrel.* (Old-fashioned.) □ *The guests at the king's feast drank mugs of mead.* □ *The host ordered a hogshead of the best wine to be opened.*
 • **keg**   a medium-sized *barrel;* often, a *barrel* for containing beer. □ *Along with the wine, the feasters consumed many kegs of beer and ale.* □ *On my way home from work, I picked up a keg of beer for the party.*

barricade   See the entry for *barrier.*

barrier   (*noun*) something that keeps you from going ahead. □ *The construction workers put up a barrier to keep traffic out of the street.* □ *The fallen rock formed a barrier across the tunnel.*
 • **barricade**   a *barrier* that someone puts up deliberately. □ *The revolutionaries erected a barricade and fired at the soldiers from behind it.* □ *We made our furniture into a barricade across the doorway.*

• **blockade**   a *barrier* that someone puts up around an enemy. □ *Ships could not get through the blockade around the coastline.* □ *The smuggler brought food through the blockade.*

• **obstacle**   a *barrier;* anything that makes it difficult for you to go ahead. □ *I didn't see the large obstacle until my car hit it.* □ *Charlie's objections formed an obstacle to my plan.*

• **obstruction**   a *barrier* across your way. □ *The obstruction in the storm drain was composed of dead leaves and twigs.* □ *There's some kind of obstruction in Donald's lungs that makes it hard for him to breathe.*

barter   See the entry for *trade.*

base   See the entry for *bottom.*

bash   See the entry for *party.*

bashful   See the entry for *shy.*

baste   See the entry for *sew.*

batch   See the entry for *group.*

bathe   See the entry for *clean².*

batter   See the entries for *beat¹, pound.*

battle   See the entry for *fight.*

bauble   See the entry for *jewel.*

bawl   See the entry for *cry.*

be anxious   See the entry for *worry.*

be attired in   See the entry for *wear.*

be clothed in   See the entry for *wear.*

be contingent   See the entry for *depend.*

be dubious about   See the entry for *doubt.*

be fond of   See the entry for *like.*

be partial to   See the entry for *prefer.*

be sorry   (*verb*) to wish you had not done something; to wish that something were not happening. (Often with *for* in the former case.) □ *Eddie called to tell me he was sorry for being rude.* □ *I'm sorry that you're not feeling well.*

• **lament**   to say that you *are sorry* about something. (Formal.) □ *The magazine article lamented the disappearance of the rain forests.* □ *"I wish I hadn't spent my money so carelessly," Helen lamented.*

• **regret** to feel bad because you *are sorry for (or about)* something. □ *Fran soon regretted her temper tantrum.* □ *George regretted having to fire his employee.*

• **repent** to *be sorry for* something and never want to do it again. (Often with *of.*) (Formal.) □ *Irene repented her former wild lifestyle.* □ *The murderer repented of his crime.*

be victorious See the entry for *win.*

beam See the entry for *smile.*

bear (*verb*) to accept something; to not oppose something; to put up with something. □ *How can you bear that constant noise?* □ *Jim bore the pain of his injury quietly and bravely.*

• **abide** to *bear* something patiently. (Usually in negative phrases like *can't abide something* or *won't abide something.*) (Formal.) □ *Dad can't abide dirt on the carpet.* □ *Kay loves old TV shows, but Laura can't abide them.*

• **endure** to *bear* something for a long time. □ *All week long, Mark had to endure his friends teasing him.* □ *It was difficult for Nancy to endure her sudden poverty.*

• **stand** to *bear* something successfully; to *bear* something at all. (Informal.) □ *Philip could stand having a blood sample taken, but he couldn't stand getting a shot.* □ *I can't stand the way he treats me.*

• **suffer** to *bear* something even though it causes you pain; to allow something to happen. (Somewhat old-fashioned.) □ *Why should I suffer such outrageous treatment?* □ *Rita suffered her friends to treat her like a fool.*

• **tolerate** to *bear* something. (Formal.) □ *The teacher would not tolerate gum-chewing in her classroom.* □ *I don't enjoy classical music, but I can tolerate it.*

• **withstand** to *bear* something; to survive something difficult. □ *The farmer's family withstood the cruel winter.* □ *They feared that the fragile young garden plants could not withstand the harsh weather.*

beast See the entry for *animal.*

beat[1] (*verb*) to hit someone or something over and over again. □ *Beating the dog won't teach her to obey.* □ *The bully beat Stanley with a club.*

• **batter** to *beat* someone or something rapidly and violently. □ *Baseball-sized hail battered the car as it drove through the storm.* □ *Someone jumped me from behind and began to batter me with his fists.*

• **buffet** to *beat* someone or something; to slap someone or something over and over again. □ *Fierce winds buffeted the flimsy island hut.* □ *Our hero buffeted the evil knight with the flat of his sword.*

• **pelt** to *beat* someone or something; to throw things at someone or something over and over again. ☐ *Cold rain pelted me as I stepped out the door.* ☐ *The class pelted the substitute teacher with wads of paper.*

• **pummel** to *beat* someone or something very hard. ☐ *Stanley tripped the bully and began to pummel him when he fell.* ☐ *Jane was so frustrated that she began to pummel her desk.*

[→see also: *hit*]

beat² (*verb*) to win against your opponent; to get the better of your opponent. (Informal.) ☐ *The home team beat the visitors by six runs.* ☐ *Surprisingly, the unknown candidate beat the incumbent senator.*

• **conquer** to *beat* someone powerfully; to use force to *beat* someone. ☐ *The invading army soon conquered the country.* ☐ *It will be difficult to conquer such a powerful foe.*

• **defeat** to *beat* someone. (Formal.) ☐ *The football team was defeated, 21–7.* ☐ *Government troops finally defeated the invading army in a decisive battle.*

• **overcome** to *beat* someone or something after a difficult fight. ☐ *Through dedication, hard work, and good luck, Bill overcame the poverty he was born into.* ☐ *Betty tried to overcome her shyness by forcing herself to go out and meet people.*

• **triumph over** to *beat* someone or something gloriously and decisively. ☐ *The general announced that his army had triumphed over the enemy.* ☐ *The basketball team triumphed over its long-standing rival.*

• **trounce** to *beat* someone quickly and overwhelmingly. ☐ *The football team was trounced, 42-0.* ☐ *The candidate trounced her opponent, who only got fifteen votes.*

[→see also: *win*]

beautiful (*adjective*) very pleasant to look at. ☐ *The flowers in Henry's garden are very beautiful this year.* ☐ *Donna has beautiful eyes.*

• **comely** physically *beautiful;* handsome. (Formal.) ☐ *All the young men in town agreed that Helen was a comely lass.* ☐ *She has a comely face, but she frowns too much.*

[→contrasting word: *ugly*]

• **gorgeous** *beautiful* and splendid. ☐ *The movie star wore a gorgeous diamond necklace.* ☐ *She lives in a gorgeous house with twelve bedrooms.*

• **lovely** *beautiful,* graceful, and appealing. ☐ *What a lovely statue!* ☐ *Eddie has such lovely handwriting.*

• **pretty** *beautiful* and charming. ☐ *Fran has a pretty smile; it lights up her whole face.* ☐ *George has a pet finch, a pretty little bird.*

beckon See the entry for *signal.*

before (*preposition*) earlier; preceding in time or in order. ☐ *Give me a call before you come over.* ☐ *We lived in Texas before we moved here.*

• **formerly**   before; in the past. □ *Formerly, Irene was a secretary, but now she is a teacher.* □ *Joe formerly served in the Marines.*
• **previous to**   before; at an earlier time than. □ *What jobs have you held previous to this one?* □ *Susan wanted to finish her education previous to starting a family.*
• **prior to**   before; up until. □ *Prior to the accident, Rita was a talented athlete.* □ *I always check my tire pressures prior to taking a long car trip.*

beg   (*verb*) to ask humbly for something; to ask for something as a favor. □ *Cinderella begged her stepmother to allow her to go to the ball.* □ *Tom begged me to lend him ten dollars.*
• **beseech**   to *beg* anxiously and desperately. (Formal.) □ *The prisoner beseeched her jailors to let her go.* □ *I beseech you not to hurt my children.*
• **entreat**   to *beg* desperately. (Formal.) □ *The criminal was on his knees, entreating the judge for mercy.* □ *The starving man entreated his neighbors for food.*
• **implore**   to *beg* urgently. (Formal.) □ *I implore you to help me before it's too late!* □ *Bill implored his mother to forgive him before she died.*
• **petition**   to *beg* formally; to ask for something formally. □ *Many groups petitioned Congress not to declare war.* □ *The employees got together and petitioned for a raise.*
• **plead**   to *beg* very emotionally. (Usually with *with*.) □ *Art, with tears streaming down his face, pleaded with us not to sell the house.* □ *"Please, please, don't sell the house," he pleaded.*
[→see also: *ask for*]

begin   (*verb*) to take the first step in doing something; to start. □ *When Ben heard the gunshot, he began to run.* □ *Carrie began taking flute lessons when she was ten years old.* □ *School will begin next Tuesday.*
• **commence**   to *begin.* (Formal.) □ *The meeting will commence promptly at three o'clock.* □ *When everyone is seated, you may commence taking the test.*
• **initiate**   to *begin;* to take the very first step; to get something started. (Formal.) □ *We will initiate this meeting by calling the roll.* □ *Donald has initiated a new business.*
• **set out**   to *begin* a project or a trip. (Sometimes with *upon.*) □ *The Wright brothers set out to build a flying machine.* □ *Early in the morning, Edith set out upon her journey.*
• **start**   to *begin;* to *begin* working; to make something, like a machine, *begin* working. □ *Fran started knitting a sweater yesterday.* □ *The lawn mower won't start.* □ *It's so cold that I can't start the car.*
[→see also: *launch*]

behavior   (*noun*) the way you act. □ *Dad praised us for our good behavior.* □ *George had no excuse for his rude behavior.*

• **conduct**   the way you usually act; the way you act in a particular situation. □ *Her conduct throughout the trial has been exceptional.* □ *Helen's outrageous conduct must be punished.*

• **deportment**   the way you usually act; the way you carry yourself. (Formal.) □ *The school trained all its students in good deportment.* □ *The young man's deportment clearly showed that he was educated, well-bred, and somewhat proud.*

• **manners**   the way you act when you are with other people; your ability to follow the rules for being polite. □ *It's not good manners to interrupt people.* □ *Kathy learned her elegant table manners by watching what her elegant friends did at meals.*

behindhand   See the entry for *late.*

being   See the entry for *animal.*

belabor   See the entry for *stress².*

belief   See the entry for *idea.*

believe¹   (*verb*) to be sure that something is true. □ *Carl believes that there is life on other planets.* □ *Donna believes everything she reads in the paper.*

• **hold**   to *believe* something firmly. □ *My parents held that children should not speak until spoken to, and that was how they brought me up.* □ *The English teacher holds that Shakespeare was the greatest writer that ever lived.*

• **maintain**   to continue to *believe* something. □ *Despite his friends' scoffing, Eddie maintained that his house was haunted.* □ *Throughout her whole life, Grandma maintained that eating six apples a day kept her healthy.*

• **think**   to *believe* something because you have considered it carefully. (See also the main entry for *think.*) □ *I think that most TV programs are silly.* □ *Fran thinks it's dangerous to talk on the phone during a thunderstorm.*

believe²   (*verb*) to feel that something is true; to feel that someone is telling you the truth. □ *George believes in reincarnation.* □ *I believe Susan when she says she didn't steal the money.*

• **credit**   to feel that something is likely to be true. (Formal.) □ *I can't credit the rumors that say that Susan is the culprit.* □ *Helen heard that the president was going to resign, but she could not credit it.*

• **have faith**   to feel that something is true or good even though you may not have any proof. (Sometimes with *in.*) □ *I have faith that Jim will get well eventually.* □ *Kay has faith in Laura's ability to solve the problem.*

• **trust**   to feel that something is true; to feel sure that something will happen. (See also the main entry for *trust*.) □ *I trust that the coming new year will be better than the old.* □ *Irene trusted her sister's advice.*

believe in   See the entry for *trust*.

belittle   See the entry for *ridicule*.

belligerent   (*adjective*) unfriendly and eager to fight; fond of fighting. □ *The belligerent watchdog snapped at anyone who walked by.* □ *Larry, who was in a belligerent mood, started punching Mark for no reason at all.*
• **combative**   ready and eager to fight. (Formal.) □ *The combative stranger challenged our hero to a fencing match.* □ *Nancy has a strong combative streak and will fight on the least excuse.*
• **contentious**   irritatingly fond of fighting or arguing. □ *The contentious old man picked a fight with the waiter.* □ *Sue isn't usually contentious, but today she's arguing with everyone.*
• **pugnacious**   fond of fighting. (Formal.) □ *Ralph's pugnacious spirit makes it impossible for him to walk away from a fight.* □ *"Just try and make me!" was Steve's pugnacious answer.*
• **quarrelsome**   eager to fight or argue about anything, even unimportant things. □ *The quarrelsome brothers seem to argue all the time.* □ *The waiter was feeling quarrelsome and answered the customer rudely.*

bellow   See the entry for *yell*.

belly   See the entry for *stomach*.

bellyache   See the entry for *complain*.

belongings   See the entry for *property*.

below   (*preposition*) lower than; at a lower level than. □ *Put that book on the shelf below the dictionary.* □ *The plane flew below the clouds.*
• **beneath**   directly *below*; covered by. □ *The marble rolled beneath the table.* □ *The floor beneath the carpet had not been swept.*
• **under**   *below*; less than. □ *Sam hid under the bed.* □ *We can drive to Maggie's house in under three hours.*
• **underneath**   directly *below*; covered by. □ *I found the book I wanted underneath a pile of other books.* □ *Tom burrowed underneath the covers.*

bemoan   See the entry for *grieve*.

bend   See the entry for *bow*.

beneath   See the entry for *below*.

Benedict Arnold   See the entry for *traitor*.

beneficent   See the entry for *generous*.

benefit[1] (*noun*) something that is good or helpful to you. □ *One benefit of owning a dog is that it can warn you of intruders.* □ *There are many benefits to regular exercise.*

• **advantage** something that is helpful to you. □ *Jan's long legs gave her an advantage in running races.* □ *Being able to speak French was a real advantage for Bill when he was traveling in Canada.*

• **asset** something that you have that is valuable. □ *Art's ability to type proved to be an asset when he was looking for a job.* □ *Mary is cheerful and enjoys meeting people, which is an asset in her work as a nurse.*

• **boon** something that is good for you; something that is very useful or helpful. (Formal.) □ *Strangely enough, the death of Charlie's uncle turned out to be a boon, because he left Charlie a great deal of money.* □ *The new computer system was a real boon to all the employees; it helped them work much more efficiently.*

benefit[2] (*verb*) to be good for someone or something; to get something that is good for you. □ *Growing up on a farm benefited Leroy; it taught him to work hard.* □ *Donald's grades benefited from all the hours he spent studying.*

• **gain** to get something that is good for you; to end up having more than when you started. □ *Eddie's friend convinced him that, in the long run, he would not really gain anything by stealing.* □ *By helping his neighbor, Fred gained a friend.*

• **profit** to get something that is good for you; to make money. (Usually with *from.*) □ *George profited immensely from going to summer school; not only did he learn new skills, he met many new friends.* □ *Helen didn't think that selling her business would profit her very much.*

• **serve** to be helpful to someone or something. □ *Mom's advice served me well when I left home and started out on my own.* □ *The old car had served Irene very well, and she was sorry to see it go.*

benign See the entry for *harmless.*

bent See the entry for *crooked.*

berate See the entry for *scold.*

beseech See the entry for *beg.*

bestow See the entry for *give.*

betray (*verb*) to tell a secret someone trusted you with; to tell a bad thing someone did; to turn someone in. □ *Jay betrayed Kay's trust; he told her secret to everyone.* □ *Larry betrayed his own brother to the police.*

• **rat on** to *betray* someone to the authorities. (Slang.) □ *Give me that candy bar, or I'll rat on you to the teacher.* □ *When he saw the police coming, the criminal knew that someone must have ratted on him.*

• **report**   to turn someone in; to *betray* someone to the authorities, especially secretly. □ *Morris begged the teacher not to report him to the principal.* □ *Someone reported Nancy for having too many cats in her apartment.*

• **squeal on**   to *betray* someone to the authorities, either because you have been threatened or because you expect a reward. (Slang.) □ *I won't squeal on my buddies, no matter what you do to me!* □ *The police offered to let the thief go free if he would squeal on the other members of the gang.*

• **tell on**   to *betray* someone to the authorities. (Juvenile.) □ *If you don't stop making fun of the teacher, I'm going to tell on you!* □ *My sister told on me for drawing on the wall with crayons.*

better   See the entry for *improve*.

bewilder   See the entry for *confuse*.

biased   See the entry for *unfair*.

bicker   See the entry for *argue²*.

big   (*adjective*) of great size. □ *We bought a big box of popcorn and ate it through the whole movie.* □ *Fourteen people sat around the big table.*

• **enormous**   unusually *big*. □ *Dinosaurs were enormous animals.* □ *Colleen baked an enormous batch of brownies for the party.*

• **giant**   very *big*; as big as a giant. □ *The giant oak tree was hundreds of years old.* □ *A giant map of the United States covered one wall of the room.*

• **gigantic**   extremely *big*; as *big* as a giant. □ *Gigantic waves crashed against the shore.* □ *A gigantic boulder tumbled down from the top of the cliff.*

• **huge**   extremely *big*. □ *A huge smile broke across Cindy's face.* □ *Mary has a huge collection of photographs.*

• **immense**   *big*, high, or broad. (Formal.) □ *Immense clouds began to gather on the horizon.* □ *The police searched an immense area, trying to find the lost boy.*

• **large**   *big*; ample. □ *The house was large enough for ten people.* □ *A large crowd gathered to watch the juggler perform.*

[→contrasting word: *small*]

bijou   See the entry for *jewel*.

billow   See the entry for *wave*.

bind   (*noun*) a choice between two unpleasant options; a difficult situation. (Informal.) □ *Tom got himself into a bind, promising to be at Sue's party when he had already said he would go to Phil's that evening.* □ *I'm* *in a real bind; I've burned the main course and my guests will be arriving any minute!*

   • **dilemma**   a choice between two unpleasant options. ☐ *Roger's dilemma was that he had to choose between telling a lie and offending his family.* ☐ *The two TV shows I really want to see are both on at the same time. What a dilemma!*

   • **predicament**   a difficult situation; a problem. ☐ *Tom locked his keys in the car, which put him in quite a predicament.* ☐ *Jan's habit of spending more than she earned got her into many predicaments.*

   • **quandary**   a difficult and perplexing situation. ☐ *Susan was in a quandary about what to tell her parents.* ☐ *Since several of my friends were quarreling with each other, I was in a quandary over which ones to invite to the party.*

bite   (*verb*) to sink your teeth into something. ☐ *Andrew hungrily bit into the apple.* ☐ *The vicious dog bit the child.*

   • **chomp**   to *bite* deeply into something; to chew something. (Informal.) ☐ *Everyone chomped happily away at the fried chicken.* ☐ *The rat chomped into the piece of cheese.*

   • **nibble**   to *bite* something lightly and repeatedly. ☐ *Emily nibbled her cookie and sipped at her tea.* ☐ *The squirrel nibbled at the crust of bread.*

   • **nip**   to *bite*; to pinch something with your teeth. ☐ *The kitten nipped its brother's ear.* ☐ *The dog nipped my arm but didn't break the skin.*

[→see also: *chew*]

biting   See the entry for *sarcastic.*

bitter   See the entry for *sour.*

bizarre   See the entry for *peculiar.*

blackguard   See the entry for *villain.*

blame   (*verb*) to think or say that someone or something did something bad. ☐ *Why do you always blame me when something goes wrong?* ☐ *We blamed the rain for ruining the picnic.*

   • **accuse**   to *blame* someone publicly. (Usually with *of.*) ☐ *My boss accused me of stealing paper clips.* ☐ *Susan was accused of the murder, but I don't think she did it.*

   • **charge with**   to *blame* someone formally or legally. ☐ *They arrested Susan and charged her with murder in the first degree.* ☐ *"What crime are you charging me with?" she asked.*

   • **condemn**   to *blame* someone severely and seriously. (Sometimes with *for.*) ☐ *Don't condemn me until you've heard my side of the story.* ☐ *Helen's friends condemned her for walking out on her husband.*

• **hold responsible**   to *blame* someone and expect that person to fix whatever he or she did wrong. □ *I hold you responsible for the mess you made, and I expect you to clean it up.* □ *The Harrises held me responsible for anything that happened to their house while I was watching it for them.*

blameless   See the entry for *innocent.*

bland   See the entry for *mild¹.*

blandish   See the entry for *flatter.*

blank   See the entry for *empty¹.*

blanket   See the entry for *cover.*

blaze   See the entry for *burn².*

blaze up   See the entry for *flare.*

bleed   See the entry for *empty².*

blemish   See the entry for *flaw.*

blend   See the entry for *mix.*

blissful   See the entry for *happy.*

blithe   See the entry for *cheerful.*

blizzard   See the entry for *storm.*

bloat   See the entry for *inflate.*

block   (*verb*) to get in the way of someone or something; to try to stop someone or something. □ *A tree fell across the road and blocked our way.* □ *The star's bodyguard blocked all attempts to get to him.*
   • **bar**   to *block* something deliberately or officially. □ *Anyone under the age of twenty-one is barred from buying liquor in this state.* □ *The judge barred the journalists from the courtroom.*
   • **hinder**   to *block* someone or something from going forward. (Formal.) □ *Irene was hindered by having one leg in a cast.* □ *David's shyness seriously hindered his social life.*
   • **impede**   to *block* or slow down someone or something. (Formal.) □ *Ellen's three large suitcases impeded her as she tried to get up the stairs.* □ *Exhaustion impeded my thinking.*
   • **obstruct**   to *block* something by putting a barrier in the way. □ *Fred stopped his car in the middle of the street to talk to a friend who was driving in the opposite direction; this obstructed traffic for blocks on both sides.* □ *A giant snowdrift obstructed the sidewalk.*
   [→contrasting word: *help;* see also: *frustrate*]

blockade   See the entry for *barrier*.

blood-curdling   See the entry for *terrifying*.

blow   See the entry for *spend*.

blow up   See the entry for *inflate*.

blue   (*adjective*) the color of the clear daytime sky. □ *Frank has blue eyes.* □ *Gayle wanted blue carpeting in her room.*
   • **azure**   blue. (Poetic.) □ *The ship set out over the azure waves.* □ *After the storm, we welcomed the sight of the azure sky.*
   • **indigo**   dark *blue*. □ *The ink in my new pen isn't exactly blue, and it's not exactly black; it's indigo.* □ *The cloth was dyed a deep indigo.*
   • **navy**   very dark *blue*, so dark that it is almost black. (Usually used to describe cloth or clothing.) □ *The school uniform was a navy jacket and gray pants.* □ *The dress was white with navy polka dots.*
   • **turquoise**   bright greenish-*blue*. □ *The tropical sea was a beautiful turquoise color.* □ *Jennifer's turquoise boots looked quite dramatic with her yellow outfit.*

blunder   See the entry for *mistake*.

blur   (*verb*) to make it hard to see the outlines of something. □ *The dirt and moss on the gravestone blurred the inscription.* □ *Drops of rain fell on the page and blurred the writing.*
   • **obscure**   to *blur* something by covering it up or darkening it. (Formal.) □ *The heavy snow obscured the lines on the highway.* □ *Darkness obscured the landscape.*
   • **smear**   to *blur* something by spreading something on it or making it spread out. □ *I'm afraid I smeared the painting by touching it while it was still wet.* □ *The criminal smeared his license plate with mud.*
   • **smudge**   to *blur* something by rubbing it or rubbing something on it. □ *My elbow bumped against the chalkboard, smudging what was written there.* □ *Kevin smudged the mirror with his greasy fingers.*

blush   (*verb*) to have your face turn red because you are embarrassed or upset. □ *Lillian blushed when the teacher scolded her.* □ *His friends' teasing made Mark blush.*
   • **color**   to *blush*. (Old-fashioned.) (See also the main entry for *color*.) □ *Jan colored when her friends asked her if she liked Tom.* □ *When Tom asked her to marry him, Jan colored and said yes.*
   • **flush**   to *blush* suddenly; to have your face turn red for any reason. □ *Sue flushed, more angry than she had ever been in her life.* □ *Phil's face had been flushed all day; I suspected that he had a fever.*
   • **redden**   to *blush*; to turn red. □ *Roger reddened to the tips of his ears when his father praised him.* □ *The sky reddened as the sun set.*

boast   See the entry for *brag*.

boat   (*noun*) a vehicle for traveling on the water. □ *We rented a boat to go fishing on the lake.* □ *You can only reach the island by boat.*
   • **barge**   a large, flat *boat* that travels on a river and carries cargo. □ *The heavily laden barge moved slowly up the river.* □ *The barge delivered coal to many riverside towns.*
   • **craft**   any small *boat*. □ *The tiny craft barely made it through the ocean storm.* □ *The captain brought his craft to a safe landing at the dock.*
   • **ship**   a large *boat* that travels on an ocean. □ *Before there were airplanes, people had to cross the oceans on ships.* □ *There were all kinds of ships in the harbor, from battleships to luxury cruise ships.*
   • **vessel**   any large *boat*. □ *This ship is smaller than many oceangoing vessels.* □ *No responsible captain would ever put to sea in such a worn-out, leaky old vessel.*
   • **yacht**   a luxurious *boat* used for pleasure. □ *Although the million-aire owned three beautiful mansions, he preferred to live on board his yacht.* □ *The yacht had bedrooms for six people, and a fully equipped kitchen as well.*

bob   See the entries for *bow, trim*.

bobble   See the entry for *grope*.

body   See the entry for *person*.

bog   See the entry for *swamp*.

bogus   See the entry for *fake*.

boil   (*verb*) to make a liquid so hot that it bubbles; to be hot enough to bubble. (See also the entry for *cook*.) □ *The cook boiled the vegetables.* □ *If you let the soup get too hot, it will boil.*
   • **simmer**   to *boil* gently for a long time. □ *Simmer the sauce over low heat for five to ten minutes.* □ *The shrimp simmered in a mixture of butter and spices.*
   • **steep**   to soak in a hot liquid for a long time. (See also the main entry for *steep*.) □ *Let the potatoes steep in the sauce, so that they will absorb the flavor.* □ *After the teabag has steeped in the water for a while, take it out and discard it.*
   • **stew**   to *boil* slowly. □ *She stewed the tomatoes until they almost looked like tomato sauce.* □ *The goulash must stew for several hours.*

boiling   See the entry for *hot*.

bold   See the entries for *courageous, vivid²*.

bolster   See the entry for *support*.

bolt   See the entry for *steal away.*

bona fide   See the entry for *real.*

bonds   (*noun*) something fastened around your wrists or ankles to keep you from escaping. □ *The prisoner struggled against her bonds.* □ *The bonds were so tight that her hands grew numb.*
>   • **chains**   *bonds* made out of heavy chain. □ *The slaves were kept in chains throughout the entire ocean voyage.* □ *The soldiers captured the enemy general and put him in chains.*
>   • **fetters**   *bonds* made out of metal. (Formal or poetic.) □ *Though his body was trapped in fetters, our hero's spirit soared free.* □ *The prisoner's fetters made it impossible for him to walk.*
>   • **handcuffs**   *bonds* that are fastened around your wrists with a lock. □ *The police officer put handcuffs on the suspect.* □ *No one knew how the magician was able to escape from the handcuffs.*
>   • **irons**   *bonds* made out of iron. (Usually used in the phrase *in irons.*) □ *The captain had the drunken sailor clapped in irons.* □ *We have the prisoner in irons; he cannot escape.*
>   • **manacles**   metal *bonds* fastened around your wrists. (Formal.) □ *The heavy manacles rubbed the prisoner's wrists raw.* □ *The jailor put him in manacles and threw him into a prison cell.*
>   • **restraints**   *bonds* that are used to keep you from hurting yourself or someone else. □ *The doctors put the suicidal patient in restraints.* □ *Carrie had been acting calmly, so she was released from her restraints.*
>   • **shackles**   *bonds* that fasten you to something else, such as a wall or another person. □ *Shackles bound prisoners to the dungeon wall.* □ *All the members of the road gang were chained to each other with shackles.*

book   (*noun*) a group of pages bound together. □ *That big brown book contains all the Grimms' fairy tales.* □ *Paperback books are sold at the newsstand.*
>   • **brochure**   a *book* with paper covers and only a few pages, especially one that advertises something. □ *According to this travel brochure, San Antonio is a fun place to visit.* □ *The college sent me a brochure describing the classes they offer.*
>   • **pamphlet**   a *book* with paper covers and only a few pages. □ *The pamphlet about the presidential candidate tells you everything he plans to do if he is elected.* □ *This pamphlet will guide you to all the historic sites in town.*
>   • **tome**   a *book* with a very large number of pages. □ *The dictionary was an impressive tome that I could scarcely lift by myself.* □ *Eddie wrote a scholarly tome about seashells.*
>   • **volume**   a *book*; one of a group of *books* that go together. □ *This is a beautiful volume, with the title stamped in gold on a red leather cover.* □ *I found the answer in a volume of the encyclopedia.*

bookkeeper   See the entry for *clerk*.

boom   See the entry for *rumble*.

boon   See the entry for *benefit¹*.

boorish   See the entry for *rude*.

boost   See the entry for *lift*.

border   See the entry for *boundary*.

boring   (*adjective*) not exciting or interesting. □ *The book was so boring that I didn't finish reading it.* □ *Fran loves horse races, but George thinks they're boring.*

    • **dull**   unchanging and therefore *boring*. □ *Harry leads such a dull life, every day exactly the same.* □ *This TV show is getting dull; they never seem to have any new story ideas.*

    • **tedious**   repetitive and therefore *boring*. □ *Irene thought that going to school was very tedious.* □ *Jim's job at the factory seems awfully tedious.*

    • **tiresome**   so *boring* that it makes you feel tired. □ *Kay knows how to knit, but she thinks it's tiresome and never does it.* □ *This rainy weather is getting awfully tiresome.*

    • **uninteresting**   not interesting; *boring*. □ *The teacher gave an uninteresting lecture about good manners.* □ *Laura thought the conversation was uninteresting, so she left the room.*

    [→contrasting word: *interesting*]

boss   (*noun*) someone at your workplace who can give you orders. (Informal.) □ *My boss wants me to type this letter by noon.* □ *Mom's boss is always sending her on out-of-town trips.*

    • **employer**   a *boss;* the person or organization you work for. (Formal.) □ *How long have you worked for your present employer?* □ *Mark is very loyal to his employer.*

    • **head**   the *boss* of a group of people. □ *Ms. Nolan is the head of our department.* □ *Let the project head know what you plan to do.*

    • **superior**   a *boss*. (Formal.) □ *I will report your misconduct to your superior.* □ *I must inform my superior of my decision to resign.*

bossy   (*adjective*) fond of giving people orders; fond of getting your own way. (Informal.) □ *Nobody likes to work with Orlando because he's so bossy.* □ *Penny can get people to do things for her without being bossy.*

    • **forward**   determined to get your own way; overly bold. (Formal.) □ *It was very forward of Susan to call Mr. Smith by his first name.* □ *Butting into someone else's conversation is a forward thing to do.*

    • **officious**   fond of giving people orders even though it is not your place to do so. (Formal.) □ *The officious customer began to order the waiter around.* □ *"Never mind what your boss told you to do; get this file for me," was Donald's officious command.*

• **presumptuous** determined to get your own way; doing what you have no right to do. (Formal.) □ *Rita is always inviting herself to parties and doing other such presumptuous things.* □ *The student did not mean to be presumptuous, but could not resist correcting the teacher's mistake.*
• **pushy** determined to get your own way; willing to force people to do what you want. (Informal.) □ *The pushy shopper insisted on going to the front of the line.* □ *I'll do what you asked; there's no need to be so pushy.*

bother See the entry for *annoy.*

bottom (*noun*) the lowest part of something. □ *There's something sticky on the bottom of my shoe.* □ *The ship sank to the bottom of the lake.*
• **base** the *bottom* of a structure; the part of a structure that supports all the rest. □ *The base of the statue was made of black marble.* □ *The table won't tip over; it has a very solid base.*
• **floor** the surface at the *bottom* of a room. □ *John tiptoed across the floor.* □ *Be careful; the kitchen floor is slippery.*
• **foot** the *bottom* of a structure, a hill, or a mountain. □ *The baby sat at the foot of the stairs and cried.* □ *There was a small cabin at the foot of the hill.*
• **foundation** the *bottom* of a building. □ *The earthquake made the building's foundation crack.* □ *The courthouse has a strong foundation of solid stone.*

boulder See the entry for *rock¹.*

bounce See the entry for *shake.*

bound See the entry for *jump.*

boundary (*noun*) the place where one thing ends and the next begins. □ *Art lives on the boundary of a poor section of town.* □ *Do not cross the boundary into the next-door neighbor's yard.*
• **border** the exact line marking a *boundary;* an official *boundary.* □ *The fugitive hoped to cross the border without getting caught.* □ *The army gathered on the border and prepared to invade the neighboring country.*
• **brink** a steep *boundary* between a high place and a low place. □ *The car rolled to a stop right on the brink of the cliff.* □ *Bill peered over the brink of the canyon into the vast depths below.*
• **edge** a sharp *boundary.* □ *That line of pine trees marks the edge of my property.* □ *The comedian's jokes were right on the edge of good taste.*
• **fringe** the most distant, extreme part of a *boundary.* (Often used in the plural.) □ *There are several nightclubs out on the fringes of the town.* □ *The candidate represented the fringes of the party, not the people in the mainstream.*

• **limit**   a *boundary,* especially a *boundary* that you cannot or should not cross. □ *We had to stay within the limits of the house and yard when our parents were not at home.* □ *The diet puts a strict limit on how much I am allowed to eat.*

• **margin**   an area near a *boundary.* □ *There was a margin of several miles between the town and its nearest neighbor.* □ *The artist left a margin of blank canvas around all sides of her picture.*

bountiful   See the entry for *plentiful.*

bow   (*verb*) to bend your head or body in a gesture of respect; to submit to something. □ *The servant bowed and said, "Yes, sir."* □ *Sir Arthur Conan Doyle bowed to the demands of his readers and wrote more stories about Sherlock Holmes.*

• **bend**   to lean your head or body down in a gesture of respect. (Poetic.) □ *The congregation bent their heads in prayer.* □ *The gentlemen bent respectfully as they were introduced to each other.*

• **bob**   to bend down slightly and quickly. □ *Donna meant to bow gracefully, but she was so nervous she wound up bobbing up and down.* □ *Eddie bobbed his head "yes."*

• **curtsey**   to lower your body gracefully by bending the knees. (Usually only girls and women curtsey.) □ *Lady Alice curtsied to the king.* □ *The maid curtsied whenever someone gave her an order.*

• **duck**   to bend down quickly, usually to avoid something that might hit you. □ *Fred threw a snowball at me, but I ducked.* □ *Rose ducked in time to avoid the book I threw.*

• **stoop**   to bend your head or body. □ *The tall man had to stoop to get through the low doorway.* □ *George stooped down and pulled something off the bottom shelf.*

boy   See the entry for *man.*

brag   (*verb*) to talk proudly about yourself or something you own, in order to show off. □ *Sue Morris is bragging about her grandchildren again.* □ *"I scored the point that won the game," Helen bragged.*

• **boast**   to *brag* by saying exaggerated things. □ *Jim always boasts about his car, but I don't think it's anything special.* □ *"The team would never win a game if it weren't for me," Helen boasted.*

• **crow**   to *brag* triumphantly. (Informal.) □ *The coach could not resist crowing about the team's victory.* □ *"I got more Valentines than you!" Kay crowed.*

• **gloat**   to *brag* in a satisfied way; to be happy because you won and someone else lost. □ *Larry gloated over his recent promotion.* □ *"Grandma gave me the silver tea set and didn't give you anything," Mary gloated to her brother.*

brain   See the entry for *mind.*

bramble   See the entry for *bush*.

brand   See the entry for *label*.

brave   See the entry for *courageous*.

break   (*verb*) to make something fall to pieces; to fall to pieces. □ *Oh, no! I broke my favorite mug!* □ *The window broke in the storm.*
   • **crack**   to *break* something brittle; to make something *break* along a line; to *break* along a line. □ *The cook cracked the egg open.* □ *The tree branch cracked down the middle.*
   • **fracture**   to *break* something hard, especially a bone; for something hard, especially a bone, to *break*. (Formal.) □ *Mark fractured his collarbone in a skiing accident.* □ *The bone fractured in an unusual place.*
   • **shatter**   to *break* something into so many pieces that it cannot possibly be put back together; to *break* into many pieces. □ *Kathy shattered the mirror with repeated hammer blows.* □ *The glass bowl shattered on the floor.*
   • **smash**   to *break* something violently; to *break* violently. (See also the main entry for *smash*.) □ *In a fit of rage, Jane smashed all her dishes against the wall.* □ *The car rolled over the cliff and smashed to pieces on the jagged rocks below.*

break down   See the entry for *sink*.

break out   See the entry for *escape*.

breaker   See the entry for *wave*.

breakfast   See the entry for *meal*.

breeze   See the entry for *wind¹*.

bridle   See the entry for *bristle*.

brief   (*adjective*) lasting only a very little while. □ *Marty took a brief vacation.* □ *The teacher gave a few brief instructions before handing out the test.*
   • **concise**   *brief* and coming right to the point. □ *Linda wrote a concise description of what she had seen.* □ *She doesn't waste any words; everything she says is concise.*
   • **pithy**   *brief,* clever, and coming right to the point. □ *Laura told a pithy story about her adventure.* □ *I enjoy reading this author's work; his style is so pithy.*
   • **short**   *brief;* not tall; not long. □ *Everyone in the class had to give a short speech.* □ *He's too short to reach the top shelf.* □ *I will only be gone for a short while.*
   • **succinct**   compressed; *brief.* □ *Mark gave a succinct answer to every question.* □ *The instructions were clear and succinct.*

• **terse**   very *brief; too brief.* □ *"What should I do?" I asked. "Leave,"* *was Nora's terse reply.* □ *You need to give more details in this paragraph; what you have written is too terse.*
[→Note: concise, pithy, succinct, and terse are only used to describe language.]

bright   (*adjective*) giving off light. (See also the entries for smart[1], vivid[2].) □ *The moon, full and bright, lighted our way.* □ *Sue has such a bright smile.*
• **brilliant**   extremely *bright.* □ *The crown was covered with brilliant jewels.* □ *The explosion gave off a brilliant light.*
• **glaring**   painfully or uncomfortably *bright.* □ *The glaring headlights blinded the pedestrian.* □ *I woke with the glaring light of the sun hitting me right in the face.*
• **luminous**   *bright; shining from within.* □ *The snow made the landscape look luminous, even at night.* □ *The luminous candles filled the room with their soft glow.*
• **radiant**   *bright; giving off light in all directions.* (Formal.) □ *After a solid month of cloudy weather, we welcomed the radiant sunshine.* □ *Philip was so happy that his face was radiant.*

brilliant   See the entries for *bright, smart[1].*

bring   See the entry for *carry.*

bring up[1]   (*verb*) to mention something; to bring a topic into the conversation. (Informal.) □ *I'm glad you brought up that question.* □ *Everyone had forgotten about having a picnic until Rita brought it up at dinner that night.*
• **introduce**   to *bring up* a thing for the first time. □ *Everyone was in a good mood, so I thought it would be a good time to introduce my plan.* □ *Conversation was dragging, so Susan introduced the subject of recent movies.*
• **propose**   to *bring up* a thing because you think someone should do it. □ *Rita proposed that we picnic at the lake.* □ *The leader proposed having another meeting next week.*
• **submit**   to *bring up* a thing in order for people to consider it. □ *Tom submitted his idea to the group.* □ *Some people objected to the new plan Jan had submitted, so it was never carried out.*

bring up[2]   (*verb*) to care for and train a child until the child is grown up. □ *Art's parents died when he was very young, so his aunt and uncle brought him up.* □ *Mary was brought up to respect her elders.*
• **nurture**   to *bring up* someone; to feed something so that it will grow. (Formal.) □ *Art's aunt nurtured him as if he were her own.* □ *The teacher did her best to nurture her students' minds.*
• **raise**   to *bring up* a child; to care for young animals until they grow up. □ *Carrie and Donald raised five children.* □ *Eddie raises hogs on his farm.*

• **rear**   to *bring up* a child. (Somewhat old-fashioned.) □ *Fran was reared by very strict parents.* □ *After his wife died, Greg reared their three boys all by himself.*
[→see also: *teach*]

brink   See the entry for *boundary*.

brisk   See the entry for *lively*.

bristle   (*verb*) to get very angry all of a sudden. (Usually with *at*.) □ *The least little bit of teasing makes Helen bristle.* □ *Jim always bristles at the things that news commentator says.*
   • **bridle**   to *bristle* because something hurts your pride; to *bristle* because you object to something. (Usually with *at*.) □ *Jay tried to order Kay around, but she bridled at that.* □ *Larry bridled when his dad scolded him.*
   • **flare up**   to *bristle* and then suddenly calm down again. □ *Mark flared up when I called him by his old nickname.* □ *I flared up at Tom's thoughtless remark.*
   • **see red**   to get extremely angry all of a sudden. (Informal.) □ *Tom hates Fran so much that just hearing her name can make him see red.* □ *Someone scratched Phil's car, and Phil saw red.*

brittle   See the entry for *fragile*.

broad   See the entry for *wide*.

broadcast   See the entry for *publish*.

brochure   See the entry for *book*.

broil   See the entry for *cook*.

broke   See the entry for *poor¹*.

broker   See the entry for *seller*.

bronze   See the entry for *metal*.

brood   See the entry for *worry*.

brook   See the entry for *river*.

brown   (*adjective*) a dark reddish-yellowish color; the color of many kinds of wood. □ *The muddy shoes left brown tracks across the clean carpet.* □ *Bake the bread until it turns brown on top.*
   • **auburn**   a light reddish *brown*. (Usually used to describe someone's hair.) □ *Rita gets many compliments on her beautiful auburn hair.* □ *The movie star's hair is auburn, and his eyes are green.*
   • **ochre**   a very yellowish *brown*. □ *We drove through miles and miles of ochre desert landscape.* □ *That dark yellow bowl is made of ochre-colored clay.*

• **rust** a light, somewhat reddish *brown*. □ *The water that came out of the faucet had a rust color.* □ *The salesclerk suggested that I buy rust shoes to complement my olive-green outfit.*
• **sepia** a very dark *brown*. □ *I have an old sepia photograph of my great-grandfather.* □ *The picture shows bare sepia trees against pure white snow.*
• **tan** a light, somewhat yellowish *brown*. □ *Tim's tan shirt is almost the same color as his skin.* □ *I don't like the dark brown briefcase; I prefer the tan one.*

browse See the entry for *read*.

brusque See the entry for *gruff*.

brutal See the entry for *savage*.

brute See the entry for *monster*.

buddy See the entry for *friend*.

budge See the entry for *move*.

buff See the entries for *fan, polish*.

buffet See the entry for *beat¹*.

bug See the entries for *annoy, insect*.

build (*verb*) to make something out of various parts. □ *The settlers built houses down by the creek.* □ *We will need to build another bridge to carry all the traffic across the river.*
• **assemble** to *build* something fairly small; to put parts together. □ *Dad had to assemble my new bicycle before I could ride it.* □ *Jan assembled the radio out of a kit.*
• **construct** to *build* something that takes skill or special planning. □ *It took the builders seven months to construct the bridge.* □ *Terry constructed a model of the Eiffel Tower out of toothpicks.*
• **fashion** to *build* something skillfully; to make something out of some kind of material. □ *The woodcarver fashioned a fancy frame for the mirror.* □ *Art fashioned the clay into the figure of a cow.*
• **put together** to *build* something; to *build* something rather casually or carelessly. (Informal.) □ *I read the instructions but could not figure out how to put the mobile together.* □ *Jennie hastily put curtains together out of old bedsheets.*

building (*noun*) something permanently set up for people to live, work, or keep things in. □ *There are twenty-four apartments in the building where I live.* □ *City Hall is the red stone building in the center of town.*
• **construction** a *building*; any constructed thing. □ *The architect came to look at the construction she had designed.* □ *The toy is a delicate construction made of cardboard, paper, and string.*

• **edifice**   a grand *building*. (Formal.) □ *The bank was an impressive edifice, built to look as though it would last forever.* □ *The skyscraper is the most famous edifice in the city.*
• **erection**   a *building* or a monument. (Formal.) □ *The millionaire planned his mansion to be the grandest erection in the history of the state.* □ *This simple erection of white marble commemorates a great war hero.*
• **structure**   a *building;* anything built with some kind of pattern. □ *The new museum is a dramatic structure, a beautiful place to keep artistic treasures.* □ *The travelers spent the night in a flimsy structure they made of fallen branches.*

bulky   See the entry for *thick.*

bulletin   See the entry for *message.*

bumble   See the entry for *grope.*

bumbling   See the entry for *clumsy.*

bump into   See the entry for *meet.*

bunch   See the entries for *cluster, crowd, group.*

bundle   See the entry for *package.*

bungalow   See the entry for *house.*

buoyant   See the entry for *jaunty.*

burden   See the entries for *duty, load.*

bureaucrat   See the entry for *authority.*

burglarize   See the entry for *steal.*

burn¹   (*verb*) to hurt or change something by making it extremely hot. (See also the entry for *smart*².) □ *Lightning burned down a large part of the forest.* □ *I burned my arm on the hot pan.*
• **char**   to *burn* something until its whole surface is black. □ *Ben doesn't really like to roast marshmallows; he likes to char them.* □ *The covers of the book were charred in the fire, but the pages weren't harmed at all.*
• **scorch**   to *burn* something until it turns brown. □ *The curling iron was so hot that it scorched Anna's hair.* □ *I held the paper too close to the candle flame, scorching it.*
• **sear**   to *burn* something until its whole surface is dry and brown. □ *The chef seared the meat over high heat.* □ *The fierce sunlight seared our eyes.*
• **singe**   to *burn* something lightly. □ *I got too close to the fire, and the hair on my arm got singed.* □ *The forest fire singed the bark on the tree.*

burn² *(verb)* to give off light or heat the way a fire does. □ *The candle burned brightly.* □ *I can see a light burning in Carrie's window.*
- **blaze** to *burn* brightly and strongly. □ *The campfire blazed up as we added more wood.* □ *The city lights blazed on the horizon.*
- **flame** to *burn* brightly; to suddenly *burn* brightly. □ *The torches flamed as the mob approached.* □ *Donald's eyes flamed angrily.*
- **smolder** to *burn* slowly and without giving off light. □ *The coals of the fire smoldered beneath the ashes.* □ *Edith may seem calm and cheerful, but anger is smoldering under the surface.*

burning See the entry for *hot.*

burnish See the entry for *polish.*

burrow See the entries for *cave, rummage.*

burst *(verb)* to break apart suddenly. □ *If you put any more water in that balloon, it will burst.* □ *The trash bag burst and scattered trash all over the ground.*
- **bust** to *burst.* (Slang.) □ *I dropped the light bulb and it busted.* □ *It got real cold and the water pipes busted.*
- **erupt** to *burst* and spew out whatever was inside. □ *The volcano erupted, sending rivers of lava running down its sides.* □ *There are vegetables all over the ceiling because the pressure cooker erupted.*
- **explode** to *burst* violently. □ *The bomb exploded and blew a hole in the side of the building.* □ *The car tumbled down the cliff, crashed onto the rocks below, and exploded.*
- **pop** to *burst* very suddenly; to *burst,* making a loud, sharp sound. □ *The balloon popped when Art stuck a pin in it.* □ *The seed pod popped and sent seeds out onto the breeze.*
- **rupture** to *burst.* (Usually only used to describe walls or body organs bursting.) □ *The dam ruptured and water came crashing through.* □ *Bill overstrained himself and ruptured an intestine.*

bush *(noun)* a woody plant with lots of branches, shorter than a tree. □ *Carrie hid herself behind a bush.* □ *Blackberries don't grow on trees, they grow on bushes.*
- **bramble** a thorny *bush.* □ *Donald struggled through the brambles, tearing his clothes.* □ *As I was walking through the forest, I got stuck in a bramble.*
- **hedge** a long row of *bushes,* serving as a fence. □ *The front yard was surrounded by a hedge.* □ *I couldn't see the house through the tall, thick hedge.*
- **shrub** a small *bush.* □ *The gardener planted several shrubs alongside the path.* □ *Only a few hardy shrubs could grow in the desert climate.*

business See the entry for *company.*

businesslike See the entry for *organized.*

bust See the entries for *sculpture, burst.*

busy[1] (*adjective*) concentrating on doing something. □ *I can't play with you now; I'm busy.* □ *Tom was busy building something in the basement when I came in.*
- **engaged** *busy;* meeting with someone. (Formal.) □ *When I went to meet with Mary, she was engaged with someone else.* □ *The doctor cannot see you now; he is otherwise engaged.*
- **occupied** so *busy* that you cannot get away to do anything else. □ *Eddie was completely occupied with cleaning up the kitchen.* □ *Can I talk to you for a minute, or are you occupied?*
- **working** *busy* at a job or a task. □ *Fran is working and can't get away for lunch.* □ *The guide dog is not a pet; he is a working dog.*

busy[2] (*adjective*) full of things to do; having lots of things to do. □ *I had a very busy day at work.* □ *Mr. Mason doesn't have time to fool around; he's a busy man.*
- **active** *busy;* full of activity. □ *Mary leads a very active life; she's never idle.* □ *Tom is such an active person that it's hard for him to be confined to bed.*
- **hectic** extremely *busy;* so *busy* that it is difficult to do everything there is to do. □ *It was a hectic day at the store, with hundreds of customers all demanding attention.* □ *The little girl was frightened by the hectic activity in the emergency room.*
- **lively** pleasantly *busy.* (See also the main entry for *lively.*) □ *Business at the restaurant was lively.* □ *Jim had a lively time at camp.*

butter up See the entry for *flatter.*

buy (*verb*) to give money in exchange for something. □ *I need to buy a dozen eggs at the store.* □ *Kay wants a car but doesn't have enough money to buy one.*
- **invest in** to *buy* something in hopes that it will become more valuable as time goes on. □ *Mr. Jones invests in oil paintings.* □ *I decided against investing in stocks.*
- **pay for** to *buy;* to have to give something in exchange for something else. □ *You can't just leave the restaurant without paying for your meal!* □ *Driving drunk was a bad mistake, and Morris paid for it with his life.*
- **purchase** to *buy.* (Formal.) □ *I wish to purchase that set of crystal goblets.* □ *The jeweler showed Martha several pearl necklaces, but she declined to purchase any of them.*

buzz   See the entry for *hum.*

bypass   (*verb*) to go around something; to go past something without stopping. □ *If we use the back roads, we can bypass the collapsed bridge.* □ *Helen walked in the road in order to bypass the icy patches on the sidewalk.*

  • **circumnavigate**   to go around something. (Formal.) □ *The army stealthily circumnavigated the enemy camp.* □ *I decided my best policy would be to circumnavigate the hostile canine.*

  • **detour**   to go around something you want to avoid. (Usually with *around.*) □ *Ever since I fought with Sally, I detour around her house on my way to school.* □ *Rather than go straight through the bad part of town, the travelers detoured around it.*

  • **skirt**   to go around the edge of something. □ *To get around that boulder, we will have to skirt the cliff.* □ *A chain-link fence skirted the edge of the parking lot.*

  [→see also: *avoid*]

C

cabin   See the entry for *house*.

café   See the entry for *restaurant*.

cafeteria   See the entry for *restaurant*.

cage   (*noun*) a structure made to confine an animal. □ *I hope the leopard can't get out of the cage.* □ *Jay kept his pet guinea pig in a cage.*
   • **cell**   a room in a prison where a person can be confined. □ *The prisoner had been in the same cell for fifteen years.* □ *After the police arrested Kay, they put her in a cell.*
   • **coop**   a small *cage;* especially, a *cage* for chickens. □ *Larry went to the coop to see if the hens had laid any eggs during the night.* □ *Is it kind to keep the rabbit confined in such a little coop?*
   • **pen**   a fenced-in area used to confine an animal; a prison (slang). □ *The farmer shut the sheep into their pen for the night.* □ *Milt begged the judge not to send him to the pen.*

cajole   See the entry for *persuade*.

calamity   See the entry for *disaster*.

calculate   See the entry for *figure*.

calisthenics   See the entry for *exercise*.

call¹   (*verb*) to say something in order to get someone to come to you. □ *"Nancy! Lunchtime!" Mother called.* □ *We stood outside and called the dog, but he didn't come to us.*
   • **page**   to *call* for someone through several rooms. □ *A voice on the intercom paged Dr. O'Connor.* □ *If you don't find Philip in his office, please page him for me.*

• **send for** to *call* someone indirectly, for instance, by having someone else go to get him or her. ☐ *The king sent for all the knights to meet with him at the castle.* ☐ *I don't know who sent for me; I just know that someone told me to be at this address at noon.*

• **summon** to *call* someone officially or formally. (Formal.) ☐ *The lady summoned all her servants to gather in the grand ballroom.* ☐ *Rita was summoned to appear in court.*

call² (*verb*) to give a name to someone or something; to use a name for someone or something. ☐ *This is a delicious dish; what do you call it?* ☐ *My name is William, but my friends call me Bill.*

• **christen** to give a name to something officially, especially in a church ceremony; to give a name to something for the first time. (Formal.) ☐ *The queen christened the ship "The Polestar."* ☐ *The minister christened the child.*

• **dub** to give someone or something a name; to declare someone a knight. (Formal.) ☐ *Because his car was so broad and clumsy, Jim dubbed it "The Tuna Boat."* ☐ *"I dub thee Sir Thomas," said the king.*

• **name** to give a name to someone or something. ☐ *Kay and Larry discussed what to name their child.* ☐ *Mark, who is not very original, named his dog Fido.*

• **term** to give a name, especially a technical name, to something. ☐ *"Manic-depressive disorder" is what doctors term this disease.* ☐ *You may call Tom's behavior unconventional, but I term it just plain rude.*

call on See the entry for *visit*.

caller See the entry for *visitor*.

calling See the entry for *profession*.

calm (*adjective*) not disturbed or excited; peaceful. (See also the entry for *peace*.) ☐ *Sue remained calm throughout the crisis.* ☐ *It's a good day for boating; the lake looks calm.*

• **collected** *calm* and self-possessed. ☐ *When the fire alarm went off, Philip acted in a perfectly collected way.* ☐ *How can you stay so collected when everyone is making demands of you?*

• **composed** *calm;* in control of yourself. ☐ *Although Rita appeared composed, I could see she had been crying.* ☐ *Stanley had hysterics when he discovered the dead body in his garage, but he was quite composed by the time the police arrived.*

• **levelheaded** *calm* and knowing what to do even in a difficult situation. ☐ *Everyone was impressed by Tom's levelheaded reaction to the news of his business failure.* ☐ *Jan was scared, but she stayed levelheaded, carefully planning what to do next.*

• **placid** perfectly *calm;* not at all disturbed. ☐ *She was a placid person who took everything in stride.* ☐ *The ship sailed across the placid blue sea.*

• **serene**   *calm* and above it all. ☐ *Alice's serene face showed she was not afraid of dying.* ☐ *The new mother cradled her baby and smiled a serene smile.*

• **tranquil**   *calm;* very peaceful. (Formal.) ☐ *Ben was distressed by our leaving, but he became tranquil when we promised we would come again soon.* ☐ *After two days of thunderstorms, we enjoyed the tranquil weather.*

calm down   See the entry for *relax*.

camouflage   See the entry for *disguise*.

cancel   (*verb*) to put an end to something; to call something off. ☐ *I wish to cancel the order I placed yesterday.* ☐ *It snowed two feet today, so the principal canceled school.*

• **abolish**   to *cancel* something completely and forever. ☐ *Carrie is writing to urge her congressman to abolish the new tax.* ☐ *The abolitionists worked to abolish slavery.*

• **do away with**   to *cancel* something completely. ☐ *The school board decided to do away with summer vacations.* ☐ *Jim wishes they would do away with speed limits on major highways.*

• **repeal**   to *cancel* a law. ☐ *Carrie is happy now that the tax law has been repealed.* ☐ *Many people opposed the law, but the lawmakers refused to repeal it.*

• **revoke**   to *cancel* a privilege or an order. ☐ *Because Jim drives so recklessly, his driver's license has been revoked.* ☐ *The captain revoked the order he had given earlier.*

candid   See the entry for *honest*.

candidate   (*noun*) someone who wants to be chosen for some kind of job or prize. ☐ *No one can guess which candidate will win the election.* ☐ *Colleen interviewed all the candidates for the job.*

• **aspirant**   a *candidate;* someone who hopes to be chosen for something. ☐ *Today we'll find out which of the talented aspirants will win the Science Fair.* ☐ *The duke was an aspirant to the throne.*

• **contender**   a *candidate* who has a good chance of being chosen. ☐ *Pat and Terry are both contenders for first place.* ☐ *Which horse in this race is the strongest contender?*

• **contestant**   a *candidate* for winning a contest or game. ☐ *Two of the contestants were eliminated in the first round.* ☐ *Only one contestant gets a chance at the big prize.*

canister   See the entry for *container*.

canny   See the entry for *wise*.

cantankerous   See the entry for *grumpy*.

canvas   See the entry for *painting*.

canyon   See the entry for *valley*.

capability   See the entry for *ability*.

capacity   See the entry for *ability*.

caper   See the entries for *frolic, practical joke*.

capital   See the entry for *money*.

capitulate   See the entry for *give in*.

caprice   See the entry for *whim*.

capricious   See the entry for *random*.

capture   (*verb*) to catch someone and make that person your prisoner.
□ *The police officer captured the thief.* □ *A trap was set to capture the secret agent.*

> • **apprehend**   to *capture* someone, especially after a long chase. (Formal.) □ *The guards finally apprehended the runaway prisoner.* □ *The detective's report stated that she had been unable to apprehend the suspect.*
> • **arrest**   for a police officer to *capture* someone. □ *The officer arrested the bank robber before he even left the bank.* □ *When the police arrived, they arrested Mr. Jones for murder.*
> • **collar**   to *capture* or arrest someone. (Slang.) □ *I'm glad to hear that they finally collared that crook.* □ *The thief thought that he was so clever that he'd never be collared.*
> • **seize**   to *capture* someone suddenly; to grab someone or something suddenly. □ *Airport guards seized Morris and made him open up his luggage.* □ *I'm not under arrest, but all my property has been seized.* [→see also: *catch*]

car   See the entry for *vehicle*.

caravan   See the entry for *procession*.

care for   See the entry for *like*.

career   See the entry for *profession*.

carefree   See the entry for *cheerful*.

careful   (*adjective*) trying very hard to do something correctly; paying special attention so you will not make a mistake. □ *The roads are very slippery, so be very careful as you drive home.* □ *Fred was careful to follow the recipe exactly.*

> • **cautious**   careful; taking no risks. □ *The cautious truck driver decided not to try to drive through the storm.* □ *We made a cautious attempt to go around the sleeping rattlesnakes.*

• **circumspect**   *careful;* showing good judgment. (Formal.) □ *Glen said whatever came to mind, not caring what other people would think, but Helen was more circumspect.* □ *Irene wanted to get money by robbing a bank, but Jim favored a more circumspect plan.*

• **guarded**   *careful;* cautious about giving information. □ *Kay was guarded about her plan for winning the race.* □ *Larry won't tell you his secret; he's a very guarded man.*

• **prudent**   *careful;* having common sense. □ *Mark spent his money as soon as he had it, but his prudent brother made sure to save as much as he could.* □ *I don't think it's prudent to ask Jane if that's her real hair color.*

careless   (*adjective*) not caring about doing things right; making no effort to do things right. □ *If you weren't so careless, you wouldn't break things so often.* □ *Susan was very careless with her money.*

• **irresponsible**   always *careless;* not keeping your promises; not to be trusted. □ *I couldn't trust an irresponsible person to take care of my children.* □ *It was soon obvious that the new employee was thoroughly irresponsible; I would have to fire her.*

• **negligent**   guilty of being *careless;* not taking good care of something. □ *The negligent cook left things boiling on the stove while she went off to watch TV.* □ *Tom was negligent of his duties as a father.*

• **reckless**   going out of your way to be *careless;* overly daring. □ *Jim was such a reckless driver that his license was taken away.* □ *The reckless mountain climber never used a safety harness.*

• **thoughtless**   *careless* because you do not think about what you are doing. □ *I'm sorry I made such a thoughtless remark.* □ *Kay is so thoughtless; she never considers anyone's feelings.*

careworn   See the entry for *haggard.*

caring   See the entry for *kind¹.*

carp   See the entry for *complain.*

carpet   (*noun*) a heavy cloth used to cover the floor. (See also the entry for *cover.*) □ *Larry bought a brown carpet to match his brown curtains.* □ *Mary vacuumed the carpet every day.*

• **carpeting**   *carpet* that covers the floor of a whole room; material that serves as a *carpet.* □ *Nancy put wall-to-wall carpeting in her living room.* □ *We tried desperately to get the stain out of the carpeting.*

• **mat**   a small *carpet.* □ *Please put your dirty shoes on the mat by the door.* □ *I have a mat protecting the floor near the kitchen sink.*

• **rug**   a *carpet* that covers only part of a floor. □ *Kathy never let anyone walk on her beautiful Persian rug.* □ *Grandma wove a rug out of old rags.*

carpeting   See the entry for *carpet.*

carry (*verb*) to lift something and move it from one place to another. □ *Art carried the box across the room.* □ *The little boy is getting too big for his mother to carry.*

• **bring** to *carry* something to somewhere; to come with something. □ *Bring me the orange juice, will you?* □ *Ben brought doughnuts to the party.*

• **convey** to *carry* something from place to place. (Formal.) □ *This vehicle is used to convey soldiers from one base to another.* □ *The waiter conveyed our food to the table on a little wheeled cart.*

• **deliver** to *carry* something somewhere and give it to someone. □ *I waited all day for the truck to come and deliver my new couch.* □ *Carrie delivers newspapers every afternoon.*

• **take** to *carry* something from somewhere. (See also the main entry for take.) □ *I took the dirty laundry down to the washing machine.* □ *The father took his crying child out of the movie theater.*

• **transport** to *carry* a large load to somewhere. (Formal.) □ *How will we transport all our furniture to the new house?* □ *The airplane can transport two hundred people.*

carry off See the entry for *kidnap*.

carry out See the entry for *finish*.

cartoon See the entry for *picture*.

carve (*verb*) to cut into something; to cut something into slices or pieces. □ *Sue carved her name into the top of the desk.* □ *Philip carved up the turkey.*

• **chisel** to *carve* with a long, pointed metal tool called a chisel. □ *I tried to chisel a hole through the ice.* □ *The sculptor chiseled lines into the stone.*

• **engrave** to *carve* a design into something. □ *The ring was engraved with Rita's initials.* □ *The judges engraved the winner's name on the trophy.*

• **hew** to *carve* something by chopping at it. □ *Susan hewed a branch off the tree with an ax.* □ *The miners hewed coal out of the tunnel walls.*

• **incise** to *carve* deeply into something. □ *The sculptor incised his mark into the base of the statue.* □ *The artist incised a pattern into the piece of wood.*

• **whittle** to *carve* little pieces off something. □ *Tom whittled toys out of chunks of wood.* □ *Jan whittled the end of the stick down to a sharp point.*

[→see also: cut]

case (*noun*) the way things happen to be. (See also the entries for *bag*, *example*.) □ *"What would you do if you didn't have any money?" Bob asked. "Well, in that case, I'd try to get a job," Kathy replied.* □ *I would feel sorry for Bill if he had no one to help him, but that isn't the case.*

• **circumstances**   the way things happen to be for someone; how prosperous someone is. □ *I don't know what I'd do if I were in Art's circumstances.* □ *Ben's circumstances were good; he earned good money and owned his own house.*

• **condition**   the way someone's health is; how prosperous someone is. □ *Carrie went to the hospital to check on her sister's condition.* □ *Donald wanted his daughter to marry someone of good condition.*

• **position**   the way things happen to be for someone, considering what he or she might lose if things go wrong. □ *Jane told Nancy my secret, which put me in an embarrassing position.* □ *Someone in Rita's position can't afford to cause a scandal.*

• **situation**   the way things happen to be; the way things are set up. □ *The police officer told her chief about the situation at the crime scene.* □ *The situation forced Susan to choose between her family fortune and the man she loved.*

• **state of affairs**   the way things happen to be. (Formal.) □ *The ambassador's message described the chaotic state of affairs in the country.* □ *Dad saw the enormous mess we had made and calmly inquired what we had done to cause this state of affairs.*

cash   See the entry for *money.*

cask   See the entry for *barrel.*

cast off   See the entry for *shed.*

castigate   See the entry for *criticize.*

cataclysm   See the entry for *disaster.*

catapult   See the entry for *throw.*

catastrophe   See the entry for *disaster.*

catch   (*verb*) to get someone or something you have been chasing; to get a hold of someone or something. (See also the entry for *trap.*) □ *Do you think the police can catch the murderer?* □ *Joe caught the runaway horse.*

• **grab**   to get a hold of someone or something suddenly; to grip someone or something suddenly. □ *Kay grabbed my arm and pulled me into her room.* □ *Lenny grabbed the candy bar out of his brother's hands.*

• **nab**   to *catch* someone or something suddenly. (Informal.) □ *The cops nabbed me for speeding.* □ *I nabbed a piece of cheese from the refrigerator when you weren't looking.*

• **seize**   to *catch* someone or something violently; to take hold of someone or something suddenly. □ *Someone seized me by the collar and asked what I was doing there.* □ *The relay runner seized the baton when it was handed to him.*

• **snag**   to *catch* someone or something by quick action. (Informal.) □ *Mary snagged an apple from a high branch of the tree.* □ *I'll see if I can snag the waitress the next time she comes by.* [→see also: *capture, take*]

catching   (*adjective*) easily spreading from one person to another. (Informal.) □ *When Tom heard me sneeze, he asked if what I had was catching.* □ *You'll have to stay away from Sue while she has the measles; it's catching.*

• **communicable**   able to spread from one person to another. (Formal.) (Usually used to describe a disease.) □ *How can we control the spread of this communicable disease?* □ *The common cold is highly communicable.*

• **contagious**   spreading from one person to another. □ *The chicken pox was so contagious that everyone in class had caught it by the end of the month.* □ *Mike's laughter is contagious; you can't help laughing when you hear him laugh.*

• **infectious**   quickly and easily spreading from one person to another. □ *These injections offer some protection against the infectious disease.* □ *Philip's good mood was infectious.*

categorize   See the entry for *sort*.

category   See the entry for *kind²*.

cause   (*verb*) to make something happen. (See also the entry for *reason*.) □ *The icy road caused the car to slip.* □ *What did I do that caused everyone to get so mad at me?*

• **effect**   to successfully make something happen. □ *Rita's advice effected a change in Susan's behavior.* □ *The new medicine seems to have effected a cure.*

• **give rise to**   to make it possible for something to happen. □ *Tom's frequent absences from work gave rise to a number of rumors.* □ *The terrible poverty in that part of town gave rise to serious unrest.*

• **induce**   to *cause*; to persuade someone to do something. (Formal.) □ *Too large a dose of this drug may induce vomiting.* □ *Bill offered a large salary to induce Jan to work for him.*

• **inspire**   to make someone very eager to do something. □ *The leader inspired his followers to work tirelessly for his cause.* □ *Marcel's experience inspired him to write a novel.*

caustic   See the entry for *sarcastic*.

caution   See the entry for *warn*.

cautious   See the entry for *careful*.

cave   (*noun*) an open space deep underground or in the side of a hill. □ *The archaeologist found some interesting bones in the cave.* □ *The bandits hid their loot in a secret underground cave.*

• **burrow** a small *cave* dug by an animal, where the animal lives. □ *The groundhog spent the winter safe in its burrow.* □ *Although I haven't seen any prairie dogs, I've seen their burrows, so I know they live here.*
• **cavern** a large *cave*. □ *The cavern was full of spectacular rock formations.* □ *The genie led Aladdin to a cavern heaped with treasures.*
• **den** a *cave* where an animal lives. □ *I think this hole beneath the tree roots is a fox's den.* □ *The mother bear led her cubs back to their den.*
• **grotto** a *cave*. (Poetic.) □ *The children took shelter in a woodland grotto.* □ *Our hero wondered what lay within the shadowed grotto.*
[→see also: *hole*]

cave in See the entry for *collapse*.

cavern See the entry for *cave*.

cavity See the entry for *hole*.

cavort See the entry for *frolic*.

cease See the entry for *stop*.

ceaseless See the entry for *relentless*.

celebration See the entry for *party*.

cell See the entry for *cage*.

censure See the entry for *criticize*.

center (*noun*) the part in the middle of something. □ *Ben put the flower arrangement in the center of the table.* □ *The speaker stood in the center of the stage.*
• **core** the important or basic *center* of something; the *center* of an apple. □ *The discussion quickly got to the core of the problem.* □ *Carrie ate the apple and threw the core away.*
• **heart** an important, vital *center*. □ *I tried to discover what lay at the heart of Donald's unhappiness.* □ *The hotel is located in the heart of town.*
• **hub** an important or active *center*. □ *The airport is a hub for this airline.* □ *The conference room is the hub of all activity in this office.*
• **midpoint** the exact *center*. □ *Springfield was the midpoint of our journey.* □ *This intersection marks the midpoint of the downtown area.*
• **nucleus** the *center* or focus of something. □ *The new factory will form the nucleus of a thriving industrial district.* □ *The leader and her few devoted followers were the nucleus of the whole protest movement.*

ceremony (*noun*) a formal act done to mark a special occasion. □ *Everyone wore caps and gowns for the graduation ceremony.* □ *John and Marcia had an elaborate wedding ceremony.*

• **formality**   a *ceremony* that makes something official. □ *You will need to pass a test before I can give you this license, but don't worry; it's just a formality.* □ *The couple had to go through all the formalities in order to adopt the child.*

• **observance**   a traditional *ceremony*. (Formal.) □ *The family went to the synagogue for the observance of Yom Kippur.* □ *The church members marked the observance of Easter with a traditional feast.*

• **rite**   a *ceremony*, especially a religious one. (Formal.) □ *Alice was buried with all the proper funeral rites.* □ *The secret society had several strange rites.*

• **ritual**   a *ceremony* that is always performed in the same way. □ *The bride and groom went through all the rituals of exchanging rings, cutting the cake, and throwing the bouquet.* □ *The tribe performed a ritual to welcome the young people into adulthood.*

• **service**   a religious *ceremony*; a meeting for conducting formal religious worship. □ *The special holiday service always draws crowds.* □ *Jim attends church service every Sunday.*

certain   (*adjective*) feeling that something is definitely true or definitely going to happen. □ *I am certain that Marty will call me today.* □ *Kevin felt certain that he had flunked the test.*

• **assured**   calm and *certain*. □ *I felt assured that Laura would keep her promise.* □ *In the midst of all the uproar, Mark's manner was competent and assured.*

• **confident**   *certain* that something will happen or be true. □ *Alice was confident that she would win the race.* □ *Sue's confident attitude impressed me.*

• **positive**   absolutely *certain*. □ *I'm positive it won't rain this afternoon.* □ *Phil wasn't positive that he had remembered to turn off the oven.*

• **sure**   very *certain*. (Informal.) □ *I'm sure you and Todd will get along.* □ *Susan was sure she had left her scissors in her desk.*

[→consider also: *smug*]

certainly   (*adverb*) for sure; without a doubt. □ *It's certainly cold out today.* □ *Tom certainly did a good job shoveling snow off the walk.*

• **absolutely**   extremely *certainly;* without the least doubt. □ *Are you absolutely sure you remembered to feed the cat?* □ *That's absolutely the biggest limousine I've ever seen.*

• **definitely**   quite *certainly;* conclusively. □ *Jan will definitely be coming to the party.* □ *Bill is definitely the fastest runner in class.*

• **positively**   very *certainly;* truly. □ *This is positively the last time I do you a favor!* □ *Anna was positively delighted with the gift.*

• **unquestionably**   *certainly;* without question. □ *The defendant is unquestionably guilty.* □ *Unquestionably, Bill will be happy to see you.*

chagrin   See the entry for *embarrass*.

chains   See the entry for *bonds.*

challenge   See the entry for *face.*

chance   See the entries for *accident, dare, random.*

change   (*verb*) to become different; to make something different. □ *Fran has changed; she's not as cheerful as she used to be.* □ *I changed the cookie recipe, adding chocolate chips and leaving out the walnuts.*
  • **alter**   to *change* slightly; to *change* only one part. □ *Helen wanted to alter her hairstyle, so she cut bangs across the front.* □ *The director altered the ending of the movie to please the audience.*
  • **convert**   to *change* something in order to make it more useful or stylish; to *change* your religion. □ *The Smiths converted their basement into a TV room.* □ *Lillian was raised a Methodist but converted to Catholicism.*
  • **shift**   to *change* position. □ *Irene shifted her weight from one foot to the other.* □ *Jim shifted the bed to the other side of the room.*
  • **switch**   to *change* to something quite different; to replace something with something else. □ *Kevin had been driving to work, but then he switched to bicycling.* □ *We switched Ragsy's dog food for a cheaper brand, to see if he would notice.*
  • **transform**   to *change* completely. □ *The wizard transformed the prince into a swan.* □ *Laura's hard work transformed the tumbledown old house into a lovely place to live.*

changeable   See the entry for *fickle.*

chant   (*verb*) to recite something in a monotone. □ *As they danced, the tribespeople chanted a prayer to the sun god.* □ *"Eight times seven is fifty-six, eight times eight is sixty-four," the students chanted.*
  • **chorus**   for a group of people to *chant* something all together. □ *"Be good while we're away," said Mom and Dad. "We will," the children chorused.* □ *All Mark's friends chorused their approval of his speech.*
  • **drone**   to speak in a monotone. □ *The teacher droned on about the American Revolution, and I fell asleep.* □ *"I cannot disobey my master," the zombie droned.*
  • **intone**   to *chant* formally or importantly; to read or recite something in a singsong. □ *The judge intoned the oath of office, and the president repeated it after him.* □ *"Do you take this man to be your lawfully wedded husband?" the minister intoned.*
  [→consider also: *sing*]

chaos   See the entry for *disorder.*

char   See the entry for *burn¹.*

character (*noun*) a strange person. (See also the entry for *personality*.) □ *Mr. Jones is that character who lives in his garage and has twenty-two cats.* □ *Janie's a real character, always mumbling to herself.*
  • **crackpot**   a strange person with lots of crazy or impractical ideas. (Informal.) □ *The talk show host was tired of getting calls from that crackpot.* □ *My uncle the crackpot says he's invented a new kind of shoe polish.*
  • **freak**   an extremely strange and unpleasant person. (Slang.) □ *Karen's such a freak that no one wants to go near her.* □ *Larry's weird wardrobe makes him look like a freak.*
  • **oddball**   a very strange person. (Informal.) □ *Who's the oddball with the green hair?* □ *Everyone thought I was an oddball for reading so many books.*
  • **weirdo**   a strange person. (Slang; insulting.) □ *"Only a weirdo would still be playing with dolls at the age of fifteen!" Mary snorted.* □ *After Nelson killed all those people, his neighbors agreed that he had always seemed like a weirdo.*
  [→consider also: *eccentric*]

charge with   See the entry for *blame*.

charged up   See the entry for *thrilled*.

charitable   See the entry for *generous*.

charity   See the entry for *mercy*.

charlatan   See the entry for *fraud*.

charm (*noun*) a word or object that is supposed to bring you good luck. □ *Sue always carries a horseshoe-shaped charm to bring her luck.* □ *The witch doctor guaranteed that the charm would drive away evil spirits.*
  • **amulet**   an ornament that you wear as a *charm*. □ *The wizard gave our hero an amulet to wear around his neck.* □ *This amulet is supposed to keep me from getting sick.*
  • **good-luck piece**   a *charm* you can carry with you. □ *Phil has an old coin he uses as a good-luck piece.* □ *When he lost his good-luck piece, he was sure something awful would happen to him.*
  • **talisman** a *charm*. (Poetic.) □ *The warlock said that the little figurine was a powerful talisman against evil.* □ *"While you keep the talisman, no harm will befall you," he said.*

charmed   See the entry for *fascinated*.

charter   See the entry for *rent*.

chase (*verb*) to go after someone or something that is running away from you. □ *The dog chased the rabbit across the field.* □ *The police officers chased the thief.*

• **dog** to go after someone or something patiently and unstoppably. □ *The patient detective dogged the criminal for weeks.* □ *That purple car has been dogging my every move, and I want to know why!*

• **hound** to go after someone or something unstoppably; to harass someone. □ *Reporters hounded the mayor wherever she went.* □ *The students hounded their teacher until she agreed to take them to the museum.*

• **hunt** to follow or search for someone or something. □ *Police have been hunting the escaped convict across three states.* □ *Roger went out to the woods to hunt rabbits.*

• **pursue** to *chase* in order to capture someone or something. (Formal.) □ *The officers pursued the getaway car at high speed.* □ *Susan is pursuing her goal of becoming an airline pilot.*

• **stalk** to go after someone or something secretly for a long time, usually to hurt or kill. □ *The hunter stalked the bear to its den.* □ *Sally is afraid to leave her house; she thinks her ex-boyfriend is stalking her.* [→see also: *follow*]

chastise See the entry for *punish.*

chat See the entries for *talk¹, talk².*

chatty See the entry for *talkative.*

cheap (*adjective*) not costing very much money; not worth very much. □ *The food at that restaurant is tasty and cheap.* □ *What a cheap pair of shoes; they came apart the first day I wore them!*

• **cut-rate** *cheap* and sometimes of poor quality. □ *The cut-rate stereo didn't cost very much, but it sounded terrible.* □ *Dad warned me against buying cut-rate tools.*

• **inexpensive** not costing very much money. (Formal.) □ *Living in this town is quite inexpensive.* □ *The clothes were surprisingly inexpensive, when you consider how well they are made.*

• **low-priced** not costing very much money. □ *The store's commercial claims that everything there is low-priced.* □ *I decided that the best way to get low-priced furniture was to buy it at a yard sale.* [→contrasting word: *expensive*]

cheapskate See the entry for *miser.*

cheat (*verb*) to get something from someone by tricking him or her. □ *That store cheats all their customers.* □ *Bill cheated me out of my last few dollars.*

• **defraud** to *cheat* someone out of what rightfully belongs to him or her. (Usually with *of.*) (Formal.) □ *Art defrauded his sister of her inheritance.* □ *The government defrauded many people of their property.*

• **rip off** to *cheat;* to steal. (Slang.) □ *I think that salesclerk ripped me off; she didn't give me the right change!* □ *Someone broke into my house and ripped off my TV.*

• **swindle** to *cheat* someone shamefully and on purpose. □ *The professional gambler swindled many unsuspecting people out of their money.* □ *The con artist swindled people by claiming she would give their money to charity.*

check (*verb*) to look at something in order to make sure it is all right. (Informal.) □ *Will you check the soup and make sure it hasn't boiled over?* □ *I checked what I had written to see if I had made any spelling errors.*

• **examine** to *check* someone or something carefully. □ *The doctor examined the patient but couldn't find anything wrong with him.* □ *The mechanic examined the car engine, looking for loose belts.*

• **inspect** to *check* something very carefully. □ *Ben's job is to inspect all the sweaters made in the factory.* □ *Dad inspected the kitchen to make sure we had cleaned everything.*

• **scrutinize** to *check* something very carefully. (Formal.) □ *The detective scrutinized the carpet near the dead body but could not find any bloodstains.* □ *You'll have to scrutinize the computer program in order to find the problem.*

check out See the entry for *explore.*

checkmate See the entry for *frustrate.*

cheer (*verb*) to shout because you are happy about something. □ *The fans cheered every time their team scored.* □ *I cheered when my brother went up on the stage to receive his diploma.*

• **applaud** to *cheer* or clap your hands to show that you think someone did a good job. □ *The audience applauded the actress as she took her bow.* □ *We applauded after every trick the magician did.*

• **hurrah** to *cheer* by shouting "hurrah." □ *Everyone in the movie theater hurrahed when the bad guy was defeated.* □ *It had been cloudy for so long that people hurrahed when the sun came out.*

• **roar** to *cheer* loudly and enthusiastically. □ *The crowd roared as the parade went by.* □ *The band appeared onstage, and the audience roared.*

cheerful (*adjective*) full of happiness; joyful. □ *No matter how Carl is feeling, he always manages to act cheerful.* □ *Donna answered the phone with a cheerful "Hello!"*

• **blithe** very *cheerful;* brightly *cheerful.* (Old-fashioned.) □ *Edith was such a blithe child, never out of sorts.* □ *Frances sang a blithe little song as she went about her work.*

• **carefree** *cheerful* and without worry. □ *The prince lived a carefree life; every comfort was provided for him.* □ *Once George was out of debt, he felt perfectly happy and carefree.*

• **lighthearted**   *cheerful* and bouncy. □ *Harriet tried to stay lighthearted despite her poverty.* □ *The lighthearted young people spent the afternoon building snowmen and having a snowball fight.*
• **merry**   *cheerful* and lively. (Somewhat old-fashioned.) □ *Uncle Jasper's merry face and boyish sense of humor made him my favorite uncle.* □ *I recognized Kay's merry laugh.*
[→see also: *happy*]

cherish   See the entry for *treasure*.

chew   (*verb*) to grind something with your teeth. □ *Chew your food thoroughly before you swallow it.* □ *I chewed on the stringy stalk of celery.*
• **gnaw**   to bite or *chew* something tough. □ *The dog gnawed his bone.* □ *Laura gnawed at the stale dinner roll.*
• **masticate**   to *chew*. (Formal.) □ *Lady Cynthia taught her children to masticate quietly and invisibly, with their mouths closed.* □ *Mark, lost in thought, silently masticated his food.*
• **munch**   to *chew* something crunchy; to *chew* noisily. □ *Tom sat in front of the television, munching popcorn.* □ *The horses happily munched their oats.*
• **ruminate**   to *chew* something over and over again; to think about something again and again. (Formal.) □ *Cows ruminate the grass they eat, bringing it back up from their stomachs to chew it over again.* □ *Sue ruminated upon what Philip had told her.*

chew out   See the entry for *criticize*.

chic   See the entry for *stylish*.

chicken   See the entry for *cowardly*.

chief   See the entry for *main*.

child   (*noun*) a young person. □ *Rita may be just a child, but she's able to take care of herself.* □ *I lived in Texas when I was a child.*
• **juvenile**   a *child*. (Formal.) □ *The police officer arrested the juvenile and took him to the police station.* □ *Dad took the book away from me and told me that such reading material was not suitable for juveniles.*
• **kid**   a *child*. (Informal.) □ *How many kids are in your class?* □ *Steve is a bright kid.*
• **minor**   a legal term for *child*. □ *Cigarettes cannot be sold to minors.* □ *Since Alice was a minor when her parents died, she needed someone to be her legal guardian.*
• **youngster**   a *child;* anyone younger than you are. □ *Every afternoon, youngsters swarmed into the park to play on the swing set.* □ *Jan was disappointed to see that her new boss was such a youngster.*

chilling   See the entry for *terrifying*.

chilly   See the entry for *cold*.

chime   (*verb*) to make a musical sound when hit. □ *The clock chimed three times; it was three o'clock.* □ *I thought I heard the doorbell chime.*
   • **clink**   to *chime* sharply. □ *The glasses clinked against each other as I took them out of the cupboard.* □ *The dining room was filled with the sound of silverware clinking against plates.*
   • **jingle**   to *chime* repeatedly, like small bells. □ *Dad's keys jingled when he pulled them out of his pocket.* □ *Anna's long, dangling earrings jingled when she moved her head.*
   • **tinkle**   to *chime* sharply and repeatedly. □ *The icicles tinkled as they fell from the eaves.* □ *The ice-cream truck tinkled a little melody as it came down the street.*
   [→see also: *ring*]

chirp   See the entry for *squeak*.

chisel   See the entry for *carve*.

chomp   See the entry for *bite*.

choose   (*verb*) to figure out which one thing you want out of many things you could have. □ *Ben went to the store to choose a new sofa for his living room.* □ *Carrie offered me a plate of cookies; I chose a lemon one.*
   • **decide on**   to *choose;* to make up your mind about what you want even though you may not be able to get it yet. □ *Donna has decided on the kind of horse she wants, even though she can't afford a horse.* □ *After discussing it for a while, they decided on the station wagon.*
   • **pick**   to *choose* something from many possibilities. (Informal.) □ *Please pick one of the cards I am holding in my hand.* □ *I picked Wednesday as the day to have the party.*
   • **select**   to *choose* something from many possibilities, after thinking about it carefully. □ *There were so many good essays in the essay contest that the judges had a hard time selecting one winner.* □ *Grandma examined five or six tomatoes before she finally selected one.*
   • **settle on**   to *choose* something, feeling sure you will never change your mind about it. □ *Fran changed her mind several times about what to order for dinner; she finally settled on the spaghetti.* □ *George has settled on Spike as a good name for his new dog.*

choosy   See the entry for *picky*.

chop   (*verb*) to cut something by hitting it with a sharp object. □ *Helen chopped the tree down.* □ *I have to chop the baby's food into small pieces.*
   • **dice**   to *chop* something into small cubes. □ *The cook diced the onions before adding them to the stew.* □ *Dice the tomatoes into one-inch cubes.*

• **hack** to *chop* something roughly. □ *Harry hacked up the old broken chair and used it for firewood.* □ *Eddie hacked up the chicken before frying it.*

• **lop** to *chop* a large piece off something. (Usually with *off.*) □ *Irene lopped a big branch off the tree.* □ *Our hero lopped off the wicked knight's head.*

• **mince** to *chop* something into tiny pieces. □ *Mince two cloves of garlic and put them into the hot oil.* □ *The chef minced the onion very fine.*

chore See the entry for *job.*

chortle See the entry for *laugh.*

chorus See the entry for *chant.*

christen See the entry for *call².*

chronicle See the entry for *story.*

chuck See the entry for *throw away.*

chuckle See the entry for *laugh.*

chum See the entry for *friend.*

churn See the entry for *seethe.*

circular See the entry for *round.*

circulate See the entry for *publish.*

circumnavigate See the entry for *bypass.*

circumspect See the entry for *careful.*

circumstances See the entry for *case.*

cite See the entry for *refer to.*

city See the entry for *town.*

civic See the entry for *public.*

civil See the entry for *polite.*

civilization See the entry for *culture.*

claim (*verb*) to say that something is true. □ *Jim claims that he saw a flying saucer last night.* □ *The commercial claimed that this soap would get rid of any stain.*

• **allege** to *claim* something even though you have no proof of it. (Formal.) □ *Kay alleged that Susan had stolen the money.* □ *The police allege that the suspect committed the murder.*

• **assert**   to *claim* something strongly. (Formal.) ☐ *Laura forcefully asserted her opinion.* ☐ *Mark asserted that he knew how to solve the problem.*

• **declare**   to *claim* something strongly; to *claim* something publicly. ☐ *The mayor declared her intention of running for reelection.* ☐ *Tom declared his love for Jean.*

clan   See the entry for *family.*

clandestine   See the entry for *secret.*

clang   See the entry for *clash.*

clank   See the entry for *clash.*

clarify   See the entry for *explain.*

clash   (*verb*) to make a metallic noise; for things to crash into each other with a metallic noise. ☐ *The pots and pans clashed against each other as I tried to put them back in the cupboard.* ☐ *The empty cans in the recycling bin clashed as Sue carried the bin down to the curb.*

• **bang**   to make a metallic noise; to make an exploding noise. ☐ *Rita banged the car door shut.* ☐ *The old car rattled and banged its way down the street.*

• **clang**   to make a ringing, metallic noise. ☐ The metal bowl clanged when it hit the floor. ☐ The heavy door clanged shut.

• **clank**   to make a loud, flat, metallic noise. ☐ *Something in the engine clanked when Phil started the car.* ☐ *From half a mile away, I could hear the clanking of the machines in the factory.*

class   (*noun*) a meeting of people who are getting together to learn something. (See also the entry for *kind²*.) ☐ *I have to be in class at eight o'clock in the morning.* ☐ *Ms. Clark teaches the social studies class.*

• **course**   a series of *classes.* ☐ *Dad is taking a course in computer repair.* ☐ *The college offered a gourmet cooking course.*

• **lecture**   a *class* in which someone teaches by giving a speech. ☐ *On Friday, I went to a lecture about the Pyramids in Egypt.* ☐ *The professor's lecture will cover the important battles of the Civil War.*

• **section**   a *class;* the group of people who attend a *class* together. (Usually used for college classes.) ☐ *I'm in Professor Warren's section of the history class.* ☐ *Susan and Tom are in the same psychology section.*

• **seminar**   a *class* in which people discuss the subject material with each other. (Formal.) ☐ *The seminar in computer programming meets twice a week.* ☐ *All the students in that seminar usually have interesting things to say.*

classified   See the entry for *private.*

classify   See the entry for *sort.*

clean[1] (*adjective*) free from dirt. (See also the entry for *innocent*.) □ *Mom won't let me go out until I put on a clean shirt.* □ *Art keeps his house very clean.*
  • **immaculate** totally *clean*. (Formal.) □ *The kitchen was immaculate—not a spot of dirt anywhere.* □ *Ben came down to dinner wearing an immaculate white jacket.*
  • **spick-and-span** *clean* and neat. (Informal.) □ *After Carrie got through cleaning it, the bathroom was spick-and-span.* □ *The restaurant may not be elegant, but it's spick-and-span, and the food is good.*
  • **spotless** totally *clean*. □ *Donald cleaned the mirror until it was spotless.* □ *With this new detergent, my dishes come out spotless.*
  [→contrasting word: *dirty*[1]]

clean[2] (*verb*) to get all the dirt off something. □ *It took me two hours to clean my room.* □ *Edith was able to see much better after she cleaned her glasses.*
  • **bathe** to *clean* a person or an animal. □ *Helen bathes once a day.* □ *I need someone to help me bathe the dog.*
  • **cleanse** to *clean* something thoroughly. (Formal.) □ *This wonderful new soap will cleanse your skin without making it feel dry.* □ *The doctor made Irene drink lots of water to cleanse her system.*
  • **launder** to *clean* clothes. □ *The stain should come out of your pants when you launder them.* □ *George forgot to launder his red shirt separately, so all his clothes turned pink in the wash.*
  • **wash** to use water to *clean* something. □ *Wash your hands before you come to the table.* □ *Fran washed the kitchen floor.*
  [→contrasting word: *dirty*[2]]

cleanse See the entry for *clean*[2].

clear (*adjective*) plain; easy to see; easy to understand. □ *It's clear from Jim's expression that he's not having a good time.* □ *Kay made a clear statement about what she wanted.*
  • **apparent** *clear*; appearing to be true. □ *Larry's dissatisfaction with his job was apparent.* □ *I don't know what to do about Mark's apparent dislike of me.*
  • **evident** *clear*, once you know the facts. □ *It's evident that Tom is upset.* □ *It was good to see Sue's evident enjoyment of the party.*
  • **manifest** *clear*; out in the open. (Formal.) □ *Philip's jealousy was manifest in everything he did.* □ *The family was upset by the brothers' manifest hatred for each other.*
  • **obvious** so *clear* that you cannot miss it. □ *The answer to that problem should be obvious.* □ *It's obvious that Rita's in a good mood today.*

clear out See the entry for *steal away*.

clemency See the entry for *mercy*.

clerk (*noun*) someone whose job is to keep records. □ *Hand your application to the clerk, and he will file it for you.* □ *The clerk totaled up the prices of everything I'd bought.*

  • **bookkeeper** a *clerk* who keeps track of how much money has been paid out and received. □ *The bookkeeper sent bills to everyone who owed money to the company.* □ *Let the bookkeeper know how much you spent, and she will write it in the ledger.*
  • **office manager** a *clerk* who runs an office. □ *I asked the office manager to order more pens and paper.* □ *The office manager made sure that all the lights were out before he locked up the office for the night.*
  • **secretary** a *clerk* who takes care of letters and phone calls. □ *I called the office, and a secretary answered the phone.* □ *I needed the secretary to type a letter for me.*
  • **teller** a *clerk* who works in a bank and handles money. □ *The teller handed me my money and said, "Have a nice day."* □ *Susan asked the teller for change for a fifty-dollar bill.*
  • **typist** a *clerk* who types things; someone who types. □ *When Tom finished writing his report, he gave it to the typist, who typed it up.* □ *Jan is a good typist; she can type seventy words a minute.*

clever See the entry for *smart¹*.

client See the entry for *customer*.

climb (*verb*) to go higher and higher; to go higher by making a strong effort. □ *The explorer climbed the mountain.* □ *We climbed the hill to watch the sun set.*

  • **ascend** to *climb*. (Formal.) □ *Bill ascended the stairs with a candle in his hand.* □ *The balloon ascended into the air.*
  • **go up** to go higher. □ *The plane went up into the sky.* □ *Art went up the ladder one step at a time.*
  • **scale** to *climb* something steep. □ *The mountaineer scaled the cliff.* □ *The stunt man scaled the side of the skyscraper.*

cling See the entry for *stick¹*.

clink See the entry for *chime*.

clip See the entry for *cut*.

clique See the entry for *team*.

close (*verb*) to cover up an opening; to make something cover up an opening. (See also the entries for *end, near, stuffy*.) □ *Joe went into the room and closed the door behind him.* □ *Kay put the shoes back into the shoebox and closed the lid.*

• **close up**   to *close* something so that nothing can get in or out. □ *Because no one was using the swimming pool, the guard closed up the pool room.* □ *Laura closed up her desk and locked it.*

• **seal**   to *close* something very tightly, so that nothing can get in or out. □ *Mark poured the freshly made jelly into the jar and then sealed the jar shut.* □ *Nancy sealed the windows with putty, so that no cold air could get in.*

• **shut**   to *close* something, especially with a certain amount of force. □ *Sue shut the closet door.* □ *Philip reluctantly shut the book and put it aside.*

• **slam**   to *close* something forcefully, making a loud sound. □ *When my neighbor slams the door, you can hear it all through the apartment house.* □ *Rita slammed shut the trunk of her car.*

close up   See the entry for *close*.

closing   See the entry for *final*.

cloth   (*noun*) something made of woven or knitted threads. □ *Mary has a dress made of beautiful shiny cloth.* □ *Grandma made a rug out of scraps of cloth.*

    • **fabric**   *cloth* of some particular kind. □ *Harry picked out a heavy fabric for his new curtains.* □ *The sheets were made of a tightly woven fabric.*

    • **material**   *cloth;* whatever something is made of. □ *I need to buy material for the coat I want to make.* □ *The jacket was made of a nubby wool material.*

    • **textile**   woven *cloth.* (Formal.) □ *The factory produces fine textiles.* □ *The chair is upholstered with a colorful textile.*

clothing   (*noun*) things you wear to cover your body. □ *Charlie's clothing is always stylish.* □ *The beggar wore tattered clothing.*

    • **apparel**   *clothing.* (Formal.) □ *The store sells gentlemen's apparel.* □ *The knights and ladies put on their most splendid apparel for the feast.*

    • **attire**   fancy or special *clothing.* (Formal.) □ *You must wear formal attire to this dance.* □ *Donald discovered that shorts were not considered proper business attire.*

    • **garb**   special or unusual *clothing.* □ *The folk dancers wore traditional Greek garb when they danced their Greek dance.* □ *The actors were costumed in old-fashioned garb for the historical play.*

    • **garment**   a piece of *clothing.* □ *Eddie's favorite garment is his old blue sweatshirt.* □ *How long will it take for the tailor to make that garment?*

    • **outfit**   a set of *clothing* that goes together. □ *The camp counselors all wore matching outfits.* □ *Fran's ballet outfit is pink tights, pink ballet shoes, and a black leotard.*

cloud   See the entry for *mist*.

club   See the entry for *organization*.

clue   (*noun*) something that guides you to the correct solution of a problem. □ *The detective needed a clue to help him solve the murder.* □ *Glenda's note contained a clue as to where she was going.*

• **glimmer**   a faint *clue*. □ *Helen did not have even a glimmer as to how to solve the math problem.* □ *I knew Irene was planning a surprise party, but I didn't have the faintest glimmer that it was a party for me!*
• **hint**   a small or indirect *clue*. □ *The mud stains on Jim's shoes gave me a hint about where he had been.* □ *Kevin gave me a hint about what he wanted for his birthday.*
• **inkling**   a very slight *clue*. □ *I don't have the least inkling what that word means.* □ *Laura had only an inkling as to who the mysterious caller was.*
• **suspicion**   a slight *clue*; a suggestion. □ Mark didn't have the least suspicion that his friend was stealing from him. □ Tom didn't even have a suspicion as to how the machine was supposed to work.

clump   See the entry for *cluster*.

clumsy   (*adjective*) not graceful; not able to do something well. □ *The clumsy boy spilled water all over when he tried to pour some from the pitcher into the glass.* □ *Sue's so clumsy she can barely walk down the street without tripping.*

• **awkward**   physically *clumsy*; embarrassing. □ *Philip has such an awkward way of walking.* □ *It was a very awkward situation; nobody knew how to behave.*
• **bumbling**   stupid and *clumsy*. □ *My bumbling brother stepped all over my new coat and ruined it!* □ *The bumbling dishwasher managed to break more dishes than she washed.*
• **inept**   hopelessly *clumsy*; incompetent. □ *Don't go to that doctor; he's inept.* □ *Roger was fired from his job for being inept.*
• **klutzy**   *clumsy*. (Slang.) □ *I'm really klutzy today, dropping things and stumbling around.* □ *That klutzy kid got six papercuts just trying to open an envelope.*
• **maladroit**   *clumsy*. (Formal.) □ *I fear that Stanley is too maladroit to achieve his dream of becoming a magician.* □ *That maladroit waiter has spilled soup in my lap!*
• **ungainly**   physically *clumsy*; big and *clumsy*. □ *The ungainly young colt wobbled across the field.* □ *You can't fit this ungainly car into that tiny parking space.*

cluster   (*noun*) a group of similar things all gathered close together. □ *A cluster of berries grew on the bush.* □ *A cluster of medicine bottles stood next to the bathroom sink.*

• **bunch**   a *cluster;* in particular, a *cluster* of fruit or flowers. ☐ *I bought a nice bunch of grapes for dessert.* ☐ *Susan brought her mother a bunch of violets.*
• **clump**   an untidy heap or *cluster.* ☐ *Several clumps of seaweed washed up on the beach.* ☐ *The candy got stuck together in one big clump.*
• **passel**   a *cluster* of a large number of things. (Folksy.) ☐ *Tim and Henrietta had a passel of kids.* ☐ *Andy whipped up a whole passel of snacks for the party.*
[→see also: *group*]

coach   See the entry for *teach.*

coarse   See the entry for *rough².*

coat   See the entries for *cover, fur.*

coax   See the entry for *persuade.*

coddle   See the entry for *spoil¹.*

coerce   See the entry for *make².*

cohort   See the entry for *friend.*

coil   See the entry for *wind².*

coincidence   See the entry for *accident.*

cold   (*adjective*) having a very low temperature. ☐ *May I offer you something cold to drink?* ☐ *Mary's hands were very cold.*
• **chilly**   quite *cold.* ☐ *Wear a sweater; it's chilly outside.* ☐ *Carrie felt chilly when she came out of the swimming pool.*
• **cool**   somewhat *cold.* ☐ *A cool breeze blew in off the lake.* ☐ *We sat in the cool shade of the oak tree.*
• **freezing**   extremely *cold; cold* enough to freeze. ☐ *Let me in quickly; it's freezing out here!* ☐ *The night the furnace broke, the house was freezing.*
[→contrasting word: *hot*]

collaborate   See the entry for *team up.*

collaborator   See the entry for *partner.*

collapse   (*verb*) to fall apart suddenly; to make something fall apart suddenly. ☐ *I built the tower of blocks three feet high, and then it collapsed.* ☐ *Donald collapsed the tent when he tripped over the rope that held it up.*
• **cave in**   to *collapse* inward; to *collapse* under a great deal of pressure. ☐ *The roof caved in under four feet of snow.* ☐ *The flood caved in one wall of the building.*
• **crumple**   to *collapse* and wrinkle up; to crush something. ☐ *The whole front end of the car crumpled when it hit the guard rail.* ☐ *Eddie crumpled the milk carton in one hand.*

• **fall**   to *collapse;* suddenly to stop standing up. (See also the main entry for *fall.*) □ *Fran built a house of cards, but it fell when somebody breathed on it.* □ *The Byzantine Empire fell in the fifteenth century.*
• **topple**   for something tall to *collapse;* to make something tall *collapse.* □ *The ancient tower toppled in the earthquake.* □ *Lightning toppled the giant redwood tree.*

collar   See the entry for *capture.*

colleague   See the entry for *partner.*

collect   (*verb*) to bring things together into a group; to come together in a group. □ *George collected all the dirty dishes in the house and put them in the dishwasher.* □ *Dust collected under the bed.*
• **accumulate**   to *collect* things over some amount of time; for things to *collect* over some amount of time. (Formal.) □ *Helen has accumulated more than fifty model cars.* □ *Just look at all the mail that accumulated while I was on vacation!*
• **amass**   to *collect* things into a large group; to *collect* a large quantity of something. (Formal.) □ *Irene amassed a great fortune.* □ *Bill has amassed a lot of knowledge about dinosaurs.*
• **assemble**   to *collect* things into some kind of order; to come together into some kind of order. □ *Jean assembled a rock collection that's just as good as any museum's.* □ *The students assembled in the gym.*
• **gather**   to *collect* things little by little; to come together little by little. □ *Over the years, Grandpa has gathered a large number of recipes.* □ *A crowd gathered in front of the burning house.*

collected   See the entry for *calm.*

college   See the entry for *school.*

collide   (*verb*) to hit together. □ *The two cars collided because they couldn't stop in time.* □ *The ice skaters lost control and collided with each other.*
• **crash**   to *collide* violently and noisily. □ *The truck crashed into the side of the building.* □ *Kelly tried to make her toy trains crash.*
• **run into**   to *collide* at high speed. □ *The race car ran into the wall and exploded.* □ *The plane ran into the side of the mountain.*
• **smash into**   to *collide* violently; to hit against something deliberately. □ *The driver lost control of the car and smashed it into a tree.* □ *The Demolition Derby cars smashed into each other.*

collusion   See the entry for *plot.*

color   (*noun*) a visible quality that you can describe with words like *red, yellow, blue,* and so on. (See also the entry for *blush.*) □ *What color are Laura's eyes?* □ *I like the shape of that desk, but I don't like the color.*
• **hue**   color. (Poetic.) □ *The sea was a deep azure hue.* □ *The crimson hue of the lady's face showed her embarrassment.*

• **shade**   a dark or light variety of a *color*. □ *Mark's hair is a light shade of brown.* □ *Tom chose a shirt in a dark shade of blue.*
• **tinge**   a slight presence of *color*. □ *A tinge of red crept into Sue's face.* □ *The artist added a tinge of yellow to the color he was mixing.*
• **tint**   a faint or delicate *color*. □ *There was a greenish tint to Philip's blond hair when he came out of the swimming pool.* □ *The brown tint of the doll's skin looked very lifelike.*

colorful   See the entry for *vivid²*.

colors   See the entry for *flag*.

colossus   See the entry for *monster*.

column   See the entry for *post*.

comatose   See the entry for *unconscious*.

combat   See the entry for *fight*.

combative   See the entry for *belligerent*.

combine   See the entry for *mix*.

come   (*verb*) to get to a certain place; to attend a certain event. □ *Uncle Lou came to our house last night.* □ *All Rita's friends came to the party.*
• **appear**   to get to somewhere suddenly; to *come* into view suddenly. □ *All of a sudden, Susan appeared at my door.* □ *Just as the students were getting rowdy, the teacher appeared.* □ *A light appeared in the window.*
• **arrive**   to get to a certain place. (Formal.) □ *The guests began to arrive at nine o'clock.* □ *The plane will arrive at the gate in five minutes.*
• **reach**   to get to a place you had to work hard to get to; to get to a precise place. □ *We were very hot and tired by the time we reached the library.* □ *The train finally reached the station.*
• **show up**   to *come* or appear somewhere. (Informal.) □ *The party starts at eight, but you can show up anytime.* □ *Two extra people showed up for dinner, and I don't know what to feed them.*

come about   See the entry for *happen*.

come across   See the entry for *find*.

come by   See the entry for *get*.

come close to   See the entry for *approach*.

come forth   See the entry for *come out*.

come out   (*verb*) to move out of something you were inside. □ *Art came out of the room.* □ *I pounded on the bottom of the ketchup bottle, but nothing came out.*

• **come forth**   to *come out*. (Poetic.) □ *Our hero came forth out of the cave.* □ *A spurt of fire came forth from the dragon's snout.*

• **emerge**   to *come out* slowly. (Usually with *from*.) □ *Smoke emerged from the chimney.* □ *As I questioned Mary over and over, the truth gradually emerged.*

• **issue**   to *come out*; especially, to *come out* in a flood. (Usually with *from*.) (Formal.) □ *Hundreds of ants issued from the tiny crack in the wall.* □ *The bell rang, and a stream of students issued from the school.* [→see also: *appear*]

comedy   See the entry for *play¹*.

comely   See the entry for *beautiful*.

comfort   (*verb*) to make someone who is sad or in pain feel better. □ *The father comforted his crying child.* □ *Susan's friends tried to comfort her by telling her funny stories.*

• **console**   to *comfort* someone who has lost something. □ *Tim's children did everything they could to console him after his wife died.* □ *The knowledge that she had done her best consoled Jan for not winning the race.*

• **relieve**   to *comfort* someone; to make bad feelings less intense. □ *Nothing could relieve Bill's intense sorrow.* □ *Spending the day with friends relieved Art's depression.*

• **solace**   to *comfort* someone; to make it possible to forget bad feelings for a while. (Formal.) □ *Ben's beloved books solaced him whenever he felt sad.* □ *Art and Mary tried to solace each other for their brother's death.*

• **soothe**   to *comfort* someone; to calm someone down. □ *I soothed Donald by assuring him that I was still his friend.* □ *The rhythmic sound of the ocean waves soothed Eddie's anger.*

comfortable   (*adjective*) feeling content and entirely free from pain; causing someone to feel very content and free from pain. □ *Are you comfortable, or should I bring you another pillow?* □ *The seats on the train were quite comfortable.*

• **at ease**   *comfortable* and relaxed. □ *Fran felt totally at ease with her new friends.* □ *George reclined in his new armchair, happy and at ease.*

• **comfy**   *comfortable*. (Slang.) □ *Helen made herself comfy, sitting on a big pile of pillows on the floor.* □ *Irene sat down on her favorite comfy chair.*

• **cozy**   *comfortable*, warm, and safe. □ *Jim made sure that his kids were all cozy in the back seat before they started out on the long car trip.* □ *Kay's kitchen is such a cozy place.*

• **snug**   *comfortable* and safe; wrapped up or compact. □ *Laura was snug in bed, with three pillows and two thick quilts.* □ *Marcia turned the tiny space downstairs into a snug little TV room.*

comfy   See the entry for *comfortable.*

comical   See the entry for *funny.*

command   See the entries for *mastery, order.*

commanding   See the entry for *masterful.*

commence   See the entry for *begin.*

commend   See the entry for *praise.*

comment   See the entry for *say.*

commercial   (*noun*) a short program or announcement that is supposed to convince you to buy something. □ *The commercial showed the car driving through the mountains.* □ *I can't seem to stop humming the song from that commercial.*
   • **advertisement** or **ad**   a *commercial;* particularly a printed *commercial.* (*Ad* is informal.) □ *I decided to try the restaurant when I read their advertisement in the paper.* □ *The ad promised very low prices.*
   • **plug**   a short *commercial.* (Slang.) □ *The movie star agreed to do a plug for the soft drink.* □ *The plug made the movie sound really interesting.*
   • **promotion**   a *commercial;* any kind of activity intended to convince you to buy something. □ *The singer appeared in a promotion for her new album.* □ *The store offered free food as a promotion to get people to shop there.*

commiserate   See the entry for *sympathize.*

common   See the entries for *average, public, yard.*

commotion   (*noun*) a great deal of noise; a violent disturbance. □ *I heard a commotion in the street.* □ *What's all the commotion in here?*
   • **fuss**   a *commotion* over something unimportant. (Informal.) □ *Dana tends to make a fuss if she doesn't get what she wants.* □ *Eddie is always making a big fuss over nothing.*
   • **hullabaloo**   a confused *commotion.* (Informal.) □ *My neighbor's party created such a hullabaloo that I thought of calling the police.* □ *There was a tremendous hullabaloo in our town when a murder was committed there.*
   • **stink**   a *commotion* in response to something offensive. (Informal.) □ *If we forget Fran's birthday, she'll probably raise a stink.* □ *The newspapers made a big stink about the mayor's frequent vacations.*

• **to-do**   a mild *commotion*. □ *There was a to-do in the office when George announced that he was quitting.* □ *Helen caused quite a to-do when she brought the stray dog home.*

• **tumult**   a great *commotion*, especially one caused by many people. □ *When the home team finally scored, there was a tumult in the ballpark.* □ *The school was in a tumult the day the principal canceled spring vacation.*

communal   See the entry for *public*.

communicable   See the entry for *catching*.

community   See the entries for *culture, town*.

compact   See the entries for *agreement, firm*.

company   (*noun*) an organization for doing business. (See also the entry for *visitor*.) □ *Dad works for an automobile company.* □ *Helen owns her own company.*

• **business**   a *company* that engages in buying and selling. □ *Irene learned how to run a business.* □ *Joe's used-car business is doing well.*

• **concern**   a *company*. (Somewhat old-fashioned.) □ *The store was a family concern and did not hire anyone outside the family.* □ *The print shop is a thriving concern.*

• **corporation**   a technical word for a *company* organized under law, especially a *company* owned by many people. □ *Kay hoped to get a job working for a major corporation.* □ *Laura owns shares in several different corporations.*

• **firm**   a *company*, especially a *company* of lawyers or stockbrokers. (Formal. See also the main entry for *firm*.) □ *Mary got a job with a law firm.* □ *Everyone welcomed the new employee to the firm.*

comparable   See the entry for *equal*.

compassion   See the entry for *mercy*.

compel   See the entry for *make²*.

compelling   See the entry for *urgent*.

compensate   See the entry for *reward*.

compete   (*verb*) to work to get something while someone else is also working to get it; to work against someone to get something. □ *There were six swimmers competing for the gold medal.* □ *Tom and Sue competed against each other for the highest grade in the class.*

• **contend**   to *compete* against someone equally good. □ *The wrestlers contended for the championship.* □ *The two actors contended against each other for the lead role.*

• **contest**   to *compete;* to challenge or argue against someone. (See also the main entry for *contest.*) ☐ *The armies contested over the small piece of territory.* ☐ *The umpire made a call, and Philip contested it.*
• **vie**   to *compete* energetically. ☐ *Rita and Stanley constantly vie to see who can type the fastest.* ☐ *The children vied with one another for their parents' attention.*
[→see also: *challenge, fight*]

competence   See the entry for *mastery.*

competition   See the entry for *contest.*

competitive   See the entry for *aggressive.*

complacent   See the entry for *content.*

complain   (*verb*) to say you are unhappy with something. ☐ *Tim complained about the quality of the food in the cafeteria.* ☐ *Jan complained that she didn't have anything nice to wear.*
• **bellyache**   to *complain* obnoxiously; to whine. (Slang.) ☐ *Stop bellyaching about how dirty the house is and help me clean it up!* ☐ *Bill spent his whole vacation bellyaching about the weather.*
• **carp**   to *complain* in a mean way. (Informal.) ☐ *Art's mom always carps at him for the way he dresses.* ☐ *Mary would rather carp about the videos I bring home than go to the store with me and help me pick them out.*
• **gripe**   to *complain* sharply. (Slang.) ☐ *"The waiters here are so slow," Charlie griped.* ☐ *Donald griped about how long he had to stand in line for the movie.*
• **grouse**   to *complain* continuously. ☐ *Every day when he comes home, Dad spends half an hour grousing about his job.* ☐ *Ellen is always grousing about how stupid most TV shows are.*
• **grumble**   to *complain* in a low voice. ☐ *Fran grumbled about having to set the table.* ☐ *George grumbled when his allowance was cut.*

complete   See the entries for *finish, whole.*

complex   See the entry for *complicated.*

complicated   (*adjective*) difficult to figure out; made up of many parts. ☐ *The movie's story was very complicated.* ☐ *Rita didn't know how to fix the complicated machine.*
• **complex**   very *complicated; complicated* by nature. ☐ *The rules for the game were so complex that we decided not to play it.* ☐ *Through the microscope, Susan could see the complex structure of the leaf.*
• **elaborate**   designed in a *complicated* way. ☐ *In the 1700s, many women wore elaborate hairstyles that stood three or four feet high.* ☐ *The spy had an elaborate plan for escaping from prison.*

• **fancy**   *complicated;* highly decorated. (Informal.) □ *I don't need any of those fancy food processors; a knife and a cutting board work just fine.* □ *Tom made a cake with fancy decorations made of frosting.*
• **intricate**   *complicated* and delicate; put together in a *complicated* way. (Formal.) □ *Jack opened the back of the watch and showed me the intricate machinery inside.* □ *Laura embroidered an intricate pattern on the shirt.*
• **involved**   *complicated;* tangled up in a *complicated* way. □ *Mark told an involved story about how he had come to live in Baltimore.* □ *Nancy has an involved system for keeping her magazines in order.*
[→contrasting word: *simple*]

compliment   See the entry for *praise.*

comply   See the entry for *consent.*

comply with   See the entry for *obey.*

component   See the entry for *element.*

composed   See the entry for *calm.*

compound   See the entry for *mix.*

comprehend   See the entry for *understand.*

comprehensive   See the entry for *thorough.*

compulsion   See the entry for *obsession.*

compunction   See the entry for *guilt.*

compute   See the entry for *figure.*

con   See the entry for *fool².*

con artist   See the entry for *fraud.*

conceal   See the entry for *hide.*

concede   See the entry for *admit.*

conceited   (*adjective*) thinking you are better than anybody else; overly proud. □ *Art is very conceited; all he ever talks about is himself.* □ *No one likes to be around such a conceited person.*
• **arrogant**   *conceited* and demanding special treatment. (Formal.) □ *The arrogant journalist thought she was too good to have to pay attention to deadlines.* □ *Bob ordered everyone around in an arrogant way.*
• **haughty**   *conceited* and scornful. □ *The haughty customer treated the salesclerks like insects.* □ *Charles was so haughty that he didn't care if people liked him or not.*

• **snooty**   *conceited,* scornful, and rude. (Slang.) □ *Don't act so snooty; you're no better than anyone else.* □ *That store is very snooty; they say they will sell things only to "quality people."*
• **stuck-up**   *conceited* and scornful. (Slang.) □ *The teacher praises Donald so much that he's getting awfully stuck-up.* □ *Eddie's an amazingly good basketball player, but he's not stuck-up about it.*
• **vain**   *conceited* about your appearance or your talents. □ *You can tell he's vain because he's always turning to look at his reflection.* □ *Fran became very vain about her ability to play the guitar.*
[→contrasting word: *modest*]

conceivably   See the entry for *maybe.*

conceive   See the entry for *imagine.*

concentration   See the entry for *attention.*

concept   See the entry for *idea.*

concern   See the entry for *company.*

concert   (*noun*) an occasion when musicians play for an audience. □ *The band will give a concert at 7:00 P.M. on Saturday.* □ *George went to a rock concert last night.*
• **performance**   a *concert;* any occasion when someone performs for an audience. □ *The performance was canceled because the pianist was ill.* □ *What time is the performance tonight?*
• **recital**   a *concert* given by one musician or the students of one musician. □ *The opera singer gave a recital that included her favorite songs.* □ *Harold had to decide what piece he would play in the recital.*
• **show**   a *concert;* a performance including musicians, dancers, or other entertainers. (See also the main entry for *show².*) □ *Irene and Jim went downtown to eat dinner and see a show.* □ *Kay hummed the theme song from the show.*

conciliate   See the entry for *appease.*

concise   See the entry for *brief.*

conclude   (*verb*) to come to a decision or form an idea after examining all the facts. (See also the entry for *finish.*) □ *Mom said, "Since I see you watching TV, I conclude that you must have finished your homework."* □ *Noticing that Mary was avoiding him, Larry concluded that she must be upset with him.*
• **deduce**   to *conclude* something by reasoning step by step. □ *From all the clues he found in the living room, the detective deduced that the thief must have come in by the window.* □ *The veterinarian examined the cat and then deduced that it had eaten something bad.*

• **gather**   to *conclude* something on the basis of a few facts. □ *Tom gathered that Sue was happy to see him.* □ *I gather that you're finished with the book.*

• **infer**   to *conclude* something by reasoning; to reason something out. □ *Given that Philip is packing his suitcase, I infer that he is going on a trip.* □ *Rita was able to infer the real meaning of Susan's words.*

• **surmise**   to *conclude* something; to make a guess after seeing all the facts. (Formal.) □ *Tim looked at the sopping clothes in the washing machine and surmised that the machine must be broken.* □ *I surmise that Jan must have sent these flowers.*

conclusion   See the entry for *end*.

conclusive   (*adjective*) giving a definite answer; putting an end to all debate. □ *The evidence of Arnold's guilt was conclusive.* □ *The scientist showed conclusive proof that her theory was correct.*

• **decisive**   entirely *conclusive*; giving a solid decision. □ *Ben gave a decisive answer.* □ *The team won a decisive victory.*

• **definitive**   *conclusive* and final; having the last word (Formal.) □ *This is the definitive book on science-fiction movies.* □ *The expert gave a definitive answer to the question.*

• **incontrovertible**   *conclusive* and undeniable. (Formal.) □ *The experiment gave incontrovertible proof that the theory was true.* □ *The star's status as one of the greatest actors in the country is surely incontrovertible.*

concur   See the entry for *agree*.

condemn   See the entry for *blame*.

condescending   See the entry for *pretentious*.

condition   See the entry for *case*.

conduct   See the entry for *behavior*.

confederate   See the entry for *partner*.

conference   See the entry for *meeting*.

confess   See the entry for *admit*.

confidant   See the entry for *friend*.

confident   See the entry for *certain*.

confidential   See the entry for *private*.

confined   See the entry for *cramped*.

conform   See the entries for *match, obey*.

confound   (*verb*) to make someone feel very confused. □ *Charlie was able to confound his pursuers by taking a zigzag path.* □ *The mysterious object in the sky confounded the scientists; they could not explain what it was.*

• **flabbergast**   to *confound* and shock someone. (Informal.) □ *The whole town was flabbergasted when they learned that the mayor was a criminal.* □ *Fred flabbergasted Edith by asking her to marry him.*

• **floor**   to deeply *confound* and surprise someone. □ *Donna floored her family by telling them that she had won the scholarship.* □ *I was floored when I heard the unexpected news.*

• **nonplus**   to *confound* someone so much that he or she does not know what to say. □ *George's rude remark nonplussed the teacher.* □ *Helen was nonplussed when she discovered a hundred-dollar bill in her coat pocket.*

• **stagger**   to *confound* someone so much that he or she feels unsteady. □ *The doctor staggered Alice by telling her that she had a serious illness.* □ *Jim's decision to leave town staggered his friends.*

[→see also: *surprise*]

confront   See the entry for *face*.

confuse   (*verb*) to make someone feel puzzled and disturbed. □ *The movie confused me; I couldn't keep track of all the characters.* □ *Kevin was confused by the way Larry treated him.*

• **bewilder**   to *confuse* someone so much that he or she does not know what to do next. □ *These instructions seem designed to bewilder anyone who tries to follow them!* □ *Computers bewildered and frightened Mark.*

• **mystify**   to *confuse* someone completely. □ *Tom didn't understand the joke; in fact, it mystified him.* □ *The cat's strange behavior mystified her owner.*

• **perplex**   to *confuse* and upset someone. □ *The baby's constant crying perplexed his parents.* □ *No matter what she did, Sue couldn't make the radio work; this perplexed her.*

[→see also: *puzzle*]

congregate   See the entry for *get together*.

congress   See the entry for *meeting*.

conjecture   See the entry for *wonder²*.

connect   See the entry for *join*.

conquer   See the entry for *beat²*.

consent   (*verb*) to agree to something; to approve of something. (See also the entry for *agree*.) □ *Philip consented to lend his stamp collection to the library.* □ *The journalist asked if he could quote me, and I consented.*

• **accede**   to *consent* or yield to something. (Usually with *to*.) (Formal.) □ *The mayor finally acceded to the people's wish that she resign.* □ *Rita acceded to the journalist's demands for an interview.*

• **acquiesce**   to *consent* to something by not opposing it. (Often with *in*.) (Formal.) □ *We asked if we could use Mr. Richards's yard; Mr. Richards acquiesced.* □ *Susan acquiesced in our plan but would not join us in carrying it out.*

• **comply**   to *consent;* to do what someone wants you to. (Usually with *with*.) □ *Jan complied with all the rules.* □ *"Take your shoes off and leave them by the door," said Tim. I complied.*

consequence   See the entry for *result*.

conservatory   See the entry for *school*.

conserve   See the entry for *preserve*.

consider   (*verb*) to give careful thought to something. □ *Art considered buying a stereo.* □ *Ben considered carefully before making up his mind.*

• **contemplate**   to *consider* something calmly; to *consider* doing something. □ *Carrie contemplated what she had heard her brother say.* □ *Donald contemplates quitting his job.*

• **deliberate**   to *consider* by debating something in your mind. (Formal.) □ *Eddie deliberated whether or not to tell what he knew.* □ *I deliberated about going to the party but finally decided not to.*

• **think about**   to *consider* something; to *consider* whether or not you will do something. □ *Fran is thinking about trying out for the play.* □ *I'll think about what you've told me.*

considerably   See the entry for *very*.

considerate   (*adjective*) kind and careful of someone else's feelings. □ *A considerate neighbor offered to look after George while he was sick.* □ *Sending George a get-well card was a considerate thing to do.*

• **attentive**   *considerate;* making sure other people are comfortable. (Used to describe people, not actions.) □ *Helen's hosts were attentive to her every need.* □ *The attentive waitress brought fresh coffee before we had a chance to ask for it.*

• **solicitous**   *considerate;* eager to know what you can do for someone. (Formal.) □ *The nurses were very solicitous, always asking if George needed anything.* □ *Always solicitous, Grandma offered to bring me an extra blanket and a warmer pair of slippers.*

• **thoughtful**   *considerate;* providing what you think someone else will want. □ *It was thoughtful of Irene to water my garden while I was away.* □ *Jane always tries to give thoughtful gifts, ones her friends can really use.*

[→see also: *kind¹*]

console   See the entry for *comfort*.

conspicuous   (*adjective*) hard to overlook. (Formal.) □ *The orange house was the most conspicuous building on the street.* □ *There was a conspicuous swelling on one side of Kay's face.*
   • **noticeable**   conspicuous; easy to notice. □ *Larry had a noticeable limp.* □ *The most noticeable thing about Mary's new car is its bright color.*
   • **prominent**   large or important and therefore conspicuous. □ *The skyscraper was a prominent part of the city's skyline.* □ *The store window included a prominent display of fashionable shoes.*
   • **visible**   conspicuous; easy to see. □ *The dome of the capitol building is visible from anywhere in town.* □ *There was a visible change in Tom after that summer.*
   [→contrasting word: *inconspicuous*]

conspiracy   See the entry for *plot*.

constant   (*adjective*) steady and never stopping. (See also the entry for *faithful*.) □ *Otto wanted to get away from his sister's constant chattering.* □ *Watching his weight is a constant problem for Peter.*
   • **continual**   constant over a long time. □ *Her classmates' continual teasing made Rita hate to go to school.* □ *The dog made continual demands to be let in or out.*
   • **incessant**   annoyingly constant; never stopping. (Formal.) □ *Susan was wearied by the dog's incessant barking.* □ *I can't sleep through that incessant noise.*
   • **nonstop**   energetic and constant; not stopping. □ *Tim held a nonstop party all weekend long.* □ *My stay at camp was nonstop fun.*
   • **perpetual**   constant over a very long time; never slowing down or ending. □ *Keeping this house clean demands perpetual work.* □ *The doctor couldn't find a reason for the baby's perpetual crying.*
   • **unceasing**   never stopping. □ *The friends vowed unceasing loyalty to each other.* □ *Jan's attempts to get me to go jogging with her were unceasing.*

construct   See the entry for *build*.

construction   See the entry for *building*.

consume   See the entry for *eat*.

consummate   See the entry for *perfect*.

contact   (*verb*) to successfully get a message to someone. □ *We need to know whom to contact in case of an emergency.* □ *If you have any questions, please feel free to contact me.*
   • **get hold of**   to contact someone in order to talk with him or her. (Informal.) □ *I've called Bill several times, but I haven't got hold of him yet.* □ *I tried to get hold of Art at his office.*

• **get in touch with**   to *contact* someone by calling or writing him or her; to find someone and talk with him or her. □ *Mary left a number where we could get in touch with her.* □ *I'm glad I finally got in touch with you.*
• **reach**   to *contact* someone. (Informal.) □ *Where can I reach you this evening?* □ *Carrie was out hiking in the country and couldn't be reached.*

contagious   See the entry for *catching*.

container   (*noun*) something you can keep things in. □ *Donald found a container to put the leftovers in.* □ *Edith had a plastic container full of nails.*
• **canister**   a small, usually metal *container* with a lid. □ *Fran kept the coffee in a tin canister.* □ *I took some flour out of the canister and added it to the bread dough.*
• **holder**   a *container* that you can put something in while you are not using it. □ *George made a holder to keep pens and pencils in.* □ *Helen has a special holder for soft drinks in her car.*
• **receptacle**   a *container* you can use to collect things in. (Formal.) □ *Please place all trash in the refuse receptacles.* □ *Irene used the little bowl as a receptacle for used tea bags.*
• **reservoir**   a *container* for storing extra liquid. □ *The engine has an extra fuel reservoir.* □ *Rainwater was stored in the town reservoir.*
• **vessel**   a *container*, especially one for holding liquids. (Old-fashioned.) □ *The merchant sold six vessels full of olive oil.* □ *The cook poured out all the wine from the vessel.*

contaminate   See the entry for *dirty²*.

contemplate   See the entries for *consider, think*.

contemporary   See the entry for *present*.

contempt   See the entry for *disrespect*.

contend   See the entries for *argue³, compete*.

contender   See the entry for *candidate*.

content   (*adjective*) pleased with everything; not wanting anything more. □ *Jay says he is content with his present job.* □ *Kay felt content to be at home.*
• **at peace**   calm and *content*; not fighting. □ *Laura is at peace with her decision to go back to school.* □ *The two brothers are finally at peace with each other.*
• **complacent**   *content* and not worried about anything; overly satisfied. (Formal.) □ *Mark should not be so complacent about his good grades; he mustn't stop working hard.* □ *Tom settled back into his chair with a complacent expression on his face.*

• **gratified**   *content* because you have gotten something good. (Formal.) □ *Sue was gratified by her friends' reaction to her new haircut.* □ *Philip was gratified to be elected club president.*
• **satisfied**   reasonably *content;* having enough. □ *My boss is satisfied with my work.* □ *A satisfied smile broke out on Rita's face when she found out she had won.*

contentious   See the entry for *belligerent.*

contest   (*noun*) an event in which people try to win a prize. (See also the entry for *compete.*) □ *Susan entered a pie-eating contest.* □ *Tim won first place in the art contest.*
    • **competition**   a *contest* in which people must compete. □ *The library sponsored a competition for who could read the most books in a month.* □ *The singer won the talent competition.*
    • **match**   a *contest* between two people or teams. (See also the main entry for *match.*) □ *The soccer team wanted to win their next match.* □ *Jan challenged me to a tennis match.*
    • **meet**   a *contest* between a number of people or teams. (See also the main entry for *meet.*) □ *There were several events in the swim meet.* □ *I went to watch the runners in the track meet.*

contestant   See the entry for *candidate.*

continual   See the entry for *constant.*

continue   See the entry for *last.*

contort   See the entry for *distort.*

contract   See the entry for *agreement.*

contract for   See the entry for *rent.*

contradictory   See the entry for *opposite.*

contraption   See the entry for *device.*

contrary   See the entry for *opposite.*

contribute   See the entry for *supply.*

contrivance   See the entry for *device.*

contrived   See the entry for *artificial.*

control[1]   (*verb*) to be able to guide something. □ *Bill controls the family money.* □ *By moving this handle, you can control how much water comes out of the faucet.*
    • **direct**   to *control* what something is going to do next. □ *The police officer directed traffic.* □ *The teacher directed his class according to his lesson plan.*

• **govern**   to *control* something, especially through laws. □ *The elected officials did their best to govern the country.* □ *It was hard for Art to govern his temper.*

• **manage**   to *control* someone or something; to keep something running smoothly. □ *Anna went to business school in order to learn how to manage a business.* □ *He is an excellent baby-sitter and can manage the most unruly children.*

• **regulate**   to *control* how fast something can go or how much it can do; to *control* something by making rules. (Formal.) □ *This valve regulates the amount of fuel that goes into the engine.* □ *The law regulates the sale of guns.*

• **run**   to *control* the way something will go forward; to make something go forward. (See also the main entry for *run*.) □ *Mary runs a grocery store.* □ *The citizens did not like the way the president was running the country.*

control² (*verb*) to have power over something. □ *Carrie knew she couldn't control her feelings, but she tried to control her actions.* □ *The wizard thought he could control future events.*

• **engineer**   to *control* the way something is designed. □ *Donald engineered the rules of the game so that he would always win.* □ *Edith helped to engineer the way classes were taught at the special school.*

• **influence**   to *control* something indirectly. □ *Fran wanted to influence my opinion.* □ *The artist's mood always influenced the pictures she painted.*

• **manipulate**   to *control* something for your own purposes. (Formal.) □ *The leader's speech manipulated the feelings of the people who heard it.* □ *George has the ability to manipulate people to do whatever he wants.*

• **shape**   to *control* the way something is formed; to form something. □ *Helen's childhood experiences shaped the way she thought.* □ *The teacher helped to shape his students' opinions.*

convene   See the entry for *get together*.

convenient   (*adjective*) happening at a good time. □ *It was convenient for me that a tow truck came by minutes after my car broke down.* □ *What would be a convenient time for you to come see me?*

• **advantageous**   happening at a useful time; useful. □ *Irene caught an advantageous cold on the day of the test she hadn't studied for.* □ *Jay's ability to speak French was advantageous on his trip through Quebec.*

• **auspicious**   happening at a lucky time; seeming like a good omen. (Formal.) □ *Kay thought that the rainbow in the sky was an auspicious sign.* □ *The smile on Dad's face when he came home seemed auspicious.*

• **favorable** happening at a good time; encouraging. □ *Laura waited for a favorable opportunity to make her request.* □ *The weather on Saturday was favorable, so we set out on our trip.*
• **opportune** happening at just the right time. (Formal.) □ *Mark arrived on the scene at an opportune time.* □ *Grandma gave me an opportune gift of five dollars, just when I needed it.*
• **propitious** happening at a lucky time; lucky. (Formal.) □ *Nancy did not think the circumstances were propitious for going ahead with her plan.* □ *The astrologer told Tom that the stars were in a propitious position for him.*
[→see also: *useful*]

convention See the entries for *custom, meeting.*

conversation See the entry for *talk¹.*

converse See the entry for *talk².*

convert See the entry for *change.*

convey See the entries for *carry, express.*

conveyance See the entry for *vehicle.*

convince See the entry for *persuade.*

cook (*verb*) to prepare food, usually by heating it in some way. □ *Philip cooked dinner for himself.* □ *Rita did not know the best way to cook fish.*
• **bake** to *cook* something in an oven. □ *Susan baked a batch of cookies.* □ *Tim baked an apple pie.*
• **barbecue** to *cook* something on a grill, usually with a spicy sauce. □ *Jan barbecued chicken wings on the outdoor grill.* □ *Bill barbecued all kinds of meat for the party.*
• **boil** to *cook* something in hot water. (See also the main entry for *boil.*) □ *Art made soup by boiling beans.* □ *The cook boiled the potatoes and then mashed them.*
• **broil** to *cook* something on a grill. □ *It's easy to broil fish.* □ *Ben broiled some lamb chops.*
• **fry** to *cook* something in hot oil or fat. □ *Carrie fries chicken according to a secret family recipe.* □ *Donald fried some potatoes for a side dish.*
• **grill** to *cook* something with an open flame, usually on a metal grid called a grill. □ *We all waited hungrily while Bob grilled the fish we had caught.* □ *For a quick snack, cut a tomato in half, sprinkle it with spicy breadcrumbs, and grill it for five minutes.*
• **roast** to *cook* something at high heat. □ *Mom put the meat in the oven to roast.* □ *Eddie makes an unusual dish by roasting an eggplant and mashing it up with spices.*

cool   See the entry for *cold.*

coop   See the entry for *cage.*

cooperate   See the entry for *team up.*

cop   See the entry for *officer.*

cope with   See the entry for *handle.*

copious   See the entry for *plentiful.*

copy[1]   (*verb*) to act the way someone else acts; to do as someone else does. ☐ *Fran hates it when her sister copies her.* ☐ *George's children sometimes copy the way he shouts.*

   • **ape**   to *copy* someone clumsily; to *copy* someone in order to make fun of him or her. ☐ *Harold looked ridiculous, aping Helen's elegant manners.* ☐ *Irene wrote a book aping the style of romance novels.*

   • **emulate**   to *copy* someone you admire. (Formal.) ☐ *Jay tried to emulate his favorite teacher.* ☐ *Kevin's little brother adores him and emulates him in every respect.*

   • **imitate**   to *copy* someone in every detail. ☐ *Larry tried to imitate Mark's voice.* ☐ *Tom can imitate many different movie stars.*

   • **mimic**   to *copy* someone exactly; to *copy* someone in order to make fun. ☐ *The comedians mimicked the president.* ☐ *Sue is trying to annoy me by mimicking everything I say.*

copy[2]   (*verb*) to create something that is exactly like something else. ☐ *Other companies tried to copy the formula for the popular soft drink.* ☐ *The artist copied the famous painting.*

   • **duplicate**   to *copy* something. (Formal.) ☐ *I can't duplicate my great-grandmother's beautiful embroidery.* ☐ *The hairdresser was able to duplicate the movie actress's hairstyle.*

   • **replicate**   to *copy* something one or more times; to do something again exactly the same way. (Formal.) ☐ *All the networks rushed to replicate the successful TV series.* ☐ *The scientist could not replicate the exciting results of his first experiment.*

   • **reproduce**   to *copy* something precisely. ☐ *The actor was very good at reproducing the way other people behaved.* ☐ *The cages in this zoo are supposed to reproduce the natural habitat of each animal.*

   • **simulate**   to create something that looks or acts like something else. ☐ *Philip can simulate the calls of several different kinds of birds.* ☐ *Ken used sugar cubes to simulate blocks of ice when he built his model igloo.*

core   See the entry for *center.*

corporation   See the entry for *company.*

corpulent   See the entry for *fat.*

correct   See the entry for *right.*

correspond   See the entry for *match.*

corridor   See the entry for *hall.*

corrode   See the entry for *wear away.*

corrupt   (*adjective*) bad and dishonest. □ *The corrupt politician stole public money.* □ *After years of hanging out with criminals, Roger became corrupt.*
> • **crooked**   *corrupt.* (Slang. See also the main entry for *crooked.*) □ *It was hard to believe that the police officer was crooked.* □ *Stanley was well known for making crooked deals.*
> • **shady**   secretly *corrupt.* (Slang.) □ *The salesman seemed like a shady character.* □ *What kind of shady business is Stanley up to now?*
> • **unprincipled**   *corrupt;* not caring about the difference between right and wrong. □ *Mr. Jones was an unprincipled man who would do anything to make money.* □ *The judge lectured the criminal about her unprincipled way of life.*
> • **unscrupulous**   *corrupt;* willing to do bad things. (Formal.) □ *The unscrupulous storekeeper loved to cheat people.* □ *Unfortunately, the banker's unscrupulous behavior was not against the law.*

costly   See the entry for *expensive.*

costume   See the entry for *disguise.*

cottage   See the entry for *house.*

counsel   See the entry for *advise.*

count   (*verb*) to go over a group of things one by one in order to find out how many there are. □ *Jan counted the guppies in the fishbowl.* □ *Bill counted how many times the baby sneezed.*
> • **add up**   to *count* things from several groups and then figure out how many there are in all; to figure out a total number. □ *Art added up the prices of everything in his grocery cart.* □ *The baby-sitter added up the number of hours she had worked that week.*
> • **number**   to *count.* (Old-fashioned.) □ *The herdsman had so many sheep he could scarcely number them.* □ *Theodore carefully numbered the insults he received from Victor, and planned to get revenge for every one.*
> • **tally**   to *count* things by making a mark for each one; to figure out a total. (Sometimes with *up.*) □ *The prisoner tallied the days he spent in jail.* □ *I tallied up how much I'd spent that month.*

count on   See the entry for *expect.*

counter   See the entry for *answer.*

counterfeit   See the entry for *artificial.*

country (*adjective*) having to do with farming or with open land. □ *Bill preferred country life to city life.* □ *He thought country folks were the friendliest people on earth.*

  • **rural**   country; having to do with land outside the city. □ *Anna lives in a rural area.* □ *Ben was delighted with the peaceful rural landscape.*

  • **rustic**   country; plain, rough, and charming. □ *There was a rustic weather vane atop the farmhouse.* □ *The old farmer had a rustic way of speaking.*

  • **pastoral**   country. (Formal or poetic.) □ *Our hero longed to return to the pastoral home where he had grown to manhood.* □ *The artist specialized in painting pastoral scenes.*

courageous (*adjective*) willing to face danger. □ *The courageous woman dived into the freezing river to save the child who had fallen in.* □ *The general praised the soldiers for their courageous actions.*

  • **bold**   willing or eager to go forward; daring. (Formal.) □ *The bold student challenged what the teacher had said.* □ *The scientist has a bold new theory about why dinosaurs became extinct.*

  • **brave**   willing to face danger or hardship. □ *The sick boy was very brave about getting the painful treatments for his disease.* □ *The fire fighter did many brave things every day.*

  • **fearless**   not afraid to face danger; not afraid. □ *The fearless criminal performed many daring robberies.* □ *A tightrope walker must be a fearless person.*

  • **intrepid**   eager to face whatever lies ahead. (Formal.) □ *The intrepid explorers pushed on toward the North Pole.* □ *The intrepid businesswoman would risk anything on a venture if she thought it was worthwhile.*

  [→contrasting word: *cowardly*]

course   See the entries for *class, series.*

court   See the entry for *date².*

courteous   See the entry for *polite.*

courtesy   See the entry for *favor.*

covenant   See the entry for *agreement.*

cover (*verb*) to be spread over something; to spread something over something else. □ *A tablecloth covered the dining room table.* □ *Carrie covered her head with a wool scarf.*

  • **blanket**   to *cover* something with a thick layer. □ *Snow blanketed the ground.* □ *Donald blanketed the bed with quilts.*

  • **carpet**   to *cover* the ground. (See also the main entry for *carpet.*) □ *Thick grass carpeted the front yard.* □ *The field was carpeted with wildflowers.*

• **coat**   to *cover* something with a thin layer. □ *Ice coated the tree branches.* □ *The candy maker coated the peppermints with chocolate.*
• **shroud**   to *cover* something so that it is hidden. □ *Fog shrouded the old house.* □ *White sheets shrouded all the furniture inside.*
• **wrap**   to *cover* something all over; to wind around something. □ *Edith wrapped the present in pretty paper.* □ *Fran wrapped a bandage around her wounded hand.*

cover up   See the entry for *hide*.

covert   See the entry for *secret*.

covet   See the entry for *want*.

covetous   See the entry for *greedy*.

cowardly   (*adjective*) afraid of facing danger. □ *George was too cowardly to ask his boss for a raise.* □ *Helen let her friend take all the blame, which was a cowardly thing to do.*
• **chicken**   cowardly. (Juvenile.) □ *Are you going to take the dare, or are you chicken?* □ *Henry likes Alice, but he's too chicken to say so to her face.*
• **craven**   very *cowardly*. (Old-fashioned.) □ *The craven knight ran from the battle.* □ *Such a craven deed was not worthy of a knight.*
• **fainthearted**   *cowardly*; too willing to give up. □ *Jay's friends thought he was too fainthearted to be a doctor.* □ *Vincent made a fainthearted attempt to write a novel, but never finished it.*
• **spineless**   *cowardly*. (Slang.) □ *That spineless girl never sticks up for herself.* □ *Kevin had a reputation for being spineless, so he never got picked to be on anyone's football team.*
[→contrasting word: *courageous*]

cower   See the entry for *wince*.

coy   See the entry for *shy*.

cozy   See the entry for *comfortable*.

crack   See the entries for *break, joke*.

crackle   See the entry for *rustle*.

crackpot   See the entry for *character*.

cradle   See the entry for *hug*.

craft   See the entry for *boat*.

crag   See the entry for *mountain*.

cram   See the entry for *pack*.

cramped   (*adjective*) too small; very crowded. □ *A family of ten lived in the cramped two-room apartment.* □ *The shower stall was too cramped to stand up in.*

   • **confined**   cramped; hard to move around in. □ *The kennel owner kept dozens of dogs in that confined little pen.* □ *The backseat of the car was much too confined a space for three little kids on such a long trip.*

   • **narrow**   not wide and therefore cramped. □ *A narrow stairway led up to the attic.* □ *The car couldn't fit through the narrow alley.*

   • **restricted**   cramped; holding you in. □ *The secretary had a very restricted space in which to work.* □ *Sam had a very restricted upbringing and was not allowed to do many of the fun things his classmates did.*

   [→consider also: *uncomfortable*]

crank   See the entry for *fraud*.

crash   See the entry for *collide*.

crass   See the entry for *rude*.

crater   See the entry for *hole*.

crave   See the entry for *want*.

craven   See the entry for *cowardly*.

craving   See the entry for *hunger*.

crazy   (*adjective*) not in your right mind; not making any sense. (Informal.) □ *Where does Mark get his crazy ideas?* □ *My aunt sometimes acts crazy, dancing around in the street and shouting at people.*

   • **demented**   completely crazy. (Formal.) □ *The demented old man claimed that he was Julius Caesar.* □ *I could make no sense out of the demented things he said.*

   • **deranged**   wildly crazy. □ *Jane became deranged after her children were killed.* □ *Oliver had a deranged plan for becoming King of the United States.*

   • **insane**   crazy. (Formal.) □ *The doctors agreed that Peter was insane and should be hospitalized.* □ *Only an insane person could do such a thing.*

   • **lunatic**   crazy. (Poetic.) □ *Our hero was dismayed by the lunatic ravings of the princess.* □ *The lord and lady had a lunatic son whom they kept confined in the castle.*

   • **mad**   crazy. (Formal; somewhat old-fashioned.) □ *Although this character in the play is supposed to be mad, she often says the most sensible things.* □ *The members of the rock band were famous for their mad behavior.*

   • **nutty**   crazy. (Slang.) □ *Don't listen to my sister; she's nutty.* □ *Ronald's always doing nutty things, like dyeing his hair green.*

creak   See the entry for *squeak*.

crease   (*verb*) a sharp fold or deep line. (See also the entry for *fold*.) ☐ *Susan made a crease down the middle of the paper.* ☐ *Fold the piece of cardboard along the crease.*

- **furrow**   a deep line; a trench. ☐ *The plow made a furrow in the earth.* ☐ *I could tell from the furrows in Tim's brow that he was thinking deeply.*
- **groove**   a fairly wide *crease*. ☐ *The sliding door fits into a groove in the floor.* ☐ *Jan's knife cut a groove into the piece of wood.*
- **wrinkle**   an irregular *crease*. ☐ *I have to iron the wrinkles out of my good shirt.* ☐ *Bill has wrinkles at the corners of his eyes.*

create   See the entry for *make¹*.

creative   (*adjective*) good at making things; cleverly thought up. ☐ *The creative baby-sitter made up lots of new games for kids to play.* ☐ *Art has such creative ideas for making things out of wood.*

- **ingenious**   good at making or doing things in clever ways; showing cleverness. ☐ *The ingenious child fixed the toy, using just a rubber band and a paper clip.* ☐ *Ben has an ingenious way of washing the dishes.*
- **inventive**   good at making useful or unusual things. ☐ *This writer is an inventive storyteller.* ☐ *The inventive cook came up with several new recipes.*
- **resourceful**   good at making things with whatever is available. ☐ *The resourceful campers made a stove out of an old coffee can they found.* ☐ *The children were very resourceful and could invent games from simple things like rocks and string.*

creature   See the entry for *animal*.

credit   See the entries for *believe²*, *money*.

creek   See the entry for *river*.

cretin   See the entry for *fool¹*.

crew   See the entry for *team*.

crime   (*noun*) an action that is against the law. ☐ *Stealing a horse used to be considered a very serious crime.* ☐ *Charles committed a crime.*

- **felony**   a major *crime*. ☐ *Dan was given a long prison sentence as punishment for his felony.* ☐ *Breaking into someone's house is a felony in this state.*
- **infraction**   a very minor *crime*; the breaking of a rule. ☐ *Edith parked her car illegally, and had to pay a fine for this infraction.* ☐ *Fred had committed so many infractions of school rules that the principal suspended him.*

• **misdemeanor**   a minor *crime.* □ *The police arrested George and charged him with a misdemeanor.* □ *Since Helen's crime was only a misdemeanor, the punishment was not very severe.*

• **offense**   a *crime;* any wrongdoing. □ *It was Irene's first offense, so she was not sent to jail.* □ *Jay didn't know what offense he had committed to make all his friends avoid him.*

[→Note: *felony, infraction, misdemeanor,* and *offense* are all legal terms.]

criminal   (*noun*) someone who commits a crime. □ *The police officer chased the criminal.* □ *I heard on the radio that a dangerous criminal had escaped from prison.*

• **crook**   a *criminal;* usually a thief or a gangster. (Slang.) □ *The crooks got together and planned to rob the bank.* □ *Smith was a notorious crook who ran a crime ring.*

• **felon**   someone who has committed a major crime. □ *The judge sentenced the felon to fifty years in prison.* □ *The book describes Jones's fall from respected businessman to convicted felon.*

• **offender**   a *criminal;* a wrongdoer. □ *The judge was lenient with the young offender.* □ *Mom had to decide how to punish the offender.*

[→consider also: *thief, murderer*]

crimp   See the entry for *fold.*

crimson   See the entry for *red.*

cringe   See the entry for *wince.*

crinkle   See the entry for *rustle.*

crisis   See the entry for *emergency.*

critical   (*adjective*) pointing out the faults of someone or something, especially in order to make someone feel bad. □ *I thought the teacher was too critical of the story Maria wrote.* □ *Tom tends to make critical comments about the gifts people give him.*

• **cutting**   sharply *critical.* □ *Sue was crushed when Philip made a cutting remark about her new hairstyle.* □ *Roger often says cutting things about people he's jealous of.*

• **derogatory**   *critical;* pointing out that something is not very good. (Formal.) □ *Susan would not have said such derogatory things about the painting if she had known that she was speaking to the person who painted it.* □ *"The old bat" is the derogatory way Todd refers to his mother.*

• **disparaging**   *critical;* intending to cut someone down. □ *The actor made disparaging remarks about everyone else who was in the movie with him.* □ *Wendy spread disparaging gossip about Victor.*

[→Note: *cutting, derogatory,* and *disparaging* are used to describe language, not people.]

criticize   (*verb*) to point out someone's faults; to tell someone what he or she did wrong. □ *Art wished his sister would quit criticizing the way he dressed.* □ *The newspaper article criticized the president's actions.*

• **castigate**   to *criticize* someone very severely. □ *The father castigated his son for his disrespectful behavior.* □ *Ben's boss castigated him for failing to get the report typed in time.*

• **censure**   to *criticize* someone formally or publicly. □ *The head of the zoo censured the zookeeper for taking such poor care of the animals.* □ *The mayor was censured by the press.*

• **chew out**   to *criticize* someone roughly. (Slang.) □ *Mom really chewed me out when I didn't come home on time.* □ *I already feel bad enough about losing the money; you don't have to chew me out.*

• **rag on**   to *criticize* someone endlessly. (Slang.) □ *All Charlie ever does is rag on his friends.* □ *Quit ragging on me and let me tell my side of the story!*

crook   See the entry for *criminal.*

crooked   (*adjective*) not straight. (See also the main entry for *corrupt.*) □ *The old tree had a crooked trunk.* □ *Rachel limped on her crooked leg.*

• **awry**   *crooked* but supposed to be straight; not working properly. □ *The door is awry and won't shut properly.* □ *Something went awry with our plan.*

• **bent**   *crooked;* folded over at an angle. □ *The old man walked with a bent back.* □ *How can you knit with those bent knitting needles?*

• **twisted**   *crooked;* turned or wrenched around and around. □ *Arthritis left Richard's fingers twisted and stiff.* □ *A wreath of twisted pine branches decorated the door.*

cross   See the entry for *grumpy.*

crow   See the entry for *brag.*

crowd   (*noun*) a large group of people. □ *The crowd in the stadium cheered.* □ *A crowd gathered to watch the juggler.*

• **bunch**   a *crowd;* a group. (Informal.) □ *A bunch of kids stood outside the movie theater.* □ *Susan isn't part of the usual bunch I hang around with.*

• **horde**   a disorganized *crowd.* (Formal.) □ *A horde of shoppers burst into the store the minute it opened.* □ *Hordes of fans chased after the rock star's limousine.*

• **mob**   a violent or disorganized *crowd.* □ *The mob outside the prison didn't want to wait till sunrise to hang Sneaky Pete.* □ *The angry mob wanted the mad scientist to destroy the monster he had created.*

• **multitude**   a *crowd.* (Poetic.) □ *The leader addressed the multitude that had gathered to hear him speak.* □ *A multitude of mourners came to the president's funeral.*

• **throng**   a *crowd* packed tightly together. (Formal.) □ *The happy throng of wedding guests threw rice at the bride and groom.* □ *Throngs of people stood on the sidewalk, waiting for the parade to appear.*
[→see also: *group*]

crude   See the entry for *rough¹*.

cruel   (*adjective*) fond of causing pain; causing pain on purpose. □ *The cruel man thought it was fun to throw rocks at his dog.* □ *Locking your brother in the closet was a cruel thing to do.*
• **merciless**   willing to cause pain; without mercy. □ *The merciless judge always gave the severest punishment possible.* □ *Tim's merciless teasing made Jan cry.*
• **ruthless**   not caring if you have to cause pain; willing to do anything to get what you want. □ *The ruthless dictator had all his enemies killed.* □ *The teacher was ruthless when it came to grading exams.*
• **unkind**   not trying to avoid causing pain. □ *Bill made an unkind remark about his friend's weight.* □ *Either Art is very thoughtless, or he's really unkind.*
[→see also: *savage*]

crumple   See the entry for *collapse*.

crunch   See the entries for *crush, emergency*.

crush   (*verb*) to flatten something by pressing on it. □ *I crushed the empty cereal box and put it in the trash.* □ *Ben stepped on the little plant, crushing it.*
• **crunch**   to *crush* something that makes a crackling noise. □ *The machine in the junkyard crunches cars into cubes of metal.* □ *Carrie crunched up the styrofoam cup.*
• **grind**   to *crush* something into small pieces; to *crush* something by rubbing it between hard surfaces. □ *The mill ground the wheat into flour.* □ *Donald ground up the coffee beans.*
• **mash**   to *crush* something into a pulp. □ *Eddie mashed the avocados to make guacamole.* □ *Fran got impatient with the clay bowl she was working on and mashed it flat.*
• **pulverize**   to *crush* something until it turns to dust. (Formal.) □ *The bricks were pulverized when the steamroller ran over them.* □ *George pulverized the piece of concrete by beating on it with a sledgehammer.*
[→see also: *smash, trample*]

cry   (*verb*) to show a strong feeling by shedding tears. □ *Helen cried at the end of the movie.* □ *Jay was so upset that he cried.*
• **bawl**   to *cry* loudly. (Informal.) □ *Keith's mother spanked him, and he bawled.* □ *The kid kept bawling all afternoon.*

• **snivel**   to *cry* and sniff in a whiny way. □ *Larry sniveled because he wasn't invited to the skating party.* □ *I hate the way Mary snivels when she's feeling sorry for herself.*
• **sob**   to *cry* hard. □ *"I miss my parents," Tom sobbed.* □ *Sue sobbed with frustration.*
• **weep**   to *cry.* (Poetic.) □ *Somewhere in the enormous house, a child was weeping.* □ *Phyllis wept all through her husband's funeral.*
• **whimper**   to *cry* softly in a whiny way. □ *The hungry baby whimpered.* □ *"I don't want to get a tetanus shot," Alice whimpered.*

cuddle   See the entry for *hug.*

culture   (*noun*) the way a group of people lives; the rules a group of people lives by; a group of people who share a way of life. □ *Susan spent a year in France to learn about French culture.* □ *In many ancient cultures, animal sacrifices were common.*
• **civilization**   a great or important *culture.* □ *Thousands of years ago, a great civilization flourished in Sumeria.* □ *The archaeologist studied the ancient civilization of the Maya.*
• **community**   a group of people who share a *culture.* □ *The politician was well respected in the Latino community.* □ *The library has an important function in our community.*
• **society**   the system a group of people lives by; a group of people who share such a system. □ *Society cannot allow criminals to go unpunished.* □ *In American society, belching is not considered polite.*

cunning   See the entry for *sneaky.*

cure   (*noun*) something that gets rid of a sickness. □ *Rest and regular meals were the cure for Art's illness.* □ *The scientist was looking for a cure for cancer.*
• **antidote**   a *cure* for poison. □ *The doctor injected Ben with an antidote for the poison he had swallowed.* □ *Playing out in the snow was a good antidote to the winter blues.*
• **remedy**   a *cure;* something that gets rid of a problem. □ *Aspirin is a popular remedy for headaches.* □ *Carrie felt there could be no remedy for her broken heart.*
• **treatment**   the use or application of a *cure.* □ *The doctor thought that treatment with eyedrops would get rid of the redness in Donald's eye.* □ *Eddie is undergoing treatment for rabies.*

curious   (*adjective*) wanting to know more. □ *The curious boy peeked into the room where he was not supposed to go.* □ *Fran is very curious and wants to know how everything works.*
• **inquiring**   *curious;* asking about things. □ *The scientist had an inquiring mind.* □ *Helen gave me an inquiring look when I said I wasn't friends with Irene anymore.*

• **inquisitive**   *curious;* wanting to find things out. (Formal.) ☐ *The inquisitive child never tired of asking questions.* ☐ *The inquisitive reporter soon found out the mayor's secret.*

• **nosy**   *curious* about something that is none of your business; prying. ☐ *The nosy man used binoculars to spy on his neighbors.* ☐ *George asked me a lot of nosy questions.*

curl   See the entry for *wind²*.

currency   See the entry for *money*.

current   See the entries for *electricity, present*.

curtsey   See the entry for *bow*.

custom   (*noun*) something that someone always does in a particular situation; something that people have done for generations. ☐ *It is Jay's custom to eat at the same restaurant every Friday night.* ☐ *We have a family custom of eating black-eyed peas on New Year's Day.*

• **convention**   a *custom* that everyone is supposed to follow. ☐ *The convention at that school is for students to address the teachers as "sir" and "ma'am."* ☐ *According to polite convention, you must say "excuse me" before you leave the table.*

• **institution**   an important, long-established, or official *custom*. ☐ *The Super Bowl party is an institution at Kay's house.* ☐ *Our town has made the Fourth of July picnic into an institution.*

• **practice**   a *custom;* something that someone is in the habit of doing. (See also the main entry for *practice*.) ☐ *Naming children after their parents or grandparents is a common practice.* ☐ *Larry makes a practice of walking his dog twice a day.*

• **tradition**   an old, respected *custom*. ☐ *Giving birthday presents is a tradition in this country.* ☐ *The wedding guests followed the tradition of painting "Just Married" on the newlyweds' car.*

customary   See the entry for *familiar*.

customer   (*noun*) someone who pays for something. ☐ *Only a few customers came into the store.* ☐ *Mary is the bakery's best customer.*

• **client**   a *customer* for someone's services. ☐ *The lawyer had a meeting with his client.* ☐ *The social worker spoke with his new client.*

• **patient**   the *customer* of a doctor or dentist. (See also the main entry for *patient*.) ☐ *Several patients were waiting to see the doctor.* ☐ *The patient said she had a bad toothache.*

• **patron**   a *customer* who supports an institution. ☐ *The librarian gladly helped the library patrons.* ☐ *George is a patron of the symphony; he attends all their concerts.*

cut   (*verb*) to separate something the way a knife does. ☐ *Helen cut the potato into four pieces.* ☐ *The broken glass cut my foot.*

• **clip**   to *cut* with scissors or shears; to *cut* something very short. □ *Irene clipped the article from the newspaper.* □ *Dad clipped the dog's hair.*

• **sever**   to *cut* something off completely. □ *Jim's thumb was severed in an accident with an electric saw.* □ *Kay severed all connections with her family.*

• **slash**   to *cut* something with a long, sweeping motion. □ *The cat's claws slashed at the dog.* □ *Laura angrily slashed up the fabric.*

• **slice**   to *cut* a thin piece off something; to make a sharp cut on something. □ *Mark sliced the fresh loaf of bread.* □ *Tom sliced off the end of the banana.*

• **slit**   to *cut* something lengthwise; to make a long, narrow cut in something. □ *Sue slit the envelope and took the letter out.* □ *Philip slit the bicycle tire and let the air leak out.*

• **snip**   to *cut* off a small piece of something with scissors or shears. (Sometimes with *off.*) □ *Rita finished her sewing and snipped the thread.* □ *The gardener snipped a rose off the rosebush.*
[→see also: *carve*]

cut-rate   See the entry for *cheap.*

cute   (*adjective*) pretty and charming. □ *What a cute baby!* □ *Susan's new outfit is awfully cute.*

• **adorable**   cute and lovable. □ *Tim was an adorable child.* □ *Jan thought the doll was adorable.*

• **attractive**   cute; pleasant to look at. □ *There was an attractive display in the store window.* □ *Bill is an attractive guy.*

• **sweet**   cute; dainty and pleasing. □ *The sleeping kittens looked so sweet.* □ *Doesn't Johnny look sweet in his little sailor suit?*

cutting   See the entry for *critical.*

D

dab See the entry for *wipe*.

dainty See the entry for *fragile*.

dally See the entry for *dawdle*.

damage (*verb*) to hurt something permanently; to hurt something so badly that it no longer works. □ *Art damaged the radio by accidentally dropping it in a sink full of water.* □ *I'm afraid Ben will damage his health if he doesn't get more sleep.*

> • **deface** to *damage* the way something looks. □ *Vandals defaced the building.* □ *Carrie defaced the movie star's picture by drawing rabbit ears on it.*
>
> • **maim** to *damage* someone; to make someone crippled. □ *The car accident maimed Eddie for life.* □ *Fred's leg was maimed in a football game.*
>
> • **mar** to *damage* the surface of something. (Formal.) □ *Don't mar the coffee table by setting wet glasses on it.* □ *Donald took every precaution against marring the finish of his new car.*
>
> • **mutilate** to *damage* someone or something severely or viciously. □ *Someone mutilated this book, cutting out all the pictures and scribbling on the pages.* □ *Gina's face was mutilated in the car accident.*
>
> [→see also: *hurt*]

damp See the entry for *wet*.

dangerous (*adjective*) likely to hurt something. □ *The police officer agreed to go on the dangerous mission.* □ *Knives are dangerous and should be handled carefully.*

> • **hazardous** *dangerous;* full of risks. □ *The bad weather made driving hazardous.* □ *The refugees made a hazardous journey through the mountains.*

• **perilous**   *dangerous.* (Poetic.) □ *Our hero took on the perilous task of slaying the dragon.* □ *The little raft shot toward the perilous rapids.*
• **unsafe**   *dangerous;* not safe. □ *The construction site is a very unsafe place to play.* □ *Research showed that the car was unsafe.*

dangle   See the entry for *hang.*

dank   See the entry for *humid.*

dare   (*verb*) to be willing to try something dangerous. □ *Susan never dared talk back to her parents.* □ *Our hero dared to challenge the evil wizard.*
• **chance**   to try something uncertain. □ *Tom knew this might be his only opportunity to escape, so he decided to chance it.* □ *If we take the back roads, we'll have to chance getting lost.*
• **gamble on**   to bet; to try something dangerous, hoping you will win. □ *Jan gambled money on her favorite basketball team.* □ *Bill was gambling on my being in a good mood when he asked to borrow my car.*
• **risk**   to be willing to lose something. □ *Art risked everything he had to start his own business.* □ *The daredevil risked his life for every stunt.*
• **venture**   to try something dangerous; to try. (Formal.) □ *Ben was not willing to venture his life savings on such an uncertain investment.* □ *Carrie timidly ventured a question.*

darkness   (*noun*) the absence of light; an area without light. □ *Donald lifted the curtain and peered out into the darkness of the night.* □ *Eddie turned out the light, leaving the room in gloomy darkness.*
• **dusk**   the *darkness* that comes just after the sun sets or just before it rises. □ *It was hard to see things in the dusk.* □ *The dusk made everything look gray.*
• **shade**   an area without sunlight. □ *We sat in the cool shade of the oak tree.* □ *There was a little shade on the other side of the hill.*
• **shadow**   a *darkness* caused by a person or object coming in front of the light. □ *The plane cast a shadow as it flew overhead.* □ *Why is my shadow on the sidewalk so much taller than I am?*
• **twilight**   the *darkness* just after the sun sets. □ *George and Helen took a walk in the twilight.* □ *I could see lights coming on in all the houses as twilight fell.*

darn   See the entry for *sew.*

dart   See the entry for *hurry.*

dash   See the entry for *hurry.*

data   See the entry for *information.*

date[1]   (*noun*) a plan to get together with someone, usually someone of the opposite sex. □ *Jay and Kay went out on a date.* □ *Larry was too shy to ask Mary for a date.*

• **appointment**   a plan to get together with someone. □ *I made an appointment with Ms. Jones for a job interview.* □ *I can't see you at two o'clock; I have a dentist appointment.*
• **engagement**   a formal plan to get together with someone. □ *Sue had several social engagements for the weekend.* □ *Tom couldn't come to the party because he had another engagement.*
• **rendezvous**   a plan to get together with someone secretly. (Formal.) □ *One of the spies was late to the rendezvous.* □ *The two lovers had their rendezvous in the park at midnight.*

date²   (*verb*) to get together often with someone; to be sweethearts with someone. □ *Philip and Rita are dating.* □ *Susan used to be my girlfriend, but now she's dating someone else.*
• **court**   to try to get someone to marry you. (Old-fashioned.) □ *Tom courted Jan for several months.* □ *The gentleman sent roses to the lady he was courting.*
• **go out with**   to *date*. (Informal.) □ *Who is Susan going out with now?* □ *Tina went out with her boyfriend on Friday night.*
• **go steady with**   to *date* someone exclusively. (Informal.) □ *Jan has been going steady with Bill for almost a month now.* □ *Mom says I'm too young to go steady with anyone.*
• **see**   to *date* someone casually. (Informal. See also the main entry for *see*.) □ *Art's seeing several young women right now.* □ *Ben is seeing someone he met when he was on vacation.*

dated   See the entry for *old-fashioned*.

dawdle   (*verb*) to waste time. □ *Stop dawdling and get ready for school!* □ *Donald dawdled along on his way to the dentist, looking in every shop window along the street.*
• **dally**   to *dawdle*; to put off doing something. (Formal.) □ *Don't dally on your way to Grandma's house.* □ *We dallied until it was almost too late.*
• **loiter**   to *dawdle* by going slowly; to be doing nothing. □ *The group of kids loitered in the hallway after the bell rang.* □ *Edith spent the whole day loitering in the park.*
• **take one's time**   to *dawdle*; to work slowly. (Informal.) □ *The mailman sure is taking his time about delivering my mail!* □ *There is no time limit on the test, so take your time and work carefully.*
• **tarry**   to *dawdle*; to wait too long. (Old-fashioned.) □ *Nancy tarried outside, watching the sun set, even after she had finished her chores.* □ *You must not tarry, or you'll miss the train.*
[→see also: *wait, delay*]

dawn   (*noun*) the earliest part of the morning, when the sky is just beginning to grow light. □ *Eddie stayed up till dawn.* □ *Fran had to get up before dawn to get to work on time.*

• **daybreak**   *dawn.* (Formal.) □ *The farmer rose at daybreak and began his daily chores.* □ *The birds began to sing at daybreak.*
• **first light**   *dawn.* (Poetic.) □ *Our hero roused himself at first light and made ready for his journey.* □ *The church members gathered at first light for the Easter service.*
• **sunrise**   *dawn;* the time when the sun first appears above the horizon. □ *The clouds lit up brilliantly at sunrise.* □ *The sky grew light; it was almost sunrise.*
• **sunup**   *dawn;* the time when the sun appears above the horizon. □ *The sheriff was going to hang the horse thief at sunup.* □ *George worked from sunup to sundown to finish the book he was writing.*

daybreak   See the entry for *dawn.*

daydream   See the entry for *dream.*

daze   (*noun*) a feeling of not being able to think clearly. □ *Helen was in a daze after she got the bad news.* □ *Irene walked down the street in a daze.*
• **reverie**   a *daze;* a pleasant, dreamy state. (Formal.) □ *Hearing the old song, Jay fell into a reverie.* □ *The slam of the door interrupted Kay's reverie.*
• **stupor**   a heavy *daze,* close to unconsciousness. □ *Sam was left in a stupor after the bookcase fell on him.* □ *Mary has been watching TV for six hours in some kind of stupor.*
• **trance**   a *daze;* a sleepy feeling of not being in control of your body. □ *Sybil went into a trance and said she was talking to ghosts.* □ *The hypnotist put Tim into a trance.*

deadly   (*adjective*) able to cause death. □ *The vial was filled with a deadly poison.* □ *The racecar driver knew that making a mistake could be deadly.*
• **fatal**   unstoppably *deadly;* killing; causing death. □ *The victim received a fatal blow on the head.* □ *How did the fatal dose of poison get into Tom's drink?*
• **lethal**   *deadly* by nature. □ *This snake's bite can be lethal.* □ *The secret agent was trained to use anything—even a ballpoint pen—as a lethal weapon.*
• **terminal**   *deadly.* (Used to describe sicknesses.) □ *The doctor said that Peter's condition was terminal.* □ *I'm afraid Rick has a terminal disease.*

deafening   See the entry for *loud.*

deal with   See the entry for *handle.*

dealer   See the entry for *seller.*

debacle   See the entry for *failure.*

debate   See the entry for *argue¹*.

debilitate   See the entry for *weaken*.

debonair   See the entry for *jaunty*.

decay   See the entry for *spoil²*.

deceive   See the entry for *fool²*.

decent   See the entry for *proper*.

decide on   See the entry for *choose*.

decipher   See the entry for *figure out*.

decisive   See the entry for *conclusive*.

deck   See the entry for *decorate*.

declare   See the entries for *announce, claim*.

decline   See the entry for *refuse*.

decode   See the entry for *figure out*.

decorate   (*verb*) to improve something by adding something to it. □ *Susan decorated the cake with roses made of frosting.* □ *Debra decorates her letters with funny stickers.*
   • **adorn**   to *decorate* something; to fasten beautiful things to something. □ *The sweater was adorned with little pink bows.* □ *The princess adorned her hair with diamond ornaments.*
   • **deck**   to *decorate* something lavishly. □ *Anthony decked the walls of his room with flags of many different countries.* □ *The shopping center was decked with holiday decorations.*
   • **embellish**   to *decorate* something in order to make it more beautiful. (Formal.) □ *Tim embellished his signature by drawing swirly loops beneath it.* □ *Jan embellished the collar of her blouse with colorful embroidery.*
   • **ornament**   to *decorate* something; to add beauty to something. □ *Several beautiful illustrations ornamented the book.* □ *Bill ornamented the room with a few little vases of flowers.*

decoy   See the entry for *trap*.

decrease   (*verb*) to grow less; to get smaller. □ *The town's population has decreased over the last ten years.* □ *The amount of water in my canteen decreased steadily.*
   • **diminish**   to *decrease* a little at a time. □ *Art's fear of computers diminished the more he worked with them.* □ *As we got farther and farther from the source of the radio signal, the strength of the signal diminished.*

• **dwindle**   to *decrease* gradually; to get much smaller. □ *The number of people in the club dwindled until only two members were left.* □ *Public interest in the story dwindled, so the newspapers stopped covering it.*

• **reduce**   to make something *decrease*. □ *The price of the coat has been reduced.* □ *Mary is trying to reduce the amount of television she watches.*

• **shrink**   to *decrease* greatly; to get very small. □ *The balloon shrank as the air was let out of it.* □ *Don't wash that shirt in hot water; it will shrink!*

• **wane**   to *decrease* after having been great. □ *Carrie's enthusiasm waned.* □ *In the middle of the month, the moon began to wane.*

dedicated   (*adjective*) serious about something; loyal and faithful to someone or something. □ *Donald is dedicated to his work.* □ *The leader had many dedicated followers.*

• **ardent**   passionately *dedicated;* enthusiastic. □ *Terri is an ardent Sherlock Holmes fan.* □ *Many women were ardent admirers of the movie actor.*

• **avid**   eager and *dedicated.* □ *Eddie is an avid reader; he must read at least one book a week.* □ *Fran spends her weekends in avid pursuit of outdoor sports.*

• **earnest**   honestly *dedicated;* serious and sincere. □ *George was not a brilliant student, but he had an earnest desire to learn.* □ *It was easy to trust the earnest young woman.*

• **fervent**   warmly *dedicated;* passionate and sincere. □ *Harry is a fervent believer in ESP.* □ *Irene made a fervent declaration of her love for Jim.*

• **wholehearted**   entirely *dedicated.* □ *Kay's wholehearted belief in the benefits of health food leads her to eat some very strange things.* □ *Laura gave her wholehearted support to her country.*

deduce   See the entry for *conclude.*

deed   See the entry for *act.*

deep   See the entry for *thick.*

deface   See the entry for *damage.*

defame   See the entry for *slander.*

defeat   See the entries for *beat², failure.*

defect   See the entries for *abandon, flaw.*

defend   See the entry for *protect.*

defer   See the entry for *delay.*

deference   See the entry for *respect¹.*

definite   See the entry for *exact*.

definitely   See the entry for *certainly*.

definitive   See the entry for *conclusive*.

deform   See the entry for *distort*.

defraud   See the entry for *cheat*.

defy   See the entry for *disobey*.

degree   See the entry for *grade*.

dehydrated   See the entry for *dry*.

dejected   See the entry for *sad*.

delay   (*verb*) to make someone or something late. (See also the entries for *keep, wait*.) □ *Bad weather delayed the plane's landing.* □ *Mom was delayed by the heavy traffic and didn't get home for dinner.*
  • **defer**   to *delay* something deliberately. (Formal.) □ *The furniture store allowed me to defer payment for my new sofa until the first of next month.* □ *We will defer the celebration until the guest of honor can be with us.*
  • **postpone**   to *delay* something until another time. □ *The students were relieved when the teacher postponed the test.* □ *The game had to be postponed until the weather improved.*
  • **put off**   to *delay*. (Informal.) □ *You can't put off your homework forever.* □ *I decided to put off doing the dishes until tomorrow.*
  • **stall**   to *delay* something that ought to go ahead. □ *When Smith got up to leave, Jones tried to stall him.* □ *Quit stalling and get to work.*
  [→see also: *dawdle, wait*]

delectable   See the entry for *delicious*.

deliberate   See the entries for *argue¹, consider*.

delicate   See the entries for *fragile, tricky*.

delicious   (*adjective*) pleasing to the taste or smell. □ *George cooked a delicious meal.* □ *The orange was delicious.*
  • **delectable**   delightfully *delicious*. □ *There were several delectable cheeses available.* □ *The baking bread filled the house with a delectable smell.*
  • **luscious**   sweet, rich, and *delicious*. □ *Dessert was a luscious ripe pear.* □ *The cupcakes were covered with luscious buttery frosting.*
  • **palatable**   tasting pleasant enough. □ *Although the stew looked disgusting, it was quite palatable.* □ *They don't even make palatable coffee at that diner.*

• **scrumptious**   quite *delicious*. (Informal.) □ *Thanks for lunch; it was scrumptious!* □ *Helen made some really scrumptious brownies for the bake sale.*
• **tasty**   *delicious*. (Informal.) □ *Irene was searching for a tasty and nutritious snack.* □ *The cookbook had recipes for several tasty soups.*

delight   See the entry for *pleasure*.

delight in   See the entry for *enjoy*.

deliver   See the entries for *carry, save*.

delude   See the entry for *fool²*.

deluge   See the entry for *flood*.

delusion   See the entry for *illusion*.

delve into   See the entry for *explore*.

demand   (*verb*) to say that something must be done. □ *The boss demanded that everyone attend the meeting.* □ *The angry customer demanded a refund.*
• **insist**   to *demand* firmly or persistently. (Often with *on*.) □ *Jim insisted on driving at high speed.* □ *Kevin's parents insisted that he get a haircut.*
• **require**   to *demand;* to say that something is necessary; to make something necessary. □ *I require your complete attention.* □ *The situation requires immediate action.*
[→see also: *order*]

demanding   See the entry for *hard*.

demented   See the entry for *crazy*.

demolish   See the entry for *destroy*.

demonstrate   See the entry for *show¹*.

demur   See the entry for *refuse*.

demure   See the entry for *prim*.

den   See the entry for *cave*.

dense   See the entries for *firm, thick*.

dent   (*noun*) a hollow depression. □ *There's a dent in the hood of my car.* □ *The can of tomatoes was marked down because it had a dent in it.*
• **dimple**   a slight *dent;* a small depression in someone's flesh. □ *The raindrop made a dimple in the sand.* □ *You can see Laura's dimples when she smiles.*

• **impression**   a *dent;* a mark made by pressing on something. □ *The animal's feet left impressions in the snow.* □ *You can see the impression of the potter's thumb on this clay bowl.*
• **indentation**   a *dent* or notch. (Formal.) □ *Something hit the wall hard enough to leave this indentation.* □ *There was an indentation in the bark of the tree where the bird had pecked at it.*
• **nick**   a small *dent* made by something sharp. □ *The cat got that nick in his ear from fighting with other cats.* □ *The doctor had to make a nick in Mark's thumb to get the splinter out.*

depart   See the entries for *die, go.*

depend   (*verb*) to be controlled or decided by someone or something else. (Usually with *on.*) □ *We have to depend on Tom to give us a ride.* □ *The success of the operation will depend on the doctor's skill.*
• **be contingent**   to *depend.* (Formal. Usually with *on.*) □ *Sue's vacation trip was contingent on her getting enough money for a plane ticket.* □ *The whole plan was contingent upon Philip's approval.*
• **hang**   to be controlled by something; to *depend* on something. (Usually with *upon.* See also the main entry for *hang.*) □ *The principal said that our whole future would hang upon what we chose to do after high school.* □ *The success of the spy's mission hung upon her ability to get information back to headquarters.*
• **hinge**   to *depend* on a crucial thing. (Usually with *on* or *upon.*) □ *Whether or not Roger goes to prison may hinge upon what this witness says.* □ *Dad said his decision would hinge on how well we behaved for Aunt Shirley.*

depend on   See the entry for *trust.*

depict   See the entry for *express.*

depleted   See the entry for *spent.*

deplore   See the entry for *disapprove.*

deportment   See the entry for *behavior.*

deposit   See the entry for *put.*

deputy   See the entry for *officer.*

deranged   See the entry for *crazy.*

derision   See the entry for *disrespect.*

derogatory   See the entry for *critical.*

descendants   (*noun*) all the people descended from someone; someone's children, grandchildren, great-grandchildren, and so on. □ *None of*

Abraham Lincoln's descendants are still living. □ *A man named Walker built that house, and his descendants still live there.*
   • **issue**   descendants. (Formal.) □ *The marriage of the king and queen was without issue.* □ *Jennie's land was divided up among her issue.*
   • **offspring**   descendants; a child or children; the young of an animal. □ *Andrew and Linda worked hard to provide for their many offspring.* □ *The bird brought back food for her offspring.*
   • **posterity**   descendants, especially those who live in the distant future. (Formal.) □ *Tim wrote down the story of his life and dedicated it to his posterity.* □ *I won't use this quilt Great-Grandma made; I'll preserve it for posterity.*
   • **progeny**   descendants of a person or an animal. (Formal.) □ *The mother cat was very protective of her progeny.* □ *Andrew and Linda's progeny had scattered across the country.*

describe   See the entry for *express.*

desert   See the entries for *abandon, wilderness.*

deserve   (*verb*) to be worthy of something. □ *I hope Irene gets the prize; she deserves it.* □ *Jay deserves to be punished.*
   • **earn**   to get something because you have worked for it. □ *Kay earned a hundred dollars from her part-time job this week.* □ *Larry's bravery earned our respect.*
   • **have the right to**   to *deserve* a privilege; to be granted a privilege by law. □ *Mark has the right to eat some of these cookies, because he helped me bake them.* □ *Tom seems to think he has the right to be rude to people.*
   • **merit**   to *deserve* something. (Somewhat formal.) □ *The teacher tried to give each paper the grade it merited.* □ *Sue did such poor work that she didn't merit a promotion.*

design   See the entries for *mean², pattern.*

designate   See the entry for *show³.*

desire   See the entry for *want.*

desist   See the entry for *stop.*

desolate   See the entry for *lonely.*

despairing   See the entry for *desperate.*

desperate   (*adjective*) having no hope; caused by a feeling of hopelessness. □ *The desperate man turned to stealing to feed his family.* □ *The child gave a desperate cry for help.*
   • **despairing**   giving up hope. □ *"What am I going to do?" Philip asked in a despairing voice.* □ *Losing her job put Rita in a despairing mood.*

• **despondent**   depressed because you feel there is no hope. (Formal.) □ *Susan has been despondent since her best friend moved away.* □ *As he thought of all the work he had to do, Tim got a despondent look on his face.*

• **hopeless**   without hope. □ *The doctor says that Tom's case is hopeless.* □ *There's nothing we can do; it's hopeless.*

[→see also: *excited*]

despicable   See the entry for *mean¹*.

despise   See the entry for *hate*.

despondent   See the entry for *desperate*.

despot   See the entry for *autocrat*.

destiny   See the entry for *luck*.

destitute   See the entry for *poor¹*.

destroy   (*verb*) to tear down something completely; to put a violent end to something. □ *The invading army destroyed the city.* □ *The accident destroyed John's hopes of becoming an athlete.*

• **demolish**   to *destroy* something violently or deliberately. (Formal.) □ *The wreckers demolished the old building.* □ *The car was totally demolished in the crash.*

• **ruin**   to *destroy* something; to make something useless. □ *I worked on the drawing all day, and then my brother ruined it with his dirty fingerprints.* □ *Wendy's angry outburst ruined the party.*

• **wreck**   to *destroy* something, sometimes violently. □ *Anna wrecked the plan for Ben's surprise party by telling Ben about it.* □ *Jim skidded his car into a wall and wrecked it.*

detach   See the entry for *remove*.

detached   See the entry for *removed*.

detain   See the entry for *keep*.

detect   See the entry for *find*.

determine   See the entry for *learn¹*.

determined   See the entries for *persistent, relentless*.

detest   See the entry for *hate*.

detour   See the entry for *bypass*.

develop   See the entry for *grow*.

deviate   See the entry for *swerve*.

device (*noun*) something made for a particular purpose. □ *Kay uses this device to curl her eyelashes.* □ *The new kitchen device is supposed to make it easy to cut up vegetables.*

• **apparatus** a complex *device.* (Formal.) □ *The scientist built a special apparatus for the experiment.* □ *Jack fixed the delicate apparatus inside the watch.*

• **contraption** an odd or newfangled *device.* (Informal.) □ *This contraption is for cleaning your dog's teeth.* □ *The vacuum cleaner came with a number of contraptions for cleaning upholstery and curtains.*

• **contrivance** a cleverly designed *device;* a clever system or plan. □ *Instead of a pocket calendar, Kay has some kind of computerized contrivance for keeping track of her appointments.* □ *Larry used a number of contrivances to try to get the baby to eat vegetables.*

• **mechanism** a *device;* a part of a machine. □ *This camera has a special mechanism that allows you to take your own picture.* □ *Mary tried to fix the mechanism that made the VCR go.*

devilish See the entry for *evil.*

devious See the entry for *sneaky.*

devoted See the entry for *faithful.*

devotee See the entry for *fan.*

devotion See the entry for *love.*

devour See the entry for *eat.*

dice See the entry for *chop.*

dicker See the entry for *bargain.*

dictate See the entry for *order.*

dictator See the entry for *autocrat.*

die (*verb*) to cease to be alive. □ *My grandfather died before I was born.* □ *Nancy was very sad when her dog died.*

• **depart** to *die;* to leave life. (Formal.) □ *Our beloved friend departed this life two days ago.* □ *Tom has not been the same since his wife departed this world.*

• **expire** to *die;* to breathe your last breath. (Old-fashioned.) □ *With a final puff of smoke, the dragon expired.* □ *The child looked toward heaven and expired in his mother's arms.*

• **pass away** to *die;* to leave life. □ *When did Paula pass away?* □ *I read in the newspaper that the great musician has passed away.*

• **pass on** to *die;* to go on to the afterlife. □ *Regina sold the house after her mother passed on.* □ *Stuart passed on at the age of forty-three.*

• **perish** to *die,* usually in a catastrophe. □ *Hundreds of people perished in the flood.* □ *The gifted poet perished in the war.*

different (*adjective*) not the same. □ *There were several different kinds of fruit juice to choose from.* □ *Art looked different with his new glasses.*

   • **disparate** entirely *different;* not compatible. (Formal.) □ *It was strange that two people from such disparate backgrounds could become good friends.* □ *How could you confuse something written by Ernest Hemingway with something by William Faulkner? Their writing styles are so disparate!*

   • **dissimilar** *different* in some respect. □ *The brothers had dissimilar personalities.* □ *These books are by the same author, but they are quite dissimilar.*

   • **distinct** entirely *different* and separate from one another. □ *I tried to convince Bill that Mexico and New Mexico were two distinct places.* □ *The detective showed that the killer had not just one but three distinct reasons for wanting the victim dead.*

   • **divergent** headed in *different* directions. (Formal.) □ *We were close friends when we were younger, but our lives went on divergent paths.* □ *Ben and Carrie had divergent opinions about the movie.*

   • **separate** *different;* apart from one another. □ *The kids all wanted separate bedrooms.* □ *You will need three separate kinds of yarn to make this sweater.*

[→contrasting word: *same*]

differentiate See the entry for *distinguish.*

difficult See the entry for *hard.*

difficulty See the entry for *problem.*

diffident See the entry for *shy.*

diffuse See the entry for *emit.*

dig (*verb*) to turn over or move dirt. (See also the entry for *poke.*) □ *Donald dug until the hole was very deep.* □ *When Edith was digging in the garden, she found an old bottle.*

   • **excavate** to *dig* in order to find something that was buried. □ *The archaeologist excavated the ancient city.* □ *After the earthquake, many people helped excavate the buildings that had been destroyed.*

   • **mine** to *dig* in order to get metal, coal, or precious stones. □ *Coal is mined in this area of the country.* □ *Many companies used to mine copper here.*

   • **quarry** to *dig* in order to get stone; to cut stone out of the earth. □ *Workers quarried giant stone blocks to build the Pyramids.* □ *The sculptor used only marble that was quarried in a special place in Italy.*

dignified   See the entry for *grand.*

dilemma   See the entry for *bind.*

diligent   See the entry for *persistent.*

dilly-dally   See the entry for *waver.*

diluted   See the entry for *watery.*

dim   See the entry for *faint.*

dimension   See the entry for *size.*

diminish   See the entry for *decrease.*

dimple   See the entry for *dent.*

dine   See the entry for *eat.*

diner   See the entry for *restaurant.*

dinner   See the entry for *meal.*

dip   See the entry for *submerge.*

diplomatic   See the entry for *tactful.*

direct   See the entries for *control¹, lead, order.*

dirt   (*noun*) the upper layer of the earth; the material that plants grow in; anything that makes things dirty. □ *The dirt near my aunt's house is red.* □ *Fran's hands were covered with dirt.*
   • **earth**   the material that plants grow in. □ *The farmer planted the seeds in the earth.* □ *Rain fell on the parched earth.*
   • **ground**   the upper layer of the earth. □ *The ground was frozen so hard that I couldn't dig into it.* □ *George sat down on the ground.*
   • **soil**   *dirt;* especially, rich *dirt* that is good for growing plants. □ *You must have a certain kind of soil to grow really hot peppers.* □ *The farmer used a plow to turn up the soil.*

dirty¹   (*adjective*) covered or smudged with dirt or stains. □ *Harold was careful not to get his good shirt dirty.* □ *By the time she finished eating, the baby's face was really dirty.*
   • **filthy**   extremely or disgustingly *dirty.* □ *Irene's hair was filthy; she hadn't washed it in a month.* □ *Jay refused to use the filthy washroom at the gas station.*
   • **grimy**   oily and *dirty;* very stained. □ *Kay's hands were really grimy from working on the car engine.* □ *Laura threw the grimy rag into the washing machine.*
   • **grubby**   quite *dirty.* (Informal.) □ *My jeans got grubby from my kneeling down to work in the garden.* □ *The cat came in from outside with his white paws all grubby.*

• **soiled**   stained, smudged, or *dirty*. ☐ *Mark dabbed at the soiled rug, trying to get it clean.* ☐ *The old man wore a soiled, ragged coat.*
[→contrasting word: *clean¹*]

dirty²   (*verb*) to make something unclean. ☐ *Tom's muddy footprints dirtied the carpet.* ☐ *Sue didn't want to dirty her hands helping to clean the kitchen.*

• **contaminate**   to make something unclean and unhealthy. (Formal.) ☐ *The gas leaked out of the factory and contaminated the air.* ☐ *Our parents thought that reading bad books would contaminate our minds.*
• **foul**   to make something nasty and unclean. ☐ *A terrible smell fouled the air.* ☐ *Oil from all the motorboats fouled the water in the lake.*
• **pollute**   to make something unclean, unsafe, or unusable. ☐ *Industrial waste polluted the river.* ☐ *Car exhaust pollutes the air.*
• **taint**   to make something unclean or unsafe by adding something very unpleasant. ☐ *Dangerous bacteria tainted the milk.* ☐ *The constant rumors tainted the mayor's reputation.*
[→contrasting word: *clean²*]

disallow   See the entry for *forbid*.

disappear   (*verb*) to become invisible; to go away entirely. ☐ *The magician made the flowers disappear.* ☐ *I thought I saw a dog in my backyard, but when I looked again, it had disappeared.*

• **dissolve**   to *disappear* a tiny bit at a time. ☐ *The picture on the TV screen dissolved into blackness.* ☐ *The sugar dissolved in the hot water.*
• **fade**   to *disappear* gradually. ☐ *The ghost faded from our sight.* ☐ *The balloon slowly faded into the distance.*
• **vanish**   to *disappear* quickly. ☐ *The strange light in the sky vanished as suddenly as it had appeared.* ☐ *When I got to my parking spot, I discovered that my car had vanished.*
[→contrasting word: *appear*]

disapprove   (*verb*) to think that someone or something is bad; to think that something should not take place. (Usually with *of.*) ☐ *Philip disapproved of what Rita did.* ☐ *Stanley's mom disapproves of the music he listens to.*

• **deplore**   to *disapprove* strongly. (Formal.) ☐ *I agree that we need more money, but I deplore your dishonest way of getting it.* ☐ *Thomas deplores the use of rough language in movies.*
• **disfavor**   to *disapprove* somewhat; not to be in favor of something. (Formal.) ☐ *Most of the members of the student council disfavored the proposal.* ☐ *Victor's parents disfavored his plan to buy a pet rabbit.*
• **frown on**   to show that you *disapprove*. ☐ *The teacher frowned on passing notes in class.* ☐ *Bill, a hard worker himself, frowned on laziness.*

disarray   See the entry for *disorder*.

disaster   (*noun*) a sudden and awful event. □ *A hundred people died in the disaster.* □ *The company lost millions of dollars in the business disaster.*
   • **calamity**   a *disaster* causing a great deal of suffering. □ *Anna's illness was a calamity for her children.* □ *One calamity after another befell the Arctic explorers.*
   • **cataclysm**   a *disaster* that changes everything; a natural *disaster* such as a flood or an earthquake. (Formal.) □ *The volcano erupted, a cataclysm that destroyed the entire city.* □ *Mom and Dad's divorce was a family cataclysm.*
   • **catastrophe**   a terrible *disaster*. □ *I had to give a speech today, and it was a catastrophe.* □ *The library was flooded, and many valuable books were lost in the catastrophe.*

disband   See the entry for *scatter*.

disburse   See the entry for *spend*.

discard   See the entry for *throw away*.

discharge   See the entry for *dismiss*.

disciple   See the entry for *student*.

discipline   (*noun*) the practice of doing everything in an orderly, controlled way. (See also the entry for *punish*.) □ *Ben may be talented, but he does not have the discipline to become a great athlete.* □ *Carrie benefited from the discipline of learning to solve math problems, even though she did not think she would use math later on in life.*
   • **self-control**   discipline; the ability to control yourself. □ *When Donald insulted Eddie, Eddie showed great self-control in not insulting him back.* □ *Fran had enough self-control to do her work even though no one was making her do it.*
   • **self-restraint**   discipline; the ability to stop yourself from doing foolish things. □ *George has no self-restraint when it comes to shopping; he just buys everything he wants.* □ *It takes a lot of self-restraint to stick to a diet.*
   • **training**   discipline; long practice at something. □ *The training Helen received as a karate student influenced her entire life.* □ *Irene's classical musical training was useful when she wanted to learn to play jazz.*

disclose   See the entry for *show²*.

disconcert   See the entry for *embarrass*.

discontent   (*noun*) a feeling of wishing things were different. □ *Jay's discontent was obvious from the way he grumbled.* □ *Kay felt a deep discontent with her job.*

• **dissatisfaction**   a feeling of not liking the way things are. ☐ *The customer expressed his dissatisfaction with the item he had bought.* ☐ *I don't understand the teacher's dissatisfaction with my work.*

• **restlessness**   a feeling of wanting to do something different. ☐ *Every spring, Laura felt a restlessness, a desire to pack her bags and travel.* ☐ *Mark's drumming fingers showed his restlessness.*

• **uneasiness**   an uncomfortable feeling that things are not right. ☐ *Nancy felt a chilling uneasiness as she walked down the dark street.* ☐ *I noticed Sue shuddering and wondered what caused her uneasiness.*

discover   See the entries for *find, learn¹.*

discreet   See the entry for *tactful.*

discriminate   See the entry for *distinguish.*

discriminating   See the entry for *picky.*

discuss   See the entry for *argue¹.*

discussion   See the entry for *talk¹.*

disdain   See the entry for *disrespect.*

disease   See the entry for *sickness.*

disfavor   See the entry for *disapprove.*

disgrace   (*noun*) a feeling of humiliation; the state of being humiliated. (See also the entry for *embarrass.*) ☐ *Philip could scarcely stand the disgrace of being yelled at in front of all his friends.* ☐ *Rita was in disgrace when her mean behavior became known.*

• **ignominy**   severe *disgrace;* complete loss of respect. (Formal.) ☐ *Susan underwent the ignominy of being led out of the building in handcuffs.* ☐ *Thomas felt that losing his job was the worst possible ignominy he could suffer.*

• **scandal**   severe *disgrace* revealed to the public. ☐ *The mayor's irresponsible behavior caused a scandal.* ☐ *Mr. Jones could not get another job because of the scandal associated with him.*

• **shame**   deep *disgrace.* ☐ *Valerie cried tears of shame when she was spanked.* ☐ *It was hard for Bill to endure the shame of being suspected of a crime.*

disguise   (*noun*) something you wear to change your appearance so that no one will recognize you. ☐ *The spy had a number of disguises he could wear.* ☐ *The king went out in disguise to talk with his people.*

• **camouflage**   something you wear so that you will blend into the background. ☐ *The soldiers wore desert camouflage so they would blend into the sandy landscape.* ☐ *The lizard's camouflage helps it disappear against the background.*

• **costume**   something you wear to change your appearance. ☐ *You have to wear a costume to the Halloween party.* ☐ *Anna has a dragon costume with claws and a long scaly tail.*
• **mask**   something you wear to cover or hide your face. ☐ *The burglar wore a black mask.* ☐ *The dancer had a feathered mask that made her look like a bird.*

disguise oneself   See the entry for *pose.*

disgust   (*verb*) to make someone feel intense dislike. ☐ *Cleaning out the fish tank disgusted Mary.* ☐ *It disgusts me when people spit on the sidewalk.*
• **nauseate**   to *disgust* someone so much that he or she feels like throwing up. ☐ *Pictures of the murder victims on the news nauseated many viewers.* ☐ *Watching Carl eat with his mouth open nauseates me.*
• **repel**   to *disgust* someone so much that he or she wants to get away. ☐ *Worms and snakes repel some people.* ☐ *Eddie was repelled by Fran's rude behavior.*
• **revolt**   to *disgust* someone strongly. ☐ *The horrible food at the restaurant revolted the diners.* ☐ *George was revolted by the smell of rotting garbage coming from his neighbor's yard.*
• **sicken**   to *disgust* someone so much that he or she feels sick; to make someone feel sick. ☐ *Mr. Smith's abuse of his dog really sickens me.* ☐ *Helen was sickened by the many pictures of starving children in the distant land.*

disinterested   See the entries for *removed, unbiased.*

dislodge   See the entry for *remove.*

disloyal   See the entry for *fickle.*

dismiss   (*verb*) to tell someone to go away and not come back; to allow someone to go. (See also the entry for *eliminate.*) ☐ *The boss dismissed his employee.* ☐ *The teacher dismissed the class for the day.*
• **discharge**   to *dismiss* a person from a job or from the military. ☐ *The soldier was discharged after she had served for three years.* ☐ *Irene was not doing a good job, so her boss discharged her.*
• **eject**   to *dismiss* someone roughly. (Formal.) ☐ *The butler ejected the unwanted guest from the house.* ☐ *The drunk diner was ejected from the restaurant.*
• **expel**   to *dismiss* someone permanently; to *dismiss* a student from school permanently. (See also the main entry for *expel.*) ☐ *George was expelled from the secret society because he had told his wife about their secret rituals.* ☐ *The principal expelled Jim for vandalizing the school.* ☐ *Keith was expelled from school.*
• **fire**   to *dismiss* a person from a job. (Informal.) ☐ *Larry was fired after he yelled at the boss one too many times.* ☐ *The company is cutting back, so they fired me.*

• **kick out**   to *dismiss* someone rudely or forcefully. (Slang.) □ *Mary got kicked out of the Model Rocket Club.* □ *If you want me to leave, you're going to have to kick me out!*

disobey   (*verb*) not to do what someone tells you; to break a rule. □ *Tom disobeyed his father.* □ *If you disobey the rules, you will be punished.*
  • **defy**   to *disobey* proudly and deliberately. □ *The rebels defied the government's laws.* □ *The students defied the unpopular teacher's authority.*
  • **flout**   to *disobey* obviously and scornfully. (Formal.) □ *Sue enjoys flouting current fashions in clothes; she wears old styles or things that don't go together.* □ *Philip openly lit a cigarette, flouting the "no smoking" rule.*
  • **scoff at**   to *disobey* scornfully; to think that something is not worth obeying. □ *Rita scoffed at the curfew and stayed out all night.* □ *Jim scoffs at the speed limit.*
  • **transgress**   to *disobey* an extremely important rule; to commit a sin. (Formal.) □ *Mother called me to her and explained that I had transgressed against good manners.* □ *The priest told Kay that she had transgressed and must atone.*
  [→see also: *rebel*]

disorder   (*noun*) confusion; lack of organization. □ *Dad sighed at the disorder of Laura's room.* □ *With the teacher out of the room, the class was in disorder.*
  • **chaos**   complete, violent *disorder*. □ *With three cooks trying to work at once, the kitchen was in chaos.* □ *After the earthquake, the city was in complete chaos.*
  • **disarray**   slight *disorder;* less than perfect order. □ *The wind left my hair in disarray.* □ *Mark's clothes were in disarray after he stopped to play soccer on the way home.*
  • **havoc**   extreme, violent *disorder*. (Formal. Sometimes in the expression *wreak havoc,* to cause extreme disorder.) □ *Tom's disruptive behavior wreaks havoc wherever he goes.* □ *The invading army left havoc behind it.*
  • **mayhem**   violent or noisy *disorder*. □ *The twenty five-year-old guests at the birthday party created plenty of mayhem.* □ *There was mayhem in the classroom when the teacher announced a surprise test.*
  • **turmoil**   *disorder* caused by violent, continuous motion. (Formal.) □ *The country was full of turmoil, and war might break out at any moment.* □ *The city was in turmoil because of the lack of food.*

disparaging   See the entry for *critical*.

disparate   See the entry for *different*.

dispatch   See the entry for *send*.

dispense   See the entry for *distribute*.

disperse   See the entries for *distribute, scatter.*

display   See the entry for *show².*

dispose of   See the entry for *throw away.*

disposition   See the entry for *personality.*

dispute   See the entry for *argue².*

disquieted   See the entry for *uneasy.*

disregard   See the entries for *ignore, skip.*

disrespect   (*noun*) a feeling that someone or something is not worth honoring. □ *Philip treated the teacher with disrespect.* □ *I felt disrespect for Rita because of the mean way she treated her friends.* □ *The art student showed great disrespect and contempt for the flag by painting it on the floor for people to walk on it.*
  • **contempt**   a feeling that someone or something is totally worthless. (Formal.) □ *Susan showed her contempt for Tim by ignoring him whenever they met.* □ *The artist has nothing but contempt for his rival's work.*
  • **derision**   a feeling that someone or something deserves to be made fun of. (Formal.) □ *Sue treated Bill with derision, mocking him to his face as well as behind his back.* □ *Art's laughter was full of derision.*
  • **disdain**   a feeling that someone or something is beneath you. □ *Mary's haughty voice showed her disdain for us.* □ *The waiter felt disdain for the sloppily dressed diners in the fine restaurant.*
  • **scorn**   a very strong feeling that someone is worthless. □ *Carrie's expression was full of scorn.* □ *Donald felt scorn for everyone who had not graduated from college.*

disrespectful   See the entry for *insolent.*

dissatisfaction   See the entry for *discontent.*

dissemble   See the entry for *lie².*

dissimilar   See the entry for *different.*

dissipate   See the entries for *scatter, waste.*

dissolve   See the entry for *disappear.*

distant   (*adjective*) not close; off in the distance. □ *Eddie's grandparents came from a distant country.* □ *Fran pointed to the distant mountains.*
  • **faraway**   very *distant.* (Somewhat poetic.) □ *Jane was a traveler from a faraway land.* □ *Hector had been to many faraway places.*
  • **far-off**   *distant* in space or time. □ *Irene dreamed of going to the far-off city.* □ *Jay planned for the far-off year when he would be able to retire.*

• **out-of-the-way**   distant and hard to get to. □ *Kay likes to go fishing in an out-of-the-way lake in the forest.* □ *Laura's favorite restaurant is an out-of-the-way place on the edge of town.*
• **remote**   extremely distant. □ *Mary lived in a remote part of the state.* □ *The probe was designed to visit the remote planets of the solar system.*

distend   See the entry for *inflate.*

distinct   See the entry for *different.*

distinguish   (*verb*) to set one thing apart from a similar thing; to perceive that two similar things are different. (Often with *between.*) □ *You can distinguish between the male cardinal and the female cardinal by their color.* □ *Carrie could not distinguish the tastes of fresh and frozen vegetables.*
• **differentiate**   to *distinguish* things that are extremely similar. (Formal. Often with *between.*) □ *The forest ranger could differentiate between all the different kinds of pine trees.* □ *What differentiates a running shoe from a basketball shoe?*
• **discriminate**   to *distinguish* between things thoughtfully and carefully. (Often with *between.*) □ *The taste test asked people to discriminate between two brands of cola.* □ *Donald can discriminate between real silk and fake silk just by looking at them.*
• **separate**   to set one thing apart from a similar thing. (Usually with *from.*) □ *The Siamese cat's unusual markings separate it from other breeds.* □ *Edith's willingness to work hard separated her from her coworkers.*
• **tell**   to *distinguish* things. (Informal. Usually with *from.* See also the main entry for *tell.*) □ *Fran could tell a cirrus cloud from a cumulus cloud.* □ *Even their parents sometimes couldn't tell the twins apart.*

distort   (*verb*) to change the shape of something drastically. □ *Some kind of technical problem distorted the TV picture.* □ *An expression of terror distorted Gina's face.*
• **contort**   to *distort* something by twisting it. □ *The acrobat contorted her body and used her feet as if they were hands.* □ *The airplane was horribly contorted by the crash.*
• **deform**   to *distort* or disfigure something. □ *A childhood illness had deformed Harold's leg.* □ *Irene deformed the clay statue she had been making.*
• **warp**   to *distort* something by making it ripple or twist; to bend or twist something out of shape. □ *Moisture warped the wooden boards.* □ *Jay left the record out in the sun, and it warped.*

distraught   See the entry for *upset.*

distress   (*noun*) a painful feeling of fear or unhappiness. □ *Kay's decision to move away caused distress to her friends.* □ *The frightened child gave a cry of distress.*

• **agony**   extreme *distress;* great physical or emotional pain. □ *Larry was in agony from the burn on his foot.* □ *Mary suffered great agony because she had to leave her children behind.*

• **anguish**   *distress* caused by grief or pain. □ *Nothing could soothe Philip's anguish over his brother's death.* □ *Rita's face showed her anguish as she admitted she had lost.*

• **anxiety**   *distress* caused by worrying. □ *Anxiety about tomorrow's test kept Tom awake all night.* □ *Sue was full of anxiety over her search for a new job.*

• **suffering**   *distress;* any kind of ongoing pain. □ *The poet's suffering inspired him to write many great poems.* □ *The doctor tried to ease the patient's suffering.*

[→see also: *hurt²*]

distribute   (*verb*) to give something out; to give out shares of something. □ *The company distributed free toothpaste samples.* □ *The bookmobile distributed books all over town.*

• **allocate**   to divide something up into shares. (Formal.) □ *Mom and Dad allocated chores to all the kids.* □ *Thomas allocated fifteen dollars of his weekly salary for entertainment.*

• **dispense**   to give out shares of something. □ *The troop leader dispensed camping equipment to all the scouts.* □ *During the drought, only a limited amount of water was dispensed to each household.* □ *The nurses dispensed both medicine and tender loving care.*

• **disperse**   to give something out to many people; to scatter something around. □ *After Vivian died, her collection of teacups was dispersed among her friends and relatives.* □ *The church dispersed the toys to a large number of needy children.*

• **dole out**   to give out charity; to give out small amounts. □ *The charity workers doled out food to the homeless.* □ *Bill doled out allowances to his children.*

• **issue**   to give something out officially. □ *The state will not issue you a driver's license until you pass this test.* □ *The boss issued a request that employees stop smoking.*

• **pass out**   to give one of something to everybody. (Informal.) □ *The teacher passed out the test and told the class to begin working.* □ *Art stood on the corner, passing out pamphlets about the end of the world.*

distrust   See the entry for *doubt.*

disturbed   See the entry for *upset.*

dive   See the entry for *fall.*

divergent   See the entry for *different.*

diverse   See the entry for *assorted.*

diversion   See the entry for *game*.

divert   See the entries for *entertain, swerve*.

divide   (*verb*) to break something into parts. □ *We divided the cake into equal shares.* □ *The thieves divided the money they had stolen.*
   • **part**   to *divide* oneself from someone; for friends or lovers to leave each other. (Formal or poetic. See also the main entry for *part*.) □ *Our hero's sword parted the dragon's head from its body.* □ *Romeo and Juliet had to part at the end of the day.*
   • **separate**   to make something go into parts; to set things apart from each other. □ *Ben separated the egg yolk from the white.* □ *This border separates the United States from Mexico.*
   • **split**   to *divide* something sharply. □ *Lightning split a branch off the tree.* □ *The jeweler split the diamond in half.*
   • **sunder**   to tear or wrench something apart. (Poetic.) □ *With a mighty stroke of the ax, our hero sundered the tree from its roots.* □ *The lovers vowed that they would never be sundered from one another.*
   [→contrasting word: *join*]

dizzy   (*adjective*) feeling as if everything is spinning around. □ *Riding on the merry-go-round in the park makes me dizzy.* □ *Carrie swung the little girl around until they both felt dizzy.*
   • **giddy**   *dizzy* from emotion; careless and flighty. □ *Happiness made Donald giddy.* □ *The giddy girl laughed and chattered, never thinking before she spoke.*
   • **light-headed**   *dizzy;* feeling as if you are going to faint. □ *Edward was light-headed from hunger.* □ *The fever made Fran feel light-headed.*
   • **motion-sick**   *dizzy* and feeling sick from riding in a vehicle. □ *Driving through the mountains made George motion-sick.* □ *Helen doesn't like carnival rides; she gets motion-sick.*
   [→see also: *groggy*]

do away with   See the entries for *cancel, eliminate*.

do in   See the entry for *kill*.

dock   (*noun*) a place where a boat can land. (See also the entry for *trim*.) □ *We went to the dock and boarded the boat.* □ *The captain piloted his boat toward the dock.*
   • **marina**   a place where many pleasure boats can land and be kept. □ *On weekends, the marina was full of people who came to sail on the bay.* □ *Irene keeps her yacht at the marina.*
   • **pier**   a structure built out into the water where boats can land. □ *Jay walked to the end of the pier and looked out over the lake.* □ *Kay tied the boat to the pier.*

• **quay** a structure built along a shoreline for boats to land on. □ *Many people waited at the quay for the boat to arrive.* □ *During the storm, high waves flooded the quay.*

• **wharf** a structure built along a shoreline for boats to land, load, or unload. □ *Laura went down to the wharf to watch the coal barge unload.* □ *Stacks of boxes stood on the wharf, waiting to be loaded on the next ship.*

doctor (*noun*) a person who is trained to care for or cure sick people. □ *The doctor told me to stick out my tongue and say "ah."* □ *Mark went to the doctor to get some medicine for his sore throat.*

　　• **pediatrician** a *doctor* for children. □ *Parents waited with their children in the pediatrician's office.* □ *Dr. Jones became a pediatrician because he likes kids.*

　　• **physician** a *doctor*. (Formal.) □ *Dr. Blank was a respected physician.* □ *Sue wanted to become a physician like her father.*

　　• **specialist** a *doctor* who has special knowledge about a particular sickness or a particular part of the body. □ *Tom went to a hearing specialist for the problem with his ears.* □ *Grandpa is being taken care of by a famous heart specialist.*

　　• **surgeon** a *doctor* who performs surgery. □ *Philip wanted only the best surgeon for the operation on his leg.* □ *A surgeon must have good eye-hand coordination.*

document (*noun*) something written or printed. □ *This document proves that I own the property.* □ *The Constitution is an important historical document.*

　　• **manuscript** a handwritten *document;* an original *document* written by the author. □ *Vincent needed someone to type the manuscript of his novel.* □ *The published version of the poem is quite different from the author's manuscript.*

　　• **paper** any *document;* a scholarly *document.* □ *The president donated all his papers to the library.* □ *Rita wrote a paper on the history of her town.*

　　• **record** an official *document.* □ *I needed to find a record of my great-grandparents' marriage.* □ *The school keeps a record of everyone's grades.*

dodder See the entry for *rock³.*

dodge (*verb*) to move aside suddenly to get away from someone or something. □ *The soldiers had to dodge bullets as they ran across the field.* □ *The soccer player dodged around the opposing team member and scored a goal.*

　　• **duck** to bend down suddenly to avoid being hit by something. □ *Susan threw a snowball at me, but I ducked.* □ *Tim isn't a very good catcher; he ducks whenever he sees the ball coming toward him.*

• **evade** to get away from someone or something in a clever way; to avoid someone or something by trickery. □ *The criminal tried to evade the police officers who were chasing him.* □ *Jan evaded all my questions.*

• **sidestep** to step or move aside in order to avoid something. □ *Bill sidestepped Art's punch.* □ *The reporter wanted the mayor to quit sidestepping the main issue.*

[→see also: *avoid, elude*]

dog See the entries for *chase, follow.*

dogged See the entry for *persistent.*

dole out See the entry for *distribute.*

dolt See the entry for *fool¹.*

dominant See the entry for *masterful.*

donate See the entry for *give.*

door See the entry for *entrance.*

dot See the entry for *spot.*

dote on See the entry for *like.*

double See the entry for *fold.*

double-crosser See the entry for *traitor.*

double-dealing See the entry for *hypocritical.*

doubt (*verb*) to be uncertain about something; to think that something may not be true. □ *I doubt that Ben was really Elvis's best friend.* □ *Carrie doubted she could finish the assignment on time.*

• **be dubious about** to think that something probably is not true. □ *Donald was dubious about Eddie's musical ability.* □ *Many people were dubious about the lady's claim to be an exiled Russian princess.*

• **distrust** to think that something is not true; to think that someone is not honest. □ *Fran distrusts a lot of the information she gets from TV news.* □ *George distrusted Helen, so he did not tell her his secret.*

• **have qualms about** to fear that something is not true or right. □ *I have qualms about letting Irene cook dinner all by herself.* □ *Irene had qualms about Jay's ability to teach school.*

• **question** to suspect that something is not true or right. □ *I question whether we really need to buy a new radio.* □ *Kay questioned Laura's right to make the decision.*

downcast See the entry for *sad.*

downy See the entry for *fluffy.*

doze   See the entry for *sleep.*

draft   See the entries for *recruit, wind¹.*

drag   See the entry for *pull.*

drain   See the entry for *empty².*

drained   See the entries for *spent, tired.*

drama   See the entry for *play¹.*

dramatic   (*adjective*) very vivid and emotional, like a drama. □ *Mark told the dramatic story of how he had broken his arm.* □ *Nancy screamed and pointed with a dramatic gesture.*
   • **histrionic**   overly *dramatic.* (Formal.) □ *Sue broke down into histrionic weeping.* □ *The judge was not moved by the criminal's histrionic pleading.*
   • **melodramatic**   *dramatic* and exaggerated. □ *Philip vowed revenge in a melodramatic speech.* □ *Quit screaming; there's no need to be melodramatic.*
   • **theatrical**   *dramatic* and artificial. □ *Rita made a theatrical entrance, sweeping into the room and crying, "Hello, darlings!"* □ *The two friends gave a theatrical display of being glad to see each other.*

dramatist   See the entry for *writer.*

drape   (*verb*) to cover something with cloth; to arrange cloth over something. □ *Susan draped the blanket over the bed.* □ *Tom draped the windows with velvet curtains.*
   • **festoon**   to arrange loops of material across something. □ *The buildings were festooned with red, white, and blue streamers for the Fourth of July.* □ *The children festooned the house with banners that said, "Welcome Home, Mom!"*
   • **garland**   to arrange ropes of leaves, flowers, or other decorations around something. □ *Jan garlanded the party room with paper streamers.* □ *The lamp posts were garlanded with ribbons.*
   • **wreathe**   to decorate or adorn something with wreaths. (Poetic.) □ *Our hero wreathed the fair lady's hair with flowers.* □ *A crown of laurel leaves wreathed the prince's brow.*

drastic   See the entry for *severe.*

draw   (*verb*) to make a picture by making lines with a pen, pencil, or crayon. (See also the entries for *attract, pull.*) □ *Bill drew a picture of his house.* □ *Anna drew a complicated design on the cover of her notebook.*
   • **outline**   to *draw* just the basic lines of something. □ *Ben outlined a plan of the bookcase he was building.* □ *Carrie just outlined the background of her picture, planning to fill it in later.*

• **sketch**   to *draw* a rough picture of something. □ *Don sketched Ed's portrait.* □ *Fran sketched the shape of an oak leaf.*

• **trace**   to *draw* by putting a transparent page over a drawing and copying it. □ *George traced the picture out of the book.* □ *Helen traced the dress pattern.*

draw near   See the entry for *approach*.

dreadful   See the entry for *awful*.

dream   (*verb*) to see imaginary things when you are asleep; to think happily about something. □ *I dreamed that I had wings.* □ *Irene dreamed of becoming a great tennis player.*

• **daydream**   to think happily about something you want; to imagine something happening. □ *Jay daydreams about being a rock star.* □ *Kay spent her time daydreaming instead of working.*

• **fantasize**   to think very vividly about something you want. □ *Laura liked to fantasize about what she would do if she won a million dollars.* □ *Mark fantasizes about being a basketball player, but he doesn't spend much time working to become one.*

• **wool-gather**   to think so much about something you want that you are not paying attention to what is happening. □ *Although Tom was bright, he spent so much time wool-gathering that he got bad grades.* □ *We can't wool-gather all day; we'd better get to work.*

dream of   See the entry for *hope*.

dredge up   See the entry for *remember*.

dribble   See the entry for *leak*.

drift   See the entry for *float*.

drill   See the entries for *lesson, practice*.

drink   (*verb*) to take in a liquid. □ *Sue needed to drink some water after spending so much time in the sun.* □ *The waitress asked if I would like something to drink.*

• **gulp**   to *drink* in big mouthfuls. □ *The thirsty woman gulped down the lemonade.* □ *Philip gulped the water.*

• **guzzle**   to *drink* greedily and in one long stretch. (Informal.) □ *The party guests quickly guzzled all the soft drinks that I had.* □ *Sip your drink slowly; don't guzzle it.*

• **imbibe**   to *drink;* to *drink* alcohol. (The former is formal; the latter, informal.) □ *The scientist monitored the amount of liquid that the animal imbibed.* □ *Rita has been known to imbibe excessively at parties.*

• **sip**   to *drink* in very small mouthfuls. □ *Susan sipped her tea.* □ *Thomas savored the ice cream soda, sipping it slowly.*

• **swallow**   to take something into your stomach through your throat. □ *Jan swallowed the cough syrup.* □ *Bill's throat was so sore that it hurt when he tried to swallow anything.*

drive   See the entry for *guide²*.

drizzle   See the entry for *rain*.

drone   See the entries for *chant, hum*.

droop   (*verb*) to hang or bend down. □ *The flag drooped in the still air.* □ *The plant needed water; its leaves drooped.*
   • **sag**   to *droop* in the middle. □ *The sofa sagged when I sat down on it.* □ *The clothesline was so loose that it sagged.*
   • **slouch**   to have a *drooping* posture. □ *Art slouched in his seat.* □ *Ben never slouches; he always stands up straight.*
   • **slump**   to *droop* down suddenly. □ *Carrie slumped over in her chair; she had fainted.* □ *The more the snowman melted, the more he slumped.*

droopy   See the entry for *limp*.

drop   See the entries for *abandon, fall*.

drop in on   See the entry for *visit*.

drove   See the entry for *herd*.

drowse   See the entry for *sleep*.

drowsy   See the entry for *sleepy*.

drug   See the entry for *medicine*.

dry   (*adjective*) without water. □ *The wood was dry and burned quickly.* □ *It had not rained for a month; the ground was very dry.*
   • **arid**   completely *dry*. (Usually used to describe a climate.) □ *Donald loves the arid desert landscape.* □ *Big trees can't flourish in such an arid climate.*
   • **dehydrated**   *dry*; having all the water removed. □ *The campers took dehydrated food because it was light and easy to carry.* □ *If you don't drink enough fluids, you will become dehydrated.*
   • **parched**   *dry* enough to crack. □ *Eddie's skin was parched from all the time he spent in the hot sun.* □ *Rain fell on the parched earth.*
   [→contrasting word: *wet*]

dry out   See the entry for *wither*.

dub   See the entry for *call²*.

dubious   See the entry for *suspicious*.

duck   See the entries for *bow, dodge*.

dull   See the entry for *boring.*

dump   See the entry for *throw away.*

dunce   See the entry for *fool¹.*

dunk   See the entry for *submerge.*

dupe   See the entry for *fool².*

duplicate   See the entry for *copy².*

duplicitous   See the entry for *hypocritical.*

dusk   See the entry for *darkness.*

duty   (*noun*) something you ought to do. □ *Parents have a duty to take care of their children.* □ *The crossing guard's main duty is to get people across the street safely.*

• **burden**   a difficult *duty.* (Old-fashioned.) □ *Fran wished someone would help her with the burden of caring for her sick mother.* □ *George felt that teaching was a burden, but he did not know what else to do for a living.*

• **obligation**   a *duty* you owe someone. □ *Helen had an obligation to help Irene, since Irene had helped her.* □ *Jay gave me the money, and said I was under no obligation to pay it back.*

• **responsibility**   a *duty* that is completely up to you. □ *It is your responsibility to feed your pets.* □ *Don't ask me to take out the trash; that's Kay's responsibility.*

dwell   See the entry for *live.*

dwindle   See the entry for *decrease.*

E

eager (*adjective*) really wanting to do something. □ *I am eager to see the new movie.* □ *Laura was eager to learn to skydive.*
   • **enthusiastic** energetically *eager.* □ *Mark was enthusiastic about going on the trip.* □ *The enthusiastic crowd cheered at everything the team did.*
   • **gung-ho** very *eager.* (Slang.) □ *The team was gung-ho and ready to win.* □ *Tom was quite gung-ho to start work on the tree house.*
   • **willing** agreeing to do something. □ *Sue is willing to loan us her drill.* □ *Philip learns quickly because he is such a willing student.*

eagerness See the entry for *enthusiasm.*

earmark See the entry for *label.*

earn See the entry for *deserve.*

earnest See the entry for *dedicated.*

earnings See the entry for *pay.*

earsplitting See the entry for *loud.*

earth See the entry for *dirt.*

easy (*adjective*) not difficult. □ *That was an easy test!* □ *Sewing is easy to do.*
   • **effortless** so *easy* it does not take any work. □ *The athlete got to the top of the wall with one effortless jump.* □ *The new vacuum cleaner is supposed to make housekeeping effortless.*
   • **elementary** very simple and therefore *easy.* (Formal.) □ *The detective thought the case was so elementary that he could solve it quickly.* □ *"If you know how to speak Spanish, learning Latin is elementary," said the Latin teacher.*

• **simple**   not complicated and therefore *easy*. □ *This is a simple problem; it should be easy to solve.* □ *To make a cake from this cake mix, just follow these four simple steps.*

eat   (*verb*) to take in solid food. □ *What did you eat for breakfast?* □ *Mark ate the sandwich.*

• **consume**   to use something up by *eating* it. (Formal.) □ *We seem to have consumed all the potato chips.* □ *The fire quickly consumed the entire forest.*

• **devour**   to *eat* hungrily and fiercely. □ *The starving man devoured the loaf of bread.* □ *The lion devoured the antelope it had killed.*

• **dine**   to *eat* dinner. (Formal.) □ *The Smiths will dine at six o'clock.* □ *We are invited to dine at Martha's house.*

• **feast**   to *eat* a big meal of many good things. □ *At Thanksgiving, we always feast.* □ *The family feasted on good things from Jane's garden.*

• **ingest**   to take something into your stomach. (Formal.) □ *Do not ingest this substance; it is poisonous.* □ *The dog had managed to ingest a piece of tinfoil.*

eat away   See the entry for *wear away*.

eatery   See the entry for *restaurant*.

eavesdrop   See the entry for *listen*.

eccentric   (*adjective*) having unusual habits. □ *The eccentric man liked to talk to trees.* □ *Tom's not crazy; he's just eccentric.*

• **erratic**   having unpredictable habits; unpredictable. □ *We knew we could not depend on Sue; she was too erratic.* □ *Philip felt worn out and confused by his erratic schedule as an ambulance driver.*

• **quirky**   having some strange habits; unpredictable. □ *The quirky teacher sometimes interrupted the class to have the students play a game.* □ *Rita's quirky housekeeping made her a difficult roommate.*

• **unconventional**   having habits different from most people's. □ *It is rather unconventional to wear socks on one's ears.* □ *The unconventional doctor sometimes prescribed sit-ups or afternoon naps instead of medicine.*

[→see also: *strange*]

echo   See the entry for *repeat*.

eclipse   See the entry for *excel*.

ecstatic   See the entry for *overjoyed*.

edge   See the entry for *boundary*.

edgy   See the entry for *nervous*.

edifice   See the entry for *building*.

educate   See the entry for *teach.*

educated   (*adjective*) having learned a lot in school; having gone up to a high level in school. □ *The magazine is written for educated people.* □ *The author compiled a list of facts that every educated person should know.*
- **erudite**   showing a great deal of knowledge about many things. (Formal.) □ *The professor made a lot of erudite jokes that no one else, not even his fellow professors, understood.* □ *Bill likes to use impressive words to show how erudite he is.*
- **informed**   knowing a great deal about what is happening in the world. □ *Carrie reads the newspaper in order to keep informed.* □ *Although the writer used veiled language, informed readers could tell that he was talking about the presidential election.*
- **knowledgeable**   knowing a great deal. □ *You should ask Donald that question; he's very knowledgeable.* □ *Eddie is very knowledgeable about popular music.*
- **learned**   having or showing a great deal of book learning. □ *Fran may be very learned, but she doesn't have much common sense.* □ *The professor gave a learned lecture about fossils.*

eerie   See the entry for *ghostly.*

efface   See the entry for *erase.*

effect   See the entries for *cause, result.*

effects   See the entry for *property.*

effervesce   See the entry for *seethe.*

effortless   See the entry for *easy.*

effusive   See the entry for *talkative.*

egg on   See the entry for *encourage.*

eject   See the entry for *dismiss.*

elaborate   See the entry for *complicated.*

elated   See the entry for *overjoyed.*

electricity   (*noun*) the kind of energy usually used to run lamps, televisions, and other appliances. □ *The battery provides electricity to run the engine.* □ *The radio runs on electricity.*
- **current**   electric power itself. □ *The power plant puts out a lot of current.* □ *Don't touch the wall outlet; you might get a shock from the current.*
- **juice**   electricity. (Slang.) □ *There's not enough juice in the battery to run the flashlight.* □ *We need a longer extension cord to get the juice to the vacuum cleaner.*

- **power**   *electricity;* the *electricity* supplied to a whole building, neighborhood, or town. □ *The whole street went dark; the power had gone out.* □ *George changed the fuse, and the power came back on.*

electrified   See the entry for *thrilled.*

elegant   See the entry for *stylish.*

element   (*noun*) something that is part of something else. □ *A mystery, a love affair, and a haunted house are all elements of the story.* □ *The show had all the elements of a successful TV program: good stories, interesting characters, and a popular star.*
- **component**   an *element* that is easy to separate from the whole. □ *The speakers are an important component of a stereo system.* □ *The mechanic had to know all the components of a car engine.*
- **factor**   an *element* that influences the whole. □ *Art's professional appearance was a factor in our decision to hire him.* □ *The cooperation of other countries was a key factor in winning the war.*
- **ingredient**   an *element* that is mixed in with others. □ *You will need the following ingredients to make the soup: navy beans, carrots, celery, and onions.* □ *Intelligence, kindness, and a sense of humor were the main ingredients in Ben's personality.*

elementary   See the entry for *easy.*

elevate   See the entry for *lift.*

eliminate   (*verb*) to remove something; to put an end to something. (Formal.) □ *Carrie had to eliminate all sweets from her diet.* □ *When Donald's cheating was discovered, his name was eliminated from the Honor Roll.*
- **dismiss**   to send someone or something away. (See also the main entry for *dismiss.*) □ *Lord Edward dismissed the servants from the room.* □ *The teacher dismissed the class early.*
- **do away with**   to put an end to something. □ *If Fran had her way, she would do away with all reruns on TV.* □ *The principal became popular after she did away with the rule against chewing gum in class.*
- **evict**   to make someone leave the place where he or she is staying. □ *Helen's landlord evicted her.* □ *The hotel owner evicted the noisy guests.*
- **get rid of**   to *eliminate* something. (Informal.) □ *I wish Mom would get rid of this ugly carpet.* □ *Irene had friends over to dinner to help her get rid of some leftovers.*
- **oust**   to force someone out of something; to remove someone from power by force. (Formal.) □ *The army ousted the dictator.* □ *The principal was ousted by the school board.*
- **remove**   to take something away; to put an end to something. (See also the main entry for *remove.*) □ *Workers came in and removed the old carpet.* □ *Vinegar removed the stain from my shirt.*

elude (*verb*) to avoid or escape from someone who is trying to catch you. □ *The fox eluded the hunters.* □ *I tried to remember the right answer, but it eluded me.*

• **evade**   to *elude* someone by trickery. □ *The boat tacked this way and that, trying to evade its pursuers.* □ *The getaway car evaded the police by dashing into a side street.*

• **give someone the slip**   to *elude* someone successfully. (Slang.) □ *When we went back to fetch the prisoner, we found that he had given us the slip.* □ *When Jay saw a salesman coming up the front walk, he gave him the slip by sneaking out through the back door.*

• **slip away**   to *elude* someone; to leave secretly. □ *Kevin slipped away while his parents were discussing how to punish him.* □ *Somehow, Lenny slipped away from the kidnappers.*

[→see also: *avoid, dodge*]

emaciated   See the entry for *thin.*

emanate   See the entry for *emit.*

emancipation   See the entry for *freedom.*

embarrass   (*verb*) to make someone feel silly or ashamed. □ *It embarrassed Mary when her parents fought in front of her friends.* □ *My sister embarrassed me by showing my baby pictures around at school.*

• **chagrin**   to make someone feel disappointed or ashamed. (Formal.) □ *Nancy was chagrined when she discovered that her blouse was inside out.* □ *Sue was chagrined by our lack of enthusiasm for her plan.*

• **disconcert**   to *embarrass*, startle, or confuse someone. □ *The door slammed, disconcerting the pianist so much that she stopped playing.* □ *The bat that flew out of my closet disconcerted me, to say the least.*

• **disgrace**   to bring shame on someone. (See also the main entry for *disgrace.*) □ *Philip has disgraced the family by committing this crime.* □ *Rita disgraced herself with her rude behavior at the party.*

• **humiliate**   to make someone feel utterly ashamed. (Formal.) □ *The teacher humiliated Stanley by criticizing him in front of the class.* □ *Day and night, Thomas plotted a way to humiliate his enemy.*

• **mortify**   to make someone feel deeply ashamed. (Formal.) □ *The little girl mortified her mother by throwing a temper tantrum right there in the restaurant.* □ *Victor was mortified when his pants split open in front of everyone.*

• **shame**   to make someone feel ashamed, especially in public. □ *Wendy shamed me by being kind to me after I had been so nasty to her.* □ *Andy's parents made him stand in the corner to shame him.*

[→consider also: *insult*]

embellish   See the entry for *decorate.*

embezzle   See the entry for *steal.*

embrace   See the entry for *hug*.

embroider   See the entry for *sew*.

emerge   See the entry for *come out*.

emergency   (*noun*) a situation requiring immediate action. ☐ *I have to go home right away; it's an emergency.* ☐ *The sirens wailed, signaling an emergency.*
> • **crisis**   a tense situation. ☐ *Ben keeps cool in a crisis and usually figures out the best thing to do.* ☐ *Many people feared that the international crisis would lead to war.*
> • **crunch**   a critical time or situation. (Slang.) ☐ *Carrie's in a financial crunch; in other words, she's broke.* ☐ *Don't hesitate to call on Donald to help you out of a crunch.*
> • **problem**   a difficult situation. (See also the main entry for *problem*.) ☐ *Eddie was having some kind of problem with his car.* ☐ *Fran never gets things done on time, which causes problems for her at work.*
> • **straits**   a difficult or upsetting situation. (Formal. Often with *dire* or *serious*.) ☐ *Their marriage was in such straits that they contemplated divorce.* ☐ *Bad planning has brought the business to these dire straits.*

eminent   See the entry for *famous*.

emit   (*verb*) to give off something, such as heat, light, or sound. (Formal.) ☐ *The distant star emitted radio waves.* ☐ *The baby emitted a piercing yell.*
> • **diffuse**   to *emit* something over a large area. ☐ *The candles diffused a golden glow throughout the room.* ☐ *The stove diffused a tremendous amount of heat.*
> • **emanate**   to be *emitted*; to flow out from somewhere. (Formal.) ☐ *Self-confidence emanated from George's face.* ☐ *The noise seems to be emanating from the basement.*
> • **radiate**   to *emit* something; to spread out from a center. ☐ *The coals radiated heat.* ☐ *Lines radiated from a point in the center of the picture.*
> • **shed**   to *emit* something; to spread something. (See also the main entry for *shed*.) ☐ *The lamp shed its light over the table.* ☐ *Helen's smile shed a friendly warmth over everyone.*
> • **transmit**   to *emit* or send a signal. ☐ *We used the radio to transmit a distress call.* ☐ *Irene's frown transmitted her uncertainty.*

emotion   See the entry for *feeling*.

empathize   See the entry for *sympathize*.

emperor   See the entry for *ruler*.

emphasize   See the entry for *stress²*.

employ   See the entry for *use*.

employer   See the entry for *boss*.

emporium   See the entry for *store*.

empress   See the entry for *ruler*.

empty[1]   (*adjective*) containing nothing or no one. □ *There's nothing in here; it's just an empty box.* □ *After the children had left, the empty classroom was quiet.*
> • **blank**   empty. (Used to describe surfaces.) □ *Jay stared at the blank piece of paper, wondering what to write.* □ *The TV screen suddenly went blank.*
> • **vacant**   empty; not lived in by anyone. □ *The children played ball in the vacant lot.* □ *The apartment next door has been vacant for months.*
> • **void**   empty. (Formal.) □ *Is the space between the stars completely void, or is there matter in it?* □ *I could not tell what John was feeling; his face was void of all expression.*
> [→contrasting word: *full*]

empty[2]   (*verb*) to remove the contents of something. □ *Kay emptied the pitcher into the sink.* □ *Laura emptied the grocery bag so that the kitten could play in it.*
> • **bleed**   to *empty* something very slowly and steadily; to let a fluid or gas out very slowly. □ *Mark bled the air out of the tires.* □ *To get maple syrup, people first bleed the sap from maple trees.*
> • **drain**   to *empty* something gradually; to use something up little by little. □ *Tom drained the water from the bathtub.* □ *Hunger drained Sue of all her energy.*
> • **evacuate**   to *empty* something forcefully and completely; to make people leave a place. (Formal.) □ *We used a pump to evacuate the water from the basement.* □ *Everyone had to evacuate the building when the fire alarm sounded.*
> • **exhaust**   to use up something completely. □ *Philip had exhausted his supply of peanut butter to make the peanut-butter cookies.* □ *The unruly children exhausted their father's patience.*

emulate   See the entry for *copy*[1].

enchanted   See the entry for *fascinated*.

encircle   See the entry for *surround*.

enclose   See the entry for *surround*.

encompass   See the entry for *surround*.

encounter   See the entries for *experience, meet*.

encourage (*verb*) to give someone courage and hope; to tell someone he or she is doing well and should continue. ☐ *Rita encouraged me to apply for the job.* ☐ *The teacher's praise encouraged Susan in her work.*

• **egg on** to *encourage* someone to do something, especially something he or she should not do. (Slang.) ☐ *Tim only put the frog in the teacher's desk because the other students egged him on.* ☐ *Jan egged Bill on to spray-paint his name on the wall.*

• **motivate** to *encourage* someone by giving reasons. (Formal.) ☐ *The boss searched for ways to motivate her employees to work harder.* ☐ *The promise of a trip to the zoo motivated the children to behave.*

• **spur** to *encourage*; to urge someone to do something. ☐ *The possibility of winning the diving match spurred Anna to practice her diving.* ☐ *Ben's interest in politics spurred him to run for student council.*

encroach upon See the entry for *invade*.

encumbrance See the entry for *load*.

end (*noun*) the last part of something. (See also the entry for *stop*.) ☐ *Carrie read to the end of the book.* ☐ *Don couldn't wait till the end of the school day.*

• **close** the *end* of something, especially a presentation such as a story or a play. (See also the main entry for *close*.) ☐ *After half an hour, Eddie's speech came to a close.* ☐ *The two friends were reunited at the story's close.*

• **conclusion** an *end*, especially one that sums things up. ☐ *The conclusion of the magazine article said that not enough was being done to help homeless people.* ☐ *I thought that the story's conclusion left a lot of loose ends.*

• **finale** the *end* of a piece of music or a show. ☐ *The finale was a spectacular song-and-dance number with fifty dancers in a chorus line.* ☐ *Fran wanted fireworks for the finale of the parade.*

• **finish** the *end* of something. ☐ *We won't know who won until the finish of the race.* ☐ *A dessert of fresh fruit made a nice finish for the meal.*

• **windup** an *end*. (Slang.) ☐ *The bored students wished the teacher's lecture would get to the windup.* ☐ *There was a nice little windup of all the story lines at the end of the movie.*

endeavor See the entry for *try*.

endorse See the entry for *approve*.

endurance See the entry for *stamina*.

endure See the entries for *bear, last*.

enemy (*noun*) someone who hates and wants to harm you. □ *George became my enemy when he insulted me in public.* □ *The two countries were enemies in the last war.*

* **adversary** someone who fights or works against you. (Formal.) □ *The great detective was the criminal mastermind's adversary.* □ *The two high school football teams had been adversaries for years.*
* **antagonist** someone who works against you. (Formal.) □ *The prince was the king's antagonist in the struggle for the crown.* □ *Helen's antagonist spoiled her plans at every opportunity.*
* **foe** an *enemy.* (Poetic.) □ *We must take arms against the foe.* □ *The evil enchantress was the most dangerous foe our hero had yet encountered.*
* **opponent** someone who is on the other side in a fight, game, or discussion. □ *The chess player had never played against this particular opponent.* □ *The tennis player shook hands with her opponent before the game began.*
* **rival** someone who competes against you for a prize. □ *Irene and Jean were rivals for Kevin's love.* □ *Laura and Mark were rivals competing for the same job.*
[→contrasting words: *friend, ally*]

energetic See the entry for *lively.*

energy (*noun*) liveliness; vigor. □ *I don't know where Danny gets the energy to run around like that all day.* □ *Rita's gestures were full of energy as she told the story.*

* **animation** energy in moving. □ *The animation in Susan's face showed that she was excited and happy.* □ *There was a great deal of animation in Ted's voice as he described the situation.*
* **pep** brisk, bouncy *energy.* (Informal.) □ *There's no stopping Becky; she's got loads of pep.* □ *Grandma doesn't like slow, sad songs; she prefers a tune with pep.*
* **spirit** emotional *energy.* □ *Jan's boss tried to frighten her, but she faced up to him with spirit.* □ *Art's reply to the insult was full of spirit.*
* **verve** energy and style. (Informal.) □ *The actress performed the role with her usual verve.* □ *The writer's style really kept me interested; it had originality and verve.*
* **vivacity** cheerful *energy;* a liveliness that attracts people. □ *Carrie's vivacity won her many friends.* □ *She had so much vivacity that she was always the center of attention.*

enervated See the entry for *tired.*

engage in See the entry for *participate.*

engaged See the entry for *busy¹.*

engagement   See the entry for *date¹*.

engaging   See the entry for *interesting*.

engineer   See the entry for *control²*.

engrave   See the entry for *carve*.

engrossed   See the entry for *absorbed*.

enhance   See the entry for *improve*.

enigmatic   See the entry for *mysterious*.

enjoy   (*verb*) to get pleasure from something. ☐ *I enjoy watching TV in the evenings.* ☐ *Donald hoped that his guests would enjoy the party.*
• **delight in**   to *enjoy* something particularly; to get special pleasure out of something. ☐ *Eddie delights in making horrible puns.* ☐ *Fran delights in visits from her grandchildren.*
• **relish**   to *enjoy* something; to *enjoy* the taste of something. ☐ *George relished the opportunity to play his music for such a friendly audience.* ☐ *Helen relished the savory Greek food.*
• **revel in**   to *enjoy* something with gusto. ☐ *Irene reveled in the dancing at the party.* ☐ *The children reveled in all the sweets their grandmother let them have.*
• **savor**   to *enjoy* something, especially a taste or smell, by taking it a little at a time. ☐ *Jay savored every moment of his vacation.* ☐ *Kay slowly sipped the cup of rich cocoa, savoring it.*
[→see also: *like*]

enjoyable   See the entry for *nice*.

enlarge   See the entry for *expand*.

enlist   See the entry for *recruit*.

enormous   See the entry for *big*.

enough   (*adjective*) the right amount. ☐ *Did you give the plants enough water?* ☐ *Five dollars should be enough to get lunch.*
• **adequate**   barely *enough*. ☐ *Some of the children were not getting adequate nutrition.* ☐ *The house was adequate for the family's needs.*
• **ample**   *enough* or more than *enough*. ☐ *She has an ample supply of money to meet her needs.* ☐ *Laura gets an ample amount of exercise.*
• **sufficient**   *enough* for your needs. ☐ *The clothing I took with me on the trip was not sufficient.* ☐ *Mark thought he had spent a sufficient amount of time on his homework.*
[→contrasting word: *insufficient*]

enraged   See the entry for *angry*.

entertain   (*verb*) to keep someone interested in a pleasant way. □ *Tom entertained us by doing impressions of famous people.* □ *The movie entertained the audience.*

• **amuse**   to *entertain* someone delightfully. □ *Sue made faces in order to amuse the baby.* □ *Philip was very amused by the joke I told.*

• **divert**   to distract someone by *entertaining* him or her. (Formal.) □ *Ken and Sue diverted themselves by playing a game of cards.* □ *Going shopping always diverted Susan.*

• **regale**   to *entertain* someone grandly. (Formal.) □ *Thomas regaled everyone with his funny stories.* □ *The king regaled the lords and ladies with a magnificent ball.*

entertainer   (*noun*) someone who entertains people for a living. □ *The popular entertainer appeared on many TV shows.* □ *The film festival celebrates the great entertainer's work.*

• **actor**   an *entertainer* who plays a part in a stage play or a movie. □ *The actor didn't like the lines he was supposed to say.* □ *The critics all agreed that he was a fine actor.*

• **performer**   an *entertainer* who is known for a particular kind of performance. □ *Of all the performers in that show, I liked the magician best.* □ *The comedian was a seasoned performer and knew what audiences liked.*

• **player**   a cast member; an *entertainer* who appears in a play. □ *After the performance, the players came down from the stage and chatted with the audience.* □ *Tom is a player in our local community theater.*

• **thespian**   an *entertainer* who performs in stage plays. (Formal.) □ *Maria is in all the school plays and hopes to become a great thespian.* □ *John Barrymore was a famous thespian in his day.*

enthuse   See the entry for *rave*.

enthusiasm   (*noun*) an energetic feeling; a passion for something. □ *Irene started the project with great enthusiasm.* □ *Jay went about the household chores with enthusiasm.*

• **ardor**   heated *enthusiasm;* passion. □ *The scientist pursued new knowledge with ardor.* □ *Kay wrote love poems filled with ardor.*

• **avidity**   eager *enthusiasm.* (Formal.) □ *Laura collected baseball cards with avidity.* □ *The teacher had never seen a student with such avidity for the subject.*

• **eagerness**   *enthusiasm;* a desire to do something. □ *Mark's eagerness to help makes him a good assistant.* □ *Tom could not hide his eagerness to get the money.*

• **zeal**   strong *enthusiasm.* □ *Debra prepared for the track meet with great zeal.* □ *All these sweaters are the result of Sue's zeal for knitting.*

• **zest**   *enthusiasm* and enjoyment. □ *The actress played the part with zest.* □ *Philip attacked the math problem with zest.*

enthusiast   See the entry for *fan.*

enthusiastic   See the entry for *eager.*

entice   See the entry for *attract.*

entire   See the entry for *whole.*

entrance   (*noun*) the place where you go in. □ *Wait for me at the entrance to the movie theater.* □ *There was a barrier across the entrance to the park.*
   • **door**   the *entrance* to a building or a room. □ *Rita knocked on the door.* □ *Someone was waiting outside the door of the house.*
   • **gate**   the *entrance* to a wall or a fence. □ *The car drove in through the gate.* □ *Susan unlatched the gate and came into the yard.*
   • **portal**   an *entrance* or door. (Poetic.) □ *Our hero guarded the castle's portal.* □ *Two stone lions stood by the portal to the mansion.*
   • **threshold**   the part of a door you step on when you go in; any *entrance.* (Formal.) □ *The groom carried his bride over the threshold.* □ *Tim stood on the threshold, not sure whether he should go in.*

entreat   See the entry for *beg.*

entrust   See the entry for *lend.*

envious   See the entry for *jealous.*

envision   See the entry for *imagine.*

ephemeral   See the entry for *temporary.*

epic   See the entry for *poem.*

episode   See the entry for *event.*

equal   (*adjective*) the same in all respects. □ *The two cups contained equal amounts of water.* □ *Jan and Bill got equal scores on the game.*
   • **alike**   the same in some respects. □ *The brothers looked alike.* □ *I can't tell those songs apart, they sound so much alike.*
   • **comparable**   the same in several respects; as good as. □ *The new computer was comparable to the old one.* □ *The houses were comparable in size, but very different in price.*
   • **equivalent**   the same for all practical purposes. □ *I would like to exchange this toaster for an equivalent one.* □ *We learned that 32 degrees Fahrenheit is equivalent to 0 degrees Celsius.*
   • **similar**   the same in many respects. □ *I want a lamp similar to the one Art has.* □ *Ben mistook his suitcase for a similar one nearby.*

equitable   See the entry for *fair.*

equivalent   See the entry for *equal.*

equivocate   See the entry for *lie²*.

era   See the entry for *time*.

eradicate   See the entry for *erase*.

erase   (*verb*) to rub something out; to rub something off a surface. □ *Carrie erased what she had written.* □ *Please erase the chalkboard.*
• **efface**   to erase or scratch something out. (Formal.) □ *The writing on the base of the statue had been effaced.* □ *Donald effaced the picture on the front of the magazine.*
• **eradicate**   to *erase* or wipe something out; to get rid of something completely. (Formal.) □ *Eddie tried to eradicate all traces of spilled tomato juice.* □ *Fran accidentally eradicated the computer file.*
• **expunge**   to *erase* completely. (Formal.) □ *The disgraced queen's name was expunged from the history of the royal family.* □ *I expunged the paragraph in the essay to which the teacher had objected.*
• **obliterate**   to *erase*; to wipe something out completely. (Formal.) □ *The workers tried to obliterate the words that had been spray-painted on the building.* □ *The waves obliterated the sand castle.*

erection   See the entry for *building*.

erode   See the entry for *wear away*.

errand   See the entry for *job*.

erratic   See the entry for *eccentric*.

error   See the entry for *mistake*.

erstwhile   See the entry for *past*.

erudite   See the entry for *educated*.

erupt   See the entry for *burst*.

escapade   See the entry for *adventure*.

escape   (*verb*) to avoid being caught; to get out or away. □ *Greg escaped from the locked room.* □ *Harry escaped his pursuers.*
• **break out**   to *escape* from a prison. (Informal.) □ *The prisoners planned to break out.* □ *When the sheriff went to see the cattle rustler, he discovered she had broken out of the cell.*
• **flee**   to *escape* by running. □ *The townspeople fled before the invading army.* □ *The cat fled when he saw the dog come into the yard.*
• **get away**   to *escape* successfully. □ *I caught the snake, but then it got away.* □ *The burglar got away from the scene of the crime.*
• **run away from**   to *escape*; to avoid someone or something. □ *Irene ran away from her husband.* □ *Jay tends to run away from responsibility.*
[→see also: *steal away*]

escort   See the entry for *accompany*.

especially   (*adverb*) to a high degree. □ *Kay seemed especially glad to see me.* □ *Laura made us an especially nice lunch.*
   • **particularly**   to a noteworthy degree. □ *The children were particularly naughty today.* □ *I particularly want to see this movie.*
   • **singularly**   to an extremely high degree. □ *The movie turned out to be singularly uninteresting.* □ *The sculptor created a singularly beautiful statue.*
   • **uncommonly**   to a rare degree. □ *Mark is an uncommonly patient person.* □ *Tom is uncommonly fond of kiwi fruit.*
   • **unusually**   to a peculiar degree. □ *An unusually large number of people came to the lecture.* □ *Sue was unusually calm all evening.*

essential   See the entry for *necessary*.

establish   See the entry for *show¹*.

esteem   See the entry for *respect²*.

estimate   See the entry for *guess*.

ethereal   See the entry for *ghostly*.

evacuate   See the entry for *empty²*.

evade   See the entries for *dodge, elude*.

even   See the entry for *flat*.

event   (*noun*) something that happens. □ *Philip's graduation was a happy event.* □ *The signing of the Declaration of Independence was an important event in American history.*
   • **episode**   one *event* in real life or in a story. □ *Until the episode when he found the fly in his soup, Roger liked that restaurant.* □ *The trip Susan took with her grandmother was a memorable episode of her childhood.*
   • **happening**   an *event*. (Often used in the plural.) □ *We heard rumors of strange happenings at City Hall.* □ *Tim told us the latest happenings with his family.*
   • **incident**   an *event*. (Somewhat formal.) □ *There were one or two incidents when Jan lost her temper.* □ *The police officer refused to discuss the robbery incident.*
   • **occurrence**   an *event*. (Formal.) □ *Bill's accident was a most unfortunate occurrence.* □ *Art wants to be prepared for every possible occurrence, including fire, flood, and earthquake.*

evict   See the entry for *eliminate*.

evidence (*noun*) something that supports your conclusions. □ *Ben says that Carrie is dishonest, but he has no evidence for it.* □ *The detective found evidence to show that the killer was a left-handed woman who limped.*

• **foundation** something on which you base your conclusions. □ *Donald's nervous behavior was the foundation for his mother's belief that he had done something wrong.* □ *Fran's argument had no logical foundation.*

• **grounds** the reasons behind your conclusions; the reasons for making an accusation. □ *Helen's poor work was sufficient grounds for firing her.* □ *On what grounds do you accuse Greg of murder?*

• **proof** something that shows your conclusions are true. □ *The footprints were proof that my dog had been in Irene's garden.* □ *Jay had no proof that the mysterious light in the sky was a flying saucer.*

evident See the entry for *clear.*

evil (*adjective*) extremely bad; wanting to cause harm. □ *The evil wizard turned our hero into an oyster.* □ *Kay refused to take part in the evil plan to kill the old man.*

• **devilish** as *evil* as the devil; mischievous. □ *The mad scientist created a devilish machine that could destroy the world.* □ *Nicky has a devilish streak in her and sometimes turns on her friends.*

• **malevolent** having or showing *evil* intentions. (Formal.) □ *The malevolent woman plotted to ruin her friend.* □ *There was a malevolent gleam in Mel's eye as he promised to take care of us.*

• **nefarious** entirely *evil* and immoral. (Formal.) □ *Many of the bank's employees were part of the nefarious scheme to defraud the depositors.* □ *The dictator came to power through nefarious means.*

• **wicked** *evil* and immoral. □ *The wicked child tried to burn the house down.* □ *Torturing small animals is wicked.*

evolve See the entry for *grow.*

exact (*adjective*) correct to a very high degree; without mistakes. (See also the entry for *actual.*) □ *Philip made an exact measurement of the doorway.* □ *What were the exact words that Ken said?*

• **definite** clear, certain, and *exact.* □ *Rita had a definite idea about which beach was the best.* □ *I asked Stanley when he could come over, but he couldn't give me a definite answer.*

• **precise** carefully *exact.* □ *The doctor made a precise incision on the patient's knee.* □ *Tim pointed to the precise spot where he had seen the bullet hole.*

• **specific** detailed and *exact.* □ *Victor gave a specific description of the car that hit him.* □ *Bill gave us very specific instructions about how to use the stove.*

exacting See the entries for *hard, strict.*

examination See the entry for *test.*

examine See the entry for *check.*

example (*noun*) a good representative of a group; one person or thing to show what others are like. □ *Art is an example of a self-educated person.* □ *The teacher used Ben's essay as an example of clear writing.*
> • **case** a situation that serves as an *example.* (See also the main entry for *case.*) □ *The TV program showed several cases of alcohol abuse.* □ *The doctors were eager to study this case of a rare disease.*
> • **instance** an *example* that helps to prove your point. (Formal.) □ *There are many instances of friendships maintained over a long distance.* □ *Carrie pointed to the rock song as an instance of music that corrupts young people.*
> • **sample** an *example* picked out to represent something. □ *I need a sample of your handwriting.* □ *If that cookie is a good sample of Donald's cooking, I can't wait to have dinner at his house!*
> • **specimen** an *example* used for scientific analysis. □ *I have a specimen of iron pyrite in my rock collection.* □ *The botanist needed a specimen of a certain kind of plant.*

excavate See the entry for *dig.*

excel (*verb*) to do extremely well; to do or be better than someone or something. □ *Eddie felt driven to excel at everything he did.* □ *The baseball team excelled last year's record.*
> • **eclipse** to do or be much better than someone or something. □ *The singer's new record eclipses everything she has done up to now.* □ *The youngest prince's good looks eclipsed his brothers'.*
> • **outdo** to do more or better than someone or something. □ *The cook has outdone herself; this meal is terrific!* □ *The sprinter vowed to outdo the standing world record.*
> • **outstrip** to do or be a great deal better than someone or something. □ *The new computer far outstrips all other models.* □ *Sales of Vincent's book soon outstripped everything else on the best-seller list.*
> • **surpass** to do or be far better than someone or something. □ *The children's misbehavior surpassed their previous unruliness.* □ *The breakfast cereal surpassed all others in both taste and nutrition.*

excellent (*adjective*) of very high quality. □ *Fran did an excellent job of painting the house.* □ *George is an excellent musician.*
> • **first-class** of the very best quality. □ *Helen is a first-class swimmer and will certainly win the race.* □ *As a teacher, Irene is first-class.*
> • **splendid** of very rich quality. □ *The movie was splendid entertainment.* □ *There is a splendid view from the top of that hill.*

• **superb** grand; of high quality. □ *Kevin cooked us a superb meal.* □ *The actor gave a superb performance.*
• **superior** of far better quality. □ *Laura's skill in writing is superior to her classmates'.* □ *You must start with superior fabric if you are going to make a superior garment.*

exceptional (*adjective*) noticeably different. (See also the entry for *strange.*) □ *Mark is a person of exceptional intelligence.* □ *Tom's artistic talent was so exceptional that we were sure he would become an artist.*
 • **extraordinary** highly *exceptional;* not at all ordinary. □ *Sue has an extraordinary way of answering the phone. She says, "What!?"* □ *It was an extraordinary movie, one of the best I've seen.*
 • **outstanding** *exceptional;* exceptionally good. □ *Philip is an outstanding student and usually gets the highest grades.* □ *Rita is the author of several outstanding mystery stories.*
 • **rare** *exceptional* and hard to find. □ *This is a rare kind of antique doll and is worth a lot of money.* □ *It is rare for such a young person to know what he wants to do in life.*
 • **remarkable** quite *exceptional;* worthy of being noticed. □ *Susan has a remarkable talent for getting into trouble.* □ *Tim's fancy calculator can do all kinds of remarkable things.*
 • **uncommon** *exceptional;* not usual. □ *It was uncommon for Jan to stay up later than ten at night.* □ *Bill's uncommon wealth allowed him to do many interesting things.*
 • **unique** *exceptional;* the only one of its kind. □ *Art hopped around on one foot, showing joy in his own unique way.* □ *This is a unique painting; so far as we know, it's the only one this artist ever did.*
 [→contrasting words: *ordinary, run-of-the-mill*]

excess See the entry for *surplus.*

exchange See the entry for *trade.*

excise See the entry for *remove.*

excited (*adjective*) very emotional. (See also the entry for *thrilled.*) □ *Ben was excited about going camping.* □ *Don't get excited; stay calm.*
 • **agitated** *excited* and disturbed. (Formal.) □ *Carrie was agitated when her brother did not come home that night.* □ *There was an agitated look on Donald's face.*
 • **frantic** *excited* enough to seem crazy. □ *Eddie made a frantic search for the car keys.* □ *Fred was frantic when he discovered he had lost the money.*
 • **frenetic** wildly *excited.* □ *It was hard to get used to the frenetic pace of city life.* □ *The frenetic woman paced back and forth across the room, wringing her hands.*

• **frenzied**   wildly, crazily *excited*. □ *The runner made a frenzied dash for the finish line.* □ *Who could be the source of those frenzied screams?*
• **wrought up**   tense and *excited*. (Formal.) □ *George was quite wrought up over the prospect of losing his girlfriend.* □ *Helen was so wrought up that she couldn't sleep.*
[→see also: *upset, desperate*]

excursion   See the entry for *journey*.

excuse   See the entry for *pardon*.

execute   See the entry for *kill*.

executive   See the entries for *authority, governmental*.

exercise   (*noun*) the activity of moving your body to keep it strong and healthy. (See also the entry for *lesson*.) □ *Irene did some kind of exercise every day.* □ *Jay would probably feel better if he got more exercise.*
• **aerobics**   *exercise* to make your heart beat faster. □ *Kay goes to the gym for aerobics.* □ *Laura does aerobics to help her lose weight.*
• **calisthenics**   *exercise* performed without equipment, such as push-ups, stretches, or jumping jacks. □ *The football team did half an hour of calisthenics at every practice.* □ *Mark did some calisthenics every morning.*
• **workout**   a session of *exercise* or an *exercise* program. □ *Swimming and weight lifting give Tom a good workout.* □ *Sue's workout includes stair climbing and muscle training.*

exhaust   See the entry for *empty²*.

exhausted   See the entry for *tired*.

exhaustive   See the entry for *thorough*.

exhibit   See the entry for *show²*.

exhort   See the entry for *urge*.

exit   See the entry for *go*.

exonerate   See the entry for *pardon*.

exorbitant   See the entry for *expensive*.

exotic   See the entry for *strange*.

expand   (*verb*) to get bigger; to make something bigger. □ *The library expanded steadily over the years.* □ *The musician learned several new pieces, expanding her repertoire.*
• **enlarge**   to *expand*; to become larger. □ *Philip wanted to enlarge his bedroom.* □ *The disease enlarged one side of Ken's head.*

• **grow**   to get bigger. (See also the main entry for *grow*.) ☐ *The city grew, taking over more and more of the neighboring towns.* ☐ *Roger's fame grew with every race he won.*

• **increase**   to get gradually bigger; to make something gradually bigger. ☐ *The number of people in the club increased.* ☐ *Susan wanted to increase the size of her muscles.*

• **swell**   to get bigger and rounder. ☐ *Tim twisted his ankle, and an hour later it had swelled hugely.* ☐ *The balloon swelled as we filled it with water.*

• **wax**   to get bigger; to become. ☐ *The moon waxed during the last part of the month.* ☐ *Victor's love for Sylvia waxed greater every time he saw her.*

[→see also: *inflate*]

expansive   See the entry for *wide*.

expect   (*verb*) to think something will happen. ☐ *Andy expects to get a present on his birthday.* ☐ *I expected you to arrive two hours ago.*

• **anticipate**   to *expect* or look forward to something. ☐ *All the students eagerly anticipated the beginning of vacation.* ☐ *Stanley was excited, anticipating his friend's visit.*

• **count on**   to *expect* something you need; to trust that something will happen. ☐ *I count on you to help me if anything goes wrong.* ☐ *Elaine was counting on her friends to provide the music for her party.*

• **reckon on**   to *expect;* to plan on something. (Informal.) ☐ *I didn't reckon on so many people coming for dinner.* ☐ *Jan had reckoned on the movie costing about five dollars, so she was upset when she found out that it cost seven-fifty.*

expedition   See the entry for *journey*.

expel   (*verb*) to force out something, often a liquid. (See also the entry for *dismiss*.) ☐ *The first-aid worker tried to expel the water from the victim's lungs.* ☐ *Molten rock, ash, and hot gases were expelled from the volcano.*

• **gush**   to force out great quantities of liquid; to pour out forcefully in great quantities. ☐ *Art's eyes gushed tears.* ☐ *Water gushed from the spigot.*

• **spew**   to violently force out quantities of something, often a liquid. ☐ *The machine spewed oil all over the room.* ☐ *The VCR made a horrible noise and started spewing tangled videotape.*

• **spurt**   to force out a liquid in a short burst; to come out in short, forceful bursts. ☐ *The teakettle spurted steam.* ☐ *Ketchup spurted out of the squeeze bottle.*

• **squirt**   to force out a small amount of liquid; to burst out in a small quantity. ☐ *Ben squirted some water onto the plants.* ☐ *Juice squirted from the grapefruit.*

[→see also: *emit*]

expend   See the entry for *spend*.

expensive   (*adjective*) costing a lot of money. □ *Carrie bought an expensive pair of shoes.* □ *I don't eat at that restaurant; it's too expensive.*
  • **costly**   very *expensive*. □ *Donald bought me a costly present.* □ *Eddie had no idea that furniture could be so costly.*
  • **exorbitant**   ridiculously *expensive*. (Formal.) □ *Fran thought that three hundred dollars was exorbitant for a dress.* □ *It was a beautiful apartment, but the rent was exorbitant.*
  • **extravagant**   *expensive;* spending too much money. □ *We can't afford such extravagant treats.* □ *The extravagant young man bought two new cars every year.*
  • **steep**   quite *expensive*. (Informal or slang. See also the main entry for *steep*.) □ *It's a nice watch, all right, but it's much too steep for me.* □ *Airplane fare was so steep that George couldn't afford to go home for the holidays.*
  [→contrasting word: *cheap*]

experience   (*verb*) to live through something; to feel something. □ *Helen had never experienced true disappointment until she failed to get into the talent show.* □ *Irene experienced a sudden feeling of dizziness.*
  • **encounter**   to *experience* something; to see or meet something; to face something. □ *Jay encountered determined opposition to his plan.* □ *Kay is the most stubborn person I've ever encountered.*
  • **go through**   to *experience* something difficult. □ *Laura went through a difficult period after her parents died.* □ *Jonathan may be only four years old, but already he's gone through a lot: he's had major surgery three times.*
  • **undergo**   to *experience* something that requires you to be strong. □ *Mark must undergo a tough examination before he can graduate.* □ *Tom has undergone a lot of suffering.*

experienced   (*adjective*) having done or lived through something many times before. □ *Sue needed an experienced waiter to help her at the restaurant.* □ *Philip is an experienced baby-sitter; I'm sure he won't have any trouble with the kids.*
  • **accomplished**   having done something many times before; skilled. □ *Rita is an accomplished pianist.* □ *Susan, an accomplished seamstress, made the suit in only two days.*
  • **practiced**   having done something many times before. □ *Thomas was a practiced liar and got everyone to believe his tall tale.* □ *Jan was practiced at getting people to do things her way.*
  • **seasoned**   *experienced;* tough; used to something. □ *The seasoned teacher was prepared for any pranks the students might pull.* □ *Even the seasoned reporter had a hard time getting the mayor to give her a straight answer.*

• **veteran** having done or lived through something before. □ *Bill was a veteran actor; he could memorize lines in his sleep.* □ *The veteran nurses in the emergency room were seldom shocked by gruesome injuries.*

expert (*noun*) someone who is very good at something; someone who knows a lot about something. □ *Art is an expert at bicycle repair.* □ *Ben asked an expert to tell him how much his pottery collection was worth.*
    • **authority** someone who knows a lot about something. (See also the main entry for *authority*.) □ *Carrie is an authority on butterflies.* □ *This book is written by the foremost authority on card games.*
    • **master** someone who is the very best at something; someone who has complete control over something. □ *Donald takes karate from a famous karate master.* □ *The reporter was a master at getting people to tell him their secrets.*
    • **virtuoso** someone who is extremely good at something. (Formal.) □ *The concert will feature a violin virtuoso.* □ *That chef is a virtuoso; she comes up with so many original dishes, all of them delicious.*

expire See the entry for *die*.

explain (*verb*) to make something clear; to give the reasons for something. □ *Eddie explained how to use the microwave.* □ *Fran overslept today, which explains why she was late to work.*
    • **account for** to give the reasons for something. □ *George had to account for his absence from class.* □ *Helen is usually a good student; I can't account for her poor performance on this test.*
    • **clarify** to make something clear. (Formal.) □ *I don't understand what you're asking for; please clarify your request.* □ *Irene tried to clarify what she meant by her remark.*
    • **illuminate** to make something clear or easy to understand. (Formal.) □ *The teacher's interesting lecture illuminated the subject we were studying.* □ *Knowing that Jay hated Kay illuminated his reasons for acting so mean to her.*

explicit See the entry for *vivid*[1].

explode See the entry for *burst*.

exploit See the entries for *adventure, use*.

explore (*verb*) to go into something carefully in order to find out more about it; to travel for the purpose of discovery. □ *The pioneers explored the wilderness.* □ *Laura played with the computer, exploring all of the things it could do.*
    • **check out** to *explore* something. (Slang.) □ *I heard that the national park was a great place to go hiking, so I decided to check it out for myself.* □ *Mark went to the car dealer's and checked out the new cars.*

• **delve into**   to *explore* something deeply and energetically. □ *Tom delved into his hero's life by reading a number of biographies.* □ *The counselor helped Sue delve into what was upsetting her.*

• **investigate**   to *explore* something systematically. □ *The reporter investigated the mayor's activities.* □ *The cats investigated their new house.*

• **probe**   to *explore* something very deeply and carefully; to find out everything you can about something. □ *The detective probed into the possible motives for the murder.* □ *Philip probed into the mysterious man's past, trying to learn his secret.*

expostulate   See the entry for *object*.

express   (*verb*) to put something into words; to show something through words or actions. □ *Rita expressed a desire to leave.* □ *Susan's grief was so deep she could hardly express it.*

• **convey**   to tell what you know to someone else; to get an idea across to someone else. (Formal.) □ *Tim tried to convey the beauty of the mountains where he had camped.* □ *Jan's drumming fingers conveyed her impatience.*

• **depict**   to tell about something in such a way that someone else can imagine how it looks or feels. (Formal.) □ *This book accurately depicts life in the Russian royal family.* □ *With a few well-chosen words, Bill depicted the town where he used to live.*

• **describe**   to tell about something in such a way that someone else can imagine exactly how it is. □ *Art described his sister so that I would recognize her when I saw her.* □ *I wish I could describe the taste of that wonderful soup.*

expunge   See the entry for *erase*.

extend   See the entry for *stretch*.

extensive   See the entry for *wide*.

exterior   See the entry for *outer*.

external   See the entry for *outer*.

extol   See the entry for *praise*.

extra   (*adjective*) more than is needed or wanted. □ *Do you have an extra sleeping bag that I could use?* □ *Much to Ben's dismay, he found he had made the sweater with an extra sleeve.*

• **additional**   *extra*; added to what you already had. □ *There are two additional guests coming to the party.* □ *The audience clapped so much that the musician came back to do a few additional songs.*

• **extraneous**   *extra* and not useful. (Formal.) ☐ *Charles carries around a lot of extraneous pens and pencils.* ☐ *Donna's speech included some extraneous jokes.*

• **spare**   *extra;* ready to be used in an emergency. ☐ *Do you have any spare parts for your bicycle?* ☐ *Eddie drove off without the spare tire.*

• **superfluous**   *extra* and not wanted. (Formal.) ☐ *It was warm enough that Fran felt her coat was superfluous.* ☐ *The newlyweds wondered what to do with the three superfluous toasters they had received as wedding gifts.*

• **supplementary**   *extra;* contributing something more. ☐ *George got supplementary income by doing yardwork for his neighbors.* ☐ *There is more information in the supplementary material at the back of the book.*

extract   See the entry for *remove.*

extraneous   See the entry for *extra.*

extraordinary   See the entry for *exceptional.*

extravagant   See the entry for *expensive.*

extreme   See the entry for *severe.*

extremely   See the entry for *very.*

eye   See the entry for *see.*

F

fable   See the entry for *story*.

fabric   See the entry for *cloth*.

fabricate   See the entry for *make¹*.

fabrication   See the entry for *lie¹*.

fabulous   See the entry for *incredible*.

façade   See the entry for *front*.

face   (*verb*) to meet someone or something bravely. (See also the entry for *front*.) □ *Helen steeled herself to face her enemy.* □ *Irene's family gave her courage to face her illness.*
    • **challenge**   to meet someone or something in competition. □ *The grocery store challenged anyone to beat their prices.* □ *Our hero challenged the Black Knight.*
    • **confront**   to meet someone face to face; to *face* someone or something bravely. □ *Jay confronted his accusers.* □ *The explorers had to confront the unknown.*
    • **stand up to**   to *face* someone or something boldly. □ *Kay stood up to the bully and wouldn't let him take her lunch money.* □ *Laura stood up to her boss and insisted that she had not made a mistake.*
    [→see also: *compete*]

factor   See the entry for *element*.

facts   See the entry for *information*.

factual   See the entry for *actual*.

fade   See the entry for *disappear*.

faded   See the entry for *pale*.

fail (*verb*) to not be able to do what you set out to do. □ *I failed to get the money.* □ *The expedition failed to reach the North Pole.*
  • **fizzle** to *fail* suddenly after a good start. (Slang.) □ *The actor's career fizzled.* □ *The party fizzled after only an hour or so.*
  • **flunk** to *fail* a test; to *fail* in school. (Slang.) □ *Mark flunked the science test.* □ *Tom flunked out of seventh grade.*
  • **fold** for a business to *fail*. (Slang. See also the main entry for *fold*.) □ *The clothing store on the corner folded.* □ *The restaurant folded after only one year.*
  • **go under** to *fail* financially. (Slang.) □ *Sue's business went under because she couldn't pay back her loans.* □ *If Philip doesn't get a job soon, his whole family will go under.*
  • **lose** to *fail* to win. (See also the main entry for *lose*.) □ *Rita lost the race.* □ *Susan is upset because she lost the art contest.*
  [→contrasting word: *win*]

failing See the entry for *quirk*.

failure (*noun*) someone or something that fails; an occasion when someone or something does not do what is expected. □ *The book was a failure; nobody bought it.* □ *Tom's failure to follow instructions was the reason he flunked the test.*
  • **debacle** a tremendous *failure*. (Formal.) □ *Jan's first public speech was a debacle; she was so nervous that she fainted.* □ *Their first battle was such a debacle that the army's morale was very low.*
  • **defeat** a *failure* to win. □ *The team's defeat did not dampen their spirit.* □ *The candidate suffered a crushing defeat on election day.*
  • **fiasco** a ridiculous *failure*. □ *Dinner at Bill's house was a fiasco; the food tasted terrible and the guests hardly talked to each other.* □ *Art's attempt to teach the dog to talk was a fiasco.*
  • **flop** a clumsy *failure*. (Slang.) □ *The movie was a big flop.* □ *Ben felt he was a flop as a teacher.*
  • **loss** a complete *failure*. (Slang.) □ *Saturday was a total loss; I didn't get anything done.* □ *Carrie realized that her attempts to get Donald to notice her were pretty much a loss.*
  [→contrasting word: *success*]

faint (*adjective*) hard to see. □ *There was some faint writing on the lid of the box.* □ *I saw faint traces of a bruise on Eddie's arm.*
  • **dim** not bright and therefore *faint*. □ *The room was dim, lit by one weak bulb.* □ *Through the dirt and dust, I could see the dim outlines of the painting.*
  • **indistinct** fuzzy and *faint*. □ *An indistinct shape moved through the fog.* □ *The photograph shows an indistinct creature swimming across the lake.*

• **obscure** *faint,* dark, or hidden. □ *A few obscure marks were all that was left of the sign that had been carved in the rock.* □ *Obscure, shadowy forms seemed to flit across the lawn.*

• **vague** *faint;* not clearly outlined. □ *In the darkness, I could see only the vague shape of the house.* □ *Fran had only a vague idea of what her uncle was like.*

fainthearted   See the entry for *cowardly.*

fair   (*adjective*) not prejudiced; not giving special favors to anyone. (See also the entries for *pale, unbiased.*) □ *The teacher tried to give fair grades.* □ *George gets everything he wants, and I never get anything. It's not fair!*

• **equitable**   *fair;* giving equal treatment to everyone. (Formal.) □ *The children made an equitable division of the things they inherited.* □ *Helen tried to settle the dispute in an equitable manner.*

• **just**   strictly *fair;* giving out justice. □ *What do you think is a just punishment for this crime?* □ *The parents wanted to be just, so they listened to both sides of their children's disagreements.*

• **right**   *fair* and morally acceptable. (See also the main entry for *right.*) □ *Since Irene ruined the pan, it's only right that she should replace it.* □ *It doesn't seem right for some people to be rich while others are desperately poor.*

fair value   See the entry for *value.*

faithful   (*adjective*) always standing by someone; able to be trusted; dependable. □ *The faithful friends helped each other through thick and thin.* □ *Our faithful old car finally broke down beyond repair.*

• **constant**   *faithful* forever. (See also the main entry for *constant.*) □ *Jay and Kevin are constant companions.* □ *Laura is the singer's most constant fan.*

• **devoted**   *faithful* and dedicated. □ *Mark is a devoted admirer of Nancy's.* □ *Sue was a devoted wife.*

• **loyal**   *faithful;* never abandoning someone. □ *The fans were loyal to their team, win or lose.* □ *The author's loyal readers would buy any book with her name on it.*

• **staunch**   strongly *faithful.* (Formal.) □ *Our hero's staunch friend offered to fight in his place.* □ *The two countries were staunch allies, always attacking each other's enemies.*

• **steadfast**   *faithful* in all circumstances. □ *Lady Cynthia's steadfast maid worked for her all her life.* □ *Philip was a steadfast believer in the benefits of taking Vitamin C.*

• **trustworthy**   *faithful* and able to be trusted. □ *The spy sent a note by a trustworthy messenger.* □ *Don't tell Rita any secrets; I don't think she's trustworthy.*

fake (*adjective*) not real. (Informal.) □ *Susan's hat was covered with fake flowers.* □ *The emerald in that ring is fake.*
   • **bogus**   obviously fake. (Slang.) □ *No one believed Eleanor's bogus claims to being the Crown Princess of Denmark.* □ *Tim put on a bogus display of being glad to see me.*
   • **false**   fake or wrong. □ *The spy wore a false mustache.* □ *Jan was using a false name.*
   • **fraudulent**   fake but being passed off as real; not honest. □ *Bill's Spanish accent was utterly fraudulent.* □ *The detective showed that some of the documents were fraudulent.*
   • **phony**   fake but being passed off as real. (Slang.) □ *Art said hello with a phony smile on his face.* □ *The dishonest dealer sold phony artwork.*
   [→contrasting word: *genuine*]

fall (*verb*) to come down from a higher place. (See the entry for *collapse*.) □ *Snow fell all morning.* □ *The glass fell off the table.*
   • **dive**   to fall fast and on purpose; to throw yourself downward. □ *The hawk dived out of the sky and snapped up the unwary rabbit.* □ *Ben dived into the pool.*
   • **drop**   to fall fast; to let go of something so that it falls. □ *The stone dropped off the edge of the cliff.* □ *I dropped the box I was carrying.*
   • **plummet**   to fall very fast. □ *The plane, out of control, plummeted to the earth.* □ *The cannonball plummeted from the sky.*
   • **plunge**   to fall fast; to push something into a liquid. □ *The rocket plunged toward the earth.* □ *Carrie plunged her hand into the bathwater.*
   • **sink**   to fall gradually. (See also the main entry for *sink*.) □ *The ship sank to the bottom of the lake.* □ *The sun sank toward the horizon.*
   • **tumble**   to fall, turning over and over. □ *Donald tumbled down the stairs.* □ *The apples tumbled out of the bag.*

fall upon   See the entry for *attack*.

false   See the entry for *fake*.

falsehood   See the entry for *lie¹*.

falter   See the entry for *stutter*.

familiar (*adjective*) well-known; frequently seen. □ *I don't know his name, but his face seems familiar.* □ *Eddie was glad to see the familiar streets of his hometown.*
   • **accustomed**   familiar; frequently done. □ *Fran was accustomed to taking a walk every afternoon.* □ *George's coffee cup stood in its accustomed place on his desk.*
   • **customary**   familiar; regularly done. □ *Helen had her customary snack at ten-thirty.* □ *It is customary to give the waiter a tip.*

• **habitual**   *familiar* and done as a habit. ☐ *Irene's habitual smoking is ruining her health.* ☐ *Jay had his habitual morning shower.*

family   (*noun*) the people you are related to by blood; the people in your household. ☐ *I spend the holidays with my family.* ☐ *How many people are in your family?*

• **clan**   a large extended *family.* ☐ *The Smith clan got together for Grandma's birthday.* ☐ *It's hard to keep track of all the people in the clan.*

• **folk**   your whole *family.* (Folksy.) ☐ *Kay's folk mostly live in Michigan.* ☐ *My folk came to America just a few generations ago.*

• **kin**   the people you are related to by blood. (Folksy.) ☐ *Laura and Mark are kin to each other.* ☐ *I met some of my distant kin at the family reunion.*

• **relations**   all the members of your *family.* ☐ *Many of Philip's friends and relations came to his wedding.* ☐ *None of Roger's relations would take him in when his parents died.*

• **relatives**   the members of your *family.* ☐ *Susan's relatives did not approve of her boyfriend.* ☐ *I'm going to visit my relatives this weekend.*

famished   See the entry for *hungry.*

famous   (*adjective*) very well known. ☐ *This is the movie that made the actor famous.* ☐ *The leader was famous for his stirring speeches.*

• **eminent**   *famous* because of a special ability; important. (Formal.) ☐ *Professor Krutch is an eminent scholar.* ☐ *The mayor and other eminent townspeople led the parade.*

• **notable**   worthy of being *famous;* worth noticing. ☐ *Several notable books were published this year.* ☐ *There are many notable players on the team this season.*

• **notorious**   *famous* for having done something bad. ☐ *Jesse James was a notorious criminal.* ☐ *Tim is notorious for putting people down.*

• **renowned**   *famous;* talked about by everyone. ☐ *The renowned explorer showed slides of her latest expedition.* ☐ *The doctor was renowned for the wonderful cures he had performed.*

• **well-known**   known by everyone. ☐ *It is a well-known saying that "The early bird gets the worm."* ☐ *Victor is well known among other stamp collectors.*

fan   (*noun*) someone who is very interested in someone or something. (Informal.) ☐ *Bill is a baseball fan.* ☐ *As the band left the concert hall, they were mobbed by their fans.*

• **aficionado**   someone who enjoys a particular pastime. (Somewhat formal.) ☐ *Art is a classical music aficionado.* ☐ *Many fine arts aficionados gathered for the opening of the museum.*

• **buff**   someone who enjoys and knows a lot about something. (Slang.) □ *Ben's an old-movie buff; he knows all the old stars.* □ *On Sunday afternoons, sports buffs had many TV programs to choose from.*
• **devotee**   someone who is very fond of someone or something. □ *The author's devotees couldn't wait for her next book to come out.* □ *Carrie, a devotee of gourmet cooking, has two shelves full of cookbooks.*
• **enthusiast**   someone who is filled with enthusiasm for something. □ *Many stamp-collecting enthusiasts came to the stamp-collecting convention.* □ *Donald loves to hike; he's a fresh-air enthusiast.*
• **freak**   someone who is passionately interested in something. (Slang.) □ *Ever since he got that computer, Eddie has become a computer-games freak.* □ *Fran is such a cat freak, not only does she have three cats, she also has toy cats, cat statues, books about cats, and cat posters!*
• **nut**   a *fan;* someone who is crazy about something. (Slang.) □ *Grace is a nut about her ham radio; she must listen to that thing twenty-four hours a day.* □ *Bill is a baseball nut who spends his weekends going to as many games as possible.*

fanciful   See the entry for *figurative.*

fancy   See the entries for *complicated, imagine, like.*

fantasize   See the entry for *dream.*

fantastic   See the entry for *incredible.*

fantasy   See the entry for *illusion.*

far-off   See the entry for *distant.*

faraway   See the entry for *distant.*

farce   See the entry for *play¹.*

fare   See the entry for *food.*

farfetched   See the entry for *improbable.*

farm   (*noun*) a place where animals or crops are raised. □ *Helen runs a hog farm.* □ *They grow soybeans on that farm.*
• **orchard**   a place where fruit trees are grown. □ *There is an apple orchard in back of the house.* □ *We went out to the apricot orchard to pick the fruit.*
• **plantation**   a large *farm* where a single thing is grown. □ *More than a hundred people worked on the cotton plantation.* □ *Workers on the rubber plantation took sap from the rubber trees.*
• **ranch**   a place where herds of animals are raised. □ *Irene raises cattle on her ranch.* □ *The sheep ranch was up on the mountain.*
• **vineyard**   a place where grapes are grown. □ *What vineyard did this wine come from?* □ *The valley was full of vineyards.*

fascinated   (*adjective*) deeply interested. □ *Jay was fascinated by the way Kay told her story.* □ *Laura had a fascinated look on her face.*

• **charmed**   *fascinated;* pleased with someone or something. □ *Mark, charmed, gazed at the little music box as it played.* □ *Nancy was charmed by Sue's graceful manners.*

• **enchanted**   *fascinated* and delighted by something. □ *Philip was enchanted by the beautiful things in the art museum.* □ *An enchanted smile spread across Rita's face as she listened to the music.*

• **hypnotized**   *fascinated;* dominated or controlled by someone or something. □ *Susan stared at the TV screen as if hypnotized.* □ *Tim, hypnotized, watched the flash of the needles as Jan knitted.*

• **intrigued**   *fascinated;* deeply curious. □ *I'm intrigued by the debate about how the Pyramids were built.* □ *Bill described the problem to his intrigued listeners.*

• **spellbound**   too *fascinated* to move; feeling as though you are under a magic spell. □ *The movie held me spellbound.* □ *The audience was spellbound as the magician performed his feats.*

• **transfixed**   too *fascinated* to move. (Formal.) □ *Anna was transfixed with terror as she saw the car spin out of control.* □ *I was transfixed by the images of poverty displayed on the TV screen.*
[→see also: *absorbed*]

fascinating   See the entry for *interesting*.

fashion   See the entries for *build, style*.

fashionable   See the entry for *stylish*.

fast   (*adjective*) moving with speed. □ *With one fast motion, the cook flipped the pancake.* □ *The fast runner won the race.*

• **quick**   *fast* and sudden. □ *I heard Ben's quick steps coming up the stairs.* □ *I tried to catch the cat, but he was too quick for me.*

• **rapid**   quite *fast*. □ *Carrie felt the rapid beating of her heart.* □ *The rapid bicyclist shot through the stalled traffic.*

• **speedy**   quite *fast;* faster than expected. □ *The speedy reader finished the book in two hours.* □ *We need a speedy solution to this problem.*

• **swift**   *fast* and graceful; happening quickly. □ *The swift cheetah easily caught up with its prey.* □ *Donald's swift thinking saved the day.*
[→contrasting word: *slow*]

fat   (*adjective*) big, heavy, and round; having a lot of fatty tissue. □ *I picked out a nice, fat peach.* □ *If Eddie doesn't stop eating so much junk food, he'll get fat.*

• **corpulent**   *fat*. (Formal.) □ *The corpulent gentleman eased himself into a chair.* □ *The weight-loss clinic promised miraculous results to its corpulent clients.*

• **heavy**   *fat; weighing a great deal.* □ *Fran has been rather heavy ever since she was a child.* □ *The desk is too heavy for me to move it by myself.*
• **obese**   extremely, unhealthily *fat.* (Formal.) □ *The doctor told her obese patient to lose weight.* □ *Climbing the stairs made the obese woman sweat heavily.*
• **overweight**   *fatter* than you should be. □ *Many people worry about being overweight.* □ *Skinny Grace thinks she's overweight!*
• **plump**   somewhat *fat.* □ *Helen was a plump baby but a skinny child.* □ *Irene's plump cheeks give a nice shape to her face.*
• **stout**   *fat* and strong-looking. □ *Everyone in Jay's family is big and stout.* □ *Kay looks stout because she has such big muscles.*
[→contrasting word: *thin*]

fatal   See the entry for *deadly.*

fate   See the entry for *luck.*

fatigued   See the entry for *tired.*

fault   See the entry for *flaw.*

faultless   See the entry for *perfect.*

favor   (*noun*) a helpful deed. (See also the entry for *prefer.*) □ *Would you do me a favor and let me use your phone?* □ *As a special favor, Laura gave me a ride to the bus station.*
• **courtesy**   a polite *favor.* (Formal.) □ *Please do me the courtesy of introducing me to your friend.* □ *Guests of the hotel may park for free as a courtesy.*
• **kindness**   a friendly *favor.* □ *Mark did me the kindness of watering my lawn when I was out of town.* □ *It would be a great kindness if you would let me borrow your drill.*
• **service**   a *favor.* (Somewhat old-fashioned.) □ *Tom was always willing to do his neighbors a service.* □ *Sue loved to perform little services, such as opening the door for someone with his arms full.*

favorable   See the entry for *convenient.*

favorite   See the entry for *popular.*

fawn on   See the entry for *flatter.*

fearless   See the entry for *courageous.*

feast   See the entry for *eat.*

feat   See the entry for *act.*

feeble   See the entry for *weak.*

feed (*verb*) to give food to a living thing; to make someone or something eat. ☐ *I feed the dog twice a day.* ☐ *Philip fed the baby.*

• **foster**   to *feed* a living thing; to help something grow. ☐ *Rita and Stanley fostered seven children, three of their own and four they adopted.* ☐ *The teacher tried to foster a love of learning in her students.*

• **nourish**   to *feed* a living thing; to be food for a living thing. ☐ *The mother bird nourished her young ones.* ☐ *This hearty soup will nourish you.*

• **sustain**   to *feed* a living thing and help it stay alive. (Formal.) ☐ *The campers took along enough food to sustain an army.* ☐ *The family had to sustain themselves on beans and cold water.*

feel (*verb*) to have an impression about something. ☐ *I feel that Tom isn't being honest.* ☐ *Jan felt that she ought to leave.*

• **intuit**   to *feel* something; to know something by instinct. (Formal.) ☐ *Although no one told him, Bill intuited that Anna disliked him.* ☐ *The dogs could intuit my uneasiness.*

• **sense**   to *feel* something; to be aware of something. ☐ *I sense that Ben is in a good mood.* ☐ *Carrie sensed that something was wrong.*

• **tell**   to *feel* something; to figure something out from what you see and hear. (Usually with *can*. See also the main entry for *tell*.) ☐ *I can tell that Donald is happy because he is whistling.* ☐ *How could you tell that Eddie was going to be late?*

feel for   See the entry for *sympathize*.

feeling (*noun*) a state of mind. (See also the entry for *hunch*.) ☐ *Fran was sunk in a feeling of intense boredom.* ☐ *Listening to music gave George a happy feeling.*

• **emotion**   a strong *feeling;* passion. (Formal.) ☐ *Anger is a powerful emotion.* ☐ *The actor's speech was filled with emotion.*

• **impression**   a vague *feeling.* (Often used in the phrases *to get the impression* and *to be under the impression.*) ☐ *I get the impression that Helen wants me to leave.* ☐ *Irene was under the impression that today would be a holiday.*

• **sensation**   a *feeling* resulting from something you sense physically. ☐ *I felt a creeping sensation as I entered the spooky old house.* ☐ *After the meal, Kay felt the pleasant sensation of having had just enough to eat.*

• **sentiment**   a refined *feeling.* ☐ *The Valentine card expressed a lovely sentiment.* ☐ *Jay flew his flag to show his patriotic sentiments.*

fellow   See the entry for *man*.

felon   See the entry for *criminal*.

felony   See the entry for *crime*.

female   See the entry for *woman*.

ferment   See the entry for *seethe*.

ferocious   See the entry for *savage*.

fervent   See the entry for *dedicated*.

festoon   See the entry for *drape*.

fetish   See the entry for *obsession*.

fetters   See the entry for *bonds*.

fiasco   See the entry for *failure*.

fib   See the entry for *lie¹*.

fickle   (*adjective*) always changing and therefore not dependable. □ *I thought that Larry was my best friend, but he turned out to be fickle.* □ *You can't expect such a fickle person to keep her promises.*
   • **changeable**   *fickle;* tending to change. □ *Mark's moods are very changeable.* □ *Tom's changeable opinions vary according to what his current girlfriend thinks.*
   • **disloyal**   *fickle* toward your friends; not loyal or trustworthy. □ *Sue's disloyal friend told all her secrets.* □ *Philip was disloyal to his own family.*
   • **inconstant**   *fickle*. (Poetic.) □ *Our hero discovered too late that he loved an inconstant woman.* □ *The queen's inconstant friends deserted her.*
   • **unreliable**   not dependable. □ *Rita was an unreliable employee, seldom doing a decent job.* □ *Susan's car is very unreliable; it seems to break down at least once a month.*
   [→contrasting words: *loyal, faithful*]

fiddle with   See the entry for *meddle*.

fidget   See the entry for *squirm*.

field   (*noun*) an open area of land, often one that is being farmed. □ *The farmer plowed the field.* □ *Corn grew tall in the fields.*
   • **grassland**   a vast, grassy, open area of land. □ *The herd of buffalo moved across the grassland.* □ *Zebras live in the grasslands of Africa.* [→see also: *yard*]
   • **meadow**   an open, grassy area of land. □ *The horses frolicked in the meadow.* □ *The meadow looked like a good place for a picnic.*
   • **pasture**   an open area of land where animals can graze. □ *The sheep are out in the pasture.* □ *Joe walked across the cow pasture.*

fiery   See the entry for *impetuous*.

fight (*verb*) to contend angrily or violently with someone. ☐ *Two kids were fighting in the playground.* ☐ *Our hero fought against his foe.*

• **battle** for armies to *fight;* to *fight* for a long time. ☐ *The two armies battled over the small piece of territory.* ☐ *The children battled for their parents' attention.*

• **combat** to *fight* with great energy and determination. ☐ *The police did everything possible to combat gang violence in the neighborhood.* ☐ *The teacher set out to combat his students' poor spelling.*

• **skirmish** to *fight* briefly; to *fight* in a small way. ☐ *Tim and Jan skirmished over who should clean the bathroom.* ☐ *The soldiers skirmished with the band of rebels.*

• **struggle** to *fight* with all your effort. (See also the main entry for *struggle.*) ☐ *Bill really struggled against his own vanity.* ☐ *The wrestlers struggled with each other.*

fight against See the entry for *rebel.*

figurative (*adjective*) using figures of speech; not literal. (Formal.) ☐ *"He flew off the handle" is a figurative way of saying that someone acted really mad.* ☐ *I was being figurative when I said that Art blew up!*

• **fanciful** *figurative* and imaginative. (Formal.) ☐ *Mary, a fanciful person, thought that the stars were little angels.* ☐ *Carrie told a fanciful story about elves and water sprites.*

• **metaphorical** *figurative;* using one thing to stand for another. (Formal.) ☐ *In this metaphorical story, the bluebird is supposed to stand for happiness.* ☐ *The author uses metaphorical language to compare the heroine to a flower.*

• **poetic** *figurative;* using the kind of language that is used in poems. ☐ *"I yearn for you, light of my life," was Donald's poetic way of expressing his feelings.* ☐ *The poetic young woman promised to climb the highest mountain to prove her love.*

[→contrasting word: *literal*]

figure (*verb*) to use numbers to get the answer to a problem; to make a prediction based on what you know. ☐ *The clerk figured the total and told me what it was.* ☐ *Eddie figured he'd be home by six.*

• **calculate** to *figure* very carefully. ☐ *Fran calculated how much butter she'd need to make six dozen cookies.* ☐ *George calculated that now was a good time to ask for a raise.*

• **compute** to *figure* precisely. ☐ *Helen computed how much she had spent on entertainment that month.* ☐ *Jay computed how many yards of fabric he would need to make the jacket.*

• **reckon** to *figure.* (Informal.) ☐ *Kay reckoned how much she could expect to get from the yard sale.* ☐ *Laura reckoned she'd better clean up the mess.*

figure out   (*verb*) to arrive at the correct meaning of something; to think something out; to understand something. □ *Can you figure out these instructions?* □ *Mark figured out what Tom wanted him to do.*

• **decipher**   to *figure out* something that is difficult to read. □ *I can't decipher Sue's handwriting.* □ *The archaeologist deciphered the symbols on the ancient monument.*

• **decode**   to *figure out* something that has a hidden meaning. □ *The parents spelled out B-I-R-T-H-D-A-Y P-R-E-S-E-N-T so that their child could not decode what they were talking about.* □ *Philip tried to decode the technical terms in the computer manual.*

• **interpret**   to *figure* something *out;* to *figure out* a meaning and explain it to someone else. □ *I interpreted Rita's gesture to mean "Go away!"* □ *Susan, who speaks Japanese, interpreted what the Japanese visitor was saying.*

• **unravel**   to *figure out* something very complicated. □ *The detective unraveled the mystery.* □ *The poem's meaning was difficult for the students to unravel.*

figurine   See the entry for *sculpture.*

filch   See the entry for *steal.*

file   See the entries for *line, sort.*

fill in for   See the entry for *replace¹.*

film   See the entry for *movie.*

filthy   See the entry for *dirty¹.*

final   (*adjective*) occurring at the end. □ *The story was resolved in the final chapter of the book.* □ *Tim had one final chance to pass the test.*

• **closing**   *final;* bringing something to an end. □ *The speaker made a few closing remarks.* □ *The closing ceremony was very impressive.*

• **last**   occurring at the end of a series. (See also the main entry for *last.*) □ *This is your last warning!* □ *Jan wanted to feed the elephant one last time before leaving the zoo.*

• **ultimate**   *final* for all time. (Formal.) □ *The court handed down its ultimate decision.* □ *What was the ultimate result of Bill's attempt to make dinner?*

[→contrasting word: *first*]

finale   See the entry for *end.*

find   (*verb*) to look for and get something; to come upon something by accident. □ *I finally found my car keys.* □ *Art found a stray kitten in the alley.*

• **come across**   to *find* something by accident. □ *If you happen to come across my glasses, please give them to me.* □ *When I went to the library to consult the encyclopedia, I came across this interesting book.*

• **detect**   to *find* out where something is; to be able to tell that something exists. ☐ *Ben detected the traces of a footprint on the carpet.* ☐ *I could detect a smell of paint thinner in the air.*

• **discover**   to *find* or learn something for the first time. ☐ *Carrie discovered a hidden passageway behind the bookshelves.* ☐ *Donald discovered that Eddie knew how to sing.*

• **locate**   to learn where something is. ☐ *Fran located the missing suitcase.* ☐ *The map helped me locate the restaurant.*

• **unearth**   to *find* something that was buried or deeply hidden. ☐ *Helen unearthed the old photo album from a pile of junk in the attic.* ☐ *George unearthed a family secret.*

[→contrasting word: *lose*]

find out   See the entry for *learn*¹.

fine   See the entry for *good*.

finicky   See the entry for *picky*.

finish   (*verb*) to bring something to an end. (See also the entry for *end*.) ☐ *Irene finished knitting the sweater.* ☐ *Jay finished the book.*

• **carry out**   to *finish* something successfully. ☐ *Kay carried out her plan to become a mechanic.* ☐ *If Larry says he will do something, you can be sure he will carry it out.*

• **complete**   to *finish* the whole of something. ☐ *Mark completed his high school education.* ☐ *Vincent finally completed the painting he was working on.*

• **conclude**   to *finish* something formally. (See also the main entry for *conclude*.) ☐ *Is there any further business before we conclude this meeting?* ☐ *The TV station played the national anthem to conclude their broadcast day.*

fire   See the entry for *dismiss*.

fired up   See the entry for *thrilled*.

firm   (*adjective*) able to stand up when pressed; tightly packed. (See also the entries for *company, stable*.) ☐ *Tom likes to sleep on a firm pillow.* ☐ *Through regular exercise, Sue developed firm muscles.*

• **compact**   tightly packed. ☐ *The sleeping bag rolled up into a compact cylinder.* ☐ *Philip wrapped everything into a compact package.*

• **dense**   heavy and tightly packed; thick. ☐ *The dense bread was full of whole grains and other wholesome ingredients.* ☐ *The forest was very dense, the trees growing close together.*

• **hard**   not giving in under pressure at all. (See also the main entry for *hard*.) ☐ *The chairs in the auditorium were hard and uncomfortable.* ☐ *It was difficult to dig in the hard, dry ground.*

• **solid**   able to stand up against pressure, tightly packed, and stable. □ *We need a solid base to put this statue on.* □ *After being on the ship for so long, Rita was glad to set foot on solid ground.*
[→contrasting words: *limp, loose*]

first-class   See the entry for *excellent.*

first light   See the entry for *dawn.*

fishy   See the entry for *suspicious.*

fit   See the entries for *healthy, satisfactory.*

fitting   See the entry for *proper.*

fix   (*verb*) to put something back together; to make something work again. (See also the entry for *prepare.*) □ *Stanley fixed the radio.* □ *The mechanic says it will take three days to fix my car.*
   • **mend**   to *fix* something torn or worn out; to put something in good condition again. □ *Tom mended the rip in his blue jeans.* □ *The bricklayers mended the old wall.*
   • **overhaul**   to *fix* something by rebuilding it completely. □ *The bicycle needs to be overhauled.* □ *Jan overhauled the rusty plumbing in her bathroom.*
   • **patch up**   to *fix* something just enough so that it will work. □ *The builder patched up the leaky ceiling.* □ *I patched up my old boots and wore them again this winter.*
   • **repair**   to *fix.* (Formal.) □ *Bill's shop repairs all appliances.* □ *I need a special tool to repair my eyeglasses.*
[→contrasting word: *break*]

fix up   See the entry for *prepare.*

fixation   See the entry for *obsession.*

fizz   See the entries for *foam, hiss.*

fizzle   See the entry for *fail.*

flabbergast   See the entry for *confound.*

flabby   See the entry for *limp.*

flag   (*noun*) a cloth with a design on it, representing a country or an organization. (See also the entry for *label.*) □ *On the Fourth of July, flags were flying from every lamppost in town.* □ *Art proudly carried the state flag in the parade.*
   • **banner**   a *flag*, especially a long *flag* with a message on it. □ *Colored banners were hung outside the store to advertise the grand opening.* □ *A banner across the front of the house read, "Welcome Home, Dad!"*

• **colors**   a *flag*. (Formal.) □ *The ship's colors waved in the breeze.* □ *As the army advanced, we saw the colors they were flying.*
•**pennant**   a small, triangular *flag,* often one that represents a sports team. □ *Ben covered his walls with college pennants.* □ *A string of bright pennants hung in front of the used car dealership.*

flag down   See the entry for *signal.*

flail   See the entry for *flap.*

flame   See the entries for *burn², flare.*

flap   (*verb*) to move up and down, as a bird's wing does. □ *The duck flapped her wings and rose into the air.* □ *The flag flapped in the breeze.*
• **flail**   to *flap* repeatedly and awkwardly. □ *The child flailed around in the shallow water, trying to swim.* □ *Charles flailed wildly, getting himself stuck deeper in the quicksand.*
• **flutter**   to *flap* quickly and repeatedly. □ *Donna fluttered her eyelashes.* □ *The flags fluttered in the high wind.*
• **stream**   to *flap* repeatedly and gracefully; to move flowingly in the air. (Poetic.) □ *Edith's long hair streamed behind her as she rode her bike.* □ *It made us feel proud to see the flag streaming in the wind.*
• **swish**   to *flap,* making a whispering noise. □ *The lasso swished through the air.* □ *The dancer's long sleeves swished as she moved.*
• **wave**   to *flap* gracefully. (See also the main entry for *wave.*) □ *The flag waved proudly above the school.* □ *The tree branches waved in the wind.*

flare   (*verb*) suddenly to burn very brightly. □ *The match flared as Fran lit it.* □ *The burner on the gas stove flared when I turned it on.*
• **blaze up**   to *flare* strongly. □ *The fire blazed up when George threw the kindling onto it.* □ *The waiter touched a match to the crepes Suzette, which blazed up with a blue flame.*
• **flame**   to *flare* intensely; to burn like a flame. □ *The torches in the castle flamed brightly.* □ *Helen's eyes flamed with anger.*
• **flash**   to *flare* briefly. □ *The diamond flashed when the light hit it.* □ *Lightning flashed, lighting up the landscape for an instant.*

flare up   See the entry for *bristle.*

flash   See the entry for *flare.*

flashy   (*adjective*) bright, attention-getting, and sometimes in bad taste. □ *Irene wears such flashy clothes.* □ *Jay's flashy new car is candy-apple red.*
• **gaudy**   *flashy* and bright-colored. □ *Why would anyone buy such a gaudy shirt?* □ *Kay decked herself out in gaudy costume jewelry.*
• **loud**   *flashy* and possibly offensive. (See also the main entry for *loud.*) □ *Those orange boots are rather loud.* □ *Larry wore a loud checked jacket that didn't even match his pants!*

• **ostentatious**   *flashy;* done to attract attention. (Formal.) □ *Mel bought an ostentatious house to show off his new wealth.* □ *Tom's living room contains an ostentatious display of his bowling trophies.*

• **showy**   too bright and *flashy.* □ *Sue wore a showy hat trimmed in parrot feathers.* □ *Philip put the picture in a showy gold frame with lots of curlicues.*

flat   *(adjective)* without any bumps or dents. (See also the entry for *mild¹.*) □ *I need a flat surface to draw on.* □ *To make the wrinkled paper flat again, Rita pressed it under a heavy book.*

• **even**   *flat* and uniform. □ *An even layer of snow covered the ground.* □ *The surface of the road was smooth and even.*

• **level**   *flat* and perfectly horizontal. □ *The legs of the table have to be all the same length so that the tabletop will be level.* □ *We need a level piece of ground to put the little swimming pool on.*

• **smooth**   *flat* and without roughness. (See also the main entry for *smooth.*) □ *The carpenter sanded the piece of wood until it was perfectly smooth.* □ *The countertop was cold and smooth.*

• **straight**   *flat;* without bends or twists. □ *Susan wanted a good, straight board to build a bookcase.* □ *I used a ruler to draw a straight line.*

flatter   *(verb)* to give someone extravagant compliments. □ *Rose kept George in a good mood by flattering him constantly.* □ *I'm not trying to flatter you; I really do think you draw well.*

• **blandish**   to *flatter* someone quite a lot. □ *Tim blandished Jan with all kinds of sweet words.* □ *I tried to blandish Bill into agreeing to sing for us.*

• **butter up**   to *flatter* someone so that he or she will be on your side. (Slang.) □ *Art thought he could get a better grade by buttering up the teacher.* □ *Why are you buttering me up? What do you want?*

• **fawn on**   to *flatter* someone slavishly. □ *The ladies-in-waiting fawned on the queen.* □ *Ben fawned on his boss, hoping for a promotion.*

• **sweet-talk**   to *flatter* someone so that he or she will do something for you. (Slang. Often used in the expression *to sweet-talk someone into something.*) □ *Carrie sweet-talked Donald into moving the heavy boxes for her.* □ *Since threatening Eddie is getting you nowhere, why not try to sweet-talk him?*

flaunt   See the entry for *show off.*

flaw   *(noun)* something wrong with someone or something; something that keeps someone or something from being perfect. □ *There is a flaw in this diamond.* □ *Fran found a flaw in George's argument.*

• **blemish**   a *flaw* on the surface. □ *I saw several blemishes in the finish of the antique desk.* □ *Helen is upset because she has a blemish on her skin.*

• **defect** a *flaw* in the way a thing was made. □ *My lawn mower has a defect and must be sent back to the factory for repairs.* □ *This shirt is poorly made and full of defects.*
• **fault** a *flaw* in someone's character; a crack or *flaw* inside something. □ *Irene's biggest fault is laziness.* □ *You can see the fault where the stone cracked.*
• **imperfection** a slight *flaw.* (Formal.) □ *There was a barely noticeable imperfection in the cloth.* □ *I see an imperfection in my drawing; let me do it over again.*

flawless See the entry for *perfect.*

fleck See the entry for *spot.*

flee See the entry for *escape.*

fleece See the entry for *fur.*

fleecy See the entry for *fluffy.*

fleeting See the entry for *temporary.*

flexible (*adjective*) able to do different things; able to bend easily. □ *Jay has to be flexible to go back and forth between his three jobs.* □ *I bent the flexible piece of wire into a circle.*
   • **adaptable** able to do whatever the situation demands. □ *This portable radio is adaptable for indoor or outdoor use.* □ *The adaptable baby-sitter could take on extra kids at a moment's notice.*
   • **adroit** good at changing from one thing to another; very capable. (Used to describe people, not things.) □ *This play needs an adroit actor who can play six different parts.* □ *Kay was adroit at making a little money go a long way.*
   • **versatile** skilled at many different things; useful in many different situations. (Formal.) □ *The versatile handyman could do everything from carpentry to electrical work.* □ *You will find a hundred uses for this versatile tool.*

flick See the entry for *movie.*

flimsy See the entry for *limp.*

flinch See the entry for *wince.*

fling See the entry for *throw.*

flit See the entry for *fly.*

float (*verb*) to hang suspended in air or liquid. □ *Laura floated lazily in the swimming pool.* □ *A feather floated on the breeze.*
   • **drift** to *float* along slowly. □ *Clouds drifted across the sky.* □ *I watched a raft drift down the river.*

• **skim** to *float* along rapidly. □ *The sailboats skimmed across the lake.* □ *The little plane skimmed through the air.*
• **waft** to *float* along gently. □ *The smell of fresh bread wafted through the house.* □ *Snow wafted down.*
[→see also: *fly*]

flock See the entry for *herd.*

flog See the entry for *whip.*

flood (*verb*) to pour in in great quantity or number. (See also the entry for *flow.*) □ *Dirty water flooded into the basement.* □ *Angry phone calls flooded the office.*
• **deluge** to *flood* heavily. (Formal.) □ *The dam burst, and floodwaters deluged the town.* □ *The radio station was deluged with requests for the song.*
• **inundate** to cover something up by *flooding.* (Formal.) □ *Thousands of tourists inundated the town.* □ *The star was inundated by fan mail.*
• **overwhelm** to defeat something by *flooding.* □ *The enormous army overwhelmed their enemy.* □ *I was overwhelmed with homework assignments.*
• **swamp** to slow someone or something down by *flooding* with people or things. (See also the main entry for *swamp.*) □ *Don't ask Mark to do any more jobs; he's already swamped.* □ *A flood of customers swamped the store.*

floor See the entries for *bottom, confound.*

flop See the entry for *failure.*

flounder See the entry for *wallow.*

flourish See the entry for *show off.*

flout See the entry for *disobey.*

flow (*verb*) to move along smoothly, like the water in a river. □ *Water flowed out of the spigot.* □ *Nancy's long hair flowed down her back.*
• **flood** to *flow* out in huge amounts. (See also the main entry for *flood.*) □ *The dam burst, and water flooded out.* □ *People flooded out of the stadium.*
• **gush** to *flow* out fast. □ *Blood gushed from our hero's wound.* □ *Water is gushing from a hole in the basement wall.*
• **pour** to *flow* steadily and without stopping. □ *Rain poured down from the sky.* □ *Apologies poured out of Sue's mouth.*
• **spill** to *flow* out and be wasted; to *flow* over the side of something. □ *Some of the juice spilled out of the glass as I carried it across the room.* □ *The stream spilled over a waterfall and into a deep pool.*

• **stream**   to *flow* steadily. □ *Tears streamed from Philip's eyes.* □ *The crowd streamed into the auditorium.*

fluffy   (*adjective*) feeling like light, puffy fur; soft and light. □ *Ken hugged the fluffy little bunny rabbit.* □ *Big, fluffy snowflakes fell from the sky.*
   • **downy**   feeling like very fine fur or feathers. □ *I touched the kitten's downy fur.* □ *The baby has such downy skin.*
   • **fleecy**   feeling like a lamb's fur; soft and white. □ *These fleecy slippers will keep your feet warm.* □ *Rita cuddled up under the fleecy blanket.*
   • **fuzzy**   feeling or looking like short, soft fur. □ *Susan watched the fuzzy caterpillar inch along the twig.* □ *Tim wrapped himself in his favorite fuzzy bathrobe.*
   • **woolly**   feeling like deep, thick fur; made of wool. □ *The buffalo had long, woolly hair.* □ *Jan knitted a woolly sweater.*

fluid   See the entry for *liquid*.

flunk   See the entry for *fail*.

flush   See the entry for *blush*.

flustered   See the entry for *upset*.

flutter   See the entry for *flap*.

fly   (*verb*) to move through the air. □ *The bird flew through the sky.* □ *The airplane flew five hundred miles.*
   • **flit**   to *fly* in short, graceful hops. □ *I watched a butterfly flit from flower to flower.* □ *The grasshopper flitted across the lawn.*
   • **glide**   to *fly* smoothly; to move along smoothly. □ *The paper airplane glided across the room.* □ *The ice-skater glided down the frozen river.*
   • **hover**   to *fly* or float above one place. □ *The helicopter hovered above the traffic jam.* □ *The bees hovered around the flower.*
   • **soar**   to *fly* up high. □ *The kite soared off into the sky.* □ *The eagle soared away.*

foam   (*verb*) to make a cluster of bubbles. □ *The root beer foamed in the glass.* □ *The water foamed at the bottom of the waterfall.*
   • **fizz**   to *foam* with a hissing sound. □ *The soft drink fizzed as I poured it out.* □ *The tablet fizzed as I dissolved it in the water.*
   • **froth**   to make a cluster of very tiny bubbles. □ *Bill beat the eggs until they frothed.* □ *The horse was worked so hard that he began to froth at the mouth.*
   • **lather**   to make a cluster of bubbles by working soap and water together. □ *Art lathered the shampoo into his hair.* □ *Ben used a shaving brush to lather the soap in his shaving mug.*

focus   See the entries for *attention, subject.*

foe   See the entry for *enemy.*

fog   See the entry for *mist.*

foible   See the entry for *quirk.*

foil   See the entry for *frustrate.*

fold   (*verb*) to bend something over on itself. (See also the entry for *fail.*) □ *Fold the paper in half.* □ *I can't get the map to fold properly.*
  • **crease**   to *fold* something and press it so there is a permanent line where you folded it. (See also the main entry for *crease.*) □ *Crease the piece of paper along the fold.* □ *Carrie put the book down carelessly, and wound up creasing several of the pages.*
  • **crimp**   to *fold* something and pinch it along the line where you folded it. □ *Donald crimped the edges of the tinfoil so that it would seal.* □ *Eddie crimped the edge of the pie dough into an attractive pattern.*
  • **double**   to *fold* something in half. □ *Double the piece of newspaper a few times and use it as a coaster.* □ *Fran doubled the fabric over so she could cut along the fold.*
  • **pleat**   to *fold* something many times, making a pattern of parallel folds. □ *George pleated the construction paper into a fan.* □ *Helen pleated the cloth and sewed it into a skirt.*

folk   See the entry for *family.*

follow   (*verb*) to go after someone or something. (See also the entry for *obey.*) □ *Follow that car!* □ *That woman seems to be following me.*
  • **dog**   to *follow* someone patiently and persistently. □ *The private eye dogged the man's footsteps.* □ *Irene dogged her enemy across two continents.*
  • **shadow**   to *follow* someone secretly. □ *The police officers were shadowing the suspect, so they knew that she had left her house.* □ *Let's shadow Jay and see where he goes.*
  • **trace**   to *follow* someone's path; to find where someone or something came from or where it went. □ *Kay traced the missing person to a downtown hotel.* □ *The police traced the gun to the store where it had been bought.*
  • **track**   to find out all the places someone or something has gone; to *follow* someone's footprints. □ *Laura used radar to track the plane.* □ *The bloodhound tracked the escaped prisoner.*
  • **trail**   to *follow* at a distance behind someone. □ *The detective trailed the suspect, taking care not to be seen.* □ *I know where Mark lives because I trailed him home.*
  [→see also: *chase*]

fondness   See the entry for *love.*

food   (*noun*) anything you eat that nourishes you. □ *David bought food at the grocery store.* □ *The starving man was in desperate need of food.*
 • **fare**   the kind of *food* that is available. (Formal.) □ *There is decent fare at that restaurant.* □ *Eddie complained about the fare at his aunt's house.*
 • **foodstuff**   any kind of *food.* (Often used in the plural.) □ *The charity gathered all kinds of foodstuffs and distributed them to the poor.* □ *Fran wondered what she could make for dinner out of the foodstuffs she had in the house.*
 • **provisions**   *food* and drink you take with you on a trip. □ *The hikers took a week's worth of provisions with them.* □ *If we don't reach civilization soon, we'll run out of provisions.*
 • **sustenance**   *food* that keeps you alive. (Formal.) □ *Trapped in her car in a vicious snowstorm, Gloria had only a few chocolate bars for sustenance.* □ *The mother bird must provide sustenance for her babies.*
 • **vittles**   *food.* (Folksy.) □ *Harold's a growing boy; he needs his vittles.* □ *Ma sure has cooked up some tasty vittles.*

foodstuff   See the entry for *food.*

fool[1]   (*noun*) someone without any sense. □ *Irene danced around on the tabletop and generally acted like a fool.* □ *Jay's such a fool he thinks the X-ray glasses he ordered will really work.*
 • **cretin**   someone without any intelligence or knowledge. □ *Larry called me a cretin because I read the map wrong.* □ *"You cretins!" said the English teacher, "haven't you ever heard of Shakespeare?"*
 • **dolt**   someone who behaves as if he or she had no sense or intelligence; a clumsy, stupid person. □ *The whole class laughed at Mary when she got the wrong answer, making her feel like a dolt.* □ *You dolt! You stomped your muddy feet across the floor you just washed!*
 • **dunce**   someone who is stupid and learns slowly. □ *Tom felt like a dunce because he couldn't figure out how to use the computer.* □ *Sue's such a dunce, she doesn't realize that Philip likes her, even though he's done so much to show it.*
 • **idiot**   someone without any sense or intelligence. □ *Don't talk to me as if I'm an idiot!* □ *Only an idiot would like this stupid TV show.*
 • **imbecile**   someone without any intelligence at all. (Formal.) □ *I felt like an imbecile when I locked my keys in the car.* □ *Imbecile! Don't leave the baby alone in the house!*
 • **moron**   someone with little intelligence. □ *These instructions are so easy that any moron could follow them.* □ *When Ken heard that it was raining cats and dogs, the moron went out to try to catch one.*
[→Note: all of these words are extremely insulting and can be offensive.]

fool[2] (*verb*) to make someone believe something that is not true. (See also the entry for *play*[2].) □ *Rita fooled me into thinking she was her twin sister.* □ *Susan's lie completely fooled her friends.*

• **con** to *fool* someone in order to get something from him or her. (Slang.) □ *Tim conned his brother into doing all the chores for him.* □ *The criminal conned Veronica out of her life savings.*

• **deceive** to *fool* someone with bad intentions. (Formal.) □ *Prince Walter has deceived us all; he's not really a prince.* □ *Andrew deceived me as to the value of the book he sold me.*

• **delude** to *fool* someone completely. □ *The advertisement deluded people by promising they would win a free vacation.* □ *Smith's fame deluded him into believing he was above the law.*

• **dupe** to *fool* someone, often a person who is easy to *fool*. □ *Once again, Betty has been duped into buying a broken-down old car.* □ *Carrie duped Donald completely; he really thought she was in love with him.*

• **hoax** to *fool* someone with a trick. □ *Readers of the magazine were hoaxed into believing that aliens really had landed on Earth.* □ *Eddie hoaxed his friends with a display of "psychic" powers.*

• **hoodwink** to *fool* someone with a trick; to *fool* someone by hiding the truth. □ *When Fran got her new vacuum cleaner home, she discovered she had been hoodwinked into buying damaged merchandise.* □ *The mayor hoodwinked the townspeople, never telling them what she was really using the money for.*

• **trick** to *fool* someone cleverly. □ *George tricked us by pretending to leave.* □ *The magician tricked the audience into looking away for an instant.*

foolish See the entry for *silly*.

foot See the entry for *bottom*.

forbearing See the entry for *patient*.

forbid (*verb*) to say that someone may not do something; to keep someone from doing something. □ *My parents forbid me to go out on school nights.* □ *As punishment, Helen was forbidden to use the computer for two weeks.*

• **bar** to absolutely *forbid* someone to do something. □ *The judge barred reporters from taking pictures in the courtroom.* □ *Because of her misdeeds, the mayor was barred from ever holding public office again.*

• **disallow** to *forbid* something; to not allow something. □ *The teacher disallowed talking during the test.* □ *Playing radios on the train is hereby disallowed.*

• **prohibit** to *forbid* something by law. (Formal.) □ *The pool rules prohibit running in the pool area.* □ *Smoking is prohibited in this building.*

[→contrasting word: *allow*]

forbidding   See the entry for *sinister*.

force   See the entry for *make²*.

forceful   See the entries for *aggressive, violent*.

forebear   See the entry for *ancestor*.

forecast   See the entry for *predict*.

forefather   See the entry for *ancestor*.

foreground   See the entry for *front*.

foreign   See the entry for *strange*.

foremost   See the entry for *supreme*.

foresee   See the entry for *predict*.

forest   (*noun*) an area where many trees grow close together. □ *The road wound through a dense forest.* □ *Deer, foxes, and bears live in the forest.*
  • **grove**   a small *forest*, often one that someone has specially planted. □ *Irene took a walk through the little grove of pine trees in back of the house.* □ *There is a grove of poplars in the park.*
  • **jungle**   an especially thick or wild *forest*. □ *It was difficult to travel through the jungle; we constantly had to cut plants out of our way.* □ *The village stood at the edge of a vast jungle.*
  • **thicket**   a small, thick *forest* with lots of undergrowth. □ *The hikers thrashed their way through the thicket.* □ *The deer bounded into the thicket, out of sight.*
  • **woods**   a thick *forest*. □ *A pleasant path went through the woods.* □ *The pioneer family built their house in the woods.*

foretell   See the entry for *predict*.

forfeit   See the entry for *give up*.

forgive   See the entry for *pardon*.

forlorn   See the entry for *lonely*.

form   See the entry for *pattern*.

formality   See the entry for *ceremony*.

former   See the entry for *past*.

formerly   See the entry for *before*.

formidable   See the entry for *awesome*.

fortitude   See the entry for *stamina*.

fortune   See the entry for *luck*.

forward   See the entry for *bossy*.

foster   See the entry for *feed*.

foul   See the entries for *dirty²*, *rotten*.

foundation   See the entries for *bottom, evidence*.

founder   See the entry for *sink*.

fracture   See the entry for *break*.

fragile   (*adjective*) easily broken. ☐ *Be careful with that figurine; it's fragile.* ☐ *Jay broke the fragile china cup by setting it down too roughly.*
   • **brittle**   hard and *fragile*; easy to snap. ☐ *The dry twigs were quite brittle.* ☐ *Kay carefully turned the brittle pages of the old book.*
   • **dainty**   *fragile* and pretty. ☐ *Laura wore a dainty pair of gold earrings.* ☐ *Just look at the dainty embroidery on the handkerchief!*
   • **delicate**   small, thin, or fine, and very *fragile*. ☐ *Mark made delicate pastries for dessert.* ☐ *Tom used a delicate brush to paint the doll's face.*

fragment   See the entry for *part*.

fragrance   See the entry for *smell*.

frail   See the entry for *weak*.

frailty   See the entry for *quirk*.

frank   See the entry for *honest*.

frantic   See the entry for *excited*.

fraud   (*noun*) someone who cheats people or pretends to be something he or she is not. ☐ *Tom claims to be a prince, but he's a total fraud.* ☐ *The faith healer was unmasked as a fraud.*
   • **charlatan**   a *fraud* who pretends to be able to do something that he or she cannot. (Formal.) ☐ *That psychic is a charlatan; he can't tell the future.* ☐ *Smith, that charlatan, is selling people his get-rich-quick schemes again.*
   • **con artist**   a *fraud* who cheats people out of their money. (Informal or slang.) ☐ *A con artist cheated Philip out of all his money.* ☐ *The con artist posed as a woman who needed money to get her car fixed.*
   • **crank**   a *fraud* with crazy ideas. (Informal.) ☐ *That crank is always calling the radio station to say that the end of the world is near.* ☐ *Roger is a harmless crank who likes to build landing platforms for UFOs.*
   • **humbug**   an obvious *fraud*. (Informal.) ☐ *Stanley promised to get me a starring part in a movie, but I didn't pay any attention to the old humbug.* ☐ *Tom's such a humbug, always trying to convince people he's found gold in his backyard.*

• **quack**   a doctor who is a *fraud;* an incompetent doctor. (Informal.) □ *Don't go to Dr. Vernon; he's a real quack.* □ *The quack prescribed dangerous medicines to his patients.*

fraudulent   See the entry for *fake.*

freak   See the entries for *character, fan, monster.*

freaky   See the entry for *peculiar.*

free   See the entries for *independent, release.*

freedom   (*noun*) the state of your being in control of what you do. □ *The prisoner yearned for freedom.* □ *Bill gave the caged bird its freedom.*
    • **emancipation**   *freedom* from slavery. (Formal.) □ *Many people worked for the emancipation of the slaves.* □ *The slaves' only hope of emancipation was if their master decided to free them upon his death.*
    • **independence**   *freedom* from someone or something else. □ *The country fought for its independence.* □ *Art's job gave him independence from his parents.*
    • **liberty**   *freedom;* in particular, physical *freedom.* □ *The police gave the prisoner his liberty.* □ *Sophia wanted the liberty to decide whether or not she would marry.*
    [→contrasting word: *bondage*]

freezing   See the entry for *cold.*

freight   See the entry for *load.*

frenetic   See the entry for *excited.*

frenzied   See the entry for *excited.*

frequently   See the entry for *often.*

fresh   See the entry for *insolent.*

fret   See the entry for *worry.*

friend   (*noun*) someone you enjoy spending time with; someone you like and trust. □ *My friend came to visit me when I was in the hospital.* □ *Ben and Carrie have been friends for years.*
    • **buddy**   a *friend* you spend a lot of time with. (Informal.) □ *Donald is out somewhere, playing with his buddies.* □ *Eddie was my special buddy at camp.*
    • **chum**   a close *friend.* (Informal; British.) □ *I say, chums, let's see what's going on in the park.* □ *Nancy got together with her chums to plan a surprise party.*
    • **cohort**   a *friend* you work with. □ *I asked my cohorts what they thought of my plan.* □ *Fran got together with her cohorts on the project for history class.*

• **confidant**   a *friend* you can tell secrets to. (Formal.) □ *George is Helen's confidant and is likely to know what she thinks about the matter.* □ *Irene told the secret only to her closest confidant.*
• **pal**   a close *friend;* a *friend* and partner. (Informal.) □ *Don't mess with my pal unless you want to mess with me.* □ *Those boys are good pals, always together.*
[→contrasting word: *enemy*]

friendly   (*adjective*) kind and easy to get along with; like a friend. □ *I was scared of meeting Jay's mother, but she turned out to be a friendly person.* □ *The librarian gave me a friendly smile.*
   • **affable**   *friendly* and easy to talk to. □ *The affable stranger struck up a conversation with me.* □ *Everyone likes Mr. Jones because he's so affable.*
   • **amiable**   *friendly* and easygoing; pleasant. □ *The amiable young woman invited me to join her for a cup of coffee.* □ *Laura greeted me in an amiable way.*
   • **genial**   *friendly,* humorous, and fun to be with. □ *The genial hostess made sure everyone was having a good time.* □ *Mark is very genial and keeps us amused with his funny stories.*
   • **sociable**   *friendly;* enjoying people's company. □ *Nancy is a sociable soul who hates to be by herself.* □ *The people at work are very sociable and made me feel welcome right away.*
   • **warm**   very *friendly* and pleasant. □ *Sue, a warm woman, made her guest feel right at home.* □ *Philip smiled a warm smile.*
[→see also: *kind¹*]

frightened   See the entry for *afraid.*

frigid   See the entry for *icy.*

fringe   See the entry for *boundary.*

frisk   See the entry for *frolic.*

fritter away   See the entry for *waste.*

frivolous   See the entry for *silly.*

frolic   (*verb*) to play, dancing around happily. □ *The children frolicked in the spring sunshine.* □ *The dog was frolicking in the newly fallen snow.*
   • **caper**   to *frolic* in a lively way. (Often with *around.*) □ *When Rita won the lottery, she capered around the house, shouting, "I won! I won!"* □ *The little girl capered around the stage before the play began.*
   • **cavort**   to *frolic* wildly. □ *The kids wore themselves out cavorting in the swimming pool.* □ *The party guests cavorted madly, leaving the house in a shambles.*
   • **frisk**   to *frolic* quickly and energetically. □ *The young horses frisked across the field.* □ *Catnip makes our cat frisk and play.*

• **romp** to *frolic* noisily and roughly. □ *Susan felt that she was too old to romp in the playground with the younger children.* □ *Tim would spend hours playing fetch with the dog, romping until they were both quite tired.*

front (*noun*) the most forward part of something. □ *There was a stain on the front of the dress.* □ *Wait for me at the front of the movie theater.*
  • **façade** the *front* of a building; outward appearance. (Formal.) □ *The bank is only one story high, but it has a two-story façade.* □ *Jan may act happy to see me, but I know it's just a façade.*
  • **face** the surface on the *front* of something. (See also the main entry for *face*.) □ *There was a colorful mural on the face of the building.* □ *Bill rolled the die and watched to see which face landed upwards.*
  • **foreground** the *front* of a picture or a view. □ *There were two human figures in the foreground of the picture.* □ *This would be a good photo if it weren't for the cars in the foreground.*

frosty See the entry for *icy*.

froth See the entry for *foam*.

frown (*verb*) to wrinkle your forehead, usually to express sadness or anger. □ *I knew I was in trouble when I saw Dad frown.* □ *Seeing the flat tire, Art frowned.*
  • **glower** to *frown* angrily. □ *I wonder why Ben is glowering at me?* □ *When Carrie went up to accept the prize, her rivals glowered at her.*
  • **grimace** to *frown* and twist up your face as if you just tasted something sour. □ *Donald twisted his ankle and grimaced from the pain.* □ *Eddie grimaced as he thought of the stupid mistake he had made.*
  • **scowl** to *frown* and lower your eyebrows. □ *Fran, scowling, concentrated on the difficult problem.* □ *Mr. Gray looked out his window and scowled at the noisy children playing in the street.*
  [→contrasting word: *smile*]

frown on See the entry for *disapprove*.

frustrate (*verb*) to keep someone from carrying out a plan. □ *Helen frustrated Irene's efforts to get Jay alone.* □ *The detective frustrated the criminal's scheme to rob the bank.*
  • **checkmate** to keep someone from ever carrying out a plan; to defeat someone by using strategy. □ *Police roadblocks checkmated Kay's plan to leave town.* □ *The general had to confess that he had been checkmated; his army could go no further.*
  • **foil** to ruin the outcome of someone's plan. (Formal.) □ *The hero foiled the villain's dastardly designs.* □ *Larry decided to stay home all day, foiling his wife's plan to prepare a surprise party for him.*

- **thwart** to keep someone from carrying out a plan by working against him or her. □ *The Republicans tried to thwart everything the Democrats proposed.* □ *My boss thwarted my plan for leaving work early.* [→see also: *block*]

fry See the entry for *cook*.

fuchsia See the entry for *red*.

fumble See the entry for *grope*.

fume See the entry for *babble*.

funds See the entry for *money*.

funny (*adjective*) making someone laugh. □ *Mark told a funny story.* □ *The picture Tom drew was very funny.*
   - **amusing** *funny;* making someone feel pleased and interested. □ *Let's watch this TV show; it sounds amusing.* □ *Sue has several amusing hobbies.*
   - **comical** very funny. □ *Philip made a comical face.* □ *Rita thought it was comical when Susan slipped on the ice.*
   - **humorous** funny. (Formal.) □ *The plot of the book takes several humorous twists.* □ *The movie was supposed to be tragic, but I thought it was quite humorous.*
   - **witty** funny and clever. □ *Tom made a witty remark.* □ *Tim is a very witty person.*

fur (*noun*) the thick, short hair of an animal. □ *The cat has fluffy gray fur.* □ *Jan petted the puppy's fur.*
   - **coat** all of an animal's fur. □ *Fido's coat was thick and glossy.* □ *The little pony had a shaggy coat.*
   - **fleece** short, fuzzy fur. □ *The lamb's fleece was yellowish white.* □ *Bill's slippers were lined with fleece.*
   - **hide** fur or skin; especially short fur and skin stripped from an animal. (See also the main entry for *hide*.) □ *The rug was made from the hides of cows.* □ *The hunter made a coat out of the deer's hide.*
   - **pelt** the thick fur and skin stripped from an animal. □ *The trappers had many pelts to sell.* □ *Art did not want baby seals to be killed for their pelts.*

furious See the entries for *angry, violent*.

furnish See the entry for *supply*.

furrow See the entry for *crease*.

furtive See the entry for *stealthy*.

fuss See the entry for *commotion*.

fussy   See the entry for *picky*.

futile   See the entry for *useless*.

fuzzy   See the entry for *fluffy*.

G

gab   See the entry for *talk²*.

gag   See the entry for *joke*.

gaggle   See the entry for *herd*.

gain   See the entries for *benefit²*, *get*.

gale   See the entry for *wind¹*.

gallery   See the entry for *hall*.

gallop   See the entry for *run*.

gamble on   See the entry for *dare*.

game   (*noun*) a contest or activity you do for fun. □ *The friends spent the afternoon playing a board game.* □ *I went to see the football game.*
    • **diversion**   a pleasant *game* that can take your mind off things. (Formal.) □ *Ben made up a treasure hunt as a diversion for his party guests.* □ *The carnival offered many interesting diversions.*
    • **pastime**   a *game* you play in your spare time. □ *Collecting stamps is a popular pastime.* □ *For Carrie, backgammon is just a pastime; for Donald, it's an obsession.*
    • **sport**   an athletic *game*. □ *Volleyball is the only sport Eddie enjoys.* □ *The favorite sport in our neighborhood is soccer.*

gang   See the entry for *organization*.

gape   See the entry for *gawk*.

garb   See the entry for *clothing*.

garbage   See the entry for *trash*.

garland   See the entry for *drape*.

garment   See the entry for *clothing*.

garner   See the entry for *harvest*.

garrulous   See the entry for *talkative*.

gasp   *(verb)* to breathe with difficulty; to breathe or speak in short bursts. □ *Fran stayed underwater for almost a minute, and then came up, gasping.* □ *"Give me some water!" George gasped.*
- **pant**   to breathe heavily and quickly. □ *After running only half a mile, I was panting for breath.* □ *The dog stuck out his tongue and panted.*
- **puff**   to breathe in short bursts. □ *I heard Helen puffing as she came up the stairs.* □ *The jogger kept on jogging, puffing as she went.*
- **wheeze**   to breathe noisily and with difficulty. □ *Irene's allergies made her wheeze.* □ *The old man wheezed in his sleep.*

gate   See the entry for *entrance*.

gather   See the entries for *collect, conclude, get together, harvest*.

gaudy   See the entry for *flashy*.

gauge   See the entry for *guess*.

gawk   *(verb)* to stare rudely at something. □ *When Jay fainted, everyone just stood there gawking.* □ *The other diners all gawked at the movie star as she entered the restaurant.*
- **gape**   to *gawk* with your mouth open; to stare in surprise. □ *Art gaped at his sister; he had never seen her dressed so beautifully before.* □ *The magician made a car disappear onstage, and the audience gaped.*
- **goggle**   to *gawk* with your eyes open very wide. □ *In the middle of class, Kay started screaming at the teacher, and everyone goggled at her.* □ *Laura's family just goggled at her when she made her announcement.*
- **ogle**   to *gawk* flirtatiously. □ *Mark ogled all the girls in the cafeteria.* □ *Tom was uncomfortable when he noticed Sue ogling him.*
- **rubberneck**   to *gawk* out of curiosity. (Slang.) □ *The cars all slowed down to rubberneck at the accident on the other side of the road.* □ *Passersby rubbernecked at the couple fighting on the sidewalk.*
  [→see also: *look, stare*]

gaze   See the entry for *look*.

gem   See the entry for *jewel*.

generous   *(adjective)* giving a great deal; ample. □ *Philip's generous friend loaned him a car.* □ *Ken receives a generous allowance.*
- **beneficent**   *generous* and kind. (Formal.) □ *The beneficent millionaire gave enough money to build a hospital.* □ *Rita gave a beneficent contribution to the youth club.*

• **charitable** helping others by being kind or *generous*. □ *The charitable woman forgave anyone who hurt her.* □ *Susan volunteers for several charitable organizations.*
• **liberal** freely *generous;* much more than enough. □ *The waiters liked the liberal customer because he left big tips.* □ *Tim spends a liberal sum on his hobby.*
• **magnanimous** greatly *generous.* (Formal.) □ *Vincent hoped that some magnanimous person would support him while he worked on his novel.* □ *It was magnanimous of Bill not to make you pay for the crystal statue you broke.*
• **munificent** grandly *generous.* (Formal.) □ *Thanks to the millionaire's munificent gift, the hospital could be built.* □ *Many charities asked Art for money, because he was known to be a munificent man.*

genial See the entry for *friendly.*

genius See the entry for *talent.*

genteel See the entry for *polite.*

gentle (*adjective*) kind and careful; trying not to cause suffering. □ *Ben was very gentle with the baby bird.* □ *Carrie tried to break the bad news with gentle words.*
• **humane** trying to keep others from suffering. □ *The animal shelter gave the animals humane treatment.* □ *Donald thought it was not humane to keep prisoners in such crowded conditions.*
• **sensitive** sympathetic to the suffering of others. (See also the main entry for *sensitive.*) □ *The sensitive counselor did not force Eddie to talk if he didn't want to.* □ *Fran is sensitive and careful not to hurt people's feelings.*
• **tender** kind, careful, and loving. □ *George made a very tender husband.* □ *Helen gave her friend's hand a tender squeeze.*
[→see also: *kind¹*]

genuine See the entry for *real.*

get (*verb*) to come to have something; to have something given to you. (See also the entry for *understand.*) □ *Where did you get that hat?* □ *Irene just got a new puppy.*
• **accept** to *get* or take something willingly. □ *Susan accepted the responsibility of taking care of the house.* □ *Tim went up to the stage to accept his award.*
• **acquire** to *get.* (Formal.) □ *The stamp collector dreamed of acquiring the rare stamp.* □ *Jay acquired a great deal of wealth.*
• **come by** to *get* something by chance. □ *I wonder how Ruby came by the rare stamps in her collection.* □ *How did you happen to come by so much money all of a sudden?*

• **gain**   to *get* something you worked for; to *get* more than you had. ☐ *Kay took the class in order to gain more knowledge.* ☐ *By helping Laura, Mark gained a friend.*

• **obtain**   to *get* something by any means. ☐ *Tom managed to obtain the computer game he wanted.* ☐ *The bookstore could not obtain the book for me.*

• **procure**   to *get* something by making an effort. (Formal.) ☐ *Sue had to go to six stores to procure the car part she needed.* ☐ *It was too late in the day to procure a copy of the morning newspaper.*

• **receive**   to *get* something; to take something in. ☐ *Jan received a letter in the mail.* ☐ *Bill received several compliments.*

[→contrasting word: *lose;* see also: *take*]

get away   See the entry for *escape.*

get hitched   See the entry for *marry.*

get hold of   See the entry for *contact.*

get in touch with   See the entry for *contact.*

get rid of   See the entries for *eliminate, throw away.*

get together   (*verb*) to come together into a group. ☐ *The gang got together every Wednesday.* ☐ *Let's get together for lunch.*

• **assemble**   to *get together* in an orderly group. ☐ *The students assembled to hear the principal's speech.* ☐ *The whole family assembled in the living room.*

• **congregate**   to *get together* in a large group. (Formal.) ☐ *The dance club is a popular place for young people to congregate.* ☐ *Several hundred people had congregated to hear the leader speak.*

• **convene**   to *get together* officially and formally; to officially start a meeting. (Formal.) ☐ *All the high-school principals convened twice a year to discuss problems in their schools.* ☐ *The club president convened the meeting.*

• **gather**   to *get together.* (Formal.) ☐ *We are gathered here today to join these people in matrimony.* ☐ *When the fire drill sounded, the students gathered outside in the parking lot.*

• **meet**   to *get together* for a particular purpose; to *get together* to discuss something. (See also the main entry for *meet.*) ☐ *The club members will meet to make up the club rules.* ☐ *Philip met with his lawyer.*

ghostly   (*adjective*) like a ghost; faint, misty, otherworldly, or weirdly chilling. ☐ *I saw a ghostly figure in the doorway of the old mansion.* ☐ *The silence in the dark forest was ghostly.*

• **eerie**   weirdly chilling. ☐ *We heard an eerie, distant wailing.* ☐ *The dry, moonlit riverbed was an eerie sight.*

• **ethereal**   misty or otherworldly; heavenly. □ *Cora was a creature of delicate, ethereal beauty.* □ *Alice dreamed that she had died and gone to an ethereal realm in the clouds.*
• **phantom**   misty and otherworldly; not real. □ *Edward saw a phantom ship, glowing palely, far out at sea.* □ *As Fran entered the abandoned house, she thought she felt the cold touch of a phantom hand against her cheek.*
• **spectral**   like a ghost or weird vision. □ *The medium invited the spectral inhabitants of the haunted house to speak to her.* □ *A spectral form glimmered on the stair landing and then disappeared.*
• **spooky**   weirdly chilling and otherworldly. (Informal.) □ *I wouldn't go into that spooky old house if you paid me a thousand dollars!* □ *Looking at these old photographs gives me a spooky feeling.*
• **wraithlike**   otherworldly; like a weird, misty vision. □ *The little girl was pale and wraithlike.* □ *Wraithlike lights danced above the swamp in the twilight.*
[→consider also: *scary*]

giant   See the entry for *big*.

gibberish   See the entry for *nonsense*.

giddy   See the entry for *dizzy*.

gift   See the entry for *talent*.

gigantic   See the entry for *big*.

giggle   See the entry for *laugh*.

girl   See the entry for *woman*.

give   (*verb*) to transfer or hand over something to someone. □ *Give me that pencil.* □ *Helen gave her old toys to her sister.*
• **bestow**   to *give* something generously. (Formal.) □ *Irene bestowed a house upon her daughter.* □ *Jay bestowed lavish gifts on Kay.*
• **donate**   to *give* something to an institution. □ *Laura donated her book collection to the library.* □ *Mark donated twenty dollars to the hurricane relief fund.*
• **present**   to *give* something formally or publicly. (See also the main entry for *present*.) □ *It is my privilege to present you with this award.* □ *The principal presented diplomas to the graduating students.*
[→contrasting word: *take*]

give in   (*verb*) to stop resisting. □ *Alice threw a tantrum right there in the store, until her father gave in and agreed to buy the toy for her.* □ *The students pestered the teacher, hoping she would give in and let class out early.*
• **capitulate**   to *give in* on certain terms. (Formal.) □ *The employees refused to work until the boss capitulated and gave them an extra fifteen-*

minute break every day. □ *Mark threatened to beat Tom up, so Tom capitulated and did Mark's homework for him.*
• **surrender** to *give in* formally; to *give in* to something much stronger than you. □ *The defeated army had to surrender.* □ *Sue surrendered to her cravings and had a hot-fudge sundae.*
• **yield** to *give in* utterly. □ *Philip yielded to Rita's continued requests.* □ *Stanley won't yield to reason; he insists on having his own way.*

give notice See the entry for *resign*.

give rise to See the entry for *cause*.

give someone some lip See the entry for *talk back to*.

give someone the slip See the entry for *elude*.

give up (*verb*) to no longer do or have something; to no longer have the right to something. □ *Tim is giving up smoking.* □ *Jan gave up her bedroom so the guest would have a comfortable place to sleep.*
• **forfeit** to have to *give up* something because you have done something wrong. □ *Jim forfeited his driver's license because of his bad driving.* □ *Bill has shown that he can't use the computer responsibly, so he has forfeited his right to use it.*
• **relinquish** to *give up* something under pressure. (Formal.) □ *It was difficult for Anna to relinquish her teddy bears as she grew up.* □ *Because no one thought his writing was very good, Vincent relinquished his hopes of becoming a famous author.*
• **sacrifice** to *give up* something dear to you in order to get something else. □ *Ben's parents had to sacrifice a lot of pleasures so they could afford to send him to school.* □ *Carrie sacrificed most of her free time to prepare for the talent show.*
• **surrender** to *give up* something to someone who has demanded it. (Formal.) □ *Donald surrendered his gun to the police officer.* □ *The smuggler had to surrender the diamonds to the customs officer.*
• **yield** to *give up* something to someone. □ *The club president yielded the floor to the treasurer.* □ *Eddie yielded the TV to his brother and went into the other room.*

glacial See the entry for *icy*.

glad See the entry for *happy*.

glance See the entry for *look*.

glaring See the entry for *bright*.

glassy See the entry for *smooth*.

glean See the entry for *harvest*.

gleeful See the entry for *happy*.

glib   See the entry for *suave*.

glide   See the entry for *fly*.

glimmer   See the entry for *clue*.

glimpse   See the entry for *see*.

glitter   See the entry for *sparkle*.

gloat   See the entry for *brag*.

globe   See the entry for *world*.

glower   See the entry for *frown*.

glue   See the entry for *stick²*.

gluey   See the entry for *sticky*.

glum   See the entry for *sad*.

glut   See the entry for *surplus*.

gnaw   See the entry for *chew*.

go   (*verb*) to travel somewhere; to travel away from somewhere. □ *Where are you going?* □ *Fran went out of the room.*
   • **depart**   to *go*. (Formal.) □ *The guests departed at ten o'clock.* □ *The plane will depart on schedule.*
   • **exit**   to *go* out or away. □ *Please put your trash in the trash containers as you exit.* □ *George exited the room.* □ *We exited the freeway at Fifth Street.*
   • **leave**   to *go;* especially, to *go* from someone or something that is important to you. □ *Helen had to leave home and find a job.* □ *I'd better leave.*
   • **retire**   to *go* from some activity; to *go* to bed. □ *The teams retired from the field at halftime.* □ *Jay brushed his teeth before he retired.*
   • **retreat**   to *go* away from some activity, particularly a fight. □ *The army, outnumbered, had to retreat.* □ *The kids were playing loudly in the living room, so Dad retreated to the kitchen.*
   • **take off**   to *go* away quickly. (Slang.) □ *I'm going to take off now so I can get home on time.* □ *Laura took off for work at seven every morning.*

go ahead of   See the entry for *pass*.

go along (with)   See the entry for *accompany*.

go along with   See the entry for *agree*.

go bad   See the entry for *spoil²*.

go forward   See the entry for *advance*.

go out with   See the entry for *date²*.

go over   See the entry for *rehash*.

go see   See the entry for *visit*.

go steady with   See the entry for *date²*.

go through   See the entry for *experience*.

go together   See the entry for *match*.

go under   See the entries for *fail, sink*.

go up   See the entry for *climb*.

goal   (*noun*) something you want to accomplish. □ *Vincent's goal is to become a famous author.* □ *Mark worked toward his goal of typing fifty words a minute.*

> • **aim**   a *goal* to which you are directing all your efforts. □ *Tom intended to be class president, and was determined to accomplish that aim.* □ *The youth center's aim is to give young people something fun and worthwhile to do after school.*
> • **object**   a *goal;* the *goal* of a game. (See also the main entry for *object.*) □ *The object in chess is to capture your opponent's king.* □ *The object of the lesson was to get students to practice long division.*
> • **point**   a *goal;* the *goal* of what someone is saying or doing. □ *Stop going off on tangents and get to the point.* □ *What was the point of making us all sit still for ten minutes?*
> • **purpose**   the *goal* of an activity; the reason for doing something. □ *The purpose of this exercise is to develop the shoulder muscles.* □ *Sue's remarks accomplished their purpose, which was to make Philip uncomfortable.*

goggle   See the entry for *gawk*.

gold   See the entry for *metal*.

goo   See the entry for *slime*.

good   (*adjective*) of decent quality; acceptable. □ *Rita did a good job.* □ *The food was good.*

> • **all right**   *good* enough. (Used only after a verb. Informal.) □ *The food was all right, but it was nothing to write home about.* □ *It wasn't a great movie, but it was all right.*
> • **fine**   quite *good*. □ *Susan gave a fine performance on the trombone.* □ *Tim is a fine writer.*
> • **OK**   *good* or correct. (Informal.) □ *Is this answer OK?* □ *Jan checked the mirror to make sure she looked OK.*

good-luck piece   See the entry for *charm*.

gore   See the entry for *stab*.

gorge   See the entry for *valley*.

gorgeous   See the entry for *beautiful*.

gossip   See the entries for *rumor, talk²*.

govern   See the entry for *control¹*.

governmental   (*adjective*) having to do with officially running a country, state, or town. □ *The mayor went out of town on governmental business.* □ *What is the name of the governmental agency that collects taxes?*
    • **administrative**   having to do with running any kind of organization. □ *Making decisions is a big part of Bill's administrative job.* □ *The administrative offices are across the street from the factory.*
    • **executive**   having to do with officially carrying out rules or laws. □ *The president is the head of the executive branch of the government.* □ *The owner made the executive decision to ban smoking in the workplace.*
    • **legislative**   having to do with making laws. □ *Congress is a legislative body.* □ *The senators debated the new legislative policy.*
    • **political**   having to do with winning power to run the government. □ *Which political party do you belong to?* □ *Art went to a political rally.*

grab   See the entry for *catch*.

gracious   See the entry for *polite*.

grade   (*noun*) a position on a scale; a year in school. □ *This restaurant serves eggs of only the highest grade.* □ *Mary is in the seventh grade.*
    • **degree**   a grade; an amount or an extent. □ *Long underwear can give you a certain degree of protection from the cold.* □ *Carrie showed a high degree of enthusiasm for the project.*
    • **level**   a grade of importance or worth. □ *Donald has a high level of intelligence.* □ *The prince did not socialize with people below his social level.*
    • **rank**   a grade; in particular, a grade in the military. □ *Eddie attained the rank of sergeant in the Army.* □ *Employees were paid according to their rank.*
    • **standing**   someone's grade with respect to other people's. □ *Fran had the highest academic standing in her class.* □ *George did not want to risk the good financial standing of his business.*

gradual   (*adjective*) slowly, a little bit at a time. □ *The mountain climbers made gradual progress up the mountain's face.* □ *The patient's recovery was gradual but steady.*
    • **incremental**   a small, precise amount at a time. (Formal.) □ *Every year, Helen saw an incremental increase in her paycheck.* □ *Irene taught the mouse to do the complicated trick in incremental steps.*

• **piecemeal**   one piece at a time. ☐ *Jay put the bike together piecemeal.* ☐ *The football player put his gear on piecemeal.*

• **progressive**   slowly, going forward bit by bit. ☐ *It was sad to watch Kay waste away with the progressive illness.* ☐ *The actors kept rehearsing, and there was progressive improvement in the show.*

• **step-by-step**   one stage at a time; presenting one stage at a time. ☐ *Laura made step-by-step progress in learning how to cook.* ☐ *Follow these easy, step-by-step instructions.*

grand   (*adjective*) great and impressive. ☐ *The millionaire lived in a grand house.* ☐ *The star of the show made a grand entrance.*

• **august**   grand and well-respected. (Formal.) ☐ *It was a privilege to study with such an august teacher.* ☐ *Mark respected the august traditions of his people.*

• **dignified**   grand and behaving very properly. ☐ *The dignified man greeted everyone with wonderful politeness.* ☐ *The actor gave a dignified bow.*

• **imposing**   grand; frighteningly impressive. ☐ *Smith had an imposing office with high ceilings and a wonderful view of the city.* ☐ *We were greeted at the door by a very imposing butler.*

• **majestic**   grand and royal-seeming. ☐ *The majestic mountain peaks were capped with snow.* ☐ *The king put on his majestic robes.*

• **noble**   grand and exalted. ☐ *Tom was descended from a noble family.* ☐ *That noble old oak tree has stood for over three hundred years.*

• **stately**   grand, lofty, and very proper. ☐ *The priest came down the aisle at a slow and stately pace.* ☐ *The queen gave her consent with a stately nod of her head.*

graphic   See the entry for *vivid¹*.

grapple   See the entry for *struggle*.

grasp   See the entry for *understand*.

grasping   See the entry for *greedy*.

grassland   See the entry for *field*.

gratification   See the entry for *pleasure*.

gratified   See the entry for *content*.

grating   See the entry for *harsh*.

gratuitous   See the entry for *unnecessary*.

grave   See the entry for *serious*.

greatest   See the entry for *supreme*.

greedy   (*adjective*) always wanting more. □ *Don't be so greedy; let everyone share.* □ *The greedy puppy ate till it was sick.*
 • **covetous**   greedy for what other people have. (Formal.) □ *Tom was covetous of Sue's video games.* □ *Philip gazed at the shiny black car with a covetous look in his eye.*
 • **grasping**   greedy; always trying to get more money or possessions. □ *The grasping shopkeeper made his fortune by cheating his customers.* □ *Not even Rita's large salary could satisfy her grasping need for more.*
 • **mercenary**   greedy; willing to do anything for money. (Formal.) □ *The king hired mercenary soldiers to fight against his enemies.* □ *The killer's motive was purely mercenary; she wanted her victim's money.*
 • **rapacious**   extremely greedy; never satisfied. (Formal.) □ *The general conquered country after country, spurred by his rapacious desire for more territory.* □ *John has a rapacious appetite.*
 [→see also: *jealous*]

green   See the entry for *yard*.

green-eyed   See the entry for *jealous*.

greet   (*verb*) to say something polite when meeting someone. □ *Susan greeted me at the door.* □ *Tim greeted Jan with a cheerful "Hi there!"*
 • **hail**   to greet someone enthusiastically. □ *Bill warmly hailed his old friend.* □ *Art and Ben hailed each other with a hearty handshake.*
 • **receive**   to greet someone and take him or her into your home. (Formal.) □ *Carrie graciously received her visitors.* □ *Donald received Eddie with a polite smile.*
 • **welcome**   to greet someone who comes to visit you. □ *Eddie stood in the front room to welcome the guests.* □ *Fran welcomed me and introduced me to the other people in the room.*

grieve   (*verb*) to be very sad about something that has happened. □ *George grieved the death of his friend.* □ *Helen grieved to see her old house in ruins.*
 • **bemoan**   to moan because you are grieving; to be sorry about something. (Formal.) □ *Ida bemoaned her husband's grave illness.* □ *Kevin bemoaned his weight gain.*
 • **lament**   to express grieving. □ *Everyone lamented the great artist's death.* □ *"All my friends have moved away," Laura lamented.*
 • **mourn**   to grieve for something that you have lost. (Sometimes with *for*.) □ *Mark mourned the disappearance of the whooping crane.* □ *Tom mourned for his grandfather.*
 • **pine**   to waste away from grieving; to miss something badly. (Often with *for*.) □ *Sue is pining for her boyfriend, who is out of town for a month.* □ *Removed from his beloved farm, Philip pined away.*

grill   See the entry for *cook*.

grim   See the entry for *serious*.

grimace   See the entry for *frown*.

grimy   See the entry for *dirty¹*.

grin   See the entry for *smile*.

grind   See the entry for *crush*.

gripe   See the entry for *complain*.

groggy   (*adjective*) dizzy, foggy, and unsteady. □ *The pills made Rita groggy.* □ *The phone rang at 2 A.M., and Susan answered in a groggy voice.*
   • **muzzy**   dizzy and not thinking clearly. (Informal.) □ *Tim was feeling muzzy from too little sleep.* □ *Somewhere in his muzzy mind, Victor realized that he had had too much to drink.*
   • **punchy**   dizzy and unsteady from exhaustion. □ *The truck driver had been on the road for twenty-four hours straight and was starting to feel punchy.* □ *After an all-day hike, Bill was very punchy and couldn't stop giggling.*
   • **woozy**   dizzy, sick, and weak. (Informal.) □ *Getting hit on the head left Art feeling woozy.* □ *Shortly after he fainted, Ben came to, but he was still too woozy to stand up.*
   [→see also: *dizzy*]

groove   See the entry for *crease*.

grope   (*verb*) to feel around clumsily, trying to grab something. □ *Carrie groped around in her purse, trying to get her keys.* □ *Donald groped for the serving fork in the back of the silverware drawer.*
   • **bobble**   to keep clumsily tossing something in the air as you try to grab it. (Informal.) □ *Eddie bobbled the ball.* □ *Fran tripped and bobbled the stack of books she was carrying.*
   • **bumble**   to move around clumsily; to do something wrong. □ *George, confused, bumbled into the women's room.* □ *The waiter bumbled and dumped soup in my lap.*
   • **fumble**   to drop something as you try to grab it; to feel at something clumsily. □ *The football player fumbled the ball.* □ *Helen's mittened fingers fumbled with the zipper on her coat.*

grotto   See the entry for *cave*.

grouchy   See the entry for *grumpy*.

ground   See the entry for *dirt*.

grounds   See the entry for *evidence*.

group   (*noun*) two or more things that belong together in some way. (See also the entry for *sort*.) □ *I always eat lunch with the same group of people.* □ *The ancient Greeks thought that a certain group of stars resembled a hunter.*

• **batch**   a *group* of similar things made at the same time. □ *Irene baked a batch of cookies.* □ *As soon as I finish painting this group of figurines, I'll be ready to do the next batch.*

• **bunch**   a large *group;* a *group* of flowers or leafy vegetables. □ *I have to do a whole bunch of chores this morning.* □ *Jay brought his girlfriend a bunch of daffodils.*

• **pair**   a *group* of two things. □ *I have a pair of cats.* □ *Kay and Larry make a lovely pair.*

• **set**   a *group* of similar things; an exclusive *group* of people who socialize with one another. (*Set* has a special meaning in mathematics.) □ *Mark bought a set of colored pencils.* □ *Janice belongs to the polo-playing set.*

[→see also: *crowd, cluster*]

grouse   See the entry for *complain*.

grove   See the entry for *forest*.

grow   (*verb*) to get bigger; to become fully developed. (Often with *into*. See also the entry for *expand*.) □ *The puppy grew into a dog.* □ *The sapling grew very slowly.*

• **develop**   to *grow* or change gradually or naturally. (Usually with *into*.) □ *With the proper training, Nancy could develop into a fine musician.* □ *The short story Vincent wrote developed into a novel.*

• **evolve**   to *grow* slowly and steadily; to *grow* into a different form. (Often with *into*.) □ *Tom's spur-of-the-moment idea evolved into an elaborate plan.* □ *Our public library has evolved from one tiny room full of books to a spacious building that houses books, magazines, videos, and tapes.*

• **mature**   to *grow* into an adult. (Formal. Often with *into*.) □ *Peter proudly watched his sons and daughters mature.* □ *Brilliant children sometimes mature into very ordinary adults.*

growl   See the entries for *rumble, snarl*.

grubby   See the entry for *dirty¹*.

gruff   (*adjective*) having abrupt or harsh manners. □ *I summoned up enough courage to ask the gruff doorman for directions.* □ *Roger may seem gruff, but underneath it all he's very nice.*

• **brusque**   having abrupt and inconsiderate manners. (Formal.) □ *"Don't bother me right now," was Susan's brusque greeting.* □ *I could tell the boss was angry by the brusque way he summoned me to his office.*

• **rough**   having harsh manners; rude. (See also the main entry for rough.) □ *The country lad felt ashamed of his rough ways when he saw the city gentleman's polished manners.* □ *The boss dismissed me with a few rough, angry words.*

• **surly**   having harsh manners; resentful. □ *Tom made a surly apology.* □ *The surly librarian was obviously not happy about helping me find my book.*

grumble   See the entry for *complain.*

grumpy   (*adjective*) in a bad or complaining mood. (Informal.) □ *Judging by her frown, Jan's feeling grumpy today.* □ *The grumpy tourist spent his whole vacation complaining.*

• **cantankerous**   grumpy and stubborn. □ *The cantankerous old horse refused to budge when I said, "Giddyap!"* □ *Bill is cantankerous when it comes to playing games; you have to play by his rules, or he goes off in a huff.*

• **cross**   angrily grumpy. (Informal.) □ *Arithmetic problems always make Art cross.* □ *Ben is cross with me because I lost his favorite pen.*

• **grouchy**   grumpy and grumbling. (Informal.) □ *The baby was grouchy when she got up in the morning.* □ *The grouchy woman yelled at the kids to shut up.*

• **irritable**   grumpy; easily upset. □ *It's difficult to work for such an irritable person.* □ *Hunger made Carrie feel quite irritable.*

• **petulant**   grumpy and whiny. □ *Donna was a very petulant child.* □ *The cat made a petulant noise when I woke her.*

guarantee   See the entry for *promise.*

guard   See the entry for *protect.*

guarded   See the entry for *careful.*

guess   (*verb*) to come to a conclusion without having all the facts. □ *Guess how old Eddie is.* □ *I guess I'll need about five dollars' worth of gas.*

• **estimate**   to guess as precisely as you can. □ *Fran estimated how much her groceries would cost.* □ *George estimated that he would have fifteen guests at the party.*

• **gauge**   to guess; to size something up. □ *Helen tried to gauge the amount of fabric she would need to make the shirt.* □ *Irene gauged how much water the tank could hold.*

• **judge**   to guess after considering carefully. (Formal.) □ *After studying the map, Jay judged that he had at least twenty more miles to go.* □ *Kay judged that Larry was in a good mood.*

guest   See the entry for *visitor.*

guffaw   See the entry for *laugh.*

guide[1] (*noun*) an experienced person who helps you do something. □ *The guide took us over the trail.* □ *Mark was our guide to the interesting world of stamp collecting.*

• **adviser** a *guide* who can tell you what you should do. □ *The president consulted his advisers before making a decision.* □ *Tom's brother was his most trusted adviser.*

• **guru** a religious *guide* or teacher; a *guide* with many followers. (Informal.) □ *Sue studied yoga with a famous guru.* □ *Ms. Smith is the latest popular dieting guru.*

• **leader** a *guide* who goes ahead to show you where to go. □ *We followed the troop leader across the river.* □ *The leader of the peace movement told her supporters what to do.*

• **mentor** a faithful, trusted *guide*. □ *The respected actress was a mentor to many young people in the theater.* □ *Mr. Smith was not just a teacher to his students; he was also a mentor.*

guide[2] (*verb*) to move someone or something in the right direction. □ *The nurse guided Tom into the doctor's office.* □ *The sign guided me to turn left.*

• **drive** to *guide* a car, a truck, or a vehicle pulled by animals. □ *Ben drove from Milwaukee to Dallas.* □ *Carrie learned how to drive the moving van.*

• **pilot** to *guide* a boat or a plane. □ *The captain piloted the boat safely through the storm.* □ *Art knew how to pilot small planes.*

• **steer** to *guide* a car or a boat. □ *Jan steered the boat toward the dock.* □ *Bill steered the car around the curve.*

guileless See the entry for *naive.*

guilt (*noun*) a bad feeling that you get after doing something wrong. □ *Guilt led Eddie to confess that he had stolen the money.* □ *Whenever Fran slept late, she was tortured by feelings of guilt.*

• **compunction** a sharp, bad feeling that you get after doing something wrong. (Formal.) □ *The murderer evidently felt no compunction at having taken a human life.* □ *George felt a twinge of compunction as he lied to his friend.*

• **remorse** a feeling of being sorry that you did something. □ *Helen was consumed with remorse for having destroyed her sister's drawing.* □ *Irene tried to express her remorse over what she had done.*

• **shame** deep *guilt*. □ *The other children laughed at Jason, and he blushed with shame.* □ *Kay's lecture made Larry feel shame for mistreating the dogs.*

guiltless See the entry for *innocent.*

gulch See the entry for *valley.*

gulp   See the entry for *drink.*

gummy   See the entry for *sticky.*

gung-ho   See the entry for *eager.*

gunk   See the entry for *slime.*

guru   See the entry for *guide.*

gush   See the entries for *expel, flow, rave.*

gust   See the entry for *wind*[1].

gut   See the entry for *stomach.*

guy   See the entry for *man.*

guzzle   See the entry for *drink.*

H

habitual See the entry for *familiar.*

hack See the entry for *chop.*

haggard (*adjective*) thin and worn out from hard work or suffering. □ *The survivors of the plane crash grew more and more haggard as the weeks passed.* □ *The doctor looked into the patient's haggard face.*
> • **careworn** worn out from suffering. □ *I wondered what made my old friend look so careworn.* □ *Mark worked to ease the burden for his careworn mother.*
> • **wan** pale and worn out from suffering. □ *The poor little girl was wan from hunger.* □ *Nancy gave me a wan smile.*
> • **wasted** thin and used up from suffering. (Old-fashioned.) □ *The starving beggar held out a wasted hand.* □ *Sophia's wasted face showed that she had been gravely ill.*

haggle See the entry for *bargain.*

hail See the entry for *greet.*

hair-raising See the entry for *terrifying.*

hale See the entry for *healthy.*

hall (*noun*) the connecting area between rooms in a building. □ *Philip went down the hall, looking for room 103.* □ *The stairway is at the end of the hall.*
> • **corridor** a long *hall.* □ *Three doors opened onto the corridor.* □ *There was a snack machine in the hotel corridor.*
> • **gallery** a wide *hall.* (Formal.) □ *Ken wandered through the marble-floored gallery on the ground floor of the mansion.* □ *Gracious, high-ceilinged rooms were connected by well-lighted galleries.*

• **passageway** a *hall;* any opening that allows you to get from one place to another. □ *Rita's apartment is at the end of the passageway.* □ *The explorers found a passageway that led them out of the cave.*

hallowed See the entry for *holy.*

hallucination See the entry for *illusion.*

halt See the entry for *stop.*

hammer See the entry for *pound.*

hand-me-down See the entry for *secondhand.*

handcuffs See the entry for *bonds.*

handle (*verb*) to do what needs to be done. (Informal.) □ *I'll handle inviting the guests if you'll handle the party decorations.* □ *Susan was confident in her ability to handle any problem that came up at work.*
   • **cope with** to *handle* someone or something successfully; to face something. □ *Tim found it hard to cope with his father's illness.* □ *Meditation helped Jan cope with stress.*
   • **deal with** to *handle* someone or something. (Informal.) □ *The waiter tried to deal with the unhappy diner.* □ *Bill left the problem for his boss to deal with.*
   • **manage** to do what needs to be done; to control people or things. □ *Five active two-year-olds were too much for the baby-sitter to manage.* □ *Anna's parents thought she was old enough to manage by herself when they went out for the evening.*
   • **take care of** to take charge of someone or something; to solve some kind of problem. (Informal.) □ *Don't worry about walking the dog; I'll take care of that.* □ *Ben took care of the problem we were having with the computer.*

handy See the entry for *useful.*

hang (*verb*) to be fastened to something above; to fasten something to something above. (See also the entry for *depend.*) □ *Several pictures hung on the wall.* □ *Carrie hung her coat from the hook.*
   • **dangle** to *hang,* moving back and forth; to *hang* something and let it move back and forth. □ *A chain dangled down from the light bulb.* □ *Donald dangled a string in front of the kitten.*
   • **suspend** to *hang* someone or something. (Formal.) □ *Eddie suspended a swing from the porch roof.* □ *The daredevil suspended himself from a helicopter.*
   • **swing** to *hang,* moving back and forth in a wide arc; to *hang* someone or something and let it move in a wide arc. □ *Monkeys swung on the tree branch.* □ *The father swung his child around.*

hang around   See the entry for *stay*.

hang-up   See the entry for *obsession*.

haphazard   See the entry for *random*.

happen   (*verb*) to come to pass. □ *A funny thing happened on my way to the theater.* □ *Fran never dreamed that such a thing could happen.*
   • **come about**   to *happen*. (Somewhat formal.) □ *George said that Helen would get a pleasant surprise this week, and it came about just that way.* □ *Irene tried to explain how it came about that she should show up just when I needed her.*
   • **occur**   to *happen*. (Somewhat formal.) □ *Jason's death occurred at four o'clock this morning.* □ *The earthquake occurred right where the seismologist predicted it would.*
   • **take place**   for something planned to *happen*. □ *The wedding will take place on Saturday.* □ *Protest demonstrations were taking place all across the country.*
   • **transpire**   to *happen* over the course of time. (Formal.) □ *It transpired that Kay did not get the job.* □ *Many interesting things transpired as a result of Laura's decision to sell her house.*

happening   See the entry for *event*.

happenstance   See the entry for *accident*.

happy   (*adjective*) very pleased or in a good mood; showing pleasure. □ *The happy painter sang as she worked.* □ *Mark did a happy little dance.*
   • **blissful**   deeply *happy*. □ *The blissful bridegroom kissed his bride.* □ *There was a blissful expression on Tom's face.*
   • **glad**   *happy;* pleased. □ *I'm glad that everything worked out all right.* □ *The student was glad to know she had passed the test.*
   • **gleeful**   rejoicing and *happy*. □ *The gleeful students ran out of the school on the last day of the school year.* □ *Sue crossed the finish line with a gleeful shout.*
   • **joyful**   deeply *happy;* wanting to celebrate. □ *Philip's graduation was a joyful day.* □ *Rita's joyful family welcomed her home after her year-long absence.*
   [→contrasting word: *sad;* see also: *cheerful*]

happy-go-lucky   See the entry for *optimistic*.

hard   (*adjective*) requiring a lot of effort. (See also the entry for *firm*.) □ *Building the garage is going to take a lot of hard work.* □ *These instructions are hard to understand.*
   • **demanding**   hard and rigorous. □ *Hiking was too demanding an activity for Susan, who preferred to sit around watching TV in her spare time.* □ *Mrs. Hall's English class is very demanding.*

• **difficult**   requiring a lot of effort or courage. □ *The explorers began the difficult climb up the mountain.* □ *It was difficult for Victor's big fingers to grasp the tiny sewing needle.*
• **exacting**   requiring a lot of care and effort. (Formal.) □ *Bill followed an exacting physical-fitness routine.* □ *Anna's exacting job leaves her exhausted.*
• **tough**   requiring a lot of effort. (Informal.) □ *This homework assignment is really tough!* □ *Shoveling snow off the driveway turned out to be a tough job.*
[→contrasting word: *easy*]

hardly   See the entry for *barely.*

hardship   See the entry for *problem.*

harm   See the entry for *hurt¹.*

harmless   (*adjective*) not causing any hurt. □ *There's no need to be scared of that snake; it's perfectly harmless.* □ *I was just making a harmless little joke.*
• **benign**   *harmless;* having or showing good intentions. (Formal. In medical terminology, *benign* also means "not deadly.") □ *Mr. Smith may look fierce, but he's quite benign.* □ *The doctor greeted me with a benign smile.*
• **innocuous**   entirely *harmless.* (Formal.) □ *Ben thought that Carrie's innocuous remark was an insult in disguise.* □ *Donald argued that violence on TV was innocuous.*
• **inoffensive**   *harmless;* not bothering anyone. □ *Why were you rude to that poor inoffensive man?* □ *I don't understand how such an inoffensive book could cause a controversy.*

harmony   See the entry for *peace.*

harp   See the entry for *nag.*

harsh   (*adjective*) hard to listen to; sharp and unpleasant. (See also the entry for *severe.*) □ *I was wakened by the harsh buzz of the doorbell.* □ *Fran thought that rock music was too harsh.*
• **grating**   very rough-sounding. □ *I heard a grating whine from under the hood of the car.* □ *There was a grating noise as the door opened on its rusty hinges.*
• **piercing**   painfully high-pitched. □ *The baby gave a piercing cry.* □ *A piercing noise came out of the radio.*
• **raucous**   loud, rough-sounding, and hard to listen to; noisy. (Formal.) □ *The dog's raucous barking lasted all night.* □ *The neighbors are holding a particularly raucous party.*
• **shrill**   high-pitched and hard to listen to. □ *When Gina gets upset, her voice gets very shrill.* □ *Helen put her fingers in her mouth and gave a shrill whistle.*

• **strident**   high-pitched, forceful, loud, and hard to listen to. □ *I could hear Irene's strident voice all the way down the hall.* □ *Kay listened patiently to Jay's strident complaints.*
[→see also: *loud*]

harvest   (*verb*) to collect and bring together something, usually crops. □ *The farmer harvested the wheat.* □ *Are the tomatoes ready to harvest?*
   • **garner**   to collect things and store them away. (Formal.) □ *Laura garnered the produce from her vegetable garden.* □ *The reporter garnered several interesting facts from the interview.*
   • **gather**   to collect and bring things together. □ *Mark went out to gather some flowers.* □ *Tom gathered the tools he would need to fix the radio.*
   • **glean**   to collect things carefully; to pick out just those things you can use; to collect something little by little. □ *Sue walked through the field, gleaning the few ears of corn that were left.* □ *All I could glean from Philip's story was the fact that someone had upset him.*
   • **pick**   to collect things that are ready or ripe. □ *Rita picked strawberries.* □ *It's not yet time to pick the peas.*
   • **reap**   to collect what you have worked for. (Formal.) □ *The farmer reaped the grain from her fields.* □ *Susan soon reaped the benefits of regular exercise.*

hasten   See the entry for *hurry*.

hate   (*verb*) to dislike someone or something intensely. □ *Tim hates his cousin.* □ *Jan hates the color of the walls in her apartment.*
   • **abhor**   to hate and want to avoid someone or something. (Formal.) □ *Bill abhors parties and never accepts invitations to them.* □ *Art abhors his sister's favorite TV show.*
   • **abominate**   to hate someone or something strongly. (Formal.) □ *Words cannot describe how I abominate that man.* □ *Don't serve brussels sprouts to Ben; he abominates them.*
   • **despise**   to hate and look down on someone or something. (Formal.) □ *We despised Charles for the cowardly way he behaved.* □ *Donald despises his boss.*
   • **detest**   to hate someone or something strongly. □ *Eddie detests cats; he thinks they're cruel.* □ *I detest the new English teacher; she's so nasty.*
   • **loathe**   to hate and feel disgust toward someone or something. □ *Dinner tonight is meatloaf, which I loathe.* □ *Fran loathes that movie.*

haughty   See the entry for *conceited*.

haul   See the entry for *pull*.

have   See the entry for *own*.

have at   See the entry for *attack*.

have faith   See the entry for *believe²*.

have faith in   See the entry for *trust*.

have in mind   See the entry for *mean²*.

have on   See the entry for *wear*.

have qualms about   See the entry for *doubt*.

have the right to   See the entry for *deserve*.

haven   See the entry for *shelter*.

havoc   See the entry for *disorder*.

hazardous   See the entry for *dangerous*.

haze   See the entry for *mist*.

head   See the entries for *boss, lead, mind*.

healthy   (*adjective*) strong and not sick. □ *You need to eat properly in order to stay healthy.* □ *The horse looked like a healthy animal.*
• **fit**   *healthy* and in good physical condition. □ *George takes a brisk walk every day to keep fit.* □ *Helen got fit by taking an exercise class.*
• **hale**   *healthy.* (Usually said of elderly people.) □ *Mr. Hall is eighty years old, but still hale and full of energy.* □ *The hale old woman said she had never been sick a day in her life.*
• **robust**   *healthy* and vigorous. □ *The robust fellow had hiked over ninety miles that week.* □ *Irene was robust enough to come through the illness all right.*
• **sound**   entirely *healthy.* (Used to describe bodies or body parts, not people.) □ *The horse's teeth seemed perfectly sound.* □ *The doctor said that Jay had a sound heart.*
• **well**   *healthy;* the opposite of *sick.* □ *We all hoped that Kay would get well quickly.* □ *How are you feeling? Are you well?*

heap   See the entry for *pile*.

hearsay   See the entry for *rumor*.

heart   See the entry for *center*.

heart-to-heart   See the entry for *talk¹*.

heave   See the entry for *throw*.

heavenly body   See the entry for *world*.

heavy   See the entry for *fat*.

hectic   See the entry for *busy²*.

hector   See the entry for *nag*.

hedge   See the entry for *bush*.

heed   See the entries for *listen, obey*.

heinous   See the entry for *atrocious*.

help   (*verb*) to make it easier for someone to do something. □ *Laura helped Mark carry the heavy box upstairs.* □ *Let me help you clean up the kitchen.*
> • **aid**   to *help* someone who needs you. (Formal.) □ *Tom sent money to aid the victims of the flood.* □ *The librarian aided me to find books about penguins.*
> • **assist**   to *help* someone, usually the person in charge of something. □ *The nurse assisted the doctor.* □ *Sue assisted Philip as he repaired the car.*
> • **succor**   to *help* and comfort someone. (Formal.) □ *The children's aunt did much to succor them after their parents were killed.* □ *Rita tried to succor the poor crying kitten.*
> [→contrasting words: *hurt, hinder*]

helpful   See the entry for *useful*.

hem in   See the entry for *surround*.

herald   See the entry for *announce*.

herd   (*noun*) a group of animals of the same kind, usually large animals. □ *The herd of buffalo thundered across the plain.* □ *Susan kept a herd of goats.*
> • **drove**   a *herd* of animals moving or being moved together. □ *The cowboy had to get the drove of cattle across the river.* □ *People came to see the movie in droves.* □ *The rancher sent a drove of sheep to market.*
> • **flock**   a group of birds or sheep. □ *A flock of sheep was grazing on the hillside.* □ *I saw a flock of sparrows flying overhead.*
> • **gaggle**   a group of geese. □ *A gaggle of geese had wandered out onto the road.* □ *Judging from the noise, there was at least a gaggle of geese out in the barnyard.*
> • **pack**   a group of dogs or wolves hunting together. (See also the main entry for *pack*.) □ *I've heard that there's a pack of wild dogs in that park.* □ *We could hear the howling of the wolf pack.*
> • **swarm**   a group of insects moving about together. □ *Tim sprinted across the lawn, pursued by an angry swarm of bees.* □ *A swarm of flies immediately settled on our picnic.*

hermit   (*noun*) someone who goes away from other people and lives alone. □ *The old hermit lived in a cave.* □ *After her husband died, Veronica became a hermit, never leaving her ruined house.*

• **loner**   someone who avoids other people. □ *Bill hasn't made any close friends; he's basically a loner.* □ *Art was a loner, moving from town to town and never putting down roots.*
• **recluse**   someone who lives shut up and hidden from people. (Formal.) □ *The writer is a recluse who never grants interviews.* □ *The movie star hated publicity so much that she became a recluse.*
• **solitary**   someone who lives alone and apart from people. (Formal.) □ *The monk was a solitary, living in his mountain cottage and never talking to anyone.* □ *Mary was perfectly content to live as a solitary.*

hesitant   See the entry for *reluctant.*

hesitate   See the entry for *wait.*

hew   See the entry for *carve.*

hibernate   (*verb*) to sleep through the winter; to sleep deeply and for a long time. □ *The bears hibernated through the winter.* □ *We found a little mouse hibernating in a hole in the wall.*
• **hole up**   to go into a hole; to go into hiding. (Informal.) □ *All the animals who had holed up during the cold weather began to show themselves again.* □ *Vincent holed up in his room, furiously writing at his novel.*
• **lie dormant**   to be inactive for a time. □ *The plants lay dormant under the layer of frost.* □ *The seeds had lain dormant for two thousand years until the archaeologist sprouted them.*
• **lie torpid**   to be sleepy and sluggish for a time. □ *The lizard lay torpid in the cold.* □ *The tiger lay torpid with the effects of the tranquilizer dart.*
• **vegetate**   to be mentally and physically inactive for a time. □ *The patient vegetated in a coma for almost a month.* □ *Carrie did nothing but vegetate in front of the TV all night.*
[→see also: *sleep*]

hide   (*verb*) to make something difficult to see or find. (See also the entry for *fur.*) □ *Donald hid the money in his shoe.* □ *Eddie hid in the closet.*
• **conceal**   to *hide* something completely. □ *Fran put down a rug to conceal the stains on the floor.* □ *George and Helen concealed the fact that they knew each other.*
• **cover up**   to *hide* something by putting it underneath something; to *hide* an event by pretending it did not happen. □ *The snow covered up the lawn.* □ *The mayor tried to cover up her dishonest activities.*
• **obscure**   to *hide* something by covering it or rubbing it out. (Formal.) □ *Several dark stains obscured the writing on the page.* □ *A veil obscured the visitor's face.*
[→see also: *stash*]

hideous See the entry for *ugly.*

high See the entry for *tall.*

high-strung See the entry for *impetuous.*

higher-up See the entry for *authority.*

highest See the entry for *supreme.*

highway See the entry for *road.*

hill (*noun*) a raised area of ground. □ *I climbed to the top of the hill to get a better look at my surroundings.* □ *The little house stood at the bottom of a hill.*
>   • **knoll** a small *hill.* □ *The picnickers spread out their cloth atop a knoll near the creek.* □ *The path led me up a gentle knoll.*
>   • **mound** a *hill,* especially a man-made one. □ *This is the burial mound of a great chief.* □ *A mound of dirt grew up next to where Laura was digging the hole.*
>   • **rise** a *hill;* any place where the ground gets higher. □ *Turn right when you get to the top of the next rise.* □ *There was a steep rise on the other side of the river.*

hinder See the entry for *block.*

hinge See the entry for *depend.*

hint See the entries for *clue, suggest.*

hire See the entry for *rent.*

hiss (*verb*) to make a long whistling noise that sounds like the letter s. □ *The snake hissed at me.* □ *Water bubbled out of the boiling pot and hissed on the stove burner.*
>   • **fizz** to *hiss* in a bubbling way. □ *Soda pop fizzed up out of the bottle.* □ *The water fizzed when I dropped the tablet in.*
>   • **sizzle** to *hiss* violently. □ *Meat sizzled on the hot coals.* □ *Rain sizzled on the burning pavement.*
>   • **sputter** to make hissing or popping noises. □ *The match sputtered as I lit it.* □ *"What—what—what!!" Mark sputtered angrily.*

histrionic See the entry for *dramatic.*

hit (*verb*) to deliver a blow to someone or something. □ *Don't hit your brother!* □ *Someone hit Tom and gave him a black eye.*
>   • **punch** to *hit* someone or something with your closed fist. □ *Sue punched down the bread dough.* □ *Paula punched Rita in the head, knocking her unconscious.*

• **slap**   to *hit* someone or something with your open hand. □ *The angry father slapped his child.* □ *The singers slapped their knees rhythmically.*

• **strike**   to *hit* someone or something forcefully. (Formal.) □ *The evil knight struck our hero across the face.* □ *Susan, frustrated, struck the wall with her fist.*

hoard   See the entry for *stash*.

hoax   See the entry for *fool²*.

hodgepodge   (*noun*) a disorderly mixture of many different kinds of things. (Informal.) □ *Tim's library is a hodgepodge of books, some good, some awful.* □ *Jan had collected quite a hodgepodge of toys.*

• **jumble**   a disorderly collection. □ *Bill tried to find a hammer among the jumble of tools in the drawer.* □ *The floor was covered with a jumble of Andrew's clothes.*

• **medley**   a mixture of things that do not ordinarily go together; a collection of tunes. □ *Ben sang a medley of popular songs from the 1950s.* □ *The sauce contained a medley of interesting flavors.*

• **mishmash**   a disorderly mixture of things. (Slang.) □ *Carrie served a mishmash of leftovers for dinner.* □ *Donald's essay was just a confused mishmash of unclear ideas.*

hogshead   See the entry for *barrel*.

hoist   See the entry for *lift*.

hold   See the entries for *believe¹, keep, own, reserve, stick¹*.

hold back   (*verb*) to keep something from going forward; to keep something in. (See also the entry for *reserve*.) □ *The police tried to hold the crowd back.* □ *Eddie held back his tears.*

• **quell**   to *hold back* and make something quiet. (Formal.) □ *The army quelled the rebellion.* □ *This ointment ought to quell the itching.*

• **repress**   to *hold back* something; to keep something down. □ *The teacher repressed her students' high spirits with a stern look.* □ *Fran had to repress a smile.*

• **restrain**   to *hold* something *back* with great effort; to keep something in. □ *Please restrain your dog.* □ *George restrained his curiosity about the stranger.*

• **suppress**   to *hold* something *back* or stop something by force; to hold something in. □ *The government suppressed all protest.* □ *Helen suppressed her laughter.*
[→see also: *stifle*]

hold dear   See the entry for *treasure*.

hold responsible   See the entry for *blame*.

holder   See the entry for *container.*

hole   (*noun*) an opening in something; an open place. □ *There's a hole in my shoe.* □ *Irene dug a hole in the backyard.*
  • **cavity**   a *hole,* especially a *hole* in a tooth. □ *The dentist found three cavities in my teeth.* □ *The bandits hid the money in a little cavity beneath the floorboards.*
  • **crater**   a large, shallow *hole.* □ *Through the telescope, Jay saw craters on the surface of the moon.* □ *The explosion left a huge crater where the building used to be.*
  • **hollow**   a shallow *hole.* □ *There was a grassy hollow in the middle of the field.* □ *Water collected in the hollow on top of the rock.*
  • **pit**   a deep *hole.* □ *The steam shovel dug a deep pit.* □ *Rust left pits all over the surface of the car.* □ *Coal is found in pits in the ground.*

hole up   See the entry for *hibernate.*

holler   See the entry for *yell.*

hollow   See the entry for *hole.*

holy   (*adjective*) having to do with a god or worshiping a god. □ *Kay was brought up to treat the Bible as a holy book.* □ *These hills were a holy place for the Native Americans who lived here.*
  • **hallowed**   *holy;* blessed or respected. (Formal.) □ *Pilgrims visited the hallowed spot where the saint was martyred.* □ *Kevin thought that universities were hallowed places where great thinkers searched for truth.*
  • **religious**   having to do with the organized worship of a god; belonging to a religion. □ *That TV station shows only religious programs.* □ *The minister had many religious duties to perform.*
  • **sacred**   dedicated to a god. □ *The priest performed the sacred rite of baptism.* □ *In Jewish schools called yeshivas, students pored over the sacred writings.*

homage   See the entry for *tribute.*

honest   (*adjective*) telling the truth; dealing in a fair way. □ *Instead of making up excuses, the honest child admitted she hadn't done her homework.* □ *Did Art get that money in an honest way?*
  • **aboveboard**   doing things openly and truthfully. □ *Ben was quite aboveboard about the car he was selling; he told me it had several problems.* □ *The shopkeeper's aboveboard dealings won him many faithful customers in the long run.*
  • **candid**   telling the truth openly. □ *The mayor made a candid statement about her plan to raise taxes.* □ *Carrie is not being candid when she says she's not upset with me.*
  • **frank**   telling the truth bluntly. □ *I'll be frank with you; I don't like your haircut.* □ *Donald wrote a frank letter expressing his doubts.*

• **sincere**   telling the truth; saying what you mean; heartfelt. ☐ *Eddie's love for Fran was sincere.* ☐ *You have my sincere good wishes.*
• **straightforward**   telling the truth simply and directly. ☐ *George gave a straightforward explanation for what he had done.* ☐ *The senator was straightforward in his dealings with the public.*
[→contrasting word: *dishonest*]

honor   See the entries for *respect¹, respect², tribute.*

hoodwink   See the entry for *fool².*

hop   See the entry for *jump.*

hope   (*verb*) to want and expect something. ☐ *I hope Helen will come for dinner.* ☐ *Irene hopes to get a good grade on her paper.*
• **aspire to**   to want to be or achieve something. ☐ *Many young actors and actresses aspire to stardom.* ☐ *Jay aspired to be a great athlete.*
• **dream of**   to *hope* for something; to imagine something. ☐ *Kay dreamed of having her own house.* ☐ *Larry stared out the window, dreaming of the coming weekend.*
• **wish**   to want something; to have a need for something. ☐ *I wish that noise would stop.* ☐ *Mark wished for the courage to tell Nancy how he felt about her.*

hopeful   See the entry for *optimistic.*

hopeless   See the entries for *desperate, useless.*

horde   See the entry for *crowd.*

horrible   See the entry for *awful.*

horrifying   See the entry for *terrifying.*

hostel   See the entry for *hotel.*

hot   (*adjective*) having much heat. (See also the entry for *spicy.*) ☐ *Sue wanted a cup of hot coffee.* ☐ *It's too hot to go running around outside.*
• **boiling**   *hot* and humid; *hot* enough to bubble. ☐ *The cook put the potatoes into the boiling oil.* ☐ *The weather was boiling all through the month of July.*
• **burning**   severely *hot;* as *hot* as fire. ☐ *The father felt his sick child's burning forehead.* ☐ *I could barely walk on the burning pavement.*
• **sweltering**   *hot* and causing you to sweat. ☐ *The explorers pushed on through the sweltering jungle.* ☐ *It was a sweltering summer day.*
• **warm**   more *hot* than cold. ☐ *Philip put the food in the oven to keep it warm.* ☐ *Are you warm enough, or would you like more blankets?*
[→contrasting word: *cold*]

hotel (*noun*) a place where people pay to stay for a short while. □ *Rita spent the weekend in a nice hotel.* □ *There were several hotels in the center of town.*

> • **hostel** a simple, cheap *hotel* for young people. □ *The hikers stopped at a hostel for the night.* □ *People who stay at this hostel must help with the chores.*
> • **inn** a *hotel*; often, a *hotel* that also serves food. (Formal.) □ *We stayed at a charming country inn.* □ *Susan got a good meal at the inn.*
> • **lodge** a *hotel*; often, a *hotel* where people stay while they pursue a sport. □ *The skiers came back to the lodge at sunset.* □ *The hunters stayed in the same lodge every year.*
> • **motel** a *hotel* with space available for cars. □ *A sign outside the motel said, "No Vacancy."* □ *We parked right outside our room in the motel.*

hotheaded See the entry for *impetuous.*

hound See the entry for *chase.*

house (*noun*) a building in which people live. □ *Tim lives in a two-story house.* □ *Come on over to my house.*

> • **apartment** a group of rooms where people live. □ *There are twenty apartments in this building.* □ *The young couple looked for a two-bedroom apartment.*
> • **bungalow** a small, one-story *house*. □ *Jan's first house was a tiny gray bungalow on a busy street.* □ *Grampa's bungalow has only one bedroom.*
> • **cabin** a small, roughly-built *house*. □ *Bill rented a cabin by the lake.* □ *The pioneer family built a cabin in the woods.*
> • **cottage** a small, cute *house*. □ *Art grew up in a pretty cottage out in the country.* □ *Ben dreamed of having a cottage in a small town somewhere.*
> • **mansion** a large, grand *house*. □ *The mansion had forty-three rooms.* □ *The millionaire built herself a mansion that looked like a royal palace.*

houseguest See the entry for *visitor.*

hovel See the entry for *shack.*

hover See the entry for *fly.*

howl See the entry for *scream.*

hub See the entry for *center.*

hue See the entry for *color.*

huffy See the entry for *indignant.*

hug (*verb*) to put your arms around and hold someone close. □ *The mother hugged her daughter.* □ *The friends, who had not seen each other for a year, hugged when they met.*

• **cradle** to *hug* someone; to hold someone in your arms. □ *The father cradled his new baby in his arms.* □ *The baby-sitter cradled the scared child.*

• **cuddle** to *hug* someone and stay close for a long time. □ *Carrie and Donald cuddled on the sofa while they watched TV.* □ *Eddie couldn't resist cuddling the cute little puppy.*

• **embrace** to *hug* someone. (Formal.) □ *The friends embraced to show that they had forgiven each other.* □ *The leaders of the two countries embraced each other.*

• **snuggle** to curl up with someone and *hug* each other. □ *The couple snuggled in front of the fire.* □ *Gina snuggled up to her mother and asked to be read a story.*

• **squeeze** to *hug* someone tight. (Informal.) □ *Harold squeezed his girlfriend.* □ *Grandma squeezed me tight and said she loved me.*

huge   See the entry for *big*.

hullabaloo   See the entry for *commotion*.

hum (*verb*) to make a steady noise that sounds like the letter *m*. □ *The car engine hummed as we drove along.* □ *Irene hummed a little tune.*

• **buzz** to make a steady noise that sounds like the letter *z*. □ *A fly buzzed around the room.* □ *The computer printer buzzed, which meant that it was out of paper.*

• **drone** to make a steady noise all on one note; to talk in a boring way. □ *Summer insects droned in the air.* □ *Somewhere in the distance, I heard a bagpipe drone.* □ *The speaker droned on and most of the audience fell asleep.*

• **whir** to move quickly, making a steady, flapping noise. □ *The flock of birds whirred into the air.* □ *An airplane motor whirred overhead.*

human being   See the entry for *person*.

humane   See the entry for *gentle*.

humbug   See the entry for *fraud*.

humid (*adjective*) slightly wet; moist. (Used to describe the air or the weather.) □ *It feels even hotter because it's so humid.* □ *It was a humid day, and everyone felt lazy.*

• **dank** unpleasantly cold and *humid*. □ *The air in the basement was dank.* □ *The stone house felt dank even in the hottest weather.*

• **muggy** extremely *humid* and warm. □ *It was so muggy out that you could see moisture waves in the air.* □ *We went out to the country to try to escape the muggy heat of the city.*

• **steamy**   very hot and *humid;* full of steam. □ *Art's hot shower left the bathroom quite steamy.* □ *It was hard for Ben to breathe the steamy tropical air.*

• **sultry**   so hot and *humid* that you sweat a lot. □ *People fanned themselves in the sultry heat.* □ *Everyone's hair went limp on that sultry day.*

humiliate   See the entry for *embarrass.*

humor   See the entry for *spoil¹.*

humorous   See the entry for *funny.*

hunch   (*noun*) an idea that you get for no obvious reason. □ *I have a hunch that Carrie didn't go out of town after all.* □ *I don't know for sure that my horse will win the race; it's just a hunch.*

• **feeling**   a vague *hunch.* (See also the main entry for *feeling.*) □ *Helen had a feeling that Irene didn't want to be disturbed.* □ *Something gives me the feeling that I'm not welcome here.*

• **intuition**   an instinctive *hunch;* the ability to know things instinctively. □ *Jay had an intuition about where to find the missing money.* □ *Kay's intuition told her not to trust Larry.*

• **premonition**   a *hunch* about something that is going to happen. (Formal.) □ *Mark had a premonition of some disaster happening on his birthday.* □ *Nancy somehow had a premonition that her sister would finally come home.*

• **presentiment**   a vague *hunch* or feeling about something that is going to happen. (Formal.) □ *Tom had a presentiment that he would lose the watch his grandfather gave him.* □ *Philip felt a strong presentiment of some joyful event, and sure enough, his mother got out of the hospital that same week.*

hunger   (*noun*) a desire or need to eat or have something. □ *Hunger drove the deer out of the woods to graze on people's lawns.* □ *Fran has a constant hunger for sweets.* □ *Marsha's hunger for attention causes her to do some strange things.*

• **appetite**   an eager desire to eat or have something. (Sometimes with *for.*) □ *I've cooked a big dinner, so I hope you have a big appetite.* □ *It's impossible to satisfy George's appetite for pasta.* □ *Nora has an insatiable appetite for learning.*

• **craving**   a strong desire to eat something. (Usually with *for.*) □ *Harry had a strange craving for pickled okra.* □ *Irene woke in the middle of the night with a strong craving for peanut butter.*

• **taste**   a desire to eat something in particular. (Usually with *for.*) □ *I have a taste for Korean food today, so I think I'll have lunch at the Korean restaurant.* □ *Jim asked if he could have apple pie for dessert, since he had a taste for it.*

hungry (*adjective*) wanting or needing something to eat. □ *Let's stop at that restaurant; I'm hungry.* □ *The baby's crying because he's hungry.*
- **famished** very *hungry* because you have not eaten for a long time. (Formal.) □ *The hikers were famished after their active day.* □ *Kay skipped lunch, so she was famished by supper time.*
- **ravenous** extremely *hungry*. (Formal.) □ *The ravenous boy ate six hamburgers.* □ *The children were afraid of the wolf, which looked ravenous.*
- **starving** very *hungry*; not having eaten for so long that you are almost dying. □ *What's for dinner? I'm starving!* □ *The starving children begged for food.*

hunt See the entry for *chase.*

hunt for See the entry for *seek.*

hurl See the entry for *throw.*

hurrah See the entry for *cheer.*

hurricane See the entry for *storm.*

hurry (*verb*) to move or act very quickly. □ *Hurry, or we'll be late to the movie!* □ *Larry hurried to get dinner ready.*
- **dart** to *hurry* directly toward something; to cross a short distance very rapidly. □ *The mouse darted into its hole.* □ *Mark darted across the road.*
- **dash** to *hurry;* to run headlong. □ *Tom had to dash to catch up with his friends.* □ *The ambulance dashed to the hospital.*
- **hasten** to *hurry.* (Formal.) □ *Sue hastened to get dressed in time for the party.* □ *Philip hastened to his neighbor's house to tell her the news.*
- **race** to *hurry* as fast as you can, as if you were in a race. □ *The bicyclist raced through the traffic.* □ *I raced home as soon as I heard Grandma was there.*
- **rush** to *hurry* so much that you are likely to make a mistake. □ *Rita rushed to get out the door in the morning, and only noticed later that she had put on two shoes that didn't match.* □ *Susan rushed around, cleaning up the living room.*

hurt[1] (*verb*) to cause pain to someone; to damage something. □ *Don't hug the baby so tight; you'll hurt her.* □ *Spilling water on the computer will hurt it.*
- **harm** to *hurt* someone or something severely. □ *The kidnaper threatened to harm the children.* □ *Looking at the sun can really harm your eyes.*
- **injure** to *hurt* someone or something. (Formal.) □ *Tim's shoulder was injured in a skiing accident.* □ *The ugly rumor injured Jan's reputation.*

• **wound**   to *hurt* a living thing by cutting. ☐ *The explosion wounded several soldiers.* ☐ *Three people were wounded in the car crash.* [→see also: *damage*]

hurt²   (*verb*) to cause pain; to be painful. ☐ *My stomach hurts.* ☐ *The doctor couldn't tell why Bill's fingers were hurting.*
   • **ache**   to *hurt* steadily. ☐ *My wrist won't stop aching; I think I sprained it.* ☐ *Art's heart ached for love of Mary.*
   • **pain**   to *hurt* sharply; to cause someone or something to suffer. (Poetic.) ☐ *Our hero's wound pained him, but he kept on his way.* ☐ *Carrie was pained by Donald's rude remarks.*
   • **throb**   to *hurt* in regular bursts. ☐ *Eddie's head throbbed.* ☐ *After her first day as a waitress, Fran's feet throbbed.*

hurtle   See the entry for *speed*.

hush-hush   See the entry for *private*.

hushed   See the entry for *quiet*.

hut   See the entry for *shack*.

hypnotized   See the entry for *fascinated*.

hypocritical   (*adjective*) not sincere; saying one thing and doing another. ☐ *George is so hypocritical; he gave Helen a lecture about how she should give to charity, but he never gives to charity himself.* ☐ *Jimmy told his mom that it was hypocritical of her to scream, "Don't scream at your sister!"*
   • **double-dealing**   pretending to think or do one thing and really thinking or doing another. ☐ *The double-dealing spy sold his country's secrets to the enemy.* ☐ *Kay caught her double-dealing boyfriend going out with another girl.*
   • **duplicitous**   pretending to think one thing and really thinking another. (Formal.) ☐ *The duplicitous man fooled us into thinking he was on our side.* ☐ *The newspaper reporter used duplicitous means to get an interview with the mayor: he pretended to admire what she had done.*
   • **insincere**   saying what you do not mean. ☐ *"I'm so sorry you can't come to my party," Larry said in an insincere voice.* ☐ *Mark is so insincere that you can't trust anything he says.*
   • **two-faced**   *hypocritical;* pretending to be one way when you are with one person, and being the opposite when you are with someone else. ☐ *The two-faced girl acted friendly to Nancy, but cut her down behind her back.* ☐ *I would never have believed Tom could be so two-faced, until I heard him talking to someone when he didn't think I could hear.*

I

icy (*adjective*) covered with ice; full of ice; as cold as ice. □ *Walk carefully; the sidewalk is icy.* □ *As Philip walked down the hot sidewalk, he yearned for an icy glass of water.*
   • **frigid** as cold as ice. (Formal.) □ *The explorers had to cope with the frigid Antarctic weather.* □ *Rita gave me a frigid smile, so I knew she was angry with me.*
   • **frosty** covered with ice or frost; very cold. □ *The windowpanes were frosty when I got up in the morning.* □ *We went to the ice cream shop for thick, frosty milkshakes.*
   • **glacial** completely covered with ice; as cold as ice. (Formal.) □ *The morning after the blizzard, I looked out over the glacial landscape.* □ *Susan was not prepared for the glacial temperatures in Minnesota in the winter.*

idea (*noun*) a thought or picture in your mind. □ *I have an idea about what to get Tim for his birthday.* □ *Jan read about some of the great philosopher's ideas.*
   • **belief** an *idea* that you feel is true. □ *It was Bill's firm belief that UFOs were visitors from other planets.* □ *Art wanted to learn more about Muslim beliefs.*
   • **concept** an *idea* about the way something is. □ *The ancient Greeks are credited with inventing the concept of democracy.* □ *Ben grew up in the tropics and had no concept of what snow must be like.*
   • **notion** a vague *idea*. □ *Grandpa has such old-fashioned notions about dating.* □ *Do you have any notion of how worried you've made me?*
   • **theory** a carefully formed *idea*. □ *There are several different theories about why the dinosaurs became extinct.* □ *The psychologist wanted to test his theory about how the mind works.*

• **thought**   an *idea;* something you think. ☐ *Carrie sat by herself, thinking sad thoughts.* ☐ *I just had an alarming thought: what if I left the oven on at home and the house burns down while I'm out?*

idiot   See the entry for *fool¹*.

idiotic   See the entry for *silly*.

idle   See the entry for *lazy*.

ignominy   See the entry for *disgrace*.

ignore   (*verb*) to pay no attention to something. ☐ *Mother told me to ignore the boys who teased me.* ☐ *Donald somehow managed to ignore the loud music from the apartment below.*
   • **disregard**   to *ignore* something on purpose. (Formal.) ☐ *Please disregard the letter I sent you earlier.* ☐ *Great danger will befall you if you disregard my warning.*
   • **neglect**   to hurt something by *ignoring* it; to not do something. ☐ *Eddie neglected his pet guinea pig so much that it almost starved to death.* ☐ *Fran neglected to brush her hair this morning.*
   • **overlook**   to *ignore* something, particularly without really meaning to. ☐ *Somehow, I overlooked the note Dad had left for me.* ☐ *George overlooked the trash can in the kitchen when he took out the garbage.*
   • **pass over**   to *ignore* someone when it is his or her turn. ☐ *The teacher passed right over Helen when she was giving our papers back.* ☐ *Not one child was passed over when Aunt Irene gave out gifts.*

illness   See the entry for *sickness*.

illogical   See the entry for *irrational*.

illuminate   See the entry for *explain*.

illusion   (*noun*) something you see or believe that does not really exist. ☐ *I thought I saw a face outside my window, but Dad convinced me that it was just an illusion.* ☐ *By typing steadily, Jay created the illusion that he was working hard.*
   • **delusion**   something you strongly believe that is not true. ☐ *Kay suffers under the delusion that someone is always following her.* ☐ *Larry had delusions that his brother was trying to kill him.*
   • **fantasy**   something you imagine that does not really exist; a dream. ☐ *Mark cherished a fantasy that he would someday be famous and could come back to his hometown and make everyone jealous.* ☐ *Nancy spent the afternoon indulging in fantasies of how she would spend a million dollars.*
   • **hallucination**   something you imagine that you see or hear. (Formal.) ☐ *Sue experienced a hallucination in which strange, fiery*

creatures danced at the edges of her vision. □ *The patient's hallucinations included voices that told him to break windows.*

• **phantasm**   an *illusion;* something that you imagine. □ *Philip insisted that the ghost we saw was unreal, a phantasm.* □ *Rita shook her head, and the spinning pinwheels of light disappeared, like the phantasms they were.*

• **vision**   something you see, imagine, or dream. □ *In the middle of the night, Susan had a vision of her dead grandmother.* □ *The children saw a vision of the Virgin Mary.*

image   See the entry for *looks.*

imagine   (*verb*) to form a picture of something in your mind. □ *Tim imagined what the characters in the book looked like.* □ *I imagine that Jan is feeling pretty sad.*

• **conceive**   to *imagine* something you have never seen or experienced. (Sometimes with *of.*) □ *The artist conceived what the space station would look like and drew a picture of it.* □ *Bill could not conceive of how much it cost to build a house.*

• **envision**   to *imagine* how something looks when you have never seen it. □ *Art envisioned the room as it would look when he was finished decorating it.* □ *Ben tried to envision what the land had looked like before people settled on it.*

• **fancy**   to *imagine* that something is true. □ *I fancied I heard a voice in the howling wind.* □ *Carrie fancies herself the best swimmer in class.*

• **picture**   to *imagine* how something looks. (See also the main entry for *picture.*) □ *The old photographs helped Donald picture his great-grandparents.* □ *It's been so long since I lived in that house that I can hardly picture it anymore.*

• **think of**   to *imagine* something; to keep something in your mind. □ *Eddie thought of a new weird beast to include in the comic book he was drawing.* □ *Fran couldn't stop thinking of that day at the beach.*

imbecile   See the entry for *fool¹.*

imbibe   See the entry for *drink.*

imitate   See the entry for *copy¹.*

immaculate   See the entry for *clean¹.*

immediate   See the entry for *sudden.*

immediately   (*adverb*) extremely quickly; at the same moment. □ *When the teacher came into the room, the students stopped laughing immediately.* □ *When the doctor heard my symptoms, he said I should get to the hospital immediately.*

• **instantaneously**   right at the same moment. (Formal.) □ *The math whiz glanced at the problem and knew the answer instantaneously.*

□ *Little rainbows appeared instantaneously when the light struck the prism.*
• **instantly**   extremely quickly. □ *George memorized the map instantly.* □ *The baby saw his mother and instantly stopped crying.*
• **promptly**   quite quickly; right on time. □ *Helen arrived promptly for her first day on the job.* □ *Irene answered all her letters promptly.*
• **right away**   very quickly; very soon; at the same moment. (Informal.) □ *Come home right away; something terrible has happened.* □ *The waiter came to my table and took my order right away.*

immense   See the entry for *big*.

immerse   See the entry for *submerge*.

impartial   See the entry for *unbiased*.

impeccable   See the entry for *perfect*.

impede   See the entry for *block*.

impel   See the entry for *make²*.

imperative   See the entry for *urgent*.

imperceptible   See the entry for *invisible*.

imperfection   See the entry for *flaw*.

impersonal   See the entry for *removed*.

impersonate   See the entry for *pose*.

impetuous   (*adjective*) acting without thinking first. (Formal.) □ *The impetuous young man suddenly quit his job and set out for Alaska.* □ *Jay's decision to marry Kay seemed rather impetuous.*
• **fiery**   easily excited; reacting violently. □ *No one wanted to anger the fiery sheriff.* □ *Laura's fiery temper blazed up and she began screaming at me.*
• **high-strung**   very nervous; quick to react without thinking first. □ *I'm afraid of what Mark will do when he gets the bad news; he's so high-strung.* □ *The high-strung animal jumped at any sudden noise.*
• **hotheaded**   angry or passionate and quick to do things without thinking. □ *The hotheaded boy tended to punch first and ask questions later.* □ *Tom is quite hotheaded and has to work to control his temper.*
• **volatile**   unpredictable; changing quickly. (Formal.) □ *The volatile situation between the two countries may lead to war.* □ *We felt uneasy around Dad because he was so volatile.*

impetus   See the entry for *reason*.

implausible   See the entry for *improbable*.

implore See the entry for *beg.*

imply See the entry for *suggest.*

impolite See the entry for *rude.*

importance See the entry for *status.*

important (*adjective*) making a big difference; having a lot of influence. □ *The signing of the Declaration of Independence was an important event in American history.* □ *The mayor is an important person in our town.*
  • **major** great and *important.* □ *Whether or not to go to college was a major decision in Sue's life.* □ *Charles Dickens was a major writer in the nineteenth century.*
  • **momentous** very *important.* (Formal.) □ *The birth of his first child was a momentous event for Philip.* □ *The demolition of the Berlin Wall symbolized the momentous changes that were taking place in Europe.*
  • **significant** *important;* very meaningful. □ *Religion is a significant part of Rita's life.* □ *"I'm going out for a walk now," Susan said, giving me a significant wink.*
  • **substantial** large or weighty and *important.* (Formal.) □ *The new job will mean substantial differences in my way of life.* □ *The professor is a substantial scholar in her field.*

importunate See the entry for *insistent.*

imposing See the entry for *grand.*

impoverished See the entry for *poor¹.*

impression See the entries for *dent, feeling.*

impressive See the entry for *awesome.*

improbable (*adjective*) probably not real; not likely. □ *Susan gave an improbable account of what had happened to her homework paper.* □ *It seems improbable that Tim has lost his way.*
  • **farfetched** *improbable* and absurd. □ *Jan's explanation seemed rather farfetched.* □ *Bill told some farfetched story about being bitten by a vicious cow.*
  • **implausible** *improbable;* hard to believe. (Formal.) □ *The plot of the movie seemed very implausible.* □ *Bill's theory about UFOs is downright implausible.*
  • **preposterous** *improbable* and very absurd. (Informal.) □ *Do you expect me to believe that preposterous story?* □ *Art told a bunch of preposterous lies.*
  • **unlikely** *improbable;* not likely to happen or exist. □ *Ben is afraid he'll flunk the test, but I think that's unlikely.* □ *Carrie is an unlikely person to run for office.*

improve   (*verb*) to raise the quality of something. □ *Donald took night-school courses to improve his chances of getting a good job.* □ *A fresh coat of paint improved the house's appearance tremendously.*

　• **better**   to *improve* something; to make something better. □ *Eddie bettered his physical condition through exercise and a healthful diet.* □ *Fran constantly strove to better herself.*

　• **enhance**   to *improve* something by adding to it. (Formal.) □ *Gina used makeup to enhance her natural coloring.* □ *The cook added a little salt to enhance the flavor.*

　• **upgrade**   to *improve* something by one step. □ *Helen wanted to upgrade her computer system.* □ *The school upgraded their textbooks every year, always buying the newest editions.*

impudent   See the entry for *insolent*.

impulse   See the entry for *whim*.

in   See the entry for *popular*.

in a coma   See the entry for *unconscious*.

in a trance   See the entry for *unconscious*.

in-depth   See the entry for *thorough*.

in vogue   See the entry for *stylish*.

inadequate   See the entries for *meager, poor*².

inane   See the entry for *silly*.

inaugurate   See the entry for *launch*.

incapacitate   See the entry for *weaken*.

incensed   See the entry for *angry*.

incessant   See the entry for *constant*.

incident   See the entry for *event*.

incise   See the entry for *carve*.

inclination   See the entry for *tendency*.

incline toward   See the entry for *prefer*.

income   See the entry for *pay*.

inconsequential   See the entry for *unimportant*.

inconstant   See the entry for *fickle*.

incontrovertible   See the entry for *conclusive*.

increase   See the entry for *expand.*

incredible   (*adjective*) hard to believe; too good to believe. □ *What an incredible story!* □ *I got an incredible bargain at the flea market.*
- **fabulous**   incredible and surprising; too good to believe. □ *Irene had a fabulous vacation.* □ *The food at that restaurant is simply fabulous.*
- **fantastic**   incredible; too good to be real. □ *The special effects in that movie were fantastic.* □ *Jay did a fantastic job of decorating the birthday cake.*
- **marvelous**   incredible and awe-inspiring. □ *There's a marvelous view from this window.* □ *Kay is a marvelous singer.*
- **unbelievable**   hard to believe. □ *My neighbor put out an unbelievable light display for the holidays.* □ *Cleaning the house required an unbelievable amount of work.*
- **wonderful**   incredible; very good. □ *Thanks for inviting me over; I had a wonderful time.* □ *Larry turned out to be a wonderful dancer.*

incremental   See the entry for *gradual.*

indefatigable   See the entry for *tireless.*

indentation . See the entry for *dent.*

independence   See the entry for *freedom.*

independent   (*adjective*) not under anyone else's control; ruling yourself. □ *The little country fought to be independent.* □ *Mark is an independent person.*
- **autonomous**   independent; acting alone. (Formal.) □ *You can't control your friends; they are autonomous people.* □ *The region wanted to remain autonomous, not to be ruled by the neighboring country.*
- **free**   independent; not under anyone else's control. □ *Nancy rejoiced to be free from her unhappy marriage.* □ *The colonies declared themselves free.*
- **self-governing**   ruling yourself. □ *Each state is self-governing in some respects.* □ *Indian reservations are self-governing areas within the United States.*
- **sovereign**   independent; having the right to rule yourself. (Formal.) □ *The Soviet Union split up into several sovereign nations.* □ *Each sovereign state has the right to make its own laws.*

indicate   See the entries for *show³, suggest.*

indication   See the entry for *sign.*

indifferent   (*adjective*) not caring one way or the other. (Formal.) □ *I asked Sue which dress she preferred; she was indifferent.* □ *The judge seemed indifferent to the prisoner's pleas for mercy.*

• **apathetic** not having any feelings one way or the other. (Formal.) □ *Philip is very apathetic when it comes to politics.* □ *When asked what he wanted to do on Saturday, Roger gave an apathetic shrug.*

• **lukewarm** not caring very much; not very interested. □ *Susan was lukewarm about the idea of having a party.* □ *The participants in the game gave a lukewarm show of enthusiasm.*

• **nonchalant** casual; not caring one way or the other. □ *Tim may act nonchalant, but I know he'll die if he doesn't get that prize.* □ *I was impressed by the tightrope-walker's nonchalant air.*

• **uncaring** not caring; heartless. □ *It's no use asking for charity from such an uncaring person.* □ *The uncaring teacher did nothing to help the students learn.*

• **uninterested** not caring; not having any interest. □ *Jan was uninterested in the TV show the rest of us were watching.* □ *Bill flipped through the book with an uninterested expression.*

indignant (*adjective*) angered by something you think is wrong. (Formal.) □ *Art was indignant at the salesclerk's rudeness.* □ *I tried to apologize, but Ben turned away with an indignant snort.*

• **huffy** displaying that you are *indignant;* offended. (Informal.) □ *Don't get huffy with me; I'll get to you when it's your turn.* □ *Carrie started acting huffy when the police officer asked to see her identification.*

• **piqued** sharply *indignant.* □ *Donna has failed to do her chores again, and I'm getting seriously piqued with her.* □ *Answering so many calls for Eddie made Fran feel piqued.*

• **provoked** *indignant* and annoyed. □ *The cat, provoked by George's teasing, lashed out with her claws.* ▣ *I am provoked with Helen; she hasn't answered any of my letters.*

[→see also: *angry*]

indigo See the entry for *blue.*

indispensable See the entry for *necessary.*

indistinct See the entry for *faint.*

indistinguishable See the entry for *invisible.*

individual See the entries for *person, personal.*

indolent See the entry for *lazy.*

induce See the entry for *cause.*

indulge See the entry for *spoil¹.*

inept See the entry for *clumsy.*

inexpensive See the entry for *cheap.*

inexplicable   See the entry for *mysterious*.

infectious   See the entry for *catching*.

infer   See the entry for *conclude*.

inferior   See the entry for *poor²*.

inflamed   See the entry for *sore*.

inflate   (*verb*) to fill something with air or any other gas. □ *Irene inflated the balloon with helium.* □ *The child inflated his lungs and then let out a tremendous yell.*
> • **bloat**   to fill something with air or fluid; to puff something up. □ *All the fluids Jay had to drink made him bloat up.* □ *Kay's stomach bloated after she ate the green peppers.*
> • **blow up**   to *inflate*. (Informal.) □ *Laura blew up balloons for the children.* □ *Mark needed a pump to blow up his bicycle tire.*
> • **distend**   to *inflate* something so much it stretches; to swell up and stretch. (Formal.) □ *The disease distended Fred's abdomen.* □ *The goldfish ate until their stomachs distended.*
> [→see also: *expand*]

influence   See the entry for *control²*.

inform   See the entry for *tell*.

information   (*noun*) news or knowledge about something. □ *Sue filled out the job application, giving information about other jobs she had had.* □ *Philip looked in the encyclopedia for information about Venezuela.*
> • **data**   *information*, particularly *information* gathered from a scientific experiment. □ *The scientist stored her data in the computer.* □ *Rita gathered data about how fast the different plants grew.*
> • **facts**   true *information*. □ *The reporter tried to separate the facts from the gossip.* □ *If you think Susan is guilty, then you don't know the facts in her case.*
> • **intelligence**   *information* gathered secretly. □ *The spy was sent to gather intelligence in the foreign country.* □ *Tim got his intelligence about what went on next door by watching his neighbors through his binoculars.*

informed   See the entry for *educated*.

informer   See the entry for *traitor*.

infraction   See the entry for *crime*.

infrequently   See the entry for *seldom*.

infringe on   See the entry for *invade*.

ingenious   See the entry for *creative*.

ingenuous   See the entry for *naive*.

ingest   See the entry for *eat*.

ingredient   See the entry for *element*.

inhabit   See the entry for *live*.

initial   See the entry for *preliminary*.

initiate   See the entries for *begin, launch*.

injure   See the entry for *hurt¹*.

inkling   See the entry for *clue*.

inn   See the entry for *hotel*.

innocent   (*adjective*) not having done anything wrong; not containing any evil; not guilty. (See also the entry for *naive*.) □ *Art protested that he was innocent of any crime.* □ *I watched the children play their innocent games.*
   • **blameless**   utterly *innocent;* not responsible for anything wrong. (Formal.) □ *Ben led a blameless life.* □ *You ought not to punish her; she is blameless.*
   • **clean**   *innocent;* having no record of wrongdoing. (Slang. See also the main entry for *clean¹*.) □ *"I'm clean! Let me go!" Carrie howled as the police officer frisked her.* □ *Donald swore that he had been clean ever since he got out of prison.*
   • **guiltless**   entirely *innocent;* never having done something. (Poetic.) □ *Our hero had to prove that he was guiltless of this foul murder.* □ *Eddie was guiltless of any knowledge of the conspiracy.*
   • **unoffending**   *innocent* and not bothering anyone. □ *The police arrested everyone in the house, including several unoffending neighbors.* □ *How could anyone carry on so about these poor, unoffending children?*
   [→contrasting word: *guilty*]

innocuous   See the entry for *harmless*.

innovative   See the entry for *new*.

inoffensive   See the entry for *harmless*.

inquire   See the entry for *ask*.

inquiring   See the entry for *curious*.

inquisitive   See the entry for *curious*.

insane   See the entry for *crazy*.

inscribe   See the entry for *write*.

insect (*noun*) a small invertebrate animal, usually with six legs. □ *All kinds of insects clustered around the porch light.* □ *Entomologists study insects.*
> • **bug** an *insect.* (Slang.) □ *We walked down to the lake, swatting at the bugs that tried to bite us.* □ *There's a weird-looking bug crawling up the bathroom wall.*
> • **mite** a very small *insect.* □ *The bedclothes were infested with tiny, biting mites.* □ *The dog's fur was crawling with mites.*
> • **pest** a bothersome or harmful *insect;* any small, bothersome animal. □ *This insecticide is guaranteed to kill most garden pests.* □ *The farmer kept a cat to kill pests.*

insensible See the entry for *unconscious.*

insignificant See the entry for *unimportant.*

insincere See the entry for *hypocritical.*

insinuate See the entries for *refer to, suggest.*

insipid See the entry for *mild¹.*

insist See the entry for *demand.*

insistent (*adjective*) asking for or demanding something over and over. □ *Fran was insistent that I should come over and look at the leak in her ceiling.* □ *I could not ignore the insistent knocking at my door.*
> • **importunate** pleading for something over and over in an annoy-ing way. (Formal.) □ *The importunate job candidate called George every day, begging for an interview.* □ *The student's importunate whining did not convince the teacher to change her grade.*
> • **persistent** doing something over and over; not stopping. (See also the main entry for *persistent.*) □ *Helen made persistent attempts to get Irene's attention.* □ *The reporter's persistent questions annoyed the mayor.*
> • **reiterative** doing something over and over; repeating. (Formal.) □ *Jay made reiterative requests for a refund.* □ *Someone knocked on Kay's door, despite her reiterative orders that no one should disturb her.*
> • **tenacious** doing or trying something over and over; not giving up; not letting go. (Formal.) □ *Vincent was tenacious in his quest for fame.* □ *The tenacious puppy held fast to the slipper, no matter how hard I tugged at it.*

insolent (*adjective*) deliberately rude to someone in authority. □ *Larry was sent to the principal's office for his insolent remarks to the teacher.* □ *Dad spanked me for being insolent.*
> • **disrespectful** insolent; not showing respect. □ *It is considered disrespectful to hang the flag upside down.* □ *The disrespectful child told his grandfather to shut up.*

• **fresh**   *insolent.* (Slang.) ☐ *"Do it yourself," was Mark's fresh reply to his father's request.* ☐ *Don't be fresh with me, young lady!*
• **impudent**   mockingly *insolent.* (Formal.) ☐ *The impudent girl thumbed her nose right in the teacher's face.* ☐ *With an impudent grin, Nancy asked me if I had a good time on my date.*
• **irreverent**   *insolent* toward religion or other serious things. (Formal.) ☐ *The atheist made an irreverent remark about the Bible.* ☐ *Tom was shocked by the comic's irreverent jokes about the president.*
[→see also: *rude*]

inspect   See the entry for *check.*

inspire   See the entry for *cause.*

instance   See the entry for *example.*

instantaneously   See the entry for *immediately.*

instantly   See the entry for *immediately.*

instinctive   See the entry for *automatic¹.*

institute   See the entries for *launch, school.*

institution   See the entry for *custom.*

instruct   See the entry for *teach.*

instrumentalist   See the entry for *musician.*

intellect   See the entry for *mind.*

intelligence   See the entry for *information.*

intelligent   See the entry for *smart¹.*

intend   See the entry for *mean².*

intense   See the entry for *sharp.*

intensive   See the entry for *thorough.*

intent   See the entry for *absorbed.*

intention   See the entry for *reason.*

intercede   See the entry for *intervene.*

interest   See the entry for *attention.*

interesting   *(adjective)* holding your attention. ☐ *There's a very interesting program on TV tonight.* ☐ *The lecture was interesting; I learned a lot.*
• **absorbing**   deeply, powerfully *interesting.* ☐ *Philip found the video game completely absorbing.* ☐ *To Rita, nothing was so absorbing as gossiping about her friends.*

• **engaging**   delightfully *interesting*. □ *The play was an engaging little comedy.* □ *Susan can be very engaging when she puts her mind to it.*
• **fascinating**   *interesting* and attractive. □ *I think stamp collecting is boring, but it's fascinating to Tim.* □ *Sue and Bill had a fascinating conversation about movies.*
[→contrasting word: *boring*]

interfere   See the entry for *meddle*.

intermittent   See the entry for *sporadic*.

interpose   See the entry for *intervene*.

interpret   See the entry for *figure out*.

interrogate   See the entry for *ask*.

intervene   (*verb*) to come between people or groups who are fighting. (Formal. Usually with *in.*) □ *I never intervene in my brothers' fights.* □ *Some people thought that the United States should intervene in the war.*
• **intercede**   to negotiate between people or groups who are fighting; to *intervene* on someone's behalf. (Formal. Often with *for.*) □ *Seeing that the students were ready to come to blows over their disagreement, the teacher interceded.* □ *Dad won't listen to my side of things unless Mom intercedes for me.*
• **interpose**   to come between or put something between two things. (Formal.) □ *Art interposed a rake between the two quarreling cats.* □ *The stone blocks fitted together so precisely that one could not interpose a thin knife blade between them.*
• **step in**   to go into the middle of a fight or discussion. □ *Do you mind if I step into the debate here?* □ *Ben decided that the fight had gone on long enough and it was time for him to step in.*
[→see also: *bargain, mediate*]

interview   See the entry for *talk¹*.

intimate   See the entry for *suggest*.

intimidate   See the entry for *threaten*.

intimidating   See the entry for *awesome*.

intone   See the entry for *chant*.

intrepid   See the entry for *courageous*.

intricate   See the entry for *complicated*.

intrigued   See the entry for *fascinated*.

introduce   See the entry for *bring up¹*.

introductory   See the entry for *preliminary*.

intuit   See the entry for *feel.*

intuition   See the entry for *hunch.*

inundate   See the entry for *flood.*

invade   (*verb*) to go into someone else's territory and take it over. □ *The Allies invaded France on D-Day.* □ *Hundreds of thousands of tourists invaded the seaside resort.*

   • **encroach upon**   to go just over the border into someone else's territory; to go past the usual limit. (Formal.) □ *The guerrillas further encroached upon government territory.* □ *Carrie never allowed her sister to encroach upon her half of the bedroom.*

   • **infringe on**   to go just over the border into someone else's territory; to ignore someone's rights. □ *My neighbor has infringed upon my yard by planting that flower bed there.* □ *The smoker felt that "no smoking" areas infringed on his freedom.*

   • **raid**   to go briefly into someone else's territory and take things. □ *The fugitive lived by hiding in the woods all day and raiding neighboring farms by night.* □ *The police raided the house, looking for illegal drugs.*

   • **trespass upon**   to go into someone else's territory. □ *Donald threatened to send an attack dog after anyone who trespassed upon his property.* □ *The star hated the way the reporters trespassed upon his privacy.*

inventive   See the entry for *creative.*

invest in   See the entry for *buy.*

investigate   See the entry for *explore.*

invigorate   See the entry for *revive.*

invisible   (*adjective*) not able to be seen. □ *The model airplanes hung from the ceiling by invisible threads.* □ *Carbon monoxide is an invisible, poisonous gas.*

   • **imperceptible**   not able to be seen, felt, or heard. (Formal.) □ *Eddie gave me an almost imperceptible nod.* □ *The problem was caused by an imperceptible hole in the water pipe.*

   • **indistinguishable**   too small to be seen; not able to be sensed; not able to be distinguished from something else. (Formal.) □ *Fran pointed to an indistinguishable spot on her painting and said, "The picture is ruined!"* □ *Now I know why this diamond ring was so cheap; the diamond is practically indistinguishable!*

   • **unseen**   not seen; not able to be seen. □ *Music came from some unseen source.* □ *George believes that unseen powers guide his life.*

involuntary   See the entry for *automatic¹.*

involved   See the entry for *complicated.*

invulnerable   See the entry for *safe.*

iota   See the entry for *whit.*

irate   See the entry for *angry.*

irk   See the entry for *annoy.*

irons   See the entry for *bonds.*

irony   (*noun*) saying or writing one thing to mean the opposite. □ *"Vincent is such a terrific writer," Helen said with heavy irony.* □ *I detected a certain irony in Irene's voice as she complimented me on my new outfit.*
> • **parody**   a humorous or mocking imitation of something. □ *The movie used parody to point out the faults of modern education.* □ *Jay gave a cruel parody of Kay's limp.*
> • **sarcasm**   using *irony* to hurt someone. □ *"I'm having a wonderful time," Laura said with obvious sarcasm.* □ *Mark's sarcasm hurt my feelings.*
> • **satire**   using *irony* in a sharp way; a piece of sharp mockery. □ *The political comedian used a lot of satire to poke fun at the current administration.* □ *The book is a satire of romance novels.*

irrational   (*adjective*) not making sense; not reasonable. (Formal.) □ *Tom became irrational, insisting that wristwatches gave off mind-control beams.* □ *Sue has an irrational belief in carrot juice as a cure for every ill.*
> • **illogical**   not making sense; not reasonably following from what you already know. (Formal.) □ *Philip's argument was illogical and convinced no one.* □ *Because Rita knew that old photographs were all in black and white, she came to the illogical conclusion that all black and white photographs must be old.*
> • **unreasonable**   not reasonable. □ *Susan is being unreasonable, refusing to listen to anything I say.* □ *The employees grew tired of the boss's unreasonable demands.*
> • **unsound**   not following from what you already know; not reasonable; not stable. □ *The teacher criticized the unsound reasoning in my essay.* □ *The doctors concluded that Philip was unsound in his mind.*

irresponsible   See the entry for *careless.*

irreverent   See the entry for *insolent.*

irritable   See the entry for *grumpy.*

irritate   See the entry for *annoy.*

issue   See the entries for *come out, descendants, distribute.*

item   See the entry for *thing.*

J

jab See the entry for *poke*.

jagged See the entry for *rough²*.

jam See the entry for *pack*.

jar See the entry for *shake*.

jaunty (*adjective*) showing happiness, energy, and style. □ *Tim swung his backpack over his shoulder in a jaunty way.* □ *Jan tilted her hat at a jaunty angle.*

  • **buoyant** happy and energetic. □ *Bill was in a buoyant mood.* □ *Nothing could depress Art's buoyant spirits.*

  • **debonair** energetic, stylish, and charming. □ *Ben is a debonair young man.* □ *The star gave the crowd a debonair wave and a smile.*

  • **sprightly** happy, lively, and quick. □ *The sprightly girl was always eager to try new amusements.* □ *The novel is written in a pleasant, sprightly style.*

jealous (*adjective*) not wanting anyone else to have what you think should be yours. □ *The jealous man never let his girlfriend out of his sight.* □ *Carrie was jealous of the other good writers in the class.*

  • **envious** wanting what someone else has. □ *People looked at Donald's new car with envious eyes.* □ *I'm envious of anyone with that much talent.*

  • **green-eyed** jealous; very much wanting what someone else has. (Slang.) □ *Eddie flaunted his leather jacket in front of his friends and watched them grow green-eyed.* □ *I felt a trifle green-eyed when I saw Fran's lovely apartment.*

  • **monopolizing** keeping someone or something to yourself. □ *George was a monopolizing speaker who never let other people get a word in edgewise.* □ *Helen was utterly monopolizing of her new stereo.*

• **possessive**   not letting anyone else enjoy what you have. ☐ *Irene's possessive boyfriend doesn't want her to talk to other men.* ☐ *Jay is possessive of his books and won't loan them out.*
[→see also: *greedy*]

jerk   See the entry for *tug*.

jettison   See the entry for *shed*.

jewel   (*noun*) a very valuable stone, such as a diamond, sapphire, or ruby. ☐ *The crown was set with many rare jewels.* ☐ *Emeralds were Kay's favorite jewels.*
   • **bauble**   a small, unimportant *jewel* or piece of jewelry. ☐ *The princess had a little gold bauble to play with.* ☐ *Laura was fond of her costume-jewelry baubles.*
   • **bijou**   a *jewel* set in a fine piece of jewelry. (Formal. The plural is *bijoux*.) ☐ *I was dazzled by Mary's diamond bijoux.* ☐ *Tom brought his wife a pretty bijou for her birthday.*
   • **gem**   a *jewel* that has been cut or polished. ☐ *The ring was set with a single gem.* ☐ *The lady was decked out in all kinds of glittering gems.*
   • **precious stone**   any *jewel*. ☐ *The hills were mined for precious stones.* ☐ *The natural history museum has an interesting collection of precious stones.*

jiggle   See the entry for *shake*.

jingle   See the entry for *chime*.

jittery   See the entry for *nervous*.

job   (*noun*) a piece of work. (See also the entry for *profession*.) ☐ *Let me finish this job in the kitchen, and I'll come help you.* ☐ *Cutting down this tree is going to be a big job.*
   • **chore**   a small, routine *job*; a tedious *job*. ☐ *The children could not go out to play until they finished their chores.* ☐ *Cleaning the bathroom can be quite a chore.*
   • **errand**   a *job* that involves having to go somewhere. ☐ *Sue went out on an errand to the post office.* ☐ *Philip drove around running errands all afternoon.*
   • **project**   a *job* that requires special planning and usually takes a long time to complete. ☐ *Rita's latest project is building a model airplane.* ☐ *Students worked on their history projects in teams.*
   • **task**   a difficult *job*; a piece of work. ☐ *The secretary often had to perform several tasks at once.* ☐ *Mom assigned me the task of cutting up the onions.*

jog   See the entry for *run*.

join   (*verb*) to put two things together so that they work as one. □ *Susan joined the chair legs to the seat.* □ *A coupling joined the railroad cars together.*
- **attach**   to *join* things, using some kind of fastener. □ *The flight attendant attached my plane ticket to my boarding card.* □ *Tim's mittens were attached to the sleeves of his coat.*
- **connect**   to *join* things loosely; to *join* together ideas in your mind. □ *Only a few threads still connected the sleeve to the shirt.* □ *I didn't connect the name in the paper with my friend.*
- **link**   to *join* things together; to *join* things together like links in a chain. □ *The friends linked arms and strode down the sidewalk.* □ *The new train line will link the city with its suburbs.*
[→contrasting words: *separate, disconnect*]

join forces   See the entry for *team up.*

join in   See the entry for *participate.*

joke   (*noun*) something said or done to make you laugh. □ *Tim told a funny joke.* □ *Jan played a practical joke on her brother.*
- **crack**   a short, mean *joke.* (Slang.) □ *Stop making cracks about Bill's cross-eye.* □ *What did you mean by that crack?*
- **gag**   a *joke;* especially, a practical *joke.* (Slang.) □ *Art thought that balancing a bucket of water over the door was a great gag.* □ *This book is full of fun gags to play on your friends.*
- **quip**   a short, very appropriate *joke.* □ *Ben, the class clown, can't resist making quips in response to everything the teacher says.* □ *I said it was raining cats and dogs; Carrie responded with some quip about being careful not to step in a poodle.*
- **witticism**   an extremely clever *joke.* (Formal.) □ *Donald made witticisms at other people's expense.* □ *Oscar Wilde was a writer famous for his witticisms.*

josh   See the entry for *tease.*

jot   See the entries for *whit, write.*

jounce   See the entry for *shake.*

journal   See the entry for *periodical.*

journalist   See the entry for *writer.*

journey   (*noun*) traveling from one place to another. □ *Eddie went on a journey back to his old hometown.* □ *The journey across the ocean took seven days.*
- **excursion**   a *journey* for pleasure. (Formal.) □ *Twelve students went on the summer excursion to Europe.* □ *The boat makes six excursions to the island every day.*

• **expedition**   an organized *journey* for a specific purpose. (Formal.) □ *The explorer organized an expedition to the North Pole.* □ *My friends and I made an expedition to the shopping mall.*
• **odyssey**   a very long *journey* to many places. (Formal.) □ *The book describes the author's odyssey through the South.* □ *Our search for just the right picture frame took us on an odyssey to every framing store in town.*
• **tour**   a *journey* to see many different sights; a *journey* to see all the sights in a particular place. □ *The bus took us on a tour of downtown Chicago.* □ *Follow the map in this pamphlet to get a tour of the museum.*
• **trek**   a difficult *journey.* □ *We went on a two-week trek through the mountains.* □ *The hikers saw interesting sights on their trek across the country.*
• **voyage**   a *journey,* usually by water or through air. □ *The adventurers made a balloon voyage across the Atlantic.* □ *The family made the voyage down the river in a houseboat.*

joy   See the entry for *pleasure.*

joyful   See the entry for *happy.*

jubilant   See the entry for *overjoyed.*

Judas   See the entry for *traitor.*

judge   See the entry for *guess.*

juice   See the entry for *electricity.*

juicy   (*adjective*) full of juice. □ *The pears were ripe and juicy.* □ *I gave the dog a nice, juicy piece of meat.*
• **moist**   full of moisture; not dry. □ *We had slices of rich, moist fruitcake for dessert.* □ *Mom dabbed at my face with a moist handkerchief.*
• **pulpy**   fleshy and full of moisture; full of pulp. □ *I mashed up the pulpy insides of the squash.* □ *Fran likes her orange juice to be very pulpy.*
• **succulent**   full of moisture or juice. □ *The fried chicken was crisp outside, tender and succulent inside.* □ *I bit into the succulent peach.*

jumble   See the entry for *hodgepodge.*

jump   (*verb*) to push yourself briefly up into the air. □ *George jumped over the fence.* □ *Helen jumped up and down, shouting, "Hooray!"*
• **bound**   to *jump* along lightly. □ *The deer bounded into the forest.* □ *The dog bounded up to me and put her paws on my chest.*
• **hop**   to *jump* quickly and lightly. □ *The cricket hopped away.* □ *Irene hopped on one foot.*
• **leap**   to *jump* a great distance. □ *The horse leaped across the ditch.* □ *The cat leaped to the top of the refrigerator.*
• **pounce**   to *jump* suddenly onto something. □ *The kitten pounced*

on the spider. □ *The lion lay on a tree branch, waiting to pounce on some unwary animal below.*

• **spring**   to *jump* in a lively way. □ *Jay sprang up from his chair to help me with the bags of groceries.* □ *The racehorses sprang out of the gate.*

• **vault**   to *jump* up high; to *jump* energetically. □ *The athlete vaulted over the bar.* □ *The burglar vaulted out of the window when he saw the family coming home.*

jumpy   See the entry for *nervous*.

jungle   See the entry for *forest*.

junk   See the entry for *trash*.

just   See the entries for *fair, only*.

just about   See the entry for *almost*.

juvenile   See the entry for *child*.

K

keen See the entry for *sharp.*

keep (*verb*) to hold back someone or something. (See also the entry for *preserve.*) ☐ *Why are you so late? What kept you?* ☐ *The teacher kept me after class to discuss my paper.*
  • **delay** to *keep* something from being on time. (See also the main entry for *delay.*) ☐ *Heavy traffic delayed Kay on her way to work.* ☐ *The train's departure was delayed for fifteen minutes.*
  • **detain** to *keep* someone or something from going away. (Formal.) ☐ *The police detained the suspect for questioning.* ☐ *I was detained at the border until my luggage could be inspected.*
  • **hold** to *keep* someone or something by force; to *keep* someone or something until a particular time. ☐ *We held the burglar locked in the bathroom until the police came.* ☐ *The book you requested is being held for you at the library.*
  • **retain** to continue to *keep* someone or something. (Formal.) ☐ *The boss decided to retain Laura as an employee.* ☐ *Please retain the receipt for your purchases.*

keep away from See the entry for *avoid.*

keg See the entry for *barrel.*

kick out See the entry for *dismiss.*

kid See the entry for *child.*

kidnap (*verb*) to capture someone by force. ☐ *The criminals planned to kidnap the mayor's son.* ☐ *Maria was kidnaped and taken to an abandoned house.*
  • **abduct** to *kidnap* someone. (Formal.) ☐ *The wealthy businessman was abducted from his office.* ☐ *The rebels abducted the president's wife.*

• **carry off**   to *kidnap* someone and take him or her away. □ *The evil knight carried off the helpless princess.* □ *The children were carried off and sold as slaves.*

• **spirit away**   to *kidnap* someone stealthily; to take someone or something stealthily away. □ *My prize German shepherd has been spirited away!* □ *Someone managed to spirit the famous painting away from the museum.*

kill   (*verb*) to cause someone or something to die. □ *The fleeing bank robber shot and killed a police officer.* □ *Tom killed flies with his trusty fly swatter.*

• **assassinate**   to *kill* a politically important person. (Formal.) □ *Someone tried to assassinate the governor.* □ *President John Kennedy was assassinated in 1963.*

• **do in**   to *kill* someone. (Slang.) □ *The criminal boss was convinced that his henchmen were planning to do him in.* □ *Tom was a heavy smoker, and lung cancer did him in.*

• **execute**   to *kill* a criminal according to the law. □ *The convicted murderer said he wanted to be executed.* □ *In the French Revolution, many of the nobility were executed at the guillotine.*

• **massacre**   to *kill* many helpless people. □ *The invading army massacred all of the town's inhabitants.* □ *The soldier could not bring himself to massacre women and children.*

• **murder**   to *kill* someone intentionally. □ *The kidnappers murdered their victim.* □ *I was shocked to learn that my neighbor had been murdered.*

• **slaughter**   to *kill* someone cruelly. □ *The housebreaker slaughtered the whole family in order to steal their TV.* □ *The man broke into the restaurant with a gun and slaughtered ten people before killing himself.*

kin   See the entry for *family.*

kind[1]   (*adjective*) pleasant and generous; wanting to make other people comfortable. □ *The kind woman bought the beggar a meal.* □ *I trusted the old man because he looked kind.*

• **caring**   showing a desire to make other people comfortable and happy. □ *Philip sent me a very caring letter when he heard I was ill.* □ *Rita felt lucky to have so many caring friends.*

• **nice**   pleasant, generous, or friendly. (See also the main entry for *nice.*) □ *Mr. Smith may look fierce, but he's really very nice.* □ *It was nice of Tim to bring flowers.*

[→see also: *considerate, friendly, gentle*]

kind[2]   (*noun*) a group of things similar in a particular way. □ *What kind of soft drink do you like best?* □ *A merganser is a kind of duck.*

• **category**   a group of things similar in a specially defined way. □ *The librarian sorted the books into categories, according to their subject matter.* □ *The contest had a special category for young people.*

• **class**   a group of things having a similar rank; a group of people having a similar social rank. (See also the main entry for *class*.) □ *The boxer was the best in his class.* □ *I felt uncomfortable among so many people from the upper classes.*

• **sort**   a group of things similar in some way. (See also the main entry for *sort*.) □ *Mom said that Veronica was not the sort of person I should be making friends with.* □ *That store sells all sorts of reading material, from newspapers to books.*

• **species**   a group of animals similar in a particular way. (Formal.) □ *The diver discovered a new species of jellyfish.* □ *The zoo keeps several different species of finches in the aviary.*

• **type**   a group of things similar in an obvious way. □ *The director was looking for an actor of the tall and muscular type.* □ *What type of movie is it: science fiction, horror, action, romance, or what?*

kindness   See the entry for *favor*.

king   See the entry for *ruler*.

klutzy   See the entry for *clumsy*.

knave   See the entry for *villain*.

knee-jerk   See the entry for *automatic¹*.

knell   See the entry for *ring*.

knock   See the entry for *tap*.

knoll   See the entry for *hill*.

knotty   See the entry for *tricky*.

knowledgeable   See the entry for *educated*.

L

label   (*verb*) to put a symbol on something so that you can identify it. □ *Bill labeled all his clothes with his initials.* □ *The jar was labeled, "Green Tea, Loose."*

  • **brand**   to *label* something by burning a symbol onto it; to *label* something in public in order to show that it is shameful. □ *The rancher branded all his cattle with a lazy Q.* □ *Art's friends stuck by him even after he was branded as a thief.*

  • **earmark**   to *label* something to show that it is special. □ *Ben earmarked the box of toys for shipment to the Children's Hospital.* □ *This money is earmarked for Carrie's school clothes.*

  • **flag**   to *label* something so that it will get attention. (See also the main entry for flag.) □ *Donald flagged the books that he wanted me to read.* □ *Go down this list and flag the names of the people who received awards.*

  • **mark**   to *label* something so that you can tell it apart from others. □ *Eddie marked the vegetarian pot pies with an extra squiggle of dough on top.* □ *Fred's courteous manners marked him as a true gentleman.*

  • **tag**   to *label* something, especially by hanging a small symbol on it. (Informal.) □ *The salesclerk tagged all the hats.* □ *I tagged my cat with the little rabies tag the veterinarian had given me.*

lackadaisical   See the entry for *listless*.

lacking   See the entry for *missing*.

lady   See the entry for *woman*.

lake   (*noun*) a body of water completely surrounded by land. □ *We took a sailboat out on the lake.* □ *Helen went swimming in the lake.*

  • **loch**   a long, narrow *lake*. (Scots dialect.) □ *The dark crags surrounding the loch were an awe-inspiring sight.* □ *The old castle overlooked the mysterious loch.*

• **pond** a small *lake*. □ *An old snapping turtle lives in the pond.* □ *The children went wading in the pond.*

• **pool** a small *lake;* a man-made body of water that people use to swim in; any body of liquid. □ *Be sure to take a shower before going in the pool.* □ *The cats had knocked the jar of molasses off the countertop, and I came home to find a dark, sticky pool of molasses covering the kitchen floor.*

• **reservoir** a man-made *lake,* used to store or collect water. □ *The town gets water from this reservoir.* □ *In the drought, even the reservoir dried up.*

lament See the entries for *be sorry, grieve.*

land (*verb*) to come to rest on the ground after flying in the air or floating on the water. □ *The boat landed at the dock.* □ *The plane landed right on time.*

• **alight** to *land* gently; to come down from any high place. □ *A butterfly alighted on my knee.* □ *The cat alighted from Irene's shoulder.*

• **set down** to *land* after flying in the air. □ *The duck set down on the surface of the water.* □ *A fly set down on my sandwich.*

• **touch down** to *land* carefully and precisely. □ *We waited breathlessly for the space shuttle to touch down.* □ *The pilot touched down so smoothly that the passengers hardly knew they had landed.*

[→see also: *arrive*]

landscape See the entries for *picture, view.*

lane See the entry for *road.*

languid See the entry for *listless.*

languish for See the entry for *miss².*

large See the entry for *big.*

lash See the entry for *whip.*

last (*verb*) to go on through time. (See also the entry for *final.*) □ *I hope Jay's bad mood will not last long.* □ *The totalitarian regime lasted for fifty years.*

• **continue** to go on without stopping. □ *The noise from downstairs continued, despite my knocking on the floor.* □ *I hope Kay will continue to practice her dancing.*

• **endure** to *last;* to go on through time despite hardships. □ *The couple went through hard times, but their marriage endured.* □ *The artist's great works endured after her death.*

• **persist** to remain strong through time; not to give up. □ *Even after Laura reassured me, some doubts persisted in my mind.* □ *Mark persisted in asking stupid questions.*

• **survive**   to live on through time; to live through hardship. □ *I think Vincent's great book is destined to survive.* □ *Nancy's father survived his heart attack.*

lasting   See the entry for *permanent.*

late   *(adjective)* not on time; occurring after the time when it was supposed to. □ *Sue was late to class.* □ *Philip's apology came too late to satisfy me.*
  • **behindhand**   *late.* (Usually used to describe a late payment.) □ *The tenant was behindhand with his rent.* □ *I was so far behindhand with my phone bills that the phone company turned off their service.*
  • **overdue**   *late;* occurring after the appointed time. □ *You must pay a fine if your library book is overdue.* □ *An explanation for Rita's strange behavior is long overdue.*
  • **tardy**   quite *late; late* for a class or an obligation. (Informal.) □ *The boss lectured the tardy employee.* □ *I ran the last block to school, hoping I would not be tardy.*
  [→consider also: *slow*]

lately   *(adverb)* in the time just past. □ *I haven't seen Susan lately.* □ *Lately Tim has been spending a lot of time in the park.*
  • **a short time ago**   a short while in the past. □ *I just read that book a short time ago.* □ *A short time ago, I spoke with Jan for the last time.*
  • **of late**   in the recent past. (Formal.) □ *What has Bill been doing of late?* □ *Art has become very subdued of late.*
  • **recently**   in the recent past; in the time just past. □ *The movie was recently released.* □ *Ben recently moved away.*

lather   See the entries for *foam, sweat.*

laud   See the entry for *praise.*

laugh   *(verb)* to make sounds to show that you are amused or happy. □ *Everyone laughed at Carrie's joke.* □ *Donna thought the other children were laughing at her clothes.*
  • **chortle**   to *laugh* in a snorting, satisfied way. □ *Eddie chortled to himself as he planned his revenge.* □ *Fran chortled and rubbed her hands.*
  • **chuckle**   to *laugh* softly. □ *That comedy show usually makes me chuckle.* □ *The friends chuckled as they reminisced about their youthful pranks.*
  • **giggle**   to *laugh* in a silly way. □ *The children whispered to each other and giggled.* □ *George giggled when Helen tickled him.*
  • **guffaw**   to *laugh* loudly and uncontrollably. □ *The joke made Irene throw her head back and guffaw.* □ *The expression on Jay's face was so funny that I guffawed helplessly.*

• **snicker** to *laugh* through your nose; to *laugh* in a mean way. □ *The kids snickered over the dirty jokes.* □ *The villain snickered as he planted the bomb.*

• **titter** to *laugh* softly in a high voice. □ *The children tittered at the raggedy boy's appearance.* □ *Miss Wilson tittered when the gentleman kissed her hand.*

launch (*verb*) to begin something grandly and publicly. □ *Kay needed money to launch her business.* □ *The company launched the new breakfast cereal with a barrage of TV commercials.*

• **inaugurate** to officially *launch* something important. (Formal.) □ *Public and private parties all across the country inaugurated the New Year.* □ *The nation inaugurated a new president.*

• **initiate** to *launch* something formally; to start something. □ *The club president initiated the meeting by calling for order.* □ *The town officials initiated an inquiry into the mayor's use of town money.*

• **institute** to *launch* something officially; to officially set something up. (Formal.) □ *The government instituted a holiday in honor of Dr. Martin Luther King, Jr.* □ *The teacher instituted a computer class at his school.*

[→see also: *begin*]

launder See the entry for *clean²*.

lavender See the entry for *purple*.

law See the entry for *rule*.

lawn See the entry for *yard*.

lax See the entry for *limp*.

lay See the entry for *put*.

lazy (*adjective*) not wanting to do any work or be active. □ *Larry is lazy and will never amount to anything.* □ *The lazy student never read anything; she asked her friends to summarize everything for her.*

• **idle** doing nothing. □ *Being idle bored Mary.* □ *The dump truck factory stood idle because there were no orders for dump trucks.*

• **indolent** always resting; not liking to work. (Formal.) □ *The indolent young man swung in his hammock all day long.* □ *I spent my vacation being happily indolent.*

• **shiftless** not willing or able to work. □ *The shiftless man refused to look for a job.* □ *Tom has no plans for the future and is altogether shiftless.*

• **slothful** working very slowly and unenthusiastically; *lazy*. □ *Tom is a slothful housekeeper, as you can tell from the gray layer of dust covering everything in his house.* □ *Energetic Philip thought it was a terrible sin to be slothful.*

lead   (*verb*) to control where something is going to go; to show someone else the way. □ *Mrs. Scott led the Girl Scout troop.* □ *The mother duck led her babies down to the water.*
- **direct**   to control what an organization is going to do; to give someone instructions. □ *The chief executive officer directs all company operations.* □ *Rita directed me to take the box up to the attic.*
- **head**   to *lead* a group or organization □ *Susan headed the protest against lengthening the school day.* □ *The detective headed an investigation into the woman's disappearance.*
- **manage**   to make sure that an organization does what it is supposed to. □ *It is Tim's job to manage this entire office.* □ *Victor wants to manage a professional baseball team someday.*

leader   See the entry for *guide¹.*

league   See the entry for *organization.*

leak   (*verb*) for a liquid to go in or out of a crack or a hole. □ *Water was leaking from the pipe.* □ *Oil had leaked out of the bottle.*
- **dribble**   for a small amount of liquid to *leak* out at a time. □ *Milk dribbled out of the baby's mouth.* □ *Motor oil was dribbling onto the pavement.*
- **ooze**   for a thick liquid to *leak* slowly and steadily. □ *Blood oozed from the cut.* □ *The tree oozed sap.*
- **seep**   to *leak* slowly and steadily. □ *Rainwater seeped gradually into the soil.* □ *Poisonous chemicals were seeping from the leaky barrels into the ground.*
- **trickle**   to *leak* slowly. □ *Only a slight amount of water trickled out of the faucet.* □ *The last few drops of soy sauce trickled out of the bottle.*

lean   See the entries for *thin, tilt.*

leaning   See the entry for *tendency.*

leap   See the entry for *jump.*

learn¹   (*verb*) to come to know something. □ *I only learned of Bill's illness yesterday.* □ *Art learned that Ben was looking for him.*
- **ascertain**   to *learn* something after gathering a great deal of information; to make sure of something. (Formal.) □ *The reporter ascertained that the mayor had used public funds to buy a yacht.* □ *Question Carrie and see if you can ascertain what she is planning to do.*
- **determine**   to *learn* or decide something after analyzing information. □ *Once I determined how much a new car would cost, I realized I couldn't afford it.* □ *The jury determined that the defendant was not guilty.*
- **discover**   to *learn* something by looking for information about it. □ *Donald has discovered my secret.* □ *Eddie discovered where Fran was hiding the keys.*

• **find out**   to *learn* something through making an effort. (Informal.) □ *I'm trying to find out what number I should call to talk to my congressman.* □ *I found out something interesting about George.*

learn²   (*verb*) to come to know a fact or have a skill. □ *Helen learned to swim when she was four years old.* □ *Irene wanted to learn how to repair TVs.*

• **acquire**   to *learn* something effortlessly. □ *Children acquire their native language without having to go to school for it.* □ *How did Jay acquire so much knowledge about Renaissance paintings?*

• **assimilate**   to *learn* something very thoroughly; to gather knowledge into your mind. (Formal.) □ *It was hard for Kay to assimilate all the facts about English grammar.* □ *The teacher presented the material at a pace that allowed her students to assimilate it.*

• **master**   to *learn* how to do something extremely well. □ *The young gymnast took weeks to master the aerial cartwheel.* □ *The homework problems helped Larry to master multiplying fractions.*

• **memorize**   to *learn* something so well that you will always have it in your memory. □ *The actor memorized his lines.* □ *The teacher made his students memorize the multiplication table up to twenty times twenty.*

• **pick up**   to *learn* something casually. (Informal.) □ *Mark picked up Spanish on his travels in Mexico.* □ *Since Nancy already knew how to roller-skate, it was easy for her to pick up skateboarding.*
[→see also: *read*]

learned   See the entry for *educated*.

lease   See the entry for *rent*.

leave   See the entry for *go*.

leave out   See the entry for *miss¹*.

lecture   See the entries for *class, speech*.

legislative   See the entry for *governmental*.

lend   (*verb*) to let someone use something of yours for a short time. □ *I asked Sue to lend me a dollar.* □ *Philip lent Rita his wristwatch.*

• **advance**   to *lend* someone something, especially money; to give someone something ahead of time. (See also the main entry for *advance*.) □ *Mom was not willing to advance me my allowance.* □ *Can you advance me ten dollars until I get paid?*

• **entrust**   to *lend* someone something important, because you trust him or her to take care of it. (Formal.) □ *The artist entrusted his paintings to the museum.* □ *Susan has entrusted me with her dog while she is on vacation.*

• **permit to borrow**   to *lend;* to let someone take something and use it for a while. □ *Would you permit me to borrow your lawn mower?* □ *The bank only permits people to borrow money on the understanding that they will pay it back with interest.*
[→consider also: *borrow*]

lesson   (*noun*) a session of learning something; something to be learned. □ *Susan has a trombone lesson today at three.* □ *The class spent the morning discussing their history lesson.*
> • **assignment**   a *lesson* that someone gives you to do. □ *The math assignment is due on Thursday.* □ *We were allowed to work in groups on the English assignment.*
> • **drill**   a *lesson* in which you practice something over and over. □ *The soldiers performed a drill with their rifles.* □ *We did arithmetic drills until the teacher was sure we could add and subtract.*
> • **exercise**   a *lesson* that gives practice. (See also the main entry for *exercise*.) □ *The swimming teacher made me do an exercise to improve my flutter kick.* □ *The singer did voice exercises for four hours every day.*

let   See the entry for *allow.*

let go   See the entry for *release.*

lethal   See the entry for *deadly.*

lethargic   See the entry for *listless.*

letter   See the entry for *message.*

level   See the entries for *flat, grade.*

levelheaded   See the entry for *calm.*

levitate   See the entry for *lift.*

liable   See the entry for *likely.*

libel   See the entry for *slander.*

liberal   See the entry for *generous.*

liberate   See the entry for *release.*

liberty   See the entry for *freedom.*

lie[1]   (*noun*) something that is said that is not true. □ *Tim said he was at home all afternoon, but I know that's a lie.* □ *Jan regretted having told a lie.*
> • **fabrication**   an elaborate *lie.* (Formal.) □ *Bill's whole story about where he got the money was a complete fabrication.* □ *The mayor dismissed the ugly rumors about her as fabrications.*

• **falsehood** a *lie;* any untrue statement. (The former is old-fashioned.) □ *How dare you utter such a falsehood, sir!* □ *That statement is a falsehood.*

• **fib** a *lie* about a small matter. □ *Art said he thought Ben's haircut was cool, which was a fib.* □ *The naughty child was always telling fibs.*

• **untruth** a *lie.* (Poetic.) □ *Our hero set out to challenge the villain who had told such a monstrous untruth.* □ *The autobiography was filled with boastful untruths and half-truths.*

lie² (*verb*) to say something that is not true deliberately. □ *The lawyer thought that the witness must be lying.* □ *Carrie lied about her age in order to get the job.*

• **dissemble** to hide the truth by pretending. (Formal.) □ *Donald dissembled his real feelings and put on a great show of being in love with Fran.* □ *Eddie dissembles so well and so often that I never know what he really thinks, or whose side he's really on.*

• **equivocate** to hide the truth by using words that have more than one meaning. (Formal.) □ *Asked if he would release the hostages soon, the terrorist leader equivocated.* □ *The politician grew skilled at equivocating, so that no one could accuse him of going back on his word.*

• **mislead** to make someone believe something that is not true deliberately. □ *When George sold me this bicycle, he misled me into thinking that it needed only minor repairs.* □ *The advertisement misled people by putting all the important information in small print at the bottom.*

• **misspeak** to say something that is not true; to say something you do not mean. □ *Helen must have misspoken when she said she would be coming over tonight.* □ *Did I say that Irene's birthday was July twentieth? I'm sorry; I misspoke. It's June twentieth.*

• **prevaricate** to avoid telling the truth. (Formal.) □ *The teacher asked Jay if he had done his homework; he prevaricated, telling her how difficult things were at home.* □ *Kay never met my eye once as she was speaking, which made me suspect she was prevaricating.*

lie dormant See the entry for *hibernate.*

lie torpid See the entry for *hibernate.*

lift (*verb*) to bring someone or something up higher. □ *The box was too heavy to lift.* □ *A sudden breeze lifted the piece of newspaper into the air.*

• **boost** to *lift* someone or something by giving it a push upwards. □ *Laura boosted me over the wall.* □ *Mark boosted the little girl into the horse's saddle.*

• **elevate** to *lift* someone or something to a higher position. (Formal.) □ *We used a helicopter to elevate the radio antenna to the top of the skyscraper.* □ *The nurse elevated the patient's feet above the level of her head.*

• **hoist**   to *lift* someone or something with a sudden effort. □ *I hoisted the toolbox onto the back of the truck.* □ *The fat man hoisted himself out of the chair.*

• **levitate**   to *lift* something without touching it; to rise up and float in midair. (Formal.) □ *The superhero used his powers to levitate the wreckage, and the trapped people were able to crawl out from underneath.* □ *The coin appeared to levitate above the surface of the table.*

• **raise**   to *lift;* to make something go higher. □ *I raised the lid of the box.* □ *Tom raised his head and looked up.*

light-headed   See the entry for *dizzy.*

lighthearted   See the entry for *cheerful.*

like   (*verb*) to have a friendly feeling for someone; to be pleased by something. □ *I like Sue.* □ *Philip likes to go to the mall on weekends.*

• **appreciate**   to *like* something and think it is good; to recognize the value of something. □ *Rita appreciates good art.* □ *Susan is learning to appreciate fine wines.*

• **be fond of**   to *like* someone or something pretty well. □ *I think Tim is fond of Jan, but I don't think he's in love with her.* □ *Bill is fond of chocolate.*

• **care for**   to *like* someone or something; to prefer someone or something. □ *Art grew to care for Mary.* □ *Would you care for any dessert?*

• **dote on**   to *like* someone excessively. □ *Charlie really dotes on his grandchildren.* □ *Donald's wife dotes on him.*

• **fancy**   to *like* or wish for something. (British.) □ *Do you think Edward fancies the new girl in class?* □ *Felicia fancied fish and chips for her dinner.*

[→see also: *enjoy*]

likely   (*adjective*) expected to happen. □ *It's likely that George will win the contest.* □ *The weatherman said that rain was likely.*

• **apt**   *likely;* tending to happen. (Formal. Usually followed by an infinitive, as in *apt to be difficult.*) □ *Helen is apt to be upset when she learns that we've broken her dish.* □ *The teacher is apt to call on me when she thinks I haven't done the assignment.*

• **liable**   strongly tending to happen. (Usually followed by an infinitive.) □ *If you keep teasing the cat, she's liable to scratch you.* □ *Irene was liable to forget things if she didn't write them down.*

• **probable**   *likely;* quite possibly true. □ *It is probable that the library has the book you need.* □ *The most probable explanation is that Jay forgot to call when he arrived home.*

limit   See the entry for *boundary.*

limp (*adjective*) not firm; soft and flexible. □ *Kay boiled the spaghetti until it was quite limp.* □ *Laura felt very limp when she came out of the steam bath.*

• **droopy** hanging down in a *limp* way. □ *Judging from his droopy eyelids, Mark needs some sleep.* □ *Long, droopy bangs hung in Nancy's eyes.*

• **flabby** not strong and therefore *limp.* (Usually used to describe muscles.) □ *Tom hadn't worked out in so long that he got flabby.* □ *The coach turned the flabby kids into a strong, spirited soccer team.*

• **flimsy** thin and *limp.* □ *The flimsy fabric tore easily.* □ *Philip wrote the letter on a flimsy piece of airmail stationery.*

• **lax** *limp* and loose; not strict. □ *Rita took a deep breath and let her stiff muscles go lax.* □ *The teacher was very lax about enforcing classroom rules.*

• **slack** *limp;* not tense. □ *I stopped pulling on the rope, and it went slack.* □ *The chain hung slack.*

line (*noun*) a group of people or things standing one behind the other or side by side. □ *The children stood in a line.* □ *I had to stand in line for an hour to get the tickets.*

• **file** a *line* of people or things standing one behind the other. (Formal.) □ *A long file of graduates stood to receive their diplomas.* □ *If all the people on earth were to form up in a file, how long do you think would it be?*

• **queue** a *line* of people or things waiting for something. (Primarily British.) □ *There was a long queue outside the post office.* □ *The computer operator brought up the next item in the queue.*

• **rank** a *line* of people or things standing side by side. (Formal.) □ *The soldiers formed up in ranks.* □ *Tim was bewildered by the ranks upon ranks of different brands of coffee at the store.*

• **row** a group of people or things standing side by side. □ *My friends and I picked desks in the same row.* □ *The director placed the dancers in two rows.*

linger See the entry for *wait.*

link See the entry for *join.*

liquefy See the entry for *melt.*

liquid (*adjective*) smoothly flowing; having a consistency like water. □ *The baby takes his aspirin in liquid form.* □ *I was entranced by the dancer's liquid movements.*

• **aqueous** like water; made with water or made of water. (Formal.) □ *Mermaids are rumored to dwell in the aqueous realms of the deep.* □ *Tim put the chemical in an aqueous solution.*

• **fluid**   smoothly flowing. □ *The horse's muscles moved in fluid ripples.* □ *The calligrapher's handwriting had a fluid grace.*

• **molten**   hot and melted and therefore smoothly flowing. □ *Molten rock spewed out of the volcano.* □ *The jeweler poured the molten silver into the mold.*

• **watery**   having the consistency of water; of water. (See also the main entry for *watery*.) □ *The first course was a thin, watery soup.* □ *The sailor was buried in a watery grave.*

list   See the entry for *tilt*.

listen   (*verb*) to attend carefully to a sound. (Usually with *to*.) □ *Jan likes to listen to music.* □ *The children gathered around to listen to the story.*

• **eavesdrop**   to *listen* secretly to a conversation. (Usually with *on*.) □ *Bill put his ear to the wall to eavesdrop on his neighbors.* □ *Art picked up the other phone and eavesdropped on his sister's conversation.*

• **heed**   to *listen* to something; to give attention to something. (Formal.) □ *Our hero heeded the old sorceress's warning.* □ *Ben said they should take extra food on the hike, but nobody heeded him.*

• **pay attention**   to attend carefully to something. □ *The students paid attention to what the teacher was saying.* □ *Carrie paid close attention as Donald changed the tire so that she would know how to do it the next time.*

listless   (*adjective*) without energy. □ *Donald seems so listless; I wonder if he's ill.* □ *Eddie replied with a listless shrug.*

• **lackadaisical**   *listless* and not interested in doing anything. (Informal.) □ *Nothing seemed to interest the lackadaisical girl.* □ *Fran was enthusiastic at first, but grew lackadaisical.*

• **languid**   *listless* and slow. □ *With a languid gesture, Ronald beckoned to the servant.* □ *The languid days of summer vacation passed all too quickly.*

• **lethargic**   sleepy and *listless*. □ *The hot weather made everyone feel lethargic.* □ *The coach tried to get some spirit into his lethargic team.*

• **sluggish**   *listless;* moving slowly. □ *The lizard grew sluggish in the cold.* □ *I sat in my car in the sluggish rush-hour traffic.*

• **torpid**   *listless;* not active; not moving. □ *The snake was not dead, it was only lying torpid.* □ *In springtime, the torpid flow of sap in the trees speeds up.*

literal   See the entry for *actual*.

litter   See the entry for *trash*.

little   See the entry for *small*.

live　(*verb*) to make your home somewhere. (Usually with *in.*) □ *Do you live in a house or an apartment?* □ *George lived in Oklahoma City for five years.*

　• **dwell**　to *live* somewhere. (Old-fashioned. Usually with *in.*) □ *The children came to the cottage where the kind old woman dwelt.* □ *Many fearsome beasts dwelt in the forest.*

　• **inhabit**　to *live* in a building or a shelter. □ *Ten people inhabited those two rooms.* □ *A family of squirrels seems to be inhabiting our attic.*

　• **occupy**　to *live* in a place; to take up a certain amount of space. □ *Helen occupies the second floor of her sister's house.* □ *A drugstore now occupies the corner where the movie theater used to stand.*

　• **reside**　to *live* somewhere for a long time. (Formal. Usually with *in.*) □ *The Ingersolls reside next door to me.* □ *Please state the address where you currently reside.*

　• **settle**　to begin to *live* somewhere; to decide on a place to *live*. (Usually with *in.*) □ *Jay's grandparents decided to settle in Wisconsin.* □ *That part of the country was not settled until 1870.*

　• **stay**　to *live* somewhere temporarily. (Usually with *at.* See also the main entry for *stay.*) □ *Kay stayed at a hotel for the night.* □ *Laura stayed with a friend while she was in New York.*

lively　(*adjective*) very active and full of life. (See also the entry for *busy².*) □ *We had a lively discussion about the new movie.* □ *Mark is so lively that it's hard to keep up with him.*

　• **brisk**　*lively* and efficient. □ *Tom set off down the sidewalk at a brisk pace.* □ *The brisk woman usually accomplished what she set out to do.*

　• **energetic**　*lively;* full of energy. □ *Sue was an energetic salesperson and sold all her band candy in two days.* □ *The guitar player was famous for his energetic solos.*

　• **vigorous**　*lively;* full of energy and strength. □ *The crowd gave a vigorous cheer for their favorite boxer.* □ *Vigorous exercise helped Philip work off his anger.*

　[→contrasting word: *tired*]

load　(*noun*) something that is carried. □ *Roger took a load of laundry down to the washing machine.* □ *The box of books was too big a load for Stanley to carry by himself.*

　• **burden**　a troublesome *load;* something troublesome that must be managed or endured. □ *Tina's large suitcase proved to be a burden on her trip.* □ *Jan refused to let her friends take care of her; she did not want to be a burden.*

　• **encumbrance**　a *load* that makes it difficult for you to do something. (Formal.) □ *Bill's armload of packages formed an encumbrance when he tried to get his house keys out of his pocket.* □ *Arnold began to think of his wife and children as encumbrances to his pursuit of happiness.*

• **freight** a *load* that is carried on a vehicle, usually for pay. □ *The truck was hauling eight tons of freight.* □ *Trains carry a great deal of the nation's freight.*

loaded See the entry for *rich.*

loath See the entry for *reluctant.*

loathe See the entry for *hate.*

locale See the entry for *place.*

locate See the entry for *find.*

location See the entry for *place.*

loch See the entry for *lake.*

lodge See the entries for *hotel, organization.*

lofty See the entry for *tall.*

loiter See the entry for *dawdle.*

lone See the entry for *single.*

lonely (*adjective*) feeling alone and wishing for company. □ *Ben is lonely because his best friend is out of town.* □ *No one offered to play with the lonely child.*
    • **desolate** *lonely* and unhappy. (Formal.) □ *Carrie was desolate without her sister's company.* □ *Donald looked out over the desolate desert landscape.*
    • **forlorn** *lonely* and neglected. (Formal.) □ *The girl sat huddled on a park bench with a forlorn expression on her face.* □ *Only a single, forlorn daffodil bloomed in my garden this year.*
    • **lonesome** *lonely; lonely* for someone or something in particular. □ *Eddie is lonesome for his girlfriend.* □ *The house feels so lonesome now that all my guests have left.*
    • **solitary** *lonely;* single; away from people. □ *Fran shuns companionship, saying she prefers to be solitary.* □ *A solitary house stood in the middle of the empty plain.*

loner See the entry for *hermit.*

lonesome See the entry for *lonely.*

long for See the entry for *miss².*

long-suffering See the entry for *patient.*

look (*verb*) to fix your eyes on something; to see. (Usually with *at.*) □ *Look at this pretty shell I found.* □ *George looked out the window.*
    • **gaze** to *look* at something steadily. □ *Helen gazed longingly at the book in the bookshop window.* □ *The gypsy gazed into the crystal ball.*

• **glance**   to *look* at something briefly. ☐ *I glanced at the person who sat down next to me.* ☐ *Irene glanced at the TV schedule but didn't see anything interesting.*

• **peep**   to *look* at something secretly. ☐ *The children peeped out through the crack in the door.* ☐ *My neighbor is always opening his curtains a slit to peep at me.*

• **peer**   to *look* at something intensely. ☐ *Jay peered at his reflection in the mirror, searching for flaws in his complexion.* ☐ *Kay peered over my shoulder as I read.*

• **stare**   to *look* at something very steadily; to *look* at someone steadily and rudely. ☐ *I stared at the instructions for building the bicycle, trying to make sense out of them.* ☐ *Laura wondered why everyone was staring at her.*

look for   See the entry for *seek.*

look like   See the entry for *seem.*

looks   (*noun*) the way something or something appears on the outside. ☐ *Mary is vain about her good looks.* ☐ *The police officer did not like the looks of the people gathered on the corner.*

• **appearance**   the way someone or something appears or seems. ☐ *Despite the dingy appearance of the restaurant, it's a clean and pleasant place to eat.* ☐ *Tom liked the town's peaceful appearance.*

• **aspect**   the way something appears or acts. (Formal.) ☐ *The clouds on the horizon had a threatening aspect.* ☐ *The hotel's somewhat menacing aspect discouraged many would-be guests.*

• **image**   the picture someone or something presents. ☐ *Sue did not think that bright-red lipstick would fit in with her dignified image.* ☐ *Philip projected an image of trustworthiness and dependability.*

loop   See the entry for *wind².*

loosen up   See the entry for *relax.*

lop   See the entry for *chop.*

loquacious   See the entry for *talkative.*

lose   (*verb*) not to be able to find someone or something. (See also the entry for *fail.*) ☐ *I lost my wristwatch, and I can't afford to buy another one.* ☐ *The little boy lost his parents in the crowd.*

• **lose track of**   not to know where someone or something is; not to watch something carefully. (Informal.) ☐ *The friends lost track of each other over the years.* ☐ *Ken lost track of how much money he had spent.*

• **mislay**   not to remember where you put something. ☐ *I seem to have mislaid my glasses.* ☐ *Rita hunted and hunted for the library book she had mislaid.*

• **misplace**   to put something somewhere and forget where it is. □ *I didn't lose the videotape; I just misplaced it.* □ *You wouldn't misplace things so often if you put them back where they belonged when you were finished with them.*
[→contrasting word: *find*]

lose track of   See the entry for *lose.*

loss   See the entry for *failure.*

loud   (*adjective*) making a great sound; not quiet. (See also the entry for *flashy.*) □ *The neighbors had a loud argument.* □ *Susan carried on in a loud voice.*
• **deafening**   so *loud* that you feel it will make you deaf. □ *There was a deafening explosion.* □ *That old car makes a deafening racket.*
• **earsplitting**   extremely *loud.* (Informal.) □ *Tim played his stereo at an ear-splitting volume.* □ *The baby emitted an ear-splitting scream.*
• **noisy**   *loud;* full of commotion. □ *The noisy dog kept everyone on the block awake.* □ *I wish the washing machine weren't so noisy.*
[→see also: *harsh*]

lousy   See the entry for *bad.*

love   (*noun*) a feeling of caring deeply for someone. □ *Jan told me of her love for Bill.* □ *For Valentine's Day, the teacher had us read poems about love.*
• **affection**   a feeling of liking someone. □ *The sisters did many little things to express their affection for each other.* □ *The cat rubbed against my legs to show his affection for me.*
• **devotion**   a feeling of wanting to do anything for someone. □ *Art praised his dog for her devotion to him.* □ *It was nice to see the father's devotion to his child.*
• **fondness**   a feeling of caring for someone or something. □ *Ben had always had a certain fondness for his cousin.* □ *Carrie's fondness for sweets was one reason for her weight gain.*

lovely   See the entries for *beautiful, nice.*

low   See the entries for *quiet, sad.*

low-down   See the entry for *mean¹.*

low-priced   See the entry for *cheap.*

loyal   See the entry for *faithful.*

luck   (*noun*) something that happens by chance; the power that makes things turn out the way they do. □ *Donald had good luck at the poker game and won a fair amount of money.* □ *It was pure luck that I ran into Eddie when I did.*

• **destiny**   the way someone's life is going to turn out. ☐ *Fran felt that it was her destiny to marry George.* ☐ *Harold fulfilled his destiny by becoming a well-loved teacher.*

• **fate**   the way someone's life is going to turn out, no matter how hard he or she fights against it; the power that guides people's lives. ☐ *Fate brought Irene and Jerry together.* ☐ *It was Kay's fate never to settle in one place for long.*

• **fortune**   the way things turn out; the power that decides who will gain and who will lose. (Formal.) ☐ *Laura met with good fortune throughout her trip abroad.* ☐ *Fortune did not favor Mark; he lost his family and his home all in one month.*

• **providence**   the divine power that decides the way things will turn out. (Formal. When capitalized, *Providence* refers to God.) ☐ *Tom worked hard and trusted to Providence for his reward.* ☐ *Tom believed that some kind providence watched over him and his loved ones.*

lukewarm   See the entry for *indifferent.*

lullaby   See the entry for *song.*

luminous   See the entry for *bright.*

lunatic   See the entry for *crazy.*

lunch   See the entry for *meal.*

lurch   See the entry for *rock².*

lure   See the entries for *attract, trap.*

luscious   See the entry for *delicious.*

luxurious (*adjective*) rich and pleasing to the senses. ☐ *The millionaire had a luxurious car with leather seats molded to fit him exactly.* ☐ *The princess dressed in gowns of the most luxurious fabrics.*

• **opulent**   grandly *luxurious; luxurious* and showing off. (Formal.) ☐ *Many silent-movie stars had opulent bathrooms, with marble, gold, or solid crystal bathtubs.* ☐ *The lady had an opulent collection of jewelry.*

• **posh**   elegant and *luxurious.* (Slang.) ☐ *Philip took his girlfriend to a posh restaurant.* ☐ *Ken thought the hotel was pretty posh.*

• **splendid**   impressively *luxurious.* ☐ *A splendid wedding feast was served.* ☐ *The actors in the play had splendid costumes made of the finest Japanese brocade.*

• **sumptuous**   overwhelmingly *luxurious;* extremely expensive. ☐ *Rita wrapped herself in the sumptuous folds of the velvet robe.* ☐ *It was hard for Susan to choose a dessert from the assortment of sumptuous pastries the waiter showed her.*

M

mad   See the entries for *angry, crazy.*

magazine   See the entry for *periodical.*

magenta   See the entry for *purple.*

magician   See the entry for *witch.*

magnanimous   See the entry for *generous.*

magnitude   See the entry for *size.*

maim   See the entry for *damage.*

main   (*adjective*) most important or essential. □ *The teacher went over the main points in the lesson.* □ *The main reason Tim went to the dance was to show off his new car.*
> • **chief**   the most important person or thing in a group. □ *The encyclopedia was my chief source of information in writing this paper.* □ *Jan's chief aim was to be popular.*
> • **primary**   first and most important. □ *Copper mining is the primary industry in this part of the country.* □ *Poverty was the primary cause of Bill's difficulties.*
> • **principal**   most important or powerful. □ *Prince Hamlet is the principal character in the play,* Hamlet. □ *Professor Moriarty was Sherlock Holmes's principal adversary.*

maintain   See the entries for *argue³, believe¹.*

majestic   See the entry for *grand.*

major   See the entry for *important.*

make[1] (*verb*) to cause something to exist; to manufacture something. □ *The refrigerator made a sudden noise.* □ *Art can make rugs out of fabric scraps.*

- **create**   to *make* something that has never existed before. □ *The cook created a tasty new sauce.* □ *Vincent creates such beautiful paintings.*
- **fabricate**   to manufacture something; to *make* something up. (Formal.) □ *The factory fabricates sinks, bathtubs, and other bathroom fixtures.* □ *Ben fabricated a story about how he had gotten the black eye.*
- **produce**   to manufacture or grow something. □ *The factory was able to produce a thousand cars a month.* □ *The farm produced corn and soybeans.*
- **turn out**   to *make* great quantities of something. (Informal.) □ *In their heyday, the factories were turning out cars at a tremendous rate.* □ *Carrie turned out dozens of handmade sweaters as birthday presents for her friends.*

make[2] (*verb*) to cause someone to do something. □ *My mother made me apologize.* □ *Donald made Eddie clean up the mess.*

- **coerce**   to *make* someone do something through pressure or force. (Formal.) □ *The army tried to coerce the president to resign.* □ *The boss coerced his employees into donating money to his favorite charity.*
- **compel**   to *make* someone do something; to *make* it necessary for someone to do something. (Formal.) □ *Hunger compelled the starving people to steal food.* □ *The speaker's earnest pleas compelled people to listen to what she had to say.*
- **force**   to use power or violence to *make* someone do something. □ *The burglar held a gun to the cashier's head and forced him to hand over all the money in the cash register.* □ *The law forced people to pay a heavy tax on gasoline.*
- **impel**   to *make* someone do something; to urge someone to do something. (Formal.) □ *Since it was a formal occasion, I felt impelled to be polite.* □ *Fran's basic honesty impelled her to tell the clerk that he had given her too much money in change.*

make a deal   See the entry for *bargain.*

make an effort   See the entry for *try.*

make fun of   See the entry for *ridicule.*

maladroit   See the entry for *clumsy.*

malady   See the entry for *sickness.*

male   See the entry for *man.*

malefactor   See the entry for *villain.*

malevolent   See the entry for *evil.*

malign   See the entry for *slander.*

maltreat   See the entry for *abuse.*

man   (*noun*) a male human being. ☐ *George is a very soft-spoken man.* ☐ *All those men are on the company baseball team.*
  • **boy**   a young male human being. ☐ *When he was a boy, Harold was shy around girls.* ☐ *Irwin's parents thought that a boy should not want to learn to sew.*
  • **fellow**   a male human being. (Informal.) ☐ *Who's the blond fellow standing by the door?* ☐ *Jay seemed like a friendly fellow.*
  • **guy**   a male human being; any person. (Slang.) ☐ *Kevin's a nice guy, but not very interesting.* ☐ *Larry went out to the movies with the guys from work.*
  • **male**   any male animal. ☐ *Mark is a fine specimen of the human male.* ☐ *The parakeet breeder needed more males to breed with her females.*

manacles   See the entry for *bonds.*

manage   See the entries for *control¹, handle, lead.*

mania   See the entry for *obsession.*

manifest   See the entry for *clear.*

manifestation   See the entry for *sign.*

manipulate   See the entry for *control².*

manner   See the entry for *style.*

manners   See the entry for *behavior.*

mansion   See the entry for *house.*

manuscript   See the entry for *document.*

mar   See the entry for *damage.*

march   See the entry for *walk.*

margin   See the entry for *boundary.*

marina   See the entry for *dock.*

mark   See the entries for *label, notice.*

marked   See the entry for *striking.*

market   See the entry for *store.*

market value   See the entry for *value.*

maroon   See the entry for *abandon.*

marry *(verb)* to become husband and wife; to make someone husband and wife. □ *Tom and Jan married in June.* □ *Philip hoped to marry Sue.* □ *The minister married the couple.*

   • **get hitched** to *marry.* (Slang; folksy.) □ *What do you know; Andy and Cora went off and got hitched!* □ *"Whaddya say we get hitched?" the eloquent young man asked his sweetheart.*

   • **tie the knot** to *marry.* (Slang.) □ *After going out with each other for six years, Rita and Stanley finally tied the knot.* □ *The young couple tied the knot in an elaborate church ceremony.*

   • **wed** to *marry.* (Poetic.) □ *Our hero desired to wed the fair lady.* □ *The couple sent a note of thanks to the minister who wedded them.*

marsh See the entry for *swamp.*

marvel See the entry for *wonder¹.*

marvelous See the entry for *incredible.*

mash See the entry for *crush.*

mask See the entry for *disguise.*

masquerade See the entry for *pose.*

massacre See the entry for *kill.*

master See the entries for *expert, learn².*

masterful *(adjective)* powerful; able to make someone or something obey. □ *Roger had a masterful personality.* □ *With a masterful tug on the reins, Susan brought the unruly horse under control.*

   • **authoritative** easily able to get people to obey; having expert knowledge. (Formal.) □ *The teacher called for silence in his most authoritative tone of voice.* □ *This is an authoritative book on stamp collecting.*

   • **commanding** powerful; in control. □ *The sergeant had a commanding stare that could reduce rebellious soldiers to whimpering obedience.* □ *The queen gave a commanding gesture, and the prisoner was taken off to the dungeon.*

   • **dominant** most powerful; leading or ruling everyone or everything. (Formal.) □ *Vic's dominant personality made him a good football coach.* □ *The dominant opinion was that Tom was much too lazy.* [→see also: *bossy*]

mastery *(noun)* the highest possible level of skill. □ *The violin player's mastery of his instrument astonished the audience.* □ *Everything the chef cooked showed her mastery of the culinary arts.*

   • **ability** skill. (See also the main entry for *ability.*) □ *Art's boss praised his typing ability.* □ *The writer's storytelling ability held her readers fascinated.*

• **command**   control and skill. □ *The Japanese visitor had an excellent command of the English language.* □ *The gymnast's routine displayed her command of many difficult gymnastic moves.*
• **competence**   sufficient skill. (Formal.) □ *Ben's enemies questioned his competence to do the job.* □ *The students in the writing class had to demonstrate their writing competence by turning in a final paper.*
• **proficiency**   ease and skill. (Formal.) □ *Carrie has a high level of proficiency in math.* □ *Proficiency in the use of computers is necessary for this job.*

masticate   See the entry for *chew.*

mat   See the entry for *carpet.*

match   (*verb*) to be alike; to be equal. (See also the entry for *contest.*) □ *The number on the key matches the number of the locker.* □ *Donald's socks don't match.*
• **conform**   to *match* a rule or a standard; to be in agreement with a rule or standard. (Formal.) □ *Every restaurant must conform to these standards of cleanliness.* □ *The students had to conform to the school dress code.*
• **correspond**   to *match* in some respect. □ *The initials on the suitcase corresponded with the first letters of Eddie's first and last names.* □ *The information in the newspaper story did not correspond with the facts.*
• **go together**   to *match* or to belong with each other. (Informal.) □ *Fran insisted on having shoes and a purse that went together.* □ *In our family, watching TV and eating popcorn just naturally seemed to go together.*
• **tally**   to *match* in several respects. □ *The criminal's description tallies with that man's appearance.* □ *The two witnesses' stories tallied on all the important points.*

material   See the entries for *cloth, stuff.*

matter   See the entry for *stuff.*

mature   See the entry for *grow.*

mauve   See the entry for *purple.*

maxim   See the entry for *saying.*

maybe   (*adverb*) not for certain; might be. □ *Maybe Dad will loan us the money.* □ *Maybe George already found the missing book.*
• **conceivably**   *maybe;* imaginably. (Formal.) □ *Helen might conceivably have left already.* □ *Irene has more placemats than she could conceivably need.*
• **perhaps**   might be. □ *Perhaps Jay wasn't invited to the party.* □ *Kay is perhaps the nicest person I know.*

• **possibly**   might happen to be. □ *Could you possibly have put the keys in your pocket?* □ *This is quite possibly the worst day of my life.*

mayhem   See the entry for *disorder.*

meadow   See the entry for *field.*

meager   (*adjective*) very little; not enough. □ *The travelers shared their meager food supplies.* □ *Scrooge paid Bob Cratchit a meager salary.*
  • **inadequate**   not enough. □ *The family had inadequate fuel to heat their house through the winter.* □ *Laura felt that words were inadequate to express her deep feelings.*
  • **measly**   pitifully little or few. (Informal.) □ *How am I supposed to feed ten people with one measly little chicken?* □ *Mark went out to see what kind of present he could buy with his two measly dollars.*
  • **paltry**   shamefully little; worthless. □ *Tom sold his bike for the paltry sum of fifty cents.* □ *I only scored a paltry seventy-two points on the exam.*
  • **scanty**   very little or few; sparse. □ *It was a bad year; the harvest was scanty.* □ *As Tom grew older, his hair got scanty.*

meal   (*noun*) food served or eaten at one time. □ *The cook served up an excellent meal.* □ *The hikers made a meal off the wild berries they found.*
  • **breakfast**   a *meal* eaten in the morning. □ *Philip had cereal for breakfast.* □ *Rita usually served a big breakfast of pancakes, eggs, and fruit.*
  • **dinner**   a *meal* eaten in the afternoon or evening. □ *Susan ate her dinner in front of the evening news on TV.* □ *Tim invited his friends over for dinner.*
  • **lunch**   a *meal* eaten at noontime. □ *Jan packed a couple of sandwiches for lunch.* □ *Bill ate lunch in a restaurant.*
  • **repast**   a *meal;* a generous *meal.* (Formal.) □ *The picnickers enjoyed their repast of fried chicken, deviled eggs, potato salad, and brownies.* □ *When we returned from our moonlight swim, we had a midnight repast of fruit and iced tea.*
  • **snack**   a small *meal* eaten between other meals. □ *Art had a snack when he got home from school.* □ *The leftover pizza made a delicious snack.*
  • **supper**   a *meal* eaten in the evening. □ *What's for supper?* □ *Supper will be late because Ben is not home yet.*

mean¹   (*adjective*) selfish, spiteful, or cruel. □ *Carrie played a mean trick on me.* □ *Donna is a mean girl.*
  • **despicable**   shamefully *mean.* (Formal.) □ *It was despicable of Eddie to cheat his own sister.* □ *Lying to your friend was a despicable thing to do.*

• **low-down**   very *mean*. (Slang.) □ *Fred is a low-down good-for-nothing disgrace!* □ *That low-down sneak stole her grandfather's life savings.*
• **nasty**   *mean* or unpleasant. □ *Gina is always making nasty remarks about me behind my back.* □ *Helen is being nasty to everyone today.*
• **unkind**   deliberately *mean* or inconsiderate. □ *Irene resented Jay's unkind teasing.* □ *The children were unkind to the new student in the class.*

mean²   (*verb*) to have something as a purpose; to set out to do something. □ *Kay meant to find out what was in the sealed room.* □ *I didn't mean to hurt your feelings.*
• **aim**   to set out to do something. (Always with *to*.) □ *Larry aimed to become the school's champion wrestler.* □ *Mark was aiming to get elected class president.*
• **design**   to set out or plan to do something. (Formal.) □ *The scheming vizier designed to marry the princess and ascend to the throne.* □ *By inviting all the most popular girls to her party, Paula designed to become popular herself.*
• **have in mind**   to have something as a purpose; to be thinking of something. (Informal.) □ *Sue has in mind buying a new car.* □ *When Rita talked about going to a concert, she had an evening at the symphony in mind; Stanley, on the other hand, thought of heavy metal.*
• **intend**   to have something as a purpose; to plan to do something. □ *I intend to get to know Jan better.* □ *Bill didn't intend to ruin the evening, but that's just what he wound up doing.*

meander   See the entry for *wander*.

meaningless   (*adjective*) without meaning or sense. □ *Art babbled a meaningless string of words.* □ *The symbols on the sign were meaningless to me, but my friend knew that they meant "No Entry."*
• **absurd**   *meaningless*; foolish. □ *Ben started belly dancing on top of the coffee table, and Carrie laughed at his absurd antics.* □ *The plot of the movie was downright absurd.*
• **pointless**   *meaningless*; without any point. □ *It's pointless to yell at the ticket seller; the train has already left, and she can't make it come back.* □ *Donald told some pointless story about how he bought his wristwatch.*
• **senseless**   *meaningless*; without sense. □ *Grief for his dead brother led Eddie to do a number of senseless things.* □ *It would be senseless to drop out of school just because you failed one class.*

means   See the entry for *way*.

measly   See the entry for *meager*.

mechanism   See the entry for *device*.

mechanized   See the entry for *automatic²*.

meddle   (*verb*) to get involved in something that is none of your business. □ *Fran told George again and again not to meddle in her affairs.* □ *Helen couldn't resist going into the kitchen and meddling with the things that were cooking on the stove.*
- **fiddle with**   to *meddle* with something; to toy with something. (Informal.) □ *Irene fiddled with Jay's wristwatch until she broke it.* □ *Quit fiddling with the remote control.*
- **interfere**   to *meddle* in something where you are not wanted. □ *My parents are always interfering in my business.* □ *The neighbors were quarreling violently, and I was scared to interfere.*
- **mess with**   to *meddle* with something. (Slang.) □ *Who's been messing with my bicycle?* □ *Don't mess with things that don't concern you.*
- **obtrude**   to *meddle* in something forcefully; to push yourself in where you are not wanted. (Formal. Usually with *on* or *upon*.) □ *I hate to obtrude upon my neighbor's privacy, but I really must borrow a cup of sugar.* □ *Without a word of apology, the stranger obtruded upon our conversation.*

mediate   (*verb*) to come in to settle an argument or a fight. (Often with *between*.) □ *The father mediated between his quarreling children.* □ *The diplomat tried to mediate between the warring factions.*
- **arbitrate**   to *mediate* and decide in someone's favor. (Formal. Often with *between*.) □ *The bosses and the workers wanted someone to arbitrate between them.* □ *Kay felt as though she had to arbitrate between her divorced parents.*
- **negotiate**   to help fighting people or groups talk to one another and reach decisions. (Formal.) □ *The ambassador was able to negotiate a peace treaty.* □ *It was hard for Laura to negotiate between her friends without taking sides.*

medication   See the entry for *medicine*.

medicine   (*noun*) something you use to treat, prevent, or cure a sickness. □ *I need some cough medicine.* □ *Are you taking any medicine for your headaches?*
- **drug**   a powerful kind of *medicine*; any chemical that has powerful effects on your body. □ *Penicillin is a useful drug.* □ *The speaker said that alcohol was a drug that could impair the ability to think clearly.*
- **medication**   *medicine* for a specific problem. □ *The ointment contains medication for the baby's rash.* □ *Make sure that Mark takes his medication.*

• **prescription**   *medicine* that a doctor orders you to take; a doctor's order for *medicine*. □ *The doctor gave me a prescription for painkillers.* □ *There were several different drugs listed in the prescription.*

mediocre   See the entry for *poor²*.

meditate   See the entry for *think*.

medley   See the entry for *hodgepodge*.

meet   (*verb*) to see or get together with someone. (See also the entries for *contest, get together*.) □ *I met Tom outside the shopping mall.* □ *What time shall we meet?*
  • **bump into**   to *meet* someone by chance. (Informal.) □ *I bumped into Rita the other day.* □ *Susan bumped into an old friend at the grocery store.*
  • **encounter**   to *meet* someone and have dealings with him or her; to *meet* someone by chance. (Formal.) □ *I encountered Sue in the hallway outside my office and inquired as to her business there.* □ *Philip encountered a long line of people at the post office.*
  • **run across**   to *meet* someone or something. □ *If you run across Jan at the dance studio, tell her I said hi.* □ *Tim ran across a picture of his grandfather in the old newspapers he was looking at.*
  • **run into**   to *meet* someone by chance. (Informal.) □ *Guess whom I ran into at lunch?* □ *Bill and Art ran into each other several times that week.*

meeting   (*noun*) an occasion when people get together to discuss or do something. □ *The model airplane club held a meeting every Thursday after school.* □ *Ben has to go to a meeting tonight.*
  • **conference**   a *meeting* for the purpose of discussing a particular subject. □ *My teacher wanted to have a conference with my parents.* □ *Carrie attended a conference on the subject of ESP.*
  • **congress**   a formal *meeting* of many people for the purpose of deciding things. □ *Many local stamp-collecting clubs sent representatives to the national stamp-collecting congress.* □ *The political party held a congress to decide what would be in their platform.*
  • **convention**   a *meeting* of many people. □ *Every science-fiction fan from hundreds of miles around came to the science-fiction convention.* □ *All the lodge brothers went to the lodge's annual convention.*
  • **rally**   a *meeting* of many people who are enthusiastic about something. □ *The political party held a rally to show that they had a lot of support.* □ *All the students had to attend the pep rally before the football game.*

melodramatic   See the entry for *dramatic*.

melody   See the entry for *tune*.

melt (*verb*) to become liquid; to make something liquid. □ *The ice melted when the sun came out.* □ *Donald melted butter in the saucepan.*

• **liquefy** to *melt* something completely; to *melt* completely. (Formal.) □ *You must have extremely high temperatures to liquefy metal.* □ *The plastic liquefied in the hot sun.*

• **soften** to *melt* something until it is soft. □ *Soften the butter, then cream the sugar into it.* □ *Eddie softened the eraser by kneading it in his warm hands.*

• **thaw** to *melt* the ice from something. □ *In the spring, the soil will thaw.* □ *Thaw out the frozen vegetables before you put them in the casserole.*

memo See the entry for *message*.

memorize See the entry for *learn²*.

menace See the entry for *threaten*.

menacing See the entry for *sinister*.

mend See the entry for *fix*.

mention See the entry for *say*.

mentor See the entry for *guide*.

mercenary See the entry for *greedy*.

merchant See the entry for *seller*.

merciless See the entry for *cruel*.

mercy (*noun*) kind treatment. □ *The jailer showed mercy to his prisoner and made sure he had enough to eat.* □ *Someone finally had mercy on that poor homeless beggar and gave her a place to stay.*

• **charity** love of other human beings; generous giving to the poor. □ *Fran knew she only had a home because of her sister's charity.* □ *George was well known for his charity to those less fortunate than himself.*

• **clemency** mercy; gentleness in the use of power. (Formal.) □ *The convicted criminal begged the judge to show clemency in sentencing him.* □ *The principal was praised for her clemency in dealing with the troublesome student.*

• **compassion** feeling for someone's sorrow or suffering. □ *The nurse's compassion for her patients was obvious.* □ *Helen sent money to the tornado fund out of compassion for the people who had lost their homes.*

• **pity** a feeling of being sorry for someone's suffering. □ *Irene took pity on the crying child and tried to help him find his parents.* □ *Jay took in the stray dog out of pity for its obvious misery.*

• **sympathy** a feeling of being able to identify with someone else's suffering. □ *Kay had a lot of sympathy for Laura, because she had been* *through the exact same thing.* □ *When Mark lost his job, his friends expressed their sympathy.*

merely See the entry for *only.*

merit See the entries for *deserve, value.*

merry See the entry for *cheerful.*

mess with See the entry for *meddle.*

message (*noun*) information that you send to someone. □ *Mr. Smith is not in right now; may I take a message?* □ *The detective found a message scratched on the wall of the murder room.*
  • **bulletin** a *message* that gives the latest news. □ *We interrupt this program for a news bulletin.* □ *Sue called us from the hospital with periodic bulletins about her mother's condition.*
  • **letter** a written *message.* □ *Philip wrote a letter to the president of the company.* □ *I got a letter from Rita today.*
  • **memo** a *message* sent to people in an office. □ *The boss sent everyone a memo about proper business attire.* □ *The memo listed the dates when staff meetings would be held.*
  • **note** a short written *message.* □ *Mom left me a note telling me to put dinner in the oven at six.* □ *Susan wrote a note to the mail carrier and left it by the mailbox.*

messy (*adjective*) not in order; confused. □ *The bathroom was really messy after Tim took his bath.* □ *I can't find anything in this messy closet.*
  • **sloppy** careless and therefore *messy.* □ *The sloppy young man left his dirty clothes all over the house.* □ *Jan did a sloppy job of gluing the bowl back together.*
  • **slovenly** lazy and therefore *messy.* (Formal.) □ *Bill is an appallingly slovenly housekeeper.* □ *Art's mother criticized him for his slovenly appearance.*
  • **squalid** dirty, poor, and *messy.* (Formal.) □ *The family lived in a squalid shack.* □ *Ben grew up in squalid surroundings.*
  • **unkempt** *messy* in your personal appearance. □ *Carrie came to work with her hair unkempt.* □ *The children in the orphanage looked unhealthy and unkempt.*
  • **untidy** *messy;* not cleaned up. □ *Donald hates to leave his desk untidy.* □ *Eddie just left his tools in an untidy heap.*

metal (*adjective*) made of a shiny, inanimate substance. □ *Fran kept the matches in a little metal box.* □ *The metal door clanged shut.*
  • **aluminum** made of a shiny, whitish *metal* of the kind often used to make cans. □ *The aluminum cans go in a separate recycling bin.* □ *The aluminum bicycle was strong but light.*

• **bronze** made of a brownish *metal* compounded of copper and tin. □ *The bronze statue had a deep golden glow.* □ *The museum has several ancient bronze vessels from China.*
• **gold** made of a valuable, yellowish *metal.* □ *The china plates had gold rims.* □ *George gave his fiancée a gold ring.*
• **silver** made of a valuable, whitish *metal.* □ *I inherited the silver brooch from my great-aunt.* □ *Helen has a silver dollar.*
• **steel** made of a strong, bluish *metal* compounded of iron and carbon. □ *The bridge was built with steel girders.* □ *The swordsmith forged a steel sword.*
• **tin** made of a whitish *metal.* □ *The tinsmith repaired the family's tin pots and pans.* □ *The tin fork was easy to bend.*

metaphorical See the entry for *figurative.*

method See the entry for *way.*

methodical See the entry for *organized.*

metropolis See the entry for *town.*

midpoint See the entry for *center.*

midriff See the entry for *stomach.*

mighty See the entry for *strong.*

mild¹ (*adjective*) gentle; not sharp. □ *The sauce isn't spicy; it's quite mild.* □ *Irene gave a mild reply to Jay's angry demand.*
• **bland** boringly *mild.* □ *The potato was awfully bland without salt.* □ *While Kay was sick, she could only eat bland food.*
• **flat** *mild;* tasteless; said of fizzy drinks, without bubbles. (See also the main entry for *flat.*) □ *Larry thinks everything tastes flat if it's not covered with red pepper sauce.* □ *The cola went flat.*
• **insipid** *mild,* dull, and tasteless or boring. (Formal.) □ *Without the spices, the stew was quite insipid.* □ *The poem was written in the most insipid language.*

mild² (*adjective*) gentle; not extreme. □ *The teacher exercised only mild discipline upon his students.* □ *The weather was mild and pleasant while I was in Minnesota.*
• **moderate** staying in the middle; not extreme. □ *Mark holds very moderate political views.* □ *There was a moderate amount of rainfall this year.*
• **temperate** never going to extremes. (Formal.) □ *Many people have moved here to enjoy the temperate climate.* □ *The two opponents managed to conduct a temperate debate.*

mimic See the entry for *copy¹.*

mince See the entry for *chop*.

mind (*noun*) the part of a person that thinks and feels. ☐ *There was no contest in Tom's mind as to who should get the prize.* ☐ *Sue has the sort of mind that delights in solving puzzles.*

  • **brain** the organ in your head that allows you to think and feel. ☐ *The professor set his formidable brain to solving the problem.* ☐ *An injury to the brain can impair a person's ability to think or act.*

  • **head** the capacity to think calmly. (Informal. Mostly in the expressions *keep one's head* and *lose one's head*.) ☐ *Philip kept a cool head throughout the crisis.* ☐ *She has a good head for business.*

  • **intellect** mind; understanding. ☐ *The scientist was a person of great intellect.* ☐ *Susan's swift intellect allowed her to understand the whole situation after she saw just a few clues.*

  • **wits** sense. ☐ *The baby-sitter kept his wits about him and called the ambulance at once.* ☐ *Tim is running around and screaming; he seems to have lost his wits altogether.*

mine See the entry for *dig*.

minor See the entries for *child, unimportant*.

minute See the entry for *small*.

miracle See the entry for *wonder¹*.

mire See the entry for *slime*.

miscellaneous See the entry for *assorted*.

misdemeanor See the entry for *crime*.

miser (*noun*) someone who hoards his or her money. ☐ *Jan was a miser from an early age; she saved all her allowance and never spent a penny if she could help it.* ☐ *The old miser never gave to charity.*

  • **cheapskate** someone who hates to spend money; someone who wants to do everything cheaply. (Slang.) ☐ *Bill is such a cheapskate that he'll buy the lowest quality things so long as they don't cost much.* ☐ *That cheapskate gave me her cast-off dress as a birthday present.*

  • **Scrooge** someone who hoards money like the character of Ebenezer Scrooge in Charles Dickens's *A Christmas Carol*. ☐ *Art's a real Scrooge when it comes to paying his employees.* ☐ *It's no use trying to get that old Scrooge to loan you any money.*

  • **skinflint** someone who will do anything to save money. (Slang.) ☐ *Ben was a skinflint who preferred to mend hopelessly ragged old clothing rather than buy something new.* ☐ *He was such a skinflint that he shivered all winter rather than spend money to heat his apartment.*

• **tightwad**   someone who hates to spend money. (Slang.) □ *Dad turned into a tightwad whenever I asked for a raise in my allowance.* □ *Carrie says she's frugal, but I say she's a tightwad.*

miserable   See the entry for *sad*.

mishmash   See the entry for *hodgepodge*.

mislay   See the entry for *lose*.

mislead   See the entry for *lie²*.

misplace   See the entry for *lose*.

miss¹   (*verb*) to pass over something that you should notice. □ *Donald missed a spot when he was cleaning the kitchen table.* □ *I tried to give a gift to every child, but I guess I must have missed one.*
  • **leave out**   to pass over something on purpose. □ *Eddie left out Fran when he was inviting people to the party.* □ *The tomato sauce would be tastier if you left out all the oregano.*
  • **neglect**   to pass over something out of carelessness. □ *George neglected his chores all week.* □ *Helen neglected to feed her cat.*
  • **overlook**   to pass over something; to ignore something. □ *Somehow, Irene overlooked the instruction booklet that came with the calculator.* □ *The teacher said she would overlook the fact that Jay was late to class.*

miss²   (*verb*) to feel sad because someone or something is not with you. □ *I miss my friend since she moved away.* □ *Kay missed the old pine tree that used to grow outside her window.*
  • **languish for**   to *miss* someone or something so much that you waste away. (Formal or poetic.) □ *Our hero grew wan and despairing, languishing for his ladylove.* □ *I am languishing for love of you, my darling.*
  • **long for**   to *miss* someone or something intensely; to want someone or something intensely. □ *Larry longed for his father while he was away.* □ *I long for the day when I will be finished with school.*
  • **pine for**   to *miss* someone or something so much that you are sad all the time. □ *The dog seems to be pining for his old home.* □ *Mark pined for his old friends.*
  • **yearn for**   to *miss* someone or something very intensely; to want someone or something very intensely. □ *Tom yearned for Jan, but dared not express his feelings.* □ *The exile yearned for his family and his homeland.*

missing   (*adjective*) gone; not in the proper place. □ *The second volume of the encyclopedia seems to be missing.* □ *When did you first notice that the money was missing?*
  • **absent**   *missing*; not present. □ *Sue was absent from class this morning.* □ *A number of people were absent from work yesterday.*

• **away**   *missing;* gone to somewhere else. □ *I took care of my neighbor's house while he was away.* □ *Philip was away for almost a year.*
• **lacking**   *missing;* needed. (Formal.) □ *The horse returned, but the rider was lacking.* □ *Several pages are now lacking from this book.*

misspeak   See the entry for *lie².*

mist   (*noun*) a collection of tiny water droplets in the air; anything that makes things look blurry. □ *A thin mist lay along the ground in the early morning.* □ *A mist appeared in Rita's vision as her eyes filled with tears.*
   • **cloud**   a puffy mass of *mist,* especially one that hangs in the sky. □ *A threatening, dark cloud grew on the horizon.* □ *I think that big white cloud looks like a rhinoceros.*
   • **fog**   a thick *mist* at ground level. □ *The cars drove slowly through the fog.* □ *The fog was so thick that I couldn't see the houses across the street.*
   • **haze**   a thin *mist.* □ *A haze of pollution hung over the city.* □ *A moist haze blurred the outlines of the trees in the park.*
   • **vapor**   a thin *mist* formed from any liquid. □ *The teakettle sent up a plume of vapor.* □ *The attendant at the filling station had to breathe gasoline vapor all day long.*

mistake   (*noun*) an act of doing something wrong. □ *I made a mistake on the homework problem.* □ *Susan decided that trusting Tim had been a mistake.*
   • **blunder**   a major *mistake.* □ *Bill's computer blunder erased a lot of important information.* □ *The mayor made his first political blunder shortly after taking office.*
   • **error**   a *mistake;* a failure to get the right answer. □ *Victor's essay contained several grammatical errors.* □ *I tried to find the error in my solution to the math problem.*
   • **slip**   a *mistake* you did not mean to make. (Informal.) □ *Don't worry; everyone makes occasional slips.* □ *I didn't mean to say that; it was a slip of the tongue.*

mistreat   See the entry for *abuse.*

misuse   See the entry for *abuse.*

mite   See the entry for *insect.*

mix   (*verb*) to put things together. □ *Mix all the ingredients together and pour the batter into the greased cake pan.* □ *Art's happiness was mixed with regret.*
   • **alloy**   to *mix* different metals; to *mix* or melt things together. □ *The artist alloyed copper and tin to make bronze.* □ *Cowardice and greed were alloyed in Bill's personality.*

• **amalgamate** to *mix* different things; to form one thing out of many. (Formal.) □ *Several different kinds of rock were amalgamated to form this cliff.* □ *The different companies agreed to amalgamate, and now they are a single corporation.*

• **blend** to *mix* things smoothly and completely. □ *I blended the milk into the batter.* □ *The artist blended blue and red to form a deep purple.*

• **combine** to *mix;* to put things together in any way. □ *Two movers had to combine their strength to lift the sofa.* □ *The tailor combined different fabrics to make this garment.*

• **compound** to *mix* things into one whole. (Formal.) □ *The new drug was compounded of aspirin and caffeine.* □ *The mayor accused the reporter of compounding her story out of lies and hearsay.*

mob See the entry for *crowd.*

mock See the entry for *ridicule.*

mode See the entry for *style.*

moderate See the entry for *mild².*

moist See the entries for *juicy, wet.*

mollify See the entry for *appease.*

molten See the entry for *liquid.*

momentous See the entry for *important.*

monarch See the entry for *ruler.*

money (*noun*) objects or material used for buying and selling; coins and bills. □ *Carrie saved a certain amount of money every month.* □ *Donald counted the money in his wallet.*

• **capital** the *money* stored up by a person or a company. (Formal.) □ *Eddie needed capital to start his business.* □ *The company had amassed an enormous amount of capital.*

• **cash** *money* in the form of coins and bills. □ *I don't have any cash with me.* □ *Fran had to pay in cash, since the store would not accept a check or a credit card.*

• **credit** a promise to pay *money* at a later time. □ *George bought the TV on credit.* □ *The store would not let me have any more credit.*

• **currency** anything used as *money,* especially coins and bills. (Formal.) □ *Salt has been used as currency in some lands.* □ *On what form of currency does Abraham Lincoln's picture appear?*

• **funds** an amount of *money.* □ *Helen did not have sufficient funds in her bank account to cover the check she wrote.* □ *Irene lacked funds and had to borrow money to pay her rent.*

moneyed   See the entry for *rich.*

monopolizing   See the entry for *jealous.*

monsoon   See the entry for *storm.*

monster   (*noun*) an unusually large or frightening creature; anything unusually large or strange. ☐ *I dreamed that a glowing monster crawled up the side of my house.* ☐ *The watermelon grew to be quite a monster.*
  • **brute**   a big, vicious *monster.* (Poetic.) ☐ *Our hero sought to slay the brute that lurked in the forest.* ☐ *A maiden was chained to the rock and left for the brute to devour.*
  • **colossus**   an enormous *monster.* ☐ *The superhero had to fight a colossus who was fifty feet tall.* ☐ *The new skyscraper is a colossus of plexiglas and steel.*
  • **freak**   a very strange *monster.* ☐ *The mutant freak had four arms and worms for hair.* ☐ *The farmer proudly displayed his garden freak: a potato that looked just like the president.*
  • **monstrosity**   anything as large or strange as a *monster.* ☐ *The town hall was an ugly monstrosity encrusted with terra cotta ornaments.* ☐ *The cow gave birth to a two-headed calf, but the monstrosity only lived for a few minutes.*

monstrosity   See the entry for *monster.*

monstrous   See the entry for *atrocious.*

monument   See the entry for *sculpture.*

mop   See the entry for *wipe.*

moron   See the entry for *fool[1].*

mortal   See the entry for *person.*

mortify   See the entry for *embarrass.*

mote   See the entry for *spot.*

motel   See the entry for *hotel.*

motion picture   See the entry for *movie.*

motion-sick   See the entry for *dizzy.*

motivate   See the entry for *encourage.*

motive   See the entry for *reason.*

mound   See the entries for *hill, pile.*

mount   See the entry for *mountain.*

mountain (*noun*) a very high rise in the ground. □ *The town was nestled at the foot of a mountain.* □ *There was a splendid view from the top of the mountain.*

• **crag** a jagged *mountain;* a jagged part of a *mountain.* □ *The mountain climbers feared they would never be able to scale the crag.* □ *I saw the silhouettes of the distant crags as the sun set behind them.*

• **mount** a poetic word for *mountain;* when capitalized, the name of a *mountain.* □ *Mount McLoughlin was covered with snow.* □ *Our hero looked up at the forbidding mount he was to climb.*

• **peak** a high *mountain;* the highest part of a *mountain.* □ *The peaks in the distance are the Rocky Mountains.* □ *The mountain climbers celebrated when they reached the peak.*

• **volcano** a *mountain* that sometimes erupts with molten lava. □ *The Hawaiian islands were formed from volcanoes.* □ *The film showed bright orange lava cascading down the side of a volcano.*

mourn See the entry for *grieve.*

mouth off See the entry for *talk back to.*

move (*verb*) to change position; to make something change position. □ *Move, so I can see the TV screen.* □ *Jay moved the chair from one side of the room to the other.*

• **budge** to *move* in any way. (Informal. Usually in negative phrases like *did not budge* or *could not budge.*) □ *Kay asked Larry to get out of her way, but he didn't budge.* □ *I pushed against the piano with all my might, but I couldn't budge it an inch.*

• **shift** to *move* from one place to another. □ *I shifted the canned goods onto a higher shelf.* □ *The cloud had shifted halfway across the sky in just a few minutes.*

• **stir** to *move* your body. □ *I called Mark's name, and he stirred in his sleep.* □ *Tom whistled for his dog, but the dog didn't stir.*

movie (*noun*) a show that is recorded and displayed on film. □ *We went to see a movie on Friday night.* □ *What did you think of the new movie?*

• **film** a *movie.* (Somewhat formal.) □ *Sue enjoys modern French films.* □ *The director had made several respected films.*

• **flick** a *movie.* (Slang.) □ *The horror flick turned out to be pretty funny.* □ *Philip doesn't like those old black-and-white flicks.*

• **motion picture** a *movie.* (Formal.) □ *The book was made into a motion picture.* □ *This is the most spectacular motion picture of the year.*

muck See the entry for *slime.*

muffle See the entry for *stifle.*

muggy See the entry for *humid.*

mull See the entry for *think.*

multitude   See the entry for *crowd.*

mumble   See the entry for *sigh.*

munch   See the entry for *chew.*

municipality   See the entry for *town.*

munificent   See the entry for *generous*

mural   See the entry for *painting.*

murder   See the entry for *kill.*

murmur   See the entry for *sigh.*

muse   See the entry for *think.*

musical   See the entry for *play¹.*

musician   (*noun*) someone who sings or makes music on an instrument. □ *Rita is in charge of hiring musicians for the dance.* □ *Susan is a talented musician.*

> • **accompanist**   a *musician* who plays background music for someone else's performance. □ *The singer nodded to his accompanist to signal that she should begin to play.* □ *A drummer was the accompanist for our modern dance class.*
>
> • **instrumentalist**   a *musician* who plays an instrument. □ *Who is the instrumentalist playing in that song?* □ *The singing group wanted an instrumentalist to back them up.*
>
> • **performer**   a *musician;* anyone who performs. □ *The cellist was a seasoned performer who knew what audiences liked.* □ *Many young performers competed for chairs in the All-State Orchestra.*
>
> • **soloist**   a *musician* who plays or sings by him- or herself. □ *The piano soloist played beautifully.* □ *Timothy often sang as a soloist in his church choir.*
>
> • **virtuoso**   an extremely skilled *musician.* □ *Everyone wanted tickets for the violin virtuoso's concert.* □ *Victor has enough talent to be a real virtuoso.*

musty   See the entry for *stuffy.*

mute   See the entry for *stifle.*

mutilate   See the entry for *damage.*

mutiny   See the entry for *rebel.*

mutter   See the entry for *sigh.*

muzzle   See the entry for *stifle.*

muzzy   See the entry for *groggy.*

mysterious   (*adjective*) hard to understand or explain; full of mystery. □ *Bill is acting very mysterious; do you suppose he has a secret?* □ *I could not interpret the mysterious symbol painted on the door.*

   • **enigmatic**   hard to understand or figure out. (Formal.) □ *Art looked at me with an enigmatic smile.* □ *"The mice will tell you," was Ben's enigmatic reply.*

   • **inexplicable**   impossible to explain. □ *The more I thought about Carrie's dislike of Donald, the more inexplicable it seemed.* □ *Eddie was troubled by his dog's inexplicable whining.*

   • **mystifying**   very hard to understand; utterly confusing. □ *The magician performed a number of mystifying tricks.* □ *The end of the movie was mystifying; I couldn't tell if the boy got the girl or not.*

   • **puzzling**   confusing and hard to understand. □ *The doctor found Fran's illness quite puzzling.* □ *The fact that George is in love with Helen helps to explain his puzzling behavior whenever she is around.*

mystify   See the entry for *confuse*.

mystifying   See the entry for *mysterious*.

N

nab   See the entry for *catch*.

nag   (*verb*) to continually tell someone that he or she is not doing things right. (Informal.) □ *Irene's dad nagged her to pick up her room, which only made Irene let her room get messier and messier.* □ *Quit nagging me about the money; I'll pay you back eventually.*

   • **harp**   to nag someone about the same thing over and over. (Informal.) □ *Jay is always harping at me to act more cheerful.* □ *The teacher started harping about spelling errors in our history reports.*

   • **hector**   to bully someone by nagging him or her. □ *As club president, Kay hectored the rest of us so much that we secretly decided to vote her out of the club.* □ *Mom hectored me about my grades to the point where I seriously considered running away from home.*

   • **scold**   to nag someone; to blame someone with angry words. (See also the main entry for *scold*.) □ *Laura scolded me for missing our appointment.* □ *The boy's father scolded him.*

naive   (*adjective*) not knowing anything about the way the world works. □ *Mark was naive enough to think that the actor must be as kind and gentle as the character he played on TV.* □ *The naive girl believed that her lover would divorce his wife for her.*

   • **guileless**   naive; not wanting or able to fool anybody. (Formal.) □ *Tom's guileless expression makes it easy to trust him.* □ *Sue is as guileless as a baby.*

   • **ingenuous**   honest in a naive way. (Formal.) □ *When asked why she had thrown her mother's dress in the trash, the little girl's ingenuous reply was, "So Mommy wouldn't get mad at me for tearing it."* □ *Philip has an ingenuous faith in the promises made by advertisements.*

• **innocent**   *naive;* not guilty of anything. (See also the main entry for *innocent.*) □ *I was afraid the innocent child would get into trouble in the city.* □ *Ken blew up at me when I asked him the innocent question, "Where were you all night?"*

• **unsophisticated**   *naive,* overly simple, or without polished manners. □ *I explained to my cousin that it was considered unsophisticated to stare up at the city skyscrapers.* □ *In Rita's unsophisticated view of the world, there is always a good guy and a bad guy.*

• **unworldly**   *naive;* concerned with honesty and virtue and therefore not caring how the world works. (Formal.) □ *The unworldly man never cared about making money, only about being good.* □ *Susan is too unworldly for her own good; people are always taking advantage of her.*

name   See the entry for *call².*

nap   See the entry for *sleep.*

narrative   See the entry for *story.*

narrow   See the entry for *cramped.*

nasty   See the entry for *mean¹.*

nature   See the entry for *personality.*

nauseate   See the entry for *disgust.*

navy   See the entry for *blue.*

near   (*adjective*) not far from; not far. (See also the entry for *approach.*) □ *The boy knew his mother was near.* □ *I felt the wind change when the storm was near.*

• **adjacent**   right next to; right alongside. (Formal.) □ *The restaurant is adjacent to the hotel.* □ *All I can see from my window is the adjacent building.*

• **close**   near to. (See also the main entry for *close.*) □ *Timothy stood close to me.* □ *We live close to the airport.*

• **nearby**   not very far. □ *I heard the nearby crying of a child.* □ *Does the theater have a nearby parking lot?*

nearby   See the entry for *near.*

nearly   See the entry for *almost.*

neat   (*adjective*) clean and in order. □ *Jan keeps her desk very neat.* □ *Everyone notices Bill's neat appearance.*

• **orderly**   in the proper order; liking to do things in the proper order. □ *Art's tools are put away in an orderly fashion.* □ *Ben is an orderly person and must have everything just so.*

• **shipshape**   in strict order, as things are on board a ship. □
*Everything in the restaurant was shipshape, ready for the restaurant
inspector's visit.* □ *The car was shipshape when I got it back from the
mechanic; even the windows had been washed.*
• **tidy**   clean, trim, and in order. □ *Carrie keeps her room very tidy.*
□ *We pitched in, and soon the kitchen was all tidy.*
[→contrasting word: *messy*]

necessary   (*adjective*) very important; impossible to do without. □
Tomato juice is a necessary ingredient in this recipe. □ *Is it necessary to make
so much noise?*
• **essential**   *necessary;* so important that things will not be complete
without it. □ *Water is essential for every living organism.* □ *Being able
to get along with others is an essential skill.*
• **indispensable**   absolutely *necessary;* so important that you cannot
do without it. □ *The bookkeeper's calculator was an indispensable tool
in her job.* □ *Donald's skill at building things made him indispensable
to the theater company.*
• **needed**   *necessary;* so important that you must have it. □ *The
students could not learn their lessons without the needed books.* □ *Your
assistance is badly needed.*
• **vital**   *necessary;* so important that nothing will thrive without it.
□ *The school nurse plays a vital role in our school.* □ *The president's
support was vital for the passage of the bill.*
[→see also: *urgent*]

needed   See the entry for *necessary.*

needle   See the entry for *tease.*

needless   See the entry for *unnecessary.*

needy   See the entry for *poor¹.*

nefarious   See the entry for *evil.*

neglect   See the entries for *ignore, miss¹.*

negligent   See the entry for *careless.*

negotiate   See the entries for *bargain, mediate.*

neighborhood   See the entries for *area, town.*

nervous   (*adjective*) very excited and fearful. □ *The nervous performers
waited their turn to go onstage.* □ *Taking tests makes me nervous.*
• **edgy**   *nervous* about waiting for something to happen. □ *Everyone
in the doctor's waiting room seemed edgy.* □ *The candidates were edgy
on the eve of the election.*

• **jittery**   so *nervous* that you feel shaky. □ *Fran's quavery voice showed how jittery the job interview had made her.* □ *Eddie gave a jittery laugh.*

• **jumpy**   *nervous* and easy to startle. □ *George was so jumpy that any sudden noise could make him twitch.* □ *The jumpy soldier fired his weapon by mistake.*

• **tense**   strained and *nervous.* (See also the main entry for *tense.*) □ *Being around Helen makes me feel tense.* □ *The atmosphere in the operating room was tense as the surgeon made the first incision.*

new   (*adjective*) never seen or done before. □ *Have you read the author's new book?* □ *Irene invented a new tuna fish recipe.*

• **innovative**   *new;* done in a *new* way. (Formal.) □ *The school uses innovative teaching methods.* □ *This innovative diet plan helps you lose weight without feeling hungry!*

• **original**   *new* and clever or striking; not copied. □ *The clothing designer created several highly original styles.* □ *There is a show of original artwork at the museum.*

• **novel**   entirely *new; new* and unusual. □ *The company came up with a novel way of advertising their product.* □ *Jay has discovered a novel use for socks; he wears them as earmuffs.*

newspaper   See the entry for *periodical.*

nibble   See the entry for *bite.*

nice   (*adjective*) quite agreeable. (See also the entry for *kind¹.*) □ *Kay had a nice time at the party.* □ *Laura served us a nice lunch.*

• **enjoyable**   *nice;* easy to enjoy. □ *The movie was enjoyable.* □ *We spent our vacation pursuing such enjoyable activities as swimming, hiking, and soaking up the sun.*

• **lovely**   very *nice;* excellent. □ *I thanked my hosts for a lovely evening.* □ *"Studying your spelling would be a lovely way to spend the afternoon," said Mother.*

• **pleasant**   *nice;* giving pleasure. □ *I had a pleasant conversation with Mark.* □ *The background music was very pleasant.*

nick   See the entry for *dent.*

nimble   See the entry for *agile.*

nip   See the entry for *bite.*

no-man's-land   See the entry for *wilderness.*

noble   See the entry for *grand.*

nodding   See the entry for *sleepy.*

noisy   See the entry for *loud.*

nonchalant   See the entry for *indifferent*.

nonessential   See the entry for *unnecessary*.

nonplus   See the entry for *confound*.

nonsense   (*noun*) something that does not make any sense. □ *Fred was talking some nonsense about the Pyramids having been built by extraterrestrials.* □ *George told his children some delightful nonsense by way of a bedtime story.*

> • **gibberish**   disordered *nonsense; nonsense* spoken rapidly. □ *Helen dismissed the politician's opinions as pure gibberish.* □ *Irene spouted gibberish.*
>
> • **rubbish**   offensive *nonsense.* □ *The critic said the book was dangerous rubbish.* □ *Jay says I've been ignoring him, but that's rubbish.*
>
> • **twaddle**   complete *nonsense.* (Slang.) □ *Kay was tired of seeing twaddle about celebrities on the front page of the newspaper.* □ *Almost everything Larry says is pure twaddle.*

nonstop   See the entry for *constant*.

normal   See the entry for *average*.

nosy   See the entry for *curious*.

not quite   See the entry for *almost*.

notable   See the entry for *famous*.

note   See the entries for *message, notice*.

noteworthy   See the entry for *striking*.

notice   (*verb*) to give your attention to something; to see something. (See also the entry for *attention*.) □ *I noticed a spot on the carpet.* □ *Laura wanted everyone to notice her new sneakers.*

> • **mark**   to *notice* something. (Old-fashioned.) □ *"Mark that light shining through the trees," the sorceress said to our hero.* □ *Mark my words; you'll come to regret your rash action!*
>
> • **note**   to *notice* and remember something. □ *Mary noted the rich quality of everything in Sue's house.* □ *I noted Tom's haggard expression and wondered what caused it.*
>
> • **observe**   to *notice* something and look at it carefully. □ *The detective observed a tiny bloodstain on the windowsill.* □ *The veterinarian observed the dog's behavior.*
>
> [→see also: *see*]

noticeable   See the entry for *conspicuous*.

notify   See the entry for *tell*.

notion   See the entry for *idea*.

notorious   See the entry for *famous*.

nourish   See the entry for *feed*.

novel   See the entry for *new*.

novelist   See the entry for *writer*.

noxious   See the entry for *poisonous*.

nucleus   See the entry for *center*.

nudge   See the entry for *push*.

number   See the entries for *count, song*.

nurture   See the entry for *bring up*[2].

nut   See the entry for *fan*.

nutty   See the entry for *crazy*.

O

obese See the entry for *fat*.

obey (*verb*) to do what you are told to do. □ *Sue was brought up to obey her parents.* □ *The soldier obeyed orders.*
> • **comply with** to do what a rule or an order says. □ *The restaurant was shut down because it did not comply with health regulations.* □ *I had to comply with my boss's request.*
> • **conform** to do precisely as something or someone says; to be in agreement with a rule or standard. (Usually with *to* or *with*.) □ *The students here must conform to the dress code.* □ *The new building must conform to the standards for a dwelling.*
> • **follow** to *obey*; to act according to what something or someone says. (See also the main entry for *follow*.) □ *Follow the instructions carefully.* □ *We followed Philip's orders.*
> • **heed** to pay attention to or *obey* someone or something. (Formal.) □ *Rita heeded the signs that said "No Swimming."* □ *Susan heeded the warning printed on the back of the spray can.*

object (*verb*) to speak out against something. (Often with *to*. See also the entries for *goal, thing*.) □ *I objected to Timothy's plan.* □ *The babysitter said it was bedtime; the children objected.*
> • **expostulate** to *object* insistently or energetically; to try to reason with someone. (Formal. Usually with *with*.) □ *No matter how Jan expostulated with him, Bill insisted that he was right.* □ *Art is stubborn; it's useless to expostulate with him.*
> • **protest** to *object* strongly; to refuse to go along with something. □ *"I protest this treatment!" the man shouted as the waiters hustled him out of the restaurant.* □ *When the principal announced that classes would be held on Saturday, the students protested by refusing to show up.*

• **take exception to**   to *object;* to be offended by something. □ *The words Ben said seemed reasonable, but I took exception to his tone of voice.* □ *Carrie took exception to the way the blind character was portrayed on the TV comedy.*

objective   See the entry for *unbiased.*

obligation   See the entry for *duty.*

obliterate   See the entry for *erase.*

oblivious   See the entry for *unaware.*

obscure   See the entries for *blur, faint, hide.*

observance   See the entry for *ceremony.*

observe   See the entries for *notice, say, watch.*

observer   (*noun*) someone who watches something. □ *Donald came to the classroom as an observer, to see what methods the teacher used.* □ *At parties, Eddie is usually a mere observer of the others' antics.*
   • **onlooker**   an *observer* who does not participate in the action. □ *The couple began to quarrel, making their dinner guests unwilling onlookers to their unhappy relationship.* □ *The street performer began to juggle in front of a small group of interested onlookers.*
   • **spectator**   an *observer* of a public event. □ *More than ten thousand spectators came to see the show.* □ *Fran did not go onstage when the magician asked her to; she preferred to remain a spectator.*
   • **witness**   an *observer* of a crime or a promise. □ *The police officer questioned the witness as to the attacker's appearance.* □ *I was a witness at my friend's wedding.*
   [→consider also: *audience*]

obsession   (*noun*) something you cannot stop doing or thinking about. □ *George is always tidying his house; he has an obsession with neatness.* □ *Helen's obsession with the rock star led her to send him letters every day.*
   • **compulsion**   something you cannot stop doing; something you feel forced to do. □ *Irene has to rearrange the furniture every Friday; it's a compulsion with her.* □ *Jay felt a strong compulsion to know how the story turned out.*
   • **fetish**   something you cannot stop thinking about; something you are excessively devoted to. □ *Kay has a sandal fetish; she has over a hundred pairs of them.* □ *Larry will only go out with girls with long hair; it's a kind of fetish he has.*
   • **fixation**   something you cannot stop thinking about. □ *Mark has a fixation on the end of the world; that's all he ever reads or thinks about.* □ *Judging from the photos she takes, this photographer has a fixation on bathroom sinks.*

• **hang-up** a problem or worry that you cannot get rid of. (Slang.) □ *Tom has a hang-up about being late, so he leaves at least an hour early for everything.* □ *My dad had some kind of hang up with pets, so we were never allowed to have any, not even a goldfish.*

• **mania** something you always do or think about with excessive enthusiasm; a craze. (Formal.) □ *Sue's interest in stamp collecting has developed into a positive mania.* □ *Philip became a victim of the national skateboarding mania.*

obsolete See the entry for *old-fashioned.*

obstacle See the entry for *barrier.*

obstinate See the entry for *stubborn.*

obstruct See the entry for *block.*

obstruction See the entry for *barrier.*

obtain See the entry for *get.*

obtrude See the entry for *meddle.*

obvious See the entry for *clear.*

occasional See the entry for *sporadic.*

occupation See the entry for *profession.*

occupied See the entry for *busy¹.*

occupy See the entry for *live.*

occur See the entry for *happen.*

occurrence See the entry for *event.*

ochre See the entry for *brown.*

odd See the entry for *peculiar.*

oddball See the entry for *character.*

ode See the entry for *poem.*

odor See the entry for *smell.*

odyssey See the entry for *journey.*

of late See the entry for *lately.*

off and on See the entry for *sporadic.*

offender See the entry for *criminal.*

offense See the entry for *crime.*

office manager   See the entry for *clerk*.

officer   (*noun*) a member of a police force. □ *I asked the officer how to get to Third Street.* □ *The officer arrested the suspect.*
  • **cop**   an *officer*. (Slang.) □ *We ought to call a cop.* □ *Why are all those cops gathered in front of the house?*
  • **deputy**   an *officer* who works for the sheriff. □ *The gunslinger got in trouble with the deputy.* □ *The sheriff made everyone in town a deputy and sent them all out to search for the killer.*
  • **patrolman**   an *officer* who walks or patrols a beat. □ *The patrolman was friendly with all the kids on the block.* □ *The patrolman noticed something suspicious happening at the drugstore.*
  • **policeman** or **policewoman**   any police *officer*. □ *The policewoman came to get information about the robbery.* □ *The fleeing suspect shot at and wounded two policemen.*
  • **trooper**   an *officer* who patrols in a car or motorcycle; an *officer* of the state police. □ *The trooper flashed his lights to get me to pull over.* □ *The troopers came to the scene of the highway accident.*

official   See the entry for *authority*.

officious   See the entry for *bossy*.

offspring   See the entry for *descendants*.

often   (*adverb*) many times. □ *I often stop for a cup of coffee on my way home from work.* □ *Rita often wondered what college was like.*
  • **frequently**   many times, at short intervals. □ *Susan frequently visits her parents.* □ *Timothy works out frequently.*
  • **recurrently**   time and time again. (Formal.) □ *Jan had made the same mistake recurrently.* □ *Bill tells that story recurrently.*
  • **regularly**   many times, at regular intervals. □ *Art regularly goes out to the movies.* □ *The newspaper appears on our doorstep regularly.*
  [→contrasting word: *seldom*]

ogle   See the entry for *gawk*.

OK   See the entries for *approve, good*.

old   See the entry for *secondhand*.

old-fashioned   (*adjective*) out of date; in an old style. □ *The children loved to dress up in Grandma's old-fashioned hats and shoes.* □ *Ben lamented that common courtesy was becoming old-fashioned.*
  • **antiquated**   old-fashioned; no longer useful. (Formal.) □ *The writer still used his antiquated manual typewriter.* □ *The plumbing in the old house was quite antiquated.*

• **archaic**   *old-fashioned;* no longer in general use. (Formal.) □ *Carrie puzzled over the archaic language of the original King Arthur stories.* □ *The historical romance was littered with archaic phrases.*
• **dated**   in a noticeably old style; not the latest style. □ *The fashions of five years ago look quite dated today.* □ *Donna wears her hair the same way she did when she was sixteen, which looks dated now.*
• **obsolete**   no longer useful. □ *The factory could not afford to replace their obsolete machinery.* □ *Cassette tapes made 8-track tapes obsolete.*
• **old-time**   in a pleasant old style; from the old days. □ *The little town held an old-time fair, with prizes for the best livestock, the best cherry preserves, and the best vegetables.* □ *We went to see an old-time melodrama, complete with helpless heroine, dastardly villain, and dashing hero.*
• **outmoded**   in an old style; not up to date. □ *The new computer was quickly outmoded.* □ *Grandpa's way of thinking is hopelessly outmoded.*
• **quaint**   in a curious or amusing old style. □ *The old professor used many quaint expressions, like "pray tell."* □ *We laughed at the quaint costumes our ancestors wore in the old family pictures.*

old saw   See the entry for *saying.*

old-time   See the entry for *old-fashioned.*

omen   See the entry for *sign.*

ominous   See the entry for *sinister.*

omit   See the entry for *skip.*

on guard   See the entry for *alert.*

onlooker   See the entry for *observer.*

only   *(adverb)* nothing but. □ *I have only five dollars.* □ *Only three people were invited.*
• **just**   precisely, no more than; nothing but. □ *Eddie just wanted to go home.* □ *Just be quiet and listen to me!*
• **merely**   no more than. □ *Fran managed to upset George merely by asking what time it was.* □ *You merely push this button, and the machine will begin to make french fries.*
• **simply**   no more and no less than. □ *I'm simply dying to read the new mystery story.* □ *It's easy; simply follow the instructions printed on your screen.*

ooze   See the entries for *leak, slime.*

operate   See the entry for *use.*

opponent   See the entry for *enemy.*

opportune   See the entry for *convenient.*

opposite   (*noun*) something that is exactly different or opposed to something else. □ *Loud is the opposite of soft.* □ *Whatever you ask Helen to do, she does the opposite.*

- **contradictory**   an *opposite* that cancels out something else. □ *I think all teachers must be smart, but Irene believes the contradictory.* □ *I don't know what to do; the boss just gave me an order that is the contradictory of one he gave five minutes ago.*
- **contrary**   an entirely different *opposite.* (Often in the expression *on the contrary,* just the opposite.) □ *Jay doesn't hate Kay; quite the contrary, in fact.* □ *I don't hate my job. On the contrary, I'm very happy with it.*
- **reverse**   an *opposite* that is exactly backwards. □ *Laura thinks that people don't notice her, but exactly the reverse is true.* □ *Mark's beliefs about UFOs are now the reverse of what they were last year.*

oppressive   See the entry for *stuffy.*

optimistic   (*adjective*) feeling that everything will turn out well. □ *Tom is optimistic that we will have good weather for the picnic.* □ *Sue plastered the walls of her room with optimistic slogans.*

- **happy-go-lucky**   carefree because you feel that everything will turn out well. (Informal.) □ *Philip is never depressed; he's a happy-go-lucky sort of person.* □ *Ken's happy-go-lucky attitude got him through the hard times.*
- **hopeful**   expecting or wishing that everything will turn out well. □ *We were all hopeful that Rita would recover.* □ *"Things are bound to get better," Susan said with a hopeful smile.*
- **positive**   expecting that everything will turn out well. □ *Tim tried to practice positive thinking.* □ *Can somebody think of a positive way to look at this situation?*
- **upbeat**   confident that everything will turn out well; cheerful. □ *Though the team lost the first game of the series, their mood was upbeat.* □ *Jan tried to cheer herself up by playing upbeat music.*
[→contrasting word: *pessimistic*]

opulent   See the entry for *luxurious.*

oration   See the entry for *speech.*

orchard   See the entry for *farm.*

order   (*verb*) to tell someone to do something. (See also the entry for *arrange.*) □ *My boss ordered me to attend this meeting.* □ *The sergeant ordered the soldiers to dig a trench.*

• **command**   to *order* authoritatively. ☐ *The king commanded his knights to assemble in the great hall.* ☐ *Tom would do anything Jan commanded.*

• **dictate**   to *order* strictly. (Formal.) ☐ *Politeness dictates that you thank your hostess, even if you had a miserable time.* ☐ *Bill dictated his own special set of rules for playing Monopoly.*

• **direct**   to *order* someone to do something; to control the way something is done. ☐ *The sign directed us to turn left.* ☐ *The head librarian directs everything that goes on in the library.*

[→see also: *demand*]

orderly   See the entries for *neat, organized.*

ordinary   See the entry for *average.*

organization   (*noun*) a group of people who come together for a purpose. ☐ *Are you a member of this organization?* ☐ *The organization was dedicated to protecting wildlife.*

• **association**   an official *organization.* ☐ *The local storekeepers formed a business association.* ☐ *Art attended a meeting of the Parent-Teacher Association.*

• **club**   an *organization* for people who share an interest. ☐ *Ben joined a photography club.* ☐ *The members of the model rocket club exchanged ideas for making better model rockets.*

• **gang**   an *organization* for doing violence or committing crimes; a group of friends. (Slang) ☐ *The police suspected that a gang was responsible for the recent robberies in the neighborhood.* ☐ *Carrie was hanging out with the usual gang.*

• **league**   an *organization* of people, groups, teams, or countries. (Formal.) ☐ *Many people joined the league for banning the sale of alcohol.* ☐ *The League of Nations was a precursor of the United Nations.*

• **lodge**   an *organization* with secret rules and practices. ☐ *Donald is Grand Master of his lodge.* ☐ *The lodge meets in a building with their secret symbol painted on the door.*

• **society**   a social *organization;* an *organization* of people with something in common. ☐ *Eddie belongs to a classical music society.* ☐ *The town historical society preserves town records and artifacts that belonged to the earliest settlers.*

[→see also: *team*]

organize   See the entry for *arrange.*

organized   (*adjective*) doing things in a careful and logical way; having everything in its proper place. ☐ *Fran is an organized person; she has her whole day planned out.* ☐ *George likes to keep everything in his closet organized.*

• **businesslike**   *organized,* efficient, and proper, as a good business is supposed to be. ☐ *The secretary filed the forms in a businesslike way.* ☐ *I was impressed by Helen's businesslike manner.*

• **methodical**   always doing things in a particular, *organized* way. ☐ *Irene is a methodical cook and follows every recipe precisely.* ☐ *Jay has a methodical system for cleaning the house.*

• **orderly**   *organized;* having everything in order; doing everything in a certain order. ☐ *The teacher would not dismiss the class until the children were lined up in an orderly fashion.* ☐ *Kay's room was neat and orderly.*

• **systematic**   *organized;* doing things according to a system. ☐ *The doctor made a systematic investigation of Laura's symptoms.* ☐ *Our systematic search of the house failed to turn up the missing items.*

original   See the entry for *new.*

ornament   See the entry for *decorate.*

ornery   See the entry for *stubborn.*

ostentatious   See the entry for *flashy.*

oust   See the entry for *eliminate.*

out cold   See the entry for *unconscious.*

out-of-the-way   See the entry for *distant.*

outcome   See the entry for *result.*

outdistance   See the entry for *pass.*

outdo   See the entry for *excel.*

outer   *(adjective)* on the surface or edge that faces out. ☐ *The house's outer appearance was drab and run-down.* ☐ *The tree was still alive beneath its outer coating of ice.*

• **exterior**   *outer;* not interior. (Formal.) ☐ *The exterior finish on the car was not very good.* ☐ *The building suffered only exterior damage from the explosion.*

• **external**   *outer;* not internal. (Formal.) ☐ *The patient suffered severe external injuries.* ☐ *Mark was careful to give no external sign of his surprise.*

• **outside**   *outer;* not inside. ☐ *The recluse had no contact with the outside world.* ☐ *The outside surface of the window was covered with tiny pockmarks.*

• **outward**   *outer;* not inward. ☐ *Tom put on an outward show of being happy for Sue, but really he was jealous of her.* ☐ *The Petersons' outward appearance was of a stable, well-adjusted family.*

• **superficial**   no deeper than the *outer* surface. (Formal.) ☐ *Rita's grief was obviously superficial.* ☐ *It's just a superficial cut; you won't need stitches.*

outfit   See the entry for *clothing.*

outlandish   See the entries for *peculiar, strange.*

outline   See the entry for *draw.*

outlook   See the entry for *point of view.*

outmoded   See the entry for *old-fashioned.*

outrageous   See the entry for *atrocious.*

outside   See the entry for *outer.*

outstanding   See the entry for *exceptional.*

outstrip   See the entries for *excel, pass.*

outward   See the entry for *outer.*

overcome   See the entry for *beat².*

overdue   See the entry for *late.*

overhaul   See the entry for *fix.*

overjoyed   (*adjective*) extremely happy. ☐ *Susan was overjoyed when Tim asked her out.* ☐ *I am overjoyed to see you again.*
   • **ecstatic**   so happy that you are beside yourself; full of happiness and joy. ☐ *I gather from Jan's ecstatic expression that she got good news.* ☐ *When he won the contest, Bill was ecstatic.*
   • **elated**   so happy that you feel uplifted; joyful; very happy. ☐ *The little boy was clearly elated, having gotten what he wanted for his birthday.* ☐ *Art was elated to learn that he was going to become a father.*
   • **jubilant**   showing great happiness. ☐ *The jubilant supporters of the winning candidate carried him down the street on their shoulders.* ☐ *The crowd gave a jubilant shout when the home team won.*

overlook   See the entries for *ignore, miss¹.*

overtake   See the entry for *pass.*

overweight   See the entry for *fat.*

overwhelm   See the entry for *flood.*

own   (*verb*) to be the owner of something; to have something in your possession. (See also the entry for *personal.*) ☐ *Ben owns only one pair of shoes.* ☐ *Carrie does not own that car; she rents it.*

• **have** to *own* or control something. □ *Donald has over a hundred books.* □ *I wish I had a computer.*
• **hold** to *own* something. (Poetic.) □ *The king held all the land between the mountains and the sea.* □ *Our hero swore he would gladly forfeit all the goods he held, if only the lady would look on him with favor.*
• **possess** to *own* something; to have complete control of something. (Formal.) □ *Whenever Edward saw a beautiful piece of art, he ardently wished to possess it.* □ *Alice swore that Gerald would never possess her heart.*

own (up) See the entry for *admit.*

P

pacify See the entry for *appease*.

pack (*verb*) to put something tightly into a container. (See also the entries for *bag, herd*.) □ *Helen packed a week's worth of clothes into her suitcase.* □ *Irene packed the container full of ice cream.*
- **cram** to force too large an amount of something into a container. □ *We managed to cram one more suitcase into the trunk of the car.* □ *Jay crammed the entire hamburger into his mouth.*
- **jam** to force something into a container. (Informal.) □ *See if you can jam those last few books into the box.* □ *Kay jammed a tape into the tape player, breaking it.*
- **stuff** to push something into a container. (Informal. See also the main entry for *stuff*.) □ *I stuffed the blankets back into the linen closet.* □ *Laura stuffed the notebooks into her backpack.*

package (*noun*) something that is packed or wrapped. □ *I got a package in the mail.* □ *On the morning of his birthday, there were a number of brightly wrapped packages waiting by Mark's place at the table.*
- **bundle** a *package* containing a number of things. □ *Tom donated a bundle of old clothes to the homeless shelter.* □ *Sue had a bundle of pencils.*
- **packet** a small *package*. □ *This packet contains information about the museum.* □ *Philip opened the packet of instant soup.*
- **parcel** a *package*, especially one that is going to be sent. (Formal.) □ *Grandma sent me a parcel of goodies.* □ *Rita found a parcel wrapped in brown paper on her doorstep.*

packed See the entry for *thick*.

packet See the entry for *package*.

pact See the entry for *agreement*.

page   See the entry for *call¹*.

pageant   See the entry for *procession*.

pain   See the entry for *hurt²*.

painful   See the entry for *sore*.

painting   (*noun*) a picture done in paint. □ *The artist did a painting of the rocky coast.* □ *That painting looks so realistic that it could almost be a photograph.*
  • **canvas**   a *painting* on a stretched piece of cloth called *canvas*. (Formal.) □ *There were a number of old canvases hanging on the walls of the formal dining room.* □ *The museum has purchased several canvases from that artist.*
  • **mural**   a large *painting* on a wall. □ *A mural on the bathroom wall depicted bright-colored sea creatures.* □ *The children painted a mural on one wall of the classroom.*

pair   See the entry for *group*.

pal   See the entry for *friend*.

palatable   See the entry for *delicious*.

pale   (*adjective*) light in color. □ *Susan's dress was pale yellow.* □ *Tim is looking quite pale.*
  • **faded**   having turned *pale*. □ *It was hard to read the faded writing on the old letters.* □ *The shirt looked faded after just a few washings.*
  • **fair**   not dark; light; having a naturally *pale* complexion. (See also the main entry for *fair*.) □ *Jan gets sunburned easily because her skin is so fair.* □ *As a baby, Bill had fair hair, but it got darker as he grew up.*
  • **pallid**   unhealthily *pale*. (Poetic.) □ *When our hero saw how pallid the lady's face had grown, he knew her life was fading.* □ *The kind nurse stroked the sufferer's pallid brow.*
  • **sallow**   *pale* and yellowish. □ *Anna hated her sallow complexion.* □ *Ben grew sallow from working indoors all the time.*

pallid   See the entry for *pale*.

palm   See the entry for *steal*.

paltry   See the entry for *meager*.

pamper   See the entry for *spoil¹*.

pamphlet   See the entry for *book*.

panorama   See the entry for *view*.

pant   See the entry for *gasp*.

paper   See the entry for *document.*

parade   See the entries for *procession, show off.*

paramount   See the entry for *supreme.*

parcel   See the entry for *package.*

parched   See the entry for *dry.*

pardon   (*verb*) to let a wrongdoer go without punishing him or her; to say that a wrongdoer may go without punishment. □ *Pardon me for interrupting you.* □ *Carrie pardoned Donald's rudeness, knowing he was under a lot of pressure.*
> • **absolve**   to *pardon* someone who has committed a sin; to *pardon* someone completely. (Formal.) □ *Eddie went to confession, and the priest absolved him.* □ *Fran generously absolved George of all blame.*
> • **excuse**   to *pardon* someone; to free someone from having to do something; to be a sufficient reason for someone to be *pardoned.* □ *Because Helen had a broken arm, the teacher excused her from gym class.* □ *Nothing could possibly excuse the boy's cruelty toward his playmate.*
> • **exonerate**   to *pardon* or free someone from blame. (Formal.) □ *Irene was accused of the theft, but her friends had faith that she would be exonerated.* □ *This new evidence exonerates you completely.*
> • **forgive**   to *pardon* someone and not have hard feelings toward him or her. □ *Jay forgave Kay for not inviting him to the party.* □ *I'm sorry, darling; forgive me.*

pare   See the entry for *trim.*

parody   See the entry for *irony.*

parrot   See the entry for *repeat.*

part   (*noun*) something less than a whole; something divided from the whole. (See also the entry for *divide.*) □ *Laura flipped through the book, only reading the juicy parts.* □ *Mark gave me part of his sandwich.*
> • **fragment**   a *part* broken off something. □ *The little figurine lay in fragments on the floor.* □ *The archaeologist found a fragment of a clay tablet.*
> • **piece**   a *part* separated from the whole. □ *Tom sewed the pieces of the shirt together.* □ *Sue cut herself a large piece of cake.*
> • **portion**   a *part*; food served for one person. □ *That restaurant serves generous portions of food.* □ *Philip always gave a portion of his income to charity.*
> • **section**   a *part* divided from the rest. □ *The next section of the book is about the history of stamp collecting.* □ *Divide the circle into four equal sections.*

participate (*verb*) to share in what others are doing. □ *All club members must participate in keeping the clubhouse clean.* □ *We invited Rita to participate in the volleyball game.*
- **engage in** to *participate;* to be busy at doing something. □ *The dinner guests engaged in a lively conversation.* □ *Susan is engaged in putting her new stamps into her stamp album.*
- **join in** to *participate* willingly or enthusiastically. (Informal.) □ *The singer wanted the audience to join in on the chorus.* □ *Let's pick a game that everyone can join in.*
- **take part** to *participate* equally; to take or have a share in doing something. □ *Tina's mother, sisters, and aunts all took part in sewing the quilt for her.* □ *Jan was feeling depressed and didn't want to take part in the festivities.*
[→see also: *team up*]

particle See the entry for *whit.*

particular See the entry for *picky.*

particularly See the entry for *especially.*

partisan See the entry for *supporter.*

partner (*noun*) someone who works with you. □ *You may work with a partner on this history project.* □ *Bill had to consult his business partner before making any important decisions.*
- **associate** a companion, *partner,* or friend. □ *The detective questioned the murder victim's friends, family, and associates.* □ *I don't know Art all that well; we are business associates.*
- **collaborator** someone who works closely with you. (Formal.) □ *The composer and the lyricist were collaborators on the songs for the musical.* □ *The scientist met with his collaborators on the experiment.*
- **colleague** someone who works equally with you or who does the same kind of work. (Formal.) □ *The novelist went to Writers Guild meetings in order to chat with her colleagues.* □ *The professor disagreed with his respected colleague.*
- **confederate** someone who works with you to trick people or commit crimes. (Formal.) □ *The gambler had a confederate among the other poker players.* □ *The organized crime boss refused to give the police the names of his confederates.*
[→contrasting word: *rival*]

party (*noun*) an occasion when people get together to eat, drink, and have fun. □ *Can you come to my birthday party?* □ *Ben holds parties every Friday night.*
- **bash** a big *party.* (Slang.) □ *Carrie's got a big Valentine's Day bash planned.* □ *The house was littered with the remains of the previous night's bash.*

• **celebration**   a *party* to celebrate something. □ *Donald and Eva's children planned a celebration of their fiftieth anniversary.* □ *When Fran graduated from college, we held a little celebration.*

• **reception**   a *party* to honor a special person or event. □ *There was plenty of food and dancing at the wedding reception.* □ *A hundred people attended the reception for the guest of honor.*

• **shindig**   a large, informal *party*. (Slang) □ *The Grants prepared an enormous shindig with tons of food and drink.* □ *The veterans' hall usually puts on quite a shindig for New Year's Eve.*

pass   (*verb*) to go by or past someone or something. □ *Helen passed the post office and turned right at the next street.* □ *Irene passed me in the street and didn't even say hello.*

• **go ahead of**   to *pass* something and continue on in front of it. □ *I allowed Jay to go ahead of me in the line.* □ *I was going the speed limit, but all the other cars were going ahead of me.*

• **outdistance**   to *pass* something or go farther than it. (Formal.) □ *The runner quickly outdistanced everyone else in the race.* □ *The baseball player had already outdistanced all previous home run records.*

• **outstrip**   to *pass* something and go far beyond it. (Formal.) □ *The record's sales this year outstripped even last year's.* □ *Kay outstripped everyone else in class in the number of books she read during the school year.*

• **overtake**   to come up from behind something and *pass* it. □ *The police car soon overtook the getaway vehicle.* □ *The lion overtook the fleeing zebra foal.*

pass away   See the entry for *die.*

pass on   See the entry for *die.*

pass out   See the entry for *distribute.*

pass over   See the entries for *ignore, skip.*

passageway   See the entry for *hall.*

passel   See the entry for *cluster.*

passing   See the entry for *temporary.*

past   (*adjective*) happening earlier in time; from an earlier time. □ *Larry was sorry for his past mistakes.* □ *The hard times are past; things are going to get better now.*

• **erstwhile**   from an earlier time and no longer happening; *past.* (Somewhat formal.) □ *It humiliated Mark to see his erstwhile girlfriend going out with his best buddy.* □ *Nancy seems to have gotten rid of her erstwhile shyness.*

• **former** from an earlier time and no longer happening. ☐ *Otto still felt loyalty to the sports teams from his former hometown.* ☐ *Philip had forgotten his former promise to help with the cooking.*
• **previous** from an earlier time; from the time right before now. ☐ *What was the name of your previous employer?* ☐ *Rita had had several previous allergy attacks, but this one was the worst of all.*
[→contrasting word: *future*]

paste See the entry for *stick²*.

pastime See the entry for *game*.

pastoral See the entry for *country*.

pasture See the entry for *field*.

pat See the entry for *tap*.

patch up See the entry for *fix*.

path See the entry for *road*.

patient (*adjective*) calmly waiting for something; calmly enduring something. (See also the entry for *customer*.) ☐ *Just be patient; dinner will be ready in half an hour.* ☐ *The patient teacher would explain things over and over until he was sure that all the students understood.*
• **forbearing** calmly enduring something. (Formal.) ☐ *Sarah was forbearing with her wayward grandson.* ☐ *Thomas's wife must be a very forbearing woman.*
• **long-suffering** calmly enduring something unpleasant for a long time. ☐ *Jan's long-suffering friends listened to the details of her latest love trouble.* ☐ *The secretary, a long-suffering person, dealt politely with floods of rude callers.*
• **persevering** calmly working for something; not giving up. ☐ *Bill is so persevering I am sure he will succeed.* ☐ *Only the most persevering students get through that tough class.*
[→see also: *persistent*]

patrician See the entry for *aristocratic*.

patrolman See the entry for *officer*.

patron See the entry for *customer*.

patronizing See the entry for *pretentious*.

pattern (*noun*) shapes and colors put together in a special way. ☐ *I tried to draw the pattern of stripes in the cat's fur.* ☐ *The wallpaper had a pleasant pattern of green leaves.*
• **arrangement** something put together in a special way. ☐ *The centerpiece was a lovely arrangement of fall flowers.* ☐ *A haphazard arrangement of pictures covered the walls.*

• **design**   a *pattern* created with care. ☐ *The design of the building allowed each worker to have a special, private space.* ☐ *I liked the design on the fabric.*

• **form**   a *pattern;* the shape of something. ☐ *Art was fascinated by the hexagonal form of snowflakes.* ☐ *Ben made a pancake in the form of a snowman.*

• **structure**   the way parts are put together. ☐ *I looked at the structure of the leaf under the microscope.* ☐ *The structure of the picnic table allows it to be folded up and carried like a suitcase.*

pause   See the entry for *wait.*

pay   (*noun*) the money you get for working. (See also the entry for spend.) ☐ *Carrie collected her pay at the end of every week.* ☐ *Donald wanted a job with higher pay.*

• **earnings**   the money you get for working. ☐ *Eddie added up his earnings from the paper route.* ☐ *The baseball player's earnings were well over a million dollars a year.*

• **income**   any money you get. (Formal.) ☐ *Fran has income from stocks.* ☐ *You must pay tax on all your income.*

• **salary**   the money you get for working for a week, a month, or a year. ☐ *It's a stressful job, but the salary is good.* ☐ *What is your annual salary?*

• **stipend**   money you get regularly. (Formal.) ☐ *George receives a monthly stipend from his father.* ☐ *The scholarship paid Helen's college tuition, plus a small stipend.*

• **wage**   the money you get for working a certain amount of time. ☐ *The hourly wage is $5.50.* ☐ *The boss promised an increase in my wages.*

pay attention   See the entry for *listen.*

pay for   See the entry for *buy.*

peace   (*noun*) freedom from all conflict; quiet; stillness. ☐ *The two warring countries were finally at peace.* ☐ *I loved the peace out in the woods.*

• **calm**   freedom from disturbance. (See also the main entry for calm.) ☐ *Irene felt a deep calm.* ☐ *The storm passed, and calm settled over the valley.*

• **harmony**   freedom from conflict; complete agreement. ☐ *Jay and Kay were able to work together in harmony.* ☐ *Laura was glad to come home to the harmony of her family life.*

• **tranquility**   freedom from disturbance or upset. ☐ *Mark found tranquility by learning to meditate.* ☐ *The baby-sitter wished for a moment of tranquility, but her active charges kept her busy the whole time.*

peak   See the entry for *mountain.*

peal   See the entry for *ring*.

pebble   See the entry for *rock¹*.

peculiar   (*adjective*) extremely unusual. □ *Tom has a peculiar habit of standing on one foot when he feels nervous.* □ *Sue's white eyeshadow looks quite peculiar.*
- **bizarre**   flamboyantly unusual. □ *Philip hung his walls with bizarre pictures of wizards and dragons.* □ *Rita wore a bizarre costume made entirely of bottle caps.*
- **freaky**   disturbingly unusual. (Outdated slang.) □ *This freaky guy started following me and singing love songs from old musicals.* □ *Philip lives in this freaky house where everything's painted black.*
- **odd**   unusual; not fitting in. □ *The man in the tuxedo looked rather odd among all•the bluejeaned people at the concert.* □ *Teasing a girl is an odd way of showing you like her.*
- **outlandish**   wildly unusual. □ *Susan told an outlandish story about why she was late for work.* □ *Ted's orange cowboy boots look outlandish with his conservative business suit.*
- **strange**   unusual or unnatural. (See also the main entry for *strange*.) □ *I heard strange noises in the attic.* □ *Our English guest was eager to try strange American foods like pizza and barbecued chicken.*
- **weird**   disturbing and unusual. (Informal.) □ *Bill is certainly acting weird today.* □ *Do my glasses make me look weird?*

pediatrician   See the entry for *doctor*.

peep   See the entry for *look*.

peer   See the entry for *look*.

pelt   See the entries for *beat¹, fur*.

pen   See the entry for *cage*.

penalize   See the entry for *punish*.

pennant   See the entry for *flag*.

pep   See the entry for *energy*.

perfect   (*adjective*) entirely complete and without any problems or mistakes. (See also the entry for *practice*.) □ *Art drew a perfect circle.* □ *The crooks were planning the perfect robbery.*
- **consummate**   the very best possible; without mistakes. (Formal.) □ *The critics praised the violinist's consummate skill.* □ *The governor was a consummate politician, promising nothing but getting credit for everything.*

• **faultless** without any faults or mistakes. □ *Juan was impressed with Charles's faultless Spanish pronunciation.* □ *The singer gave a faultless performance.*

• **flawless** without any flaws or mistakes. □ *Donald wanted a flawless diamond for his girlfriend's engagement ring.* □ *Edith's makeup was flawless.*

• **impeccable** entirely without problems or mistakes. (Formal.) □ *Fran decorated her home in impeccable taste.* □ *George's manners are impeccable.*

performance See the entry for *concert.*

performer See the entries for *entertainer, musician.*

perhaps See the entry for *maybe.*

perilous See the entry for *dangerous.*

period See the entries for *stage, time.*

periodical (*noun*) a publication that comes out at regular intervals. (Formal.) □ *Does the library carry this periodical?* □ *Helen liked to read the latest periodicals.*

• **journal** a serious or scholarly *periodical.* □ *The scientist published her results in a respected journal.* □ *The stamp-collecting society publishes a quarterly journal.*

• **magazine** a *periodical,* usually one that contains many pictures and comes out every week or month. □ *Irene couldn't wait for the new issue of her favorite fashion magazine.* □ *The mayor was interviewed in a national news magazine.*

• **newspaper** a *periodical* giving the latest news, usually one that comes out every day or week. □ *Jay read the newspaper every morning.* □ *There was a story about Kay in the local newspaper.*

• **serial** a *periodical;* any publication or story that comes out in a series. (Formal.) □ *You will find that publication on the shelf with the other serials.* □ *Laura was addicted to a TV serial.*

perish See the entry for *die.*

permanent (*adjective*) not for a short time only; staying in place for a long time. □ *Mark is a permanent resident of the hotel.* □ *The townsfolk put up a statue as a permanent tribute to their beloved mayor.*

• **lasting** staying or existing for a very long time. □ *Tom and Jim had a lasting friendship.* □ *Philip's injured leg was a lasting reminder of the car accident.*

• **perpetual** always staying in place or existing; never stopping or changing. (Formal.) □ *The monument was a perpetual symbol of the people's gratitude to the fallen soldiers.* □ *The students grew tired of the teacher's perpetual criticism.*

• **stable**   always staying in place; never moving or changing. (See also the main entry for *stable*.) □ *The Robertsons seem to be a stable family.* □ *The building is quite stable; not even an earthquake should be able to shake it.*
[→contrasting word: *temporary*]

permit   See the entry for *allow*.

permit to borrow   See the entry for *lend*.

perpetual   See the entries for *constant, permanent*.

perplex   See the entry for *confuse*.

persevering   See the entry for *patient*.

persist   See the entry for *last*.

persistent   (*adjective*) continuing; not giving up. (See also the entry for *insistent*.) □ *There was a persistent knocking at the door.* □ *I tried to ignore Susan's question, but she was persistent.*
• **determined**   having decided never to give up. □ *The reporter was determined to get the information somehow.* □ *The determined cat tried everything to get at the goldfish.*
• **diligent**   working hard and never giving up. (Formal.) □ *Tim is a diligent worker.* □ *The diligent student spent a week preparing for the test.*
• **dogged**   never giving up, despite all obstacles. □ *The dogged detective followed the criminal's trail for months.* □ *Nothing could discourage Victor's dogged pursuit of a date with the movie star.*
• **resolute**   having strongly made up your mind not to give up. (Formal.) □ *The mountain climber looked up at the peak with a grim, resolute expression.* □ *The resolute man vowed he would have revenge.*
• **tenacious**   clinging to something; never giving up. (Formal.) □ *The puppy had a tenacious grip on the slipper.* □ *The tenacious salesman refused to leave the customer alone until he bought something.*
[→see also: *patient*]

person   (*noun*) any man, woman, boy, or girl. □ *Bill is a decent person.* □ *How many people came to the party?*
• **body**   a *person*. (Folksy.) □ *Working in the garden all day can really tire a body out.* □ *Mrs. Hall is a fun-loving old body.*
• **human being**   a *person;* a member of the human race. □ *There are billions of human beings on the planet.* □ *How could anyone torture another human being like that?*
• **individual**   a *person* different from all other people. □ *Ben was not a terribly thoughtful individual.* □ *The police officers watched the suspicious individual.*

• **mortal**   a *person;* any creature who must eventually die. (Poetic.) □ *Our hero was the bravest of mortals, but the silver-scaled dragon struck fear into even his heart.* □ *Carrie was disappointed to discover that the rock star was a mere mortal like anyone else.*

personal   (*adjective*) belonging to someone; not for sharing with everyone. □ *Donald took all his personal belongings from his desk at work and left the office.* □ *This towel is for Eddie's personal use and shouldn't be touched by anyone else.*

   • **individual**   belonging to a particular person. □ *Everyone got an individual serving of jam in a little plastic container.* □ *The teacher tried to find out about her students' individual interests.*

   • **own**   belonging to someone. (See also the main entry for *own*.) □ *Each child had his or her own bedroom.* □ *I want to do this in my own way.*

   • **private**   not for sharing with everyone. (See also the main entry for *private*.) □ *Fran's private opinion was that George was too bossy.* □ *Helen's diary is strictly private.*

personality   (*noun*) the way someone is; the personal qualities that make one person different from all others. □ *People like Irene for her delightful personality.* □ *Jay has a domineering personality.*

   • **character**   all the qualities of someone or something; how moral someone is. (See also the main entry for *character*.) □ *Judge Sue by her character, not by the way she looks.* □ *The politician said his opponent was lacking in character.*

   • **disposition**   the way someone acts and thinks. (Formal.) □ *The child's sunny disposition made it easy to like her.* □ *Kay has such a quarrelsome disposition that it's hard to talk to her without getting into a fight.*

   • **nature**   the way someone naturally is; someone's inborn qualities. □ *Larry's not in a bad mood; he's just grumpy by nature.* □ *I'm afraid that Mary's trusting nature will get her into trouble.*

   • **temperament**   the way someone tends to react. (Formal.) □ *It is almost impossible to train a dog with such a vicious temperament.* □ *Tom has a very excitable temperament.*

perspective   See the entry for *point of view*.

perspire   See the entry for *sweat*.

persuade   (*verb*) to get someone to do or believe something. □ *I persuaded Philip to loan us his car.* □ *Rita persuaded Susan not to go on the trip.*

   • **cajole**   to *persuade* someone through flattery. □ *Tim cajoled Jan into cooking Thanksgiving dinner by saying how much everyone loved her cooking.* □ *Bill pleaded and cajoled until Art agreed to appear in the talent show.*

• **coax** to *persuade* someone gently. □ *The mother coaxed the little child to walk down the stairs.* □ *We finally coaxed shy Ben to come out and meet the guests.*

• **convince** to *persuade* someone by reasoning with him or her. □ *The statistics about smoking and lung disease convinced Carrie to give up her cigarettes.* □ *Donald convinced me that he was the right person for the job by telling me about his qualifications.*

• **talk into** to *persuade* someone by talking to him or her; to *persuade* someone to do something he or she does not really want to do. □ *Eddie talked Fran into donating some used clothing to the thrift shop.* □ *How could I have let George talk me into taking care of his dogs for two whole weeks?*

• **wheedle** to *persuade* someone through constant flattery. □ *Howard kept wheedling Irene until she agreed to marry him.* □ *Smooth-talking Jay wheedled twenty dollars out of me.*

perturbed See the entry for *upset.*

peruse See the entry for *read.*

pest See the entry for *insect.*

pester See the entry for *annoy.*

petition See the entry for *beg.*

petrified See the entry for *afraid.*

petulant See the entry for *grumpy.*

phantasm See the entry for *illusion.*

phantom See the entry for *ghostly.*

phase See the entry for *stage.*

phenomenon See the entry for *wonder¹.*

phony See the entry for *fake.*

physician See the entry for *doctor.*

pick See the entries for *choose, harvest.*

pick up See the entry for *learn².*

picky (*adjective*) insisting on only the best; wanting only a certain kind. (Informal.) □ *Kay was very picky about the kind of job she would take.* □ *Laura is a notoriously picky eater.*

• **choosy** wanting only the best. (Informal.) □ *The choosy shopper felt all the tomatoes in the pile before she finally selected one.* □ *Mark is so choosy about the girls he'll go out with that he never goes out with anyone.*

• **discriminating**   wanting only the very best. (Formal.) □ *The most discriminating people shop at our store.* □ *This television series will appeal to the discriminating viewer.*

• **finicky**   willing to take only a certain kind. □ *The finicky baby refused to eat anything but pureed apricots.* □ *Tom is very finicky about shoes; he'll only wear his favorite brand.*

• **fussy**   liable to be upset unless you get just what you want. (Informal.) □ *Our teacher is awfully fussy about neatness and will lower our grades if we turn in messy papers.* □ *The fussy diner sent his soup back to the kitchen three times.*

• **particular**   wanting only a certain kind; wanting things done a certain way. (Formal.) □ *Sue is quite particular about whom she invites to her home.* □ *Philip is particular about the way he wants his eggs cooked.*

picture   (*noun*) a representation on a flat surface of something in the real world; a design made by drawing, painting, or photography, for instance. (See also the entry for *imagine*.) □ *Ken drew a picture of a race car.* □ *Rita has a picture of her family on her desk.*

• **cartoon**   an exaggerated or simple, and often funny, *picture*. □ *We laughed at Susan's cartoon of the teacher.* □ *The political cartoon used a donkey to stand for the Democratic Party.*

• **landscape**   a *picture* of a view. □ *Vincent painted a beautiful western landscape.* □ *Tim bought a landscape to hang in his living room.*

• **portrait**   a *picture* of a person. □ *Bill had his portrait taken.* □ *A portrait of the president hung in the post office.*

piece   See the entry for *part*.

piecemeal   See the entry for *gradual*.

pier   See the entry for *dock*.

pierce   See the entry for *stab*.

piercing   See the entry for *harsh*.

pig-headed   See the entry for *stubborn*.

pigeonhole   See the entry for *sort*.

pile   (*noun*) a collection of things, tumbled together one on top of the other. □ *When Art finished sawing through the board, there was a little pile of sawdust on the floor.* □ *Ben threw his clothes onto the pile of laundry.*

• **heap**   a shapeless *pile*. □ *The children left their toys in a heap.* □ *The king had heaps of golden coins in his treasure house.*

• **mound**   a rounded *pile*. □ *Carrie pushed the sand up into a mound.* □ *The blue china bowl held a mound of mashed potatoes.*

• **stack**   an orderly *pile*, each thing right on top of the thing below it. □ *Donald served up a tall stack of pancakes.* □ *Eddie checked out a whole stack of books from the library.*

pillar   See the entry for *post*.

pilot   See the entry for *guide²*.

pine   See the entry for *grieve*.

pine for   See the entry for *miss²*.

piquant   See the entry for *spicy*.

piqued   See the entry for *indignant*.

pit   See the entry for *hole*.

pitch   See the entries for *rock², throw*.

pithy   See the entry for *brief*.

pity   See the entry for *mercy*.

pivot   See the entry for *turn*.

placate   See the entry for *appease*.

place   (*noun*) a particular region or point. (See also the entry for *put*.) □ *Put the hammer back in the same place where you found it.* □ *Fran thought that New Mexico was the most beautiful place on earth.*
> • **locale**   a special or interesting *place*; a *place* in which a story is set. (Formal.) □ *The photographer often traveled to exotic locales to get pictures.* □ *The locale of every story that author writes is a fictional town in the Old West.*
> • **location**   a *place*, especially one where something has been put. □ *The convenience store has moved to a new location.* □ *"What is your present location?" the control tower asked the pilot.*
> • **site**   the *place* where something interesting happened or is located. □ *The statue marks the site where the general made his famous speech.* □ *The millionaire selected a mountaintop site for his new mansion.*
> • **spot**   a specific *place*. (See also the main entry for *spot*.) □ *I can't quite reach the spot that itches.* □ *George showed the police the exact spot where he was attacked.*
> [→see also: *area*]

placid   See the entry for *calm*.

plan   (*noun*) a step-by-step outline for what is to be done. □ *The mayor had a plan for attracting more tourists to the town.* □ *We did everything according to plan.*
> • **agenda**   a formal *plan* for a meeting. □ *After the treasurer gave her report, we went to the next item on the agenda.* □ *What should we put on the agenda for our next meeting?*

• **program** a formal or strict *plan;* a *plan* or schedule for a performance. ☐ *Helen follows a strenuous exercise program.* ☐ *Tonight's program will include Beethoven's Fifth Symphony.*

• **scheme** a secret *plan;* a *plan* for doing something bad. ☐ *Irene cooked up a scheme for getting Jay out of the club.* ☐ *The police thwarted the bankrobbers' scheme.*

• **strategy** a careful, clever *plan.* ☐ *The general had a strategy for the attack.* ☐ *The coach explained the strategy we should use in the second half.*

[→see also: *plot*]

planet See the entry for *world.*

plant See the entry for *put.*

plantation See the entry for *farm.*

plaster See the entry for *stick².*

platitude See the entry for *saying.*

play¹ (*noun*) a story that actors present onstage. ☐ *George Bernard Shaw wrote a play about Joan of Arc.* ☐ *Kay wanted the leading role in the class play.*

• **comedy** a funny *play.* ☐ *The play was supposed to be a comedy, but it didn't make me laugh even once.* ☐ *The new comedy had the audience laughing until the tears came to their eyes.*

• **drama** a serious *play.* ☐ *This compelling drama tells the story of five sisters and their mean-spirited mother.* ☐ *Is this play a comedy or a drama?*

• **farce** a broadly funny *play,* usually involving slapstick. ☐ *Slamming doors and mistaken identities were key elements in the farce.* ☐ *We knew the farce was a success when we heard the audience laughing.*

• **musical** a *play* that includes songs. ☐ *My Fair Lady is Laura's favorite musical.* ☐ *To appear in this musical, you must be able to sing as well as act.*

• **show** any *play,* movie, or television program. (See also the main entry for *show².*) ☐ *The show will open on Friday.* ☐ *We went out to dinner and a show.*

play² (*verb*) to use something just for fun; to use something unseriously. (Usually with *with.*) ☐ *Mark played with his new dump truck.* ☐ *Don't play with the tape deck; it's not a toy.*

• **fool** to meddle with something for fun. (Usually with *with.* See also the main entry for *fool².*) ☐ *Kids shouldn't fool with knives.* ☐ *Tom had a good time fooling with the computer.*

• **toy** to use someone or something for fun; to treat someone or something like a toy. (Usually with *with*.) □ *Sue toyed with the end of her ponytail.* □ *Philip isn't really in love with Rita; he's just toying with her.*

• **trifle** to use something just for fun; to use something frivolously. (Formal. Usually with *with*.) □ *The lady was trifling with our hero's affections.* □ *The sorcerer's apprentice learned not to trifle with magic spells.*

player See the entry for *entertainer*.

playwright See the entry for *writer*.

plead See the entry for *beg*.

pleasant See the entry for *nice*.

pleasure (*noun*) intense enjoyment. □ *Susan got the most pleasure out of sailing on the lake.* □ *It gives me great pleasure to introduce Ms. Smith.*

• **delight** happiness and *pleasure*. □ *An expression of pure delight spread over Tim's face as he relaxed, listening to the music.* □ *Jan is such an enthusiastic student that it is a delight to be her teacher.*

• **gratification** *pleasure* that fills a need; happiness and satisfaction. (Formal.) □ *Seeing Bill graduate gave his parents some gratification for everything they had sacrificed to keep him in school.* □ *Art lived only for the gratification of his senses, never stopping to think about higher things.*

• **joy** intense happiness and *pleasure*. □ *Ben's joy at seeing his friend again was written all over his face.* □ *The charity workers brought joy to many poor households that holiday season.*

pleat See the entry for *fold*.

pledge See the entry for *promise*.

plentiful (*adjective*) more than enough. □ *We have a plentiful supply of pencils.* □ *Water is plentiful in this part of the country.*

• **abundant** very *plentiful*. □ *The millionaire was not willing to share his abundant wealth with anyone.* □ *There is an abundant growth of wild strawberries in the forest.*

• **ample** all that you need. □ *Grandma made sure we had ample food for the trip.* □ *This amount of cloth should be ample for making two pairs of pants.*

• **bountiful** *plentiful;* very generous. □ *The farmer's harvest that year was bountiful.* □ *The hunters found a bountiful supply of game in the hills.*

• **copious** all that you could possibly need; very many. □ *The bride and groom received copious gifts from their family and friends.* □ *Carrie has a copious supply of cloth napkins.*

plight   See the entry for *problem.*

plod   See the entry for *walk.*

plot   (*noun*) a secret plan to do something evil or illegal. □ *Who was involved in the plot to blow up the town hall?* □ *Donald was always seeing signs of a vast plot against him.*
>   • **collusion**   secret cooperation to do something evil, deceitful, or illegal. (Formal.) □ *Bugsy didn't act alone; he and Mitch were operating in collusion.* □ *The candidate lost the election as a result of his collusion in the crime.*
>   • **conspiracy**   a secret organization for doing something evil or illegal. □ *The grocery-store owners formed a conspiracy to keep food prices high.* □ *Mr. Green's trusted secretary was a member of the conspiracy against his life.*
>   • **racket**   a plan or method for defrauding people. (Slang.) □ *Bugsy had a very nice betting racket going, until the police found out.* □ *I got a letter saying I had won a vacation home in Florida, but I figured it must be some kind of racket.*
>   • **scheme**   a secret, clever plan to do something evil or illegal. □ *Helen tried to get me involved in a get-rich-quick scheme.* □ *Irene had worked out a whole scheme for getting her brother's money.*
>   [→see also: *plan*]

pluck   See the entry for *tug.*

plug   See the entry for *commercial.*

plummet   See the entry for *fall.*

plump   See the entry for *fat.*

plunge   See the entries for *fall, submerge.*

pocket   See the entry for *take.*

poem   (*noun*) an arrangement of words in lines that uses striking language, and often rhymes or has rhythm. □ *Jay had to memorize a poem by Henry Wadsworth Longfellow.* □ *Kay wrote a poem for her boyfriend.*
>   • **epic**   a long *poem* that tells a story. □ *The Greek poet Homer is famous for his two epics,* The Iliad *and* The Odyssey. □ *Vincent is working on an epic about his recent trip to Montana.*
>   • **ode**   a *poem* about an important person or thing. □ *John Keats wrote an ode about the painting on a Grecian urn.* □ *The ode was the poet's tribute to his dead friend.*
>   • **quatrain**   a *poem* four lines long. □ *The teacher asked all the students to compose a quatrain in honor of Mother's Day.* □ *The poet expressed a great depth of feeling in just a simple quatrain.*

• **rhyme**   a rhyming *poem.* □ *Laura found it very helpful to know the little rhyme that begins "Thirty days hath September." □ The birthday card had a nice rhyme inside.*

• **verse**   a great *poem;* poetry in general. (Poetic.) □ *We spent a week studying the verses of Coleridge. □ The critic thought that the actors were not doing justice to Shakespeare's immortal verse.*

poet   See the entry for *writer.*

poetic   See the entry for *figurative.*

point   See the entry for *goal.*

point of view   (*noun*) a particular way of thinking about or reacting to something. □ *Before you get angry at Tom, try to look at things from his point of view. □ The popular children's author was good at writing from a child's point of view.*

• **outlook**   point of view; a particular way of responding to things. □ *Philip has such a gloomy outlook. □ Rita maintained a cheerful outlook even during the hardest times.*

• **perspective**   a particular way of looking at or thinking about something. □ *The men on the debating team asked Susan to give them a woman's perspective on the issue. □ Teaching class for a day gave Tim a chance to see things from the perspective of a teacher.*

• **standpoint**   a particular way of thinking about things, influenced by having a particular opinion. □ *Many people found the movie offensive from a religious standpoint. □ From a purely artistic standpoint, it is fortunate that the artist suffered so much, since suffering inspired her greatest work.*

point out   See the entry for *show³.*

pointed   (*adjective*) coming to a point; making a point. □ *Jan used a pointed stick to draw a picture in the dirt. □ The witch's costume included a tall, pointed hat. □ Rose made a pointed mention of how late it was growing.*

• **barbed**   coming to a sharp and dangerous point; making a mean or hurtful point. □ *The fence was made of barbed wire. □ The scorpion stings with its barbed tail. □ Ken made a number of barbed remarks just to hurt my feelings.*

• **sharp**   coming to a fine point or edge; stinging. (See also the main entry for *sharp.*) □ *Bill needed a good, sharp needle to sew with. □ The knife didn't cut very well because it wasn't very sharp. □ Linda grew tired of her mother's sharp criticisms.*

• **spiked**   coming to a long, sharp point; having a long, sharp point. □ *Anna's new shoes had spiked heels. □ The soldiers wore spiked helmets.*

pointless   See the entry for *meaningless.*

poisonous (*adjective*) containing poison; very harmful. □ *Ben kept the drain opener and other poisonous household chemicals out of the children's reach.* □ *Many poisonous mushrooms look similar to harmless ones.*
• **noxious**   very harmful; very bad-smelling. (Formal.) □ *As the car idled, the noxious exhaust fumes filled the garage.* □ *Carrie used some kind of noxious preparation to strip the old paint off the kitchen table.*
• **toxic**   very poisonous. (Formal.) □ *Toxic chemicals were seeping into the ground from the city dump.* □ *The lead paint used in the old building was highly toxic and had to be removed.*
• **venomous**   poisonous; able to hurt or kill you if it bites you. □ *Are rattlesnakes venomous?* □ *Donald got very sick from the bite of a venomous spider.*

poke (*verb*) to push at or against someone or something with something pointed. □ *Eddie poked me in the ribs.* □ *Fran poked at the lizard with her walking stick.*
• **dig**   to *poke* deeply into something. (See also the main entry for *dig*.) □ *The rider dug his spurs into the horse's side.* □ *George dug his elbow into his attacker's stomach.*
• **jab**   to *poke* something sharply. □ *The doctor jabbed me with the needle and gave me a shot.* □ *Helen jabbed her finger into the air as she lectured.*
• **prod**   to *poke* something hard or repeatedly. □ *The bank robber prodded the teller with his gun.* □ *Irene prodded me with her foot to get me to stop talking.*
[→see also: *stab*]

pole   See the entry for *post*.

policeman   See the entry for *officer*.

policewoman   See the entry for *officer*.

policy   See the entry for *rule*.

polish (*verb*) to rub something to make it smooth and shiny. □ *Jay polished the silver teapot.* □ *Kay polished her glasses with her handkerchief.*
• **buff**   to *polish* something gently. □ *Laura buffed her nails.* □ *The jeweler buffed the ring with a soft cloth.*
• **burnish**   to *polish* something with a hard, smooth tool. □ *The potter burnished the clay pot with a smooth stone.* □ *The leather had been burnished to a mirror-like gloss.*
• **shine**   to *polish* something until it is very bright. (*Shined* is the past tense of *shine* when it is used in this sense.) □ *The soldier had to shine his shoes for inspection.* □ *Mark shined his belt buckle so that it glittered.*
• **wax**   to *polish* something by rubbing wax on it. □ *Tom loved to spend the afternoon waxing his car.* □ *Otto used a mop to wax the hardwood floor.*

polished   See the entry for *smooth*.

polite   (*adjective*) having or showing good manners. □ *What a polite child!* □ *Sending a thank-you note is the polite thing to do, even if you did not like the gift.*

• **civil**   *polite* but not friendly. □ *The rivals had a hard time being civil to one another.* □ *Philip restrained his dislike for Rita and gave a civil reply to her question.*

• **courteous**   *polite* and dignified. □ *The salesclerk was very courteous to all the customers.* □ *The reporter sent a courteous letter, requesting an interview with the governor.*

• **genteel**   *polite* and well-bred. □ *Susan admired Tim's genteel manners.* □ *Jan shocked her genteel friends by telling a raunchy joke.*

• **gracious**   *polite*, friendly, and generous. □ *The gracious host made sure all of his guests were enjoying themselves.* □ *It's very gracious of you to offer to help.*

• **well-mannered**   *polite*. (Usually used to describe young people.) □ *Bill praised the well-mannered little boy.* □ *My friend did her best to appear well-mannered in front of my parents.*

[→contrasting word: *rude*; see also: *tactful*]

politic   See the entry for *tactful*.

political   See the entry for *governmental*.

pollute   See the entry for *dirty²*.

pond   See the entry for *lake*.

ponder   See the entry for *wonder²*.

pool   See the entry for *lake*.

poor¹   (*adjective*) having little or no money. □ *Art's family was very poor when he was growing up.* □ *The woman was so poor that she didn't know how she would get her next meal.*

• **broke**   having no money at all. (Slang.) □ *I can't go to the movies with you; I'm broke.* □ *Ben spends his money as soon as he gets it, so he's always broke.*

• **destitute**   having nothing at all. (Formal.) □ *The earthquake left Carrie destitute; it destroyed her home, which was all she had.* □ *Donald was shocked to see how destitute his neighbors were.*

• **impoverished**   having very little. (Formal.) □ *Impoverished as he was, Eddie found enough money to give to charity.* □ *The impoverished college students pooled their money to buy a textbook to share.*

• **needy**   not having enough of something. □ *Fran took food to needy families.* □ *There were so many needy children that the charity workers despaired of being able to help them all.*

[→contrasting word: *rich*]

poor² (*adjective*) of low quality; not good. □ *George's grades were poor.* □ *The carpenter did extremely poor work.*

> • **inadequate**   not good enough. (Formal.) □ *Helen thought that her performance on the test was inadequate.* □ *Irene did an inadequate job of cleaning the bathroom.*
> • **inferior**   not as good as something else. (Formal.) □ *This is an inferior brand of detergent; it didn't get my laundry clean at all!* □ *The writing in this essay is inferior to your previous work.*
> • **mediocre**   neither good nor bad. □ *The new restaurant looked elegant, but the food was mediocre.* □ *Jay is a mediocre ballplayer.*
> • **shoddy**   of low quality; worn out or carelessly made. (Informal.) □ *Kay's new radio turned out to be a shoddy piece of goods.* □ *If Larry is so well-to-do, why does he wear such a shoddy old coat?*

pop   See the entry for *burst*.

popular   (*adjective*) liked by most people. □ *Mary is the most popular girl in the sixth grade.* □ *Soccer is a popular sport in our neighborhood.*

> • **favorite**   liked better than others. □ *Mark Twain is Tom's favorite author.* □ *The children had pizza, their favorite food, for dinner.*
> • **in**   accepted by many people; accepted by the most important people. (Slang.) □ *After Sue got her hair cut short, she discovered that short hair was no longer in.* □ *Philip desperately wanted to be part of the in crowd.*
> • **well-liked**   liked by many people. (Usually used to describe a person.) □ *Rita is well liked at work.* □ *Many of her former students came back to visit the well-liked teacher.*

portal   See the entry for *entrance*.

portentous   See the entry for *sinister*.

portion   See the entry for *part*.

portrait   See the entry for *picture*.

pose   (*verb*) to pretend to be someone you are not. (Formal. Usually with *as*.) □ *Susan posed as my sister.* □ *The reporter posed as a TV repairman in order to get into the house.*

> • **disguise oneself**   to dress up and pretend to be someone you are not. (Usually with *as*.) □ *The spy wore a drab suit and glasses to disguise herself as an ordinary office worker.* □ *Tim stole a postal uniform and disguised himself as a letter carrier.*
> • **impersonate**   to pretend to be a particular person. (Formal.) □ *The actor impersonated Elvis Presley.* □ *Jan impersonated the teacher very humorously.*

• **masquerade**   to pretend to be someone you are not, often in a showy way. (Formal. Usually with *as*.) □ *The con artist was masquerading as a member of the Swedish royal family.* □ *Bill dressed up in a white lab coat and masqueraded as a doctor.*

posh   See the entry for *luxurious*.

position   See the entry for *case*.

positive   See the entries for *certain, optimistic*.

positively   See the entry for *certainly*.

possess   See the entry for *own*.

possessive   See the entry for *jealous*.

possibly   See the entry for *maybe*.

post   (*noun*) a piece of wood, metal, or stone stuck upright in the ground. (See also the entry for *publish*.) □ *The cowboy hitched his horse to a post.* □ *The fence was made of barbed wire strung between wooden posts.*
   • **column**   a *post* that is a decorative part of a building. □ *There were six white marble columns across the face of the building.* □ *These granite columns mark the entrance to the tomb.*
   • **pillar**   a solid *post*. □ *The statue stood atop a tall pillar.* □ *Stone pillars held up the roof of the great hall.*
   • **pole**   a tall, narrow *post*. □ *Twelve flags flew from twelve poles in front of the building.* □ *The electrician climbed up the telephone pole.*
   • **stake**   a short, narrow *post* used to mark a spot or hold something down. □ *The diligent Boy Scout hammered the tent stake into the hard ground.* □ *The construction workers put stakes where the corners of the building would be.*

posterity   See the entry for *descendants*.

postpone   See the entry for *delay*.

potentate   See the entry for *ruler*.

pouch   See the entry for *bag*.

pounce   See the entry for *jump*.

pound   (*verb*) to beat on something over and over. □ *Ben pounded the nail into the wall.* □ *Carrie pounded on the door with her fist.*
   • **bang**   to *pound* something that makes a loud or metallic noise. □ *I wonder why my neighbor is banging on the wall like that.* □ *Donald enthusiastically banged the drum.*
   • **batter**   to *pound* someone or something until it is hurt or ruined. □ *The boxer battered his opponent with his fists.* □ *The storm battered the little boat but could not sink it.*

• **hammer** to *pound* with a hammer or as if you were using a hammer. □ *Eddie hammered the metal flat.* □ *Fran hammered on the coconut but couldn't get it to crack.*

• **thump** to *pound* something that makes a dull sound. □ *George angrily thumped the sofa pillows.* □ *Helen's feet thumped on the steps.*

pour See the entries for *flow, rain.*

power See the entries for *ability, electricity.*

powerful See the entry for *strong.*

powerless See the entry for *weak.*

practical joke (*noun*) a joke that is played on someone. □ *Pulling a chair out from under someone is Irene's favorite practical joke.* □ *Jay put sugar in the salt shaker as a practical joke.*

• **antics** funny movements or actions. □ *We laughed at Kay's antics.* □ *The clown amused the children with her antics.*

• **caper** a wild *practical joke.* □ *Larry and Mark were planning to steal the bust of Lincoln from in front of the auditorium, and they wanted me to join in on the caper.* □ *Tom thought that egging Sue's car would be a great caper.*

• **prank** a *practical joke* done to irritate someone. □ *The only prank Philip ever played was to call people up and ask, "Is your refrigerator running?"* □ *Tipping over outhouses was a popular prank, back when most people had them.*

• **trick** a *practical joke* done to fool someone. □ *When Rita gave me a box of candy, I suspected it was a trick; sure enough, a toy snake popped out of it when I opened the lid.* □ *Susan wanted to play a trick on Tim.*

practically See the entry for *almost.*

practice (*verb*) to do something over and over again to learn to do it well. (See also the entry for *custom.*) □ *Jan practiced the dance step until she got it right.* □ *The pianist practiced for eight hours every day.*

• **drill** to make someone *practice* something in a disciplined way. □ *The sergeant drilled the soldiers relentlessly.* □ *The teacher drilled the students in their multiplication tables.*

• **perfect** to *practice* something to get it exactly right; to remove all faults or mistakes from something. (See also the main entry for *perfect.*) □ *Bill wanted to perfect his recipe for vegetable soup.* □ *The pitcher worked to perfect his curve ball.*

• **rehearse** to *practice* something you are going to perform. □ *The actors rehearsed the scene for weeks.* □ *Anna stood before the mirror, rehearsing her speech.*

• **work at**   to *practice* something with a lot of effort. □ *Mary worked at her Spanish by having conversations with Spanish speakers.* □ *Charles knew he needed to work at his spelling.*

practiced   See the entry for *experienced.*

praise   (*verb*) to say that someone or something is good. □ *Donna's parents praised her for saving her money.* □ *The teacher praised everyone for working so hard on the history project.*
   • **applaud**   to *praise* someone enthusiastically and publicly. □ *The townspeople applauded the mayor's decision to lower taxes.* □ *The newspaper applauded the man for his bravery in rescuing the drowning boy.*
   • **commend**   to *praise* someone formally. (Formal.) □ *Mr. Edwards sent me a letter commending me for my efforts.* □ *Felicia commended her sister's good judgment.*
   • **compliment**   to *praise* someone directly. □ *Gina complimented Harry on his new haircut.* □ *I compliment you on your good taste in decorating.*
   • **extol**   to *praise* someone very enthusiastically. (Formal.) □ *The book critic extolled the writer's skill.* □ *The commercial extolled the car's many luxurious features.*
   • **laud**   to *praise* someone highly. (Formal or poetic.) □ *Song and story lauded our hero's exploits.* □ *Before presenting the award to Sue, the principal lauded her academic achievements.*
   [→contrasting word: *condemn*]

prank   See the entry for *practical joke.*

prate   See the entry for *babble.*

precarious   See the entry for *shaky.*

precious stone   See the entry for *jewel.*

precipitate   See the entry for *sudden.*

precipitous   See the entry for *steep.*

precise   See the entry for *exact.*

predicament   See the entries for *bind, problem.*

predict   (*verb*) to know or say what is going to happen in the future. □ *The old farmer predicted that it was going to be a bitterly cold winter.* □ *The psychic predicted that the movie star would get married.*
   • **forecast**   to *predict* something; for an expert to *predict* something. □ *The weather bureau is forecasting rain tonight.* □ *The commentators were forecasting an election victory for the incumbent.*
   • **foresee**   to *predict* what you are sure will happen. □ *I foresee hard times ahead for us.* □ *No one could have foreseen that John would lose his job.*

• **foretell**   to say what is going to happen in the future. □ *Everything happened to Kevin just as the gypsy foretold.* □ *Larry was sure that Nostradamus's cryptic poem had foretold World War II.*
• **prophesy**   to *predict* solemnly. (Formal.) □ *I prophesy a happy future for the bride and groom.* □ *Mary prophesied that her older son would come to no good.*

prefer   (*verb*) to like something better than something else. □ *I'll have coffee, but Nancy prefers tea.* □ *Tom prefers to spend his spare time reading.*
• **be partial to**   to *prefer* something. (Informal.) □ *Jane must be partial to yellow. She wears it every day.* □ *Ken grew up in China, so he's quite partial to Chinese food.*
• **favor**   to *prefer* something or think it is better than other things. (See also the main entry for *favor.*) □ *Roger favors sports programs on TV.* □ *Stanley favored spending the day in the library.*
• **incline toward**   to tend to choose something because you *prefer* it. □ *Thomas wants to take the train into town, but I incline toward driving.* □ *Victor inclined toward going to college after he finished high school.*

prejudiced   See the entry for *unfair.*

preliminary   (*adjective*) coming before the main thing; done to prepare. □ *I have a few preliminary remarks before we begin the meeting.* □ *In the preliminary negotiations, the diplomats agreed on a place to meet to negotiate the actual treaty.*
• **initial**   done right at the beginning; first. □ *The initial stage of designing the new toy will involve interviewing hundreds of children to see what they like to play with.* □ *The initial tests showed that the drinking water was safe.*
• **introductory**   *preliminary;* leading to something else. □ *The article's introductory paragraph interested me.* □ *The speaker gave a short introductory lecture before beginning the slide show.*
• **preparatory**   done to prepare. (Formal.) □ *The professor gave us a few preparatory instructions before we began to dissect the earthworms.* □ *The cook needed to take preparatory steps to get the vegetables ready to steam.*

premonition   See the entry for *hunch.*

preparatory   See the entry for *preliminary.*

prepare   (*verb*) to get something ready. □ *I put snow tires on the car to prepare it for winter.* □ *Wendy prepared the guest room for her friend to spend the night.*
• **fix**   to *prepare* food. (See also the main entry for *fix.*) □ *Art fixed us a nice lunch.* □ *Will you fix me a sandwich?*

• **fix up**   to *prepare* something by mending or arranging it. (Informal.) □ *Ben fixed up his old pants so he could wear them again.* □ *Carrie really fixed up that broken-down house.*

• **ready**   to *prepare* something to be used right away. (Formal.) □ *Our hero told his squire to ready their horses.* □ *Donald readied himself for the journey.*

preposterous   See the entry for *improbable.*

prescription   See the entry for *medicine.*

present   (*adjective*) at this time; existing right now. (See also the entries for *give, show²*.) □ *What is your present address?* □ *Eddie reached his present height when he was seventeen years old.*

• **contemporary**   happening or existing in the same period of time. (Formal.) □ *The gallery featured work by the best contemporary artists.* □ *Fran will only listen to contemporary music.*

• **current**   happening or existing now; up-to-the-minute. □ *Do you have the current issue of this magazine?* □ *George's current popularity is likely to decrease.*

• **recent**   happening or existing right now or not very long ago. □ *Helen's recent decision to move away came as a shock to her friends.* □ *The recent fire left the house a complete wreck.*

presentiment   See the entry for *hunch.*

preserve   (*verb*) to take care of something so that it will last a long time. □ *Irene preserved her family photos in a picture album.* □ *The museum preserves a number of antique automobiles.*

• **conserve**   to use something sparingly so that you will still have some at a later time. □ *To conserve electricity, turn out the lights when you leave a room.* □ *The hikers ate sparingly, to conserve their dwindling food supply.*

• **keep**   to have something for a long time. (See also the main entry for *keep.*) □ *Jay kept the pictures his children drew in kindergarten.* □ *Kay kept her love letters in a locked box.*

• **save**   to hold on to something for a long time; to put something away carefully in order to have it for a long time. (See also the main entry for *save.*) □ *Laura saved the programs from every play she ever attended.* □ *Mark saves his old clothes to use as rags.*

[→see also: *stash*]

pressing   See the entry for *urgent.*

pressure   See the entry for *stress¹.*

prestige   See the entry for *status.*

presume   See the entry for *assume.*

presumptuous   See the entry for *bossy.*

pretentious   (*adjective*) acting as if you are more important than you really are. (Formal.) □ *Tom says that using big words makes one sound pretentious, but I beg to differ.* □ *The pretentious woman talked of nothing but the exclusive clubs she belonged to.*
> • **condescending**   treating other people as less worthy than you. □ *"You may take my coat," Sue said in a condescending tone.* ⊔ *Philip's condescending way of explaining things makes me angry.*
> • **patronizing**   treating other people as on a lower level than you; acting as though you are doing other people a favor. □ *"Your little apartment is really quite nice,"* was *Rita's patronizing remark.* □ *Susan acts very patronizing toward her younger brother.*
> • **superior**   thinking or acting as if you are on a high level. □ *Tim puts on superior airs just because he won the math prize.* □ *"You wouldn't understand," said Jan, sounding superior.*

pretty   See the entry for *beautiful.*

prevail   See the entry for *win.*

prevaricate   See the entry for *lie².*

previous   See the entry for *past.*

previous to   See the entry for *before.*

prey   See the entry for *victim.*

prick   See the entry for *stab.*

prickle   See the entry for *smart².*

prim   (*adjective*) excessively proper or formal. □ *The prim young lady sat perfectly still, with her hands folded in her lap.* □ *Bill had a prim dislike of off-color jokes.*
> • **demure**   modest and proper. □ *Anna chose a demure blue dress to wear to the party.* □ *The little girl made a demure curtsey.*
> • **prissy**   excessively proper and rigid. (Informal.) □ *Mary is so prissy, she thinks "The Three Little Pigs" is too violent for children.* □ *"I was brought up to respect my elders," Charles said with a prissy little smile.*
> • **stiff**   so proper that you seem awkward. □ *It was a formal occasion, and everyone felt stiff.* □ *Donna gave her guests a stiff speech of welcome.*

primary   See the entry for *main.*

principal   See the entry for *main.*

print   See the entries for *publish, write.*

prior to   See the entry for *before.*

prissy   See the entry for *prim*.

private   (*adjective*) secret; not public. (See also the entry for *personal*.)
□ *These are private family matters, not to be shared with your friends.* □
Linda and Felicia looked for a place where they could have a private conversation.
> • **classified**   officially secret; known only by a few people. □ *The
> classified documents were kept locked up in a safe.* □ *Only the highest
> government officials could get to the classified information.*
> • **confidential**   known only by a few people; not to be told to
> everyone. (Formal.) □ *I'm going to tell you something, but I want you
> to keep it confidential.* □ *Gina wondered whom she could trust to advise
> her on this confidential matter.*
> • **hush-hush**   secret. (Slang.) □ *Harold and Sue's wedding was a
> hush-hush affair.* □ *Jane told Jill to keep their secret strictly hush-hush.*
> [→contrasting word: *public*]

prize   See the entry for *treasure*.

probable   See the entry for *likely*.

probe   See the entry for *explore*.

problem   (*noun*) something that is difficult to solve or overcome. (See
also the entry for *emergency*.) □ *I'm having a problem getting the oven to
heat properly.* □ *Will it cause a problem if I'm late to work today?*
> • **adversity**   a *problem* that you must fight hard to get through.
> (Formal.) □ *Kevin showed great courage in the face of adversity.* □ *Larry
> and Mary stayed friends through every adversity.*
> • **difficulty**   a *problem* that you must work hard or be strong to get
> through. □ *I'm having difficulty hearing you; can you speak up?* □
> *Nancy's lack of popularity contributed to her difficulties at school.*
> • **hardship**   a *problem* that causes much suffering. □ *The journey
> to the West was full of hardships.* □ *Tom's losing his job was a great
> hardship for his family.*
> • **plight**   a very sad or pitiful *problem;* a pitiful situation. (Old-
> fashioned.) □ *Jane had great sympathy for the hungry child's plight.*
> □ *Left without friends, family, or home, Richard was truly in a sorry
> plight.*
> • **predicament**   an amusing, minor, or temporary *problem*. (For-
> mal.) □ *I'm in a bit of a predicament; I seem to have lost my wallet.*
> □ *The kitten tangled herself up in the ball of yarn, and we laughed at
> her predicament.*
> • **trial**   a *problem* that requires a lot of strength to get through. □
> *Keeping his temper was quite a trial for the hotheaded boy.* □ *His child's
> fatal illness was the greatest trial of Stanley's life.*

• **trouble**   an upsetting *problem;* an upsetting time. ☐ *Many people told Thomas their troubles.* ☐ *A visit from Victor usually means trouble.*

procedure   See the entry for *way.*

proceed   See the entry for *advance.*

procession   (*noun*) a line of people, vehicles, or animals, traveling steadily forward. ☐ *A procession of bridesmaids walked down the aisle ahead of the bride.* ☐ *A procession of ants went from the anthill to the spilled soda and back.*

  • **caravan**   a *procession* of people going on a journey. ☐ *The caravan of traders set out for the East.* ☐ *The caravan moved slowly across the desert.*

  • **pageant**   a showy or colorful *procession.* ☐ *The school put on a pageant of costumes from other lands.* ☐ *The prince's ball was a pageant of wealth and splendor.*

  • **parade**   a *procession* to celebrate something; a military *procession.* ☐ *Did you see the Fourth of July parade?* ☐ *The parade passed by the reviewing stand, where the president saluted the passing soldiers.*

proclaim   See the entry for *announce.*

procure   See the entry for *get.*

prod   See the entry for *poke.*

prodigy   See the entry for *wonder¹.*

produce   See the entry for *make¹.*

profession   (*noun*) what a person is educated to do for a living. ☐ *Wendy thought that being a veterinarian must be an interesting profession.* ☐ *Dr. Jones is a member of the medical profession.*

  • **calling**   what a person chooses to do for a living. ☐ *The pastor did not want to do anything undignified or otherwise inappropriate to his calling.* ☐ *I believe Ben has finally found his calling as a TV announcer.*

  • **career**   the kind of work a person does or wants to do throughout his or her life. ☐ *Is it necessary to have a college degree to pursue a career in banking?* ☐ *Carrie trained for a career in real estate.*

  • **job**   what a person does for a living. (Informal. See also the main entry for *job*.) ☐ *Donald got a job at the restaurant.* ☐ *Eddie's first job was delivering newspapers.*

  • **occupation**   the kind of work a person does for a living. (Formal.) ☐ *What is your occupation?* ☐ *Fran felt ashamed of her occupation as a housekeeper.*

  • **vocation**   what a person does for a living. (Formal.) ☐ *For some people, acting is a hobby, but for George, it's a vocation.* ☐ *Helen had a natural talent for styling hair, so she made it her vocation.*

• **walk of life**   the kind of work a person does. (Formal.) □ *Irene was a teacher, and most of her friends were from the same walk of life.* □ *The members of our church come from all walks of life.*

proficiency   See the entry for *mastery.*

profit   See the entry for *benefit².*

progenitor   See the entry for *ancestor.*

progeny   See the entry for *descendants.*

program   See the entry for *plan.*

progress   See the entry for *advance.*

progressive   See the entry for *gradual.*

prohibit   See the entry for *forbid.*

project   See the entry for *job.*

prominent   See the entry for *conspicuous.*

promise   (*verb*) to seriously and sincerely say that you will do or not do something. □ *Jay promised Kay that he would call home every night.* □ *Laura promised to clean up the living room.*
    • **assure**   to *promise;* to say you are certain about something. □ *I assure you that I won't forget.* □ *The captain assured the passengers that there was no cause for alarm.*
    • **guarantee**   to *promise* officially, formally, or enthusiastically. □ *The company guarantees that this wristwatch will work under water.* □ *If you go on this trip with me, I guarantee you'll have a good time.*
    • **pledge**   to *promise* solemnly. □ *The friends pledged their eternal loyalty.* □ *The new citizens pledged to defend their adopted country.*
    • **swear**   to *promise* by taking an oath. □ *The detective swore she would track down the criminal.* □ *I swear I'll never do it again.*
    • **vow**   to *promise* solemnly or religiously. □ *The bride and groom vowed to stand by each other in good times and bad.* □ *Our hero vowed revenge against the evil knight.*

promote   See the entry for *advertise.*

promotion   See the entry for *commercial.*

prompt   See the entry for *urge.*

promptly   See the entry for *immediately.*

pronounced   See the entry for *striking.*

proof   See the entry for *evidence.*

prop up   See the entry for *support.*

propensity   See the entry for *tendency*.

proper   (*adjective*) socially correct; correct for the situation. □ *Mark did not think it was proper for children to call adults by their first names.* □ *I don't have the proper tool to fix the sink.*
> • **appropriate**   correct for the situation. □ *Tom searched for an appropriate birthday card for his friend.* □ *Sue's formal gown was quite appropriate for the elegant party.*
> • **decent**   socially and morally correct. □ *The townsfolk were decent people and did their best to help the homeless man.* □ *Philip knew that the only decent thing to do was admit to having broken the window and offer to pay for it.*
> • **fitting**   precisely correct for the situation. □ *The evening of comedy was a fitting tribute to the great comic actor.* □ *Since Rita had loved the old house more than anyone, it seemed fitting that she should inherit it.*
> • **right**   appropriate for the situation. (See also the main entry for *right*.) □ *Susan tried to decide what was the right thing to do.* □ *We had just the right number of eggs to make a batch of pancakes.*
> • **seemly**   dignified and socially correct. (Formal.) □ *The grand lady did everything in the most seemly fashion.* □ *Mom and Dad thought it was not seemly to kiss in public.*

property   (*noun*) things that you own; in particular, land or buildings that you own. □ *Tim shouted to the intruder, "Get off my property!"* □ *This whole building is the property of Mr. Vance.*
> • **assets**   anything valuable that you own, including money. (Formal.) □ *Bill's assets were very limited.* □ *Anna's assets included stocks, bonds, and real estate.*
> • **belongings**   personal items that you own. □ *Mary put all of her belongings in a suitcase and left in the middle of the night.* □ *The tornado destroyed all of Charlie's belongings.*
> • **effects**   anything that you own. (Formal.) □ *The landlord asked the tenant to remove all of her effects from the apartment.* □ *The detective found several mysterious letters in the dead man's effects.*

prophesy   See the entry for *predict*.

propitiate   See the entry for *appease*.

propitious   See the entry for *convenient*.

proportion   See the entry for *size*.

propose   See the entry for *bring up¹*.

protect   (*verb*) to keep someone or something from harm. □ *The raincoat protected me from the nasty weather.* □ *Linda tried to protect her children from the violence in their neighborhood.*

• **defend**   to *protect* someone or something from an enemy. □ *The soldier was willing to die to defend her country.* □ *Felicia learned to defend herself against attackers.*

• **guard**   to *protect* someone or something from intruders; to prevent someone or something from escaping. □ *The officer's job was to guard the museum during the night.* □ *Two armed men guarded the prisoner.*

• **safeguard**   to *protect* someone or something from all possible harm. □ *The inoculation will safeguard you against the disease.* □ *Gina wanted a good way to safeguard her money.*

• **shield**   to *protect* someone or something by putting something between it and harm. □ *Harold used his body to shield his daughter from the falling rocks.* □ *The safety glasses shielded the welder's eyes.*

protected   See the entry for *safe*.

protégé   See the entry for *student*.

protest   See the entry for *object*.

prove   See the entry for *show¹*.

proverb   See the entry for *saying*.

provide   See the entry for *supply*.

providence   See the entry for *luck*.

provisional   See the entry for *temporary*.

provisions   See the entry for *food*.

provoked   See the entry for *indignant*.

prudent   See the entry for *careful*.

prune   See the entry for *trim*.

pry   See the entry for *snoop*.

public   (*adjective*) for everyone to know or use. □ *It is now public knowledge that the mayor intends to resign.* □ *Sue visited the public library.*

• **civic**   for all citizens to use; having to do with a town or city. (Formal.) □ *The civic center will host some interesting events.* □ *I feel a sense of civic pride when I look at our beautiful, peaceful town.*

• **common**   for everyone to share. □ *It was in the townspeople's common interest to put up more streetlights on the main roads.* □ *At dinner, everyone ate out of a common dish.*

• **communal**   for everyone to share equally. □ *On the kibbutz, child care is communal.* □ *The roommates put their money in a communal bank account.*

publicize   See the entry for *advertise*.

publish (*verb*) to make something public; to distribute information to many people. □ *The newspaper published a story about the governor.* □ *Jane had made the remark in private and did not expect to see it published.*

• **broadcast** to make something public by putting it on radio or television. □ *Pictures of the murder victim were broadcast on the evening news.* □ *The radio station will broadcast the president's message at seven o'clock.*

• **circulate** to tell or hand something around to many people. □ *Kevin circulated a rumor about Larry.* □ *Mary went from door to door, circulating a pamphlet about the need for a new school in the neighborhood.*

• **post** to put a message in a public place. (See also the main entry for *post*.) □ *The teacher posted our final grades on the classroom door.* □ *Nancy posted signs about her lost dog all over town.*

• **print** to make many copies of a written message and distribute them to many people. □ *The reporter asked her editor to print the story.* □ *The magazine printed several shocking pictures.*

[→see also: *distribute*]

puce See the entry for *red*.

puff See the entry for *gasp*.

pugnacious See the entry for *belligerent*.

pull (*verb*) to bring something toward you; to move something, usually with effort. □ *Sam pulled Jane into the room.* □ *The cowboy pulled his gun out of the holster.* □ *The girl pulled the door open for her mother.*

• **drag** to *pull* something with difficulty. □ *The little girl dragged the heavy sack across the floor.* □ *The horse dragged the cart uphill.*

• **draw** to *pull* something smoothly along. (See also the main entry for *draw*.) □ *Roger drew a little book out of his pocket.* □ *The magician can draw a rabbit out of his sleeve.*

• **haul** to *pull* something heavy over a distance. □ *The little car was hauling an enormous trailer.* □ *Stanley hauled his son out of the swimming pool.*

• **tow** to *pull* something heavy along behind you. □ *The tugboat towed the ship into the dock.* □ *Thomas towed the Great Dane along by its leash.*

[→contrasting word: *push*; see also: *tug*]

pulpy See the entry for *juicy*.

pulsate See the entry for *vibrate*.

pulverize See the entry for *crush*.

pummel See the entry for *beat¹*.

punch See the entry for *hit*.

punchy   See the entry for *groggy*.

puncture   See the entry for *stab*.

pungent   See the entry for *spicy*.

punish   (*verb*) to deal with someone severely as a penalty for wrong-doing. □ *Victor must be punished for lying to me.* □ *Wendy's mom punished her by grounding her for a week.*

> • **chastise**   to *punish* someone physically; to *punish* someone by speaking sharply. (Formal.) □ *Art beat his dog to chastise it for dirtying the carpet.* □ *We could hear the shrill sound of Mr. Bonner's voice as he chastised the unruly student.*
>
> • **discipline**   to control someone by *punishing* or threatening to *punish* him or her. (See also the main entry for *discipline*.) □ *The Clarks never discipline their children, who are very wild as a result.* □ *The coach disciplined Donald for beating up his teammate.*
>
> • **penalize**   to *punish* someone by taking something away. (Formal.) □ *The drunk driver was penalized by having her driver's license taken away.* □ *The team was penalized for kicking the ball out of bounds.*

pupil   See the entry for *student*.

purchase   See the entry for *buy*.

purloin   See the entry for *steal*.

purple   (*adjective*) a blend of red and blue. □ *Sunset turned the clouds purple.* □ *Edith wore purple eyeshadow.*

> • **lavender**   pale *purple*. □ *Fran wrote me a note on lavender stationery.* □ *The walls were painted a delicate lavender shade.*
>
> • **magenta**   bright, reddish *purple*. □ *Gina's magenta lipstick certainly was attention-getting.* □ *Helen's car isn't exactly red, and it isn't exactly purple; it's magenta.*
>
> • **mauve**   pale, grayish *purple*. □ *The mauve carpet went well with the gray walls.* □ *Irene chose a subdued mauve dress.*
>
> • **violet**   bluish *purple*. □ *The violet color of Jane's shirt brings out the blue in her eyes.* □ *Kay liked to write in violet ink.*

purpose   See the entry for *goal*.

pursue   See the entry for *chase*.

push   (*verb*) to force someone or something away from you. □ *Laura pushed her plate away.* □ *Mark pushed Tom out of the room.*

> • **nudge**   to *push* something gently. □ *Sue nudged her chair toward Philip's.* □ *Rita nudged me to get my attention.*

• **ram**   to *push* something with great force and violence. □ *Susan's car rammed into the wall.* □ *The soldiers used a tree trunk to ram the gate open.*

• **shove**   to *push* something suddenly and violently. □ *Tim shoved his brother off the couch.* □ *Jan shoved the box out of the window and watched it crash to the sidewalk below.*

• **thrust**   to *push* something with great force. □ *Our hero thrust the sword into the dragon's belly.* □ *Bill tried to hold the door shut, but Art thrust it open.*

[→contrasting word: *pull*]

push-button   See the entry for *automatic²*.

pushy   See the entry for *bossy*.

put   (*verb*) to bring something to a certain position and leave it there. □ *Put your cup on the table.* □ *Ben put his wallet in his pocket.*

• **deposit**   to *put* something in a safe place; to *put* something permanently in a place. (Formal.) □ *Carrie deposited her money at the bank.* □ *The river deposited mud along its banks.*

• **lay**   to *put* something down on a place. □ *Donald laid the book on his desk.* □ *Eddie laid his head on Fran's shoulder.*

• **place**   to *put* something down precisely. (See also the main entry for *place*.) □ *George placed the centerpiece in the exact center of the table.* □ *Helen placed her glass on a coaster.*

• **plant**   to *put* something solidly in a place. □ *The dog planted himself in front of the door and refused to budge.* □ *Irene planted a stake in the ground to show where her property began.*

• **set**   to *put* something carefully in a place. □ *Jay set his wet boots on a piece of newspaper.* □ *Set the coffee table in front of the sofa.*

• **situate**   to *put* something permanently or strategically in a place. (Formal.) □ *Kay wanted to situate her restaurant close to downtown.* □ *The town is situated near a river.*

put back   See the entry for *replace²*.

put off   See the entry for *delay*.

put together   See the entry for *build*.

putrid   See the entry for *rotten*.

puzzle   (*verb*) to make someone feel confused; to be very difficult for someone to figure out. □ *Art's symptoms puzzled the doctor.* □ *Ben's strange behavior really puzzles me.*

• **baffle**   to *puzzle* someone thoroughly. □ *This brain-teaser has baffled everyone I know.* □ *The villain did his best to baffle the detective.*

• **stump** to *puzzle* someone so much that he or she cannot go on. □ *I don't know how to finish this math problem; I'm stumped.* □ *The last question stumped all the contestants on the game show.*

• **stymie** to *puzzle* someone a great deal; to be impossible for someone to figure out. (Informal.) □ *The detective was stymied by the absence of clues.* □ *Carrie stymied her friends; they couldn't figure out how she did the magic trick.*

puzzling See the entry for *mysterious*.

Q

quack   See the entry for *fraud.*

quail   See the entry for *wince.*

quaint   See the entry for *old-fashioned.*

quake   See the entry for *vibrate.*

quality   See the entry for *value.*

quandary   See the entry for *bind.*

quarrel   See the entry for *argue².*

quarrelsome   See the entry for *belligerent.*

quarry   See the entries for *dig, victim.*

quatrain   See the entry for *poem.*

quay   See the entry for *dock.*

queen   See the entry for *ruler.*

quell   See the entry for *hold back.*

query   See the entry for *ask.*

question   See the entries for *ask, doubt.*

questionable   See the entry for *suspicious.*

queue   See the entry for *line.*

quick   See the entry for *fast.*

quiet (*adjective*) at a low volume; not noisy. (See also the entry for *reserved*.) ☐ *The only sound was the quiet rustling of the leaves.* ☐ *Donald tried to be very quiet as he opened the door.*

• **hushed** calm and quiet. ☐ *The visitors at the Lincoln Monument spoke in hushed voices.* ☐ *There were a few hushed whispers from the back of the room.*

• **low** very quiet. ☐ *Eddie sang a lullaby very low.* ☐ *Keep your voice low; I'm trying to concentrate.*

• **soft** gentle and quiet. ☐ *The kitten's soft purring was a pleasant sound.* ☐ *I heard Fran's soft footsteps coming upstairs.*

quip See the entry for *joke*.

quirk (*noun*) a strange way of acting. ☐ *George's hatred of bananas is an interesting quirk.* ☐ *Helen loved Jay in spite of his many quirks.*

• **failing** a fault or weakness in someone's personality. ☐ *Kay's lack of patience is her chief failing.* ☐ *Laura was only human, and therefore had her failings.*

• **foible** a harmless weakness in someone's personality. (Formal.) ☐ *Mark's gambling was not a mere foible, but a serious problem.* ☐ *Tom forgave Sue's foibles, and she forgave his.*

• **frailty** a weakness in someone's personality. (Old-fashioned.) ☐ *Philip had an obvious frailty: he would do anything to win the approval of his friends, even if he knew it was wrong.* ☐ *An interest in the gruesome and sensational is a common human frailty.*

quirky See the entry for *eccentric*.

quit See the entry for *stop*.

quite See the entry for *very*.

quiver See the entry for *vibrate*.

quiz See the entry for *test*.

R

race   See the entry for *hurry.*

racket   See the entry for *plot.*

radiant   See the entry for *bright.*

radiate   See the entry for *emit.*

rag on   See the entry for *criticize.*

ragged   See the entry for *shabby.*

raid   See the entry for *invade.*

rain   (*verb*) for water to fall in drops from the clouds. □ *It rained all afternoon.* □ *Take your umbrella; it looks like it might rain.*
   • **drizzle**   to *rain* in very small drops. □ *It's not raining very hard; it's just drizzling.* □ *It drizzled just enough to discourage me from going out.*
   • **pour**   to *rain* heavily. □ *All of a sudden, it began to pour, and everyone outside was drenched.* □ *It poured for two whole days, and the streets flooded.*
   • **shower**   to *rain* for a short time; to pour down constantly. □ *The weather report says it may shower later today.* □ *Everyone at the parade was showered with confetti.*
   • **sprinkle**   to *rain* gently; to *rain* off and on. □ *Grandpa wouldn't let us go outside, even though it was only sprinkling.* □ *It sprinkled for a few minutes and then seemed to let up.*

raise   See the entries for *bring up², lift.*

rally   See the entries for *meeting, revive.*

ram   See the entry for *push.*

ramble   See the entry for *wander.*

ranch   See the entry for *farm.*

rancid   See the entry for *rotten.*

random   (*adjective*) in no order at all; with no plan. □ *The screen showed a random pattern of dots.* □ *Rita picked a few random words from the newspaper article.*
> • **arbitrary**   not planned; not for any reason. (Formal.) □ *The contest judges evidently made an arbitrary decision; the prize certainly did not go to the best contestant.* □ *The tornado destroyed houses in an arbitrary fashion.*
> • **capricious**   not for any reason; according to someone's whim. (Formal.) □ *Susan's father is capricious and sometimes punishes her for no reason at all.* □ *I never know what to expect from that capricious girl.*
> • **chance**   not planned; completely by accident. □ *It was a chance meeting between two strangers.* □ *I made a chance remark about Tim, and Jan told me that she knew him.*
> • **haphazard**   in no order at all. □ *Bill left the books in a haphazard pile.* □ *Art's haphazard way of throwing things into his desk makes it very hard for him to find them.*

rank   See the entries for *grade, line, rotten.*

ransack   See the entry for *rummage.*

rant   See the entry for *babble.*

rap   See the entry for *tap.*

rapacious   See the entry for *greedy.*

rapid   See the entry for *fast.*

rapt   See the entry for *absorbed.*

rare   See the entry for *exceptional.*

rarely   See the entry for *seldom.*

rascal   See the entry for *villain.*

rasp   See the entry for *scrape.*

rat on   See the entry for *betray.*

rather   See the entry for *very.*

rational   See the entry for *reasonable.*

rationale   See the entry for *reason.*

rattle   See the entry for *shake.*

ratty See the entry for *shabby.*

raucous See the entry for *harsh.*

rave (*verb*) to praise someone or something with great enthusiasm. (Informal. Often with *about.* See also the entry for *babble.*) ☐ *Fran raves about Eddie's cooking.* ☐ *"This is a stupendous play," the critic raved.*

　• **enthuse** to *rave* in an overly vigorous and possibly insincere manner. (Informal. This word—a verb made from the noun *enthusiasm*—is objected to by some people and should be avoided in writing.) ☐ *Art enthused about the new book.* ☐ *Ben likes his job and is always enthusing about his boss.*

　• **gush** to *rave* on and on. ☐ *"This is simply the very best party I've ever been to," Carrie gushed.* ☐ *Donald gushed over the way I had decorated the living room.*

　• **rhapsodize** to *rave* passionately and in glowing or poetic terms. (Formal.) ☐ *George can rhapsodize for hours about his new girlfriend.* ☐ *The teacher rhapsodized about Helen's work in chemistry class.*

ravenous See the entry for *hungry.*

ravine See the entry for *valley.*

raw See the entry for *sore.*

reach See the entries for *achieve, come, contact, stretch.*

read (*verb*) to take in the meaning of written words. ☐ *Ben read the sign.* ☐ *Carrie sat in the armchair, reading a book.*

　• **browse** to *read* a little bit here and a little bit there, according to what interests you. ☐ *Donald browsed through the magazine.* ☐ *I browsed around in the new book; it looked interesting, so I bought it.*

　• **peruse** to *read* very carefully. (Formal.) ☐ *Eddie perused the document before signing it.* ☐ *Fran perused the morning paper as she drank her coffee.*

　• **skim** to *read* just enough to get the idea. ☐ *On the night before the biology test, George skimmed the chapter on amphibians.* ☐ *I didn't read the letter very carefully; I just skimmed it.*

　• **study** to learn something by *reading;* to *read* something in order to memorize it. ☐ *Helen studied the history of St. Louis.* ☐ *Irene needs us to be quiet while she studies for the test.*

ready See the entry for *prepare.*

real (*adjective*) actually existing or true. ☐ *There was real sympathy in Jay's eyes.* ☐ *Kay is a real friend.*

　• **authentic** *real;* exactly what it claims to be. (Formal.) ☐ *The experts tried to decide if the painting was an authentic work of Van Gogh.* ☐ *The skilled actress makes pretended emotion seem authentic.*

• **bona fide** *real;* in good faith. □ *The shop owner assured me that this little table is a bona fide antique.* □ *After ten years of training, Laura was finally a bona fide doctor.*

• **genuine** *real* and not fake. □ *I wonder if the diamond in that ring is genuine.* □ *Mark shows a genuine interest in learning to play the flute.*

really See the entry for *very.*

reap See the entry for *harvest.*

rear See the entry for *bring up².*

reason (*noun*) something that explains an action or feeling; a statement of a cause. □ *Tom had a good reason for not telling Sue where he had been.* □ *Philip's reason for leaving the party was that he suddenly felt sick.*

• **cause** a person or thing that makes something happen; the *reason* something happens. (See also the main entry for *cause.*) □ *Stress seems to be the cause of Rita's headaches.* □ *Susan's gossiping was the cause of a lot of misery.*

• **impetus** the cause that triggers an action. (Formal.) □ *His friends' encouragement served as a powerful impetus to Tim to keep up with his artwork.* □ *The impetus behind Bill's sudden burst of studying was a desire to impress Jan.*

• **intention** the *reason* for doing something; a plan. □ *Anna's intention in moving away had been to make it impossible for her family to pry into her business.* □ *I know your intentions were good, but you really did mess everything up.*

• **motive** a *reason* for doing something; sometimes, the *reason* for committing a crime. □ *Mary's motive in calling me up was evidently to find out everything I know about Charlie.* □ *The police wondered what the motive for the murder had been.*

• **rationale** a well-thought-out *reason* for acting a certain way. (Formal.) □ *The mayor explained her rationale for raising taxes.* □ *Donna's rationale for shutting her friends out of her life was that they didn't need her problems in addition to their own.*

reasonable (*adjective*) making good sense. □ *Jane's suggestion seems reasonable.* □ *Gina is a reasonable person and will understand why you can't help her right now.*

• **rational** *reasonable* and well thought out; able to think clearly. (Formal.) □ *Harold developed a rational argument against selling the house.* □ *Alan has a very rational mind.*

• **sensible** *reasonable* and practical; full of common sense. □ *Jenny has a sensible plan for getting enough money for college.* □ *Kevin was too sensible to do anything so rash.*

• **sound** *reasonable* in all respects. □ *Larry has several sound reasons for wanting to quit his job.* □ *The old woman was frail, but still of sound mind.*

rebel   (*verb*) to fight the authorities; to try to overthrow the authorities. □ *The teacher wanted to keep the whole class after school, but the students rebelled.* □ *Slaves were horribly punished for rebelling against their master.*
• **fight against**   to struggle to overthrow someone or something. □ *The rebels were fighting against the government.* □ *Gun owners joined together to fight against gun control.*
• **mutiny**   to *rebel*, especially for sailors or soldiers to *rebel* against officers. □ *The captain treated the sailors so harshly that they mutinied.* □ *Some of the soldiers wanted to mutiny against their general.*
• **revolt**   to fight against a leader or a government. □ *The colonists revolted against the king.* □ *The peasants were starving and likely to revolt if any more taxes were imposed upon them.*
[→see also: *disobey*]

rebuke   See the entry for *scold.*

recall   See the entry for *remember.*

recant   See the entry for *take back.*

recapitulate   See the entry for *rehash.*

receive   See the entries for *get, greet.*

recent   See the entry for *present.*

recently   See the entry for *lately.*

receptacle   See the entry for *container.*

reception   See the entry for *party.*

recital   See the entry for *concert.*

recite   See the entry for *repeat.*

reckless   See the entry for *careless.*

reckon   See the entry for *figure.*

reckon on   See the entry for *expect.*

recluse   See the entry for *hermit.*

recollect   See the entry for *remember.*

recommend   See the entry for *advise.*

recompense   See the entry for *reward.*

reconciled   See the entry for *resigned.*

record   See the entries for *document, write.*

recruit (*verb*) to convince people to join an organization, particularly the army or navy. □ *Mary recruited her friends to help her paint the house.* □ *The army needed to recruit more soldiers.*

• **draft** to make someone join an organization, particularly the army or navy. □ *Tom was drafted and served in the navy.* □ *The boss drafted several employees to work on his pet project.*

• **enlist** to sign up, or make someone sign up; to join an organization, particularly the army or navy. □ *When war broke out, many patriotic people enlisted in the armed forces.* □ *Sue enlisted her family's help to take care of her children while she worked.*

• **win over** to convince someone to join you or to support your side. □ *The speaker's passionate words won many people over.* □ *After reading that magazine article in support of vegetarianism, I'm completely won over.*

recurrently See the entry for *often.*

red (*adjective*) the color of blood. □ *We picked red, ripe cherries from the tree.* □ *There was a red mark on Philip's face where Rita had hit him.*

• **crimson** deep, dark *red.* □ *A crimson stain spread across the bandage on Susan's arm.* □ *The little girl's party dress was made of crimson velvet.*

• **fuchsia** bright, purplish *red.* □ *The flowers blossomed a bright fuchsia.* □ *Tina dyed her hair fuchsia, just to be different.*

• **puce** dark, dull *red.* □ *Jan screamed until her face was puce.* □ *The walls of that depressing room were puce.*

• **scarlet** very bright *red.* □ *Wendy chose a scarlet shade of nail polish.* □ *The king wore a scarlet robe.*

• **vermilion** bright, orangey *red.* □ *The vermilion tomatoes made a nice contrast to the pale green lettuce.* □ *We admired the vermilion hue of the sunset sky.*

redden See the entry for *blush.*

reduce See the entry for *decrease.*

refer to (*verb*) to mention something; to bring something to someone's attention. □ *The politician referred to her opponent's drinking problem.* □ *The letter referred to all the favors Anna had done for me in the past.*

• **allude to** to *refer to* something indirectly. □ *When I asked why she didn't trust me, Mary alluded to the money I still owed her.* □ *Charlie alluded to a secret that he shared with Donna.*

• **cite** to *refer to* something briefly; to mention someone or something as an example. (Formal.) □ *Linda recommended giving Fred a medal for heroism, citing his brave rescue of the people in the burning building.* □ *Gina cited Emmy Noether and Sophia Kovalevsky as two important women mathematicians.*

• **insinuate**   to mention something indirectly and slyly; to hint. □ *Harold insinuated that I had cheated him.* □ *The newspapers insinuated that the movie star would be getting a divorce soon.*
• **suggest**   to bring something to someone's mind indirectly. (See also the main entry for *suggest*.) □ *Are you suggesting that I'm not a good driver?* □ *The results of the experiment suggested that babies learn to recognize faces very early in life.*

refined   See the entry for *aristocratic*.

reflect   See the entry for *think*.

reflex   See the entry for *automatic[1]*.

refresh   See the entry for *revive*.

refuge   See the entry for *shelter*.

refuse   (*verb*) to say no to something. (See also the entry for *trash*.) □ *I refuse to give Alan any more money until he proves he can manage it wisely.* □ *Jenny refused to listen to me.*
• **decline**   to *refuse* politely. (Formal.) □ *We asked Kevin to run for student body president, but he declined.* □ *Larry declined the invitation.*
• **demur**   to *refuse*; to hesitate to accept. (Formal.) □ *Mary was offered the prize, but she modestly demurred.* □ *"Speech! Speech!" we cried, but the guest of honor demurred.*
• **say no**   to *refuse*. (Informal.) □ *Don't be afraid to ask for favors; the worst someone can do is say no.* □ *Nancy asked three different people to go to the movies with her, but they all said no.*
• **turn down**   to *refuse* an offer. □ *Otto turned down the job offer.* □ *Jane asked me so nicely that I didn't have the heart to turn her down.*

regale   See the entry for *entertain*.

regard   See the entries for *respect[2]*, *watch*.

region   See the entry for *area*.

regress   See the entry for *revert*.

regret   See the entry for *be sorry*.

regular   See the entry for *average*.

regularly   See the entry for *often*.

regulate   See the entry for *control[1]*.

regulation   See the entry for *rule*.

rehash (*verb*) to say or explain something again and again. (Informal.) □ *Roger and Stanley just keep rehashing that old debate about censorship.* □ *A well-written conclusion should do more than rehash what was said in the rest of the paper.*

• **go over** to explain or examine something carefully. □ *The librarian went over the instructions for the computer catalog.* □ *Thomas went over my math homework with me.*

• **recapitulate** to say again what you have already said; to sum up. (Formal.) □ *The teacher recapitulated the main points of the lesson.* □ *The speaker recapitulated her argument at the end of her speech.*

• **reiterate** to say something again and again. (Formal.) □ *Let me reiterate: as I've said many times already, there is no such thing as a stupid question.* □ *The doctor reiterated his warning against eating too much salt.*

• **restate** to say something again; to say something again in different words. □ *Victor had to restate his request three times before the clerk understood it.* □ *Please restate your opinion in simpler language.*

rehearse See the entry for *practice.*

reinstate See the entry for *replace².*

reiterate See the entry for *rehash.*

reiterative See the entry for *insistent.*

relapse See the entry for *revert.*

relate See the entry for *tell.*

relations See the entry for *family.*

relatives See the entry for *family.*

relax (*verb*) to stop feeling tense. □ *Wendy watched TV to relax after work.* □ *Art relaxed when he saw that Ben wasn't angry at him.*

• **calm down** to stop feeling tense and upset; to stop acting upset; to make someone stop feeling tense and upset. □ *Calm down! I'm sure we can find someone to fix the leak.* □ *Carrie calmed her mother down.*

• **loosen up** to stop feeling tense; to become more easygoing. (Informal.) □ *Donald needs to loosen up if he wants people to like him.* □ *That teacher used to be very strict, but he's loosened up a lot lately.*

• **unbend** to stop feeling tense or acting stiff. □ *Eddie's constant friendship and encouragement helped Fran unbend.* □ *When George saw that we liked him just the way he was, he gradually unbent.*

• **unwind** to stop feeling tense gradually. (Informal.) □ *Doing yoga helps Helen unwind.* □ *Dad unwound a lot on family vacations.*
[→contrasting word: *tense up*]

relay   See the entry for *send*.

release   (*verb*) to let someone or something go free. □ *Harold released my arm.* □ *Irene released Jay from their engagement.*
   • **free**   to *release* someone or something that is trapped or imprisoned. (Formal.) □ *Kay's friends petitioned the government to free her from prison.* □ *Laura tried to free herself, but the ropes were tied too tightly.*
   • **let go**   to *release* someone or something that you are holding or imprisoning; to *release* your grip on something. (Informal.) □ *Mark caught a lizard, but then he let it go.* □ *Let me go!*
   • **liberate**   to *release* someone or something that is imprisoned or enslaved. (Formal.) □ *The Founding Fathers sought to liberate the country from British tyranny.* □ *The new government promised to liberate all political prisoners.*
   • **set free**   to *release* a captive. □ *After nursing the wolf back to health, Tom took it out to the woods and set it free.* □ *Sue begged the kidnappers to set her free.*

relentless   (*adjective*) never stopping or giving up. □ *The detective's relentless pursuit of the murderer paid off in the end.* □ *The reporter was relentless when it came to asking for interviews.*
   • **ceaseless**   never stopping. □ *I am tired of my neighbor's loud, ceaseless music.* □ *Philip and Rita's arguments were ceaseless.*
   • **determined**   never giving up; committed to doing something. □ *Susan was determined to get an A on the test.* □ *Tim put a lot of determined effort into learning his lines for the school play.*
   • **unremitting**   never stopping, giving up, or relaxing. (Formal.) □ *The movie star hated his fans' unremitting curiosity about his love life.* □ *That summer, Jan entertained an unremitting stream of visitors.*
   [→see also: *stubborn*]

relieve   See the entry for *comfort*.

religious   See the entry for *holy*.

relinquish   See the entry for *give up*.

relish   See the entry for *enjoy*.

reluctant   (*adjective*) not wanting to do something; hesitating to do something. □ *I am reluctant to ask Bill for help.* □ *We had Anna's reluctant cooperation.*
   • **hesitant**   hesitating to do something. □ *Mary was hesitant to go to another of Charlie's parties, considering what a terrible time she had had at the last one.* □ *The kitten made a hesitant motion toward the food dish.*
   • **loath**   very *reluctant*. (Formal.) □ *Donna is always loath to say what she really thinks.* □ *Linda was loath to spend money on anyone but herself.*

• **squeamish**   too proper to do something; feeling slightly sick. □ *Jane felt squeamish about kicking George out of the club just because he had moved to the wrong side of town.* □ *Harold hates gory movies because he is squeamish.*
• **unwilling**   not wanting to do something; refusing to do something. □ *Alan was unwilling to take the risk.* □ *Jenny became an unwilling participant in the robbery.*

rely on   See the entry for *trust.*

remain   See the entry for *stay.*

remainder   See the entry for *rest.*

remark   See the entry for *say.*

remarkable   See the entry for *exceptional.*

remedy   See the entry for *cure.*

remember   (*verb*) to call something back to mind. □ *Kevin remembered what a good time he had had at the beach last summer.* □ *Laura remembered having put her glasses down on the coffee table.*
• **dredge up**   to *remember* something with great effort. (Informal.) □ *I remember the title of the book, but I just can't dredge up the author's name.* □ *Mary tried to dredge up the tune to the old song.*
• **recall**   to make an effort to *remember* something; to call something back to mind. □ *Nancy wistfully recalled the last time she had danced with Tom.* □ *I know we've met before, but I'm afraid I can't recall your name.*
• **recollect**   to *remember;* to gather up a memory of something. □ *Jane recollected that she had tried guava jelly before and didn't like it.* □ *Can you recollect what city Ken moved to?*
[→contrasting word: *forget*]

remorse   See the entry for *guilt.*

remote   See the entry for *distant.*

remove   (*verb*) to take a piece off something; to take something from somewhere. (See also the entry for *eliminate.*) □ *Roger removed the mud from his shoe.* □ *The mechanic removed the car's front wheels.*
• **detach**   to *remove* something by separating it from the whole. □ *Stanley easily detached the table legs.* □ *Detach the top portion of the page by tearing along the dotted line.*
• **dislodge**   to *remove* something that is firmly stuck; to drive or force something out of place. □ *Thomas hit me so hard that he dislodged one of my teeth.* □ *Victor used tweezers to dislodge the splinter from his thumb.*

• **excise** to *remove* something by cutting it out. (Formal.) ☐ *Wendy excised the rotten part of the potato.* ☐ *The writer excised a paragraph from her essay.*

• **extract** to *remove* something completely; to take something out. ☐ *The dentist extracted the tooth.* ☐ *Art used a paper clip to extract the pits from the cherries.*

• **take away** to *remove* something and move it to another place. ☐ *A truck came and took away the dead tree branches that the storm had scattered on the street.* ☐ *The housekeeper took away the dirty towels.*

• **take out** to *remove* something that was inside. ☐ *Carrie reached into her pocket and took out a dollar bill.* ☐ *Ben's mother came and took him out of class early for a doctor appointment.*

removed (*adjective*) not interested; not emotionally involved. ☐ *Donald seemed strangely removed all throughout his trial.* ☐ *Eddie kept himself removed from family quarrels.*

• **apathetic** not involved; not caring. (Formal.) ☐ *Fran was surprised that her friends were so apathetic to the problems of poor people.* ☐ *George was not enthusiastic, as his apathetic expression clearly showed.*

• **detached** emotionally *removed*; not influenced by others. ☐ *The reporter knew he should remain detached, but he couldn't help getting angry at the person he was interviewing.* ☐ *Patients thought the doctor was very cold because of the detached way she examined them.*

• **disinterested** not emotionally involved; not biased; fair. ☐ *The speaker was alarmed to see so many disinterested faces in the audience.* ☐ *We need a disinterested person to listen to our argument and decide who is right.*

• **impersonal** not emotionally involved; not warm or friendly. ☐ *Helen sent me an impersonal letter.* ☐ *Irene hated answering machines; she thought them very impersonal.*

• **uninvolved** not emotionally involved; not participating. ☐ *Jay felt uninvolved in the story the movie was telling.* ☐ *Kay preferred to remain uninvolved in Laura's plot against Mark.*

[→see also: *indifferent, haughty*]

rend See the entry for *tear*.

rendezvous See the entry for *date¹*.

renew See the entry for *revive*.

renowned See the entry for *famous*.

rent (*verb*) to pay someone in order to use something he or she owns; to let someone use something you own for money. ☐ *Tom rented an apartment and moved in at the first of the month.* ☐ *Sue rented her house to Philip.*

• **charter**   to *rent* a large vehicle and someone to drive or pilot it. □ *The club chartered a bus to travel to the convention.* □ *We asked the captain if he would charter his boat.*

• **contract for**   to make a formal agreement to *rent* something or to do something. □ *Ken contracted for the office space.* □ *The movie star contracted for two more films with the studio.*

• **hire**   to pay money for the use of something or for someone's services. □ *Rita hired Susan to cook for her.* □ *Tim hired a limousine to take him to the airport.*

• **lease**   to *rent* something for a certain period of time. □ *Jan leased the apartment for a year.* □ *Bill leased his car to Anna.*

repair   See the entry for *fix.*

repast   See the entry for *meal.*

repay   See the entry for *reward.*

repeal   See the entry for *cancel.*

repeat   (*verb*) to say what has already been said. □ *The reporter repeated the news bulletin.* □ *I repeat, come out with your hands up!*

• **echo**   to *repeat* what someone else has said, especially right after he or she says it. □ *Mary echoed Charlie's demand for more money.* □ *Donna's words echoed the warning Linda had given me earlier.*

• **parrot**   to *repeat* something without understanding it. □ *Jane has no opinions of her own; she just parrots everything her mother says.* □ *Gina parroted what she had read in the book.*

• **recite**   to *repeat* something you have memorized. □ *Harold recited a poem by Walt Whitman.* □ *Alan recited the multiplication tables.*

repel   See the entry for *disgust.*

repent   See the entry for *be sorry.*

repercussion   See the entry for *result.*

replace¹   (*verb*) to put something in the place of something else. □ *Jenny wanted to replace her pickup truck with a newer model.* □ *Kevin replaced the worn-out carpet in his room.*

• **fill in for**   to work in the place of someone or something else. (Informal.) □ *The waiter asked his friend to fill in for him on Saturday afternoon.* □ *An unfamiliar person was filling in for the usual newscaster.*

• **substitute**   to put something in place of something else; to take the place of someone or something else. (Usually with *for*, in the latter case.) □ *Larry substituted bread crumbs for graham cracker crumbs in the recipe.* □ *Mary is substituting for Nancy at third base.*

• **supplant**   to take someone else's place by force. (Formal.) □ *The general supplanted the dictator.* □ *The king feared that his son would supplant him.*

replace² *(verb)* to put something in its place again. □ *Tom replaced the flour canister in the cupboard.* □ *Jane was careful to replace the book in the same position on the shelf.*

   • **put back**   to *replace* something. (Informal.) □ *Ken put the coat back on the rack.* □ *Roger saw me trying to sneak the candy out of the jar, so I put it back.*

   • **reinstate**   to *replace* a person in his or her old office; to put something back in power. (Formal.) □ *Stanley was reinstated as head of the company.* □ *The new principal reinstated the school's old, strict dress code.*

   • **restore**   to *replace* someone or something that was gone for a long time. □ *The exiled queen was restored to the throne.* □ *Thomas was very happy to have his house restored to him.*

   • **return**   to *replace* something; to put something back in the place where it started. □ *Wendy played with the parakeet for a while, then returned it to its cage.* □ *Victor returned the book to the library.*

replicate   See the entry for *copy*².

reply   See the entry for *answer*.

report   See the entry for *betray*.

repress   See the entry for *hold back*.

reprimand   See the entry for *scold*.

reprisal   See the entry for *revenge*.

reproach   See the entry for *scold*.

reproduce   See the entry for *copy*².

reprove   See the entry for *scold*.

repulsive   See the entry for *ugly*.

repute   See the entry for *status*.

request   See the entry for *ask for*.

require   See the entry for *demand*.

requisition   See the entry for *ask for*.

rescue   See the entry for *save*.

resemble   See the entry for *seem*.

reserve   *(adjective)* to keep something for the use of a particular person. □ *The waiter reserved a table for the Smiths.* □ *This seat is reserved for the mother of the bride.*

• **hold**   to *reserve;* to keep something in possession. ☐ *The tickets were being held at the box office.* ☐ *Please hold this book for me when it comes in.*

• **hold back**   to *reserve* something for a future time. (See also the main entry for *hold back.*) ☐ *Irene held back a few cupcakes to eat after the party.* ☐ *I gave my brothers most of the seashells I had found, but I held back a few to give to my best friend.*

• **set aside**   to *reserve* something for a special purpose. ☐ *Jay set aside a certain amount of money every month for the car he wanted to buy.* ☐ *Kay set aside the clothes that needed mending.*

• **withhold**   to *reserve* something; to keep something from someone. ☐ *Laura withheld her son's allowance.* ☐ *The information was withheld from the public.*

reserved   (*adjective*) keeping your thoughts and feelings to yourself. ☐ *Art is usually quite reserved and hates to gossip.* ☐ *Ben's reserved manner makes it hard to get to know him.*

• **quiet**   *reserved;* not saying much. (See also the main entry for *quiet.*) ☐ *Carrie is such a quiet person; one never knows what she is thinking.* ☐ *Donald seemed very quiet and dignified.*

• **reticent**   very *reserved;* not liking to say anything about yourself. (Formal.) ☐ *Eddie is so reticent that he is almost bashful.* ☐ *Fran was reticent about her recent operation.*

• **retiring**   *reserved;* staying away from people. ☐ *The retiring author preferred not to make public appearances.* ☐ *George tried to coax his shy, retiring cousin out for a walk.*

• **unobtrusive**   *reserved;* not forcing yourself on anyone. (Formal.) ☐ *The guests scarcely noticed the butler's unobtrusive presence.* ☐ *The reporter observing the meeting tried to be as unobtrusive as possible.*

reservoir   See the entries for *container, lake.*

reside   See the entry for *live.*

residue   See the entry for *rest.*

resign   (*verb*) to say you are going to leave a job or a project. ☐ *Mark resigned from his job.* ☐ *Tom resigned as club president.*

• **abdicate**   for a monarch to *resign* from the throne. (Formal.) ☐ *Edward VIII abdicated in 1936.* ☐ *The queen was forced to abdicate.*

• **give notice**   to *resign* and say how long you will remain in your present job before you leave. ☐ *Sue's fellow workers were so upset by the way she was treated that they all gave notice.* ☐ *I hereby give notice that I will resign.*

• **step down**   to *resign* from a high office. ☐ *The school board asked the principal to step down.* ☐ *Because his health was failing, the Supreme Court justice decided to step down.*

• **withdraw**   to *resign* from a contest.   ☐ *The senatorial candidate withdrew.*   ☐ *The runner had to withdraw from the race.*

resigned   (*adjective*) deciding to endure something patiently.   ☐ *Philip was resigned to a life of hard work and no recognition.*   ☐ *With a resigned sigh, Rita agreed to baby-sit her little brother again that night.*
  • **accepting**   *resigned;* deciding not to oppose something.   ☐ *We admired Susan's accepting attitude toward her illness.*   ☐ *Tim thought that people in the city would be more accepting toward his differences.*
  • **reconciled**   *resigned;* deciding that something is for the best.   ☐ *Jan was reconciled to her poverty.*   ☐ *Bill slowly became reconciled to his friend's moving away.*
  • **submissive**   *resigned;* mildly enduring anything that happens. (Formal.)   ☐ *Anna's employees were outwardly submissive, but inwardly they all rebelled against her.*   ☐ *Mary gave a meek, submissive nod.*

resolute   See the entry for *persistent.*

resound   See the entry for *ring.*

resourceful   See the entry for *creative.*

respect[1]   (*noun*) high esteem.   ☐ *Charlie earned our respect by his hard work and honesty.*   ☐ *I hold Donna in the highest respect.*
  • **deference**   a display of *respect.* (Formal.)   ☐ *Linda treated her teacher with great deference.*   ☐ *Jane bowed to Gina as a show of deference.*
  • **honor**   deep *respect; respect* for a very worthy or high-ranking person.   ☐ *The president's courage won the people's honor.*   ☐ *The Veteran's Day holiday is in honor of those who have served their country.*
  • **reverence**   worshipful *respect.* (Formal.)   ☐ *Howard handled the ancient statue with reverence.*   ☐ *The congregation knelt and offered up a prayer full of reverence.*
  • **veneration**   adoring, worshipful *respect.* (Formal.)   ☐ *The flag is the object of many people's veneration.*   ☐ *Alan's admiration for Elvis Presley bordered on veneration.*

respect[2]   (*verb*) to think that someone is very worthy.   ☐ *Kevin was brought up to respect his elders.*   ☐ *I respect Larry for speaking his mind.*
  • **esteem**   to feel deeply that someone is worthy.   ☐ *Mary's friends esteem her highly.*   ☐ *The author's works were very much esteemed.*
  • **honor**   to feel awed by someone's great worth; to show that you think someone is very worthy.   ☐ *The artist was not greatly honored during her lifetime.*   ☐ *The statue honors the memory of our beloved mayor.*
  • **regard**   to estimate someone's worth.   ☐ *I regard Nancy very highly.*   ☐ *Tom's parents regarded him as a shiftless boy.*

respond   See the entry for *answer.*

responsibility See the entry for *duty*.

rest (*noun*) what is left; those that are left. □ *Philip let me have the rest of the potato salad.* □ *The star gave autographs to three people, and the rest of us had to go away with nothing.*
  • **balance** the part that has not been used or spent. (Formal.) □ *Ken stayed with his father for the first week in April and spent the balance of the month at his mother's.* □ *After you pay the rent, you can do what you like with the balance of your money.*
  • **remainder** the part that remains. □ *Rita spent the remainder of the day relaxing.* □ *Add two tablespoons of the sugar to the dough and sprinkle the remainder on top.*
  • **residue** the part that is left after some has been taken away. (Formal.) □ *After the taxes were all paid, the residue of Susan's estate was only five hundred dollars.* □ *The water evaporated, leaving a white, chalky residue on the glass.*
  [→see also: *surplus*]

restate See the entry for *rehash*.

restaurant (*noun*) a place to buy and eat a meal. □ *Tim ate lunch in a restaurant.* □ *That restaurant serves good fried chicken.*
  • **café** a small, informal *restaurant*. □ *The lovers met for dinner at a sidewalk café.* □ *The café specialized in rich desserts.*
  • **cafeteria** a *restaurant* where people serve themselves. □ *Most of the workers at the plant eat lunch in the cafeteria.* □ *At the cafeteria, I picked up a tray and got in line for the food.*
  • **diner** a small *restaurant* with inexpensive food. □ *We stopped at the diner for a cup of coffee.* □ *The cook at the diner knows the kind of food that truckers like.*
  • **eatery** a small *restaurant* with inexpensive food served quickly. (Informal.) □ *There's a little eatery on the corner where we could have a snack.* □ *The friends usually had breakfast at the neighborhood eatery.*

restlessness See the entry for *discontent*.

restore See the entry for *replace²*.

restrain See the entry for *hold back*.

restraints See the entry for *bonds*.

restricted See the entry for *cramped*.

result (*noun*) something that happens because of something else. □ *Jan's injury was the result of a fall down the stairs.* □ *Bill decided to turn left at the corner of Third Street and got lost as a result.*
  • **aftermath** all the *results* of something; disastrous *results*. □ *The aftermath of the flood brought poverty and hunger to those who had lost*

their homes. □ *Anna got Mary very, very angry, and then didn't stay to see the aftermath.*

• **consequence** an important *result.* (Sometimes used in the plural.) □ *One consequence of Charlie's gossiping was that Donna decided not to trust him anymore.* □ *Linda was afraid to face the consequences of having lied to her friend.*

• **effect** a direct *result* of something. □ *The medicine had the desired effect on the patient.* □ *The effect of any leavening, such as yeast or baking powder, is to make dough rise.*

• **outcome** the final *result* of something. □ *What was the outcome of your discussion with Frank? Will he give us the money?* □ *The outcome of the experiment was not what the scientist expected.*

• **repercussion** an indirect *result;* an unforeseen *result.* (Often used in the plural.) □ *The mayor knew that raising taxes would have many repercussions.* □ *Gina's moving away had repercussions for all of her friends.*

retain See the entry for *keep.*

retaliation See the entry for *revenge.*

reticent See the entry for *reserved.*

retire See the entry for *go.*

retiring See the entry for *reserved.*

retort See the entry for *answer.*

retract See the entry for *take back.*

retreat See the entries for *go, shelter.*

retribution See the entry for *revenge.*

retrieve See the entry for *save.*

return See the entries for *answer, replace².*

reveal See the entry for *show².*

revel in See the entry for *enjoy.*

revenge (*noun*) hurting someone in return for wrong done to you. □ *More than anything else, Howard wanted revenge on Alan.* □ *Jenny showed Kevin's baby pictures to all his friends; he took revenge by publishing her baby pictures in the newspaper.*

• **reprisal** doing violence to someone in return for violence to you; an act of violently punishing someone for wrongdoing. (Formal.) □ *The government swore that if their country was invaded, they would execute the hostages in reprisal.* □ *If anyone rebelled, the army swiftly made reprisal.*

• **retaliation**   doing the same thing to someone as was done to you. □ *Larry would have made fun of Mary, but he feared her retaliation.* □ *Nancy toilet-papered Tom's house, so he toilet-papered hers in retaliation.*
• **retribution**   punishment in return for wrongdoing. (Formal.) □ *Jane thought of killing Ken as an act of retribution.* □ *Roger's suffering seemed a fitting retribution for the suffering he had caused others.*
• **vengeance**   punishment in return for a hurt to you. (Formal or poetic.) □ *From that moment on, our hero lived only for vengeance.* □ *The teacher treated the students so badly that they all dreamed of vengeance.*

reverberate   See the entry for *ring.*

reverence   See the entry for *respect¹.*

reverie   See the entry for *daze.*

reverse   See the entry for *opposite.*

revert   (*verb*) to go back to the way you used to be. (Formal.) □ *I thought Stanley was finally becoming considerate, but he seems to have reverted.* □ *Whenever Thomas went home, he reverted to the Tennessee accent of his childhood.*
• **backslide**   to *revert* gradually. □ *Without his friend to keep him steady, the drunkard backslid into his old hard-drinking ways.* □ *Victor truly tried not to be so lazy, but he couldn't stop himself from backsliding now and then.*
• **regress**   to *revert*; to go backwards. (Formal.) □ *When Wendy felt shy, she would regress into baby talk.* □ *The hypnotist claimed to help people regress into previous lives.*
• **relapse**   to *revert* suddenly; to grow suddenly worse. □ *The doctor tried to figure out why the patient had relapsed.* □ *Art thought he was free of his gambling problem, but seeing lottery tickets for sale made him relapse.*

revive   (*verb*) to get new energy; to give someone or something new energy or bring someone or something back to life. □ *Ben revived from his faint.* □ *Carrie revived the old family custom of singing songs around the piano.*
• **invigorate**   to give someone new energy. (Formal.) □ *The brisk walk invigorated me.* □ *Donald thought a cold shower would invigorate him.*
• **rally**   to give someone new enthusiasm; to show new energy or enthusiasm. □ *The coach's speech rallied the team.* □ *We were afraid that Eddie would not survive the operation, but he rallied suddenly and came through with flying colors.*

• **refresh** to give someone or something new energy or strength; to make someone or something more lively. □ *Fran was refreshed by a good night's sleep.* □ *A good watering will refresh those poor droopy plants.*

• **renew** to start something again; to make something like new. □ *Encouraged by the smile she gave him, George renewed his attempts to get Helen to go out with him.* □ *Irene renewed the decorations in the living room.*

revoke See the entry for *cancel.*

revolt See the entries for *disgust, rebel.*

revolve See the entry for *turn.*

reward (*verb*) to give someone something in return for what he or she has done. □ *Jay will reward anyone who brings back his lost dog.* □ *Laura did not expect to be rewarded for her honesty.*

• **compensate** to give someone something of exactly equal value in return for what he or she has done; to give someone something equal to what he or she has lost. (Formal.) □ *The employer amply compensated his employees for the time they spent working late.* □ *Mark's delightful personality compensates for his less-than-gorgeous looks.*

• **recompense** to give someone something equal to what he or she has lost. (Formal.) □ *The wonderful experiences Tom had during his year abroad recompensed him for the many difficulties.* □ *No amount of life insurance money could recompense Sue for the loss of her husband.*

• **repay** to give someone something in return; to pay someone back. □ *How can I ever repay you for saving my life?* □ *Philip repaid the trust I placed in him.*

rhapsodize See the entry for *rave.*

rhyme See the entry for *poem.*

rich (*adjective*) having a great deal of money or property. □ *Lots of rich people live in that neighborhood.* □ *Ken said he'd rather be rich than famous.*

• **affluent** quite *rich.* (Formal.) □ *Rita's family was very affluent, and she was used to the best of everything.* □ *Susan's clothing made her appear to be an affluent woman.*

• **loaded** very *rich.* (Slang.) □ *We'll get Tim to lend us the money; he's loaded.* □ *Jan grew up poor, but now she's loaded.*

• **moneyed** very *rich;* having a great deal of money. □ *Sailing a yacht is a pastime for the moneyed few.* □ *The moneyed family had a butler and two maids.*

• **wealthy** *rich.* (Formal.) □ *The wealthy woman had a number of suitors.* □ *Although Bill was wealthy, he lived very simply.*

• **well-heeled**   quite *rich.* (Slang.) □ *Anna must be pretty well-heeled since her grandmother left her all that money.* □ *The well-heeled young man invited his friends for a weekend at his country house.*
[→contrasting word: *poor*]

ridicule   (*verb*) to laugh at someone or something; to make someone feel ashamed by making jokes about him or her. □ *It's mean to ridicule the way someone speaks.* □ *Mary ridiculed Charlie when he told her he loved her.*
   • **belittle**   to make someone or something seem little or not important. (Formal.) □ *The critic belittled the movie's artsy style.* □ *Donna belittled everyone who spoke out against her.*
   • **make fun of**   to *ridicule.* (Informal.) □ *Linda's making fun of me!* □ *The parody made fun of a well-known TV show.*
   • **mock**   to *ridicule* someone or something meanly or spitefully. □ *Jane mocked Gina's attempts to write poetry.* □ *Harold mocked Alan's elegant manners.*
   [→see also: *tease*]

ridiculous   See the entry for *silly.*

rifle   See the entry for *rummage.*

right   (*adjective*) precisely true; morally proper. (See also the entries for *fair, proper.*) □ *Did I get the right answer?* □ *It isn't right to take things that don't belong to you.*
   • **accurate**   free from any error; exactly true. (Formal.) □ *Jenny gave an accurate description of the car.* □ *Kevin's calculations appear to be accurate.*
   • **correct**   free from any error. □ *You will score five points for each correct answer.* □ *Larry's guess was correct.*
   • **true**   agreeing precisely with the facts. □ *We could hardly believe that Mary's story was true.* □ *The reporter wanted to know if the rumor was true.*
   • **valid**   true; well-grounded. □ *Nancy's illness was a valid excuse for not coming to school.* □ *Tom raised several valid objections to the plan.*
   [→contrasting words: *incorrect, wrong*]

right away   See the entry for *immediately.*

rigid   See the entry for *strict.*

ring   (*verb*) to make a musical sound, like a bell. □ *The doorbell rang.* □ *The children's laughter rang through the halls.*
   • **knell**   to *ring* solemnly. □ *The church bell knelled for Jane's funeral.* □ *I heard the distant bell knelling and wondered what disaster had occurred.*

• **peal**   to *ring* loudly and clearly. □ *The wedding bells pealed joyfully.* □ *The bells were pealing in celebration.*
• **resound**   to *ring* loudly; to echo over and over again. (Poetic.) □ *As the curtain fell, the audience's applause resounded throughout the theater.* □ *Roger's happy shout resounded across the hills.*
• **reverberate**   to *ring* out, echoing over and over; to vibrate in waves. (Formal.) □ *Thunder reverberated through the mountains.* □ *The shock of Stanley's death reverberated throughout his circle of friends.*
• **toll**   to *ring* out a signal. □ *The clock in the town hall tolled five.* □ *The bell tolled once for every person who had died in the accident.* [→see also: *chime*]

rip   See the entry for *tear.*

rip off   See the entry for *cheat.*

ripple   See the entry for *wave.*

rise   See the entry for *hill.*

risk   See the entry for *dare.*

rite   See the entry for *ceremony.*

ritual   See the entry for *ceremony.*

rival   See the entry for *enemy.*

river   (*noun*) a body of water that flows along naturally. □ *We let our raft float down the river.* □ *The town is on the west bank of the Mississippi River.*
• **brook**   a very small *river.* □ *Thomas waded across the little brook.* □ *A brook ran through the field.*
• **creek**   a small *river.* □ *Victor's all muddy because he fell into the creek.* □ *The heavy rains made the creek swell up.*
• **stream**   a *river;* any quantity of liquid that flows along. □ *Wendy sat beside the stream and listened to the sound of the water.* □ *A stream of milk poured out of the pitcher.*

road   (*noun*) a clearly marked, often paved, way from one place to another. □ *This road goes right through the middle of town.* □ *The traveler went wherever the road led him.*
• **alley**   a narrow *road,* usually one that runs behind or between buildings. □ *Art took the trash out to the bin in the alley.* □ *The alley was only wide enough for one car to go through.*
• **highway**   a major *road* on which cars and trucks can travel. □ *The truck zoomed down the highway.* □ *The traffic on the highway was very heavy that morning.*

• **lane** a narrow *road;* a strip of *road* wide enough for a single vehicle. □ *There were only a few houses on the winding country lane.* □ *That car is not staying in its lane.*
• **path** a *road* for people to walk on. □ *Ben followed the path into the woods.* □ *There was a well-worn path connecting the two houses.*
• **street** a busy *road.* □ *Carrie's house is just down the street.* □ *Turn right on the third street from the corner.*
• **trail** a long *road;* a primitive *road.* □ *The pioneers guided their covered wagons along the trail.* □ *We hiked the whole length of the trail, up to the top of the mountain.*

roam See the entry for *wander.*

roar See the entries for *cheer, yell.*

roast See the entry for *cook.*

rob See the entry for *steal.*

robust See the entries for *healthy, strong.*

rock¹ (*noun*) a large piece of mineral. □ *That patch of ground is too full of rocks for us to use it as a garden.* □ *Donald threw a rock at the dog.*
• **boulder** a large *rock.* □ *Eddie climbed to the top of the boulder.* □ *That boulder blocks the entrance to the cave.*
• **pebble** a tiny *rock.* □ *Fran collected the prettiest pebbles from the beach.* □ *The children played a game with a handful of pebbles.*
• **stone** a small *rock.* □ *George skipped a stone across the lake.* □ *Helen used a stone as a hammer to crack the nut open.*

rock² (*verb*) to swing back and forth. □ *Irene rocked the baby in her arms.* □ *The train rocked gently from side to side, and Jay gradually fell asleep.*
• **lurch** to *rock* unsteadily; to move unsteadily. □ *The car suddenly lurched sideways.* □ *As the roller coaster plunged downward, my stomach lurched.*
• **pitch** to *rock* violently. □ *The little boat pitched from side to side in the storm.* □ *The high wind made the plane pitch alarmingly.*
• **sway** to *rock* widely or sweepingly. □ *The singers swayed in time with the song.* □ *The trees were swaying in the wind.*

rock³ (*verb*) to move unsteadily from side to side. □ *The glass rocked back and forth and then fell over.* □ *The table rocked on its uneven legs.*
• **dodder** to move shakily, weakly, and unsteadily. □ *Shaken and confused, Kay doddered down the street.* □ *The old lady doddered up the steps.*
• **totter** to be unsteady enough to fall over. □ *Laura tottered, on the verge of fainting.* □ *We watched, horrified, as the burning building tottered and fell.*

• **wobble**   to move from side to side quickly and unsteadily. □ *The chair wobbled so much I thought it would break.* □ *The loose wheel wobbled as the car picked up speed.*

rogue   See the entry for *villain.*

romp   See the entry for *frolic.*

root around   See the entry for *rummage.*

rot   See the entry for *spoil².*

rotate   See the entry for *turn.*

rotten   (*adjective*) spoiled and bad-smelling. □ *Mark found nothing in the bin but a few rotten potatoes.* □ *Tom cut out the rotten parts of the apple.*
  • **foul**   disgustingly bad-smelling. □ *What's that foul smell?* □ *Somebody wash the dog; he's getting really foul!*
  • **putrid**   completely decomposed and bad-smelling. (Formal.) □ *A putrid slime had gathered at the bottom of the refrigerator.* □ *The police found the putrid remains of several dead chickens.*
  • **rancid**   spoiled and sour. (Said of milk, butter, or oil.) □ *Just one sip of the milk told me it was rancid.* □ *Sue spoiled the cookies by using rancid butter in them.*
  • **rank**   extremely bad-smelling. (Formal.) □ *Rank weeds had taken over the garden.* □ *Philip's room was filled with the rank odor of unwashed gym clothes.*

rotund   See the entry for *round.*

rough¹   (*adjective*) not finished; hastily or sloppily made. □ *Rita wrote a rough draft of her essay.* □ *Susan gave me a rough estimate of how much the repairs would cost.*
  • **crude**   rough; not finely made. □ *Tim made a crude drawing of a truck.* □ *They constructed a crude shelter out of cardboard boxes.*
  • **rudimentary**   not finished; only begun to be formed. (Formal.) □ *The child made a rudimentary sculpture of a cat.* □ *Jan had only the most rudimentary idea of how a bicycle works.*
  • **unfinished**   not finished. □ *The symphony was left unfinished at the composer's death.* □ *The door was made of unfinished lumber.*

rough²   (*adjective*) not smooth; raspy. (See also the entries for *gruff, violent.*) □ *Bill felt the rough surface of the coconut.* □ *The tree's bark was very rough.*
  • **coarse**   rough; not fine-textured. □ *Anna made a shirt out of coarse cloth.* □ *The carpenter used coarse sandpaper to smooth the board.*
  • **jagged**   rough and having many sharp points. □ *The broken bottle had a jagged edge.* □ *The sun set behind the jagged mountain range.*

• **rugged**   *rough* and strong. □ *Mary needed hiking boots with rugged soles.* □ *Donna admired the rugged features of Charlie's face.*

• **uneven**   *rough;* not regular or level. □ *The car shook as it speeded over the uneven road surface.* □ *Linda tripped over the uneven floorboards.*

round   (*adjective*) curved; shaped like a circle or a ball. □ *Jane has a round face.* □ *Is your table square or round?*

• **circular**   *round* like a circle. □ *Give me the hat with the circular brim.* □ *The car's headlights were perfectly circular.*

• **rotund**   *round* and plump. (Formal.) □ *We laughed at the way the rotund hippopotamus waddled into the water.* □ *Gina ate until she was quite rotund.*

• **spherical**   shaped like a ball. □ *A spherical balloon floated across the sky.* □ *Howard rolled a spherical ball of snow.*

rove   See the entry for *wander*.

row   See the entry for *line*.

rubberneck   See the entry for *gawk*.

rubbish   See the entry for *nonsense*.

rude   (*adjective*) not polite; displaying bad manners. □ *The rude boy thumbed his nose at me.* □ *It's rude to talk during the movie.*

• **boorish**   clownishly *rude*. □ *Alan's boorish behavior embarrassed his friend.* □ *The boorish diner belched loudly and often during the meal.*

• **crass**   extremely *rude* or foul-mouthed. □ *I thought the jokes on that TV show were really crass.* □ *The man made a crass remark as the women walked by.*

• **impolite**   *rude;* not polite. □ *It's impolite to leave the table before others are finished eating.* □ *Jenny noticed Kevin's impolite stare.*

• **uncouth**   untrained and therefore *rude*. (Formal.) □ *I felt very uncouth in comparison with Larry's polished manners.* □ *In the church sanctuary, a group of tourists joked and laughed and were generally uncouth.*

• **vulgar**   not refined and therefore *rude;* obscene. □ *Mary had the vulgar habit of blowing her nose on her sleeve.* □ *Nancy made a vulgar comment about the man's backside.*

[→contrasting word: *polite;* see also: *insolent*]

rudimentary   See the entry for *rough¹*.

rug   See the entry for *carpet*.

rugged   See the entry for *rough²*.

ruin   See the entry for *destroy*.

rule (*noun*) a statement of what to do and what not to do. □ *In our house we have a rule against wearing outdoor shoes on the carpet.* □ *We read the rules of the game before we started to play.*

• **act**   a *rule* passed by legislators. (See also the main entry for *act*.) □ *The Civil Rights Act of 1964 created the Equal Employment Opportunity Commission.* □ *Congress passed the Alien and Sedition Acts in 1798.*

• **law**   an official or formal *rule*. ⊔ *The town council passed a law against dumping garbage in vacant lots.* □ *Speeding is against the law.*

• **policy**   a *rule* that is supposed to be followed all the time; a statement that guides how you behave. □ *You must pay in cash; that's the store policy.* □ *The company had a policy that forbade dating between employees.*

• **regulation**   an official *rule* for controlling something. (Formal.) □ *The soldier did not have his belt buckle polished according to regulation.* □ *School regulations absolutely prohibit smoking.*

• **statute**   an official *rule* passed by legislators. (Formal.) □ *The new state statute requires every car to pass an emissions test.* □ *The sale of drugs is controlled by federal statute.*

ruler (*noun*) someone who governs a country with absolute power. □ *Augustus Caesar was the ruler of Rome from 27 B.C. to A.D. 14.* □ *Queen Victoria was a beloved ruler.*

• **emperor**   the male *ruler* of an empire. □ *Charlemagne was crowned emperor in A.D. 800.* □ *The Roman emperors ruled countries as far away as England.*

• **empress**   the female *ruler* of an empire; the wife of an emperor. □ *Catherine became empress of Russia in 1762.* □ *The Empress Josephine was Napoleon's wife.*

• **king**   a male *ruler* of royal blood. □ *Who was the king of France in 1789?* □ *The Pyramids are the tombs of Egyptian kings.*

• **monarch**   a *ruler* of a kingdom or an empire. □ *Tsar Nicholas II was the last Russian monarch.* □ *In 1547, the ten-year-old monarch Edward VI ascended the English throne.*

• **potentate**   a *ruler* who has great power. (Formal.) □ *Many foreign potentates attended the prime minister's funeral.* □ *The potentates of the warring countries met to discuss peace terms.*

• **queen**   a female *ruler* of royal blood. □ *When her half-sister Mary I died, Elizabeth became queen.* □ *The queen was crowned in Westminster Abbey.*

• **sovereign**   a *ruler* with absolute authority. (Formal.) □ *The nobles bowed before their sovereign.* □ *Catherine proved to be a very capable sovereign.*

[→see also: *leader, autocrat*]

rumble (*verb*) to make a deep, rolling sound. □ *The car rumbled down the rough road.* □ *Thunder rumbled in the distance.*

• **boom** to make a deep, resonant sound. □ *We heard cannons booming.* □ *The bass drum boomed.*

• **growl** to make a deep, snarling sound. □ *Tom's stomach was growling.* □ *The jeep growled up the hill.*

• **thunder** to make a loud, rolling sound, like thunder. □ *The children thundered up the stairs.* □ *I heard a jet plane thunder overhead.*

ruminate See the entries for *chew, wonder²*.

rummage (*verb*) to go through everything as you look for something. (Sometimes with *through*.) □ *Jane rummaged through the desk drawer.* □ *Ken rummaged around in his pockets.*

• **burrow** to dig deeply; to dig around looking for something. □ *Some small animal has burrowed beneath the tree roots.* □ *Rita burrowed into the closet in search of her snow boots.*

• **ransack** to disrupt everything as you look for something. □ *The burglars completely ransacked my apartment.* □ *Stanley ransacked the library in his search for information about Billy the Kid.*

• **rifle** to hunt through something that does not belong to you and take things from it. □ *Thomas rifled through Victor's papers, looking for the secret map.* □ *Wendy rifled her mother's wallet but found only a few dollars.*

• **root around** to *rummage;* to dig here and there looking for something. □ *I rooted around in the bedclothes, in search of the missing sock.* □ *Art rooted around in the cupboard, but couldn't find the baking soda.*

[→see also: *seek*]

rumor (*noun*) a story passed from person to person; a story that may or may not be true. □ *I heard a rumor that Ben is moving away.* □ *Carla said that Donald is in love with Linda, but that's just a rumor.*

• **gossip** information about people that may or may not be true. □ *Fran gave me all the latest gossip.* □ *The friends met for coffee and gossip every afternoon.*

• **hearsay** *rumor;* something you have heard and that may or may not be true. □ *It's only hearsay, but George might be getting married.* □ *The reporter's story was entirely based on hearsay.*

• **scandal** talk about a person that may hurt that person's reputation. □ *Helen was the subject of neighborhood scandal for weeks.* □ *Irene feared public scandal if she went to the clinic for help with her alcoholism.*

run (*verb*) to go fast by taking rapid, leaping steps. (See also the entries for *control¹, series*.) □ *Jay ran all the way to school.* □ *Kay ran up the stairs.*

• **gallop**   to *run* the way a horse does, taking big jumps. □ *The horse galloped across the meadow.* □ *Laura galloped happily onto the soccer field.*

• **jog**   to *run* at a moderate pace, taking bouncing steps; to exercise by *running* at a moderate pace. □ *We jogged along the beach.* □ *Mark jogs five miles every evening.*

• **scamper**   to *run* lightly from place to place. □ *The kitten scampered after the ball of string.* □ *The children scampered off to find the ice-cream truck.*

• **scurry**   to *run* or hurry with tiny little steps. □ *The mouse scurried into its hole.* □ *I saw a squirrel scurry across the lawn with a nut in his mouth.*

• **sprint**   to *run* as fast as you can. □ *Tom sprinted toward the finish line.* □ *Sue sprinted after the departing bus.*

• **trot**   to *run* or walk fast with bouncing steps. □ *The horse trotted along the bridle path.* □ *The dog trotted up, expecting me to give her a treat.*

[→see also: *walk*]

run across   See the entry for *meet.*

run away from   See the entry for *escape.*

run-down   See the entry for *shabby.*

run into   See the entries for *collide, meet.*

rupture   See the entry for *burst.*

rural   See the entry for *country.*

rush   See the entry for *hurry.*

rust   See the entry for *brown.*

rustic   See the entry for *country.*

rustle   (*verb*) to make swishing sounds or cause something to make swishing sounds. □ *The leaves rustled in the breeze.* □ *Philip rustled the pages of his book.*

• **crackle**   to make many small, popping sounds. □ *The fire crackled in the fireplace.* □ *The ice crackled as we stepped on it.*

• **crinkle**   to make many small, sharp, metallic sounds or cause something to make such sounds. □ *The plastic crinkled as I opened the package.* □ *Ken crinkled the candy wrapper, much to the annoyance of the people sitting near him at the theater.*

ruthless   See the entry for *cruel.*

S

sack   See the entry for *bag*.

sacred   See the entry for *holy*.

sacrifice   See the entry for *give up*.

sad   (*adjective*) full of sorrow or grief. □ *Rita looks awfully sad.* □ *The clown had a sad face.*
- **dejected**   very *sad* and depressed. (Formal.) □ *Her first several weeks in the new school, Susan felt lonely and dejected.* □ *There was a dejected slump to Tim's shoulders as the coach ordered him off the field.*
- **downcast**   acting or appearing *sad* and subdued. (Formal.) □ *Jan, usually lively and cheerful, was downcast that day.* □ *The children were utterly downcast when they heard that their uncle would not be able to visit after all.*
- **glum**   sad and gloomy. □ *The awful weather made everyone feel glum.* □ *Bill's hilarious jokes soon changed our glum expressions.*
- **low**   sad and listless. (Informal.) □ *Anna was very low after losing the contest.* □ *Mary always cheers me up when I'm feeling low.*
- **miserable**   intensely *sad;* full of misery. □ *Charlie has been miserable ever since his girlfriend left him.* □ *Between a bad cold and her bad grades, Donna felt thoroughly miserable.*
- **unhappy**   sad; not happy. □ *I hate to see you so unhappy.* □ *Linda's job made her unhappy, so she quit.*
[→contrasting word: *happy*]

safe   (*adjective*) free from danger. □ *Inside the house, we were safe from the storm.* □ *The bank was a safe place to keep my money.*
- **invulnerable**   completely *safe* from attack; not able to be hurt. (Formal.) □ *Within his sturdy armor, the knight was invulnerable.* □ *The army attacked from an invulnerable position.*

• **protected** kept *safe* by someone or something. □ *Felicia stayed in the cave, protected from the wind.* □ *The car's finish was protected against rust.*

• **secure** strong and *safe.* □ *The guard made sure the building was secure.* □ *I need a secure place to store my suitcase.*

safeguard See the entry for *protect.*

sag See the entry for *droop.*

salary See the entry for *pay.*

sallow See the entry for *pale.*

sample See the entry for *example.*

sanction See the entry for *approve.*

sap See the entry for *weaken.*

sarcasm See the entry for *irony.*

sarcastic (*adjective*) nasty and scornful; meant to hurt someone's feelings. □ *There was a sarcastic tone in Gina's voice as she complimented me on my clothes.* □ *Almost everything Harold says is sarcastic.*

• **acerbic** bitterly, acidly *sarcastic.* (Formal.) □ *Sue's acerbic criticism of her friends did not make her popular.* □ *I thought the writer's acerbic style was very funny.*

• **biting** sharply *sarcastic.* □ *"At least I don't go back on my promises," was Jenny's biting reply.* □ *The skit was a biting satire of the presidential candidates.*

• **caustic** sharply *sarcastic;* very critical. (Formal.) □ *Mark Twain was well known for his witty but caustic commentaries on human foolishness.* □ *The actor made several caustic remarks about his rival.*

• **sharp** painfully *sarcastic;* pointed; angry or impatient. (See also the main entry for *sharp.*) □ *Kevin said a few sharp things about me, making sure I overheard.* □ *The little boy was upset by his mother's sharp words.*

• **stinging** *sarcastic;* causing emotional pain. □ *Larry delivered a stinging insult.* □ *I felt I did not deserve such a stinging lecture on my faults.*

sass See the entry for *talk back to.*

satire See the entry for *irony.*

satisfactory (*adjective*) meeting all the requirements in terms of quality. (See also the entry for *enough.*) □ *This carpenter does satisfactory work.* □ *Mary is a satisfactory student.*

• **adequate** meeting the requirements well enough. □ *A one-bedroom apartment should be adequate for us.* □ *Nancy did an adequate job of fixing the car.*

• **fit** meeting the requirements; ready; appropriate. □ *Tom argued that Jane was not a fit mother for their children.* □ *Roger fixed up the spare bedroom until it was fit for the fussiest possible guest.*

• **suitable** meeting the requirements well enough; appropriate. □ *We tried to find a suitable room for our meeting.* □ *Is this movie suitable for children?*

satisfied See the entry for *content.*

saturated See the entry for *wet.*

saunter See the entry for *walk.*

savage (*adjective*) wild and cruel; not civilized. □ *The savage animal tore its victims limb from limb.* □ *Many savage forms of punishment were common in the olden days.*

• **brutal** forceful and cruel. □ *The brutal dictator killed everyone who opposed him.* □ *Stanley received a brutal beating.*

• **ferocious** fierce and cruel. □ *That tiger certainly looks ferocious.* □ *We were caught in the middle of a ferocious storm.*

• **vicious** violent and cruel; cruel and wicked. □ *Thomas loved to play vicious practical jokes.* □ *Only a vicious person could have committed these horrible murders.*

[→see also: *cruel*]

save (*verb*) to bring someone or something out of danger. (See also the entry for *preserve.*) □ *"Somebody save me!" cried the man who had fallen overboard.* □ *The kitten was about to fall into the hole, but I saved her.*

• **deliver** to bring someone or something into safety. □ *The police officers delivered the hostages from their captivity.* □ *The prisoner prayed for someone to deliver her.*

• **rescue** to bring someone or something out of extreme, immediate danger. □ *The search party rescued the freezing hikers.* □ *Wendy dove into the river to rescue the drowning child.*

• **retrieve** to bring someone or something back. □ *I had to go back to the library to retrieve the gloves I had left there.* □ *Art retrieved his kids from the shopping mall.*

savor See the entry for *enjoy.*

say (*verb*) to express something in words. □ *"I would like a tomato,"* Anna said. □ *Mary said that she would be home at five.*

• **comment** to *say* something about what you are seeing or hearing. □ *"That actress doesn't look good in polka dots," Charles commented as we watched the movie.* □ *Donna asked the teacher to comment on her writing style.*

• **mention**   to *say* something briefly; to bring up a subject. □ *Linda mentioned her plans to go to Florida.* □ *Frank mentioned that he would be seeing Gina on Saturday.*

• **observe**   to *say* that you have noticed something. □ *"Harold seems upset," Sue observed.* □ *Jenny said good night, observing that it was getting late.*

• **remark**   to briefly *say* what you think. □ *"Lousy weather we're having," Kevin remarked.* □ *Larry remarked that kids seemed to be getting ruder all the time.*

• **state**   to *say* something; to *say* something for the record. (Formal.) □ *Mary stated that she had not been in contact with her brother for several years.* □ *Please state your full name.*

say no   See the entry for *refuse.*

saying   (*noun*) an expression, especially one that has come down through time. □ *"You can't teach an old dog new tricks" is a well-known saying.* □ *Ben Franklin put his favorite sayings into* Poor Richard's Almanack.

• **adage**   an old *saying.* (Formal.) □ *Nancy filled out her tax form, thinking of the well-known adage about death and taxes.* □ *As the months went by, Tom discovered the truth of the adage that time heals all wounds.*

• **maxim**   a *saying* that expresses a truth; a short rule for how to behave. (Formal.) □ *"Children should be seen and not heard" was a maxim my parents often quoted.* □ *Jane lived her life according to maxims like "Least said, soonest mended" and "Silence is golden."*

• **old saw**   an old, often-used *saying.* (Informal.) □ *Please don't quote that old saw about leading a horse to water!* □ *Granny seems to have an old saw for every occasion.*

• **platitude**   a *saying* that has been overused; a dull old *saying.* (Formal.) □ *She tried to comfort her daughter with platitudes like "there are other fish in the sea."* □ *The politician's speech was full of platitudes and empty of any real promises.*

• **proverb**   a well-known *saying.* □ *Ken felt confident that he would win, but he forgot the proverb "There's many a slip 'twixt the cup and the lip."* □ *The proverb "Don't look a gift horse in the mouth" originated from the fact that you can tell a horse's age by looking at its teeth.*

scale   See the entry for *climb.*

scamper   See the entry for *run.*

scandal   See the entries for *disgrace, rumor.*

scanty   See the entry for *meager.*

scarcely   See the entries for *barely, seldom.*

scared   See the entry for *afraid.*

scarlet   See the entry for *red.*

scatter (*verb*) to go off in all directions; to make things go off in all directions. □ *The flock of chickens scattered when they heard the noise.* □ *Roger scattered flour over the surface of the dough.*
- **disband**   to become *scattered*. (Formal.) □ *The club disbanded in January.* □ *The rock group decided to disband.*
- **disperse**   to *scatter;* to spread things around a large area. (Formal.) □ *The crowd gradually dispersed.* □ *After Stanley died, his book collection was dispersed among his friends.*
- **dissipate**   to *scatter;* to make something dissolve or disappear. (Formal.) □ *The gust of wind dissipated the pile of leaves.* □ *When the sun came up, the fog dissipated.*
[→contrasting word: *gather*]

scenery   See the entry for *view.*

scent   See the entry for *smell.*

scheme   See the entries for *plan, plot.*

school (*noun*) a place for teaching and learning. □ *Which grade school did you attend?* □ *Thomas visited his old school.*
- **academy**   a specialized *school.* (Formal.) □ *Victor took tap lessons at a dance academy.* □ *For high school, Wendy attended a private academy.*
- **college**   a *school* offering advanced education. □ *Art planned to go to college when he finished high school.* □ *Ben took a photography class at the local community college.*
- **conservatory**   a *school* for music education. □ *The violinist trained at a famous conservatory.* □ *The singer had to audition to get into the conservatory.*
- **institute**   a *school* for a specialized subject; an organization for researching a particular topic. □ *Carrie learned to repair computers at a technical institute.* □ *The National Institute for Mental Health supports many research projects.*
- **seminary**   a *school* for training priests, ministers, or rabbis. □ *Donald attended a Methodist seminary.* □ *Eddie had his heart set on going to the seminary and becoming a priest.*
- **university**   a *school* for higher learning. □ *Fran is a student at the state university.* □ *The university has a very large library.*

scintillate   See the entry for *sparkle.*

scoff at   See the entry for *disobey.*

scold (*verb*) to find fault with someone in an angry way. (See also the entry for *nag.*) □ *Fran scolded the puppy for soiling the carpet.* □ *Dad scolded me for coming home late.*

• **berate**   to *scold* someone very angrily. (Formal.) □ *The teacher berated his students for their poor performance on the test.* □ *I was afraid that George would berate me for having dented his beautiful new car.*
• **rebuke**   to disapprove; to *scold* someone in a serious way. (Formal.) □ *The preacher rebuked his congregation for their sins.* □ *Mother sternly rebuked me for setting such a bad example for my sister.*
• **reprimand**   to *scold* someone formally. □ *The principal reprimanded Helen in front of the whole school.* □ *Irene was late every day this week, so the boss reprimanded her.*
• **reproach**   to blame someone for doing wrong; to express disapproval of someone. □ *My conscience reproached me for forgetting Jay's birthday.* □ *Kay reproached Laura for making fun of Mark.*
• **reprove**   to express disapproval of someone in order to convince him or her to do better. (Formal.) □ *My friends' disappointed faces silently reproved me for acting so stuck-up.* □ *Whenever I went wrong, Grampa gently reproved me.*
• **upbraid**   to blame someone for doing wrong. □ *Tom upbraided his sister for getting tar on his new bike.* □ *Sue upbraided Philip until he looked completely miserable.*

scope   See the entry for *size.*

scorch   See the entry for *burn¹.*

scorn   See the entry for *disrespect.*

scoundrel   See the entry for *villain.*

scour   See the entry for *scrape.*

scourge   See the entry for *whip.*

scowl   See the entry for *frown.*

scrape   (*verb*) to rub a surface with something sharp or rough; to remove something by rubbing it with something sharp or rough. □ *The car scraped against the tree.* □ *Ken scraped the skin off the potato.*
• **abrade**   to wear down a surface by rubbing it with something rough. (Formal.) □ *The gritty cleanser abraded the bathtub's smooth surface.* □ *Rita needed to get the burned food off without abrading the shiny copper pot.*
• **rasp**   to *scrape* something with a rough surface or tool; to drag a file called a *rasp* along a surface. □ *The cat's tongue rasped against my skin.* □ *The carpenter rasped the piece of wood until it was the right shape.*
• **scour**   to clean or polish a surface by rubbing it with something rough. □ *Susan scoured the kitchen floor with a scrub brush.* □ *Tim thoroughly scoured the pots and pans.*

• **scuff** to make a mark on a surface by dragging something across it. □ *Jan's boots scuffed the floor.* □ *Don't drag the chair along the floor like that; you'll scuff it.*

scrawl See the entry for *write.*

scream (*verb*) to make a shrill, high-pitched cry. □ *"Leave me alone!" Bill screamed at the top of his lungs.* □ *A cold hand touched Anna from behind, and she screamed.*
> • **howl** to make a long, loud cry; to yell or shout. □ *We could hear wolves howling in the forest.* □ *Mary howled with laughter.*
> • **shriek** to make a loud, shrill cry. □ *Everyone shrieked as the roller coaster plunged downward.* □ *"I will have vengeance!" the woman shrieked.*
> • **wail** to make a long, sad cry. □ *The widower wept and wailed at his wife's funeral.* □ *The wind wailed through the trees.*
> [→see also: *yell, cry*]

screech See the entry for *squeak.*

scribble See the entry for *write.*

Scrooge See the entry for *miser.*

scrumptious See the entry for *delicious.*

scrutinize See the entry for *check.*

scuff See the entry for *scrape.*

sculpture (*noun*) a figure made out of stone, wood, metal, or other materials. □ *Michaelangelo's David is a famous sculpture.* □ *Vincent made an abstract sculpture out of old tires and beer bottles.*
> • **bust** a *sculpture* of a person's head and shoulders. □ *A bust of Plato stood by the library door.* □ *Charles looked into the eyes of the bust of Alexander the Great and wondered what kind of person he was.*
> • **figurine** a small, decorative *sculpture,* usually depicting a person or an animal. □ *Donna collects animal figurines.* □ *A graceful china figurine of a ballerina stood on the shelf.*
> • **monument** something built in memory of a person or event (sometimes a *sculpture*). □ *In front of the town hall is a monument to those who died serving their country.* □ *Linda wanted to visit the Washington Monument.*
> • **statue** a *sculpture* depicting a person or an animal. □ *Leonardo planned a giant statue of a horse.* □ *In front of the museum is a statue of Louis IX.*

scurry See the entry for *run.*

seal See the entry for *close.*

sear   See the entry for *burn¹*.

search for   See the entry for *seek*.

seasoned   See the entry for *experienced*.

secondhand   (*adjective*) used before by someone else. □ *Frank bought all his furniture secondhand.* □ *Gina hated having to wear secondhand clothes.*
> • **hand-me-down**   *secondhand;* handed down from one person to another. □ *I got a lot of hand-me-down shirts from my brother.* □ *Harold was grateful for the hand-me-down tools from his father.*
> • **old**   *secondhand* or used over a long time; not new. □ *Sue made curtains out of old sheets.* □ *I can't wear this old suit; it's a decade out of style!*
> • **used**   *secondhand;* used before by someone else. (Often used to describe merchandise.) □ *Jenny bought a used car.* □ *Who left this used tissue on the desk?*

secret   (*adjective*) hidden from others; not public. □ *Whenever club members met, they gave the secret handshake.* □ *The movie star wanted a secret place to spend her honeymoon.*
> • **clandestine**   deliberately *secret; secret* and for an evil purpose. (Formal.) □ *The rebels made clandestine attempts to assassinate the president.* □ *The gang held clandestine meetings in an empty warehouse.*
> • **covert**   *secret;* not out in the open. (Formal.) □ *The spy's covert activities were gradually brought to light.* □ *No one suspected Kevin's covert plans to leave town.*
> • **underground**   *secret;* hidden from the authorities. □ *Larry published an underground newspaper that criticized the government severely.* □ *Bugsy was a member of an underground crime network.*

secretary   See the entry for *clerk*.

secrete   See the entry for *stash*.

section   See the entries for *class, part*.

secure   See the entry for *safe*.

see   (*verb*) to use your eyes to look at something. (See also the entry for *date²*.) □ *I saw a dark shape move across the lawn.* □ *Can you see the hot-air balloon up in the sky?*
> • **eye**   to *see* something and study it carefully. □ *Mary eyed the last piece of cake.* □ *Nancy eyed me suspiciously.*
> • **glimpse**   to *see* something for just an instant. □ *I glimpsed something shiny at the bottom of the pool.* □ *Tom glimpsed a bright red bird in the tree outside his window, but when he went to take a closer look, it had flown away.*

• **view**   to *see* something; to *see* something and pay attention to it. (Somewhat formal. See also the main entry for *view*.) ☐ *Philip invited his friends over to view the slides he took on his vacation.* ☐ *Many people came to view the Egyptian exhibits in the museum.*

see red   See the entry for *bristle*.

seedy   See the entry for *shabby*.

seek   (*verb*) to try to find something. (Formal.) ☐ *Police are currently seeking the fugitive.* ☐ *Alexander sought his long-lost parents.*
   • **hunt for**   to *seek* or go after something. ☐ *Ken went through the cupboard, hunting for the last can of cream of broccoli soup.* ☐ *Roger hunted for his old friend's phone number.*
   • **look for**   to *seek* something; to look everywhere to try to find something. (Informal.) ☐ *From the way Stanley is pawing through his dresser drawers, I'd say he's looking for something.* ☐ *Thomas went to every toy store in town, looking for the doll his daughter wanted.*
   • **search for**   to *seek* something carefully and painstakingly. ☐ *We all searched for the missing necklace.* ☐ *The townspeople went out with flashlights to search for the lost child.*

seem   (*verb*) to appear to be a certain way. ☐ *Victor seems like a nice man.* ☐ *The clouds seem to be blowing away.*
   • **appear**   to *seem* a certain way on the surface; to be a certain way, as far as anyone can see. ☐ *Wendy appeared happy, but I suspected she was just putting on a show.* ☐ *This appears to be Art's handwriting.*
   • **look like**   to *seem* a certain way; to be a certain way as far as you can tell by looking. ☐ *The table looked like an antique, but it was only a reproduction.* ☐ *It looks like rain.*
   • **resemble**   to *seem* very similar to something else. ☐ *The vinyl floor tiles resembled marble.* ☐ *Ben strongly resembles his father.*

seemly   See the entry for *proper*.

seep   See the entry for *leak*.

seethe   (*verb*) to bubble steadily, as if boiling; to be disturbed or upset. ☐ *The liquid in the witch's cauldron seethed, sending up a vile odor.* ☐ *When Charlie saw Donna with her new boyfriend, he seethed inwardly.*
   • **churn**   to bubble or turn violently. ☐ *The pool at the bottom of the waterfall churned constantly.* ☐ *Linda was so upset that her stomach churned.*
   • **effervesce**   to bubble up and hiss in a lively way; to fizz; to bubble up with energy. (Formal.) ☐ *Champagne is aged in bottles to make it effervesce.* ☐ *The lively young woman simply effervesced that night.*
   • **ferment**   to bubble constantly, as if worked on by yeast. ☐ *Wine is obtained by fermenting the juice of grapes.* ☐ *Ideas and speculations fermented in the inventor's active brain.*

seize   See the entries for *capture, catch, take.*

seldom   (*adverb*) hardly ever; only once in a great while. □ *I seldom go out for dinner.* □ *Frank seldom forgets to send his sister a birthday card.*
   • **infrequently**   seldom; not frequently. □ *Gina watched the news so infrequently that she wasn't sure who was president.* □ *Harold missed work infrequently.*
   • **rarely**   seldom; almost never. □ *Sue rarely invites people over.* □ *Jenny scolded her children so rarely that it really upset them when she did it.*
   • **scarcely**   seldom; hardly at all. □ *We scarcely hear from Kevin anymore.* □ *Larry scarcely ever missed a basketball game.*
   [→contrasting word: *often*]

select   See the entry for *choose.*

self-assertive   See the entry for *aggressive.*

self-control   See the entry for *discipline.*

self-governing   See the entry for *independent.*

self-restraint   See the entry for *discipline.*

seller   (*noun*) someone who sells something. □ *The buyer and the seller agreed on a price.* □ *Mary is a seller of rare old books.*
   • **broker**   a person who buys and sells things for other people. □ *Nancy needed a trustworthy broker to buy stock for her.* □ *The livestock broker made a good profit at the cattle auction.*
   • **dealer**   a person who buys and sells things; someone who sells a particular brand of items. □ *Hundreds of antique dealers gathered at the flea market.* □ *Tom took his car to the car dealer for repairs.*
   • **merchant**   a person who buys and sells things; a storekeeper. □ *The local merchants decorated their stores for the holidays.* □ *The merchant was waiting for a new shipment of picture frames.*
   • **trader**   a *seller;* someone who trades. □ *The trappers took the furs to the trader in town and exchanged them for food and tobacco.* □ *Jane is a trader in fine works of art.*
   • **vendor**   a *seller* on a small scale; a peddler; a formal term for *seller.* □ *We bought a snack from the hot-pretzel vendor.* □ *The vendor's name should appear on the receipt.*

seminar   See the entry for *class.*

seminary   See the entry for *school.*

send   (*verb*) to cause something or someone to go from one place to another. □ *Roger sent me a letter.* □ *Stanley sent me to an office down the hall.*

• **dispatch**   to *send* something officially or quickly. (Formal.) □ *The officer dispatched the latest news to his superiors.* □ *I dispatched the package at 2:34 P.M. today.*

• **relay**   to *send* something to the next person or place along the way. □ *Thomas relayed the news about Gramma to his sister.* □ *I relayed the gift for Victor to Wendy, who in turn will relay it to Art, who will give it to Victor.*

• **transmit**   to *send* a message. (Formal.) □ *The ship transmitted a distress call.* □ *The coach transmitted the signal to bunt.*

send for   See the entry for *call¹.*

sensation   See the entries for *feeling, wonder¹.*

sense   See the entry for *feel.*

senseless   See the entry for *meaningless.*

sensible   See the entry for *reasonable.*

sensitive   (*adjective*) easily hurt or offended; easily influenced. (See also the entry for *gentle.*) □ *Ben is very sensitive and takes offense at the slightest things.* □ *The sensitive child had nightmares about the pictures of starving children she had seen on the news.*

• **testy**   easily angered; impatient. (Informal.) □ *Carrie is feeling rather testy because things aren't going well at work.* □ *Don't ask Donald for anything right now; he's real testy and would probably just yell at you.*

• **thin-skinned**   easily hurt or angered. (Informal.) □ *Once Eddie discovered that Fran was thin-skinned, he couldn't resist teasing her constantly.* □ *It's hard for George to take criticism because he is so thin-skinned.*

• **touchy**   nervous and easily upset. (Informal.) □ *My, you're touchy today!* □ *Don't ask Helen about her diet; she's gained a few pounds and is kind of touchy about it.*

[→see also: *irritable*]

sentiment   See the entry for *feeling.*

separate   See the entries for *different, distinguish, divide.*

sepia   See the entry for *brown.*

sequence   See the entry for *series.*

serene   See the entry for *calm.*

serial   See the entry for *periodical.*

series   (*noun*) a group of things or events coming one after the other. □ *The TV station presented a series of programs about the English royal family.* □ *The artist made a series of paintings of the same building.*

• **course** an unbroken *series* in which one thing leads to the next. □ *Irene described the course of events that brought her to New York City.* □ *Jay had to take a course of tests before he could attend the school.*

• **run** a *series* of similar things; an unbroken *series*. (See also the main entry for *run*.) □ *There was a run of really terrible movies at the local theater.* □ *Kay had a run of bad luck.*

• **sequence** an orderly or connected *series* of things; an order. □ *Laura took a sequence of classes in American history.* □ *Mark arranged his family pictures in their proper sequence.*

• **string** a *series*; a group of things connected like beads on a string. □ *A string of losing bets left Tom without any money.* □ *A whole string of doctors had not been able to cure Sue.*

• **succession** a *series*; a group of things following each other in order. (Formal.) □ *We lived in a succession of apartments, each one a bit more run-down than the last.* □ *The football player got a succession of injuries that season.*

• **train** a connected *series*, especially a *series* of events; a group of things one following another. □ *A train of coincidences brought Philip and me together.* □ *A bizarre train of events led to the capture of the criminal.*

serious (*adjective*) deeply concerned; not joking. □ *No, I mean it! I'm serious!* □ *Ken was in a serious mood after his talk with Rita.*

• **grave** very *serious*; not joking in the least. (Formal.) □ *Father's face was very grave as he asked us who had taken the money.* □ *Susan was a grave young woman who seldom smiled.*

• **grim** so *serious* as to seem frightening. □ *The prisoner did not like the grim look on the judge's face.* □ *Tim is very friendly, despite his grim appearance.*

• **solemn** extremely *serious* and somber. □ *Jan read the prayer in a solemn voice.* □ *I could tell from Bill's solemn expression that something awful had happened.*

sermon See the entry for *speech*.

serve See the entry for *benefit²*.

service See the entries for *ceremony, favor*.

serviceable See the entry for *useful*.

set See the entries for *group, put*.

set aside See the entry for *reserve*.

set down See the entry for *land*.

set free See the entry for *release*.

set out See the entry for *begin*.

settle   See the entry for *live*.

settle on   See the entry for *choose*.

sever   See the entry for *cut*.

severe   (*adjective*) overly strict or punishing. □ *Anna gives her children such severe punishments.* □ *The principal was very severe with the disrespectful students.*

> • **drastic**   extremely *severe;* going to extremes. □ *The doctor had to take drastic measures to save the patient's life.* □ *To keep Mary from seeing Charlie anymore, her parents took the drastic step of sending her to school five hundred miles away.*
> • **extreme**   *severe;* going to the outermost limits. □ *Grounding the child for six months is a bit extreme, don't you think?* □ *Donald's extreme stinginess has not won him many friends.*
> • **harsh**   very *severe;* overly rough. (See also the main entry for *harsh*.) □ *Eddie's parents are very harsh with him.* □ *Such harsh punishments as whipping and branding may have discouraged some people from wrongdoing.*
> • **stern**   grim, uncompromising, or *severe.* □ *The teacher enforced stern discipline on her students.* □ *Mom looked stern when she heard where we had spent the afternoon.*

sew   (*verb*) to fasten pieces of something (usually fabric) with needle and thread. □ *Fran sat by the window, sewing.* □ *George sewed a patch onto his jeans.*

> • **baste**   to *sew* something temporarily, with big stitches. □ *Helen basted the shirt, tried it on, made a few adjustments, and then sewed it together.* □ *Just baste the hem for now; we'll finish it later.*
> • **darn**   to fill in a hole by *sewing.* □ *Irene carefully darned the heels of her socks.* □ *Jay darned the holes in the blanket.*
> • **embroider**   to *sew* designs on something. □ *Kay embroidered her purse with gold thread.* □ *Laura embroidered her initials on the pocket.*
> • **stitch**   to *sew,* with emphasis on pushing the needle and thread through the fabric over and over. □ *It was hard to stitch the stiff fabric together.* □ *Mark stitched up a cute little suit for his baby cousin.*

shabby   (*adjective*) very worn out. □ *I tried to clean the old sofa, but it looked as shabby as ever.* □ *The man's shabby clothes showed that he was poor.*

> • **ragged**   *shabby* and torn; in rags. □ *The puppy chewed on the blanket until it was quite ragged.* □ *The beggar had only a ragged coat to protect her from the cold.*
> • **ratty**   *shabby* and tattered. (Informal.) □ *Tom should be ashamed to go out in public in such a ratty T-shirt.* □ *Sue's ratty old tennis shoes were the most comfortable footwear she owned.*

• **run-down** *shabby;* not taken good care of. ☐ *The barn in back of the house was completely run-down.* ☐ *The main street of the little town was lined with run-down storefronts.*

• **seedy** poor and *shabby.* ☐ *Philip stayed in a seedy hotel that was very cheap.* ☐ *That seedy old man is the town drunk.*

• **threadbare** so *shabby* that it is worn down to threads. ☐ *The rug is really getting threadbare.* ☐ *Ken asked me to mend his threadbare shirt.*

• **worn** *shabby;* old and showing signs of use. ☐ *Those shoes are so worn that they look like they're coming apart.* ☐ *Rita opened the worn cover of her favorite book.*

shack (*noun*) a small, crude house. ☐ *Susan built a little shack to stay in when she fished at the lake.* ☐ *The wind whistled through the thin walls of the shack.*

• **hovel** a poor, squalid *shack.* (Formal.) ☐ *The poor family scarcely had enough fuel to heat their hovel.* ☐ *Tim hated to walk past the hovels in the poor part of town.*

• **hut** a primitive *shack.* ☐ *Jan lived in a grass hut on the island.* ☐ *The hermit lived in a little hut made of twigs.*

• **shanty** a poor *shack;* a small house that is not really adequate for people to live in. ☐ *The refugees built shanties out of cardboard and scrap metal.* ☐ *Bill was shocked and depressed to see the shanty his poor brother lived in.*

shackles See the entry for *bonds.*

shade See the entries for *color, darkness.*

shadow See the entries for *darkness, follow.*

shady See the entries for *corrupt, suspicious.*

shake (*verb*) to move someone or something rapidly from side to side or up and down. ☐ *Anna shook the dice in the dice cup.* ☐ *Mary took Charlie by the shoulders and shook him.*

• **bounce** to make something spring up and down; to spring up and down. ☐ *Donna bounced the basketball on the floor.* ☐ *The baby bounced up and down on the rocking horse.*

• **jar** to cause someone or something to *shake;* to have a bad effect on someone or something. ☐ *Linda's elbow jarred the table, and the glasses all fell over.* ☐ *The shocking news jarred Frank.*

• **jiggle** to *shake* someone or something lightly. ☐ *Gina jiggled the door handle, but the door wouldn't open.* ☐ *Howard jiggled the plug in the socket, and the lamp came on.*

• **jounce** to *shake* something up and down; to push something so that it *shakes.* ☐ *We jounced the car by pushing on the trunk.* ☐ *Sue jounced the diving board, and Jenny fell off it into the water.*

• **rattle** to move something up and down or side to side, so that it makes a noise. □ *Kevin rattled his birthday present and wondered for the twentieth time what it could be.* □ *Larry rattled the aspirin bottle.*
• **wiggle** to move something quickly back and forth. □ *Mary wiggled the key in the lock.* □ *Nancy wiggled her fingers.*

shaky (*adjective*) not balanced; ready to fall. □ *That table looks kind of shaky; I think one of the legs is weak.* □ *Tom felt very shaky after he gave his speech.*
• **precarious** not balanced; easily made to fall. (Formal.) □ *The cat meowed helplessly from his precarious perch at the top of the tree.* □ *I tried not to upset the precarious balance of the house of cards.*
• **unstable** ready to fall; not stable. □ *The vase was narrow at the bottom and wide at the top, which made it very unstable.* □ *Jane's unstable emotions were hard to deal with sometimes.*
• **unsteady** ready to fall; not steady. □ *The tightrope walker wobbled across the rope with unsteady steps.* □ *Don't lean against that wall; it's unsteady.*

shame See the entries for *disgrace, embarrass, guilt.*

shanty See the entry for *shack.*

shape See the entry for *control².*

sharp (*adjective*) very severe, alert, or cutting. (See also the entries for *pointed, sarcastic, smart¹.*) □ *The detective's sharp eyes caught every detail.* □ *I felt a sharp pain in my stomach.*
• **acute** very *sharp;* severe, concentrated, or focused. (Formal.) □ *Roger suffered an acute twinge of nausea.* □ *Ken pays acute attention to details.*
• **intense** very severe and concentrated. □ *For the first few weeks in his new home, Victor's loneliness was intense.* □ *Stanley felt uneasy under Thomas's intense stare.*
• **keen** cutting; concentrated. □ *Wendy's keen mind saw the solution to the problem at once.* □ *Art felt a keen desire to go back home.*

shatter See the entry for *break.*

shave See the entry for *trim.*

shed (*verb*) to let a covering drop off. (See also the entry for *emit.*) □ *The pony was shedding his winter coat.* □ *The tree shed its autumn leaves.*
• **cast off** to throw a covering off. □ *Ben woke and sat up, casting off the blankets.* □ *Our hero cast off his cloak as he entered the hall.*
• **jettison** to push or throw something out. (Formal.) □ *The sailors had to jettison the cargo in order to keep the boat afloat.* □ *The airplane jettisoned the bomb.*

• **slough**   to let a covering, especially dead skin, drop off you. (Usually with *off*.) □ *The snake sloughed off its dead skin.* □ *Carrie sloughed off her wet, dirty clothes and slipped gratefully into the hot bath.* [→see also: *throw away*]

sheer   See the entry for *steep*.

shell out   See the entry for *spend*.

shelter   (*noun*) a place that is safe and protected. □ *The hikers built a shelter for the night.* □ *Where can we find shelter from the storm?*
    • **haven**   a peaceful *shelter*. (Formal.) □ *The library was a haven for Donald.* □ *The little cabin in the mountains was a pleasant haven, where telephones and TVs were completely absent.*
    • **refuge**   a *shelter* where you can hide. (Formal.) □ *Eddie had a refuge in a corner of the attic, where he would go when he needed to be alone.* □ *The fox fled to a refuge where the hunters could not find him.*
    • **retreat**   a *shelter* where you can be alone or escape from your troubles. □ *Fran takes vacations in her woodland retreat.* □ *The camp is a retreat for artists and writers.*

shield   See the entry for *protect*.

shift   See the entries for *change, move*.

shiftless   See the entry for *lazy*.

shifty   See the entry for *sneaky*.

shindig   See the entry for *party*.

shine   See the entry for *polish*.

ship   See the entry for *boat*.

shipshape   See the entry for *neat*.

shiver   See the entry for *vibrate*.

shock   See the entry for *surprise*.

shoddy   See the entry for *poor²*.

shoot   See the entry for *speed*.

shop   See the entry for *store*.

short   See the entry for *brief*.

shout   See the entry for *yell*.

shove   See the entry for *push*.

show[1]   (*verb*) to make it clear that something is true. □ *George must show that he can be trusted before we tell him our secret.* □ *The experiment showed that plants grown in the dark are not as healthy as those grown in the light.*
   • **demonstrate**   to do something that makes it clear that something is true. (Formal.) □ *Helen demonstrated that she knew how to use the VCR.* □ *The chemistry teacher demonstrated that the litmus paper would turn red in vinegar.*
   • **establish**   to make it clear beyond a doubt that something is true. □ *Nicholas Copernicus established that the planets revolve around the sun.* □ *The police wanted to establish that Irene had taken the money.*
   • **prove**   to make it clear that something is true by giving convincing evidence or presenting a logical argument. □ *The tire tracks in the snow proved that Jay's car had been at the scene that day.* □ *The author wanted to prove that Columbus was not the first European to reach America.*

show[2]   (*verb*) to put something out in the open, so that it can be seen. (See also the entries for *concert, play*[1].) □ *Kay showed me the story she had written.* □ *I showed the doctor the cut on my leg.*
   • **disclose**   to tell something openly; to bring something into the open. (Formal.) □ *Laura would not disclose the source of her information.* □ *Mark disclosed that he had been aware of the secret plan all along.*
   • **display**   to put something out in the open in such a way that it attracts attention. □ *Tom displayed his collection of model cars on his bookshelves.* □ *The quilt displayed Sue's fine needlework.*
   • **exhibit**   to put or bring something out for many people to see. □ *The museum will exhibit paintings by Rembrandt.* □ *Philip exhibited his scar to all his buddies.*
   • **present**   to formally bring something to everyone's attention. (See also the main entry for *present*.) □ *Rita presented a slide show about whales.* □ *The stamp-collecting club will present a lecture on how to get started collecting stamps.*
   • **reveal**   to bring something hidden out into the open. □ *Susan revealed that she was the missing heiress.* □ *The customs officer lifted up the lining of the smuggler's suitcase, revealing a mass of glittering diamonds.*

show[3]   (*verb*) to bring something to someone's attention. □ *Show me which person you are talking about.* □ *Tim showed Jan the stamp he wanted to buy.*
   • **designate**   to *show* something to someone; to pick something out specially. □ *Anna designated the dessert she wanted by pointing at it.* □ *The teacher designated Bill to supervise the class while she stepped out of the room.*

• **indicate**   to *show* something to someone indirectly. (Formal.) □ *Please indicate which movie you would prefer to see.* □ *Mary nodded to indicate her agreement.*

• **point out**   to *show* or call attention to something, especially by pointing at it. (Informal.) □ *Charlie pointed out the best Mexican restaurants in town.* □ *Donna pointed out that it was too cold to go for a long walk.*

• **specify**   to *show* exactly what you mean. (Formal.) □ *Which kind of house pets will you allow? Please specify.* □ *In her speech, Linda specified how she would improve things for the student body if she were elected class president.*

show off   (*verb*) to display something boastfully. □ *Frank is showing off his gymnastics out on the lawn.* □ *Gina couldn't wait to show off her new video game.*

• **flaunt**   to *show* something *off* very boldly. □ *Howard flaunted his wealth by getting the best and most expensive kind of everything.* □ *Bill liked to wear sleeveless shirts in order to flaunt his shapely arm muscles.*

• **flourish**   to wave something in the air to *show* it *off.* □ *Jenny flourished her A+ test paper in front of her parents.* □ *"Look what I got!" Larry said, flourishing his new wristwatch.*

• **parade**   to make a great show of something; to *show* something *off.* □ *Mary paraded her grandchildren in front of her guests.* □ *Nancy will parade out her stamp albums at the least excuse.*

• **vaunt**   to *show off* your accomplishments; to brag. (Formal.) □ *Tom's mantelpiece vaunted a large collection of trophies.* □ *Jane's parents vaunted her good grades so much that she sometimes thought that was the only reason they loved her.*

show up   See the entry for *come.*

shower   See the entries for *rain, spray.*

showy   See the entry for *flashy.*

shred   See the entry for *tear.*

shrewd   See the entry for *wise.*

shriek   See the entry for *scream.*

shrill   See the entry for *harsh.*

shrink   See the entry for *decrease.*

shrivel   See the entry for *wither.*

shroud   See the entry for *cover.*

shrub   See the entry for *bush.*

shudder   See the entry for *vibrate*.

shun   See the entry for *avoid*.

shut   See the entry for *close*.

shy   (*adjective*) not liking to go out and meet people; not liking to socialize. ☐ *Ken felt shy in such a big crowd.* ☐ *The shy little girl could not even be persuaded to say hello.*
- **bashful**   shy and sensitive. ☐ *The bashful child hid his face in his father's coat.* ☐ *Roger is very bashful and blushes at just about anything.*
- **coy**   pretending to be *shy*. ☐ *Stanley is being coy, refusing to show off his artwork.* ☐ *The coy young woman would blush and giggle whenever her suitor came near.*
- **diffident**   shy; not confident. (Formal.) ☐ *Thomas isn't haughty; he's so quiet because he's diffident.* ☐ *Victor was diffident about his ability to win the race.*
- **timid**   shy; afraid of people. ☐ *The timid puppy hid whenever we had company.* ☐ *Don't be so timid; nobody here is going to hurt you.*
[→contrasting word: *bold*]

sicken   See the entry for *disgust*.

sickness   (*noun*) the condition of being unhealthy; something that makes you unhealthy. ☐ *Sickness kept Wendy out of school for a whole month.* ☐ *The winter brought colds and flu and a variety of other sicknesses.*
- **ailment**   something that makes you unhealthy. (Old-fashioned.) ☐ *Sophia wondered what ailment could be robbing her of all her vigor.* ☐ *Chicken pox is a common childhood ailment.*
- **disease**   a severe *sickness;* a particular condition that makes you sick. ☐ *The doctor told Ben that he had heart disease.* ☐ *Many people in my family have a disease called diabetes.*
- **illness**   the condition of being ill; something that makes you ill. ☐ *Carrie missed a day of work due to illness.* ☐ *The new medicine cured Donald's illness.*
- **malady**   a *sickness;* something that makes you feel bad. (Poetic.) ☐ *Evangeline suffered from a malady that made it impossible for her to walk.* ☐ *Heaviness filled our hero's limbs; some strange malady had overtaken him.*

sidestep   See the entry for *dodge*.

sigh   (*verb*) to let out a long, deep breath because you are sad, tired, happy, etc. ☐ *Fran burrowed into the warm bed and sighed happily.* ☐ *I heard George sigh and wondered what the matter was.*
- **mumble**   to speak in a low voice; to speak in a way that is hard to hear or understand. ☐ *Helen mumbled something about being late*

to work and dashed out the door. □ *Don't mumble like that; I can't understand you.*

• **murmur** to make a low, confused sound; to speak smoothly in a low voice. □ *"There, there," Irene murmured, soothing the child.* □ *The low wind murmured in the trees.*

• **mutter** to complain in a low voice; to complain in a way that is hard to hear or understand. □ *"I hate computers," Jay muttered as he tried to get the program to work.* □ *The angry customer left the store, muttering under her breath.*

• **whisper** to speak in a very low voice; to speak softly or make a soft shushing noise. □ *I have a secret; I'll whisper it to you.* □ *"What's this play about?" Kay whispered to me as the curtain rose.*

sign (*noun*) something that shows you the way things are. □ *I looked at my neighbor's house to see if there were any signs of her being at home.* □ *The green shoots of the daffodils were the first signs of spring in Laura's backyard.*

• **indication** a slight *sign;* a hint. (Formal.) □ *The car gave no indication of being out of gas; it just suddenly sputtered to a stop.* □ *Mark's clenched hands were an indication of how anxious he felt.*

• **manifestation** an outward *sign.* (Formal.) □ *Tom's raised eyebrow was the only manifestation of his surprise.* □ *The little black spot on the rind of the orange was a manifestation of the rot within.*

• **omen** a *sign* that shows what is going to happen. □ *Sue thought that the rainbow was a good omen.* □ *A black cat crossed Philip's path; he regarded this as a bad omen.*

• **symptom** a *sign* of a sickness or a problem. □ *Rita's runny nose was the main symptom of her cold.* □ *The students' unwillingness to learn was a symptom of the school's problems, not the cause of them.*

• **token** an outward or symbolic *sign.* (Poetic.) □ *Susan gave Tim a ring as a token of her affection.* □ *The mayor gave the governor the key to the city, as a token of the trust she placed in him.*

signal (*verb*) to get someone's attention or give someone a message by making gestures. □ *The bicyclist signaled that she was about to turn left.* □ *The librarian signaled for us to be quiet.*

• **beckon** to *signal* someone to come to you. □ *Jan beckoned the waitress to her table.* □ *Bill beckoned from across the room.*

• **flag down** to *signal* a passerby to stop. (Informal.) □ *Anna flagged down a police officer and asked for help.* □ *Mary stood by her broken-down car, trying to flag down a passing motorist.*

• **wave** to *signal* someone by moving your hand or arm back and forth. (See also the main entry for *wave.*) □ *Charlie waved good-bye.* □ *Donna waved at me from the train window.*

significant   See the entry for *important*.

silly   (*adjective*) not sensible. □ *Frank told all kinds of silly jokes to get me to laugh.* □ *It was silly of me to go running out in the snow in my good clothes, but I enjoyed myself.*
> • **foolish**   *silly;* like a fool. □ *Why is Linda acting so foolish?* □ *Gina is a foolish woman for letting Harold use all her money.*
> • **frivolous**   *silly* and overly playful; not serious. (Formal.) □ *Harold bought a toy car, a box of candy, and a number of other frivolous things.* □ *Sue thought that playing cards was a frivolous pastime that should be discouraged.*
> • **idiotic**   extremely *silly;* dangerously foolish. □ *It was idiotic of Jenny to stick a knife in the toaster while it was still plugged in.* □ *I made several idiotic mistakes when I was learning to use the computer.*
> • **inane**   *silly* and stupid. (Formal.) □ *The jokes in that movie were all quite inane.* □ *Kevin gave some inane excuse for not arriving on time.*
> • **ridiculous**   outrageously *silly.* □ *Larry wore a ridiculous hat with a battery-operated propeller on top.* □ *The story in that book is so unbelievable that it's ridiculous.*
> [→see also: *absurd*]

silver   See the entry for *metal*.

similar   See the entry for *equal*.

simmer   See the entry for *boil*.

simple   See the entry for *easy*.

simply   See the entry for *only*.

simulate   See the entry for *copy²*.

sincere   See the entry for *honest*.

singe   See the entry for *burn¹*.

single   (*adjective*) one and only. □ *There was only a single dollar left in my wallet.* □ *I have a single request: please wash your own dishes!*
> • **lone**   one and only; solitary. □ *A lone oak tree grew in the middle of the field.* □ *Mary was the lone survivor of the plane crash.*
> • **singular**   one, only, unique, or unusual. □ *Each snowflake has a singular pattern.* □ *Nancy's teachers were amazed by her singular talent for writing.*
> • **sole**   one and only. (Formal.) □ *The king made the princess his sole heir.* □ *Tom's need for money was the sole reason he stayed at his hateful job.*

singular   See the entry for *single*.

singularly   See the entry for *especially*.

sinister   (*adjective*) evil-looking; promising evil to come. □ *The sinister old house stood at the top of a steep hill.* □ *"I'll take good care of you," Jane said with a sinister smile.*

 • **forbidding**   dangerous-looking. □ *The children stood at the edge of a dark, forbidding forest.* □ *The old man's shaggy eyebrows gave his face a forbidding look.*

 • **menacing**   making a threat; promising evil or danger to come. □ *The dog gave a menacing growl.* □ *The group of teenagers followed after Jane in a menacing way.*

 • **ominous**   promising danger; looking like a bad sign. (Formal.) □ *The thunderclouds on the horizon looked ominous.* □ *There was an ominous frown on the principal's face when I entered his office.*

 • **portentous**   looking like a bad sign; looking like a sign of things to come. (Formal.) □ *Every night, the portentous howling of the wolves got closer to our cabin.* □ *We feared that Ken's being fired was portentous.*

 • **threatening**   making a threat; promising harm to come. □ *Shoot him if he makes a threatening move.* □ *Rita gave her sister a threatening poke.*

sink   (*verb*) to stop floating; to go lower and lower; to fail. (See also the entry for *fall*.) □ *The boat sank in the middle of the lake.* □ *Susan sank down into a chair.*

 • **break down**   to fail or collapse suddenly. □ *I can't get to work; my car broke down.* □ *Tim broke down in tears.*

 • **founder**   to fail or *sink* after coming up against an obstacle. □ *The ship hit an iceberg and foundered.* □ *Lacking money, the project foundered.*

 • **go under**   to fail or *sink*. (Informal.) □ *We watched helplessly as the drowning man went under for the third time.* □ *The movie house went under because not enough people came to see the shows.*

sip   See the entry for *drink*.

site   See the entry for *place*.

situate   See the entry for *put*.

situation   See the entry for *case*.

size   (*noun*) bigness; how big something is. □ *What size pan should I use for the soup?* □ *Jan was amazed by the size of the ostrich egg.*

 • **dimension**   how long, wide, tall, or far around something is. (Often used in the plural.) □ *The box is two feet long in its largest dimension.* □ *We need a tablecloth of the proper dimensions for our table.*

 • **magnitude**   how big or great something is. (Formal.) □ *No one had ever seen an explosion of such magnitude before.* □ *This is a problem of great magnitude.*

• **proportion**   how big something is, compared to something else. (The plural, *proportions,* is a formal word for *size.*) □ *The proportion of boys to girls in this school is roughly two to one.* □ *The millionaire built a house of enormous proportions.*

• **scope**   how far something reaches. □ *Bill does not understand the scope of the problem.* □ *I had a lot of respect for the scope of Anna's learning.*

sizzle   See the entry for *hiss.*

skate   See the entry for *slide.*

sketch   See the entry for *draw.*

skid   See the entry for *slide.*

skim   See the entries for *float, read.*

skinflint   See the entry for *miser.*

skinny   See the entry for *thin.*

skip   (*verb*) to leave someone or something out. (Informal. See also the entry for *steal away.*) □ *I think we skipped Mary when we went around the room introducing ourselves.* □ *If you are familiar with using a camera, you may skip the next chapter.*

• **disregard**   to pay no attention to something. □ *Please disregard my previous order.* □ *Charlie disregarded the warnings on the label.*

• **omit**   to leave something out. (Formal.) □ *When she rewrote her essay, Donna omitted the paragraph about the American Revolution.* □ *Linda omitted to tell me that she had lost my wristwatch.*

• **pass over**   to leave something out; to *skip* something. □ *I somehow passed over the part of the instructions that tells how to turn the machine on.* □ *Frank passed over the cheaper brands of coffee and got the most expensive kind in the store.*

skirmish   See the entry for *fight.*

skirt   See the entry for *bypass.*

slack   See the entry for *limp.*

slam   See the entry for *close.*

slander   (*verb*) to hurt someone's reputation by saying something bad and untrue about him or her. □ *Gina slandered Harold behind his back.* □ *Sue claimed that the newspaper slandered her by saying she cheated on her taxes.*

• **bad-mouth**   to *slander* or find fault with someone. (Slang.) □ *I got tired of hearing Jenny bad-mouth her ex-boyfriend, so I made up an excuse to leave.* □ *Kevin bad-mouths me every chance he gets.*

• **defame**   to *slander* someone openly; to harm someone's reputation. (Formal.) □ *Larry tried to defame his opponent in all his speeches.* □ *Mary's friends maintained that she had been wrongfully defamed.*
• **libel**   to *slander* someone; in legal terminology, to *slander* someone in print. □ *The court had to decide if the newspaper story had libeled the mayor.* □ *The star's fans thought that the new biography libeled their idol.*
• **malign**   to *slander* someone meanly or viciously. (Formal.) □ *I don't understand why Nancy has been maligning me.* □ *Those people have nothing better to do than gossip and malign their neighbors.*
• **smear**   to *slander* someone publicly, especially by telling lies about him or her. (Slang.) □ *The politician planned to smear his opponent.* □ *The attempt to smear the mayor in the public press did not succeed.*
• **vilify**   to *slander* or curse someone. (Formal.) □ *Tom stomped up and down the room, vilifying his rival.* □ *The minister kept preaching on the street corner, although passersby vilified him.*

slant   See the entry for *tilt.*

slap   See the entry for *hit.*

slash   See the entry for *cut.*

slaughter   See the entry for *kill.*

sleek   See the entry for *smooth.*

sleep   (*verb*) to be asleep; to rest in an inactive, unconscious state. □ *Jane slept for nine hours last night.* □ *Don't make a noise; the baby is sleeping.*
• **doze**   to *sleep* very lightly. □ *Ken dozed in front of the TV.* □ *I was just beginning to doze off when the telephone rang.*
• **drowse**   to be on the verge of *sleeping.* □ *Roger drowsed in his hammock, listening to the birds sing.* □ *The cats drowsed by the fire.*
• **nap**   to *sleep* for a short period. □ *Stanley napped during his lunch hour.* □ *Thomas read a book while the children napped.*
• **slumber**   to *sleep.* (Poetic.) □ *Our hero slumbered on, never hearing the dragon's approach.* □ *Victor tried not to disturb the child as she slumbered.*
• **snooze**   to *sleep* lightly. (Slang.) □ *I started to snooze during the long lecture.* □ *Wendy snoozed through the whole movie.*

sleepy   (*adjective*) ready to fall asleep. □ *Art was very sleepy; he could barely keep his eyes open.* □ *Why do I have to go to bed if I'm not sleepy?*
• **drowsy**   quite *sleepy;* right on the verge of being asleep. □ *The drowsy child rubbed his eyes.* □ *"No, I'm not asleep," Ben said in a drowsy voice.*
• **nodding**   so *sleepy* that your head nods. □ *The children were nodding, so I sent them to bed.* □ *It was three A.M. by the time the meeting was over, and everyone was nodding.*

• **somnolent**   *sleepy;* causing sleepiness. (Formal.) □ *Carrie nudged her somnolent sister, saying, "Wake up, sleepyhead!"* □ *My eyes felt heavy as the somnolent music droned on.*

slender   See the entry for *thin.*

sleuth   See the entry for *snoop.*

slice   See the entry for *cut.*

slick   See the entries for *smooth, suave.*

slide   (*verb*) to move easily along a smooth surface; to make something move easily along a smooth surface. □ *The penguin slid down the ice into the water.* □ *Donald slid the book across the table.*
  • **skate**   to *slide* along on skates or as if you were wearing skates. □ *Eddie skated around the rink.* □ *The dancers moved so smoothly they appeared to skate across the floor.*
  • **skid**   to *slide* out of control as you try to stop or turn. □ *The car skidded on the wet road.* □ *The bicycles skidded around the corner.*
  • **slip**   to *slide* and lose your balance. □ *I slipped on the newly waxed floor.* □ *Fran slipped her hand into the glove.*
  • **slither**   to *slide* along the way a snake does. □ *A garter snake slithered into view.* □ *The slippery fabric slithered through my fingers.*

slight   See the entry for *small.*

slightly   See the entry for *barely.*

slim   See the entry for *thin.*

slime   (*noun*) an unpleasantly slippery or sticky substance. □ *The snail left a trail of slime.* □ *The lettuce was so old it had decayed into a pool of slime.*
  • **goo**   an unpleasantly sticky substance. (Slang.) □ *George puts some kind of goo on his hair to make it stand up like that.* □ *The plumber put white goo around the edge of the bathtub to keep it from leaking.*
  • **gunk**   a dirty, sticky substance. (Slang.) □ *I don't know why Helen puts that makeup gunk on her face.* □ *Wash that gunk off your hands before you come to the table.*
  • **mire**   a sticky substance like thick mud. □ *The car was stuck in the mire.* □ *Our feet sank into the mire as we picked our way across the swamp.*
  • **muck**   sticky, damp manure; any sticky filth. □ *Irene cleaned the muck out of the gerbil cage.* □ *Don't let the dog in; he's been rolling around in the muck.*
  • **ooze**   a slippery, sticky substance like soft mud. □ *Jay went wading in the river, letting the ooze squish between his toes.* □ *A strange brown ooze was trickling down the wall.*

• **sludge**   a slippery substance like the mud deposited by a river. □ *The river dried up into a ribbon of sludge.* □ *After the flood was over, everything in the house was covered with sludge.*

sling   See the entry for *throw.*

slip   See the entries for *mistake, slide, trip.*

slip away   See the entry for *elude.*

slippery   See the entry for *smooth.*

slit   See the entry for *cut.*

slither   See the entry for *slide.*

slope   See the entry for *tilt.*

sloppy   See the entry for *messy.*

slosh   See the entry for *wallow.*

slothful   See the entry for *lazy.*

slouch   See the entry for *droop.*

slough   See the entries for *shed, swamp.*

slovenly   See the entry for *messy.*

sludge   See the entry for *slime.*

sluggish   See the entry for *listless.*

slumber   See the entry for *sleep.*

slump   See the entry for *droop.*

sly   See the entry for *sneaky.*

small   (*adjective*) not big; little in size. □ *When Kay was a small child, she would hide under her mother's chair.* □ *I would like a small glass of milk, please.*
> • **little**   small; not important. □ *Laura lives in a cute little house.* □ *I can't be bothered with your little problems right now.*
> • **minute**   extremely small; so small you can hardly see it. (Formal.) □ *There is a minute amount of fruit juice in that soft drink.* □ *Mark can't stand to see even a minute scratch on his car.*
> • **slight**   small, thin, or not very important. □ *Tom is a slight man, but very strong.* □ *Sue felt a slight dislike for her new acquaintance.*
> • **tiny**   very small and delicate. □ *Philip touched the baby's tiny hand.* □ *The spy used a tiny camera concealed in his coat button.*
> • **wee**   very small. (Folksy; Scots dialect.) □ *The dolls had their own wee tea set.* □ *I haven't tasted oatmeal since I was a wee laddie.*
> [→contrasting word: *big*]

smart[1]   (*adjective*) able to learn or understand things quickly; showing great intelligence. (Informal.) □ *The smart kid quickly figured out how to start the car.* □ *Rita was smart enough to stay away from Stanley when he was in a bad mood.*

• **bright**   very *smart*. (See also the main entry for *bright*.) □ *Tim was so bright that he was allowed to skip the fourth grade.* □ *Jan is bright when it comes to schoolwork, but not so bright when it comes to dealing with people.*

• **brilliant**   outstandingly *smart*. □ *The brilliant scientist made an important discovery.* □ *Bill came up with a brilliant solution to the problem.*

• **clever**   smart at practical things. □ *She was out of milk, so the clever cook substituted fruit juice in the muffins, and nobody knew the difference.* □ *Anna fixed her bicycle in a clever way.*

• **intelligent**   smart. (Formal.) □ *The newspaper bragged that it was written for intelligent people.* □ *Mary made an intelligent decision.*

• **sharp**   smart and alert. (Informal. See also the main entry for *sharp*.) □ *You can't fool Charlie; he's pretty sharp.* □ *The sharp salesperson could tell what kind of approach to take with any given customer.*
[→contrasting word: *stupid;* see also: *wise*]

smart[2]   (*verb*) to give a sharp, tingling pain. □ *Donna's poison ivy really smarted.* □ *"Ouch! That smarts!" said Linda as I put disinfectant on her cut.*

• **burn**   to give a hot, tingling pain. (See also the main entry for *burn*[1].) □ *My leg burned where I had scraped it.* □ *Frank's skin burned from the cold.*

• **prickle**   to give a tingling feeling or a tingling, pricking pain. □ *Gina's scalp prickled with fear.* □ *The burrs prickled where they touched my skin.*

• **sting**   to give a quick, piercing, tingling pain. □ *The whip stung as it cut into Harold's back.* □ *Sue was stung by a wasp.*

smash   (*verb*) to flatten something violently, especially by stepping on it or hitting it. (See also the entry for *break*.) □ *I smashed the soft drink cans before putting them in the recycling bin.* □ *The sandwich got smashed from being in my backpack.*

• **squash**   to smash something into a pulp. (Informal.) □ *Jenny squashed the spider with her heel.* □ *Kevin accidentally sat on the cupcakes, squashing them.*

• **squelch**   to defeat someone or something violently and completely; to step on something that makes a sucking sound. □ *Larry's scorn squelched Mary's enthusiasm.* □ *Nancy squelched through the swamp.*

• **squish** to *smash* or mash something soft. (Informal.) □ *Tom squished the clay through his fingers.* □ *Jane squished the piece of bread out flat.*
[→see also: *crush*]

smash into See the entry for *collide*.

smear See the entries for *blur, slander*.

smell (*noun*) the quality of a thing that you can sense with your nose. □ *The room was filled with the smell of baking bread.* □ *There's a horrible smell in the refrigerator.*
   • **aroma** an unusual or pleasant *smell*. □ *Ken woke to the aroma of brewing coffee.* □ *We walked through the woods, breathing in the piney aroma of the trees.*
   • **fragrance** a pleasant or delicate *smell*. (Formal.) □ *The notepaper had a faint, flowery fragrance.* □ *Roger liked the fragrance of Susan's special perfume.*
   • **odor** a strong *smell*. □ *A pungent odor of skunk wafted in through the window.* □ *I smelled a sharp odor, as of something burning.*
   • **scent** a *smell* that something gives off. □ *The baby's hair had a pleasant scent.* □ *My dog picked up the scent of another dog on my clothes.*
   • **stench** a strong, unpleasant *smell*. □ *The locker-room stench was overpowering.* □ *From a hundred yards away, we could smell the stench of the filthy stable.*
   • **whiff** a faint *smell* that you detect only for a moment; a puff of *smell*. □ *I caught a whiff of frying garlic from the kitchen.* □ *Thomas's sensitive nose detected a whiff of woodsmoke on the breeze.*

smidgen See the entry for *whit*.

smile (*verb*) to express pleasure by turning up the corners of your mouth. □ *The salesclerk smiled and said, "May I help you?"* □ *Victor's jokes always make me smile.*
   • **beam** to *smile* broadly and happily. □ *Wendy just beamed when she saw Art at the door.* □ *Ben's parents beamed as he went to accept his diploma.*
   • **grin** to *smile* broadly, usually because you think something is funny. □ *"I've got a surprise for you," Carrie said, grinning.* □ *Donald grinned evilly as he teased his sister.*
   • **smirk** to *smile* in a self-satisfied way. □ *Eddie smirked at himself in the mirror.* □ *"I'm so sorry you didn't win," Fran smirked.*
[→contrasting word: *frown*]

smirk See the entry for *smile*.

smolder See the entry for *burn²*.

smooth (*adjective*) without bumps; without any roughness. (See also the entries for *flat, suave.*) □ *George sanded the wood until it was perfectly smooth.* □ *Helen ran her hand along the smooth concrete wall.*
  • **glassy** very *smooth* and shiny, like glass. □ *The boat lay still on the glassy surface of the lake.* □ *The glassy tabletop had taken a lot of polishing.*
  • **polished** made *smooth* by polishing. □ *Irene had a collection of polished rocks.* □ *The polished leather gleamed in the light.*
  • **sleek** glossy and *smooth.* □ *The horse had a sleek coat.* □ *Jenny shook her sleek hair.*
  • **slick** *smooth* and slippery. □ *I slipped on the slick marble floor.* □ *The wet stepping-stones were very slick.*
  • **slippery** *smooth* or oily and therefore hard to grasp; easy to slip over or upon. □ *Kay couldn't keep hold of the slippery frog.* □ *Be careful on that icy sidewalk; it's slippery.*

smother See the entry for *stifle.*

smudge See the entry for *blur.*

snack See the entry for *meal.*

snag See the entry for *catch.*

snap See the entry for *snarl.*

snare See the entry for *trap.*

snarl (*verb*) to make an ugly sound and show one's teeth. □ *The lion snarled, and everyone leaped back from its cage.* □ *"Leave me alone," Laura snarled.*
  • **bark** to express anger by giving loud, sharp cries, the way a dog does; to speak very sharply and angrily. □ *The neighbor's dog barked all night.* □ *The sergeant barked out orders.*
  • **growl** to express anger or hostility by making a low, rumbling sound. □ *The cat growled as I came near.* □ *Mark growled at everybody today; he's in a really bad mood.*
  • **snap** to express anger or hostility by biting at the air; to speak angrily and impatiently, in short bursts. □ *The dog snapped at my hand.* □ *"Get it yourself," Tom snapped.*

sneaky (*adjective*) like a person who doesn't want to be seen. (Informal.) □ *When I said I hated potatoes, my sneaky father made potato pancakes and didn't tell me what they were made of until I had eaten them.* □ *There was a sneaky look in Sue's eyes as she promised to keep the money safe.*
  • **cunning** sneaky and clever. □ *The cunning thief was never caught.* □ *Philip had a cunning plan for getting out of prison.*
  • **devious** sneaky; tricking people dishonestly. (Formal.) □ *The devious boy told his parents he was going to his friend's house to study,*

when really they were going to a rock concert. □ *Ken is devious by nature; I doubt he tells his true plans to anyone.*
• **shifty**   appearing to be *sneaky;* full of tricks. (Informal.) □ *Rita's shifty eyes never met mine.* □ *Susan was involved in some kind of shifty business involving used TVs.*
• **sly**   *sneaky* and crafty; cleverly dishonest. □ *Don't trust him; he has a sly face.* □ *The reporter asked a number of sly questions to trick the mayor into telling the truth.*
• **underhanded**   *sneaky.* (Used to describe methods or projects, not people.) □ *Rumor had it that the mayor had won the election by underhanded means.* □ *The criminal tried to make an underhanded deal with the judge.*
• **wily**   *sneaky;* clever and full of schemes. □ *Police despaired of catching the wily bank robber.* □ *The wily reporter tried several different tricks to get the mayor to tell the truth.*
[→see also: *stealthy*]

snicker   See the entry for *laugh.*

snip   See the entry for *cut.*

snivel   See the entry for *cry.*

snoop   (*verb*) to watch someone sneakily; to eavesdrop on someone. (Informal. Usually with *into* or *on.*) □ *My sister always snoops on my phone conversations.* □ *Tim was snooping outside the door.*
• **pry**   to *snoop;* to try to find out things that are none of your business. (Usually with *into.*) □ *Jan is always prying into my affairs!* □ *I don't mean to pry, but are you and your girlfriend fighting a lot?*
• **sleuth**   to *snoop* as if you were a detective. □ *Bill sleuthed around Anna's house for several days.* □ *The reporter had been sleuthing into the mayor's past.*
• **spy on**   to *snoop* into someone's affairs; to secretly get information from an enemy, especially an enemy country. □ *My neighbor is spying on me with binoculars!* □ *Mary was sent to spy on the Russians.*
• **stick one's nose into**   to *snoop* or meddle where you are not welcome. (Informal.) □ *Don't stick your nose into what doesn't concern you.* □ *The anonymous note told Charlie to stop sticking his nose into Donna's business.*

snooty   See the entry for *conceited.*

snooze   See the entry for *sleep.*

snug   See the entry for *comfortable.*

snuggle   See the entry for *hug.*

soak up   See the entry for *absorb.*

soaked See the entry for *wet.*

soar See the entry for *fly.*

sob See the entry for *cry.*

sociable See the entry for *friendly.*

society See the entries for *culture, organization.*

soft See the entry for *quiet.*

soften See the entry for *melt.*

soggy See the entry for *wet.*

soil See the entry for *dirt.*

soiled See the entry for *dirty[1].*

solace See the entry for *comfort.*

sole See the entry for *single.*

solemn See the entry for *serious.*

solicit See the entry for *ask for.*

solicitous See the entry for *considerate.*

solid See the entries for *firm, stable.*

solitary See the entries for *hermit, lonely.*

soloist See the entry for *musician.*

somnolent See the entry for *sleepy.*

song (*noun*) a piece of music with words set to a tune. □ *Linda sang a song in the talent show.* □ *A love song was playing on the radio.*
    • **anthem** the official *song* of a group or a country; a patriotic *song.* □ *"La Marseillaise" is the French national anthem.* □ *"We Shall Overcome" became the anthem of the civil rights movement.*
    • **aria** in an opera, a *song* sung by one person. □ *The heroine sang an aria about her hopeless love for the hero.* □ *The soprano sang a beautiful aria from* Faust.
    • **ballad** a romantic *song;* a simple, traditional *song* that tells a story. □ *The lounge singer crooned a popular ballad.* □ *"Barbara Allen" is a very old English ballad about a cruel woman.*
    • **lullaby** a *song* for lulling a child to sleep. □ *The father sang his children a lullaby.* □ *The soothing lullaby quickly put the baby to sleep.*
    • **number** a *song* that is part of a performance. (Slang.) □ *For my next number, I'd like to do an old hit from the 1950s.* □ *The singer changed costumes after every number.*
    [→see also: *tune*]

soothe See the entry for *comfort.*

sophisticated See the entry for *suave.*

sopping See the entry for *wet.*

sorcerer See the entry for *witch.*

sore (*adjective*) hurt; very sensitive. □ *Frank's muscles were sore from lifting weights the previous day.* □ *My mouth was sore after my visit to the dentist.*

> • **inflamed** swollen, red, and *sore.* (Formal.) □ *Gina's cut grew more and more inflamed.* □ *Harold, who is allergic to mosquitoes, was covered with inflamed bites.*
> • **painful** *sore;* causing pain. □ *The splinter was very painful.* □ *Sue had a painful rash.*
> • **raw** scraped and *sore.* □ *Jenny's elbow was raw and bleeding.* □ *There was a raw patch of skin under Kevin's runny nose.*
> • **tender** *sore;* painful when touched. □ *Larry's bruised shin was tender for several days.* □ *Mary put lotion on her tender, sunburned skin.*

sort (*verb*) to put things in a specific order. (See also the entry for kind².) □ *I sorted the books according to size.* □ *Nancy sorted the stamps into three different piles.*

> • **alphabetize** to *sort* things according to the alphabet; to put things in alphabetical order. □ *Tom alphabetized the names on the class list.* □ *I need to alphabetize these files.*
> • **categorize** to *sort* things into categories; to put something in a category. □ *The teacher categorized all her students as either "bright" or "slow."* □ *How would you categorize this book? Is it fiction or nonfiction?*
> • **classify** to *sort* things into different kinds or classes. □ *The geologist classified the rock samples she had collected.* □ *The contestants in the spelling bee were classified into age groups.*
> • **file** to *sort* things and put them in files; to put something in the proper file. □ *The clerk filed the bills that had come in that day.* □ *I filed Jane Andrews' address under A in my address book.*
> • **group** to *sort* things into groups. (See also the main entry for group.) □ *The troop leader grouped the scouts into four patrols.* □ *The decorator grouped several ornaments together on the mantelpiece.*
> • **pigeonhole** to *sort* things into a series of slots or holes; to put something in a strict category; to put something aside and forget about it for a while. □ *Most people pigeonholed Ken as shy and sweet, never knowing how nasty he could be.* □ *I wrote a complaining letter to the owner of the restaurant, but I think he just pigeonholed it.*

sound See the entries for *healthy, reasonable.*

sour (*adjective*) tasting acidy and sharp, like a lemon; the opposite of *sweet*. □ *The rhubarb pie tasted sour.* □ *The sour candy really made my mouth pucker.*

> • **acid** as *sour* as acid; burningly *sour*. □ *Too much vinegar gave an acid taste to the salad dressing.* □ *How can you drink that acid grapefruit juice?*
> • **bitter** harshly *sour;* exceedingly, unpleasantly *sour*. □ *Roger thought the turnip greens were too bitter to eat.* □ *Stanley could still taste the bitter aspirin on his tongue.*
> • **tart** sharply *sour;* pleasantly *sour*. □ *Thomas likes his lemonade tart.* □ *Victor made a tart cherry pie.*

sovereign See the entries for *independent, ruler.*

spare See the entry for *extra.*

sparkle (*verb*) to give off light in quick flashes. □ *Wendy's eyes sparkled with excitement.* □ *The water from the sprinkler sparkled in the sunlight.*

> • **glitter** to give off light in quick, brilliant flashes. □ *Art's diamond ring glittered.* □ *The broken glass glittered on the pavement.*
> • **scintillate** to give off light in a stream of quick flashes. (Formal.) □ *The frost scintillated in the light of the streetlamps.* □ *Moonlight scintillated on the surface of the lake.*
> • **twinkle** to give off light in flashes. □ *Tiny lights twinkled in the decorated trees.* □ *The stars twinkled in the midnight sky.*

speak See the entry for *talk².*

specialist See the entry for *doctor.*

species See the entry for *kind².*

specific See the entry for *exact.*

specify See the entry for *show³.*

specimen See the entry for *example.*

speck See the entry for *spot.*

spectator See the entry for *observer.*

spectral See the entry for *ghostly.*

speculate See the entry for *wonder².*

speech (*noun*) a formal talk given in front of a group. □ *The politician gave a speech.* □ *Ben's speech made the audience cheer.*

> • **address** a *speech*, especially a *speech* given on a formal occasion. □ *We watched the president's inaugural address.* □ *The headmaster gave an opening address.*

• **lecture**   a *speech* that is meant to teach something. ☐ *The teacher gave a lecture about the ancient Egyptians.* ☐ *Carrie went to hear a lecture about UFOs.*

• **oration**   a *speech* given on a solemn occasion or a grand topic. (Formal.) ☐ *Daniel Webster was famous for the eloquence of his orations.* ☐ *The speaker gave a two-hour oration at the great man's funeral.*

• **sermon**   a *speech* on a religious or moral subject. ☐ *The minister's sermons were often pretty interesting.* ☐ *Donald gave me a sermon about my thoughtlessness.*

• **talk**   a *speech,* especially a scholarly or informative *speech.* (See also the main entry for *talk*¹.) ☐ *The professor will give a talk about the causes of the War of 1812.* ☐ *I heard Eddie's talk about aphids at the Garden Club.*

speed   (*verb*) to go as fast as possible; to go very fast. ☐ *We sped down the highway at ninety miles an hour.* ☐ *Fran sped home, running at top speed.*

• **hurtle**   to *speed* headlong. ☐ *The rocket hurtled through space.* ☐ *The car hurtled past the surprised bystanders and crashed into the side of the building.*

• **shoot**   to *speed* along with great force. ☐ *I was standing in the hallway when George shot past, yelling "Fire!"* ☐ *Helen shot out of the school building the instant the bell rang.*

• **streak**   to *speed* along so fast that you look like a blur as you go by. ☐ *The racecar streaked past.* ☐ *The fighter planes streaked across the sky.*

• **whiz**   to *speed* along with a buzzing sound. (Informal.) ☐ *The bullet whizzed by my head.* ☐ *The baseball whizzed past the second baseman and out into left field.*

• **zoom**   to *speed* along with a humming sound. (Informal.) ☐ *Cars zoomed by on the road below us.* ☐ *The plane zoomed down the runway.* [→see also: *rush*]

speedy   See the entry for *fast.*

spellbound   See the entry for *fascinated.*

spend   (*verb*) to use money for something. ☐ *Irene spent forty dollars at the grocery store.* ☐ *Jay spends an awful lot of money on clothes.*

• **blow**   to *spend* a large sum of money; to *spend* a large sum of money foolishly. (Slang.) ☐ *Kay blew a hundred bucks on her shopping spree.* ☐ *I blew my whole paycheck on a new sound system.*

• **disburse**   to *spend* or pay out money in an orderly, official way. (Formal.) ☐ *The town council disbursed a large sum of money for building the new town hall.* ☐ *The company disbursed paychecks twice a month.*

• **expend**   to *spend* all your money; to use up anything completely. (Formal.) ☐ *Laura expended her entire allowance on tickets to the movies.* ☐ *Mark expended too much energy in quarreling with his brother.*

• **pay**   to *spend* a certain sum of money. (See also the main entry for *pay*.) □ *How much did you pay for that TV set?* □ *Tom paid twenty dollars for the book he wanted.*

• **shell out**   to *spend* a certain sum of money. (Slang.) □ *How much did you shell out for dinner?* □ *The store wanted me to shell out two hundred dollars for one pair of shoes!*

spent   (*adjective*) completely used; completely worn out; exhausted. □ *Sue felt entirely spent after the ten-mile hike.* □ *Philip's patience was completely spent.*

• **depleted**   partially used; made less. (Formal.) □ *Our depleted supplies could not possibly carry us through the winter.* □ *His strength was so depleted that he could barely get out of his chair.*

• **drained**   used; emptied; exhausted. □ *Rita was drained by the end of a typical work day.* □ *The gas tank was drained completely dry.*

• **used up**   completely used or consumed. (Informal.) □ *The corn oil was all used up.* □ *The hard school year left Susan a used-up wreck.*

• **wasted**   used up for no good reason. □ *Tim regretted the wasted hours he had spent watching TV.* □ *Our trip down to the department store was wasted, since they didn't have what we wanted.*

spew   See the entry for *expel*.

spherical   See the entry for *round*.

spick-and-span   See the entry for *clean¹*.

spicy   (*adjective*) having a sharp or interesting flavor; flavored with spices. □ *Jan had another spicy gingersnap.* □ *Bill likes spicy dishes, especially curries.*

• **hot**   having a sharp, burning flavor. (See also the main entry for *hot*.) □ *This salsa is too hot for me!* □ *The chile peppers made the casserole quite hot.*

• **piquant**   having a sharp, interesting flavor. (Formal.) □ *The fish was served with a pleasantly piquant sauce.* □ *Anna liked the piquant flavors of Cajun cooking.*

• **pungent**   having a sharp flavor or smell. □ *I could smell the pungent odor of bleu cheese.* □ *Mary introduced me to kim chee, a hot and pungent kind of pickled cabbage made in Korea.*

• **tangy**   having a sharp, sour flavor. □ *Charlie has a secret recipe for tangy barbecue sauce.* □ *Donna added grapefruit juice to the punch to make it tangy.*

[→contrasting word: *mild¹*]

spiked   See the entry for *pointed*.

spill   See the entry for *flow*.

spin   See the entry for *turn*.

spineless   See the entry for *cowardly*.

spirit   See the entry for *energy*.

spirit away   See the entry for *kidnap*.

splash   See the entry for *spray*.

splendid   See the entries for *excellent, luxurious*.

split   See the entry for *divide*.

splutter   See the entry for *stutter*.

spoil¹   (*verb*) to give someone, especially a child, everything he or she wants; to indulge someone too much. □ *Grandpa always spoiled us.* □ *Linda was spoiled by doting parents.*
> • **baby**   to do everything for someone, the way you would for a baby. □ *Don't baby Frank; let him clean up after himself!* □ *Gina liked to be babied when she was sick.*
> • **coddle**   to be very gentle with someone; to take care of someone too much. □ *Harold coddled his pet dog, which grew fat and snappish as a result.* □ *Everyone spoke to me in soft voices, patted my hand, and coddled me in the most annoying way.*
> • **humor**   to make someone feel better by doing exactly what he or she wants. □ *If we humor Sue's crazy whims, maybe she'll calm down.* □ *Jenny said she wanted her room painted black, so I humored her.*
> • **indulge**   to do whatever someone wants; to fulfill someone's wish. □ *Kevin indulged his girlfriend by wearing the suit that she liked.* □ *This may sound like a silly request, but please indulge me.*
> • **pamper**   to do everything for someone; to indulge someone in everything. □ *That hotel really pampers people who stay there; anything you want, they'll bring to your room.* □ *The movie star had a whole staff of people to pamper her, from her masseuse to her manicurist.*

spoil²   (*verb*) to get sour or moldy and therefore unfit for eating; to decompose. □ *I left the milk out overnight, and it spoiled.* □ *The fruit felt so mushy that Larry knew it had spoiled.*
> • **decay**   to decompose; to be eaten away by bacteria. (Formal.) □ *The abandoned tent gradually decayed until only moldy shreds of cloth were left.* □ *The pile of garbage on the lawn was decaying.*
> • **go bad**   to decompose enough to be unfit for eating. □ *We can't have the chili for lunch; it's gone bad.* □ *The eggs quickly went bad in the heat.*
> • **rot**   to decompose; to be eaten away by mold or bacteria. □ *The old log is rotting and no longer makes a sturdy bridge across the creek.* □ *The potatoes rotted in the warm dark of the cupboard.*

sponge   See the entry for *wipe*.

sponsor See the entry for *supporter*.

spontaneous See the entry for *automatic¹*.

spooky See the entry for *ghostly*.

sporadic (*adjective*) happening only now and then; happening at irregular intervals. (Formal.) ☐ *I get sporadic letters from Mary.* ☐ *Those sporadic flashes of light might be a signal.*
   • **intermittent** happening at irregular intervals; not constant. (Formal.) ☐ *Nancy's intermittent temper tantrums could be very alarming.* ☐ *The radio signal was intermittent; we could not hear all of the words.*
   • **occasional** happening only every so often; happening now and then. ☐ *Tom takes occasional trips to Florida.* ☐ *Jane never made anything fancy for dinner, apart from the occasional cheese soufflé.*
   • **off and on** happening only now and then. (Informal.) ☐ *Our friendship was off and on through the years.* ☐ *It was fun to read about the movie stars' off-and-on engagement.*
   • **unsteady** happening at irregular intervals; not constant or steady. ☐ *An unsteady stream of people came to the library throughout the weekend.* ☐ *Roger could find only unsteady work; he longed for a permanent job.*

sport See the entries for *game, wear*.

spot (*noun*) a small mark or stain. (See also the entry for *place*.) ☐ *What's that red spot on your face?* ☐ *I can't get that blue spot to wash out of my shirt.*
   • **dot** a very small round mark. ☐ *Stanley drew a dot on the map to show his hometown.* ☐ *The fabric was white with red dots.*
   • **fleck** a very small mark or particle. ☐ *The mashed potatoes were covered with black flecks of pepper.* ☐ *The rock had a lot of shiny gold flecks in it.*
   • **mote** a very small particle. (Mostly in the expression *dust mote*, a small particle of dust.) ☐ *Dust motes swirled through the sunbeam.* ☐ *Thomas couldn't stand to see a single mote of dust on the surface of his coffee table.*
   • **speck** a small particle. ☐ *Victor wiped the last speck of dirt off the countertop.* ☐ *I picked a speck of lint off my sleeve.*

spotless See the entry for *clean¹*.

spray (*verb*) to throw fine droplets of a liquid over something. ☐ *I sprayed the plants with water.* ☐ *Wendy sprayed paint on the bicycle.*
   • **shower** to steadily throw droplets of a liquid over something; to pour out a large amount of something. ☐ *The sprinkler system showered water on everything in the greenhouse.* ☐ *Art showered Ben with compliments.*

• **splash**   to dash a great deal of a liquid on something. □ *The children played in the pool, splashing each other.* □ *I splashed salad dressing onto the salad.*
• **sprinkle**   to scatter droplets of a liquid over something; to scatter small particles over something. □ *Carrie sprinkled soy sauce on her food.* □ *Donald sprinkled cleanser on the bathtub.*
[→see also: *squirt*]

spread   See the entry for *stretch*.

sprightly   See the entry for *jaunty*.

spring   See the entry for *jump*.

sprinkle   See the entries for *rain, spray*.

sprint   See the entry for *run*.

spry   See the entry for *agile*.

spur   See the entry for *encourage*.

spurt   See the entry for *expel*.

sputter   See the entry for *hiss*.

spy on   See the entry for *snoop*.

squabble   See the entry for *argue²*.

squad   See the entry for *team*.

squalid   See the entry for *messy*.

squander   See the entry for *waste*.

squash   See the entry for *smash*.

squeak   (*verb*) to make a short, high-pitched noise. □ *The door squeaked as I opened it.* □ *I heard a mouse squeak, I know I did!*
• **chirp**   to make a short, musical, high-pitched sound. □ *Early in the morning, the birds began to chirp.* □ *A single blackbird sat on the fence, chirping her heart out.*
• **creak**   to make a drawn-out, high-pitched noise; to *squeak* loudly. □ *The step creaked as I tiptoed down the stairs.* □ *Eddie opened the gate, and the rusty hinges creaked.*
• **screech**   to make a harsh, drawn-out, high-pitched noise. □ *The car screeched to a stop.* □ *"Get out of here!" Fran screeched.*
• **squeal**   to make a shrill, drawn-out noise. □ *The piglet squealed as I picked it up.* □ *I need a shopping cart whose wheels don't squeal.*

squeal   See the entry for *squeak*.

squeal on   See the entry for *betray*.

squeamish   See the entry for *reluctant.*

squeeze   See the entry for *hug.*

squelch   See the entry for *smash.*

squirm   (*verb*) to turn and twist. □ *I tried to hold the puppy, but it was squirming too hard.* □ *The audience squirmed in their seats during the gory scene in the movie.*

   • **fidget**   to twist or move around because you are bored or impatient. □ *The kids fidgeted while Dad lectured.* □ *Sit still; don't fidget.*
   • **twitch**   to move with quick jerks or spasms. □ *One corner of George's eyelid was twitching.* □ *Helen twitched with nervousness.*
   • **wiggle**   to move rapidly back and forth; to twist around rapidly. □ *I wiggled out of Grandma's embrace.* □ *Irene wiggled in the chair, trying to get comfortable.*
   • **wriggle**   to *squirm* in a lively way. □ *Mary wriggled out of her sleeping bag.* □ *When we lifted up the rotting log, we saw a number of worms and grubs wriggling on the ground where it had been.*
   • **writhe**   to twist and turn violently. □ *The prisoner writhed in his bonds but could not get free.* □ *The cat writhed as I picked it up, lashing out with its claws.*

squirrel away   See the entry for *stash.*

squirt   See the entry for *expel.*

squish   See the entry for *smash.*

stab   (*verb*) to jab someone or something with a sharp object. □ *The murderer stabbed his victim with a bread knife.* □ *Jay stabbed the last bite of meat with his fork.*

   • **gore**   to *stab* someone or something with a horn or a tusk. □ *The bull tried to gore the matador.* □ *The zookeepers sawed off the ends of the elephant's tusks so it couldn't gore anybody.*
   • **pierce**   to *stab* someone, breaking the skin; to *stab* through the surface of something. □ *The cactus spines pierced my skin.* ⊡ *My scissors could not pierce the thick fabric.*
   • **prick**   to *stab* someone or something very lightly. □ *The nurse pricked my finger to draw blood.* □ *Laura pricked herself as she was sewing.*
   • **puncture**   to make a hole in something by *stabbing* it; to make a small hole in something. □ *A nail punctured the tire.* □ *The dog bit me, puncturing the skin.*
   • **stick**   to *stab* someone or something with a fine, sharp object, such as a needle. (See also the main entry for *stick.*) □ *The doctor stuck me with the hypodermic needle.* □ *I stuck the pincushion full of pins.*
   [→see also: *poke*]

stable (*adjective*) not likely to move or change; not likely to fall or collapse. (See also the entry for *permanent*.) □ *Make sure the ladder is stable before you climb up it.* □ *Mark grew up in a loving, stable family.*

• **firm** strong and *stable*. (See also the main entry for *firm*.) □ *The house was built on a firm foundation and did not collapse during the earthquake.* □ *Tom was a firm supporter of the Republican Party.*

• **solid** heavy and *stable*. □ *The construction workers prepared a solid gravel base before paving over it.* □ *Sue built a solid wall around her property.*

• **steady** balanced and *stable;* regular and lasting. □ *Philip held the chair steady while I stood up on it.* □ *A steady stream of customers came into the store all day.*

stack See the entry for *pile*.

stage (*noun*) a level; a step in a process. □ *Ken is at the beginning stage of his career.* □ *Rita was in the last stages of the illness.*

• **period** a *stage* in someone's life or career; an amount of time specially marked out in some way. □ *During that period, Picasso used a lot of blue in his pictures.* □ *The years after the American Civil War were a difficult period in our nation's history.*

• **phase** a *stage* in the development of someone or something. □ *Susan went through a phase where she dyed her hair a different color every day.* □ *The tiny legs forming on the tadpole showed that it was entering a new phase.*

• **state** a way of being; a condition. □ *Right after the operation, Tim was in a confused state.* □ *Jan was ashamed of the messy state her apartment was in.*

stagger See the entries for *confound, trip*.

stake See the entry for *post*.

stalk See the entry for *chase*.

stall See the entry for *delay*.

stamina (*noun*) the strength to continue doing something difficult for a long time. (Formal.) □ *A marathon runner must have stamina.* □ *I was amazed by the lecturer's stamina; he talked for three hours straight!*

• **endurance** the power to do something or put up with something for a long time. □ *The runner built up her endurance by running a greater distance every day.* □ *My neighbor kept turning his music up until it was beyond my endurance.*

• **fortitude** strength; the courage to continue doing something. (Formal.) □ *The Arctic expedition required a great deal of fortitude.* □ *The ballet dancer's friends admired her fortitude and patience for the demanding routine.*

• **staying power**   the power to continue for a long time. □ *The years have proved that our friendship has staying power.* □ *Many movies have been pooh-poohed by critics when they first came out, only to display remarkable staying power in years that followed.*

stammer   See the entry for *stutter.*

stamp on   See the entry for *trample.*

stand   See the entry for *bear.*

stand up to   See the entry for *face.*

standing   See the entry for *grade.*

standpoint   See the entry for *point of view.*

stare   See the entry for *look.*

start   See the entry for *begin.*

startle   See the entry for *surprise.*

startling   See the entry for *unexpected.*

starving   See the entry for *hungry.*

stash   (*verb*) to hide something for future use. (Informal.) □ *I stashed the money in my inside pocket.* □ *Bill stashed a few chocolate bars in his underwear drawer.*
   • **hoard**   to save and store something away. □ *Anna hoards pennies; she must have thousands of them.* □ *Mary hoarded scraps of material, saying she was planning to make a quilt.*
   • **secrete**   to hide something. (Formal.) □ *The spy had secreted the poison capsule in a special compartment in his shoe.* □ *I secreted the note from Charlie inside my wallet.*
   • **squirrel away**   to hide or store something for future use. (Informal.) □ *Donna checks out books from the library and then squirrels them away in her room.* □ *Linda had squirreled away more than three hundred snapshots in shoeboxes in her closet.*
   • **stow**   to put something away in a safe or hidden place. □ *I stowed my suitcase under my seat.* □ *Frank stowed the computer manual in his desk drawer.*
   [→see also: *hide, preserve*]

state   See the entries for *say, stage.*

state of affairs   See the entry for *case.*

stately   See the entry for *grand.*

statue   See the entry for *sculpture.*

status (*noun*) someone's position or state; the level of respect someone gets; social or professional standing. □ *What is your marital status: single, married, divorced, or widowed?* □ *Gina found that elegant clothes can give a certain amount of status.*

- **importance** value; how important someone or something is. □ *As mayor, Harold has a lot of importance in this town.* □ *The scientists did work of tremendous importance.*
- **prestige** the level of admiration someone gets; reputation or influence. □ *Sue's prestige rose after her picture appeared in the paper.* □ *The professor's work brought her great prestige.*
- **repute** the level of respect someone gets; reputation. (Formal.) □ *Jenny is a person of good repute.* □ *The author's books were held in high repute.*

statute See the entry for *rule.*

staunch See the entry for *faithful.*

stay (*verb*) to continue to be in some place; to continue to be a certain way. (See also the entry for *live.*) □ *Stay here till I get back.* □ *The light stayed on for hours.*

- **abide** to *stay* somewhere; to make your home somewhere. (Old-fashioned.) □ *Tom's love for Jan abided in his heart.* □ *Karen left her old home and went to abide in a little cottage by herself.*
- **hang around** to *stay* or wait somewhere. (Slang.) □ *Larry hung around after the parade to see the fireworks.* □ *Hang around for a few minutes, OK?*
- **remain** to *stay* somewhere; to continue being a certain way. □ *The house that Mary's parents built remained even after they passed away.* □ *Nancy remained cheerful despite her disappointment.*

staying power See the entry for *stamina.*

steadfast See the entry for *faithful.*

steady See the entry for *stable.*

steal (*verb*) to take something that does not belong to you. □ *Jane stole five dollars from her mother's purse.* □ *Tom stole my idea!*

- **burglarize** to break into a place and *steal* things. □ *Someone burglarized my apartment while I was away.* □ *The thieves burglarized two houses on the same block.*
- **embezzle** to *steal* from the place where you work. □ *Roger was caught embezzling money from the cash register.* □ *The banker embezzled over ten thousand dollars.*
- **filch** to *steal*, especially to *steal* something small. (Informal.) □ *Stanley filched a cookie from the cookie jar.* □ *Thomas filched a pencil here, a pad of paper there.*

• **palm**   to *steal* something by hiding it in your hand. □ *Victor palmed the money that was lying on the table.* □ *Wendy, on a dare, palmed a package of gum from the grocery store.*
• **purloin**   to *steal* something. (Formal.) □ *Someone has been purloining books out of the library.* □ *Art purloined several computer programs from his friend.*
• **rob**   to *steal* from someone; to waylay someone and *steal* the things he or she is carrying or go into someone's house and *steal* things. □ *Ben was robbed at gunpoint.* □ *The bandits robbed the stagecoach.*

steal away   (*verb*) to leave secretly. □ *Ron stole away from the playground when the teacher wasn't looking.* □ *Our neighbors stole away in the middle of the night, taking all the furniture in the apartment with them.*
• **abscond**   to *steal* away or escape and go into hiding. (Usually with *with*.) □ *The burglar absconded with all the jewelry in Mom's jewelry box.* □ *Josie tried to abscond with the cookie jar, but Aunt Linda caught her.*
• **bolt**   to escape from someone who has caught you or from a trap or imprisonment. □ *The deputies discovered that the prisoner had bolted from the jail during the night.* □ *The suspect bolted before the police officers could handcuff him.*
• **clear out**   to *steal* away and take all your things with you. □ *When the detective arrived at Helen's house, he discovered that she had cleared out weeks ago.* □ *The thief decided to clear out before the law caught up with him.*
• **skip**   to *steal* away in order to escape from your responsibilities. (Informal or slang. See also the main entry for *skip*.) □ *Kevin skipped town when people began to suspect what he had done.* □ *Laura skipped out rather than face the consequences of her wrongdoing.*
[→see also: *escape*]

stealthy   (*adjective*) secret and sly. □ *Mark padded up the stairs with a stealthy tread.* □ *From the stealthy way Tom went into the house, I guessed that he was up to no good.*
• **furtive**   appearing to be *stealthy*; secretly guilty. □ *Sue gave a furtive glance at the closet, thus giving away her friend's hiding place.* □ *Philip's furtive manner made me suspicious.*
• **surreptitious**   acting *stealthy*; trying to hide from the authorities. (Formal.) □ *Ken gave a surreptitious tug at Mary's sleeve.* □ *Susan's surreptitious purchase of banned records soon got her into trouble.*
• **underhanded**   dishonest and *stealthy*. (Used to describe methods or projects, not people.) □ *The mayor used underhanded tactics to defeat his opponent in the election.* □ *The car salesman's underhanded dealings were exposed on the news.*
[→see also: *sneaky*]

steamy See the entry for *humid*.

steel See the entry for *metal*.

steep (*adjective*) sloping sharply. (See also the entries for *boil, expensive*.) □ *The car could barely get up the steep hill.* □ *We hiked up the steep trail.*
  • **precipitous** high and *steep*, like a cliff (Formal.) □ *The waterfall descended from a precipitous height.* □ *The mountain climbers inched their way up the precipitous side of the glacier.*
  • **sheer** extremely *steep*; sloping straight up or down. □ *The castle stood atop a sheer cliff.* □ *There was no way to get up the sheer walls of the canyon.*

steer See the entry for *guide²*.

steer clear of See the entry for *avoid*.

stench See the entry for *smell*.

step-by-step See the entry for *gradual*.

step down See the entry for *resign*.

step in See the entry for *intervene*.

stern See the entry for *severe*.

stew See the entries for *boil, worry*.

stick¹ (*verb*) to be fastened firmly, as if with glue. (See also the entry for *stab*.) □ *The tape won't stick to the wall.* □ *The bandage stuck to my fingers and wouldn't come off.*
  • **adhere** to *stick* fast; to remain attached. (Formal.) □ *This decal will adhere to any clean, dry surface.* □ *The glue adhered to the piece of plastic.*
  • **cling** to *stick* or hang onto tightly. □ *The dough clung to my fingers, no matter how I tried to scrape it off.* □ *Barnacles clung to the ship's hull.*
  • **hold** to *stick*; to remain firmly fastened. □ *Now that we've glued the teacup back together, I hope the glue will hold.* □ *Tim was amazed at how well the rubber cement held.*

stick² (*verb*) to fasten things together with a sticky substance. □ *Jan stuck the stamp to the envelope.* □ *Bill stuck a sign on the door.*
  • **affix** to *stick* one thing onto another; to fasten one thing firmly to another. (Formal.) □ *Please affix this decal to the windshield of your automobile.* □ *The clerk affixed price tags to the merchandise.*
  • **glue** to *stick* things together with glue or something gluey. □ *I glued the toy horse's leg in place.* □ *Anna glued the broken cup back together.*

• **paste**   to *stick* things together with paste. □ *Mary pasted pictures on the front of her notebook.* □ *I pasted a label on the box.*

• **plaster**   to *stick* things all over a surface, so that the surface is completely covered. (Informal.) □ *Charlie plastered the walls of his room with posters.* □ *Donna plastered bandages all over her arm, to make her wound look worse than it really was.*

stick one's nose into   See the entry for *snoop*.

sticky   (*adjective*) thick and clingy, like glue or soft dough. □ *I've got something sticky on the bottom of my shoe.* □ *The sticky piece of tape wouldn't come off my fingers.*

• **gluey**   as *sticky* as glue; having the consistency of glue. □ *Linda tried to pull her feet from the gluey mud.* □ *I poured the gluey molasses into the gingerbread batter.*

• **gummy**   thickly *sticky; sticky* and squishy. □ *The piecrust was gummy and tasteless.* □ *Frank dropped a gummy dollop of rubber cement onto the page.*

• **tacky**   *sticky*; easy to stick things to. □ *Let the glue dry until it is tacky.* □ *This specially treated tacky cloth will pick up dirt and sawdust from the surface of the wood.*

stiff   See the entry for *prim*.

stifle   (*verb*) to make someone quiet; to suppress someone or something; to cut the air off from someone or something. □ *Gina put her hand over Harold's mouth to stifle his eager questions.* □ *The town's unbending ideas of proper behavior stifled the free spirits of its young people.*

• **muffle**   to make something quiet by covering it up. □ *How can we muffle the noise from the engine?* □ *A plush carpet muffled our footsteps.*

• **mute**   to make someone or something quieter. □ *Worshipers muted their voices as they entered the synagogue.* □ *The thick walls muted any sound from within.*

• **muzzle**   to fasten an animal's mouth shut so that it will be quiet and not bite; to force someone to be quiet. □ *That dog is dangerous and should be muzzled.* □ *The mayor muzzled all protest by threatening to jail anyone who spoke out.*

• **smother**   to kill someone by making it hard for him or her to breathe; to take the air away from something. □ *The murderer smothered his victim with a pillow.* □ *The picnickers poured dirt on the campfire to smother it.*

[→see also: *hold back*]

sting   See the entry for *smart²*.

stinging   See the entry for *sarcastic*.

stink   See the entry for *commotion*.

stipend   See the entry for *pay*.

stir   See the entry for *move*.

stitch   See the entry for *sew*.

stomach   (*noun*) the middle section of the body, below the chest and above the hips; the organ in the middle section of the body that aids in the digestion of food. ☐ *Tom's bathing suit showed off his muscular stomach.* ☐ *Something I ate made my stomach hurt.*
  • **belly**   the middle section of the body. ☐ *Grampa has a big, fat belly.* ☐ *Jenny felt horrible cramps in her belly.*
  • **gut**   the middle section of the body; the abdomen; the place where instincts are felt. (Informal.) ☐ *Kevin punched Larry right in the gut.* ☐ *Something bad is going to happen; I can feel it in my gut.*
  • **midriff**   the middle section of the body, especially when exposed by the way clothes are cut. (Formal.) ☐ *Many bathing suits are designed to display a bare midriff.* ☐ *Mary's costume drew attention to her trim midriff.*
  • **tummy**   the *stomach*. (Slang.) ☐ *Nancy tickled the baby's tummy.* ☐ *The little boy complained that his tummy hurt.*

stomp on   See the entry for *trample*.

stone   See the entry for *rock¹*.

stoop   See the entry for *bow*.

stop   (*verb*) to leave off doing something; to quit doing something. ☐ *Stop making so much noise!* ☐ *The store stopped selling my favorite shampoo.*
  • **cease**   to *stop* completely. (Formal.) ☐ *At midnight, the guns ceased firing.* ☐ *Tom ceased to feel any affection for Jane.*
  • **desist**   to *stop*; to refrain from doing something. (Formal.) ☐ *My neighbor is playing loud music again; I wish she would desist.* ☐ *The mayor did everything she could think of to get the reporters to desist.*
  • **end**   to *stop* or finish doing something; to draw to a close. (See also the main entry for *end*.) ☐ *The professor ended his lecture with a joke.* ☐ *The vacation ended much too soon.*
  • **halt**   to *stop* going forward. ☐ *The army halted just this side of the border.* ☐ *Ken halted construction of his toolshed.*
  • **quit**   to *stop* or give up doing something. (Informal.) ☐ *Rita quit smoking last year.* ☐ *Quit bothering me.*
  • **terminate**   to *stop*; to bring something to an end. (Formal.) ☐ *The landlord and the tenant agreed to terminate the lease on the apartment.* ☐ *This program will terminate in five seconds.*

store   (*noun*) a business where things are sold. □ *I need to go to the shoe store.* □ *Stanley bought bread and eggs at the grocery store.*
- **emporium**   a *store* that sells many different things. (Old-fashioned.) □ *The dry-goods emporium carried everything from calico cloth to ammunition.* □ *McMurphy's Feed and Seed Emporium carried everything a farmer might need.*
- **market**   a large *store*, especially one where food is sold; any place where people come together to buy and sell. □ *You can get fresh fruit cheap at the open-air market on the weekends.* □ *Thomas bought socks, a quilt, and an antique lamp at the flea market.*
- **shop**   a small *store*, usually selling only one kind of thing. □ *Victor owns a dress shop that has all the latest styles.* □ *The gourmet food shop had all kinds of exotic items.*

storm   (*noun*) an episode of violent weather. □ *The weather map shows a storm coming in from the west.* □ *The storm brought down the power lines.*
- **blizzard**   a *storm* with a great deal of snow and strong wind. □ *The blizzard snowed us in; we were stuck in the house for two days.* □ *After the blizzard, the whole landscape was a blanket of white.*
- **hurricane**   a *storm* with strong winds and heavy rain. □ *The hurricane destroyed many expensive beach houses.* □ *The TV news showed film of palm trees being torn out by the roots in the hurricane.*
- **monsoon**   a tropical *storm* with heavy wind and rain; any very heavy rain. □ *The monsoon brought terrible floods.* □ *The rain is really coming down out there—what a monsoon!*
- **tempest**   a windstorm with rain, hail, or snow. (Poetic.) □ *Our hero bravely traveled on through the tempest, heedless of the mighty wind that felled trees before him.* □ *The ship was destroyed in the tempest.*
- **tornado**   a *storm* that develops as a funnel-shaped cloud and brings extremely high winds. □ *We huddled in our basement, hoping to stay safe from the tornado.* □ *The tornado passed through the center of town, ripping buildings apart as it went.*

story   (*noun*) an account of something that happened; a made-up account. □ *Wendy told us the story of how she came to the United States.* □ *Alice's Adventures in Wonderland was Art's favorite story.*
- **anecdote**   a short, usually amusing *story*. □ *Ben returned from his travels with a stack of snapshots and a large supply of interesting anecdotes.* □ *Carrie entertained us with anecdotes about her family.*
- **chronicle**   a *story* that tells things in the order they happened; a history of something. (Formal.) □ *Donald would give perfect strangers the most detailed chronicle of his illness.* □ *The newspapers gave a fairly accurate chronicle of the events.*
- **fable**   an imaginative or symbolic *story*. □ *The Spanish conquistadores had heard fables of a city made of gold.* □ *The author wrote pretty fables for children.*

• **narrative**   a *story* told by someone; a *story* of connected events. □ *Several parts of Eddie's narrative seemed hard to believe.* □ *The book contains narratives by people who say they have seen UFOs.*

• **tale**   a *story* told by someone. (Poetic.) □ *Our hero listened, spellbound, to the old man's tale.* □ *I'll tell you a tale to freeze your blood.*

• **yarn**   an imaginative *story*; a *story* full of adventure. (Slang.) □ *It was fun to listen to Uncle Bill's hunting yarns.* □ *That whole story about me going to the Antarctic, that was just a yarn.*

stout   See the entry for *fat.*

stow   See the entry for *stash.*

straight   See the entry for *flat.*

straightforward   See the entry for *honest.*

strain   See the entries for *stress¹, tune.*

straits   See the entry for *emergency.*

strange   (*adjective*) very different from what you are used to; not familiar. (See also the entry for *peculiar.*) □ *Fran had never eaten much German food, so the idea of wurst and sauerkraut seemed strange to her.* □ *George was lost in a strange city, with no idea how to get to the bus station.*

• **alien**   from another place or another culture, and therefore *strange.* (Formal.) □ *The American custom of hugging and kissing one's friends was alien to Ming-li.* □ *The immigrants took everything they could carry and left to make their home in an alien land.*

• **exceptional**   *strange;* unusual or unique. (See also the main entry for *exceptional.*) □ *Helen shows exceptional intelligence.* □ *This is a movie of exceptional quality.*

• **exotic**   *strange* and exciting or interesting. □ *Irene was eager to sample the exotic food in the Japanese restaurant.* □ *Jenny liked to wear exotic clothing, like harem pants or saris.*

• **foreign**   from another country or another culture, and therefore *strange.* □ *A foreign student is visiting our school this year.* □ *Do you know any foreign languages?*

• **outlandish**   ridiculous and *strange.* □ *Kay has the outlandish habit of breaking everything in sight when she's upset.* □ *Laura put on outlandish makeup: bright orange lipstick and false eyelashes three inches long.*

• **unfamiliar**   *strange;* not familiar. □ *I gradually learned my way around the unfamiliar city.* □ *Mark had been away so long that his old hometown looked unfamiliar.*

• **unusual**   *strange;* not usual. □ *Quiet, orderly family dinners were unusual in our house.* □ *The teacher showed an unusual amount of patience.*

strategy   See the entry for *plan*.

streak   See the entries for *speed, stripe*.

stream   See the entries for *flap, flow, river*.

street   See the entry for *road*.

stress[1]   (*noun*) great pressure or force; anxiety that comes from having to face too many problems. □ *Don't put too much stress on that joint or the chair will break.* □ *Tom's life was so full of stress that he got an ulcer.*

   • **pressure**   a great deal of force pressing on something; anxiety that comes from someone expecting a lot from you. □ *To demonstrate that the car could stand up to pressure, the ad showed an elephant stepping on it.* □ *Sue felt pressure to succeed, because she knew her family was depending on her.*

   • **strain**   too much force pulling on something; anxiety that comes from working too intensely. □ *I put too much strain on the rope, and it snapped.* □ *Philip's health gave way under the strain of medical school.*

   • **tension**   force pulling something tight; a feeling of being over-strained or very anxious. □ *The tension on the tightrope needs to be just right, not too tight and not too loose.* □ *Rita massaged her neck, trying to get rid of the tension in the muscles.*

stress[2]   (*verb*) to say a word with extra force or put strong emphasis on an idea. □ *"Susan doesn't know," Tim said, stressing* Susan. □ *The speaker stressed that the time for action was now.*

   • **accentuate**   to do something with extra force; to exaggerate something. (Formal.) □ *Jan's makeup accentuated her large brown eyes.* □ *Italic type was used to accentuate the main points in the article.*

   • **belabor**   to *stress* an idea or a point excessively. (Formal.) □ *The teacher endlessly belabored the importance of neatness.* □ *The author made her point in the first paragraph, and went on to belabor it in the rest of the essay.*

   • **emphasize**   to *stress* something you say; to put emphasis on something. □ *Let me emphasize that there is no need to panic.* □ *Bill's coat emphasized his broad shoulders.*

   • **underscore**   to *stress* an idea; to give extra force to a point. □ *Speech after speech underscored the importance of registering to vote.* □ *The pictures Anna showed underscored what she had said about the extreme poverty in the area.*

stretch   (*verb*) to reach out; to make something longer. □ *Mary stretched her hand out for the keys.* □ *Charles stretched the fabric across the frame.*

   • **extend**   to *stretch;* to cover a certain area. (Formal.) □ *Donna extended her arm, and I saw that it was covered with scratches.* □ *The forest extends twenty-five miles to the north.*

• **reach** to *stretch* out to a certain point; to be long enough to get to a certain point. □ *Linda reached across the table to get the milk.* □ *The new rail line will reach all the way to the airport.*

• **spread** to *stretch* out or expand to a certain size; to cover a certain area. □ *Frank spread the sheet over the bed.* □ *The desert spread out before the travelers.*

stretched tight See the entry for *tense.*

strict (*adjective*) following the rules exactly. □ *Mrs. Hall is a very strict teacher.* □ *We did everything according to a strict schedule.*

• **exacting** insisting that others follow the rules exactly; punishing those who do not follow the rules. □ *Howard obeyed his exacting father.* □ *The players thought that the coach was too exacting.*

• **rigid** following the rules exactly; not flexible. □ *The rigid librarian forbade talking in the library, even to tell people that it was on fire.* □ *Students had to follow a rigid dress code.*

• **stringent** insisting that others follow the rules exactly; very *strict.* □ *Tom's parents hoped that the stringent discipline of a military academy would improve his behavior.* □ *Jenny was a stringent baby-sitter who never let her charges snack or stay up late.*

strident See the entry for *harsh.*

strike See the entry for *hit.*

striking (*adjective*) unusual; very attention-getting. (See also the entry for *vivid¹.*) □ *Kevin's arched eyebrows are his most striking feature.* □ *The racecar's elegant design was quite striking.*

• **marked** *striking;* easy to notice. (Somewhat old-fashioned.) □ *Larry showed a marked dislike for Mary's company.* □ *There was a marked formality in the letter I received from Nancy.*

• **noteworthy** *striking* and worth noticing. □ *The article listed the scientist's noteworthy accomplishments.* □ *What were the noteworthy events of last year?*

• **pronounced** exaggerated and therefore *striking.* □ *Tom walked with a pronounced limp.* □ *I was puzzled by the pronounced coldness in Jane's greeting.*

string See the entry for *series.*

stringent See the entry for *strict.*

strip See the entry for *stripe.*

stripe (*noun*) a long narrow area of a different color. □ *The tiger has black stripes.* □ *Roger painted a gold stripe down the side of his black car.*

• **band** a broad *stripe.* □ *The purple team shirt had a yellow band across the chest.* □ *The river was a blue band through the green landscape.*

• **bar**   a broad *stripe* or one of a series of *stripes.* □ *The flag had two blue bars crossed on a red background.* □ *The shadow of the tree cast a black bar across the lawn.*

• **streak**   an irregular *stripe.* □ *The bicycle tire left a long black streak on the kitchen floor.* □ *A few streaks of light showed above the horizon.*

• **strip**   a long narrow piece of something. □ *A narrow strip of grass grew in front of the house.* □ *Stanley tore a strip of fabric off his shirt.*

• **swath**   a *stripe* or broad piece of something. □ *Thomas mowed one swath across the lawn and then gave up.* □ *Victor draped himself in swaths of white fabric and pretended to be a ghost.*

strive   See the entry for *try.*

stroll   See the entry for *walk.*

strong   (*adjective*) having great force or power. □ *I need a strong person to help me lift this.* □ *Wendy felt a strong liking for Art.*

• **athletic**   strong and muscular; good at sports. □ *Carrie has an athletic build.* □ *Ben is quite athletic; he plays soccer, basketball, and baseball.*

• **mighty**   very *strong;* having tremendous power of any kind. □ *With a mighty heave, we lifted the iron box.* □ *Donald gave a mighty laugh.*

• **powerful**   strong; having any kind of power. □ *Eddie displayed his powerful arm muscles.* □ *The king was very powerful.*

• **robust**   strong and enduring; able to survive. □ *Fran is a robust young person; camping out is not going to hurt her.* □ *George is in robust good health.*

• **sturdy**   strong and solid; not easy to hurt or break. □ *Exercise and proper nutrition build sturdy bodies.* □ *I need something sturdy to stand on to reach the light.*

structure   See the entries for *building, pattern.*

struggle   (*verb*) to fight with great effort; to work very hard. (See also the entry for *fight.*) □ *Helen struggled against her mother's rigid rules for years.* □ *The explorers struggled up the side of the mountain.*

• **grapple**   to *struggle,* holding on to your opponent; to seize your opponent and *struggle.* (Usually with *with.*) □ *Our hero and the Black Knight grappled at the edge of the abyss.* □ *Irene grappled with her conscience about keeping the secret.*

• **tussle**   to *struggle* roughly or playfully with someone. (Informal.) □ *Jay got so tired of tussling with his brother for everything that he left home.* □ *The father tussled with his small children, all of them laughing.*

• **wrestle**   to *struggle* hard; to *struggle,* trying to pin down your opponent. □ *The two men wrestled until someone put a stop to the fight.* □ *I wrestled the bicycle up the stairs.*

stubborn (*adjective*) insisting on doing what you want; refusing to do what someone else wants. □ *The stubborn man would not take advice from anyone.* □ *This old car is a really stubborn machine; it only runs when it wants to.*

  • **obstinate** very *stubborn*. (Formal.) □ *Don't be so obstinate; please, change your mind.* □ *Kay replied with an obstinate shake of her head.*

  • **ornery** *stubborn* and bad-tempered. (Folksy.) □ *I just can't get that ornery mule to giddyap.* □ *Laura had a reputation for being ornery and independent.*

  • **pig-headed** very *stubborn;* foolishly *stubborn.* (Slang.) □ *My pig-headed sister insisted on turning right, even though I told her it was the wrong direction.* □ *Mark wouldn't change his pig-headed opposition to Tom's marriage.*

stuck-up See the entry for *conceited.*

student (*noun*) someone who studies or learns. □ *How many students attend this school?* □ *Sue is a high-school student.*

  • **disciple** someone who learns from and follows a particular teacher. □ *The disciples all gathered for a special supper.* □ *The mystic attracted disciples by promising them wisdom and peace of mind.*

  • **protégé** someone who is protected and taught by a particular person; someone who is being trained to be like his or her teacher. □ *Philip cared for his protégé as if she were his daughter.* □ *The dancer taught all of her dances to her most promising protégé.*

  • **pupil** someone who studies at a particular school or from a particular teacher. (Formal.) □ *The teacher gave his pupils a lengthy homework assignment.* □ *The principal felt responsible for every pupil in the school.*
  [→consider also: *follower*]

study See the entry for *read.*

stuff (*noun*) raw material; any substance; a collection of things. (Informal. See also the entry for *pack.*) □ *The pastry was filled with some kind of sweet stuff.* □ *Someone went into my room and messed up all my stuff.*

  • **material** the *stuff* out of which something is made. □ *What kind of material will you need to build the garage?* □ *The author's life was the raw material for many of her most-beloved books.*

  • **matter** solid, tangible *stuff;* the *stuff* that the physical universe is made of. □ *All matter is made of molecules, and all molecules are made of atoms.* □ *The strange greenish matter we found in the leaf pile turned out to be a slime mold.*

  • **substance** a particular kind of *stuff;* material with particular qualities. □ *The statue was not made of marble at all, but of a manmade substance.* □ *The study showed that caffeine could be a dangerous substance when used in excess.*

stuffy (*adjective*) without fresh air; without enough air. □ *Open a window; it's stuffy in here.* □ *Ken tried hiding in the closet, but it was too stuffy.*

* **close**   warm and *stuffy*. (See also the main entry for *close*.) □ *As more and more people crowded into the auditorium, the air grew heavy and close.* □ *It was summertime, and Sophia's room was close even with the blinds drawn.*
* **musty**   moldy-smelling, dusty, and *stuffy*. □ *I found a musty old armchair in the basement.* □ *Rita loves the musty smell of old houses.*
* **oppressive**   so *stuffy* that you feel weak or sick. (Formal.) □ *We fanned ourselves in the oppressive heat.* □ *With the windows open, the room was too cold; with them closed, the heat from the steam pipes made it oppressive.*
* **unventilated**   *stuffy*; not letting air in or out. □ *Ten people were packed into one unventilated room.* □ *You can't put the guinea pig in an unventilated box; he'll suffocate!*

stumble   See the entries for *stutter, trip*.

stump   See the entry for *puzzle*.

stunt   See the entry for *act*.

stupor   See the entry for *daze*.

sturdy   See the entry for *strong*.

stutter (*verb*) to speak haltingly, repeating some sounds over and over again. □ *"I'm s-s-s-sorry," Susan said, stuttering as usual.* □ *The other kids made fun of Tim because he stuttered.*

* **falter**   to speak haltingly, especially from being embarrassed or afraid. □ *"I, um, I mean, I didn't—yes, sir," Jan faltered, as her boss glared at her.* □ *I faltered out an excuse for my lateness.*
* **splutter**   to speak in a confused way; to speak in little, spitting bursts. □ *"B-b-b-but you can't!" Bill spluttered.* □ *Anna spluttered protestingly, but we left anyway.*
* **stammer**   to say something haltingly or nervously, repeating some sounds over and over again. □ *"How d-d-d-o y-yuh-yuh-you di-di-do?" Mary stammered.* □ *Blushing, Charlie stammered an invitation to the dance.*
* **stumble**   to make a mistake in speaking; to speak in a confused way. □ *The speaker stumbled, consulted her notes, and began the sentence again.* □ *Donna was so upset that she stumbled as she was giving the speech she had memorized.*

style (*noun*) the way something is done; the way someone chooses to behave or to present himself or herself. □ *The artist has a unique painting* *style.* □ *Linda's friends tried to copy her style, but they never seemed as elegant as she was.*

• **fashion**   a particular *style;* the currently popular *style.* □ *The carpenter joined the boards together in an unusual fashion.* □ *These clothes are not in the latest fashion.*

• **manner**   a *style* or method of doing something. □ *Frank always speaks in a learned manner.* □ *Gina drooped her eyelids in a flirtatious manner.*

• **mode**   *style;* the way something is. □ *It was hard for the teacher to abandon his lecturing mode and simply converse.* □ *Bicycling was Harold's favorite mode of transport.*

stylish   (*adjective*) doing everything in the currently popular way; appearing in the currently popular style. □ *Sue has such stylish clothes.* □ *The magazine gave advice on how to be stylish.*

• **chic**   extremely tasteful and *stylish.* □ *The new hairstyle makes you look very chic.* □ *At one time, it was considered chic to shop at this department store.*

• **elegant**   rich, beautiful, and *stylish.* □ *I admired the elegant decor of Kevin's living room.* □ *It was an elegant meal, elegantly served.*

• **fashionable**   *stylish;* in the latest fashion. □ *Kevin would wear whatever was fashionable, whether or not it looked good on him.* □ *The ski resort was a fashionable place to spend a winter vacation.*

• **in vogue**   very *stylish;* in the very latest fashion. □ *When exercising came in vogue, all my friends started going to the gym.* □ *White lipstick was in vogue that summer.*

stymie   See the entry for *puzzle.*

suave   (*adjective*) having very polished manners. □ *Larry is elegant and suave.* □ *The waitress gave us a suave apology for keeping us waiting for our food.*

• **glib**   *suave* and good at saying the right thing. □ *The glib salesman was never at a loss for words.* □ *Her many years in politics had made the mayor very glib.*

• **slick**   extremely and obviously *suave;* so *suave* as to seem untrustworthy. (Slang.) □ *Mary's boyfriend seems a little slick to me; I hope she won't be sorry she got involved with him.* □ *Nancy's slick manner left a bad impression.*

• **smooth**   *suave* and good at convincing people. (See also the main entry for *smooth.*) □ *Tom's smooth talk got him past the door guard into the exclusive party.* □ *She's so smooth that she can get anything she wants.*

• **sophisticated**   very cultured, experienced, and *suave.* □ *Jane, wanting to appear sophisticated, tried to drink espresso coffee but could barely choke it down.* □ *He was a sophisticated man who enjoyed fine dining and the fine arts.*

subject (*noun*) the thing that is talked or thought about. □ *Ken was the subject of our discussion.* □ *The book's subject was water pollution.*
- **focus** the thing that someone wants to concentrate on. □ *The writer tried not to lose his focus on current politics in his discussion of history.* □ *The focus of the program was the extinction of the rhinoceros, although other endangered species were discussed.*
- **theme** the main *subject* of conversation or writing. □ *The theme of the story had to do with the importance of being yourself.* □ *Loneliness is a theme in many of the songs Roger writes.*
- **thrust** the main point that someone is trying to make. □ *The thrust of the magazine story was that more research should be done about global warming.* □ *As far as I could tell, the thrust of Stanley's remarks was that he doesn't think Thomas can be trusted.*
- **topic** the *subject* of conversation or writing. (Formal.) □ *Victor will give a lecture on the topic of daily life in South Africa.* □ *The teacher assigned everyone a topic to write about.*

submerge (*verb*) to push something completely down into a liquid. □ *The submarine submerged itself in the ocean.* □ *After the flood, the whole town was completely submerged in water.*
- **dip** to put something briefly into a liquid and pull it out again. □ *Wendy dipped the strawberry in chocolate.* □ *I dipped my toe into the swimming pool to check the temperature.*
- **dunk** to push something briefly into a liquid. (Informal.) □ *Art dunked the stale doughnut in his cocoa.* □ *Ben's friends picked him up and dunked him in the pond.*
- **immerse** to push something down into a liquid; to sink something down. (Formal.) □ *I immersed the dirty pot in the sudsy water.* □ *Carrie was immersed in thought.*
- **plunge** to push or drop something (or oneself) forcefully into a liquid, a place, or a condition. □ *The kids eagerly plunged into the swimming pool.* □ *Donald plunged his hand into the bowl of nuts.*

submissive See the entry for *resigned.*

submit See the entry for *bring up¹.*

substance See the entry for *stuff.*

substantial See the entry for *important.*

substitute See the entry for *replace¹.*

succeed See the entry for *win.*

succession See the entry for *series.*

succinct See the entry for *brief.*

succor See the entry for *help.*

succulent   See the entry for *juicy*.

sudden   (*adjective*) happening all at once, without any warning. □ *There was a sudden, loud crash from the kitchen.* □ *The sudden movement frightened the cat.*

> • **abrupt**   happening quickly and without any warning. □ *We came to an abrupt stop.* □ *Eddie's abrupt dismissal from his job came as a shock.*
> • **immediate**   happening right away. □ *When I call for you, I expect an immediate response.* □ *Fran's wound needs immediate treatment.*
> • **precipitate**   happening too fast. (Formal.) □ *George had only known Helen for two weeks, so his proposal of marriage seemed rather precipitate.* □ *Irene made the precipitate assumption that she knew Mr. Jones well enough to call him by his first name.*

suffer   See the entry for *bear*.

suffering   See the entry for *distress*.

sufficient   See the entry for *enough*.

suggest   (*verb*) to indirectly tell someone what to do; to express something indirectly. (See also the entries for *advise, refer to*.) □ *I suggest you ask Kay's permission before you use her wristwatch.* □ *Laura suggested a way we might solve the problem.*

> • **hint**   to say something very indirectly. □ *Mark hinted that he would like a bicycle for his birthday.* □ *Tom hinted that I should leave the room.*
> • **imply**   to say something indirectly. □ *Sue said that Philip was a wonderful person, and I thought that implied that she knew him.* □ *"Ken was once really good at dancing," said Rita, implying that he wasn't anymore.*
> • **indicate**   to show or point to something indirectly. □ *The teacher indicated her displeasure by giving us a pop quiz.* □ *The gas gauge indicates that we are almost out of fuel.*
> • **insinuate**   to say something indirectly and sneakily. □ *Susan insinuated that Tim was a liar.* □ *"Oh, Jan knows all about jails," Bill said, insinuating that she had been in prison.*
> • **intimate**   to say something politely and indirectly; to hint something delicately. (Formal.) □ *Our host intimated that it was time to bring the party to a close.* □ *Anna intimated that she would like to visit Palm Springs.*

suitable   See the entry for *satisfactory*.

sultry   See the entry for *humid*.

summon   See the entry for *call¹*.

sumptuous   See the entry for *luxurious*.

sunder   See the entry for *divide*.

sunrise   See the entry for *dawn*.

sunup   See the entry for *dawn*.

superb   See the entry for *excellent*.

superficial   See the entry for *outer*.

superfluity   See the entry for *surplus*.

superfluous   See the entry for *extra*.

superior   See the entries for *boss, excellent, pretentious*.

supper   See the entry for *meal*.

supplant   See the entry for *replace¹*.

supplementary   See the entry for *extra*.

supply   (*verb*) to give or produce something that is needed. (Usually with *with*.) □ *Mary supplied the plans for building the bookcase, and I supplied the labor.* □ *The garden supplies us with fresh vegetables all summer long.*
    • **contribute**   to give a share of something that is needed. □ *Charles contributed money to the charity.* □ *Donna contributed several pies to the bake sale.*
    • **furnish**   to *supply* someone with something; to give something. (Formal. Usually with *with*.) □ *Linda's parents furnished all their children with matched sets of luggage.* □ *The company will furnish you with all the writing materials you may need.*
    • **provide**   to give something that someone needs or can use; to *supply* something at no charge. (Usually with *with*.) □ *Grandma provided me with new clothes for the school year.* □ *Frank cooked most of the food, but Gina provided the dessert.*

support   (*verb*) to help keep someone or something strong or standing up; to approve of or endorse something. □ *Only the flimsy walls supported the roof of the shack.* □ *I support Howard's plan to go to night school.*
    • **bolster**   to help keep someone or something strong. □ *Sue's friends bolstered her when she felt like quitting.* □ *Jenny's accurate prediction of the plane crash bolstered Kevin's belief in her psychic abilities.*
    • **prop up**   to help keep someone or something from falling. □ *I used a stick to prop up the lid of the garbage dumpster.* □ *Larry propped Mary up in bed with a number of pillows.*
    • **sustain**   to help keep someone or something alive or continuing. □ *Nancy's faith in me sustained me through the tough times.* □ *The farmer could not raise enough food to sustain his family.*
    • **uphold**   to help something continue; not to strike something down. □ *The school upheld the tradition of reciting the Pledge of Allegiance every morning.* □ *The court upheld its previous decision.*

supporter   (*noun*) someone who believes in and helps a person or cause. □ *Supporters of the new law were loudly attacked by its opponents.* □ *The candidate's ideas may seem crazy, but he has many loyal supporters.*

　• **adherent**   someone who believes in a cause. □ *Tom was an adherent of gun control.* □ *The plan to abolish the government found some adherents.*

　• **backer**   someone who helps pay for a project. (Informal.) □ *The inventor needed a backer to pay for manufacturing his invention.* □ *The backers of the Arctic expedition were alarmed when they lost touch with the explorers.*

　• **partisan**   someone who is devoted to a person or a cause, especially a political party. □ *The club soon divided into Jane's partisans versus Ken's.* □ *Roger is a staunch partisan of the Democratic Party.*

　• **sponsor**   someone who pays for a project. □ *Who are the sponsors of this TV program?* □ *Stanley wrote to the sponsor who was paying his school tuition and let her know that he was doing well.*

suppose   See the entry for *assume*.

suppress   See the entry for *hold back*.

supreme   (*adjective*) the very greatest; above all the rest. □ *She was an opera singer of supreme talent.* □ *The soldier made the supreme sacrifice, laying down his life for his country.*

　• **foremost**   the very first or most important. □ *Professor Thompson is one of the foremost scholars at the university.* □ *Victor's foremost loyalty is to his family.*

　• **greatest**   the largest or most important. □ *Many consider* Moby Dick *Melville's greatest work.* □ *He was the greatest baseball player of his day.*

　• **highest**   above all the rest. □ *I hold her in the highest esteem.* □ *Wendy aspired to the highest office in the land.*

　• **paramount**   the very most important. (Formal.) □ *Your mission is of paramount importance.* □ *The pilot's duty to transport passengers safely is paramount.*

sure   See the entry for *certain*.

surfeit   See the entry for *surplus*.

surgeon   See the entry for *doctor*.

surly   See the entry for *gruff*.

surmise   See the entry for *conclude*.

surpass   See the entry for *excel*.

surplus   (*noun*) an extra amount. □ *Not only did we have enough material, we wound up with a large surplus.* □ *We ate as much of the pasta as we could, and stored the surplus in the refrigerator.*

• **excess**   a *surplus;* the amount that is left over. ☐ *I've poured as much juice into the pitcher as it will hold; what should I do with the excess?* ☐ *No, I don't need any more magazines; I have an excess of them as it is.*

• **glut**   a large *surplus;* more than can possibly be used. ☐ *Tomatoes are so cheap, there must be a tomato glut.* ☐ *There was a glut of computer programmers, so Art had a hard time finding a programming job.*

• **superfluity**   a *surplus* or overflow. (Formal.) ☐ *Ben had a superfluity of houseguests and a scarcity of spare beds, so several of his friends had to sleep on the floor.* ☐ *Carrie's closet was bursting with a superfluity of clothes.*

• **surfeit**   an excessive *surplus;* too much of something, especially food. ☐ *A surfeit of rich pastries made Donald feel sick.* ☐ *Eddie indulged himself in a surfeit of TV watching.*

[→see also: *rest*]

surprise   (*verb*) to make someone feel disbelief and wonder because of something unexpected. ☐ *Bill surprised his wife by making breakfast for her.* ☐ *It surprised Maria to see her picture on the front page of the newspaper.*

• **amaze**   to *surprise* someone greatly. ☐ *The power of this new detergent will amaze you.* ☐ *Edith's test scores amazed her mother.*

• **astonish**   to *surprise* someone so much that he or she does not know what to think. ☐ *Fred's rudeness astonished Joe.* ☐ *I was astonished by the results of the experiment.*

• **astound**   to *surprise* someone seriously. ☐ *The truth about Irene astounded everyone.* ☐ *We were astounded by Jenny's bravery.*

• **shock**   to *surprise* someone very violently or unpleasantly. ☐ *The gruesome scenes in the movie shocked me.* ☐ *We were shocked by our friend's sudden death.*

• **startle**   to *surprise* someone suddenly. ☐ *You startled me; I didn't realize there was someone else in the room.* ☐ *We were startled to hear that Mary had left town.*

[→see also: *confound*]

surrender   See the entries for *give in, give up.*

surreptitious   See the entry for *stealthy.*

surround   (*verb*) to go completely around someone or something; to be placed completely around someone or something. ☐ *The police surrounded the house.* ☐ *Fran was surrounded by people staring at her.*

• **encircle**   to *surround* someone or something with a circle. ☐ *A deep moat encircled the castle.* ☐ *George encircled Helen in his arms.*

• **enclose**   to *surround* someone or something tightly; to shut someone or something up inside. ☐ *Irene enclosed a photograph in the envelope.* ☐ *Jay was enclosed in a windowless room.*

• **encompass** to *surround* or contain something. (Formal.) □ *The county borders encompass two hundred square miles of farmland.* □ *The little island was encompassed by an empty expanse of ocean.*

• **hem in** to *surround* someone or something tightly; to *surround* someone and keep him or her from moving very far. □ *The wild ponies, who were used to galloping across endless open spaces, were now hemmed in by an electric fence.* □ *The police managed to hem in the fugitive, moving in on him from all sides.*

survive See the entry for *last*.

suspend See the entry for *hang*.

suspicion See the entry for *clue*.

suspicious (*adjective*) seemingly dishonest; possibly evil. □ *Kay is acting awfully suspicious.* □ *There were several suspicious stains on Laura's skirt.*

• **dubious** *suspicious;* causing doubt; possibly dishonest. □ *Mark told a dubious story about where he got the money.* □ *The gemstones are of dubious authenticity.*

• **fishy** very *suspicious.* (Slang.) □ *There's something awfully fishy going on around here.* □ *Tom seems to be involved in some kind of fishy business.*

• **questionable** *suspicious;* causing you to question its honesty or goodness. □ *The store made questionable claims in its advertisements.* □ *Sue is a person of questionable background.*

• **shady** secret and *suspicious.* (Informal.) □ *The mayor was accused of making shady deals with local businesspeople.* □ *Philip seems like a shady character.*

sustain See the entries for *feed, support*.

sustenance See the entry for *food*.

swab See the entry for *wipe*.

swallow See the entry for *drink*.

swamp (*noun*) an area of spongy ground or shallow water. (See also the entry for *flood*.) □ *You can't build on that land; it's all swamp.* □ *We waded through the swamp, mud up to our knees.*

• **bog** an area of deep, spongy mud. □ *Odorous gases rose from the bog.* □ *The archaeologist found an ancient piece of cloth perfectly preserved in a bog.*

• **marsh** an area of spongy ground and abundant plant and animal life. □ *The duck hunters waited in the marsh.* □ *This kind of grass will grow only in a marsh.*

• **slough**   an area of deep mud or shallow water. (Folksy.) □ *Roger fell down in the slough and got covered in slime.* □ *Two of our cattle got stuck in the slough.*

• **wetlands**   an area of wet ground. □ *Stanley fought to keep a shopping center from being built in an area of wetlands.* □ *The wetlands are a fragile habitat for many different kinds of wildlife.*

swarm   See the entry for *herd*.

swath   See the entry for *stripe*.

sway   See the entry for *rock²*.

swear   See the entry for *promise*.

swear by   See the entry for *trust*.

sweat   (*verb*) to give off moisture through your skin. (Informal.) □ *Thomas sweated from nervousness as he waited his turn to go onstage.* □ *The exercises really made me sweat.*

• **lather**   for an animal to *sweat* so much that a foam forms on its skin. □ *Victor drove the horse till it lathered.* □ *The intense heat made the cow lather.*

• **perspire**   to *sweat*. (Formal.) □ *Wendy perspired a great deal and had a hard time getting the stains out of her clothes.* □ *It was such a hot day that even lying in his hammock made Art perspire.*

• **swelter**   to *sweat* because you are very hot; to *sweat* because the weather is hot and moist. □ *The air conditioning was broken, and everyone in the building sweltered.* □ *Ben sweltered in his heavy coat.*

sweet   See the entry for *cute*.

sweet-talk   See the entry for *flatter*.

swell   See the entry for *expand*.

swelter   See the entry for *sweat*.

sweltering   See the entry for *hot*.

swerve   (*verb*) to change course suddenly. □ *The truck suddenly swerved and hit the car in the next lane.* □ *The bicyclist swerved to avoid broken glass on the sidewalk.*

• **deviate**   to move off your original or planned course. (Formal.) □ *You must not deviate from the route I marked on the map.* □ *The speaker deviated from her original topic.*

• **divert**   to change the course of something. □ *We will divert the stream so that it flows into the bean field.* □ *The signs diverted traffic onto a side road.*

• **veer**   to turn suddenly. □ *Carrie strode along for several blocks, then suddenly veered into an alley.* □ *The plane veered sharply.*
• **zigzag**   to turn one way and then another. (Informal.) □ *The car zigzagged down the slippery road.* □ *I zigzagged along through the forest.*
[→consider also: *turn*]

swift   See the entry for *fast*.

swindle   See the entry for *cheat*.

swing   See the entry for *hang*.

swish   See the entry for *flap*.

switch   See the entry for *change*.

sympathize   (*verb*) to feel sorry for someone; to have sympathy for someone else's pain. (Usually with *with*.) □ *When Donald's father died, his friends sympathized with him.* □ *I just lost my job, too, so I can sympathize.*
• **commiserate**   to share in someone else's pain; to have sympathy for someone else. (Formal. Usually with *with*.) □ *While the contest winner enjoyed his victory, the losers commiserated with each other.* □ *We visited Fran's hospital room to commiserate with her after her surgery.*
• **empathize**   to feel someone else's pain. (Usually with *with*.) □ *Eddie empathized with the main character in the movie.* □ *The mother empathized with everything her sick child was suffering.*
• **feel for**   to feel sorry for someone. □ *I really feel for you; I wish I could help you.* □ *George felt for the victims of the earthquake after seeing how their homes had been destroyed.*
[→consider also: *identify with*]

sympathy   See the entry for *mercy*.

symptom   See the entry for *sign*.

systematic   See the entry for *organized*.

T

tacky See the entry for *sticky*.

tactful (*adjective*) carefully polite; able to do and say the right things. □ *Helen made the tactful suggestion that perhaps we ought to leave Irene by herself for a while.* □ *Rather than tell Jay that he had picked an ugly suit, the tactful saleswoman merely said, "It doesn't quite make you look your best."*
  • **diplomatic** very skilled at being *tactful*; able to say things without upsetting people. □ *Kay told Laura that she thought they could accomplish more by working separately, which was a diplomatic way of saying that she couldn't stand to work with her.* □ *Mark is very diplomatic; I'm sure he can smooth over the quarrel.*
  • **discreet** *tactful*; showing good judgment in what you say; keeping secret things properly hidden. □ *Tom wanted a discreet housekeeper, one who wouldn't blab his secrets all over the neighborhood.* □ *The embarrassing book arrived in the mail, covered in a discreet wrapper.*
  • **politic** *tactful*; saying only the things that will help your cause. (Formal.) □ *Sue judged that it would be politic to flatter Philip.* □ *Rita made a politic show of interest in Susan's speech.*
  [→see also: *polite*]

tag See the entry for *label*.

taint See the entry for *dirty²*.

take (*verb*) to get hold of or receive something. (See also the entry for *carry*.) □ *Who took the apple I left on the table?* □ *Linda took the job that Frank offered her.*
  • **appropriate** to suddenly *take* something from someone else, usually for an emergency or a special purpose. (Formal.) □ *Mom and Dad appropriated my room for our guests.* □ *"I've got to go out to the mailbox," Gina said, appropriating my umbrella.*

• **pocket**   to *take* something and put it in your pocket; to *take* something secretly. □ *Harold pocketed the five-dollar bill he found on the sidewalk.* □ *Sue quietly pocketed the pair of earrings she found by the bathroom sink.*

• **seize**   to *take* something by force; to grab something suddenly. □ *The general seized territory belonging to another country.* □ *Jenny seized me by the arm.*
[contrasting word: *give*]
[→see also: *get, grab*]

take away   See the entry for *remove.*

take back   (*verb*) to say that you did not mean something you said before. (Informal.) □ *I shouldn't have said you were stupid; I take it back.* □ *Tim twisted Jan's arm, insisting that she take back what she had said.*

• **recant**   to *take* something *back* openly; to say that you no longer believe something. (Formal.) □ *Bill once believed in UFOs, but he has since recanted.* □ *Anna gave a speech in which she recanted her former views.*

• **retract**   to *take* something *back* formally, especially in print. □ *Faced with a lawsuit for libel, the newspaper decided to retract their accusations against Mary.* □ *I wish to retract my earlier statement.*

• **withdraw**   to *take back* an objection or a suggestion. □ *When we told Charlie he could be the leader, he withdrew his objection to the plan.* □ *I saw that Donna was taking her responsibilities as club president more seriously, so I withdrew my suggestion that she resign.*

take care of   See the entry for *handle.*

take exception to   See the entry for *object.*

take for granted   See the entry for *assume.*

take in   See the entry for *absorb.*

take off   See the entry for *go.*

take one's time   See the entry for *dawdle.*

take out   See the entry for *remove.*

take part   See the entry for *participate.*

take place   See the entry for *happen.*

tale   See the entry for *story.*

talent   (*noun*) an unusual ability; the ability to do something easily and very well. □ *Kevin has a talent for acting.* □ *Larry showed musical talent, so his parents made him take piano lessons.*

• **aptitude** the ability or willingness to do something easily and well. (Formal.) □ *Mary showed an early aptitude for math.* □ *Every room in Nancy's house displayed her aptitude for decorating.*

• **genius** the ability to do something original extremely well. □ *Tom has a genius for computer programming.* □ *The author's genius shone in every word he wrote.*

• **gift** an unusual ability, especially one that you have not trained for; a special ability that seems to have been given to you by a higher power. □ *"It's a gift," Jane shrugged when her friends asked how she learned to sing so well.* □ *That painter has a marvelous gift for capturing facial expressions.*

talisman See the entry for *charm.*

talk¹ (*noun*) an occasion on which people speak to one another for a while; an exchange of words and thoughts. (See also the entry for *speech.*) □ *The teacher wanted to have a talk with my parents.* □ *Ken called, and we had a nice long talk.*

• **chat** an informal, friendly *talk.* □ *I've enjoyed our little chat.* □ *Roger unplugged his telephone so that nothing would interrupt our chat.*

• **conversation** a *talk;* an occasion during which people speak back and forth. □ *The conversation was on a topic that didn't interest me.* □ *The detective taped his conversation with the suspect.*

• **discussion** a *talk* in which people discuss or debate something. □ *The club members held a discussion about where to have the next meeting.* □ *Stanley and Thomas were having a lively discussion out in the living room.*

• **heart-to-heart** an intimate *talk;* a *talk* in which people share deep feelings. (Informal.) □ *Ever since my heart-to-heart with Victor, I feel I understand him more.* □ *Wendy and Art stayed up all night, drinking coffee and having a real heart-to-heart.*

• **interview** a formal *talk* in which one person asks questions and another answers them. □ *I watched the TV interview with the rock star.* □ *The reporter wanted an interview with the mayor.*

talk² (*verb*) to speak to someone; to use spoken language. □ *Ben liked to talk about what happened at work each day.* □ *It was exciting when the baby began to talk.*

• **chat** to *talk* informally and in a friendly way. □ *Charlie stayed after class, chatting with his friends.* □ *I chatted with Donna for a while before getting back to work.*

• **converse** to *talk* back and forth with someone. (Formal.) □ *Linda and Frank conversed about the weather.* □ *The more I conversed with Gina, the more interesting I found her.*

• **gab** to *talk* energetically; to *talk* unstoppably. (Slang.) □ *Stop gabbing with Harold; I need to use the phone!* □ *What does Sue do all day besides gab with her neighbors?*

• **gossip** to *talk* with someone and exchange the latest news; to spread rumors. □ *Jenny gossips about all her friends.* □ *Kevin and Larry could gossip for hours.*

• **speak** to *talk*. (Formal.) □ *I would like an opportunity to speak with you.* □ *The teacher spoke sharply.*

talk back to (*verb*) to respond rudely to someone in authority. (Informal.) □ *Mary's in trouble for talking back to the teacher.* □ *Dad would spank us if we talked back to him.*

• **give someone some lip** to *talk back to* someone; to be rude to someone in authority. (Slang.) □ *Don't give me any of your lip.* □ *Nancy gave the police officer some lip when he told her she was speeding.*

• **mouth off** to *talk back to* or use bad language to someone. (Slang.) □ *Tom made the mistake of mouthing off to the principal and got suspended.* □ *Jane wanted to mouth off to her boss, but she didn't dare.*

• **sass** to *talk back to* someone; to show disrespect to someone. (Slang.) □ *That fresh boy sassed his mother.* □ *The more Susan's mother punished her, the more she sassed.*

[→see also: *retort*]

talk into See the entry for *persuade*.

talkative (*adjective*) fond of talking; talking a great deal. □ *When Thomas is in a talkative mood, he'll keep me on the phone for an hour at a time.* □ *The talkative suspect told the detective all she wanted to know.*

• **chatty** talking informally; fond of talking informally. □ *Victor wrote me a long, chatty letter from camp.* □ *My chatty friend Wendy will talk about anything!*

• **effusive** giving out a flood of talk; gushing. (Formal.) □ *Art's effusive greeting seemed rather insincere.* □ *Ben was embarrassed by Carrie's effusive praise.*

• **garrulous** very fond of talking or telling stories; talking unstoppably. □ *The garrulous old man told endless stories about his youth.* □ *Donald was so garrulous that no one else got a chance to talk.*

• **loquacious** talkative. (Formal.) □ *I soon wearied of listening to my loquacious friend.* □ *A time limit on the debate kept the politicians from being too loquacious.*

tall (*adjective*) rising far up; the opposite of *short*. □ *Do you think Eddie will grow as tall as his brother?* □ *We waded through the tall grass in the vacant lot.*

• **high** *tall*. (Usually used to describe buildings or mountains.) □ *A high mountain range rose up to our left.* □ *The new skyscraper is a hundred stories high.*

• **lofty** very *tall;* reaching far up. (Poetic.) □ *Our hero vowed to scale the lofty peak.* □ *Fran had lofty ambitions.*

• **towering**   very *tall* and impressive; as *tall* as a tower. □ *The castle stood atop a towering cliff.* □ *I looked up at the towering thunderclouds building on the horizon.*
[→contrasting word: *short*]

tally   See the entries for *count, match.*

tan   See the entry for *brown.*

tangy   See the entry for *spicy.*

tap   (*verb*) to make a noise by hitting something lightly; to hit something lightly. □ *Helen tapped her foot in time to the music.* □ *George tapped me on the shoulder.*
   • **knock**   to make a noise by hitting something firmly. □ *Is someone knocking at the door?* □ *I knocked on the wall to get my neighbor to turn the music down.*
   • **pat**   to hit or touch something lightly with your open hand. □ *Irene patted the horse's neck.* □ *Jay patted the dough into a circle.*
   • **rap**   to make a noise by hitting something sharply. □ *The teacher rapped on her desk for attention.* □ *The police officer rapped on the car window.*

tardy   See the entry for *late.*

target   See the entry for *victim.*

tarry   See the entry for *dawdle.*

tart   See the entry for *sour.*

task   See the entry for *job.*

taste   See the entry for *hunger.*

tasty   See the entry for *delicious.*

taunt   See the entry for *tease.*

taut   See the entry for *tense.*

teach   (*verb*) to help someone learn; to show someone how to do something. □ *Kay teaches sixth-grade English.* □ *Laura taught me how to play the guitar.*
   • **coach**   to *teach* someone closely; to carefully prepare someone to do something. □ *Mark coached the actors in their British accents.* □ *Tom's mother coached him as to how he was to behave at the formal party.*
   • **educate**   to *teach*; to help someone learn all the things he or she will need to know. □ *The parents tried to educate their children the best they could.* □ *Sue was educated at the University of Arizona.*
   • **instruct**   to *teach* or give someone directions for doing something. (Formal.) □ *The sergeant instructed the soldiers in marksmanship.* □

When you have assembled the box, tell me, and I will instruct you as to what to do next.

• **train**   to *teach* someone a skill; to help someone prepare to do something. □ *Philip trained his dog to shake hands.* □ *Rita's parents trained her to keep a clean house.*

• **tutor**   to *teach* someone privately; to give someone extra help in learning a particular subject. □ *Susan tutors people who want to learn to read.* □ *Tim isn't doing well in history; he could use someone to tutor him.*

team   (*noun*) a group of people who work together; a group of people who play a sport together on the same side. □ *A team of safety inspectors went over every inch of the building.* □ *Jan is on the basketball team.*

• **band**   a group of people who go around together. (Somewhat old-fashioned or poetic.) □ *Our hero went forth with his merry band of followers.* □ *A dangerous band of thieves was abroad in the countryside.*

• **clique**   an exclusive group of people who go around together. □ *Everyone wanted to be part of Bill's clique.* □ *Anna's friends formed a snobbish clique.*

• **crew**   a group of people who work together, especially on a ship or plane. □ *The ship's crew made ready to sail.* □ *The crew of flight attendants was polite and efficient.*

• **squad**   a small, organized group of people who work together, especially in the military. □ *The captain sent a squad out to patrol.* □ *On Saturday mornings, the family formed a housecleaning squad.*
[→see also: *organization*]

team up   (*verb*) to join together and work with one another. □ *The teacher allowed students to team up on the homework assignment.* □ *Sam teamed up with several of his friends to form a lawn-mowing business.*

• **collaborate**   to work together on a project. (Formal.) □ *The composer and the lyricist collaborated to write a musical.* □ *Several reporters collaborated on this story.*

• **cooperate**   to work together; to help one another. □ *If Charlie would cooperate with me, things would go much more smoothly.* □ *Donna and Linda cooperated to wash the dishes; Donna washed, and Linda rinsed and dried.*

• **join forces**   to join together to work better or have more strength. □ *The two countries joined forces against their common enemy.* □ *Frank's friends joined forces to convince him to go on vacation.*

tear   (*verb*) to pull something apart; to be pulled apart. □ *I bent over too far, and my pants tore.* □ *Gina tore the piece of paper in half.*

• **rend**   to *tear* something violently. (Poetic.) □ *The Black Knight threatened to rend our hero limb from limb.* □ *The explosion rent the heavy gate asunder.*

• **rip** to *tear* something violently or energetically. □ *The high wind ripped branches from all the trees.* □ *The cat's claws ripped the piece of fabric.*

• **shred** to *tear* something into thin strips. □ *Howard shredded the secret document so that no one could read it.* □ *The barbed wire shredded my coat as I tried to get it free.*

tease (*verb*) to try to upset someone by repeatedly saying or doing something annoying. □ *Sue teased her sister mercilessly.* □ *Jenny teased the puppy until it bit her.*

• **bait** to *tease* someone viciously; to persecute someone. □ *The other boys baited Kevin, trying to pick a fight.* □ *Larry constantly baited Mary by saying horrible things about her parents.*

• **josh** to *tease* someone playfully. (Slang.) □ *Don't get mad; I was just joshing you.* □ *Nancy joshed Tom about his new girlfriend.*

• **needle** to *tease* or annoy someone with sharp remarks. □ *Jane needled me so much about my lack of a job that I stopped talking to her.* □ *Roger finally needled his brother into punching him.*

• **taunt** to *tease* someone cruelly; to insult someone or call someone names. □ *The other kids taunted Stanley because of his grubby, ragged appearance.* □ *"Boy, did you get a bad grade!" Thomas taunted.*
[→see also: *ridicule*]

technique See the entry for *way*.

tedious See the entry for *boring*.

teeter See the entry for *waver*.

tell (*verb*) to let someone know something; to give information to someone. (See also the entries for *distinguish, feel*.) □ *Tell me what the problem is.* □ *Victor told his friends that he would be late.*

• **inform** to give information to someone; to *tell* someone something. (Formal.) □ *The note informed me that I still owed the store seven dollars.* □ *Wendy informed me that she was my new boss.*

• **notify** to officially *tell* someone the news. (Formal.) □ *The teacher notified my parents that I was failing in science.* □ *The landlord asked me to notify him thirty days before moving out.*

• **relate** to *tell* someone what happened; to *tell* a story. (Formal.) □ *Art related his strange experience to a group of interested listeners.* □ *If you ask Ben how he's feeling, he's liable to relate the story of all his latest illnesses.*
[→see also: *advise*]

tell on See the entry for *betray*.

teller See the entry for *clerk*.

temperament See the entry for *personality*.

temperate   See the entry for *mild²*.

tempest   See the entry for *storm*.

temporary   (*adjective*) lasting only a short time; not lasting forever. □ *I took a temporary job with the phone company.* □ *Carrie's blindness was temporary; she soon regained her sight.*
- **ephemeral**   lasting only a very short time. (Formal.) □ *We enjoyed the ephemeral beauty of the blossoming apple trees.* □ *Donald did not realize that youth was ephemeral; middle age, when it came, was a surprise to him.*
- **fleeting**   lasting only for a moment; passing by very quickly. □ *I got only a fleeting glimpse of the bird before it flew away.* □ *Another fleeting summer vacation sped by.*
- **passing**   not lasting forever; soon to go away. □ *Eddie's desire to be a chef was just a passing whim.* □ *Fashion trends are passing things, thank goodness.*
- **provisional**   lasting only a short time; lasting only until something else is set up. □ *After the revolution, a provisional government took control until elections could be held.* □ *The tent was our provisional shelter while the house was being rebuilt.*
- **transient**   not lasting; passing through. □ *Fran was curious about the transient occupants of the hotel where she worked.* □ *George's love for Helen proved to be transient.*
- **transitory**   lasting only a short time; moving on. (Formal.) □ *The singer's fame was transitory.* □ *Irene grew disappointed at how transitory every pleasure seemed.*

[→contrasting word: *permanent*]

tenacious   See the entries for *insistent, persistent*.

tendency   (*noun*) a thing that someone or something is likely to do; a thing that someone or something tends to do. □ *That chair has a tendency to wobble.* □ *Jay was embarrassed by Kay's tendency to fall asleep during movies.*
- **inclination**   a *tendency* or preference. (Formal.) □ *Laura's inclination to bully her sisters caused a lot of fights.* □ *Mark went against his frugal inclinations and bought the more expensive stereo.*
- **leaning**   a *tendency* or preference; a thing that someone leans toward doing. □ *Tom's political leanings are very conservative.* □ *I preferred symphonies to sports events, but Sue had the opposite leaning.*
- **propensity**   a *tendency*; a thing that someone or something favors doing. (Formal.) □ *The teacher knew about Philip's propensity for cheating.* □ *Rita did her best to get rid of her propensity for overeating.*

tender   See the entries for *gentle, sore*.

tense (*adjective*) pulled as tight as possible; strained. (See also the entry for *nervous*.) □ *Susan tried to relax her tense muscles.* □ *Tim gave me a tense smile.*

 • **stretched tight** pulled out as far as it will go; pulled tight. □ *The fabric was stretched tight over the seat of the chair.* □ *Make sure the drumhead is stretched tight before you fasten it on.*
 • **taut** pulled tight and firm. □ *Jan pulled the rope taut.* □ *"You're late," Bill said in a taut voice.*
 • **tight** pulled snug; not loose. □ *Anna tried to struggle free, but her bonds were tied up tight.* □ *The lid is on too tight; I can't get it off.* [→see also: *firm*]

tension See the entry for *stress*[1].

term See the entry for *call*[2].

terminal See the entry for *deadly*.

terminate See the entry for *stop*.

terrestrial sphere See the entry for *world*.

terrible See the entry for *awful*.

terrified See the entry for *afraid*.

terrifying (*adjective*) extremely frightening. □ *Someone painted terrifying threats all over Mary's door.* □ *The newspaper gave the terrifying facts about the murder.*

 • **blood-curdling** so *terrifying* that it makes your blood run cold. □ *I heard a blood-curdling yell from the other end of the parking lot.* □ *A high, shrill, blood-curdling noise stopped us in our tracks.*
 • **chilling** so *terrifying* that it makes you feel cold. □ *Charlie received a chilling hint of what would happen if he kept trying to solve the mystery.* □ *Donna entered the room and saw a chilling sight: a headless body sitting in her favorite chair.*
 • **hair-raising** so *terrifying* that the hair stands up on the back of your neck. □ *The author was famous for his hair-raising stories.* □ *We sat around the fire telling ghost stories, each more hair-raising than the last.*
 • **horrifying** *terrifying*; causing you to feel horror. □ *Horrifying pictures from the war zone began appearing on the news.* □ *Linda came to the horrifying realization that she was alone in the snowbound cabin, unable to communicate with the outside world.*
 [→consider also: *frightening*]

terse See the entry for *brief*.

test   (*noun*) a way to measure how well someone or something can do. □ *We have to take a science test tomorrow.* □ *The car passed all its safety tests.*

• **audition**   a *test* of the ability of a performer, such as an actor or a musician; a *test* to see if someone is good enough to be in a show. □ *Dozens of actors came to the audition.* □ *The violinist did well at her audition.*

• **examination**   a formal *test,* either written or given out loud. □ *To get into the school, you must pass an entrance examination.* □ *The final examination will contain six essay questions.*

• **quiz**   a small *test.* □ *The history teacher gives a quiz every week.* □ *Frank asked me so many questions I felt as though he was giving me a quiz.*

• **trial**   a *test;* an occasion on which you try to prove something. □ *The scientist hoped that the next trial of the experiment would proceed smoothly.* □ *Your first three months on the job will be a trial to see how well you can do.*

testy   See the entry for *sensitive.*

textile   See the entry for *cloth.*

thaw   See the entry for *melt.*

theatrical   See the entry for *dramatic.*

theme   See the entry for *subject.*

theory   See the entry for *idea.*

thespian   See the entry for *entertainer.*

thick   (*adjective*) having a heavy texture; measuring a lot from top to bottom or side to side; closely packed. □ *It was hard to stir the thick cake batter.* □ *A thick quilt covered the bed.*

• **bulky**   thick and awkward; large or heavy and awkward. □ *I hate to wear this bulky sweater, but it's warm.* □ *Gina wrestled the bulky package up the stairs.*

• **deep**   measuring a lot from top to bottom. □ *A deep layer of snow covered the ground.* □ *Our footprints were muffled by the deep pile of the carpet.*

• **dense**   having a heavy, closely packed texture. □ *The chocolate cake was dense and rich.* □ *We picked our way through the dense forest.*

• **packed**   firmly stuffed; dense. □ *You will need half a cup of packed brown sugar.* □ *We slid easily over the packed snow.*

thicket   See the entry for *forest.*

thin (*adjective*) not having much flesh on the body; the opposite of *fat*. (See also the entry for *watery*.) ☐ *Harold is short and thin.* ☐ *Sue exercises in order to stay thin.*
- **emaciated** so *thin* that the bones stand out; extremely *thin*. (Formal.) ☐ *The starving people looked emaciated.* ☐ *The sick man reached out an emaciated arm for his medicine.*
- **lean** *thin* and muscular. ☐ *The lean athlete jogged onto the field.* ☐ *As they hiked across the country, Jenny and Kevin grew tanned and lean.*
- **skinny** awkwardly *thin*. (Informal.) ☐ *Larry was a skinny kid, but to look at him now, you'd never know it.* ☐ *Mary was ashamed of her skinny legs.*
- **slender** elegantly, pleasingly *thin;* quite *thin*. ☐ *Nancy is slender enough to be a model.* ☐ *Almost anything looked good on Sue's slender figure.*
- **slim** quite *thin;* gracefully *thin*. ☐ *Jane has such beautifully slim ankles.* ☐ *Ken is as slim as a ballet dancer.*
[→contrasting word: *fat*]

thin-skinned See the entry for *sensitive*.

thing (*noun*) something you can see, hear, touch, taste, or smell; anything that exists or can exist. ☐ *What's that orange thing on the shelf?* ☐ *Roger bought many expensive things.*
- **article** an inanimate *thing;* a *thing* belonging to a certain category. (Formal.) ☐ *Stanley put a few necessary articles in his suitcase and was out the door within minutes.* ☐ *A winter coat can be a very expensive article of clothing.*
- **item** one of a number of *things;* one in a series of *things*. (Formal.) ☐ *I ordered several items from the catalog.* ☐ *Thomas went down the items on the list, one by one.*
- **object** a tangible *thing;* something that can be sensed. (See also the main entry for *object*.) ☐ *Victor could barely see the large, dark object lying across the road.* ☐ *Wendy filled her home with beautiful art objects.*

think (*verb*) to consider something carefully in your mind. (Usually with *about*. See also the entry for *believe¹*.) ☐ *Art thought about taking a trip to Australia.* ☐ *Ben thought about the speech he had to give.*
- **contemplate** to *think* calmly about something; to pay long and careful attention to something. ☐ *Carrie contemplated quitting her job.* ☐ *Donald contemplated the painting for several minutes.*
- **meditate** to *think* calmly; to *think* for a long time. (Usually with *on*.) ☐ *Eddie meditated on the words he had just read.* ☐ *Fran meditated, staring out the window.*
- **mull** to *think* about something over and over; to ponder something. ☐ *I mulled over my last conversation with George and wondered*

what I had said to upset him. □ *Helen sat alone, mulling how to get the best revenge.*
• **muse**   to *think* deeply and seriously. □ *Irene mused about her new acquaintance. Was he as pleasant as he seemed?* □ *I mused about my possible future.*
• **reflect**   to *think* calmly and seriously. (Usually with *on* or *upon*.) □ *You should stop to reflect before you take such a serious action.* □ *On New Year's Eve, Jay reflected upon the last year's events.*
[→see also: *wonder*²]

think about   See the entry for *consider*.

think of   See the entry for *imagine*.

thorny   See the entry for *tricky*.

thorough   (*adjective*) including everything; taking care of everything. □ *We gave the house a thorough cleaning.* □ *Kay did a thorough job of organizing those papers.*
• **comprehensive**   including everything. (Formal.) □ *The book contains comprehensive information about birds native to this area.* □ *Students must take a comprehensive examination in all subjects.*
• **exhaustive**   including or considering absolutely everything. (Formal.) □ *Laura made an exhaustive list of all her valuables.* □ *We will need an exhaustive description of the missing woman.*
• **in-depth**   including everything important; going into great detail. □ *The news program presented an in-depth story on the scandal.* □ *I read an in-depth interview with the president of the company.*
• **intensive**   including everything; highly concentrated. □ *Mark learned French in four weeks of intensive study.* □ *This project will require intensive research.*

thought   See the entry for *idea*.

thoughtful   See the entry for *considerate*.

thoughtless   See the entry for *careless*.

thrash   See the entry for *whip*.

threadbare   See the entry for *shabby*.

threaten   (*verb*) to say that you will hurt someone; to act as if you are going to hurt someone. □ *Tom threatened to tell on me if he caught me stealing again.* □ *Tom threatened his little sister, so she said nothing about what he had done.*
• **intimidate**   to make someone afraid by *threatening* him or her. □ *The principal tried to intimidate the tough student.* □ *Philip's loud, rough way of speaking intimidates many people.*

• **menace** to *threaten* someone; to make someone afraid of what you are going to do. □ *Ken menaced me with his switchblade.* □ *The dog menaced the intruder by growling and showing his teeth.*

threatening See the entry for *sinister*.

threshold See the entry for *entrance*.

thrilled (*adjective*) so full of joy that you feel a tingle; excited and happy. □ *Rita was thrilled to receive the award.* □ *I could tell from Susan's thrilled expression that she was enjoying the roller-coaster ride.*
• **aroused** so full of emotion that you feel ready for action. □ *The soldiers fought bravely, their patriotism fiercely aroused.* □ *My aroused curiosity would not let me rest until I discovered the truth.*
• **charged up** full of emotion and energy. (Slang.) □ *Charged up with the cheers of the spectators, the team burst onto the field.* □ *Listening to good dance music always makes me feel charged up.*
• **electrified** surprised and full of violent emotion. □ *The startling news left us electrified.* □ *Tim's electrified face showed that I had, indeed, surprised him.*
• **excited** full of strong emotion and energy. (See also the main entry for *excited*.) □ *I tried to calm the excited children.* □ *The dog gave a series of excited barks.*
• **fired up** full of eagerness; excited and ready for action. (Slang.) □ *The politician was all fired up and ready to give her best speech ever.* □ *I had been all fired up for the party, so I was disappointed when it was called off.*

throb See the entry for *hurt*².

throng See the entry for *crowd*.

throw (*verb*) to send something through the air with force. □ *Throw me the keys.* □ *Jan threw a pillow at her sister.*
• **catapult** to use a lever to *throw* something. □ *Bill used a spoon to catapult a dollop of mashed potatoes across the room.* □ *The soldiers catapulted steel bolts over the wall into the besieged city.*
• **fling** to *throw* something energetically. □ *Anna flung the door open.* □ *Mary flung her pencil aside impatiently.*
• **heave** to *throw* or push something with great effort. □ *We heaved the box up onto the truck.* □ *Charlie heaved his suitcase onto the shelf.*
• **hurl** to *throw* something violently. □ *We hurled snowballs at our opponents.* □ *Donna hurled curses at the fleeing man.*
• **pitch** to *throw* something in a particular direction. □ *I pitched my shoes into the closet.* □ *Eddie pitched the ball toward the plate.*
• **sling** to *throw* with a sweeping motion, as if with a slingshot. □ *Fran slung her backpack over her shoulder.* □ *George slung the little boy onto his back.*

• **toss**   to *throw* something lightly or effortlessly. ☐ *Helen tossed the toy into the air and caught it.* ☐ *Toss me that book, will you?*

throw away   (*verb*) to put aside or take away something useless; to toss something out. ☐ *Should I keep this old pair of shoes, or should I throw it away?* ☐ *I can't believe you're throwing away perfectly good food.*

   • **chuck**   to *throw* something *away*; to toss something aside. (Slang.) ☐ *We chucked everything we couldn't fit in the car.* ☐ *Sue chucked the apple core into the trash can.*

   • **discard**   to *throw* something *away*. (Formal.) ☐ *Remove and discard the plastic wrapper.* ☐ *Jenny discarded four or five drafts of her essay before producing one she liked.*

   • **dispose of**   to *throw away* something permanently; to put something useless where it belongs. ☐ *The murderer wondered how to dispose of the body.* ☐ *Please dispose of this moldy bread.*

   • **dump**   to *throw* something *away*; to take away something useless and drop it somewhere. ☐ *I dumped the used dishwater.* ☐ *I dumped the moldy leftovers onto the compost heap.*

   • **get rid of**   to *throw* something *away* or do away with something. ☐ *Get rid of this junk, will you?* ☐ *Kevin tried to get rid of his troublesome visitor.*

thrust   See the entries for *push, subject.*

thump   See the entry for *pound.*

thunder   See the entry for *rumble.*

thwart   See the entry for *frustrate.*

ticklish   See the entry for *tricky.*

tidy   See the entry for *neat.*

tie the knot   See the entry for *marry.*

tight   See the entry for *tense.*

tightwad   See the entry for *miser.*

tilt   (*verb*) to be higher on one side than the other; to make something higher on one side than the other. ☐ *The table tilts because one leg is shorter than the others.* ☐ *Larry tilted up his cup to get the last drop of orange juice.*

   • **lean**   to hang more to one side than the other. ☐ *The shack leaned a little to one side.* ☐ *Mary leaned against the car.*

   • **list**   to move so that one side is higher than the other. (Nautical.) ☐ *The boat listed heavily; the sailors tried to right her.* ☐ *The old car listed to one side.*

   • **slant**   to have one side higher than the other; to make one side higher than the other. ☐ *The lines of Nancy's handwriting slanted upwards.* ☐ *Tom slanted the book so that the light fell on it.*

• **slope**   to go up or down at an angle. □ *A hill sloped gently upward in back of the house.* □ *Jane's dress showed off the way her shoulders sloped.*

time   (*noun*) a part of the past, present, or future. □ *At that time, Ken was planning to become a librarian.* □ *The writer uses language from an earlier time.*

• **age**   a *time* in history. □ *It was a chaotic age in the history of Europe.* □ *Roger decorated his room in the style of the Victorian Age.*

• **era**   an important *time* in history. □ *This house dates from the era of the American Civil War.* □ *The book discusses American politics in the Eisenhower era.*

• **period**   a *time* during which something particular was going on. □ *Stanley's childhood was an important period of his life.* □ *A period of anxiety followed Thomas's decision to move to Memphis.*

timid   See the entry for *shy.*

tin   See the entry for *metal.*

tinge   See the entry for *color.*

tinkle   See the entry for *chime.*

tint   See the entry for *color.*

tiny   See the entry for *small.*

tip off   See the entry for *warn.*

tired   (*adjective*) needing rest; lacking energy. □ *I'm too tired to play basketball tonight.* □ *If you don't get enough sleep tonight, you'll be tired in the morning.*

• **drained**   lacking energy or enthusiasm. □ *Waiting through Uncle Warren's surgery left us all feeling drained.* □ *The whole team seemed completely drained after soccer practice yesterday.*

• **exhausted**   thoroughly *tired.* □ *Rachel was exhausted after her first day at work.* □ *Jim was so exhausted that he fell asleep at six o'clock last night.*

• **enervated**   completely lacking energy. (Formal.) □ *The actors were utterly enervated after the long rehearsal.* □ *I always feel enervated on hot, humid days.*

• **fatigued**   *tired* from too much exertion. (Formal.) □ *The young lady appears to be fatigued from the long walk.* □ *We will continue with our sightseeing tomorrow, since we feel too fatigued to do any more today.*

• **weary**   *tired* from too much of something. □ *Louise grew weary of her patient's constant demands.* □ *After studying all weekend, Edgar longed to rest his weary brain.*

• **worn out**   too *tired* to continue. □ *George is always worn out at the end of a workweek.* □ *The dog doesn't want to play anymore; she's all worn out.*

[→contrasting words: *lively, energetic*]

tireless   (*adjective*) never stopping or losing energy. □ *The lawyer was tireless in her quest for justice.* □ *I commend Victor's tireless efforts on behalf of the club.*

> • **indefatigable**   unstoppable; full of energy. □ *The criminal could not escape the indefatigable detective.* □ *The indefatigable reporter usually got the stories he went after.*
>
> • **unflagging**   never slowing down or losing energy. □ *The author was grateful for her readers' unflagging enthusiasm for her works.* □ *Whatever else might happen, I knew I had Wendy's unflagging loyalty.*
>
> • **unwearying**   never needing rest. □ *The athlete's unwearying pursuit of excellence won her a great deal of admiration.* □ *Aunt Wendy grew tired of playing, but the kids were unwearying.*

tiresome   See the entry for *boring.*

titter   See the entry for *laugh.*

to-do   See the entry for *commotion.*

token   See the entry for *sign.*

tolerate   See the entry for *bear.*

toll   See the entry for *ring.*

tome   See the entry for *book.*

topic   See the entry for *subject.*

topple   See the entry for *collapse.*

tornado   See the entry for *storm.*

torpid   See the entry for *listless.*

toss   See the entry for *throw.*

total   See the entry for *whole.*

totter   See the entry for *rock³.*

touch down   See the entry for *land.*

touchy   See the entry for *sensitive.*

tough   See the entry for *hard.*

tour   See the entry for *journey.*

tout   See the entry for *advertise*.

tow   See the entry for *pull*.

towering   See the entry for *tall*.

town   (*noun*) a large group of houses and buildings where people live. □ *Danville is a cute little town.* □ *I'm from a small town in Arizona.*
   • **city**   a large, busy, and important *town*. □ *Chicago is the biggest city in Illinois.* □ *Art grew up in the city of Los Angeles.*
   • **community**   a *town* or part of a *town* where the people have some things in common. □ *The town where I grew up was a close-knit community.* □ *There is a flourishing Hispanic community in our town.*
   • **metropolis**   a very large *town*. (Formal.) □ *Ben felt overwhelmed by the hustle and bustle of the metropolis.* □ *From the plane, I could see the lights of the metropolis spread out below me.*
   • **municipality**   a *town* that governs itself. (Formal.) □ *The town library exchanged books with libraries in other municipalities.* □ *Your house is outside the border of this municipality.*
   • **neighborhood**   a part of a *town*. □ *It was a quiet neighborhood of hard-working people.* □ *I heard that this neighborhood is not safe after dark.*
   • **village**   a small *town*. □ *Carrie took a picture of the quaint village nestled in the valley.* □ *Only two hundred people lived in the village.*

toxic   See the entry for *poisonous*.

toy   See the entry for *play²*.

trace   See the entries for *draw, follow*.

track   See the entry for *follow*.

trade   (*verb*) to give one thing for another. □ *The trappers traded their fur for flour, sugar, and coffee.* □ *I'll trade you my peanut butter and jelly for your tuna salad.*
   • **barter**   to *trade* goods or services instead of using money. □ *Donald and Eddie bartered with each other, Donald agreeing to fix Eddie's car if Eddie would give him his portable TV.* □ *When Fran visited Russia, she was able to barter her American blue jeans for some nice souvenirs.*
   • **exchange**   to *trade*; to replace one thing with another. (Formal.) □ *George and Helen exchanged phone numbers.* □ *I would like to exchange this coat for one in a larger size.*
   • **traffic**   to *trade* or sell something as a business. (Usually with *in*.) □ *The store traffics in exotic kinds of coffee.* □ *Rumor had it that Jones trafficked in drugs.*

trader   See the entry for *seller*.

tradition   See the entry for *custom*.

traffic   See the entry for *trade.*

trail   See the entries for *follow, road.*

train   See the entries for *series, teach.*

training   See the entry for *discipline.*

traitor   (*noun*) a person who betrays someone or something. □ *Kay considered Larry a traitor for blabbing her secret to everyone.* □ *The traitor sold his country's secrets to the enemy.*
  • **Benedict Arnold**   a *traitor,* especially one who betrays his country, as Benedict Arnold did in the American Revolution. (Slang.) □ *What a Benedict Arnold that guy is, for selling state secrets!* □ *They should put that Benedict Arnold in jail for a hundred years.*
  • **double-crosser**   a *traitor* who fools you into thinking that he or she is on your side. (Informal or slang.) □ *"You dirty double-crosser!" the crime boss hissed. "You were working for the cops all along!"* □ *The spy turned out to be a double-crosser, telling secrets from both countries.*
  • **informer**   a *traitor* who tells secrets to the authorities. □ *An informer told the police where to find the crime boss.* □ *To save her own skin, the thief turned informer and betrayed her friends.*
  • **Judas**   a *traitor,* like Judas Iscariot, who betrayed Jesus. □ *Mark's former friends regarded him as a Judas for publishing private things about them in the paper.* □ *Some Judas betrayed the rebel leader, who was caught and killed.*
  • **turncoat**   a *traitor;* someone who goes over to the other side. □ *Tom is a turncoat for going to play ball with the other team.* □ *Kirkland first fought for the Americans in the Revolutionary War, but then the turncoat joined the British side.*

trample   (*verb*) to destroy something or mash it flat by stepping on it repeatedly. □ *The hat was blown onto the sidewalk, where it was quickly trampled by pedestrians.* □ *The stampeding horses trampled down the fence.*
  • **stamp on**   to step on something heavily or forcefully. □ *We stamped on the last few burning coals to put them out.* □ *Sue threw the letter on the floor and stamped on it angrily.*
  • **stomp on**   to step on something forcefully. (Slang.) □ *I stomped on the aluminum cans before I put them in the recycling bin.* □ *Philip stomped on the accelerator, and the car zoomed forward.*
  • **tread on**   to step on something heavily. (Formal.) □ *Passersby trod on the poor little flower, not noticing it was there.* □ *I always seem to tread on people's feelings by saying exactly the wrong thing.*
  [→see also: *crush*]

trance   See the entry for *daze.*

tranquil   See the entry for *calm.*

tranquility   See the entry for *peace*.

transfixed   See the entry for *fascinated*.

transform   See the entry for *change*.

transgress   See the entry for *disobey*.

transient   See the entry for *temporary*.

transitory   See the entry for *temporary*.

transmit   See the entries for *emit, send*.

transpire   See the entry for *happen*.

transport   See the entry for *carry*.

trap   (*verb*) to capture someone or something; to keep something from escaping. ☐ *Ken trapped a number of rabbits that day, so he had rabbit stew for supper.* ☐ *The police trapped the fleeing criminal in a rundown barn.*
  • **catch**   to capture someone or something after a chase. (See also the main entry for *catch*.) ☐ *The cat caught the mouse.* ☐ *I tried to run away, but Rita caught me.*
  • **decoy**   to capture someone or something by a trick. ☐ *The police officer pretended to want to buy drugs, thus decoying the pusher into trying to sell him some.* ☐ *The kidnappers sent a forged message to decoy their victim into the abandoned house.*
  • **lure**   to capture someone or something by offering something attractive. ☐ *I lured the cat into the cage with a dish of tuna.* ☐ *Photos of gorgeous food in the restaurant window lured people inside.*
  • **snare**   to capture someone or something quickly or cleverly. ☐ *Susan used a piece of string to snare the pesky squirrel.* ☐ *Tim's good looks and lovely manners snared many a girl.*

trash   (*noun*) something that is no longer useful; something of poor quality. (Informal.) ☐ *After the party, we picked up the trash and threw it away.* ☐ *Why do you watch that trash on TV?*
  • **garbage**   trash. (Formal.) ☐ *The bins were overflowing with garbage.* ☐ *Jan loves to read romance novels, though she knows they're garbage.*
  • **junk**   trash; something useless. ☐ *Piles of rusty old junk stood in the front yard.* ☐ *That broken old jewelry is just junk; why do you save it?*
  • **litter**   trash that has been left out in the open. ☐ *It was sad to see so much litter in the park.* ☐ *There is a fine for leaving litter at the side of the road.*
  • **refuse**   trash, especially trash left over from preparing or eating food. (See also the main entry for *refuse*.) ☐ *The beggar was so hungry she would go through the restaurant's refuse, looking for something to eat.* ☐ *Put this refuse on the compost heap.*

• **waste**   *trash* that is left over from doing or using something. (See also the main entry for *waste*.) □ *Bill just threw the kitchen waste into the backyard, where it rotted and stank.* □ *Anna built a bookcase out of the boards, bricks, and other waste from the construction across the street.*

tread   See the entry for *walk*.

tread on   See the entry for *trample*.

treasure   (*verb*) to consider something very valuable and keep it safe. □ *Mary treasured the movie star's autograph.* □ *I treasure our friendship.*
  • **cherish**   to consider something very valuable or special. □ *Charlie cherished the memory of his summer in Italy.* □ *Donna drew me a picture, which I cherish to this day.*
  • **hold dear**   to consider something valuable; to think that something is worth a great deal. □ *I hold you very dear.* □ *Linda held her photo albums dear and scarcely let anyone else touch them.*
  • **prize**   to consider something valuable; to think that something is one of the best things you have. □ *Frank prized his car and spent most of his free time taking care of it.* □ *Gina prized her children.*

treatment   See the entry for *cure*.

trek   See the entry for *journey*.

tremble   See the entry for *vibrate*.

trespass upon   See the entry for *invade*.

trial   See the entries for *problem, test*.

tribute   (*noun*) a show of respect or appreciation. □ *The show was a tribute to the comedian's thirty years of entertainment.* □ *Harold wrote the book as a tribute to his father.*
  • **accolade**   a show of appreciation or admiration. □ *Sue's work brought her the highest accolades.* □ *The ad for the movie boasted of the critic's accolade.*
  • **homage**   a show of deep respect. □ *Jenny paid homage to her teacher and mentor.* □ *The program was an homage to the great movie director.*
  • **honor**   deep respect and admiration; an award. □ *The soldier had received every honor it was possible to get.* □ *I give this donation in honor of my parents' wedding anniversary.*

trick   See the entries for *fool², practical joke*.

trickle   See the entry for *leak*.

tricky (*adjective*) requiring special skill to solve. □ *This is a very tricky puzzle.* □ *Resolving the quarrel between Kevin and Larry will be tricky.*
• **delicate**   requiring very special care to solve. □ *I undertook the delicate task of getting the sisters to say how they really felt without hurting each other's feelings.* □ *The diplomat did her best at the delicate negotiations.*
• **knotty**   complex and difficult to solve. □ *We ran into some knotty problems early on.* □ *The debaters struggled with the knotty question.*
• **thorny**   dangerous and difficult to solve. □ *Gun control was a thorny issue in that election.* □ *Mary and her father have a thorny relationship.*
• **ticklish**   requiring special care to solve; sensitive. □ *The inheritance was a ticklish point with the cousins.* □ *The reporter handled the ticklish subject quite well.*
[→see also: *complicated*]

trifle   See the entry for *play²*.

trim   (*verb*) to cut a little bit off something. □ *Trim off the ends of these carrots.* □ *Nancy trimmed her fingernails.*
• **bob**   to cut something short, especially hair. □ *Tom bobbed the horse's tail.* □ *In the 1920s, many women bobbed their hair.*
• **dock**   to cut a piece off something. (See also the main entry for *dock.*) □ *The boss docked Jane's wages.* □ *The teacher docked my grade because I turned the paper in late.*
• **pare**   to cut something down a little. □ *I pared the skin off a potato.* □ *Roger carefully pared an inch off the bottom of the door.*
• **prune**   to cut branches off something. □ *Stanley spent the afternoon pruning the hedges.* □ *That tree needs to be pruned.*
• **shave**   to cut a little off the surface of something; to cut all the hair off someone's skin. □ *Thomas shaved a little wood off the edge of the door.* □ *Victor shaved his face.*

trip   (*verb*) to make a wrong step; to bump against an obstacle and lose your balance. □ *Wendy tripped and fell.* □ *Pull in that broom handle so no one will trip over it.*
• **slip**   to slide, losing your balance. □ *I slipped on the icy sidewalk.* □ *I just waxed the floor; be careful not to slip.*
• **stagger**   to walk unsteadily; to take an unsteady step. □ *From the way that guy staggers, I'd say he was drunk.* □ *Carrie punched Donald, and he staggered.*
• **stumble**   to make a wrong step; to walk clumsily. □ *Art stumbled over the rocky path.* □ *Ben stumbled along, exhausted.*

triumph   See the entry for *win*.

triumph over   See the entry for *beat²*.

trivial   See the entry for *unimportant*.

trooper   See the entry for *officer*.

trot   See the entry for *run*.

trouble   See the entry for *problem*.

trounce   See the entry for *beat²*.

truck   See the entry for *vehicle*.

trudge   See the entry for *walk*.

true   See the entry for *right*.

trumpet   See the entry for *announce*.

trust   (*verb*) to feel sure that someone or something will act in a certain way; to feel sure that someone or something will be on your side. (See also the entry for *believe²*.) □ *I trust that Eddie will keep his promise.* □ *You can trust Fran; she's very honest.*
  • **believe in**   to feel sure that something is true. □ *George believes in the basic goodness of people.* □ *Do you believe in ghosts?*
  • **depend on**   to expect someone or something to help you. □ *I depend on you to be here on time.* □ *Helen kept going only because she knew a lot of people were depending on her.*
  • **have faith in**   to feel very sure about something. □ *I have faith in your ability to win.* □ *Irene felt she could do anything, because her friends had faith in her.*
  • **rely on**   to expect someone or something to help you; to use the help of someone or something often. □ *The blind woman relied on her seeing-eye dog.* □ *Jay relies on the money he gets from his parents.*
  • **swear by**   to expect someone or something to do the job; to have confidence in someone or something. (Folksy.) □ *Gramma swears by that brand of soap.* □ *Kay swears by her doctor, though no one else seems to have much faith in his opinions.*

trustworthy   See the entry for *faithful*.

try   (*verb*) to do your best to do something; to give yourself a chance to do something. □ *I don't know if I can finish the book today, but I'll try.* □ *Laura had never tried skateboarding.*
  • **attempt**   to do your best to do something. (Formal.) □ *I attempted to calm Mark down.* □ *Tom attempted to sing the tenor part.*
  • **endeavor**   to work to do something. (Formal.) □ *The waiter endeavored to be polite even to the rudest customers.* □ *We endeavored to put up the tent in the high wind.*

• **make an effort**   to put some work into doing something. □ *Sue made an effort to be friendly to the new girl.* □ *Your grades won't improve if you don't make an effort to study.*
• **strive**   to work or strain to do something. (Formal.) □ *The librarian always strove to be helpful.* □ *The runner strove to better her previous record.*
• **undertake**   to intend to do something; to set out to do something. (Formal.) □ *Philip undertook the mending of all his old clothes.* □ *When I undertook this project, I didn't know how much work it would require.*

tug   (*verb*) to pull something sharply. □ *Ken put his arms into the sweater and then tugged it down over his head.* □ *I tugged on the rope.*
• **jerk**   to pull or move something sharply. □ *Rita jerked her arm from my grip.* □ *Susan jerked the door open.*
• **pluck**   to pull something out sharply. □ *Tim plucked a feather from the bird's tail.* □ *I plucked the letter from the envelope.*
• **yank**   to pull something suddenly or violently. □ *Jan tried to yank out her loose tooth.* □ *Bill yanked Anna's long braid to get her attention.*
[→see also: *pull*]

tumble   See the entry for *fall*.

tummy   See the entry for *stomach*.

tumult   See the entry for *commotion*.

tune   (*noun*) a piece of music. □ *Mary hummed a sad tune.* □ *I remember the words to the song, but I can't remember how the tune goes.*
• **air**   a *tune*. (Old-fashioned.) □ *Charlie whistled a lively Scottish air.* □ *The band played a patriotic air to encourage the soldiers.*
• **melody**   a pleasing *tune*. □ *The flute played a haunting melody.* □ *The composer wrote many beautiful melodies.*
• **strain**   a familiar *tune;* the *tune* of a song. (Formal. Often used in the plural.) □ *As the parade approached, we could hear the strains of "Yankee Doodle."* □ *The tune is made up of several variations on a single strain.*
[→see also: *song*]

turmoil   See the entry for *disorder*.

turn   (*verb*) to move around a center; to go around and around. □ *Donna turned in her sleep.* □ *I switched the machine on, and the gears began to turn.*
• **pivot**   to *turn* around a fixed center. □ *The dancer pivoted on one foot.* □ *The door pivots on its hinges.*
• **revolve**   to *turn* around and around an object. (Usually with *around*.) □ *The moon revolves around the earth.* □ *Everything at the Edwardses' seems to revolve around what the oldest son wants.*

• **rotate** to *turn* around your own center. □ *It takes one day for the earth to rotate completely.* □ *The wheel is stuck; it won't rotate.*
• **spin** to *turn* rapidly around and around. □ *The pinwheel spun in the breeze.* □ *The shocking news made my head spin.*
• **twirl** to *turn* gracefully. □ *The ice skater's skirts flared out as she twirled.* □ *The drum major twirled his baton.*
• **whirl** to *turn* wildly around and around □ *The dead leaves whirled in the wind.* □ *The children whirled around and around on the merry-go-round.*

turn down See the entry for *refuse*.

turn out See the entry for *make¹*.

turncoat See the entry for *traitor*.

turquoise See the entry for *blue*.

tussle See the entry for *struggle*.

tutor See the entry for *teach*.

twaddle See the entry for *nonsense*.

twilight See the entry for *darkness*.

twine See the entry for *wind²*.

twinkle See the entry for *sparkle*.

twirl See the entry for *turn*.

twist See the entry for *wind²*.

twisted See the entry for *crooked*.

twitch See the entry for *squirm*.

two-faced See the entry for *hypocritical*.

type See the entry for *kind²*.

typist See the entry for *clerk*.

tyrant See the entry for *autocrat*.

U

ugly (*adjective*) unpleasant to look at. □ *Why do you want a poster of that ugly movie star?* □ *I think lime green is an ugly color.*
   • **hideous** extremely *ugly*. □ *Frank wore a really hideous tie today; it looked as though he had spilled something on it.* □ *The artist painted a nightmare scene full of hideous monsters.*
   • **repulsive** so *ugly* it makes people want to move away. □ *Gina's so fat it's repulsive.* □ *I can't stand the repulsive noises Harold makes while he eats.*
   • **unattractive** somewhat *ugly*; not attractive. □ *Sue may be unattractive, but she's so much fun to be with that you never notice it.* □ *Someone should tell Jenny that so much makeup is unattractive.*
   [→contrasting word: *beautiful*]

ultimate See the entry for *final*.

unanticipated See the entry for *unexpected*.

unattractive See the entry for *ugly*.

unavailing See the entry for *useless*.

unaware (*adjective*) not paying attention to something; not knowing that something is happening. □ *The teacher was unaware of how much the students disliked him.* □ *I was unaware that Kevin was ill.*
   • **absent** *unaware* of everything around you; so *unaware* that you seem as though you are not there. □ *I can tell Larry's not paying attention to the lecture; just look at the absent expression on his face.* □ *Mary would often grow absent while her parents chatted over dinner.*
   • **oblivious** completely *unaware* of everything around you. □ *Nancy was playing a video game, oblivious to her surroundings.* □ *Tom somehow managed to be oblivious to Jane's enormous crush on him.*

• **unmindful**   *unaware* of something; not obeying something. ☐ *Our hero rushed onto the mountain path, unmindful of the sheer drop to one side.* ☐ *Unmindful of the safety rules, Ken began to work on the chemistry experiment without putting on his safety goggles.*

unbelievable   See the entry for *incredible*.

unbend   See the entry for *relax*.

unbiased   (*adjective*) not prejudiced; not leaning toward either side of an argument. ☐ *We want an unbiased person to settle this question.* ☐ *A good reporter is supposed to remain unbiased.*
   • **disinterested**   not involved in an argument; not prejudiced. ☐ *A disinterested party should decide how to divide the money up.* ☐ *The jury heard the case with a disinterested coolness.*
   • **fair**   not leaning toward either side of an argument; just. (See also the main entry for *fair*.) ☐ *Roger tried to give a fair decision.* ☐ *I'm sure the judge will be fair.*
   • **impartial**   not prejudiced; not having a preference for either side of an argument. ☐ *Dad remained impartial during all of our arguments.* ☐ *The program gave an impartial presentation of both sides of the issue.*
   • **objective**   not emotionally involved in an argument; not taking sides. ☐ *The reporter tried to remain objective, but found herself sympathizing with the victims of the crime.* ☐ *The writer uses an objective tone, but it's pretty obvious that he is not in favor of gun control.*
   • **without interest**   not prejudiced; not involved in an argument. (Formal.) ☐ *Do you swear that you are without interest in this matter?* ☐ *Stanley is completely without interest in the case; he will gain nothing, no matter who wins.*

uncaring   See the entry for *indifferent*.

unceasing   See the entry for *constant*.

uncommon   See the entry for *exceptional*.

uncommonly   See the entry for *especially*.

unconscious   (*adjective*) not knowing or aware of what is going on around you; not able to sense anything that is going on around you. ☐ *The boxer was knocked unconscious.* ☐ *The paramedics lifted the unconscious man into the ambulance.*
   • **comatose**   deeply *unconscious* because of a sickness or an injury. (Formal.) ☐ *Thomas remained comatose for many hours after his operation.* ☐ *The doctor was alarmed when the patient became comatose.*
   • **in a coma**   in a deeply *unconscious* state. ☐ *While Victor was in a coma, his family gathered around him, trying to wake him up.* ☐ *She has been in a coma for almost six months.*

• **in a trance**   in an *unconscious* or hypnotized state. ☐ *While the medium was in a trance, she spoke in the dead woman's voice.* ☐ *Wendy was so shocked that she appeared to be in a trance.*

• **insensible**   *unconscious;* not aware of anything. (Formal; old-fashioned.) ☐ *Upon hearing the awful news, Art sank to the floor, insensible.* ☐ *We found the insensible form of the butler thrust into the closet.*

• **out cold**   completely *unconscious,* especially as the result of being hit. (Slang.) ☐ *Ben hit me so hard that I was out cold.* ☐ *He can't answer you; he's out cold.*

unconventional   See the entry for *eccentric.*

uncouth   See the entry for *rude.*

under   See the entry for *below.*

undergo   See the entry for *experience.*

underground   See the entry for *secret.*

underhanded   See the entries for *sneaky, stealthy.*

undermine   See the entry for *weaken.*

underneath   See the entry for *below.*

underscore   See the entry for *stress².*

understand   (*verb*) to have clear knowledge of something; to make sense out of something. ☐ *I can't understand what Carrie is saying.* ☐ *Now I understand why Donald was so upset yesterday.*

• **apprehend**   to come to *understand* something. (Formal.) ☐ *The universe is far bigger than anyone can apprehend.* ☐ *It took a while for me to apprehend that Eddie was really dead, that I would never see him again.*

• **comprehend**   to *understand* something. (Formal.) ☐ *The test will measure how well students comprehend what they have read.* ☐ *Fran made a mistake because she did not comprehend the instructions.*

• **get**   to *understand* or come to *understand* something. (Slang. See also the main entry for *get.*) ☐ *Don't you get it? George is trying to make you jealous!* ☐ *I didn't really get what Helen was talking about.*

• **grasp**   to firmly *understand* something. ☐ *The idea that she was really famous was difficult for Irene to grasp.* ☐ *Jay never did quite grasp the basics of adding and subtracting fractions.*

undertake   See the entry for *try.*

unearth   See the entry for *find.*

uneasiness   See the entry for *discontent.*

uneasy (*adjective*) not able to relax; worried. □ *Being alone in the house made Kay feel uneasy.* □ *Laura's uneasy laughter showed how nervous she felt.*

• **anxious**   uneasy; full of nervousness or anxiety. □ *The anxious man wrung his hands.* □ *"They should have been here an hour ago," Tom said in an anxious voice.*

• **apprehensive**   uneasy because you feel that something bad is going to happen. (Formal.) □ *I couldn't help feeling apprehensive as the day for my operation drew near.* □ *Mark took an apprehensive step closer to the edge of the cliff.*

• **disquieted**   made uneasy. □ *The mysterious noise left us all feeling disquieted.* □ *From the minute I entered the house, I could tell that my family was disquieted.*

uneven   See the entry for *rough²*.

unexpected (*adjective*) surprising; not expected. □ *The evening was enlivened by the unexpected arrival of several guests.* □ *The plot of the movie took several unexpected turns.*

• **startling**   unexpected and sudden. □ *Sue made the startling announcement that she had just gotten married.* □ *Philip's sudden laugh was very startling.*

• **unanticipated**   unexpected; not waited or planned for. □ *The project was stalled by an unanticipated difficulty.* □ *Ken's unanticipated growth spurt left him with no clothes that fit.*

• **unforeseen**   unexpected; nothing you knew about ahead of time. □ *The team's rise to the championship was completely unforeseen.* □ *The unforeseen loss of her job made Rita feel very depressed.*

unfair (*adjective*) not right; favoring one side of an argument. □ *You're always taking Susan's side! It's unfair!* □ *I think you're being unfair when you say that Tim is lazy.*

• **arbitrary**   unfair or random; done according to a whim. □ *As a child, Jan received arbitrary punishments.* □ *The judge's decision seemed arbitrary.*

• **biased**   unfair; strongly favoring one side. □ *Bill's mother thinks he's brilliant, but then, she's biased.* □ *The article was clearly biased in favor of the Democrats.*

• **prejudiced**   unfair; favoring one side regardless of the facts. □ *Anna would not give up her prejudiced belief that people with southern accents were stupid.* □ *I was prejudiced against action movies until I saw this one.*

• **unjust**   unfair; not giving out justice. □ *The law is unjust and should be repealed.* □ *Mary reversed her unjust condemnation of Charlie's actions.*

unfamiliar   See the entry for *strange.*

unfinished   See the entry for *rough*[1].

unflagging   See the entry for *tireless.*

unforeseen   See the entry for *unexpected.*

ungainly   See the entry for *clumsy.*

unhappy   See the entry for *sad.*

unimportant   (*adjective*) not important; not worth considering. □ *How the food looks is unimportant, as long as it tastes all right.* □ *Donna felt that her job was unimportant.*
• **minor**   *unimportant* or small; not major. □ *I had a few minor problems putting the bicycle together.* □ *He was a writer of minor importance.*
• **inconsequential**   *unimportant;* of no importance or influence. (Formal.) □ *In writing my report, I left out inconsequential details such as what I had for breakfast each day.* □ *Don't worry about what Linda says; her opinions are inconsequential, after all.*
• **insignificant**   *unimportant* or not mattering much. □ *There is only an insignificant difference between the two brands of soda pop.* □ *I made some insignificant remark about the weather.*
• **trivial**   *unimportant* and not worth taking seriously. □ *Frank is full of trivial knowledge about baseball.* □ *Compared to what I spent on my plane ticket, food was a trivial expense.*

uninterested   See the entry for *indifferent.*

uninteresting   See the entry for *boring.*

uninvolved   See the entry for *removed.*

unique   See the entry for *exceptional.*

university   See the entry for *school.*

unjust   See the entry for *unfair.*

unkempt   See the entry for *messy.*

unkind   See the entries for *cruel, mean*[1].

unlikely   See the entry for *improbable.*

unmindful   See the entry for *unaware.*

unnecessary   (*adjective*) not needed. □ *All Gina's worrying turned out to be unnecessary.* □ *Don't bring anything unnecessary on the camping trip; you'll have to carry everything you bring.*

• **gratuitous**   *unnecessary;* included for no good reason. □ *The swear words in the comedian's jokes seemed gratuitous.* □ *The movie was full of gratuitous violence.*

• **needless**   *unnecessary* and not wanted. □ *To save yourself needless wandering around, get a highway map and plan out your trip beforehand.* □ *We will have to eliminate all needless expense.*

• **nonessential**   *unnecessary;* not vital. □ *The boss had to lay off nonessential employees.* ⎿ *Harold could not afford nonessential things like going out to the movies.*

[→see also: *useless*]

unobtrusive   See the entry for *reserved.*

unoffending   See the entry for *innocent.*

unprincipled   See the entry for *corrupt.*

unquestionably   See the entry for *certainly.*

unravel   See the entry for *figure out.*

unreasonable   See the entry for *irrational.*

unreliable   See the entry for *fickle.*

unremitting   See the entry for *relentless.*

unsafe   See the entry for *dangerous.*

unscrupulous   See the entry for *corrupt.*

unseen   See the entry for *invisible.*

unsophisticated   See the entry for *naive.*

unsound   See the entry for *irrational.*

unstable   See the entry for *shaky.*

unsteady   See the entries for *shaky, sporadic.*

untidy   See the entry for *messy.*

untruth   See the entry for *lie¹.*

unusual   See the entry for *strange.*

unusually   See the entry for *especially.*

unventilated   See the entry for *stuffy.*

unwearying   See the entry for *tireless.*

unwilling   See the entry for *reluctant.*

unwind   See the entry for *relax*.

unworldly   See the entry for *naive*.

upbeat   See the entry for *optimistic*.

upbraid   See the entry for *scold*.

upgrade   See the entry for *improve*.

uphold   See the entry for *support*.

upset   (*adjective*) full of sudden emotion; not calm. ☐ *Mom was upset when I showed her my report card.* ☐ *From the way Sue is stomping around, she must be upset.*
   • **distraught**   extremely *upset; upset* enough to seem crazy. ☐ *Jenny was distraught when her father died.* ☐ *The police officer tried to get the distraught robbery victim to answer her questions.*
   • **disturbed**   upset or bothered. ☐ *After seeing the gory movie, I felt disturbed.* ☐ *Kevin came out of the room with a disturbed expression.*
   • **flustered**   somewhat *upset* and confused. ☐ *Flustered at being awakened in the middle of the night, I threw on my bathrobe and went to the door.* ☐ *Larry began to search the house, despite Mary's flustered objections.*
   • **perturbed**   alarmed and *upset.* ☐ *When Nancy was late getting home, I became perturbed.* ☐ *Tom was perturbed by all the violence he saw on TV.*
   [→see also: *excited*]

urge   (*verb*) to tell someone very strongly to do something. ☐ *Jane's friends urged her to see a doctor.* ☐ *Ken urged me to try out for a part in the play.*
   • **admonish**   to tell someone very strongly that he or she ought to do something. ☐ *Mom admonished us to clean up after ourselves.* ☐ *The teacher admonished her students, telling them to behave for the substitute.*
   • **exhort**   to tell someone strongly and emotionally that he or she ought to do something. ☐ *Endless TV commercials exhorted people to vote in the election.* ☐ *Roger exhorted me to go out and get a job.*
   • **prompt**   to tell or remind someone to do something. ☐ *A message on the computer screen prompted me to push the "return" key.* ☐ *Stanley prompted me to apologize for being late.*
   [→see also: *force*]

urgent   (*adjective*) needing attention right away. ☐ *I got an urgent phone call from my sister.* ☐ *Thomas had an urgent need for medical care.*
   • **compelling**   commanding attention. ☐ *Victor had compelling reasons for leaving town.* ☐ *Wendy told the compelling story of her escape from prison.*

• **imperative**   commanding attention; necessary. ☐ *The hikers realized that finding shelter was imperative.* ☐ *It is imperative that you be here on time.*

• **pressing**   needing to be taken care of right away. ☐ *I have several pressing matters to attend to before I can leave work today.* ☐ *The need for a good school in the town grew more and more pressing as the population increased.*

[→see also: *necessary*]

use   (*verb*) to make something work to help you; to put something into action or service. ☐ *Use a pair of pliers to pull that nail out.* ☐ *This class will teach you to use a computer.*

• **apply**   to *use* something by putting it in contact with something else; to *use* knowledge. ☐ *I applied a tire iron to the rusty bolt.* ☐ *The detective applied all his skills to the solution of the mystery.*

• **employ**   to *use* something or have someone work for you. ☐ *For this painting, the artist employed watercolors.* ☐ *The company employs sixty people.*

• **exploit**   to *use* something fully or wastefully; to take advantage of something. ☐ *For this role, the actor can exploit his talents both as an actor and as a dancer.* ☐ *Art exploited the natural riches of his land, cutting down all the trees and harvesting all the fish from the lake.*

• **operate**   to *use* a machine; to make a machine work for you. ☐ *Ben can operate a sewing machine.* ☐ *The vacuum cleaner was easy to operate.*

• **utilize**   to *use* something. (Formal.) ☐ *The job gave Carrie a chance to utilize her public speaking skills.* ☐ *The woodcarver utilized several different saws to carve the fancy decorations.*

used   See the entry for *secondhand*.

used up   See the entry for *spent*.

useful   (*adjective*) helping a lot in doing a task; able to be used for many different tasks. ☐ *The food processor turned out to be quite useful.* ☐ *Typing is a useful skill.*

• **handy**   *useful* in making a task easier; immediately available for a task. ☐ *This appointment book is a handy size; it fits right in my pocket.* ☐ *I made soup out of all the vegetables that were handy.*

• **helpful**   helping a lot; *useful* in making things easier. ☐ *The helpful librarian showed me how to find the information I needed.* ☐ *A map of Atlanta would have been helpful on my visit there.*

• **serviceable**   *useful*, sturdy, and functional; holding up through a lot of use. ☐ *My car isn't very good looking, but it's serviceable.* ☐ *I used my dad's serviceable old typewriter.*

useless (*adjective*) not useful or helpful; not leading to the result you want. ☐ *The city had changed so much that the old guidebook was now useless.* ☐ *It's useless to complain; we can't change anything that way.*

• **futile**   *useless;* without any purpose; leading to no result. ☐ *After struggling with his bonds for several minutes, the prisoner gave up his futile efforts to escape.* ☐ *It was futile to try to attract the attention of passing motorists.*

• **hopeless**   having no hope of leading to the result you want. ☐ *There was no help in sight; the situation seemed hopeless.* ☐ *Trying to fix the car in the dark was obviously hopeless.*

• **unavailing**   *useless;* not leading to the result you want. ☐ *All my attempts to contact Donald were unavailing.* ☐ *Eddie made unavailing appeals for mercy.*

• **vain**   for nothing; leading to a *useless* result. ☐ *Vincent's vain struggle for artistic fame consumed his entire life.* ☐ *Fran made a last, vain attempt to keep herself from falling.*

[→see also: *unnecessary*]

usher   See the entry for *accompany*.

usual   See the entry for *average*.

utilize   See the entry for *use*.

V

vacant See the entry for *empty¹*.

vacillate See the entry for *waver*.

vagary See the entry for *whim*.

vague See the entry for *faint*.

vain See the entries for *conceited, useless*.

valid See the entry for *right*.

valley (*noun*) a long, narrow, low area in the earth, usually between hills or mountains. □ *The farm stood in a beautiful green valley.* □ *The road wound down from the mountains into the valley.*
> • **canyon** a deep *valley*, especially one in the western United States. □ *The canyon is full of Anasazi Indian ruins.* □ *We camped that night in a secluded canyon.*
> • **gorge** a very deep *valley* with steep sides. □ *The car plummeted over the edge of the gorge and fell to the bottom.* □ *A waterfall cascaded down one side of the gorge.*
> • **gulch** a deep *valley*, especially one with a river running through it. □ *We picked our way down the sides of the gulch and waded across the river.* □ *During the summer, the gulch was dry, and no plants grew there.*
> • **ravine** a *valley* with a river running through it. □ *The nature trail led down into the ravine.* □ *George went down to the ravine to catch tadpoles.*

value (*noun*) how good, useful, or well regarded something is; how much money something can be exchanged for. □ *I consider our friendship to be of great value.* □ *The value of Helen's business is more than a million dollars.*

• **fair value** how much money something should rightfully be exchanged for. □ *I will give you fair value for anything you want to sell to me.* □ *The buyer and the seller argued about the fair value of the furniture.*

• **market value** how much money you can get for something on the market. □ *The market value of Grandma's china may not be much, but its sentimental value is enormous.* □ *Irene was able to sell the car for twice its market value.*

• **merit** how good, useful, or well regarded something is. □ *He may be a good teacher, but his merit as a friend is doubtful.* □ *Jay's artistic attempts were of little merit.*

• **quality** how good or useful something is. □ *The quality of the vegetables sold at that store is quite good.* □ *The poor quality of Kay's writing got her into trouble at work.*

• **worth** how good, useful, or well regarded someone or something is; how much money something can be exchanged for. □ *Laura has done charity work of great worth.* □ *For his old watch, Mark asked a price far above its real worth.*

van See the entry for *vehicle.*

vanish See the entry for *disappear.*

vapor See the entry for *mist.*

various See the entry for *assorted.*

varmint See the entry for *animal.*

vault See the entry for *jump.*

vaunt See the entry for *show off.*

veer See the entry for *swerve.*

vegetate See the entry for *hibernate.*

vehicle (*noun*) something that can carry people or things. □ *At rush hour, the street was choked with vehicles.* □ *It was hard to get the clumsy vehicle through the narrow streets.*

• **automobile** a *vehicle* that moves under its own power and can carry several people. (Formal.) □ *This luxury automobile is well worth the extra cost.* □ *Tom can fix any automobile ever made in the United States.*

• **car** an automobile. (Informal.) □ *Sue wished she could afford a car.* □ *Philip drove his car across the country.*

• **conveyance** any *vehicle.* (Formal.) □ *I had never ridden in a horse-drawn wagon before, but was willing to try any conveyance that would get me into town.* □ *Ken wanted an armored conveyance of some kind to take the money to the bank.*

• **truck**   a *vehicle* for carrying large quantities of things. ☐ *A truck delivered food to the cafeteria every week.* ☐ *We carried our furniture into the truck.*

• **van**   a *vehicle* for carrying people or things. ☐ *Rita rented a van to take the whole club to the forest preserve.* ☐ *The TV repairman parked his van outside the house.*

vendor   See the entry for *seller.*

veneration   See the entry for *respect¹.*

vengeance   See the entry for *revenge.*

venomous   See the entry for *poisonous.*

venture   See the entry for *dare.*

vermilion   See the entry for *red.*

versatile   See the entry for *flexible.*

verse   See the entry for *poem.*

verve   See the entry for *energy.*

very   (*adverb*) to a high degree; much. ☐ *I'm very unhappy.* ☐ *Susan did a very good job on her homework.*

• **considerably**   to a noticeable degree. ☐ *It's considerably warmer today than it was yesterday.* ☐ *Tim was considerably impressed by Jan's dancing.*

• **extremely**   to the highest possible degree. ☐ *I'm extremely eager for spring vacation to start.* ☐ *After football practice, Bill was extremely hungry.*

• **quite**   to a fairly high degree. ☐ *I'm quite comfortable, thank you.* ☐ *Anna is quite nice, once you get to know her.*

• **rather**   to a certain degree; somewhat. ☐ *Mary looks rather ill.* ☐ *I'm rather pleased at the way my sculpture turned out.*

• **really**   to a high degree; truly. ☐ *Charlie was really happy to be home.* ☐ *Are you really sure you want to do that?*

vessel   See the entries for *boat, container.*

veteran   See the entry for *experienced.*

vex   See the entry for *annoy.*

vibrate   (*verb*) to move quickly a short distance back and forth. ☐ *The violin string vibrated as the bow was drawn across it.* ☐ *You could see the bell vibrate when it was struck.*

• **pulsate**   to *vibrate* in beats or pulses. ☐ *The huge engine pulsated beneath the ship's deck.* ☐ *I heard my neighbor's stereo pulsate to the beat of the music.*

• **quake**   to *vibrate* violently. □ *Donna was quaking with fear as she entered the dentist's office.* □ *The explosion made the earth quake for miles around.*

• **quiver**   to *vibrate* slightly. □ *The kitten's whiskers quivered with curiosity.* □ *Linda's eyelids quivered, so we knew she was still alive.*

• **shiver**   to *vibrate* from cold or emotion; to shake. □ *We shivered in the cold room.* □ *The scary movie really made the audience shiver.*

• **shudder**   to *vibrate* or shake from fear or disgust. □ *Looking at insects in the zoo makes Frank shudder.* □ *Gina shuddered as she read the threatening note.*

• **tremble**   to *vibrate* from emotion. □ *The terrified child trembled in my arms.* □ *Harold's hand trembled as he aimed the gun.*

vicinity   See the entry for *area*.

vicious   See the entry for *savage*.

victim   (*noun*) a person who is hurt by someone else; a person someone picks out to hurt. □ *Sue was the victim of a robbery.* □ *The murder stalked his victim for weeks.*

• **prey**   an animal that is to be eaten by another animal; a *victim*. □ *Birds and rodents are the cat's chief prey.* □ *The spider wove a web to trap its prey.*

• **quarry**   a person or animal that is to be hunted. □ *The police knew that their quarry was headed for the abandoned building.* □ *The deer hunter moved slowly so as not to startle her quarry.*

• **target**   a person or thing that is aimed at. □ *Jenny was the target of some vicious name-calling.* □ *I aimed my gun at the target.*

vie   See the entry for *compete*.

view   (*noun*) something seen, especially from a window or a high place. (See also the entry for *see*.) □ *The fifteenth floor has a lovely view.* □ *The view out my window is my neighbor's brick wall.*

• **landscape**   a *view* of land. □ *We admired the mountain landscape.* □ *Kevin opened the curtains and saw a snowy landscape spread out around him.*

• **panorama**   a *view* that extends all the way around you. □ *From the observation deck, we could see a panorama of city lights.* □ *We stopped at a spot on the trail to enjoy the panorama of lake, forest, and hills.*

• **scenery**   an interesting *view*; what surrounds you. □ *I sat in the backseat of the car, taking in the rural scenery that we sped by.* □ *We took a trip to Arizona, and the scenery was just lovely.*

• **vista**   a *view*, especially from a high place. □ *The mountain cabin offered a spectacular vista of the entire valley.* □ *We climbed up the church tower to look at the vista from the top.*

vigilant   See the entry for *alert*.

vigorous   See the entry for *lively*.

vile   See the entry for *bad*.

vilify   See the entry for *slander*.

village   See the entry for *town*.

villain   (*noun*) someone who does evil or intends to do evil. □ *Do you think the good guy will defeat the villain?* □ *We agreed that Larry had behaved like a villain in lying to us all.*
  • **blackguard**   someone who does evil; someone with no morals. (Old-fashioned.) □ *That blackguard kissed the girl several times, yet he had no intention of marrying her!* □ *He is a blackguard who would sell his mother if he could hope to gain from it.*
  • **knave**   someone who does evil; someone who tricks people. (Old-fashioned.) □ *Sophia, not knowing Ethan for a knave, trusted him to invest her money.* □ *Too late, the townsfolk discovered that the man they had chosen for sheriff was a swindler and a knave.*
  • **malefactor**   someone who does evil; a criminal. (Formal.) □ *The police had fingerprint records of tens of thousands of malefactors.* □ *As district attorney, Mary vowed to prosecute every malefactor to the best of her ability.*
  • **rascal**   someone who plays wicked tricks. □ *Watch out for that puppy; he's a little rascal.* □ *When Nancy's dad found out about the trick she played, he called her a rascal and sent her to bed.*
  • **rogue**   someone with no morals; someone who plays tricks. □ *That rogue dared to thumb his nose at me!* □ *The salesman was a well-known rogue who would lie about anything to make a sale.*
  • **scoundrel**   someone who would dare to do any evil. □ *That scoundrel of a landlord cheats his poor tenants.* □ *Investigation showed that the mayor had been a scoundrel who used city funds for her own purposes.*

vineyard   See the entry for *farm*.

violent   (*adjective*) using unrestrained energy or strength; harmfully energetic. □ *The criminal is a violent person and should be approached with caution.* □ *We were caught out in the violent storm.*
  • **forceful**   using great force or strength. □ *Nancy gave me a forceful shove toward the door.* □ *Tom says forceful things, but never follows them up with action.*
  • **furious**   full of unrestrained energy; full of unrestrained anger. □ *My thin coat was little protection from the furious lashings of the rain.* □ *Jane's fists delivered furious blows to Ken's head.*

• **rough**   strong and unrestrained; not gentle. (See also the main entry for *rough*.) □ *Don't be so rough with him; he's only a child.* □ *The football game quickly grew rough, and the players were all left with bruises.*

violet   See the entry for *purple*.

virtuoso   See the entries for *expert, musician*.

visible   See the entry for *conspicuous*.

vision   See the entry for *illusion*.

visit   (*verb*) to spend time with someone. □ *I visit my grandparents every summer.* □ *After work, Roger visited Stanley in the hospital.*
   • **call on**   to go to someone's house to *visit*. □ *Let's call on Thomas and see if he's home.* □ *Several people called on me in the afternoon.*
   • **drop in on**   to go to *visit* someone without letting him or her know ahead of time. □ *Victor won't mind if we just drop in on him.* □ *I dropped in on Wendy on my way home.*
   • **go see**   to go to where someone is and *visit* him or her. □ *I'm going to go see my friend in New Orleans.* □ *Let's go see Art; I bet he's still up.*

visitor   (*noun*) someone who comes to spend time with you. □ *I offered my visitors some snacks.* □ *Some visitors came to the classroom to observe our class.*
   • **caller**   someone who comes to spend a brief time with you. □ *Ben gossiped with his callers for half an hour or so.* □ *Who could be at the door? I'm not expecting any callers.*
   • **company**   someone you have invited to spend time with you. (See also the main entry for *company*.) □ *Carrie was excited at the thought of having company over.* □ *Donald couldn't chat on the phone; he had company to entertain.*
   • **guest**   someone you have invited to spend time with you; someone who is staying with you for a while. □ *I am having six guests to dinner.* □ *Eddie introduced his guest to all his neighbors.*
   • **houseguest**   someone who is staying with you in your home for a while. □ *Fix up the spare room for our houseguest.* □ *Fran enjoyed being a houseguest at George's family home.*

vista   See the entry for *view*.

vital   See the entry for *necessary*.

vittles   See the entry for *food*.

vivacity   See the entry for *energy*.

vivid[1]   (*adjective*) describing things so well that it is easy to imagine them. □ Helen's letter gave a vivid account of her travels in Paraguay. □ The novel contained a vivid murder scene.

    • **explicit**   telling everything in detail. □ *Can you give a more explicit description of the person who attacked you?* □ *The explicit sex scene could not be shown on TV.*

    • **graphic**   describing everything in detail. □ *I thought the movie's graphic violence was sickening.* □ *Upton Sinclair's* The Jungle *gives graphic descriptions of what goes on in a sausage factory.*

    • **striking**   capturing your attention by showing interesting details. (See also the main entry for *striking*.) □ *The poet used very striking language to depict the old house.* □ *Irene's story was so striking that I was convinced she was telling the truth.*

vivid[2]   (*adjective*) intense, lively, and full of color. □ *His hair was a vivid red.* □ *Jay wore a vivid blue shirt.*

    • **bold**   intense; standing out. □ *The painter used very bold colors.* □ *The bold yellow letters on the blue background really got my attention.*

    • **bright**   brilliant and intense. (See also the main entry for *bright*.) □ *Bright green leaves began to come out on the trees.* □ *Kay wanted a bright color for the living room walls.*

    • **colorful**   lively; full of color. □ *Laura leafed through the colorful picture book.* □ *Mark's album was filled with colorful stamps.*

vocation   See the entry for *profession*.

void   See the entry for *empty*[1].

volatile   See the entry for *impetuous*.

volcano   See the entry for *mountain*.

volume   See the entry for *book*.

vow   See the entry for *promise*.

voyage   See the entry for *journey*.

vulgar   See the entry for *rude*.

W

waft   See the entry for *float*.

wage   See the entry for *pay*.

wail   See the entry for *scream*.

wait   (*verb*) to let time pass before something happens. □ *Wait here until I get back.* □ *Tom waited for fifteen minutes before deciding that the bus wasn't going to come.*

  • **delay**   to let time pass before you do something. (See also the main entry for *delay*.) □ *The pilot agreed to delay takeoff until the missing passenger arrived.* □ *Don't delay—send in your entry form now!*
  • **hesitate**   to let time pass before you do something, because you are not sure about doing it. □ *Sue hesitated on the curb, afraid to cross the busy street.* □ *I hesitate to wake Philip; I know he needs the rest.*
  • **linger**   to let time pass; to stay somewhere for a while before moving on. □ *Rita lingered outside with her sweetheart, not wanting to go in the house.* □ *Susan's gaze lingered on the book she wanted so badly.*
  • **pause**   to let time pass without doing anything. □ *The actors paused to let the audience's laughter die down.* □ *Tim said, "I have something to tell you," and then paused.*
  [→see also: *dawdle, delay*]

walk   (*verb*) to move along, taking one step after another. □ *Jan walked down the hallway.* □ *Bill's house isn't very far; we can walk there.*

  • **amble**   to *walk* slowly and easily. □ *The friends ambled through the park, chatting.* □ *My horse ambled slowly along.*
  • **march**   to *walk* rhythmically, taking measured steps. □ *The soldiers marched across the parade ground.* □ *The band marched in the Labor Day parade.*

• **plod**   to *walk* heavily and wearily. □ *Anna plodded home, not wanting to face her parents.* □ *The cows plodded along the trail.*

• **saunter**   to *walk* around aimlessly. □ *Mary sauntered into the classroom, ten minutes late.* □ *I sauntered down the street, looking at all the shop windows I passed.*

• **stroll**   to *walk* slowly, for pleasure. □ *We strolled along hand in hand.* □ *Charlie strolled through the mall, not really shopping for anything.*

• **tread**   to *walk*, with emphasis on putting your feet down. □ *Donna had trodden that path so many times that she could follow it in her sleep.* □ *My upstairs neighbor was treading heavily back and forth.*

• **trudge**   to *walk* wearily but steadily. □ *The hikers trudged back to camp.* □ *We trudged three miles to the library.*
[→see also: *run*]

walk of life   See the entry for *profession*.

walk out on   See the entry for *abandon*.

wallow   (*verb*) to roll around in something wet or sticky. □ *The pig wallowed in the mud.* □ *Linda wallowed in self-pity.*

• **flounder**   to thrash around helplessly in something wet. □ *I floundered in the swimming pool.* □ *The speaker floundered, trying to remember what she was supposed to say.*

• **slosh**   to splash through something wet; to make something wet splash around. □ *We sloshed down the rainy sidewalk.* □ *The dirty water sloshed in the bucket.*

• **welter**   to roll around in something wet and unpleasant. (Old-fashioned.) □ *His ankle sprained, the helpless traveler weltered in the mire of the muddy road.* □ *Frank weltered in a flood of nasty rumors.*

wan   See the entry for *haggard*.

wander   (*verb*) to travel around with no particular destination. □ *We wandered through the downtown, enjoying the sights.* □ *The butterfly wandered from flower to flower.*

• **meander**   to travel first this way and then that. □ *We gradually meandered through Ohio, stopping anyplace that looked interesting.* □ *The little brook meandered through the valley.*

• **ramble**   to travel around without stopping; to travel where you please. □ *The hobo rambled from place to place.* □ *Gina intended to ramble her whole life, never settling down.*

• **roam**   to travel a great distance. □ *Harold roamed across the state in search of a good job.* □ *Sue roamed around the world on her summer vacation.*

• **rove** to travel around with no particular destination; to travel a great distance. (Poetic.) □ *The jolly band of brigands roved from town to town.* □ *Our hero roved for many miles before he saw a human habitation.*

wane See the entry for *decrease.*

want (*verb*) to feel that you need something; to feel that you would like to have or do something. □ *I want something to eat.* □ *Jenny wants to go to the movies.*
   • **covet** to *want* something someone else has. □ *I covet Kevin's stamp collection.* □ *Larry knew that his friends coveted his sports car.*
   • **crave** to *want* something desperately, especially food. □ *I woke up in the middle of the night, craving a spinach salad.* □ *Mary craved wealth so much that she would betray her friends for it.*
   • **desire** to *want* something deeply. (Formal.) □ *The young singer desperately desired fame.* □ *The reporter wrote to the mayor to say that he desired an interview.*
   • **wish for** to *want* something or hope that you will get it; to say that you *want* something. □ *Nancy wished for her parents to stop fighting.* □ *Tom would give his daughter anything she wished for.*

warm See the entries for *friendly, hot.*

warn (*verb*) to tell of danger ahead. □ *The sign warned that the road was slippery when wet.* □ *I'm warning you; don't cross me again!*
   • **alert** to make someone aware of danger ahead. (See also the main entry for *alert.*) □ *The radio alerted its listeners that a tornado was on the way.* □ *Jane called to alert me that the detective was looking for me.*
   • **caution** to tell someone to be careful of danger ahead. □ *The weather reports caution everyone not to travel unless it is absolutely necessary.* □ *Ken cautioned me to guard against pickpockets in the outdoor market.*
   • **tip off** to tell someone of danger secretly. (Slang.) □ *When the police got to the criminal's hideout, he was gone; someone must have tipped him off.* □ *My sister tipped me off that Dad was in a bad mood.*

warp See the entry for *distort.*

wary See the entry for *alert.*

wash See the entry for *clean².*

waste (*verb*) to use something up for no good purpose. (See also the entries for *trash, wilderness.*) □ *We don't have much glue left, so don't waste any.* □ *Our trip to the store was wasted; it was closed when we got there.*

• **dissipate**   to *waste* something completely; to scatter something wastefully. □ *Roger dissipated his inheritance within a year of receiving it.* □ *Stanley tried not to dissipate his energy by thrashing around in the water while he waited for a boat to come by and rescue him.*

• **fritter away**   to *waste* something gradually, a little at a time. (Folksy.) □ *Thomas could fritter away hours at a time just gossiping with the neighbors.* □ *Haven't you got something better to do with your money than fritter it away on video games?*

• **squander**   to *waste* something stupidly. (Formal.) □ *Victor squandered his wealth at the gambling table.* □ *The farmer squandered the richness of his soil, never putting back any of the nutrients that the crops took out.*

waste away   See the entry for *wither*.

wasted   See the entries for *haggard, spent*.

wasteland   See the entry for *wilderness*.

watch   (*verb*) to pay attention to something; to look at something and pay attention to it. □ *I watched an interesting TV show last night.* □ *Watch how Wendy holds the bat, and try to imitate her.*

• **attend**   to pay attention to something. (Formal. Usually with *to*.) □ *Art attended to the instructions so that he would know how to perform the experiment.* □ *Ben never attends to a word I say.*

• **observe**   to pay close, careful attention to something. □ *Carrie observed the birds as they built a nest on her windowsill.* □ *By observing the way Donald walks, I can tell he had a bad day at school.*

• **regard**   to look at something with attention. (Formal.) □ *Eddie regarded the picture curiously.* □ *The principal regarded me in silence.*

• **witness**   to pay attention to a promise; to be prepared to say that you have seen or heard something; to see a crime happening. □ *I called on my friends to witness my vow of revenge.* □ *Did anyone witness the murder?*

[→see also: *see*]

watered-down   See the entry for *watery*.

watery   (*adjective*)   having the same consistency as water. (See also the entry for *liquid*.) □ *The punch is too watery; add some more juice.* □ *A watery fluid flowed from the animal's wound.*

• **diluted**   *watery;* having water added. □ *The chemist used diluted acid in the experiment.* □ *The tea that Fran served the children was highly diluted.*

• **thin**   *watery;* not thick or viscous. (See also the main entry for *thin*.) □ *We added water to the paint until it was thin enough to use.* □ *With the few vegetables she could afford, the poor woman made a thin soup.*

• **watered-down** *watery;* having extra water added; made less strong. ☐ *The watered-down soda pop at the restaurant tasted terrible.* ☐ *George told a watered-down version of the story to his grandmother.*
• **weak** *watery;* not strong or flavorful. ☐ *This is a weak cup of coffee.* ☐ *We made a weak solution of salt water.*
[→consider also: *runny*]

wave (*noun*) a curve in the surface of a moving liquid, especially the water in a lake or ocean. (See also the entries for *flap, signal.*) ☐ *The boat scudded across the waves.* ☐ *We jumped up and down in the swimming pool until we made waves.*

• **billow** a large ocean *wave.* ☐ *Helen loved to watch the billows from the deck, but it only made me seasick.* ☐ *The sun glittered on the billows.*
• **breaker** a *wave* that hits the shore. ☐ *The children played on the beach, letting the breakers chase them up the sand.* ☐ *The breakers grew bigger as the wind increased.*
• **ripple** a small, gentle *wave.* ☐ *Irene tossed a stone into the pond and watched the ripples spread.* ☐ *I could see ripples in the old pane of glass.*

waver (*verb*) to sway back and forth; to hesitate, trying to make up your mind. ☐ *Jay wavered between the leather jacket and the satin one.* ☐ *At a time when a firm decision was needed, the president wavered.*

• **dilly-dally** to hesitate, trying to make up your mind. (Informal.) ☐ *Kay spends too much time dilly-dallying whenever she goes to the store.* ☐ *Laura dilly-dallied over whether or not to go to the party.*
• **teeter** to sway back and forth; to go back and forth, trying to make up your mind. ☐ *Mary teetered in on her new high heels.* ☐ *Tom teetered between loyalty to his friends and doing what he knew in his heart was right.*
• **vacillate** to hesitate, trying to make up your mind; to not be sure about something. ☐ *Sue vacillated, not wanting to risk the money, and yet not wanting to pass up a chance to earn more.* ☐ *The waiter smiled calmly while the customer vacillated about what to order.*

wax See the entries for *expand, polish.*

way (*noun*) a set of steps for doing something; a particular style of doing something. ☐ *Philip taught me an easier way to make spaghetti sauce.* ☐ *Ken has a special way of tying his shoes.*

• **means** a *way* to accomplish something; anything you have to do to accomplish something. ☐ *The candidate was willing to use any means to get elected.* ☐ *The millionaire had acquired his fortune through dishonest means.*
• **method** a careful or practiced *way* to do something. ☐ *The piano teacher has a favorite method of teaching his students to read music.* ☐ *Rita followed the method shown in the book for testing the boiling candy syrup.*

• **procedure** a specific set of steps for doing something; an official or established *way* of doing something. □ *The chemistry teacher showed us the procedure we must follow in the experiment.* □ *The librarian checked in the books according to the proper procedure.*

• **technique** a *way* of doing something skillfully. □ *I admire Susan's bread-baking technique.* □ *Do you have a special technique for getting that cranky old radio to work?*

weak (*adjective*) having little strength or energy. (See also the entry for *watery*.) □ *Tim's illness left him very weak.* □ *I'm too weak to lift this.*

• **feeble** very *weak;* not vigorous. □ *It took every ounce of Jan's feeble strength to get up the stairs.* □ *Bill answered with a feeble "Yes."*

• **frail** *weak;* easy to break or damage. □ *The old man was very frail and could be badly hurt if he fell down.* □ *The frail twig snapped easily.*

• **powerless** *weak;* without power. □ *Mary had been an athlete, but the accident made her once strong legs powerless.* □ *Anna felt powerless because she was not old enough to vote.*

weaken (*verb*) to take the strength or energy away from someone or something; to make someone or something weak. □ *Charlie's illness weakened him.* □ *Donna's determination to be on the soccer team weakened when she found out how much work it would require.*

• **debilitate** to *weaken* someone or something so much that it cannot function well. (Formal.) □ *The fever debilitated me completely for several days.* □ *Shyness debilitates Linda; meeting people scares her nearly to death.*

• **incapacitate** to *weaken* someone or something so much that it cannot function at all; to make someone or something unable to function. □ *The accident incapacitated Frank until he recovered enough to get around on crutches.* □ *Blindness did not incapacitate Gina; she simply had to learn new ways of doing things.*

• **sap** to *weaken* someone or something gradually; to drain the strength away from someone or something. □ *Long hours of rehearsal sapped my enthusiasm for the play.* □ *Hunger seriously sapped the hiker's strength.*

• **undermine** to *weaken* someone or something secretly or without being noticed. □ *Working such late hours will undermine Harold's health.* □ *Sue's teasing undermined my self-confidence.*

wealthy See the entry for *rich*.

wear (*verb*) to have a piece of clothing on your body. □ *Jenny is wearing a yellow sweater.* □ *Kevin usually wears a suit to work.*

• **be attired in** to *wear* something special. (Formal.) □ *The bride was attired in white satin with seed-pearl trim.* □ *The little boy was attired only in his birthday suit as he dashed through the living room.*

• **be clothed in** to *wear* something. (Poetic.) □ *The lady was clothed in crimson velvet.* □ *Our hero was clothed in his finest raiment.*

• **have on**   to *wear* something. (Informal.) □ *I really like that tie that Larry has on.* □ *I don't want to walk across the mud; I have on my good shoes.*

• **sport**   to *wear* something proudly; to *wear* something that attracts attention. □ *Mary sported a big orange flower in her buttonhole.* □ *Nancy sported a jacket emblazoned with the name of her favorite basketball team.*

wear away   (*verb*) to take away a part of something a little at a time; to grind at something gradually over a long time. □ *Over the years, the feet of thousands of children wore away a spot in the middle of the steps leading up to the school.* □ *The river gently wore away the rock on its banks.*

• **corrode**   to *wear away* at something, especially with a chemical. (Formal.) □ *Don't leave your bicycle out in the salty air; rust will corrode it.* □ *Smog corroded the finish on Tom's car.*

• **eat away**   to *wear* something *away*, especially with a chemical. □ *The acid ate away a piece of the linoleum floor.* □ *Dry rot was eating away the wooden beams.*

• **erode**   to *wear* something *away*, especially with flowing water; to destroy something gradually. □ *The rich topsoil is eroding away.* □ *Jane's constant doubting eroded my feeling of certainty.*

weary   See the entry for *tired*.

wed   See the entry for *marry*.

wee   See the entry for *small*.

weep   See the entry for *cry*.

weird   See the entry for *peculiar*.

weirdo   See the entry for *character*.

welcome   See the entry for *greet*.

well   See the entry for *healthy*.

well-bred   See the entry for *aristocratic*.

well-heeled   See the entry for *rich*.

well-known   See the entry for *famous*.

well-liked   See the entry for *popular*.

well-mannered   See the entry for *polite*.

welter   See the entry for *wallow*.

wet   (*adjective*) having absorbed a lot of water. □ *The laundry got wet because it was left out in the rain.* □ *Coming out of the shower, Ken left wet footprints on the bathmat.*

• **damp**   slightly *wet.* □ *I wiped the table with a damp rag.* □ *Roger's skin was cold and damp.*

• **moist**   very *wet;* full of moisture. □ *The ground is nice and moist; plants should grow well here.* □ *The cake was tasty and moist.*

• **saturated**   completely *wet;* having absorbed as much water or fluid as possible. (Formal.) □ *Stanley carefully carried the saturated sponge to the sink to wring it out.* □ *My shoes are completely saturated from walking through the slush.*

• **soaked**   thoroughly *wet.* □ *The kids came in completely soaked from the water-pistol fight.* □ *Come in out of the rain; you're soaked!*

• **soggy**   too *wet;* unpleasantly *wet.* (Informal.) □ *My lunch fell in a puddle, and my sandwich is all soggy.* □ *The weather was soggy all week.*

• **sopping**   very *wet;* dripping with water. (Informal.) □ *Thomas's friends threw him in the swimming pool, and he came out sopping.* □ *Victor toweled off his sopping hair.*

[→contrasting word: *dry*]

wetlands   See the entry for *swamp.*

wharf   See the entry for *dock.*

wheedle   See the entry for *persuade.*

wheeze   See the entry for *gasp.*

whiff   See the entry for *smell.*

whim   (*noun*) a sudden desire to do something for no particular reason. □ *On a whim, Wendy painted her room purple.* □ *I want to be sure that Art's desire to become a doctor is not just a passing whim.*

• **caprice**   a playful desire to do something for no particular reason. □ *Everyone in the family tried to satisfy the youngest child's every caprice.* □ *Some strange caprice moved Ben to shave his head.*

• **impulse**   a sudden, strong desire to do something. □ *I felt an impulse to bring my mother some flowers.* □ *What impulse caused Carrie to give away all her toys?*

• **vagary**   something done for no particular reason; an unpredictable action. (Formal.) □ *The students feared the vagaries of the cruel teacher.* □ *The singer did very well at first, but then became a victim of the vagaries of popularity.*

whimper   See the entry for *cry.*

whip   (*verb*) to hit someone or something with a whip; to hit someone or something with any long, flexible object like a whip. □ *The rider whipped his horse to make it go faster.* □ *The cruel woman whipped her servants if they misbehaved.*

• **lash**   to *whip;* to tie someone or something down tightly. (Old-fashioned.) □ *The freezing rain lashed against my face.* □ *They lashed the prisoner to a chair.*

• **flog**   to *whip* someone very hard; to *whip* someone over and over. □ *In former times, criminals could be flogged.* □ *The slave begged the overseer not to flog her.*

• **scourge**   to *whip* someone severely. (Formal.) □ *The jailer scourged the prisoner until he bled.* □ *The ice storm scourged the county.*

• **thrash**   to *whip* or beat someone energetically and repeatedly. (Folksy.) □ *Do as your mother says, or I'll thrash you within an inch of your life.* □ *The boxer thrashed his opponent soundly.*

whir   See the entry for *hum.*

whirl   See the entry for *turn.*

whisper   See the entry for *sigh.*

whit   (*noun*) a very tiny thing or amount. □ *Go or don't go; it doesn't matter to me one whit.* □ *Donald showed not a whit of interest in the game.*

• **atom**   the tiniest possible thing or amount. □ *The patient teacher never showed an atom of irritation with his students.* □ *We learned that all matter is made up of atoms.*

• **iota**   a very tiny thing. □ *Eddie is not willing to change his plans one iota.* □ *When Fran received the shocking news, her expression did not change an iota.*

• **jot**   a very tiny thing. (Informal.) □ *It would help if I got a jot of cooperation from you.* □ *It doesn't matter a jot if George is mad at us.*

• **particle**   a tiny thing; a tiny bit. □ *I don't care if Helen's upset, not a particle.* □ *The water that came out of the tap contained tiny particles of rust.*

• **smidgen**   a tiny amount. (Informal.) □ *I'll have just a smidgen of chocolate sauce on my ice cream, thank you.* □ *Jay dabbed a smidgen of oil onto the bicycle chain.*

whittle   See the entry for *carve.*

whiz   See the entry for *speed.*

whole   (*adjective*) including every part. □ *I read only the first chapter, but Kay read the whole book.* □ *This picture doesn't show the whole painting, just a small part of it.*

• **complete**   including every part; including everything. □ *Laura has a complete set of socket wrenches.* □ *As soon as the builders put the roof on, the house will be complete.*

• **entire**   including every part; with nothing taken away. □ *The party-goers ate an entire gallon of ice cream.* □ *It took Mark an entire year to save enough money for a new TV.*

• **total** *complete;* including everything all added together; the sum of things added together. □ *The total number of students at this school is eight hundred.* □ *Please give me your total attention.*

wholehearted See the entry for *dedicated.*

wicked See the entry for *evil.*

wide (*adjective*) measuring a great deal from side to side. □ *Tom has a wide mouth.* □ *The river is quite wide at that point.*
  • **broad** measuring a great deal from side to side; extending far across. □ *The sidewalk was broad enough for three people to walk shoulder to shoulder.* □ *Grandpa had big, broad hands.*
  • **expansive** extremely far across; covering a great area. □ *The sailors traveled across the expansive ocean.* □ *The family farmed an expansive area of land.*
  • **extensive** reaching over a great area. □ *The forests were once extensive, but have mostly been cut down.* □ *Sue has extensive knowledge of the Russian tsars.*

wide-awake See the entry for *alert.*

wiggle See the entries for *shake, squirm.*

wilderness (*noun*) a place where everything is wild; a place where people have not settled. □ *We hiked through the wilderness, searching for a town, or at least a house.* □ *The whole area is a swampy wilderness.*
  • **badland** a harsh *wilderness;* a place that is too harsh for people to settle. (Informal. Sometimes used in the plural.) □ *The wagon train was lucky to come through the badland alive.* □ *The outlaw fled to the badlands, where no sheriff would dare to follow.*
  • **desert** a *wilderness,* especially one where there is no water. □ *The travelers feared dying of thirst in the desert.* □ *We drove through the desert, admiring the grim beauty of the rocks.*
  • **no-man's-land** a dangerous *wilderness;* a barren, dangerous place. □ *After dark, the neighborhood became a no-man's-land, silent except for gunshots and sirens.* □ *Philip wants to go to Antarctica. Why would anyone choose to visit such a no-man's-land?*
  • **waste** a barren *wilderness;* a broad, barren place. (See also the main entry for *waste.*) □ *The ship was all alone on the blue ocean waste.* □ *The enemy's bombardment left the city a rubble-filled waste.*
  • **wasteland** a completely barren place. □ *The drought turned the farm into a wasteland.* □ *Newton Minow called television a "vast wasteland."*

willing See the entry for *eager.*

wily See the entry for *sneaky.*

win (*verb*) to defeat an opponent or opponents. □ *Our team won the game.* □ *Ken won the hundred-yard dash.*

• **be victorious**   to *win*; to achieve a victory. □ *The team lost a few points early on, but in the end they were victorious.* □ *We felt proud when the U.S. Olympic hockey team was victorious.*

• **prevail**   to *win* because you are better or stronger. □ *The wrestler's friends had faith that he would prevail.* □ *Rita considered spending all her money on lottery tickets, but her good sense prevailed.*

• **succeed**   to *win*; to do what you set out to do. □ *The comedian succeeded in getting the audience to laugh.* □ *Susan wanted to succeed in her new job.*

• **triumph**   to *win* gloriously. □ *The Allies finally triumphed, and World War II came to a close.* □ *After a long, hard game, the home team triumphed.*

[→see also: *beat²*]

win over   See the entry for *recruit*.

wince (*verb*) to draw back when something hurts you. □ *I winced when the nurse gave me the injection.* □ *Tim winced as the hot water touched the cut on his arm.*

• **cower**   to hide or draw back, fearing that something will hurt you. □ *The father raised his hand, and his children cowered.* □ *The dog cowered in the closet, knowing she had done something wrong.*

• **cringe**   to draw back, fearing that something will hurt you; to draw back when something hurts or embarrasses you. □ *My brother's rude behavior made me cringe.* □ *Hearing the off-key singer, the musician cringed.*

• **flinch**   to jerk away from something that might hurt you; to jerk away when something hurts you. □ *Jan flinched when Bill made a move to slap her.* □ *Just thinking about the dentist's office makes me flinch.*

• **quail**   to draw back from something that might hurt you; to be fearful. □ *Mom's angry shouting made us quail.* □ *Our hero never quailed, but strode boldly into the dragon's cave.*

wind¹ (*noun*) a moving stream of air. □ *The leaves tossed in the wind.* □ *The storm brought high winds and freezing rain.*

• **breeze**   a light *wind.* □ *A cool breeze relieved the heat of the summer day.* □ *We felt a pleasant breeze coming off the lake.*

• **draft**   a *wind* coming into a room or building. □ *I stuffed rags in the crack under the door to stop the draft.* □ *We shut all the windows, but still felt a draft.*

• **gale**   a violent, strong *wind.* □ *My umbrella blew away in the gale.* □ *The gale created waves ten feet high.*

• **gust** a sudden strong *wind*. □ *A gust of wind blew the hat right off my head.* □ *A warm gust of air blew out of the furnace.*

wind² (*verb*) to turn something around and around; to wrap something around and around something else. □ *I wound the yarn into a ball.* □ *The opossum wound her tail around the tree branch.*
   • **coil** to *wind* something in circles; to *wind* something into a cylinder. □ *Anna coiled up the garden hose.* □ *The snake coiled around my arm.*
   • **curl** to *wind* something into a round shape; to give something a curved shape. □ *The cat curled her tail around her feet.* □ *Mary curled her hair with a curling iron.*
   • **loop** to *wind* something so that it hangs loosely. □ *I looped the dog's leash over the chair.* □ *Charlie looped the electrical cord around his shoulder.*
   • **twine** to *wind* something tightly around something else. □ *The vine twined itself around the tree.* □ *The princess twined a gold chain into her hair.*
   • **twist** to *wind* something into a spiral; to bend something so that it is no longer straight. □ *Donna nervously twisted the string around her finger.* □ *Linda twisted her body to look behind her.*

windup See the entry for *end*.

wipe (*verb*) to clean or remove something by rubbing. □ *I wiped the spilled soda pop off the floor.* □ *Frank wiped his face with his handkerchief.*
   • **dab** to clean or remove something by giving it little pats; to put something on a surface with little pats. □ *Mom dabbed at my face with a wet rag.* □ *Gina dabbed paint onto the canvas.*
   • **mop** to clean or remove something by pressing something absorbent on it; to use a mop. □ *The weeping woman mopped her streaming eyes.* □ *Will you mop the kitchen floor?*
   • **sponge** to clean or remove something by using something absorbent, like a sponge. □ *I sponged the tabletop clean.* □ *Harold sponged the water off the chair cushions.*
   • **swab** to clean or remove something by rubbing at it with something absorbent. □ *Sue swabbed out the bathroom sink.* □ *Jenny swabbed the basement's concrete floor.*

wise (*adjective*) having a lot of knowledge about the world; understanding the way things are. □ *Whenever Kevin had a problem, he asked his wise grandfather for advice.* □ *Larry is smart, but he's not very wise.*
   • **astute** having a lot of knowledge and being able to reason about things. (Formal.) □ *Mary is a pretty astute judge of whether someone is telling the truth.* □ *The detective's astute thinking was very much admired.*

• **canny**   very clever and understanding of the way things are. (Folksy.) ☐ *The canny child knew that his grandparents would let him do things his parents wouldn't.* ☐ *The students could not outwit the canny teacher.*

• **shrewd**   knowing a lot; able to figure things out quickly. ☐ *Nancy, who is quite shrewd, knew that Tom was in love with Jane before either of them knew it.* ☐ *Roger made a shrewd observation about his sister.* [→see also: *smart*]

wish   See the entry for *hope*.

wish for   See the entry for *want*.

witch   (*noun*) a woman who practices some form of magic. ☐ *The old lady was accused of being a witch.* ☐ *The witch cast a spell over the whole castle.*

• **magician**   a person who practices magic; a person who can perform tricks that look like magic. ☐ *The magician made a goldfish bowl disappear.* ☐ *A magician entertained people at Stanley's birthday party.*

• **sorcerer**   someone who practices magic; someone who can control evil spirits. ☐ *Our hero asked the sorcerer to give him a magic sword.* ☐ *The sorcerer drew strange symbols on the floor.*

• **wizard**   someone, often a man, who has magic powers. ☐ *The wizard made lightning strike the cottage.* ☐ *The quiet-looking man was in fact a powerful wizard.*

withdraw   See the entries for *resign, take back*.

wither   (*verb*) to shrink down; to get smaller and drier. ☐ *The bouquet of flowers withered overnight.* ☐ *The grass withered in the extreme heat.*

• **dry out**   to *wither*; to lose moisture. ☐ *Cover the bread tightly, or it will dry out.* ☐ *The muddy front yard gradually dried out over the next several sunny days.*

• **shrivel**   to *wither* up; to become wrinkled. ☐ *Left out in the sun, the fruit quickly shriveled.* ☐ *The heat inside the oven made the mushrooms shrivel up.*

• **waste away**   to *wither* gradually; to get weaker and weaker or thinner and thinner. ☐ *The sick man seemed to waste away.* ☐ *If you don't eat something, you'll waste away!*

withhold   See the entry for *reserve*.

without interest   See the entry for *unbiased*.

withstand   See the entry for *bear*.

witness   See the entries for *observer, watch*.

wits See the entry for *mind.*

witticism See the entry for *joke.*

witty See the entry for *funny.*

wizard See the entry for *witch.*

wobble See the entry for *rock³.*

woman (*noun*) an adult female human being. ☐ *My aunt is a very interesting woman.* ☐ *Victor married a nice woman.*
- **female** any female creature. ☐ *We need to separate the male gerbils from the females.* ☐ *Is that horse a male or a female?*
- **girl** a young female human being. ☐ *Wendy's mother looked a lot like Wendy when she was a girl.* ☐ *When Anna was just a girl, she decided she would be a veterinarian.*
- **lady** an adult female human being; an adult female human being with good manners. (A polite term.) ☐ *Please ask the lady if she knows what time it is.* ☐ *Mary was taught to act like a lady at all times.*

wonder¹ (*noun*) something unusual that makes you feel awe. ☐ *The Southwest is filled with scenic wonders.* ☐ *The book described the Seven Wonders of the World.*
- **marvel** something that makes you feel deep awe. ☐ *The little boy's expert violin playing was quite a marvel.* ☐ *The magician performed many marvels.*
- **miracle** something awesome that cannot have happened in any ordinary way. ☐ *Carrie's recovery from cancer was a miracle.* ☐ *The little girl ran out onto the highway, and it was a miracle she wasn't hit.*
- **phenomenon** something very unusual. (Formal.) ☐ *The school's transformation into a clean, quiet place of learning was a phenomenon.* ☐ *When I was up north, I observed the phenomenon of the northern lights.*
- **prodigy** something wonderful and unusual; something unlike anything ever seen before. (Formal.) ☐ *The carnival freak show included such prodigies as a bearded lady and a two-headed calf.* ☐ *The young genius was hailed as a prodigy.*
- **sensation** something that makes everyone feel surprise or awe; something that suddenly attracts everyone's interest. ☐ *The movie star's divorce caused quite a sensation.* ☐ *For biblical scholars, the discovery of the Dead Sea Scrolls was a sensation.*

wonder² (*verb*) to imagine how something might be; to debate in your mind whether something is really true. ☐ *Donald wondered about life on other planets.* ☐ *Eddie wondered if Fran was angry at him.*
- **conjecture** to debate whether something is really true. ☐ *The newspaper article conjectured about the solution to the mystery.* ☐ *George conjectures that the construction next door might be an apartment building.*

• **ponder**   to debate something in your mind; to think deeply about something. ☐ *Kay pondered what she had read.* ☐ *Laura lay awake half the night, pondering what she should do.*
[→see also: *think*]
• **ruminate**   to think about something over and over, trying to decide what it means. ☐ *I ruminated about the things I had overheard.* ☐ *Helen sat, chin in hand, quietly ruminating.*
• **speculate**   to imagine how something might be. ☐ *Irene speculated about what she would do after graduating from high school.* ☐ *Jay speculated about the source of the strange noise.*

wonderful   See the entry for *incredible.*

woods   See the entry for *forest.*

wool-gather   See the entry for *dream.*

woolly   See the entry for *fluffy.*

woozy   See the entry for *groggy.*

work at   See the entry for *practice.*

working   See the entry for *busy¹.*

workout   See the entry for *exercise.*

world   (*noun*) the earth; a particular domain, such as the *world* of sports; a body that revolves around a star. ☐ *Mark has traveled around the world.* ☐ *Tom's family is almost his whole world.*
• **globe**   a formal word for the earth; a sphere-shaped map of the earth; any sphere. ☐ *I found Indonesia on the classroom globe.* ☐ *The vegetable stand was heaped with fragrant globes of cantaloupe.*
• **heavenly body**   a sun, moon, star, or planet; any natural object in the sky that reflects or gives off light. ☐ *Sue studied the heavenly bodies through a telescope.* ☐ *The moon is the brightest heavenly body in the night sky.*
• **planet**   a body that revolves around a star. ☐ *There are nine planets revolving around the sun.* ☐ *The satellite orbited Venus and sent back pictures of that planet.*
• **terrestrial sphere**   the earth. (Poetic.) ☐ *Surely the platypus is the strangest creature in the whole terrestrial sphere.* ☐ *Our hero would never again see his love in this terrestrial sphere.*

worn   See the entry for *shabby.*

worn out   See the entry for *tired.*

worry   (*verb*) to think a great deal about a problem or about something that might happen. ☐ *When Philip was late getting home, I began to worry.* ☐ *Ken is always worrying about his grades.*

• **agonize**   to torture yourself by *worrying;* to feel anguish. ☐ *I wish Rita would quit agonizing about her looks.* ☐ *Susan agonized over whether or not to write to Tim.*

• **be anxious**   to *worry* about something that might happen. ☐ *Jan was anxious, waiting for news from home.* ☐ *There's no need to be anxious; I can take care of myself.*

• **brood**   to *worry* seriously; to *worry* over a long period of time. ☐ *Bill brooded over what the teacher had said.* ☐ *Art was a melancholy boy, always brooding about something.*

• **fret**   to *worry;* to feel irritated. ☐ *The spoiled child began to fret when her parents didn't give her the toy right away.* ☐ *First Susan agonized about writing to Tim, then she fretted about whether or not the letter had reached him.*

• **stew**   to feel upset; to *worry* intensely. (Informal.) ☐ *Ben's insult made me stew for days.* ☐ *Charlie is stewing because he wasn't invited to the party.*

worth   See the entry for *value.*

wound   See the entry for *hurt¹.*

wraithlike   See the entry for *ghostly.*

wrangle   See the entry for *argue².*

wrap   See the entry for *cover.*

wreathe   See the entry for *drape.*

wreck   See the entry for *destroy.*

wrestle   See the entry for *struggle.*

wretched   See the entry for *bad.*

wriggle   See the entry for *squirm.*

wrinkle   See the entry for *crease.*

write   (*verb*) to put words down on paper; to compose something, such as a story or a letter, on paper or a computer. ☐ *Donna wrote her name at the top of the page.* ☐ *Linda wrote an interesting story.*

• **inscribe**   to carefully *write* something on a surface; to carve writing into a surface. ☐ *Gina inscribed a line of poetry on the book she gave to Howard.* ☐ *Frank inscribed his initials on a signet ring.*

• **jot**   to *write* something quickly or hastily. ☐ *I jotted a few notes on a piece of scrap paper.* ☐ *Sue jotted down Kevin's address.*

• **record**   to *write* something so that it will be preserved. ☐ *Births and deaths were recorded in the family Bible.* ☐ *Larry recorded his thoughts in a diary.*

• **print**   to *write* carefully and clearly; to *write* in letters that look like typed letters. □ *Nancy printed the book's title on a slip of paper.* □ *Mary can print, but she can't write in cursive.*

• **scrawl**   to *write* hastily and clumsily. □ *I just had time to scrawl a note to my dad.* □ *Tom scrawled "Help!" on a piece of paper and tossed it out the window.*

• **scribble**   to *write* hastily and illegibly. □ *I can't read what Jane scribbled on the chalkboard.* □ *Ken scribbled down the numbers and quickly added them up.*

writer   (*noun*) someone who composes things on paper. □ *Roger is the best writer in my English class.* □ *Stanley wants to be a magazine writer.*

• **author**   a recognized or well-known *writer*. □ *Washington Irving was an early American author.* □ *Who is the author of* Pride and Prejudice?

• **dramatist**   a *writer* of scripts for plays or movies. □ *Lope de Vega was a seventeenth-century Spanish dramatist.* □ *The dramatist won an Academy Award for the movie script.*

• **journalist**   a *writer* of articles for newspapers or magazines. □ *The journalist wanted an interview with the mayor.* □ *Walter Lippmann was a respected journalist.*

• **novelist**   a *writer* who writes books of fiction. □ *Margaret Atwood is a novelist who also writes poetry.* □ *Everyone wanted to check the novelist's new book out of the library.*

• **playwright**   a *writer* of plays for the stage. □ *Saint Joan was written by George Bernard Shaw, the Irish playwright.* □ *Many playwrights started out as actors.*

• **poet**   a *writer* of poems. □ *Emily Dickinson is Dad's favorite poet.* □ *Because the baby was good at finding rhyming words, his parents thought he would be a poet when he grew up.*

writhe   See the entry for *squirm.*

wrought up   See the entry for *excited.*

XYZ

yacht See the entry for *boat*.

yank See the entry for *tug*.

yard (*noun*) an open area of land around a house. □ *The dog played out in the yard.* □ *Thomas put a fence around his yard.*
   • **common** an open area of land in the middle of town, where people can gather. □ *I met my neighbor strolling across the common.* □ *The market is held on the common every Saturday.*
   • **green** an open area of ground with grass growing on it. (Formal.) □ *The children frolicked on the village green.* □ *An ancient oak tree shaded the green.*
   • **lawn** an open area of ground with well-kept grass growing on it. □ *Victor mowed the lawn.* □ *The house was surrounded by a beautiful, smooth lawn.*
   [→see also: *field*]

yarn See the entry for *story*.

yearn for See the entry for *miss²*.

yell (*verb*) to make a loud sound with your voice; to call something out loudly. (Informal.) □ *"Look out!" I yelled.* □ *Why is Mom yelling at me so much today?*
   • **bellow** to *yell* out strongly, like an animal. □ *Wendy bellowed in pain.* □ *Art bellowed for us to shut up.*
   • **holler** to *yell*. (Folksy.) □ *Ben hollered when the snapping turtle bit his toe.* □ *Carrie hollered that the train was coming, so we hopped off the track.*
   • **roar** to *yell* out roughly or growlingly. □ *"Leave me alone!" Donald roared.* □ *The coach roared out instructions to the team.*

• **shout** to *yell* suddenly. □ *The crowd shouted the winner's name.* □ *"I got an A on the test!" Eddie shouted.* [→see also: *scream*]

yield See the entries for *give in, give up.*

youngster See the entry for *child.*

zeal See the entry for *enthusiasm.*

zest See the entry for *enthusiasm.*

zigzag See the entry for *swerve.*

zoom See the entry for *speed.*

NTC'S LANGUAGE DICTIONARIES

The Best, By Definition

Spanish/English
Vox New College (Thumb-index & Plain-edge)
Vox Modern
Vox Compact
Vox Everyday
Vox Traveler's
Vox Super-Mini
Cervantes-Walls

Spanish/Spanish
Diccionario Básico Norteamericano
Vox Diccionario Escolar de la lengua española
El Diccionario del español chicano

French/English
NTC's New College French and English
NTC's Dictionary of *Faux Amis*
NTC's Dictionary of Canadian French

German/English
Schöffler-Weis
Klett's Modern (New Edition)
Klett's Super-Mini
NTC's Dictionary of German False Cognates

Italian/English
Zanichelli New College Italian and English
Zanichelli Super-Mini

Greek/English
NTC's New College Greek and English

Chinese/English
Easy Chinese Phrasebook and Dictionary

For Juveniles
Let's Learn English Picture Dictionary
Let's Learn French Picture Dictionary
Let's Learn German Picture Dictionary
Let's Learn Italian Picture Dictionary
Let's Learn Spanish Picture Dictionary
English Picture Dictionary
French Picture Dictionary
German Picture Dictionary
Spanish Picture Dictionary

English for Nonnative Speakers
Everyday American English Dictionary
Beginner's Dictionary of American English Usage

Electronic Dictionaries
Languages of the World on CD-ROM
NTC's Dictionary of American Idioms, Slang, and
  Colloquial Expressions (Electronic Book)

Other Reference Books
Robin Hyman's Dictionary of Quotations
British/American Language Dictionary
NTC's American Idioms Dictionary
NTC's Dictionary of American Slang and
  Colloquial Expressions
Forbidden American English
Essential American Idioms
Contemporary American Slang
NTC's Dictionary of Grammar Terminology
Complete Multilingual Dictionary of Computer
  Terminology
Complete Multilingual Dictionary of Aviation &
  Aeronautical Terminology
Complete Multilingual Dictionary of Advertising,
  Marketing & Communications
NTC's Dictionary of American Spelling
NTC's Classical Dictionary
NTC's Dictionary of Debate
NTC's Mass Media Dictionary
NTC's Dictionary of Word Origins
NTC's Dictionary of Literary Terms
Dictionary of Trade Name Origins
Dictionary of Advertising
Dictionary of Broadcast Communications
Dictionary of Changes in Meaning
Dictionary of Confusing Words and Meanings
NTC's Dictionary of English Idioms
NTC's Dictionary of Proverbs and Clichés
Dictionary of Acronyms and Abbreviations
NTC's Dictionary of American English
  Pronunciation
NTC's Dictionary of Phrasal Verbs and Other
  Idiomatic Verbal Phrases
Common American Phrases

Polish/English
The Wiedza Powszechna Compact Polish and
  English Dictionary

For further information or a current catalog, write:
National Textbook Company
a division of *NTC Publishing Group*
4255 West Touhy Avenue
Lincolnwood, Illinois 60646-1975 U.S.A.